PISA 2009 Results: Learning Trends

CHANGES IN STUDENT PERFORMANCE SINCE 2000

(VOLUME V)

This work is published on the responsibility of the Secretary-General of the OECD. The opinions expressed and arguments employed herein do not necessarily reflect the official views of the Organisation or of the governments of its member countries.

Please cite this publication as:
OECD (2010), *PISA 2009 Results: Learning Trends: Changes in Student Performance Since 2000 (Volume V)*
http://dx.doi.org/10.1787/9789264091580-en

ISBN 978-92-64-09149-8 (print)
ISBN 978-92-64-09158-0 (PDF)

The statistical data for Israel are supplied by and under the responsibility of the relevant Israeli authorities. The use of such data by the OECD is without prejudice to the status of the Golan Heights, East Jerusalem and Israeli settlements in the West Bank under the terms of international law.

Photo credits:
Getty Images © Ariel Skelley
Getty Images © Geostock
Getty Images © Jack Hollingsworth
Stocklib Image Bank © Yuri Arcurs

Corrigenda to OECD publications may be found on line at: *www.oecd.org/publishing/corrigenda*.

Foreword

One of the ultimate goals of policy makers is to enable citizens to take advantage of a globalised world economy. This is leading them to focus on the improvement of education policies, ensuring the quality of service provision, a more equitable distribution of learning opportunities and stronger incentives for greater efficiency in schooling.

Such policies hinge on reliable information on how well education systems prepare students for life. Most countries monitor students' learning and the performance of schools. But in a global economy, the yardstick for success is no longer improvement by national standards alone, but how education systems perform internationally. The OECD has taken up that challenge by developing PISA, the Programme for International Student Assessment, which evaluates the quality, equity and efficiency of school systems in some 70 countries that, together, make up nine-tenths of the world economy. PISA represents a commitment by governments to monitor the outcomes of education systems regularly within an internationally agreed framework and it provides a basis for international collaboration in defining and implementing educational policies.

The results from the PISA 2009 assessment reveal wide differences in educational outcomes, both within and across countries. The education systems that have been able to secure strong and equitable learning outcomes, and to mobilise rapid improvements, show others what is possible to achieve. Naturally, GDP per capita influences educational success, but this only explains 6% of the differences in average student performance. The other 94% reflect the potential for public policy to make a difference. The stunning success of Shanghai-China, which tops every league table in this assessment by a clear margin, shows what can be achieved with moderate economic resources in a diverse social context. In mathematics, more than a quarter of Shanghai-China's 15-year-olds can conceptualise, generalise, and creatively use information based on their own investigations and modelling of complex problem situations. They can apply insight and understanding and develop new approaches and strategies when addressing novel situations. In the OECD area, just 3% of students reach this level of performance.

While better educational outcomes are a strong predictor of economic growth, wealth and spending on education alone are no guarantee for better educational outcomes. Overall, PISA shows that an image of a world divided neatly into rich and well-educated countries and poor and badly-educated countries is out of date.

This finding represents both a warning and an opportunity. It is a warning to advanced economies that they cannot take for granted that they will forever have "human capital" superior to that in other parts of the world. At a time of intensified global competition, they will need to work hard to maintain a knowledge and skill base that keeps up with changing demands.

PISA underlines, in particular, the need for many advanced countries to tackle educational underperformance so that as many members of their future workforces as possible are equipped with at least the baseline competencies that enable them to participate in social and economic development. Otherwise, the high social and economic cost of poor educational performance in advanced economies risks becoming a significant drag on economic development. At the same time, the findings show that poor skills are not an inevitable consequence of low national income – an important outcome for countries that need to achieve more with less.

But PISA also shows that there is no reason for despair. Countries from a variety of starting points have shown the potential to raise the quality of educational outcomes substantially. Korea's average performance was already high in 2000, but Korean policy makers were concerned that only a narrow elite achieved levels of excellence in PISA. Within less than a decade, Korea was able to double the share of students demonstrating excellence in reading literacy. A major overhaul of Poland's school system helped to dramatically reduce performance variability among

schools, reduce the share of poorly performing students and raise overall performance by the equivalent of more than half a school year. Germany was jolted into action when PISA 2000 revealed a below-average performance and large social disparities in results, and has been able to make progress on both fronts. Israel, Italy and Portugal have moved closer to the OECD average and Brazil, Chile, Mexico and Turkey are among the countries with impressive gains from very low levels of performance.

But the greatest value of PISA lies in inspiring national efforts to help students to learn better, teachers to teach better, and school systems to become more effective.

A closer look at high-performing and rapidly improving education systems shows that these systems have many commonalities that transcend differences in their history, culture and economic evolution.

First, while most nations declare their commitment to education, the test comes when these commitments are weighed against others. How do they pay teachers compared to the way they pay other highly-skilled workers? How are education credentials weighed against other qualifications when people are being considered for jobs? Would you want your child to be a teacher? How much attention do the media pay to schools and schooling? Which matters more, a community's standing in the sports leagues or its standing in the student academic achievement league tables? Are parents more likely to encourage their children to study longer and harder or to spend more time with their friends or in sports activities?

In the most successful education systems, the political and social leaders have persuaded their citizens to make the choices needed to show that they value education more than other things. But placing a high value on education will get a country only so far if the teachers, parents and citizens of that country believe that only some subset of the nation's children can or need to achieve world class standards. This report shows clearly that education systems built around the belief that students have different pre-ordained professional destinies to be met with different expectations in different school types tend to be fraught with large social disparities. In contrast, the best-performing education systems embrace the diversity in students' capacities, interests and social background with individualised approaches to learning.

Second, high-performing education systems stand out with clear and ambitious standards that are shared across the system, focus on the acquisition of complex, higher-order thinking skills, and are aligned with high stakes gateways and instructional systems. In these education systems, everyone knows what is required to get a given qualification, in terms both of the content studied and the level of performance that has to be demonstrated to earn it. Students cannot go on to the next stage of their life – be it work or further education – unless they show that they are qualified to do so. They know what they have to do to realise their dream and they put in the work that is needed to achieve it.

Third, the quality of an education system cannot exceed the quality of its teachers and principals, since student learning is ultimately the product of what goes on in classrooms. Corporations, professional partnerships and national governments all know that they have to pay attention to how the pool from which they recruit is established; how they recruit; the kind of initial training their recruits receive before they present themselves for employment; how they mentor new recruits and induct them into their service; what kind of continuing training they get; how their compensation is structured; how they reward their best performers and how they improve the performance of those who are struggling; and how they provide opportunities for the best performers to acquire more status and responsibility. Many of the world's best-performing education systems have moved from bureaucratic "command and control" environments towards school systems in which the people at the frontline have much more control of the way resources are used, people are deployed, the work is organised and the way in which the work gets done. They provide considerable discretion to school heads and school faculties in determining how resources are allocated, a factor which the report shows to be closely related to school performance when combined with effective accountability systems. And they provide an environment in which teachers work together to frame what they believe to be good practice, conduct field-based research to confirm or disprove the approaches they develop, and then assess their colleagues by the degree to which they use practices proven effective in their classrooms.

Last but not least, the most impressive outcome of world-class education systems is perhaps that they deliver high-quality learning consistently across the entire education system, such that every student benefits from excellent learning opportunities. To achieve this, they invest educational resources where they can make the greatest difference, they attract the most talented teachers into the most challenging classrooms, and they establish effective spending choices that prioritise the quality of teachers.

These are, of course, not independently conceived and executed policies. They need to be aligned across all aspects of the system, they need to be coherent over sustained periods of time, and they need to be consistently implemented. The path of reform can be fraught with political and practical obstacles. Moving away from administrative and bureaucratic control toward professional norms of control can be counterproductive if a nation does not yet have teachers and schools with the capacity to implement these policies and practices. Pushing authority down to lower levels can be as problematic if there is not agreement on what the students need to know and should be able to do. Recruiting high-quality teachers is not of much use if those who are recruited are so frustrated by what they perceive to be a mindless system of initial teacher education that they will not participate in it and turn to another profession. Thus a country's success in making these transitions depends greatly on the degree to which it is successful in creating and executing plans that, at any given time, produce the maximum coherence in the system.

These are daunting challenges and thus devising effective education policies will become ever more difficult as schools need to prepare students to deal with more rapid change than ever before, for jobs that have not yet been created, to use technologies that have not yet been invented and to solve economic and social challenges that we do not yet know will arise. But those school systems that do well today, as well as those that have shown rapid improvement, demonstrate that it can be done. The world is indifferent to tradition and past reputations, unforgiving of frailty and complacency and ignorant of custom or practice. Success will go to those individuals and countries that are swift to adapt, slow to complain and open to change. The task of governments will be to ensure that countries rise to this challenge. The OECD will continue to support their efforts.

***

This report is the product of a collaborative effort between the countries participating in PISA, the experts and institutions working within the framework of the PISA Consortium, and the OECD Secretariat. The report was drafted by Andreas Schleicher, Francesca Borgonovi, Michael Davidson, Miyako Ikeda, Maciej Jakubowski, Guillermo Montt, Sophie Vayssettes and Pablo Zoido of the OECD Directorate for Education, with advice as well as analytical and editorial support from Marilyn Achiron, Simone Bloem, Marika Boiron, Henry Braun, Nihad Bunar, Niccolina Clements, Jude Cosgrove, John Cresswell, Aletta Grisay, Donald Hirsch, David Kaplan, Henry Levin, Juliette Mendelovitz, Christian Monseur, Soojin Park, Pasi Reinikainen, Mebrak Tareke, Elisabeth Villoutreix and Allan Wigfield. Volume II also draws on the analytic work undertaken by Jaap Scheerens and Douglas Willms in the context of PISA 2000. Administrative support was provided by Juliet Evans and Diana Morales.

The PISA assessment instruments and the data underlying the report were prepared by the PISA Consortium, under the direction of Raymond Adams at the Australian Council for Educational Research (ACER) and Henk Moelands from the Dutch National Institute for Educational Measurement (CITO). The expert group that guided the preparation of the reading assessment framework and instruments was chaired by Irwin Kirsch.

The development of the report was steered by the PISA Governing Board, which is chaired by Lorna Bertrand (United Kingdom), with Beno Csapo (Hungary), Daniel McGrath (United States) and Ryo Watanabe (Japan) as vice chairs. Annex C of the volumes lists the members of the various PISA bodies, as well as the individual experts and consultants who have contributed to this report and to PISA in general.

Angel Gurría
OECD Secretary-General

Table of Contents

This book has...

Look for the *StatLinks* at the bottom left-hand corner of the tables or graphs in this book. To download the matching Excel® spreadsheet, just type the link into your Internet browser, starting with the ***http://dx.doi.org*** prefix.
If you're reading the PDF e-book edition, and your PC is connected to the Internet, simply click on the link. You'll find *StatLinks* appearing in more OECD books.

BOXES

FIGURES

TABLES

Executive Summary

The design of PISA does not just allow for a comparison of the relative standing of countries in terms of their learning outcomes; it also enables each country to monitor changes in those outcomes over time. Such changes indicate how successful education systems have been in developing the knowledge and skills of 15-year-olds.

Indeed, some countries have seen impressive improvements in performance over the past decade, sometimes exceeding the equivalent of an average school year's progress for the entire 15-year-old student population. Some of these countries have been catching up from comparatively low performance levels while others have been advancing further from already high levels. All countries seeking to improve their results can draw encouragement – and learn lessons – from those that have succeeded in doing so in a relatively short period of time.

Changes in student performance over time prove that a country's performance in reading is not set in stone. In both absolute and relative terms, educational results can improve, and they cannot be regarded either as part of fixed "cultural" differences between countries or as inevitably linked to each country's state of economic development.

Since both PISA 2000 and PISA 2009 focused on reading, it is possible to track how student performance in reading changed over that period. Among the 26 OECD countries with comparable results in both assessments, Chile, Israel, Poland, Portugal, Korea, Hungary and Germany as well as the partner countries Peru, Albania, Indonesia, Latvia, Liechtenstein and Brazil all improved their reading performance between 2000 and 2009, while performance declined in Ireland, Sweden, the Czech Republic and Australia.

Between 2000 and 2009, the percentage of low performers in Chile dropped by more than 17 percentage points, while the share of top performers in Korea grew by more than 7 percentage points.

In many countries, improvements in results were largely driven by improvements at the bottom end of the performance distribution, signalling progress towards greater equity in learning outcomes. Among OECD countries, variation in student performance fell by 3%. On average across the 26 OECD countries with comparable data for both assessments, 18% of students performed below the baseline reading proficiency Level 2 in 2009, while 19% did so in 2000. Among countries where between 40% and 60% of students performed below Level 2 in 2000, Chile reduced that proportion by the largest amount, and Mexico and the partner country Brazil also show important decreases in their share of low performers. Among countries where the proportion of students performing below Level 2 was smaller than 40% but still above the OECD average of 19%, the partner country Latvia reduced the proportion by 13 percentage points, while Portugal, Poland, Hungary, Germany, Switzerland and the partner country Liechtenstein reduced the share by smaller amounts. In Denmark, the percentage of students below Level 2 fell from an already below-average level.

The share of top performers – those students who attain reading proficiency Level 5 or 6 in reading – increased in Japan, Korea and the partner economy Hong Kong-China such that these countries now have the largest proportions of high-achieving students among the countries participating in the 2009 assessment. Several countries that had above-average proportions of top performers in 2000 saw those proportions decrease in 2009. Notable among them was Ireland, where the proportion of top performers fell from 14% to 7%, which is below the OECD average.

Between 2000 and 2009, Poland, Portugal, Germany, Switzerland and the partner countries Latvia and Liechtenstein raised the performance of their lowest-achieving students while maintaining the performance level among their highest-achieving students. Korea, Israel and the partner country Brazil raised the performance of their highest-achieving students while maintaining the performance level among their lowest-achieving students. Chile and the partner countries Indonesia, Albania and Peru showed improvements in reading performance among students at all proficiency levels.

On average, OECD countries narrowed the gap in scores between their highest- and lowest-performing students between 2000 and 2009; some also improved overall performance. In Chile, Germany, Hungary, Poland, Portugal, and the partner countries Indonesia, Latvia and Liechtenstein, overall performance improved while the variation in performance decreased. In many cases, this was the result of improvements among low-achieving students.

The gender gap in reading performance did not narrow in any country between 2000 and 2009.

The gender gap in reading performance widened in Israel, Korea, Portugal, France and Sweden, and in the partner countries and economies Romania, Hong Kong-China, Indonesia and Brazil between 2000 and 2009. The fact that girls outperform boys in reading is most evident in the proportion of girls and boys who perform below baseline proficiency Level 2. Across OECD countries, 24% of boys perform below Level 2 compared to only 12% of girls. The proportion of girls performing below this level decreased by two percentage points between 2000 and 2009, while the share of low-achieving boys did not change during the period.

Across the OECD area, the percentage of students with an immigrant background increased by an average of two percentage points between 2000 and 2009. The performance gap between students with and without an immigrant background remained broadly similar over the period. However, some countries noted large reductions in the performance advantage of students without an immigrant background. In Belgium, Switzerland and Germany, the gap narrowed by between 28 and 38 score points due to improvements in reading proficiency among students with an immigrant background. However, the gap is still relatively wide in these countries.

Across OECD countries, overall performance in mathematics remained unchanged between 2003 and 2009, as did performance in science between 2006 and 2009.

In mathematics, students in Mexico, Turkey, Greece, Portugal, Italy, Germany and the partner countries Brazil and Tunisia improved their mathematics scores considerably, while students in the Czech Republic, Ireland, Sweden, France, Belgium, the Netherlands, Denmark, Australia and Iceland saw declines in their performance. On average across the 28 OECD countries with comparable results in the 2003 and 2009 assessments, the share of students below mathematics proficiency Level 2 remained broadly similar over the period, with a minor decrease from 21.6% to 20.8%. Among the OECD countries in which more than half of students performed below mathematics proficiency Level 2 in 2003, Mexico shrunk this proportion by 15 percentage points, from 66% to 51%, by 2009 while Turkey reduced it from 52% to 42% during the same period. Meanwhile, the percentage of top performers in mathematics in those 28 OECD countries decreased slightly, from 14.7% in 2003 to 13.4% in 2009. Portugal showed the largest increase – four percentage points – in top performers in mathematics.

In science, 11 of the 56 countries that participated in both the 2006 and 2009 assessments show improvements in student performance. Turkey, for example, saw a 30 score point increase, nearly half a proficiency level, in just three years. Turkey also reduced the percentage of students below science proficiency Level 2 by almost 17 percentage points, from 47% to 30%. Portugal, Chile, the United States, Norway, Korea and Italy all reduced the share of lowest performers in science by around five percentage points or more, as did the partner countries Qatar, Tunisia, Brazil and Colombia. Performance in science declined considerably in five countries.

On average across OECD countries, the percentage of students who report reading for enjoyment daily dropped by five percentage points.

Enjoyment of reading tends to have deteriorated, especially among boys, signalling the challenge for schools to engage students in reading activities that 15-year-olds find relevant and interesting. On average across OECD countries, the percentage of students who said they read for enjoyment every day fell from 69% in 2000 to 64% in 2009. On the other hand, changes in student-teacher relations and classroom climate have generally been favourable or, at least, they have not deteriorated as many would have expected. Generally, students have become more confident that they can get help from their teachers. Across the 26 OECD countries that participated in both assessments, 74% of students in 2000 agreed or strongly agreed with the statements, "If I need extra help, I will

receive it from my teachers" or "Most of my teachers treat me fairly", while in 2009, 79% of students agreed or strongly agreed with those statements. Overall, aspects of classroom discipline have also improved. Thus there is no evidence to justify the notion that students are becoming progressively more disengaged from school.

Introduction to PISA

THE PISA SURVEYS

Are students well prepared to meet the challenges of the future? Can they analyse, reason and communicate their ideas effectively? Have they found the kinds of interests they can pursue throughout their lives as productive members of the economy and society? The OECD Programme for International Student Assessment (PISA) seeks to answer these questions through its triennial surveys of key competencies of 15-year-old students in OECD member countries and partner countries/economies. Together, the group of countries participating in PISA represents nearly 90% of the world economy.[1]

PISA assesses the extent to which students near the end of compulsory education have acquired some of the knowledge and skills that are essential for full participation in modern societies, with a focus on reading, mathematics and science.

PISA has now completed its fourth round of surveys. Following the detailed assessment of each of PISA's three main subjects – reading, mathematics and science – in 2000, 2003 and 2006, the 2009 survey marks the beginning of a new round with a return to a focus on reading, but in ways that reflect the extent to which reading has changed since 2000, including the prevalence of digital texts.

PISA 2009 offers the most comprehensive and rigorous international measurement of student reading skills to date. It assesses not only reading knowledge and skills, but also students' attitudes and their learning strategies in reading. PISA 2009 updates the assessment of student performance in mathematics and science as well.

The assessment focuses on young people's ability to use their knowledge and skills to meet real-life challenges. This orientation reflects a change in the goals and objectives of curricula themselves, which are increasingly concerned with what students can do with what they learn at school and not merely with whether they have mastered specific curricular content. PISA's unique features include its:

- Policy orientation, which connects data on student learning outcomes with data on students' characteristics and on key factors shaping their learning in and out of school in order to draw attention to differences in performance patterns and identify the characteristics of students, schools and education systems that have high performance standards.
- Innovative concept of "literacy", which refers to the capacity of students to apply knowledge and skills in key subject areas and to analyse, reason and communicate effectively as they pose, interpret and solve problems in a variety of situations.
- Relevance to lifelong learning, which does not limit PISA to assessing students' competencies in school subjects, but also asks them to report on their own motivations to learn, their beliefs about themselves and their learning strategies.
- Regularity, which enables countries to monitor their progress in meeting key learning objectives.
- Breadth of geographical coverage and collaborative nature, which, in PISA 2009, encompasses the 34 OECD member countries and 41 partner countries and economies.[2]

The relevance of the knowledge and skills measured by PISA is confirmed by studies tracking young people in the years after they have been assessed by PISA. Longitudinal studies in Australia, Canada and Switzerland display a strong relationship between performance in reading on the PISA 2000 assessment at age 15 and future educational attainment and success in the labour market (see Volume I, Chapter 2).[3]

The frameworks for assessing reading, mathematics and science in 2009 are described in detail in *PISA 2009 Assessment Framework: Key Competencies in Reading, Mathematics and Science* (OECD, 2009).

Decisions about the scope and nature of the PISA assessments and the background information to be collected are made by leading experts in participating countries. Governments guide these decisions based on shared, policy-driven interests. Considerable efforts and resources are devoted to achieving cultural and linguistic breadth and balance in the assessment materials. Stringent quality-assurance mechanisms are applied in designing the test, in translation, sampling and data collection. As a result, PISA findings are valid and highly reliable.

Policy makers around the world use PISA findings to gauge the knowledge and skills of students in their own country in comparison with those in the other countries. PISA reveals what is possible in education by showing what students in the highest performing countries can do in reading, mathematics and science. PISA is also used to gauge the pace of educational progress, by allowing policy makers to assess to what extent performance changes observed nationally are in line with performance changes observed elsewhere. In a growing number of countries, PISA is also used to set policy targets against measurable goals achieved by other systems, and to initiate research and peer-learning designed to identify policy levers and to reform trajectories for improving education. While PISA cannot identify cause-and-effect relationships between inputs, processes and educational outcomes, it can highlight the key features in which education systems are similar and different, sharing those findings with educators, policy makers and the general public.

THE FIRST REPORT FROM THE 2009 ASSESSMENT

This volume is the fifth of six volumes that provide the first international report on results from the PISA 2009 assessment. It provides an overview of trends in student performance in reading, mathematics and science from PISA 2000 to PISA 2009. It shows educational outcomes over time and tracks changes in factors related to student and school performance, such as student background and school characteristics and practices.

The other volumes cover the following issues:

- Volume I, *What Students Know and Can Do: Student Performance in Reading, Mathematics and Science,* summarises the performance of students in PISA 2009, starting with a focus on reading, and then reporting on mathematics and science performance. It provides the results in the context of how performance is defined, measured and reported, and then examines what students are able do in reading. After a summary of reading performance, it examines the ways in which this performance varies on subscales representing three aspects of reading. It then breaks down results by different formats of reading texts and considers gender differences in reading, both generally and for different reading aspects and text formats. Any comparison of the outcomes of education systems needs to take into consideration countries' social and economic circumstances and the resources they devote to education. To address this, the volume also interprets the results within countries' economic and social contexts. The chapter concludes with a description of student results in mathematics and science.
- Volume II, *Overcoming Social Background: Equity in Learning Opportunities and Outcomes,* starts by closely examining the performance variation shown in Volume I, particularly the extent to which the overall variation in student performance relates to differences in results achieved by different schools. The volume then looks at how factors such as socio-economic background and immigrant status affect student and school performance, and the role that education policy can play in moderating the impact of these factors.
- Volume III, *Learning to Learn: Student Engagement, Strategies and Practices,* explores the information gathered on students' levels of engagement in reading activities and attitudes towards reading and learning. It describes 15-year-olds' motivations, engagement and strategies to learn.
- Volume IV, *What Makes a School Successful? Resources, Policies and Practices,* explores the relationships between student-, school- and system-level characteristics, and educational quality and equity. It explores what schools and school policies can do to raise overall student performance and, at the same time, moderate the impact of

socio-economic background on student performance, with the aim of promoting a more equitable distribution of learning opportunities.

- Volume VI, *Students On Line: Reading and Using Digital Information*, (OECD, forthcoming) explains how PISA measures and reports student performance in digital reading and analyses what students in the 20 countries participating in this assessment are able to do.

All data tables referred to in the analysis are included at the end of the respective volume. A Reader's Guide is also provided in each volume to aid in interpreting the tables and figures accompanying the report.

Technical annexes that describe the construction of the questionnaire indices, sampling issues, quality-assurance procedures and the process followed for developing the assessment instruments, and information about reliability of coding are posted on the OECD PISA website (*www.pisa.oecd.org*). Many of the issues covered in the technical annexes will be elaborated in greater detail in the *PISA 2009 Technical Report* (OECD, forthcoming).

THE PISA STUDENT POPULATION

In order to ensure the comparability of the results across countries, PISA devoted a great deal of attention to assessing comparable target populations. Differences between countries in the nature and extent of pre-primary education and care, in the age of entry to formal schooling, and in the structure of the education system do not allow school grades levels to be defined so that they are internationally comparable. Valid international comparisons of educational performance, therefore, need to define their populations with reference to a target age. PISA covers students who are aged between 15 years 3 months and 16 years 2 months at the time of the assessment and who have completed at least 6 years of formal schooling, regardless of the type of institution in which they are enrolled,

■ Figure V.A ■

A map of PISA countries and economies

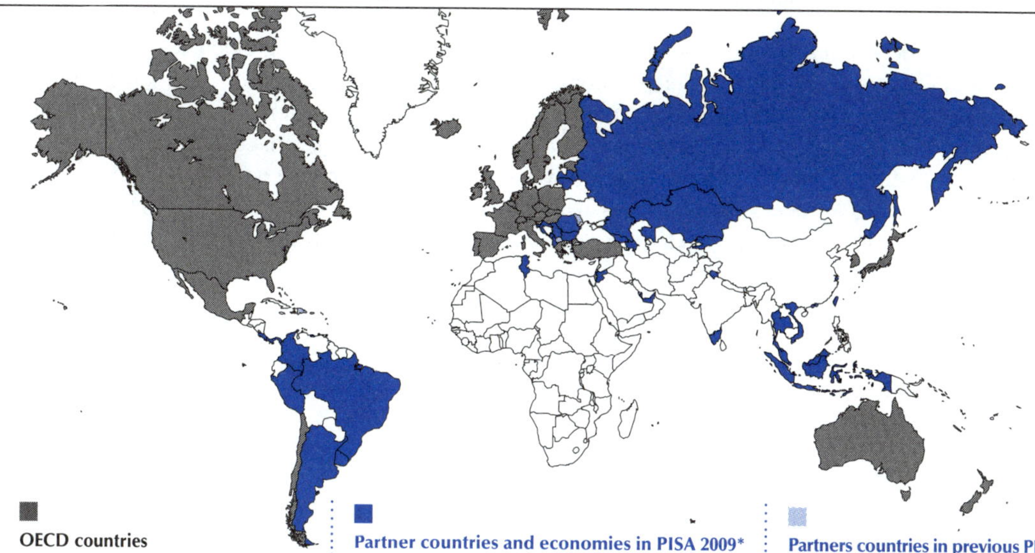

OECD countries

Australia
Austria
Belgium
Canada
Chile
Czech Republic
Denmark
Estonia
Finland
France
Germany
Greece
Hungary
Iceland
Ireland
Israel
Italy
Japan
Korea
Luxembourg
Mexico
Netherlands
New Zealand
Norway
Poland
Portugal
Slovak Republic
Slovenia
Spain
Sweden
Switzerland
Turkey
United Kingdom
United States

Partner countries and economies in PISA 2009*

Albania
Argentina
Azerbaijan
Brazil
Bulgaria
Colombia
Costa Rica*
Croatia
Georgia*
Himachal Pradesh-India*
Hong Kong-China
Indonesia
Jordan
Kazakhstan
Kyrgyzstan
Latvia
Liechtenstein
Lithuania
Macao-China
Malaysia*
Malta*
Mauritius*
Miranda-Venezuela*
Montenegro
Netherlands-Antilles*
Panama
Peru
Qatar
Romania
Russian Federation
Serbia
Shanghai-China
Singapore
Tamil Nadu-India*
Chinese Taipei
Thailand
Trinidad and Tobago
Tunisia
Uruguay
United Arab Emirates*
Viet Nam*

Partners countries in previous PISA surveys

Dominican Republic
Macedonia
Moldova

* These partner countries and economies carried out the assessment in 2010 instead of 2009.

whether they are in full-time or part-time education, whether they attend academic or vocational programmes, and whether they attend public or private schools or foreign schools within the country. (For an operational definition of this target population, see the *PISA 2009 Technical Report* [OECD, forthcoming].) The use of this age in PISA, across countries and over time, allows the performance of students to be compared in a consistent manner before they complete compulsory education.

As a result, this report can make statements about the knowledge and skills of individuals born in the same year who are still at school at 15 years of age, despite having had different educational experiences, both in and outside school.

Stringent technical standards were established to define the national target populations and to identify permissible exclusions from this definition (for more information, see the PISA website *www.pisa.oecd.org*). The overall exclusion rate within a country was required to be below 5% to ensure that, under reasonable assumptions, any distortions in national mean scores would remain within plus or minus 5 score points, *i.e.* typically within the order of magnitude of two standard errors of sampling (see Annex A2). Exclusion could take place either through the schools that participated or the students who participated within schools. There are several reasons why a school or a student could be excluded from PISA. Schools might be excluded because they are situated in remote regions and are inaccessible or because they are very small, or because of organisational or operational factors that precluded participation. Students might be excluded because of intellectual disability or limited proficiency in the language of the test.

In 29 out of the 65 countries participating in PISA 2009, the percentage of school-level exclusions amounted to less than 1%; it was less than 5% in all countries. When the exclusion of students who met the internationally established exclusion criteria is also taken into account, the exclusion rates increase slightly. However, the overall exclusion rate remains below 2% in 32 participating countries, below 5% in 60 participating countries, and below 7% in all countries except Luxembourg (7.2%) and Denmark (8.6%). In 15 out of 34 OECD countries, the percentage of school-level exclusions amounted to less than 1% and was less than 5% in all countries. When student exclusions within schools are also taken into account, there were 9 OECD countries below 2% and 25 countries below 5%. Restrictions on the level of exclusions in PISA 2009 are described in Annex A2.

The specific sample design and size for each country aimed to maximise sampling efficiency for student-level estimates. In OECD countries, sample sizes ranged from 4 410 students in Iceland to 38 250 students in Mexico. Countries with large samples have often implemented PISA both at national and regional/state levels (*e.g.* Australia, Belgium, Canada, Italy, Mexico, Spain, Switzerland and the United Kingdom). This selection of samples was monitored internationally and adhered to rigorous standards for the participation rate, both among schools selected by the international contractor and among students within these schools, to ensure that the PISA results reflect the skills of the 15-year-old students in participating countries. Countries were also required to administer the test to students in identical ways to ensure that students receive the same information prior to and during the test (for details, see Annex A4).

Box V.A **Key features of PISA 2009**

Content

- The main focus of PISA 2009 was reading. The survey also updated performance assessments in mathematics and science. PISA considers students' knowledge in these areas not in isolation, but in relation to their ability to reflect on their knowledge and experience and to apply them to real-world issues. The emphasis is on mastering processes, understanding concepts and functioning in various contexts within each assessment area.
- For the first time, the PISA 2009 survey also assessed 15-year-old students' ability to read, understand and apply digital texts.

Methods

- Around 470 000 students completed the assessment in 2009, representing about 26 million 15-year-olds in the schools of the 65 participating countries and economies. Some 50 000 students took part in a second round of this assessment in 2010, representing about 2 million 15 year-olds from 10 additional partner countries and economies.
- Each participating student spent two hours carrying out pencil-and-paper tasks in reading, mathematics and science. In 20 countries, students were given additional questions via computer to assess their capacity to read digital texts.
- The assessment included tasks requiring students to construct their own answers as well as multiple-choice questions. The latter were typically organised in units based on a written passage or graphic, much like the kind of texts or figures that students might encounter in real life.
- Students also answered a questionnaire that took about 30 minutes to complete. This questionnaire focused on their personal background, their learning habits, their attitudes towards reading, and their engagement and motivation.
- School principals completed a questionnaire about their school that included demographic characteristics and an assessment of the quality of the learning environment at school.

Outcomes

PISA 2009 results provide:

- a profile of knowledge and skills among 15-year-olds in 2009, consisting of a detailed profile for reading and an update for mathematics and science;
- contextual indicators relating performance results to student and school characteristics;
- an assessment of students' engagement in reading activities, and their knowledge and use of different learning strategies;
- a knowledge base for policy research and analysis; and
- trend data on changes in student knowledge and skills in reading, mathematics and science, on changes in student attitudes and socio-economic indicators, and in the impact of some indicators on performance results.

Future assessments

- The PISA 2012 survey will return to mathematics as the major assessment area; PISA 2015 will focus on science. Thereafter, PISA will turn to another cycle, beginning with reading again.
- Future tests will place greater emphasis on assessing students' capacity to read and understand digital texts and solve problems presented in a digital format, reflecting the importance of information and computer technologies in modern societies.

Notes

1. The GDP of the countries that participated in PISA 2009 represents 87% of the 2007 world GDP. Some of the entities represented in this report are referred to as partner economies. This is because they are not strictly national entities.

2. Thirty-one partner countries and economies originally participated in the PISA 2009 assessment and ten additional partner countries and economies took part in a second round of the assessment.

3. Marks, G.N (2007); Bertschy, K., M.A. Cattaneo and S.C. Wolter (2009); OECD (2010a).

Reader's Guide

Data underlying the figures

The data referred to in this volume are presented in Annex B and, in greater detail, on the PISA website (*www.pisa.oecd.org*).

Five symbols are used to denote missing data:

a The category does not apply in the country concerned. Data are therefore missing.

c There are too few observations or no observation to provide reliable estimates (*i.e.* there are fewer than 30 students or less than five schools with valid data).

m Data are not available. These data were not submitted by the country or were collected but subsequently removed from the publication for technical reasons.

w Data have been withdrawn or have not been collected at the request of the country concerned.

x Data are included in another category or column of the table.

Country coverage

This publication features data on 65 countries and economies, including all 34 OECD countries and 31 partner countries and economies (see Figure V.A). The data from another 10 partner countries were collected one year later and will be published in 2011.

The statistical data for Israel are supplied by and under the responsibility of the relevant Israeli authorities. The use of such data by the OECD is without prejudice to the status of the Golan Heights, East Jerusalem and Israeli settlements in the West Bank under the terms of international law.

Calculating international averages

An OECD average was calculated for most indicators presented in this report. The OECD average corresponds to the arithmetic mean of the respective country estimates.

Readers should, therefore, keep in mind that the term "OECD average" refers to the OECD countries included in the respective comparisons.

Rounding figures

Because of rounding, some figures in tables may not exactly add up to the totals. Totals, differences and averages are always calculated on the basis of exact numbers and are rounded only after calculation.

All standard errors in this publication have been rounded to one or two decimal places. Where the value 0.00 is shown, this does not imply that the standard error is zero, but that it is smaller than 0.005.

Reporting student data

The report uses "15-year-olds" as shorthand for the PISA target population. PISA covers students who are aged between 15 years 3 months and 16 years 2 months at the time of assessment and who have completed at least 6 years of formal schooling, regardless of the type of institution in which they are enrolled and of whether they are in full-time or part-time education, of whether they attend academic or vocational programmes, and of whether they attend public or private schools or foreign schools within the country.

Reporting school data

The principals of the schools in which students were assessed provided information on their schools' characteristics by completing a school questionnaire. Where responses from school principals are presented in this publication, they are weighted so that they are proportionate to the number of 15-year-olds enrolled in the school.

Focusing on statistically significant differences

This volume discusses only statistically significant differences or changes. These are denoted in darker colours in figures and in bold font in tables. See Annex A3 for further information.

Abbreviations used in this report

ESCS PISA index of economic, social and cultural status

GDP Gross domestic product

ISCED International Standard Classification of Education

PPP Purchasing power parity

S.D. Standard deviation

S.E. Standard error

Further documentation

For further information on the PISA assessment instruments and the methods used in PISA, see the *PISA 2009 Technical Report* (OECD, forthcoming) and the PISA website (*www.pisa.oecd.org*).

This report uses the OECD's StatLinks service. Below each table and chart is a url leading to a corresponding Excel workbook containing the underlying data. These urls are stable and will remain unchanged over time. In addition, readers of the e-books will be able to click directly on these links and the workbook will open in a separate window, if their Internet browser is open and running.

1

Comparing Performance over Time

This chapter describes how PISA has measured trends in reading performance between the first PISA assessment in 2000 and the latest in 2009. Since reading was the focus of both assessments, it is possible to obtain detailed comparisons of how student performance in reading changed between 2000 and 2009. The chapter also discusses the methods used for tracking trends in student performance in mathematics and science.

PISA 2009 is the fourth full assessment of reading since PISA was launched in 2000, the third assessment of mathematics since PISA 2003, when the first full assessment of mathematics took place, and the second assessment of science since PISA 2006, when the first full assessment of science took place.

Both PISA 2000 and PISA 2009 focus on reading, so it is possible to obtain detailed comparisons of how student performance in reading changed over the 2000-2009 period. Comparisons over time in the areas of mathematics and science are more limited, since there have not yet been two full assessments of either area in nine years of PISA testing.

Box V.1.1 **Interpreting trends requires some caution**

- The methodologies underlying the establishment of performance trends in international studies of education are complex (Gebhardt and Adams, 2007). In order to ensure that the measurement of reading performance in different surveys is comparable, a number of common assessment items are used in each survey. However, the limited number of such items increases the risk of measurement errors. Therefore, the confidence band for comparisons over time is wider than for single-year data, and only changes that are indicated as statistically significant in this volume should be considered robust.[1]
- Some countries have not been included in comparisons between 2000, 2003, 2006 and 2009 for methodological reasons. The PISA 2000 sample for the Netherlands did not meet the PISA response-rate standards and mean scores for the Netherlands were therefore not reported for 2000. In Luxembourg, the assessment conditions were changed in substantial ways between the 2000 and 2003 PISA surveys, thus results are only comparable between 2003, 2006 and 2009.[2] The PISA 2000 and PISA 2003 samples for the United Kingdom did not meet the PISA response-rate standards, so data from the United Kingdom are not comparable with other countries.[3] For the United States, no reading results are available for 2006.[4] The sampling weights for the PISA 2000 assessment in Austria have been adjusted to allow for comparisons with subsequent PISA assessments.[5] For the PISA 2009 assessment, a dispute between teachers' unions and the education minister had led to a boycott of PISA, which was only withdrawn after the first week of testing. The boycott required the OECD to remove identifiable cases from the dataset. Although the Austrian dataset met the PISA 2009 technical standards after the removal of these cases, the negative atmosphere in regard to educational assessment has affected the conditions under which the assessment was administered and could have adversely affected student motivation to respond to the PISA tasks. The comparability of the 2009 data with data from earlier PISA assessments can therefore not be ensured and data for Austria have therefore been excluded from trend comparisons.

Some countries did not participate in all PISA assessments. When comparing trends in reading, this volume looks at the 38 countries with valid results from the 2000 and 2009 assessments.[6] When comparing trends in mathematics, it considers 39 countries with valid results from the 2003 and 2009 assessments. PISA 2000 results in mathematics are not considered, since the first full assessment in mathematics took place in 2003. Similarly, science performance in 2009 cannot be compared to that of PISA 2000 or PISA 2003, since the first full science assessment took place in 2006. Thus, when comparing trends in science, the 56 countries with valid results from the 2006 and 2009 assessments are included. Annex A5 provides a list of countries considered in this trends analysis.

Among OECD countries, the Slovak Republic and Turkey joined PISA in 2003, Chile and Israel did not participate in the PISA 2003 assessment, and Estonia and Slovenia only participated in 2006 and 2009. The different number of OECD countries participating in successive PISA assessments is reflected through separate OECD averages that provide reference points for trend comparisons. For reading, the main reference point is the OECD average for the 26 OECD countries that participated in both PISA 2000 and PISA 2009, but for comparisons involving all four assessments, the average for the 23 OECD countries that participated in all of them is also provided. For mathematics, trends can be calculated for the OECD average in 28 OECD countries that have valid results for both PISA 2003 and PISA 2009. Thirty-three OECD countries have valid results for the 2006 and 2009 assessments in science. Annex A5 gives more details on how the OECD average was calculated for different trend comparisons presented in this volume.

Figure V.1.1 summarises trends in reading performance. The first column provides information on whether reading performance in PISA 2009 was above (blue), at (no colour) or below (grey) the average for OECD countries. Countries are sorted by the magnitude of change in reading performance from PISA 2000 to PISA 2009, which is reported in the second column. Increases in performance are indicated in blue; decreases are indicated in grey. No colour means that there was no statistically significant change in performance. In addition, the chart highlights changes in reading performance separately for boys and girls, changes in the proportion of lowest performers (below proficiency Level 2) and in the proportion of top performers (students at proficiency Level 5 or 6). The last column shows changes in the relationship between the socio-economic background of students and student performance, which provides an indication of whether equity in the distribution of educational opportunities has increased (when the relationship has weakened) or equity has decreased (when the relationship has strengthened).[7] In all cases, blue indicates positive change, grey indicates negative change, and no colour means that there has been no statistically significant change.

■ Figure V.1.1 ■

A summary of changes in reading performance

Mean score in reading 2009 is statistically significantly above the OECD average. Changes in reading and in the share of students at proficiency Level 5 or above are statistically significantly positive. Changes in the share of students below proficiency Level 2 and in the association of socio-economic background with reading is statistically significantly negative.

Mean score in reading 2009 is not statistically significantly different from the OECD average. Changes in reading, in the share of students at proficiency Level 5 or above, in the share of students below proficiency Level 2 and in the association of socio-economic background with reading are not statistically significantly different.

Mean score in reading 2009 is statistically significantly below the OECD average. Changes in reading and in the share of students at proficiency Level 5 or above are statistically significantly negative. Changes in the share of students below proficiency Level 2 and in the association of socio-economic background with reading is statistically significantly positive.

	Mean score in reading 2009	Change in reading performance between 2000 to 2009					
		All students	Boys	Girls	Share of students below proficiency Level 2	Share of students at proficiency Level 5 or above	Association of socio-economic background with reading performance
Peru	370	43	35	50	-14.8	0.4	0.1
Chile	449	40	42	40	-17.6	0.8	-7.6
Albania	385	36	35	39	-13.7	0.1	-9.9
Indonesia	402	31	23	39	-15.2	0.0	-6.9
Latvia	484	26	28	23	-12.5	-1.2	-11.0
Israel	474	22	9	35	-6.7	3.3	-8.4
Poland	500	21	14	28	-8.2	1.3	-1.5
Portugal	489	19	12	26	-8.6	0.6	-4.7
Liechtenstein	499	17	16	17	-6.4	-0.4	-13.3
Brazil	412	16	9	21	-6.2	0.8	-0.6
Korea	539	15	4	25	0.0	7.2	8.5
Hungary	494	14	11	17	-5.1	1.0	-4.2
Germany	497	13	10	15	-4.2	-1.2	-7.7
Greece	483	9	3	13	-3.1	0.6	2.0
Hong Kong-China	533	8	0	17	-0.8	2.9	-8.6
Switzerland	501	6	1	10	-3.6	-1.1	-2.3
Mexico	425	3	1	6	-4.0	-0.5	-7.3
Belgium	506	-1	0	-5	-1.2	-0.8	0.7
Bulgaria	429	-1	-8	6	0.7	0.6	-4.5
Italy	486	-1	-5	2	2.1	0.5	3.2
Denmark	495	-2	-5	-1	-2.7	-3.4	-3.2
Norway	503	-2	-5	-1	-2.5	-2.8	0.4
Russian Federation	459	-2	-6	1	-0.1	-0.0	1.4
Japan	520	-2	-6	3	3.5	3.6	c
Romania	424	-3	-18	11	-0.9	-1.5	10.7
United States	500	-5	-2	-6	-0.3	-2.4	-9.2
Iceland	500	-7	-10	-6	2.3	-0.5	5.4
New Zealand	521	-8	-8	-8	0.6	-3.0	4.9
France	496	-9	-15	-4	4.6	1.1	7.0
Thailand	421	-9	-6	-10	5.8	-0.2	-0.7
Canada	524	-10	-12	-10	0.7	-4.0	-6.4
Finland	536	-11	-12	-8	1.2	-4.0	5.8
Spain	481	-12	-14	-10	3.3	-0.9	1.5
Australia	515	-13	-17	-13	1.8	-4.9	-1.4
Czech Republic	478	-13	-17	-6	5.6	-1.9	-11.4
Sweden	497	-19	-24	-15	4.9	-2.2	7.7
Argentina	398	-20	-15	-22	7.7	-0.7	-1.7
Ireland	496	-31	-37	-26	6.2	-7.3	5.8

Countries are ranked in descending order of the change in reading performance between 2000 and 2009 for all students.
Source: OECD, *PISA 2009 Database*, Tables V.2.1, V.2.2, V.2.4 and V.4.3

StatLink http://dx.doi.org/10.1787/888932359948

In several countries, student achievement has improved markedly across successive PISA assessments since 2000 (Table V.2.1). Each of these countries offers an example of an education system that succeeded in improving its outcomes (see Chapter 2). This volume includes brief descriptions of some of the education systems that have seen marked improvements in the performance of their students in PISA. Notes on Korea (Box V.B) and Poland (Box V.C) appear between Chapters 1 and 2, notes on Portugal (Box V.D) and Turkey (Box V.E) appear between Chapters 3 and 4, a note on Chile (Box V.F) appears between Chapters 4 and 5, and a note on Brazil (Box V.G) appears after Chapter 5.

School systems differ in many ways, including their overall performance level, the socio-economic background of students and schools, the learning environment at school and how school systems are organised. Therefore, it is important to interpret changes in learning outcomes in the context of the underlying characteristics of education systems. In some of the education systems that have seen improvements or a decline in their performance, some of the changes can be attributed to changes in the demographic profile of students. For example, in some countries, student populations have become more socio-economically diverse over recent years, which, as Volume II, Overcoming Social Background, shows, can be associated with performance disadvantages such that a decline in performance may not necessarily be associated with a decline in the quality of the educational services provided, but rather with a more challenging socio-economic context. To account for such changes, observed changes in reading performance are discussed together with trend estimates that have been adjusted for changes in the demographic and socio-economic profile of students and schools. More detailed descriptions of trends in equity in learning opportunities and outcomes (see Chapter 4), and trends in the learning environment (see Chapter 5) that have been observed since 2000 are also presented in this volume.

Annex A1 provides details on how performance scales were equated and on how trends were computed. Annex A6 provides details on how performance scales were adjusted for demographic and socio-economic context. Overall, the evidence suggests that the performance trends reported in this volume are not affected by methodological choices, and that in most countries, they are not driven by changes in the demographic and socio-economic composition of the student population.

This volume also discusses trends in mathematics and science, although comparisons over time are much more limited (see Chapter 3). Figure V.1.2 below summarises trends for all three assessment areas. Countries are sorted by their reading performance in 2009. Since the trends for reading are calculated over a nine-year period for most of the countries, and over a six-year or a three-year period for some of them, the trends have been annualised to make them comparable across the three subject areas.[8] Similarly, trends for mathematics and science were also annualised as they are calculated over a six-year or three-year period for mathematics and over a three-year period for science. Although the annualised figures ensure that the magnitude of changes is comparable across subject areas, greater variability in reading trends is expected, as the longer reporting period for reading provides more opportunites to reflect changes in education systems. This has indeed been observed.

Results are reported for all countries that participated in at least two assessments. The number of years for which reading performance trends were calculated is given after the mean reading performance. Trends in mathematics were calculated over six years if a country participated from at least 2003, or over three years if a country participated in the last two assessments. All trends in science were calculated for three years between 2006 and 2009.

Among countries that scored at or above the OECD average, Portugal improved in all assessment areas, Korea and Poland improved in both reading and science, Germany improved in reading and mathematics, Hungary and Liecthenstein improved in reading, and Norway and the United States improved in science.

■ Figure V.1.2 ■

A summary of annualised performance trends in reading, mathematics and science

(light shading)	Mean score in reading 2009 is statistically significantly above the OECD average. Annualised score point changes in reading, mathematics and science are statistically significantly positive.
(dark shading)	Mean score in reading 2009 is not statistically significantly different from the OECD average. Annualised score point changes in reading, mathematics and science are not statistically significantly different from zero.
(medium shading)	Mean score in reading 2009 is statistically significantly below the OECD average. Annualised score point changes in reading, mathematics and science are statistically significantly negative.

	Mean score in reading 2009	Number of years for which PISA results are available	Reading	Mathematics	Science
Korea	539	9	1.6	0.7	5.3
Finland	536	9	-1.2	-0.6	-3.1
Hong Kong-China	533	8	1.0	0.7	2.3
Canada	524	9	-1.1	-0.9	-1.9
New Zealand	521	9	-0.9	-0.7	0.5
Japan	520	9	-0.3	-0.9	2.7
Australia	515	9	-1.5	-1.7	0.1
Netherlands	508	6	-0.8	-2.0	-0.9
Belgium	506	9	-0.1	-2.3	-1.3
Norway	503	9	-0.2	0.5	4.4
Estonia	501	3	0.1	-0.8	-1.2
Switzerland	501	9	0.7	1.2	1.7
Poland	500	9	2.4	0.8	3.4
Iceland	500	9	-0.7	-1.4	1.6
United States	500	9	-0.5	0.8	4.4
Liechtenstein	499	9	1.9	0.0	-0.7
Sweden	497	9	-2.1	-2.5	-2.7
Germany	497	9	1.5	1.6	1.6
Ireland	496	9	-3.4	-2.6	-0.1
France	496	9	-1.0	-2.3	1.0
Chinese Taipei	495	3	-0.3	-2.1	-4.0
Denmark	495	9	-0.2	-1.8	1.1
United Kingdom	494	6	-2.1	-2.6	-0.4
Hungary	494	9	1.6	0.0	-0.4
Portugal	489	9	2.1	3.5	6.2
Macao-China	487	6	-1.8	-0.3	0.1
Italy	486	9	-0.2	2.9	4.5
Latvia	484	9	2.9	-0.2	1.4
Slovenia	483	3	-3.8	-1.0	-2.4
Greece	483	9	1.0	3.5	-1.1
Spain	481	9	-1.3	-0.3	-0.1
Czech Republic	478	9	-1.5	-3.9	-4.1
Slovak Republic	477	6	1.4	-0.3	0.6
Croatia	476	3	-0.5	-2.4	-2.3
Israel	474	8	2.7	1.7	0.3
Luxembourg	472	6	-1.2	-0.7	-0.8
Lithuania	468	3	-0.5	-3.3	1.2
Turkey	464	6	3.9	3.7	10.0
Russian Federation	459	9	-0.3	-0.1	-0.4
Chile	449	8	5.0	3.2	3.1
Serbia	442	6	5.0	0.9	2.4
Bulgaria	429	8	-0.2	4.9	1.7
Uruguay	426	6	-1.4	0.8	-0.3
Mexico	425	9	0.4	5.5	2.1
Romania	424	7	-0.5	4.1	3.3
Thailand	421	8	-1.2	0.3	1.4
Colombia	413	3	9.3	3.6	4.6
Brazil	412	9	1.7	5.0	5.0
Montenegro	408	3	5.2	1.1	-3.5
Jordan	405	3	1.5	0.9	-2.2
Tunisia	404	6	4.8	2.1	5.1
Indonesia	402	8	3.9	1.9	-3.6
Argentina	398	8	-2.5	2.3	3.2
Albania	385	8	4.5	m	m
Qatar	372	3	19.8	16.7	10.0
Peru	370	8	5.3	m	m
Azerbaijan	362	3	2.9	-15.0	-3.1
Kyrgyzstan	314	3	9.8	6.9	2.5

Countries are ranked in descending order of the mean score in reading in 2009.
Source: OECD, *PISA 2009 Database*.
StatLink http://dx.doi.org/10.1787/888932359948

Notes

1. Normally, when making comparisons between two concurrent means, the significance is indicated by calculating the ratio of the difference of the means to the standard error of the difference of the means. If the absolute value of this ratio is greater than 1.96, then a true difference is indicated with 95% confidence. When comparing two means taken at different times, as in the different PISA surveys, an extra error term, known as the linking error, is introduced and the resulting statement of significant difference is more conservative.

2. For Luxembourg, changes were made in the organisational and linguistic aspects of the assessment conditions between PISA 2000 and PISA 2003 in order to improve compliance with OECD standards and to better reflect the national characteristics of the school system. In PISA 2000, students in Luxembourg had been given one assessment booklet, with the language of assessment having been chosen by each student one week before the assessment. In practice, however, a lack of familiarity with the language of assessment was a significant barrier for a large proportion of students in Luxembourg in PISA 2000. In PISA 2003 and PISA 2006, each student was given two assessment booklets – one in each of the two languages of instruction – and the student could choose his or her preferred language immediately prior to the assessment. This provided for assessment conditions that were more comparable with those in countries that have only one language of instruction and resulted in a fairer assessment of the performance of students in mathematics, science, reading and problem-solving. As a result of this change in procedures, the assessment conditions, and hence the assessment results, for Luxembourg cannot be compared between PISA 2000 and PISA 2003. Assessment conditions between PISA 2003 and PISA 2006 were not changed and therefore those results can be compared.

3. In PISA 2000, the initial response rate for the United Kingdom fell 3.7% short of the minimum requirement. At that time, the United Kingdom had provided evidence to the PISA Consortium that allowed for an assessment of the expected performance of the non-participating schools. On the basis of that evidence, the PISA Consortium concluded that the response bias was likely negligible and the results were included in the international report. In PISA 2003, the United Kingdom's response rate was such that sampling standards had not been met, and a further investigation by the PISA Consortium did not confirm that the resulting response bias was negligible. Therefore, these data were not deemed internationally comparable and were not included in most types of comparisons. For PISA 2006 and PISA 2009, more stringent standards were applied, and PISA 2000 and PISA 2003 data for the United Kingdom are therefore not included in comparisons.

4. In the United States, because of an error in printing the test booklets, some of the reading items had incorrect instructions; as a result, the mean performance in reading cannot be accurately estimated. The impact of the error on the estimates of student performance is likely to exceed one standard error of sampling. This was not the case for science and mathematics items. For details, see Annex A3.

5. As noted in the PISA 2000 Technical Report (OECD, 2002a), the Austrian sample for the PISA 2000 assessment did not cover students enrolled in combined school and work-based vocational programmes as required by the technical standards for PISA. The published PISA 2000 estimates for Austria were therefore biased (OECD, 2001). This non-conformity was corrected in the PISA 2003 assessment. To enable reliable comparisons, adjustments and modified student weights were developed to make the PISA 2000 estimates comparable to those obtained in PISA 2003 (Neuwirth, 2006, available at *http://www.oecd-ilibrary.org/education/oecd-education-working-papers_19939019*).

6. Albania, Argentina, Bulgaria, Chile, Hong Kong-China, Indonesia, Israel, Peru and Thailand delayed the PISA 2000 assessment to 2001, while Romania delayed it to 2002. Thus, for these countries, the period of time between PISA 2000 and PISA 2009 assessments is shorter.

7. The relationship between student socio-economic background and performance is captured by a slope co-efficient of the PISA index of economic, social and cultural and educational status (ESCS) in a regression explaining student reading performance (see Chapter 4).

8. Annualised trends that are reported here were calculated by dividing the change in performance by the number of years between two assessments. For example, a change in reading performance between 2000 and 2009 was divided by nine for countries that participated in the first and in the most recent assessments. For countries that participated in PISA 2003 and PISA 2009 but not in PISA 2000, the change in reading performance between 2003 and 2009 was divided by six. Similarly, for participants in PISA 2006 and PISA 2009, a change in performance was divided by three. Although annualised trends were calculated for mathematics, PISA 2000 results were not considered. For science, the change in performance between 2006 and 2009 was divided by three.

Box V.B **Korea**

In 2000, with PISA reading performance at 525 score points, Korea was already performing above the OECD average. At that time, several countries had similar or even higher performance levels, including Australia, Canada, Ireland, Japan, New Zealand and Finland, the highest-performing country that year. Nine years later, Finland has retained its top performance level, but Korea now outperforms all of the other abovementioned countries. Korea's experience demonstrates that even at the highest performance level further improvements are possible.

Despite the country's strong performance in PISA 2000, Korean policy makers considered that students' skills needed further improvement to meet the changing demands of an internationally competitive labour market. One approach was to shift the focus of the Korean Language Arts Curriculum from proficiency in grammar and literature to skills and strategies needed for creative and critical understanding and representation, along the lines of the approach underlying PISA. Diverse teaching methods and materials that reflected those changes were developed, including investments in related digital and Internet infrastructure.

Recognising reading as a key competence in the 21st century, the government also developed and implemented reading-related policies. Schools were requested to spend a fixed share of their budgets on reading education. Training programmes for reading teachers were developed and distributed. Parents were encouraged to participate more in school activities. They were also given information on how to support their children's schoolwork. In addition to that, socio-economically disadvantaged students were given support through various after-school reading, writing and mathematics courses that had been put in place at the end of the 1990s.

The new "National Human Resources Development Strategies for Korea" defined policy objectives and implementation strategies. As part of this, and following experiences with PISA and other instruments, the government established the National Diagnostic Assessment of Basic Competency (NDABC) and strengthened the National Assessment of Educational Achievement (NAEA) as measurement tools for monitoring the quality of educational achievement. These instruments were implemented to ensure that all students had attained basic competencies. The NDABC was implemented as a diagnostic tool in 2002 to measure basic competency in reading, writing and mathematics for third-grade students. These measurement tools are now used locally to diagnose the progress of elementary and middle-school students across different subjects. The NAEA programme was introduced in 1998. Following changes in educational policy in 2002, the programme has expanded its subject and grade coverage. NAEA assesses educational achievement and trends for 6th, 9th and 10th grade students in Korean Language Arts, social studies, mathematics, science and English. With the help of NAEA, the government monitors individual student performance levels and the accountability of public education.

Since 2000, Korea has seen significant improvements in both reading and science performance (see Figure V.1.2 and Tables V.2.1 and V.3.4). The proportion of top performers in reading increased in Korea by more than seven percentage points from 5.7% to 12.9% between 2000 and 2009 (see Figure V.2.5 and Table V.2.2). That is the highest observed change among countries participating in PISA. Korea also experienced improved scores in science from an already high level in 2006 (see Figure V.3.5 and Table V.3.4). Moreover, in 2006 11% of its students scored below Level 2 in science, whereas in 2009 this proportion had been reduced to 6% - nearly the lowest among the OECD countries (see Figure V.3.7 and Table V.3.5).

On the other hand, Korea is among countries that have seen the highest increase in variation of reading performance (see Figure V.4.1 and Table V.4.1). A closer look reveals that the increase was driven by improvements among high-achieving students that were not shared by low-achieving students (see Figure V.2.11 and Table V.2.3). The 2009 results from Korea also show a modest increase in the association of socio-economic background with PISA performance.

One factor that may have contributed to an increase in the number of top performers in reading is the introduction of higher standards and the demand for language literacy. Korean Language Arts as a screening subject have been strengthened in the College Scholastic Ability Test (CSAT), which students must take to get into university, especially top-ranking institutions. Depending on what subjects they intend to take at university and on their future careers, students generally select five to seven subjects on the assessment. However, almost all top-

....

ranking universities focus on Korean Language Arts, mathematics and English. The reading domain of Korean Langauge Arts, in particular, is the largest and most important part of this assessment, while NAEA/NDABC tend to evaluate the six domains of the Korean Language Arts Curriculum – listening, speaking, reading, writing, literature, and grammar – equally. This provides additional incentives for high-achieving students in Korea to spend more time studying the language arts and also mathematics and science.

Korea is also one of the countries with the highest number of students participating in after-school lessons. More than two-thirds of students participate in such lessons for remedial purposes, while nearly half of the students participate in after-school lessons for enrichment purposes in at least one of the following three subjects: science, mathematics and reading (see Volume IV, *What Makes a School Successful? Resources, Policies and Practices*, Table IV.3.17a). While private lessons are very popular in Korea among those who can afford them, after-school group classes are often subsidised, so even disadvantaged students enrol frequently. For example, as of June 2007, 99.8% of all primary and secondary schools were operating after-school programmes and about 50% of all primary and secondary students participated in after-school activities (see MEHRD, 2007). Many observers suspect that high participation rates in after-school classes in Korea may be due to cultural factors and an intense focus on preparation for university entrance examinations. PISA 2006 data show that Korean students attending schools with socio-economically advantaged students are more likely to attend after-school lessons with private teachers than students in other countries. On the other hand, disadvantaged students in Korea are more likely to attend after-school group lessons more often than students in other countries. In both cases, attending such extra lessons after school is associated with higher performance on PISA (OECD, 2010d).

The gender gap increased by 20 score points in Korea, mainly because of a marked improvement in girls' performance that was not matched by a similar trend among boys (see Figure V.2.7 and Table V.2.4). The percentage of top performers increased among girls by more than nine percentage points, while among boys it rose by slightly less than five percentage points (see Tables V.2.5 and V.2.6). Overall, the average reading performance improved only among girls, while it remained at similar levels among boys. The remarkable improvement in girls' performance was noticed not only in reading, but also in other assessment areas covered by PISA and other international or national studies. The gender gap in mathematics and science has been narrowing for a number of years, while PISA 2009 results show that the reading advantage of girls has become even greater. National assessments demonstrated that the number of girls performing at the highest levels has been gradually increasing since 2002.

Several changes could be associated with the more positive trend among girls. Since 2000, a more female-friendly science and mathematics curriculum has been gradually introduced. For instance, women who were scientists or engineers were promoted and thus became good role models for girls, a more gender-neutral language was used in textbooks, and learning materials that were considered to be more interesting for girls were introduced in science teaching. At the same time, national assessments such as the NAEA were re-developed to better monitor how girls and boys acquire skills differently and to use formats that girls prefer, including, for example, constructed response-item format. On the other hand, the trend may also be explained partly by changes in the society. Over the past few years, the family structure in Korea has changed as the number of children per household has rapidly decreased and the number of single-child families increased. While traditionally girls from larger families were unlikely to get a good education, sociologists note that parents in Korea today tend to value educating their children a great deal, regardless of gender. Smaller families along with new opportunities and incentives for learning may also explain this trend.

Korean students' lower performance in the PISA 2006 science assessment compared with the 2003 assessment prompted policy makers to integrate modern science into school programmes. Although the number of Korean students who performed below Level 2 in both mathematics and science was very small compared to other countries, Korean officials considered the overall level of science performance too low. In 2007, the Korean government decided to merge the Ministry of Science and Technology and the Ministry of Education into one ministry and to improve and strengthen science education in order to enhance creativity and problem-solving skills. Measures that have been undertaken cut across different activities, including providing new mathematics and science textbooks that are more comprehensible and more interesting for students, but also using teaching methods that encourage experimenting and inquiry-oriented science education. Recent

...

improvements in science, especially among top-performing students, could be associated with these latest policy changes. Nevertheless, larger improvements are expected at all performance levels once the new policy is fully implemented.

Box V.C **Poland**

In 2000, Poland's 15-year-old students averaged 479 score points on the PISA reading assessment, well below the OECD average of 500. More troubling for policy makers in Poland was the fact that over 23% of students had not reached the baseline Level 2 in reading. The PISA results also showed large disparities in reading performance between students attending various types of secondary schools. The mean score among students enroled in basic vocational schools – who, at that time, constituted more than one-fifth of all students – was 358 score points, while the mean score among students enroled in general academic schools was 543 score points and that of students in secondary vocational schools was around 480 score points.

Even prior to the release of the PISA results in 2000, plans were already under way in Poland to try and improve student learning outcomes. In 1998, the Polish Ministry of Education presented the outline of a reform agenda to: *i)* raise the level of education in Poland by increasing the number of people with secondary and higher-education qualifications; *ii)* ensure equal educational opportunities; and *iii)* support improvements in the quality of education. The reform was also part of a larger set of changes, including devolving more responsibilities for education to local authorities, health reforms and pension-system reforms.

The education reform envisaged changes in the structure of the education system, reorganising the school network and transportation; changes in administration and supervision methods; changes in the curriculum; a new central examination system with independent student assessments; reorganising school finances through local government subsidies; and new teacher incentives, such as alternative promotion paths and a revised remuneration system. Although not all proposed changes were finally implemented as proposed, the reform clearly changed the way schools in Poland were managed, financed and evaluated, while also affecting teaching content and methods.

The structural changes resulted in a new type of school: the lower secondary "gymnasium" with the same general education programme for all students, which became a symbol of the reform. The previous structure, comprising eight years of primary school followed by four or five years of secondary school or a three-year basic vocational school, was replaced by a system described as 6+3+3. This meant that education at primary school was reduced from eight to six years. After completing primary school, a pupil would then continue his or her education in a comprehensive three-year lower-secondary school. Thus, the period of general education, based on the same curriculum and standards for all students, was extended by one year. Only after completing three years of lower-secondary education would he or she move on to a three- or four-year upper-secondary school that provided access to higher education or to a two- or three-year basic vocational school. In the new system, each stage of education ends with a standardised national examination, which provides students, parents and teachers with feedback. Policy makers can also use the results of the examination to monitor the school system at the local or central level.

The reformers assumed that the lower secondary gymnasia would allow Poland to raise the level of education, particularly in rural areas where schools were small. The new lower secondary schools would be larger; they would also be well-equipped, with qualified teachers. Since the number of pupils in each school varies depending on the catchment area, establishing the lower secondary gymnasia involved reorganising the school network. Thus, since 2000, a number of small primary schools have been closed, with many more students travelling to larger lower secondary schools.

....

The reform postponed choosing between an upper secondary general or vocational curriculum by one year – giving all students one more year of a general lower secondary programme. The reform did not involve pre-primary education, nor did it result in lowering the age at which compulsory schooling begins (seven years); rather, it focused on primary and lower-secondary schools. In the meantime, enrolment in higher education increased from roughly half a million students before 1993 to nearly two million 15 years later (see GUS, 2009). This also changed the environment in which newly established schools operated, with more parents keen to provide their children with the best education and more students choosing schools carefully, taking into consideration future career prospects. Education became highly valued in Poland as the economic returns of a good education grew (see OECD, 2006a).

The reformers had two main arguments for proposing such changes. First, dividing education into stages would allow teaching methods and curricula to better meet the specific needs of pupils of various ages. Second, changing the structure of the education system would require teachers to adapt the curriculum and their teaching methods, encouraging teachers to change not only *what* they taught but also *how* they taught.

After years of complaints about overloaded curricula and disputes about the way forward, the concept of a core curriculum was adopted. This gave schools extensive autonomy to create their own curricula within a pre-determined general framework, balancing the three goals of education: imparting knowledge, developing skills and shaping attitudes. The curricular reform was designed not only to change the content of school education and to encourage innovative teaching methods, but also to change the teaching philosophy and culture of schools. Instead of passively following the instructions of the educational authorities, teachers were expected to develop their own teaching styles, which would be tailored to the needs of their pupils.

Introducing curricular reform based on decentralisation required implementing a system for collecting information and monitoring the education system at the same time. The reformers thus decided to organise compulsory assessments to evaluate student achievement at the end of the primary and lower secondary cycles. The results of the primary school assessments would not affect the students' school career, as completing the cycle would not depend on the results of those assessments. However, for admission to upper secondary schools, the score earned on the lower secondary gymnasium final examination would be considered together with the pupil's final marks. Both of those examinations were first administered in 2002. Schooling would culminate with the *matura* examination, first administered in 2005, which would be taken at the end of upper secondary education. All of these examinations would be organised, set and corrected by the central examination board and regional examination boards–new institutions that had been set up as part of the reform.

Introducing the national examination system not only provided an opportunity to monitor the outcomes of schools centrally in a partly decentralised system, it also changed incentives for students and teachers. It sent a clear signal to students that their success depended directly on their externally evaluated outcomes. It also made it possible to assess teachers and schools on a comparable scale across the whole country. Finally, it provided local governments with information on the outcomes of schools that were now under their organisational and financial responsibility.

After the reform, local governments became an even more important part of the Polish school system. Although by 1996 almost all primary schools were already under the responsibility of local governments, changes in the financing scheme had been introduced together with the reform. The need to reorganise the school network in order to create space for lower secondary schools provided additional incentives for local governments to increase the efficiency and the quality of their local schools. After 2000, school funds were transferred to local governments using a per-pupil formula. Those funds now constitute a large share of their budgets. After 2002, some local governments also started using results from national examinations to evaluate their schools and to shape pre-primary and upper secondary education in their local area.

The reform also introduced a new system of teacher development and evaluation. Initially, many teachers upgraded their levels of education and professional skills to meet those new requirements. But the changes only partly affected the remuneration system, which gives local governments and school principals little discretion. This, together with high employment security and other benefits contained in the so-called Teacher Charter, limited the impact of changes on the teaching profession (see OECD, 2006a).

....

The age cohorts covered by PISA in 2000, 2003 and 2006 have been affected by the reform in different ways. The first group, those assessed in 2000, was not affected by the reform. The group of 15-year-olds in 2003 that was covered by the second PISA assessment started primary school in the former system, but attended the new lower secondary gymnasia. Those students all had the same educational curricula and were not divided into different school types. The group covered by PISA 2006 had been part of the reformed educational system for most of its school career, while those assessed in 2009 had been part of that system for their entire school career.

While it is not possible to establish a causal relationship between the reform and the outcomes measured by PISA, reading performance in Poland has improved by 21 score points since 2000 (see Figure V.2.1 and Table V.2.1). The largest improvement was observed in PISA 2003, right after the reform. The PISA 2009 results suggest that the lowest-performing students appear to have benefited most from the reform. The share of students below proficiency Level 2 decreased by eight percentage points and the performance of the lowest-achieving students increased by 40 score points, while remaining at similar levels for the highest-achieving students (see Figure V.2.4 and Tables V.2.2 and V.2.3).

Additional analyses suggest that students from former vocational schools benefited most from these reforms (see Jakubowski, Patrinos, Porta, Wisniewski, 2010). Lower secondary school students assessed in 2006 with the same background as students who were in basic vocational schools in 2000 performed higher by roughly one standard deviation on the PISA reading scale. Smaller improvements were also apparent among 2006 lower secondary school students who had a similar background to those in secondary vocational schools in 2000, although the benefits to those who were similar to students in general upper secondary schools in 2000 were negligible. This suggests that the reform improved outcomes for students who would end up in former basic vocational schools under the old system and who were given a chance to acquire more general skills in newly created lower secondary schools.

Poland reduced its total variation in reading performance by 20% (see Figure V.4.1 and Table V.4.1). This was mainly achieved by reducing the differences in performance between schools and improving performance among the lowest achievers. From a relatively high level in 2000, between-school variation decreased by three-fourths to a level well below the OECD average. Moreover, by 2009, the association between a school's socio-economic background and its mean performance was three times weaker than that in 2000, although the overall impact of socio-economic background on performance remained unchanged (see Figure V.4.3 and Table V.4.3). This suggests that the school reform in Poland had the effect of distributing students from different backgrounds more evenly across schools. Nevertheless, the overall improvement in performance, larger improvements among the lowest-achieving students, and a decrease in the total variation of student performance, suggest that Poland improved markedly both with regard to its mean performance as well as to the level of equity in the distribution of learning opportunities.

2

Trends in Reading

This chapter highlights trends in reading performance between 2000 and 2009. It includes changes in performance among the lowest- and highest-achieving students, boys and girls, students with an immigrant background, socio-economically advantaged and disadvantaged students, and among countries.

CONTINUITY AND CHANGE IN THE READING LITERACY FRAMEWORK AND ASSESSMENT

Reading literacy includes a broad set of cognitive competencies, from basic decoding, through knowledge of words, grammar and linguistic and textual structures and features, to knowledge about the world. It also includes metacognitive competencies: the awareness of and ability to use a variety of appropriate strategies when processing texts. Specifically, PISA defines *reading literacy* as understanding, using and reflecting on written texts in order to achieve one's goals, acquire knowledge, develop one's potential and participate in society (OECD, 2006b). A more detailed description of the conceptual framework underlying the PISA reading assessment is provided in Volume I of this report, *What Students Know and Can Do*.

The framework and instruments for measuring reading literacy were developed for the PISA 2000 assessment. The PISA 2000 mean score for reading for 28 OECD countries was set at 500 and the standard deviation was set at 100, establishing the scale against which reading performance in PISA 2009 was compared. Two countries that participated in PISA 2000 have joined the OECD since 2000, while results for four OECD countries were excluded from comparisons over time. Thus, reading performance trends are discussed for the 26 OECD countries that participated in and had comparable results from both the 2000 and 2009 assessments. The PISA 2000 OECD average for these 26 OECD countries is now 496, while the reading performance scale remained unchanged.[1] In PISA 2003 and PISA 2006, when the focus shifted first to mathematics and then to science, reading was allocated smaller amounts of assessment time than in 2000, allowing only for an update on overall performance rather than the kind of in-depth analysis of knowledge and skills that was possible for the PISA 2000 and 2009 assessments. To ensure comparability across successive reading assessments, 41 out of the 130 PISA reading items used in the 2009 assessment were taken from the PISA 2000 assessment. These items were selected to reflect the overall balance of the framework so that the proportion of items contained in each type of task was similar. From the 41 items assessed in both 2000 and 2009, 28 reading items were also used in PISA 2003 and 2006 to assure the comparability of results for these assessments. Details of the equating methodology for reading performance trends are provided in Annex A1.

The scale on which student performance is reported is thus the same as the one used in 2000. It can be compared across all four cycles. Consequently, the proficiency levels are also the same, although in 2009 the reading scale was extended with new proficiency levels, at both the top and bottom ends of the performance distribution, to reflect the capacity of PISA 2009 to provide more detailed information about low- and high-performing students.

HOW STUDENT PERFORMANCE IN READING HAS CHANGED SINCE 2000

The OECD's average reading performance has remained similar since 2000, in relation to the 26 OECD countries that had comparable results both in the 2000 and 2009 assessments. This, in itself, is noteworthy because in recent years, most countries have increased their investment in education substantially. Between 1995 and 2007, expenditure per primary and secondary student increased by 43% in real terms, on average, across OECD countries (OECD, 2010b, Table B1.5). In the short period between 2000, when the first PISA assessment was undertaken, and 2007, increases in expenditures on education averaged around 25%; eight OECD countries increased their expenditures by between 35% and 71%. While not all these expenditures were devoted to raising the performance of students assessed in PISA, it is intriguing that in many countries, such major financial efforts have not yet translated into improvements in performance.

However, some countries have seen marked improvements in learning outcomes. Among the 38 countries that can be compared between 2000 and 2009, 13 have seen improvements in reading performance since 2000 (Figure V.2.1, see also Table V.2.1). Of the 26 OECD countries with comparable results for both assessments, seven countries have seen improvements: Chile, Israel and Poland all improved their reading performance by more than 20 score points, and Portugal, Korea, Hungary and Germany by between 10 and 20 score points. Similarly, among the partner countries, Peru, Albania, Indonesia and Latvia improved their performance by more than 20 score points, and Liechtenstein and Brazil by between 10 and 20 score points.

Four countries saw a decline in their reading performance between 2000 and 2009. Among those, student performance in Ireland decreased by 31 score points, in Sweden by 19 score points, and in Australia and the Czech Republic by 13 score points.

PISA considers only those results as statistically significant, marking them as such, where the uncertainty in measuring changes in performance implies that an increase or decrease would be identified in less than five out

of 100 replications of PISA when, in fact, there is no change. It is possible to calculate the exact percentage of replications in which a change would be reported when there is no real change. This so-called "p-value" is reported in Figure V.2.1 (see also the last column in Table V.2.1). The smaller this percentage, the more confidence one can have that the observed changes are real. The p-value allows readers to assess the reliability of observed performance differences that are not identified as statistically significant by PISA, using the stringent criteria described above. For example, the observed increase in performance is nine score points in Greece and eight score points in Hong Kong-China. This is a sizeable magnitude but the p-values for these estimates suggest that, in 28 out of 100 replications in the case of Greece and in 21 out of 100 replications in the case of Hong Kong-China, PISA could have identified such a change even if there is, in fact, no change. Because of the magnitude of the potential error, PISA does not identify these changes as statistically significant. However, readers who are satisfied with a lower level of confidence can still take these values into consideration.

■ Figure V.2.1 ■

Change in reading performance between 2000 and 2009

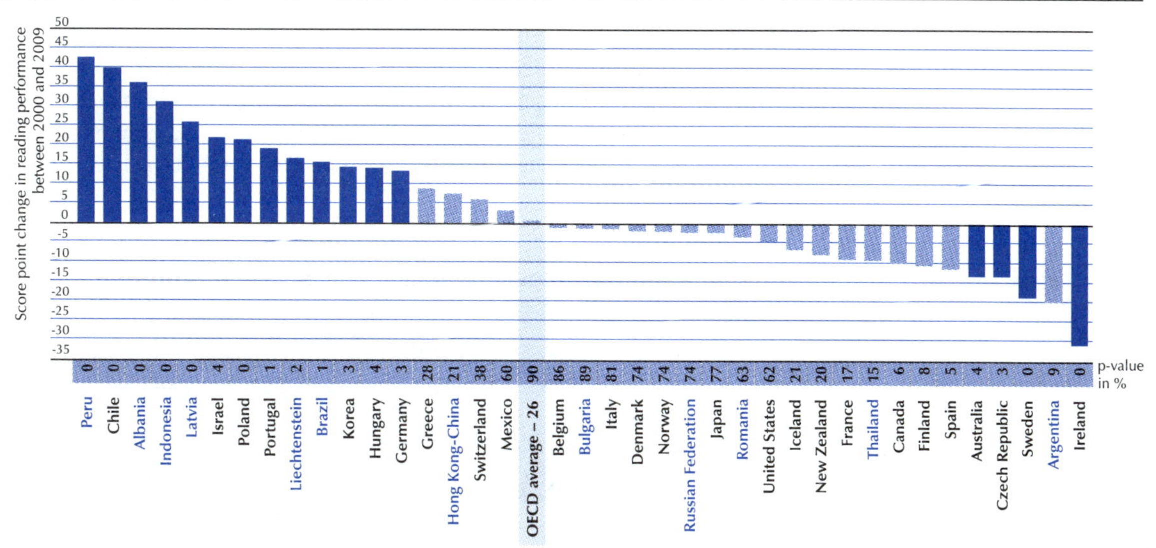

Note: Statistically significant score point changes are marked in a darker tone.
Countries are ranked in descending order of the score point change in reading performance between 2000 and 2009.
Source: OECD, *PISA 2009 Database*, Table V.2.1.
StatLink http://dx.doi.org/10.1787/888932359967

Countries differ in their absolute performance levels, so even with improvements in reading performance, some countries still perform far below the OECD average, while some countries with a decline in reading performance may still outperform many other countries. It is thus useful to examine both where countries stand and how performance has changed.

Countries towards the right of Figure V.2.2 improved their performance between 2000 and 2009, while those towards the left saw a decrease in student scores. Countries towards the top performed above the OECD average in 2009, while those towards the bottom performed below the OECD average. Countries that improved their performance between 2000 and 2009 can be classified into three groups, depending on their performance level in 2009. The first group includes countries that improved their performance but still performed below the OECD average. These countries are represented in the bottom-right corner of Figure V.2.2. The second group includes countries that improved their performance so that they now perform close to the OECD average. These countries are represented in the middle-right of Figure V.2.2. The third group contains countries that had already outperformed most of the PISA participants but still improved their performance. These countries are on the top-right part of Figure V.2.2. For countries with a white marker the changes were not statistically significant.

Among countries that scored above the OECD average in 2009, three countries improved their performance. Korea improved its performance by 15 score points from an already high level in 2000. Poland improved its performance by 21 score points and, from a country that performed below the OECD average in 2000, became a country that

scored above the OECD average in 2009. The partner country Liechtenstein improved its performance by 17 score points. More detailed discussions of the school systems in Korea and Poland are provided in Boxes V.B and V.C, respectively, which appear between Chapters 1 and 2.

Among average-performing countries in 2009, reading performance improved in Portugal, Hungary and Germany. Box V.D, which appears between Chapters 3 and 4, provides more details on reforms in Portugal.

Several countries with below-average performance in 2009 saw marked improvements. Among OECD countries, student performance in Chile increased by 40 score points and is now close to 450 score points, while student performance in Israel increased by 22 score points and is now equal to 474 score points. Chile's school system is briefly discussed in Box V.F, which appears after Chapter 4. The partner country Peru saw the largest improvement, with an increase of 43 score points, although its overall performance is still below 400 score points. Albania and Indonesia increased their performance by 30 to 40 score points, although both countries still perform at or below 400 score points. Brazil increased its performance by 16 score points and now performs above 400 score points (see Box V.G, which appears after Chapter 5). Latvia increased its performance by 26 score points and now performs at 484 score points.

A number of countries performing above the average saw a decrease in reading scores. Australia's performance declined by 13 score points but the country still ranks among the top performers in reading. Performance in Ireland and Sweden declined by 31 and 19 score points, respectively, and both countries now perform around the OECD average. The Czech Republic also saw a decline in performance and now scores below the OECD average.

■ Figure V.2.2 ■

How countries perform in reading and how reading performance has changed since 2000

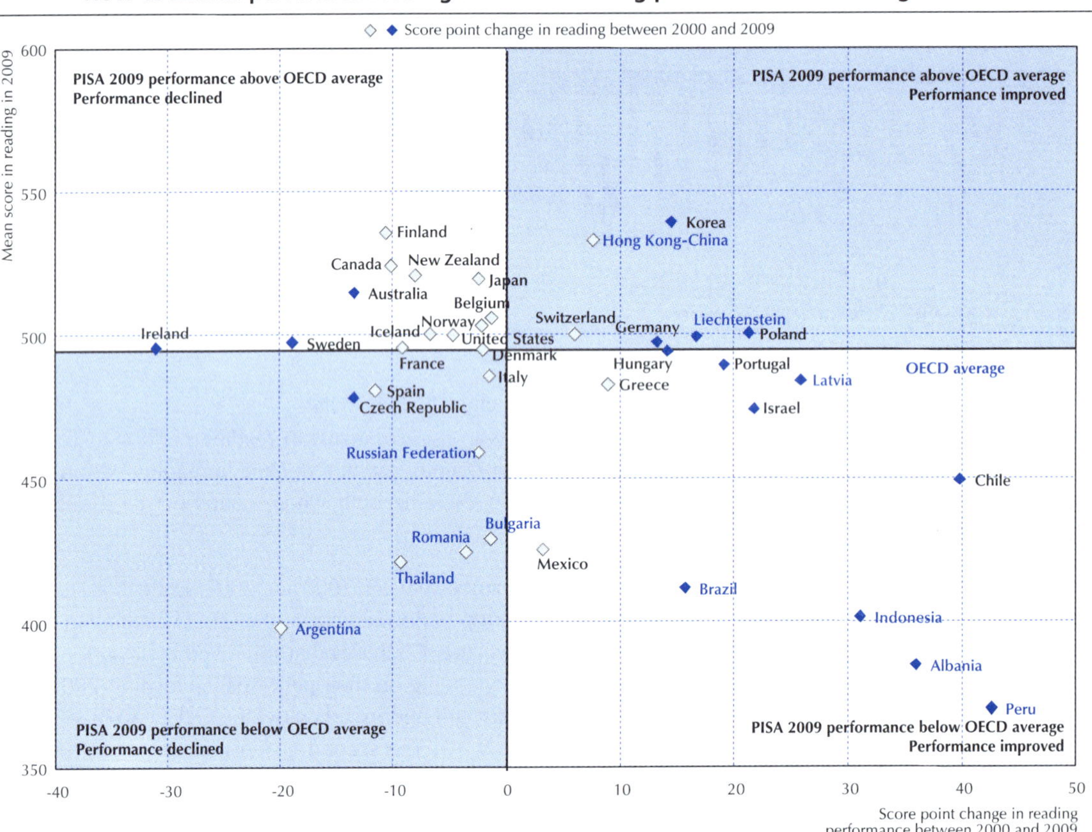

Note: Score point change in reading performance between 2000 and 2009 that are statistically significant are marked in a darker tone.
Source: OECD, *PISA 2009 Database*, Table V.2.1.
StatLink http://dx.doi.org/10.1787/888932359967

■ Figure V.2.3 ■

Multiple comparisons between 2000 and 2009

	Reading performance in 2000	Reading performance in 2009	Countries with lower performance in 2000 and similar performance in 2009	Countries with lower or similar performance in 2000 and higher performance in 2009	Countries with similar performance in 2000 and 2009	Countries with similar or higher performance in 2000 and lower performance in 2009	Countries with higher performance in 2000 and similar performance in 2009
Korea	525	539			Hong Kong-China	Japan, Canada, Ireland, New Zealand, Australia	Finland
Finland	546	536	Korea, Hong Kong-China				
Hong Kong-China	525	533			Korea	Japan, Canada, Ireland, New Zealand, Australia	Finland
Canada	534	524	Japan	Korea, Hong Kong-China	New Zealand	Australia	
New Zealand	529	521		Korea, Hong Kong-China	Japan, Canada, Australia	Ireland	
Japan	522	520		Korea, Hong Kong-China	New Zealand, Australia	Sweden, Ireland	Canada
Australia	528	515		Canada, Korea, Hong Kong-China	Japan, New Zealand	Ireland	
Belgium	507	506	Liechtenstein, Switzerland, Poland		Norway, United States	Iceland, Sweden, Ireland, France	
Norway	505	503	Liechtenstein, Germany, Switzerland, Poland		Iceland, Belgium, United States, France		Sweden, Ireland
Switzerland	494	501	Liechtenstein, Germany, Poland, Hungary		Denmark, United States	Italy Spain, Czech Republic	Iceland, Norway, Belgium, Sweden, Ireland, France
Poland	479	500			Liechtenstein, Germany, Hungary	Italy Portugal, Spain, Greece, Czech Republic	Iceland, Norway, Switzerland, Belgium, Denmark, Sweden, Ireland, United States, France
Iceland	507	500	Liechtenstein, Germany, Switzerland, Poland, Hungary	Belgium	Norway, United States, France		Sweden, Ireland
United States	504	500	Liechtenstein, Germany, Poland, Hungary		Iceland, Norway, Switzerland, Belgium, Denmark, Sweden, France	Spain, Czech Republic	Ireland
Liechtenstein	483	499			Germany, Poland, Hungary	Italy Spain, Greece, Czech Republic	Iceland, Norway, Switzerland, Belgium, Denmark, Sweden, Ireland, United States, France
Sweden	516	497	Iceland, Norway, Liechtenstein, Germany, Switzerland, Denmark, Poland, Portugal, Hungary, France	Japan, Belgium	United States		Ireland
Germany	484	497			Liechtenstein, Poland, Hungary	Italy Spain, Greece, Czech Republic	Iceland, Norway, Switzerland, Denmark, Sweden, Ireland, United States, France
Ireland	527	496	Iceland, Norway, Liechtenstein, Germany, Switzerland, Denmark, Sweden, Poland, Portugal, Hungary, United States, France	Japan, Belgium, Korea, Hong Kong-China, New Zealand, Australia			
France	505	496	Liechtenstein, Germany, Switzerland, Denmark, Poland, Portugal, Hungary	Belgium	Iceland, Norway, United States		Sweden, Ireland
Denmark	497	495	Liechtenstein, Germany, Poland, Portugal, Hungary		Switzerland, United States	Spain, Czech Republic	Sweden, Ireland, France
Hungary	480	494			Liechtenstein, Germany, Poland, Portugal	Italy Spain, Greece, Czech Republic	Iceland, Switzerland, Denmark, Sweden, Ireland, United States, France
Portugal	470	489		Poland	Latvia, Greece, Hungary	Russian Federation, Israel Spain, Czech Republic	Italy, Denmark, Sweden, Ireland, France
Italy	487	486	Latvia, Portugal, Greece	Liechtenstein, Germany, Switzerland, Poland, Hungary	Spain	Czech Republic	
Latvia	458	484			Portugal	Russian Federation, Israel	Italy, Spain, Greece, Czech Republic
Greece	474	483	Latvia, Israel	Liechtenstein, Germany, Poland, Hungary	Portugal	Russian Federation	Italy, Spain, Czech Republic
Spain	493	481	Latvia, Israel, Greece	Liechtenstein, Germany, Switzerland, Denmark, Poland, Portugal, Hungary, United States	Italy, Czech Republic		
Czech Republic	492	478	Latvia, Israel, Greece	Italy, Liechtenstein, Germany, Switzerland, Denmark, Poland, Portugal, Hungary, United States	Spain		
Israel	452	474		Latvia, Portugal		Russian Federation	Spain, Greece, Czech Republic
Russian Federation	462	459		Latvia, Israel, Portugal, Greece			
Chile	410	449				Argentina, Thailand, Bulgaria, Romania, Mexico	
Bulgaria	430	429		Chile	Thailand, Romania, Mexico	Argentina	
Mexico	422	425		Chile	Thailand, Bulgaria, Romania	Argentina	
Romania	428	424		Chile	Thailand, Bulgaria, Mexico	Argentina	
Thailand	431	421		Chile	Bulgaria, Romania, Mexico	Argentina	
Brazil	396	412				Argentina	
Indonesia	371	402					Argentina
Argentina	418	398	Indonesia	Thailand, Bulgaria, Romania, Brazil, Mexico, Chile			
Albania	349	385					
Peru	327	370					

Source: OECD, *PISA 2009 Database*.

StatLink http://dx.doi.org/10.1787/888932359967

Figure V.2.3. provides multiple comparisons of changes in the relative standing of countries in reading performance in 2000 and 2009. Countries are sorted by their performance in 2009. For each country the figure identifies a list of other countries or economies with similar performance. The first group includes comparisons between countries that had lower scores in 2000 but have similar performance levels in 2009 as the country shown in the first column. The second group includes countries with lower or similar scores in 2000 but that show higher scores in 2009. The third group includes countries whose performance was similar in 2000 and 2009. The fourth group includes countries with similar or higher scores in 2000 and lower scores in 2009. The fifth group includes countries with higher scores in 2000 and similar scores in 2009. The figure includes all 38 countries that have comparable results from the 2000 and 2009 assesments.

The chart can be used to see how the position of a country changed compared to other countries that are close in relative performance.

Mean performance summarises overall student performance in PISA. While it gives a general idea of how countries perform in comparison to others, mean performance can mask important variations in student performance. For policy makers, information about the variability of student performance is important. For example, readers interested in policies and practices relating to the most talented students might be interested in those countries in which the highest-achieving students improved their performance, or countries in which the share of high-achieving students grew. Similarly, readers interested in policies and practices relating to lower-performing students might examine more closely those countries that have seen improvements among the lowest-achieving students, or where the share of low-achieving students decreased.

Performance trends among low- and high-achieving students can be examined by considering changes in the percentage of students at each of the PISA proficiency levels. As explained in Volume I, *What Students Know and Can Do*, reading scores in 2009 are reported according to different levels of proficiency that correspond to tasks of varying difficulty. Establishing proficiency levels in reading makes it possible not only to rank students' performance but also to describe what students at different levels of the reading scale can do.

As explained in Volume I, reading proficiency Level 2 can be considered a baseline level of proficiency, at which students have learned to read and begin to demonstrate the kind of competencies that are required to use reading for learning. Students below this level may still be capable of locating pieces of explicitly stated information that are prominent in the text, recognising a main idea in a text about a familiar topic, or recognising the connection between information in the text and their everyday experience. However, they have not acquired the level of literacy that is required to participate effectively and productively in life. On average across the 26 OECD countries with comparable results for both assessments, 18.1% of students performed below Level 2 in 2009, while the corresponding percentage in 2000 was 19.3% (Table V.2.2). Although this percentage changed only slightly between the two assessments, it varied noticeably among countries.

Reducing the percentage of poorly performing students is considered one of the most important tasks for school systems in many countries, given the large economic and social costs associated with poor performance in school. Following up on students who were assessed in PISA 2000, the Canadian Youth in Transitions Survey shows that students scoring below Level 2 face a disproportionately higher risk of poor participation in post-secondary education or low labour-market outcomes at age 19, and even worse outcomes at age 21, the latest age for which these data are available (OECD, 2010a).

Figure V.2.4 shows changes in the share of students below Level 2. For each country, bars represent the percentage of students performing below Level 2 in 2009, while markers denote that share in 2000. Countries are sorted according to the percentage of students below Level 2 in 2009, with those that show fewer students at this low proficiency level are on the left.

To make comparisons of changes in the percentage of students at different proficiency levels more meaningful, countries can be grouped according to how many students in those countries performed at each level in 2000. In 2000, more than 60% of students in Peru, Albania and Indonesia performed below Level 2 (Table V.2.2). All three countries have seen a reduction in this share of more than 10 percentage points. The proportion of lower-performing students remained at relatively high levels in these countries, but this trend shows that real progress has been made in all the PISA countries where the very highest percentages of 15-year-olds have limited reading skills.

■ Figure V.2.4 ■

Percentage of students below proficiency Level 2 in reading in 2000 and 2009

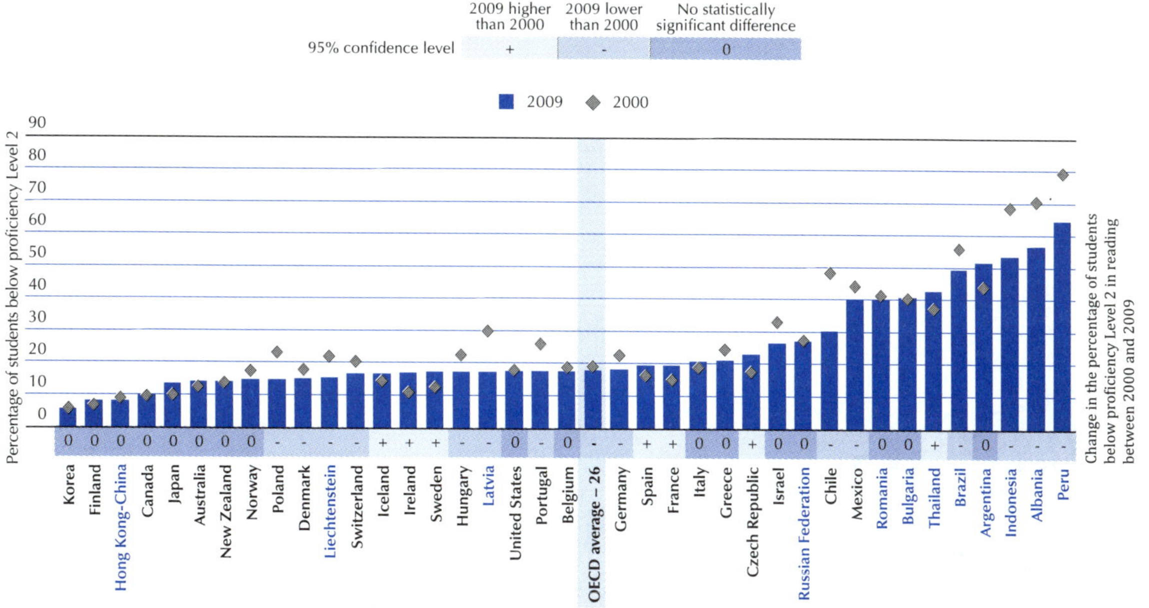

Countries are ranked in ascending order of the percentage of students below proficiency Level 2 in reading in 2009.
Source: OECD, *PISA 2009 Database*, Table V.2.2.
StatLink http://dx.doi.org/10.1787/888932359967

Among countries where between 40% and 60% of students performed below Level 2 in 2000, in Chile that proportion decreased by 18 percentage points (see Box V.F), while the proportion decreased by smaller amounts in Mexico and the partner country Brazil (see Box V.G).

Among countries where the proportion of students performing below Level 2 was smaller than 40% but still above the OECD average of 19%, the partner country Latvia reduced the proportion by 13%, while Portugal, Poland, Hungary, Germany, Switzerland, and the partner country Liechtenstein reduced it by smaller amounts (see Boxes V.D for Portugal and V.C for Poland for examples of policies that might be associated with these trends). In the partner country Thailand, the proportion of students performing below Level 2 increased by six percentage points from a relatively high level of 37%. In countries where the proportion of students performing below Level 2 was already below average in 2000, Denmark further reduced the proportion by three percentage points and now shows 15% of students below Level 2.

The proportion of students below Level 2 increased in Ireland, the Czech Republic, Sweden, France, Spain and Iceland. While this proportion is still below the OECD average in Iceland, Ireland and Sweden, it is now above average in France, Spain and the Czech Republic.

Students performing at Level 5 or 6 are frequently referred to as "top performers" in this report. These students can handle texts that are unfamiliar in either form or content. They can find information in such texts, demonstrate detailed understanding, and infer which information is relevant to the task. Using such texts, they are also able to evaluate critically and to build hypotheses, draw on specialised knowledge and accommodate concepts that may be contrary to expectations. A comparison of the kinds of tasks students at Level 5 or above are capable of suggests that those who get to this level can be regarded as potential "world class" knowledge workers of tomorrow. Thus, the proportion of a country's students reaching this level is a good indicator of its future economic competitiveness.

On average across the 26 OECD countries with comparable results for both assessments, the combined percentage of students performing at Level 5 or 6 was 9.0% in 2000 and decreased to 8.2% in 2009 (see Table V.2.2). Although the proportion of students at this level changed only slightly between the assessments, it varies considerably across countries.

Figure V.2.5 shows changes in the shares of top-performing students. For each country, blue bars represent the percentage of students performing at Level 5 or 6 in 2009, while markers denote the corresponding proportion in 2000. Countries are sorted according to the percentage of students at Level 5 or above in 2009, with countries that have the largest proportion of top performers on the left.

■ Figure V.2.5 ■

Percentage of top performers in reading in 2000 and 2009

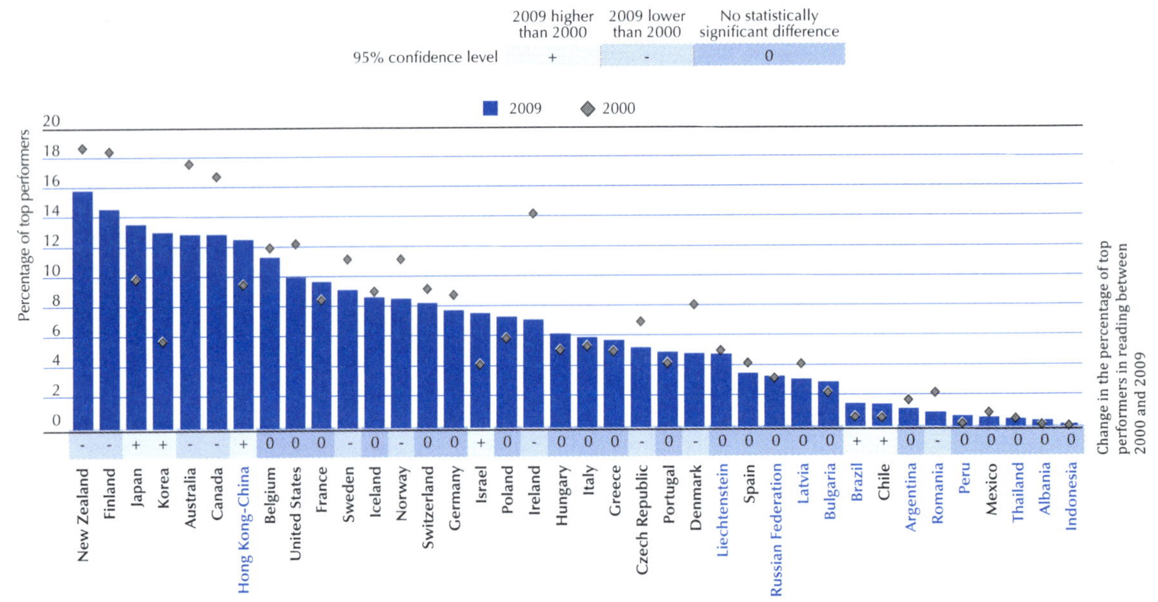

Note: Countries are ranked in descending order of top performers in reading in 2009.
Source: OECD, *PISA 2009 Database*, Table V.2.2.
StatLink http://dx.doi.org/10.1787/888932359967

The proportion of top performers increased in Japan and Korea and the partner economy Hong Kong-China to one of the higest levels among 2009 participants (Table V.2.2). In Japan, this proportion increased from nearly 10% to above 13%. In Korea, it increased by more than seven percentage points from less than 6% to almost 13%, which was the highest observed change among participating countries. Because of this improvement, Korea moved from below to above the OECD average in the percentage of top performers (see also Box V.B). In Hong Kong-China, this proportion increased by almost three percentage points to slightly more than 12%. Among countries that have relatively low proportions of top performers, the percentage of students at Level 5 or above increased by three percentage points in Israel, and by less than one percentage point in Chile and the partner country Brazil.

In several countries that had above-average proportions of top performers in 2000, this percentage decreased. The most noticeable change was in Ireland, where the proportion of top performers decreased from 14% to 7%, which is below the OECD-26 average. In Australia, Canada, Finland and New Zealand, the decrease was smaller and all these countries still have more top performers than the OECD average for the 26 countries that have comparable results from both assessments. This proportion decreased in Norway and Sweden from a similar level of 11% in 2000 to 9% in Sweden and 8% in Norway. The proportion of top performers decreased from 8% to less than 5% in Denmark and from 7% to 5% in the Czech Republic. Interestingly, in Denmark, the proportion of students below Level 2 also decreased. The partner country Romania is the only country where the proportion of top performers decreased from an already low level, from 2% to less than 1%.

While trends in proficiency levels compare the highest- and the lowest-performing students with an absolute measure, it is also possible to compare the top and bottom ends of the performance distribution relative to the average student *within* a country. This is particularly useful in countries with very low or high overall levels of student performance, in which international benchmarks for the highest- and the lowest-performing students may be less relevant. Such within-country comparisons can be facilitated by analysing the percentiles of the

student performance distribution within a country. Percentiles do not indicate what students can do; they provide quantitative information on the performance of the lowest- or the highest-achieving students relative to other students in a country.

The 90th percentile indicates the point on the PISA performance scale below which 90% of students in a country score or which only 10% of students exceed. Changes in the value of the 90th percentile show whether a country saw an increase or decrease in the performance level of its highest-performing students. Similarly, the 10th percentile indicates the point on the PISA performance scale below which only 10% of students in a country score. A change in the value of the 10th percentile indicates whether a country sees an increase or decrease in the performance level of its lowest-performing students.

The difference between the 90th and 10th percentiles can be used as a measure of the range of performance in each country. Trends in this difference show whether the variation in student performance within the country is changing.

Performance at key percentile ranks can change even if a country's mean performance remains the same.

Figure V.2.6 classifies countries into four groups (see also Table V.2.3). Countries in the top-right corner show improved performance among both their highest- and lowest-achieving students, while countries in the bottom-

■ Figure V.2.6 ■

Performance changes among the lowest- and highest-achieving students in reading between 2000 and 2009

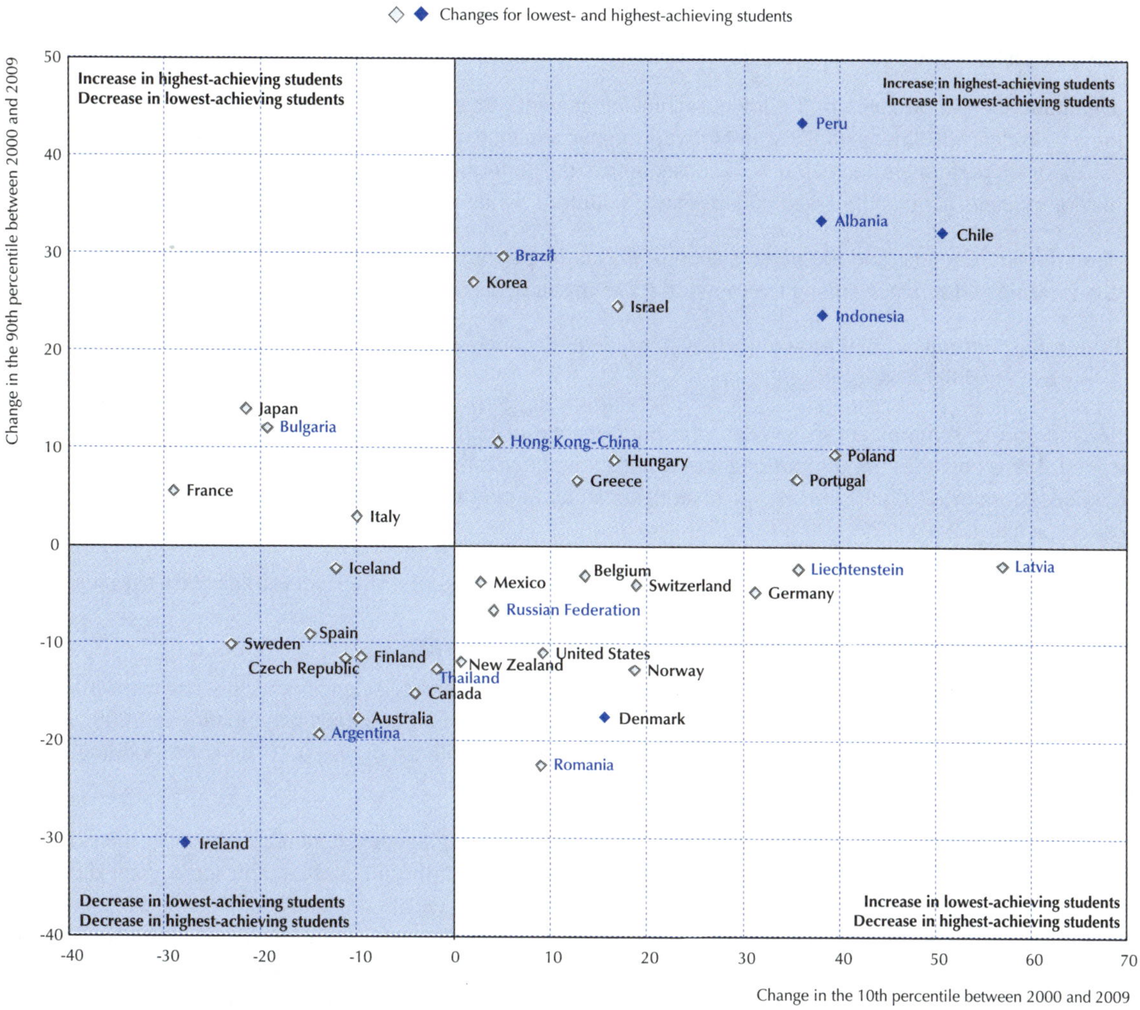

Note: Changes for both lowest- and highest-achieving students that are statistically significant are marked in darker tone.

Source: OECD, *PISA 2009 Database*, Table V.2.3.

StatLink http://dx.doi.org/10.1787/888932359967

left corner show a decline in performance among both groups of students. Countries in the top-left corner show improvements in performance among their highest-achieving students and a decline in the performance of their lowest-achieving students. In these countries, variation in performance increased because of the widening gap between the top and the bottom levels of student performance. Countries in the bottom-right corner show an improvement in performance among their lowest-achieving students and a decline among their highest-achieving students. In these countries, the variation in performance diminished. Most of the countries, however, are situated in the top-right or bottom-left corners, indicating that performance trends among their lowest- and highest-achieving students in these countries are similar. Countries indicated with blue markers showed statistically significant changes in the performance of both their highest- and lowest-achieving students. Countries indicated with white markers did not see statistically significant changes or saw them for either the highest- or the lowest-achieving students, but not for both.

Chile and three partner countries, Indonesia, Albania and Peru, all show marked improvements in reading performance among both their lowest- and highest-achieving students. These countries are also among those that show the largest improvement in mean performance and in which the percentage of students performing below Level 2 decreased. The lowest-achieving students show relatively larger improvements than the highest-achieving students in Chile and Indonesia, while in Peru and Albania both groups of students show similar levels of improvement. In short, in these countries, students across the entire performance scale improved.

Six countries – Poland, Portugal, Germany, Switzerland, and the partner countries Latvia and Liechtenstein – saw improvements in the performance of their lowest-achieving students while maintaining the performance level among the highest-achieving students.

Korea, Israel, and the partner country Brazil raised the performance of their highest-achieving students while maintaining the performance level among the lowest-achieving students.

In Denmark, the performance of the lowest-achieving students improved, while the performance of the highest-achieving students declined. Similarly, in Norway, the performance of the lowest-achieving students improved and the share of top performers decreased. As a consequence, the performance gap between the lowest- and the highest-achieving students narrowed markedly in these two countries, while their mean performance did not change.

In Australia and Canada, and the partner country Romania, performance among their highest-achieving students declined while performance among their lowest-achieving students remained largely unchanged.

In France, the performance of the lowest-achieving students declined while the performance of the highest-achieving students remained the same.

In Ireland and to some extent in Sweden, the performance of both the lowest- and highest-achieving students declined. These countries are also among those that show the greatest decrease in mean performance results and are among those in which the percentage of students at the highest proficiency levels fell while the percentage of those below Level 2 rose.

For the rest of the countries, performance among the lowest- and the highest-achieving students did not change measurably.

HOW GENDER DIFFERENCES IN READING HAVE EVOLVED

The gender gap is far wider in reading than it is in either mathematics or science, and this has been true since the first PISA assessment in 2000. Girls outperform boys in reading in all countries participating in 2009, with an average advantage of 39 score points across OECD countries (see Table V.2.4). In 2000, the corresponding gender gap was 32 score points, on average, across OECD countries.

The gender gap widened in some countries, but it did not narrow in any country. It increased by more than 20 score points in Israel and Korea and the partner country Romania. In all of these countries, the score point difference between boys and girls at least doubled. In Israel and Korea, the gap widened because of a marked improvement in girls' performance that was not matched by a similar trend among boys (see Box V.B, which discusses changes in girls' performance in Korea). The performance advantage among girls also increased in Portugal, the partner economy, Hong Kong-China, and the partner countries, Indonesia and Brazil, where the overall positive trend was due, in part, to a greater improvement among girls in comparison with boys. The gender gap also widened in France and Sweden, mainly because of a decline in boys' performance.

■ Figure V.2.7 ■

Comparison of gender differences in reading between 2000 and 2009

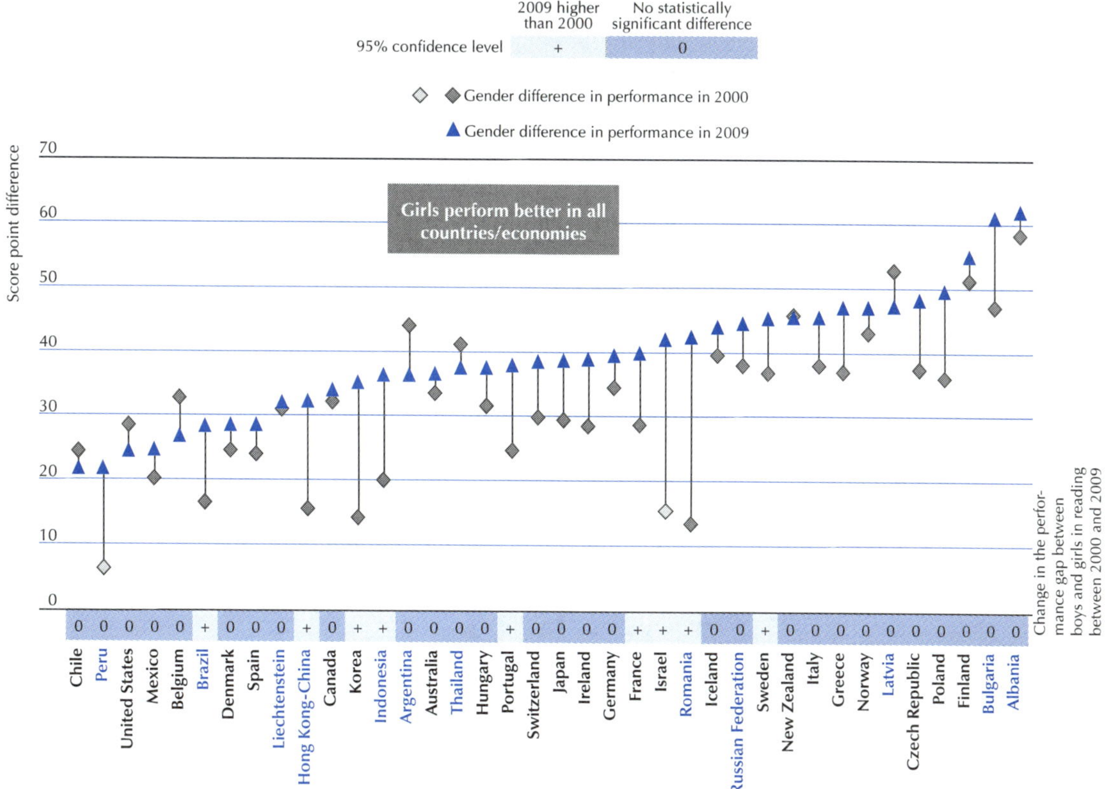

Notes: All gender differences in PISA 2009 are significant. Gender differences in 2000 that are statistically significant are marked in a darker tone.
Countries are ranked in ascending order of gender differences (girls - boys) in 2009.
Source: OECD, *PISA Database 2009*, Table V.2.4.
StatLink http://dx.doi.org/10.1787/888932359967

None of the countries where the advantage of girls increased is among those with the widest gender gaps. However, after the changes in the relative performance of boys and girls in Romania and Israel, the gender gap has become wider in these countries than on average across OECD countries, while it had previously been narrower.

In general, girls' performance advantage in reading is most pronounced in the percentage of students who perform below Level 2 (Tables V.2.5 and V.2.6). Across OECD countries, 24% of boys perform below Level 2 compared to only 12% of girls. Policy makers in many countries are already concerned about the large percentage of boys who lack basic reading skills. Therefore, any increase in this share is worth noting.

Figure V.2.8 shows changes in the percentages of boys and girls who perform below Level 2 in reading. Countries are sorted according to the overall trend among lower-performing students, with those where their numbers have fallen most shown on the left.

Across OECD countries, the percentage of girls performing below Level 2 decreased by two percentage points, while the share of lower-performing boys did not change.

In nearly all countries where there was a decrease in the percentage of students performing below Level 2, this trend was usually more apparent among girls. In Indonesia, the overall decrease in the percentage of students performing below Level 2 was around 15 percentage points; but while the percentage of girls performing below Level 2 decreased by 21 percentage points, the percentage of boys performing at that level decreased by only 9 percentage points. Similarly, in Peru and Albania, the share of girls performing below Level 2 decreased by 19 and 17 percentage points, respectively, whereas the corresponding share of boys decreased by 11 and 12 percentage points, respectively. In Israel and Brazil, the overall decrease in the share of students performing below Level 2

■ Figure V.2.8 ■

Change in the share of boys and girls who are low performers in reading between 2000 and 2009

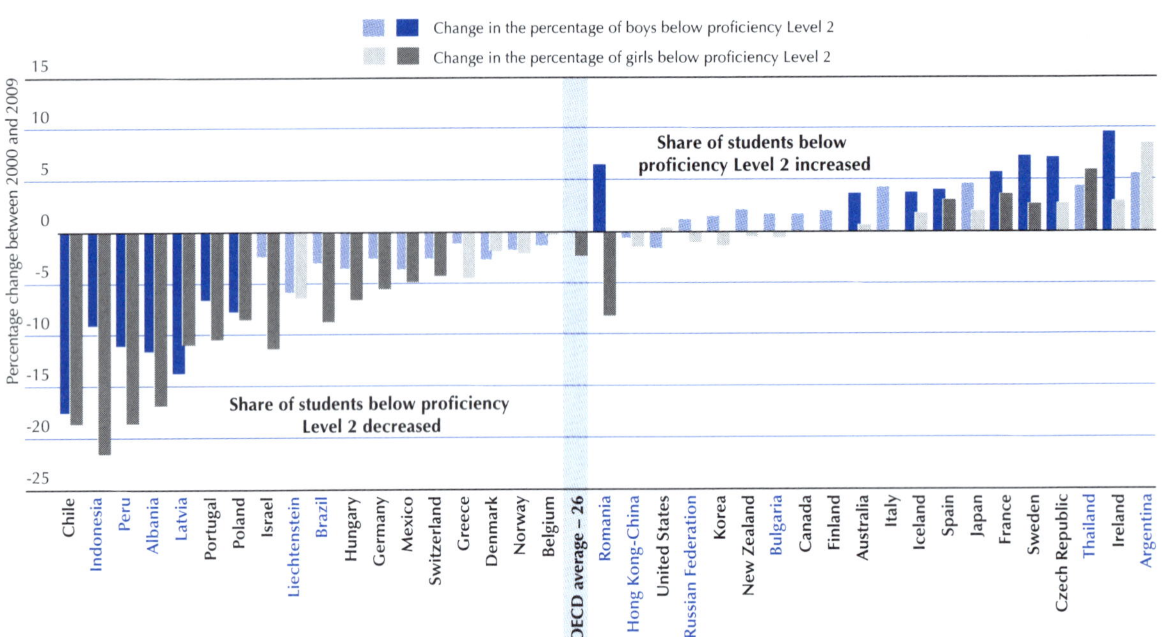

Note: Changes in the share of students below proficiency Level 2 that are statistically significant are marked in a darker tone.
Countries are ranked in ascending order of change in the percentage of all students below Level 2 on the reading scale between 2000 and 2009.
Source: OECD, *PISA 2009 Database*, Table V.2.2. Table V.2.5 and Table V.2.6.
StatLink http://dx.doi.org/10.1787/888932359967

was also mainly the result of improvements among girls, with 11 and 9 percentage points fewer girls, respectively, performing below Level 2. The decrease in the percentage of boys performing below Level 2 in these countries was more modest, at two and three percentage points, respectively.

In Chile and Poland, the percentage of boys and girls below Level 2 decreased by about the same amount.

In another set of countries, the percentage of students below Level 2 has risen. In Sweden, France and Spain, this increase has occurred for both boys and girls although it has been greater for boys. In Ireland, the Czech Republic and Iceland, only the percentage of boys with a reading proficiency below Level 2 has risen. In Thailand, on the other hand, it has risen slightly for girls but not for boys.

In most countries, changes in the percentage of top-performing students, those at reading proficiency Level 5 or 6, are quite similar among boys and girls, but in a few countries they differ noticeably (Tables V.2.5 and V.2.6). For example, while in Denmark and Romania the decrease in the percentage of top performers was almost identical among boys and girls, it differed in magnitude in Finland, Australia, Canada and Ireland. In New Zealand, only the percentage of top performers among girls decreased significantly, while in the Czech Republic and Germany, only the percentage of top performers among boys decreased significantly.

Although the percentage of top performers increased in Japan and Korea and the partner economy Hong Kong-China to similarly high levels, the increase was very different among boys and girls. In Korea, the increase was the largest when looking at all students, but also when looking separately at boys and girls. Nonetheless, the percentage of top performers increased among girls by more than nine percentage points and among boys by slightly less than five percentage points. In Hong Kong-China, the percentage of top performers among girls increased by more than six percentage points, while it did not change among boys. Similarly, in Japan, this proportion increased by almost five percentage points among girls, more than among boys. Effectively, the gap in the proportion of top performers among boys and girls widened in these countries.

CHANGES IN PERFORMANCE AND CHANGES IN STUDENT POPULATIONS

The PISA assessments continue to evolve, to capture newly emerging knowledge and skills as the learning goals and instructional practices of countries change, reflecting methodological advances. At the same time, PISA implements high technical standards and coherence in methodologies across successive assessments, ensuring that performance can be monitored reliably over time and that the samples of students are representative of the same populations.

However, in many countries the demographic and socio-economic context of student populations has changed. Thus, observed changes in learning outcomes may not only reflect changes in the quality of the educational services provided for 15-year-olds, but also changes in the composition of the student populations. For example, if migration into a country has been significant over the past ten years, it might influence learning outcomes. Similarly, if the student population has become more socio-economically diverse, then this too can influence outcomes.

This section discusses how trends are affected by changes in student populations. It also provides an overall trend line that summarises information across all PISA assessments. Annex A6 provides details on methods used in this section. It also discusses any impact that technical changes in the national samples of students may have on the comparability of student performance over time.

THE IMPACT OF CHANGES IN THE SOCIO-ECONOMIC COMPOSITION OF STUDENT POPULATIONS ON TRENDS IN READING PERFORMANCE

In the following section, changes in the age and gender composition of students, the socio-economic background of student populations, changes in the share of students who always or almost always speak the language of the assessment at home, and changes in the share of students with foreign-born parents are accounted for when interpreting changes in student performance. The corresponding demographic data for 2000 and 2009 are presented in Annex A6 where the adjustment method is also explained in detail. The data on changes in socio-economic background are provided in Table V.4.2.

Figure V.2.9 shows both the observed change in student performance and the predicted performance change if the composition of the student population in 2000 had been similar to the one in 2009, that is, if the student population in 2000 had the same age and gender composition, the same socio-economic background and the same share of

■ Figure V.2.9 ■

Changes in reading performance between 2000 and 2009

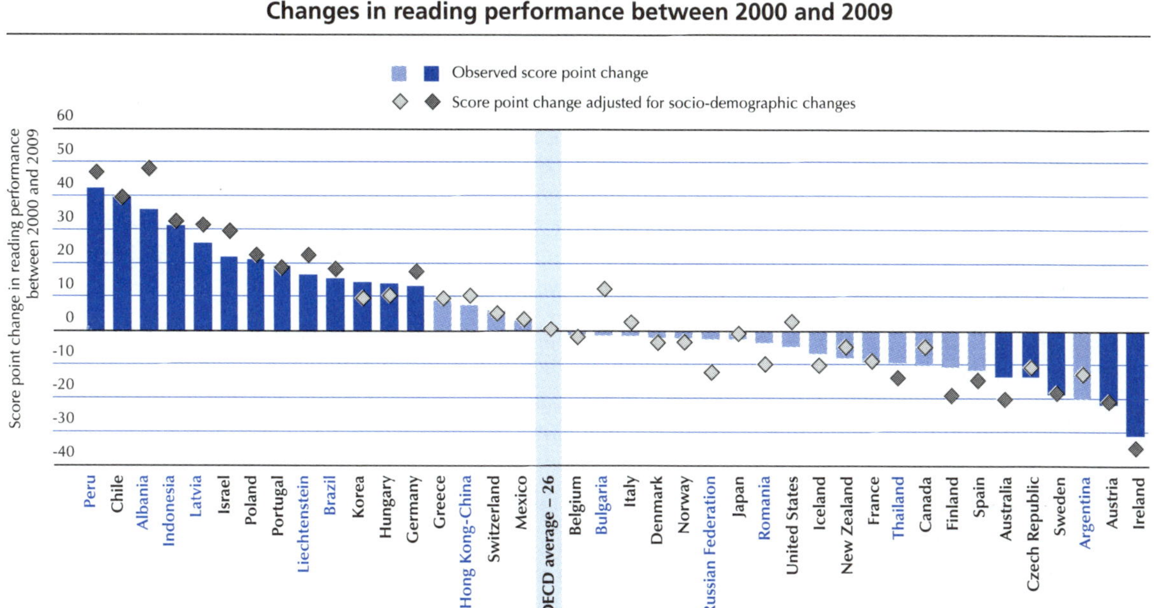

Note: Observed score point changes that are statistically significant are marked in a darker tone.
Countries are ranked in descending order of the observed score point change between 2000 and 2009.
Source: OECD, *PISA 2009 Database*, Table V.2.7.
StatLink http://dx.doi.org/10.1787/888932359967

students with an immigrant background as in 2009 (see also Table V.2.7). The observed change is represented by bars, while the predicted change adjusted for changes in the composition of the student body is denoted by markers. Countries are sorted by the observed change in reading performance.

Among countries that showed improvements in reading performance, changes in the demographic and socio-economic composition of student populations had the largest impact in Israel and the partner country Albania, where the improvement in student performance would have been seven and 12 score points larger, respectively, if the demographic and socio-economic context had been similar in 2000 and 2009 (see Tables V.2.1 and V.2.7).[2] In Germany and the partner countries Liechtenstein, Latvia and Peru, the adjusted performance improvement was larger by around five score points. In these countries, student performance would have increased more rapidly than the performance increase that was actually observed if the changes in the demographic and socio-economic composition of the student population had been accounted for. This is explained by the fact that within these countries, in 2009 the student population had a more disadvantaged background than in 2000 (see Table V.4.2 and Annex A6).

In Australia and Ireland, student performance would have declined more rapidly than actually observed if the changes in the socio-economic composition of the student population had been accounted for. In Finland, the results suggest performance decline when accounting for changes in student demographic and socio-economic characteristics. This is explained by the fact that, in 2009, the student population in these countries was more socio-economically advantaged than in 2000. In Hungary and Korea, adjusting for the socio-economic background of students reduces the estimate of a positive trend. In Thailand and Spain, the change in performance becomes negative after those adjustments, while it was insignificant without them.

ESTABLISHING AN OVERALL ESTIMATE OF READING PERFORMANCE TRENDS

Reading performance data across all PISA assessments can be combined into a single trend indicator. The results are provided in Table V.2.8 for both the observed performance of students in reading and for the performance after accounting for the above demographic and socio-economic characteristics. The resulting trends have been annualised, so the data reflect the performance changes for a single year. Annex A6 provides details on the methods used to obtain linear trends.

Figure V.2.10 compares these linear trends with annualised performance differences between 2000 and 2009. Four countries increased their reading performance when considering results from all assessments. In Korea, the linear trend suggests larger improvements, with the linear trend larger by 0.6 score points than the annualised performance difference between 2000 and 2009. This is due to rapid improvement in performance until 2006 followed by a slight decline in 2009. In the partner economy Hong Kong-China, the linear trend shows a rise of one score point per year between 2000 and 2009. After an initial decline in 2003, performance in Hong Kong-China improved in 2006 and was still higher in 2009. In Poland and Chile, linear trends also show slightly larger improvements. In Poland, this reflects a pattern similar to that seen in Korea, but with smaller changes. In Chile, the data demonstrate a large improvement between 2000 and 2006 followed by a much smaller change between the last two assessments.

For Israel and the partner countries Liechtenstein, Latvia and Brazil, the linear trends show smaller or even insignificant increases than the observed performance difference between 2000 and 2009. This is because in these countries, performance varied considerably across successive PISA assessments.

In Spain and the partner country Argentina, the linear trend is more negative than the difference in performance between 2000 and 2009. In Spain, this is due to a steady decline in performance from 2000 to 2006 and to recent improvements in 2009, with the mean performance still lower than it was in 2000. Similar patterns can be found in Argentina, with a decline between 2000 and 2006, followed by a smaller recent improvement.

COUNTRY-BY-COUNTRY COMPARISON OF READING TRENDS

Figures V.2.11, V.2.12 and V.2.13 summarise changes in the distribution of reading performance. The overall trend in mean performance between 2000 and 2009 is summarised by the dashed line, which corresponds to the linear trend discussed in the previous section. Where the dashed line is bold, mean performance has improved or declined in statistically significant ways. The constant line shows changes in the overall performance between successive PISA assessments.

Performance trends for the lowest-achieving students are represented in the bottom part of the figure. The bottom margin of the dark blue area denotes performance at the 10th percentile and the bottom dark part denotes the performance range between the 10th and 25th percentiles. The top margin of the dark blue area denotes performance at the 90th percentile and the top dark part denotes the performance range between the 90th and 75th percentile. The range between the 10th and 90th percentiles represents the variation of student performance, so the narrower the blue area, the less diverse the reading performance in a particular assessment. Changes in the range covered by the blue area demonstrate trends in performance.

In Figures V.2.11, V.2.12 and V.2.13, countries are grouped by performance so one can compare changes in the distribution of performance in any one country with countries with similar overall performance. Figure V.2.11 shows countries with mean performance above the OECD average, Figure V.2.12 countries with mean performance around the OECD average and Figure V.2.13 countries with mean performance below the OECD average.

■ Figure V.2.10 ■

Linear trends and performance differences between 2000 and 2009

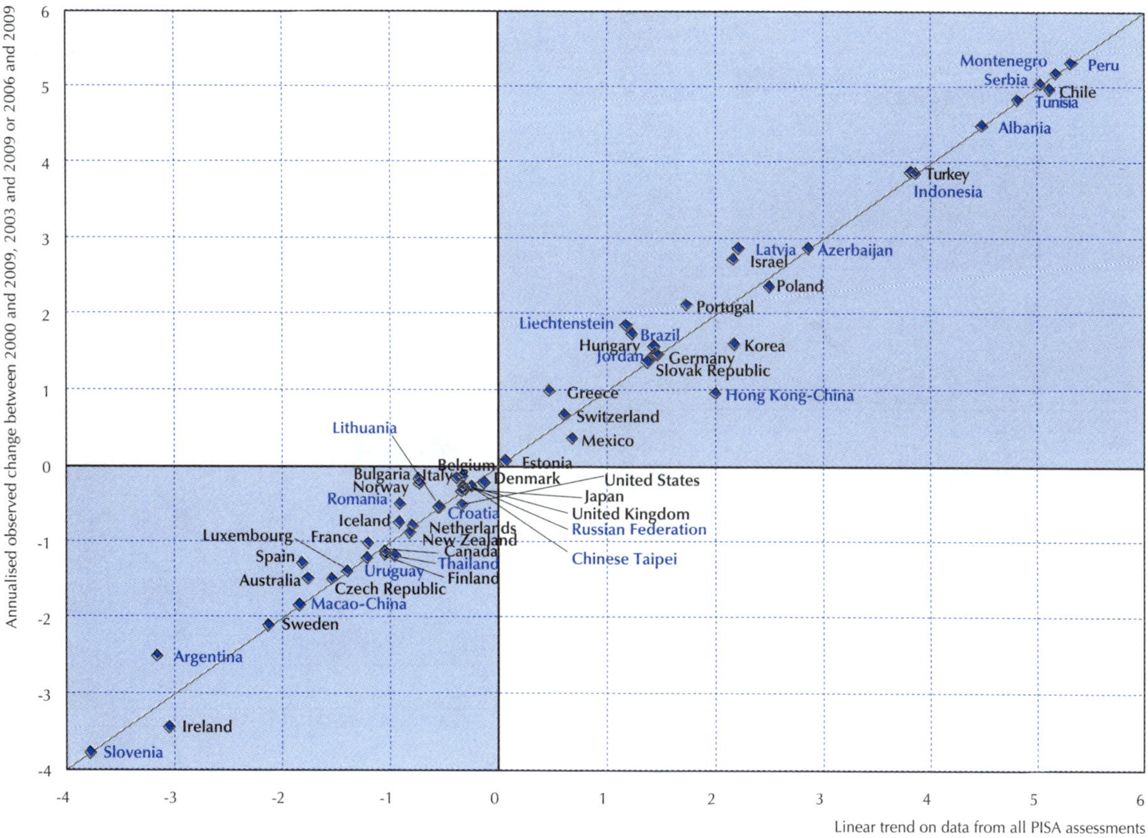

Annualised observed change between 2000 and 2009, 2003 and 2009 or 2006 and 2009

Linear trend on data from all PISA assessments

Source: OECD, *PISA 2009 Database*, Table V.2.8.

StatLink http://dx.doi.org/10.1787/888932359967

From these country-by-country figures one can see that countries differ not only in how reading performance evolved for the average student, but also how performance trends for the highest-performing and the lowest-performing students differ. For example, two OECD countries, Korea and Poland, that perform above the average, having shown huge improvements since 2000, differ not only in the average performance and the magnitude of the trends, but also in terms of how different groups of students in those countries evolved over time. Both countries improved between 2000 and 2006 and declined slightly between 2006 and 2009. Nonetheless, in both countries, overall trends are significant and positive. While the trend in Korea was largely driven by improvements among the highest-achieving students with no change among the lowest-achieving, in Poland, the lowest-achieving students

■ Figure V.2.11 [Part 1/2] ■

Trends in reading performance: countries above the OECD average

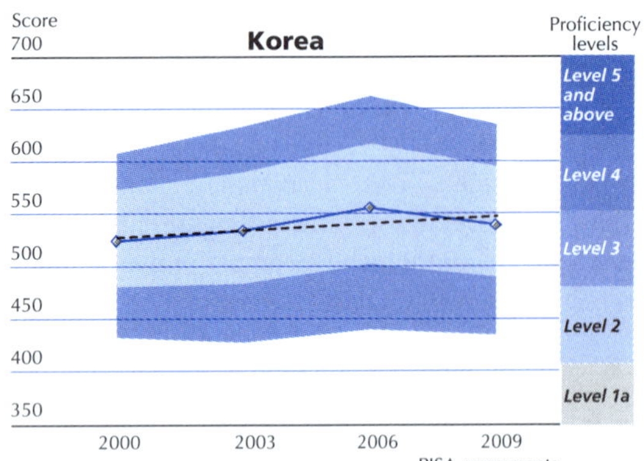

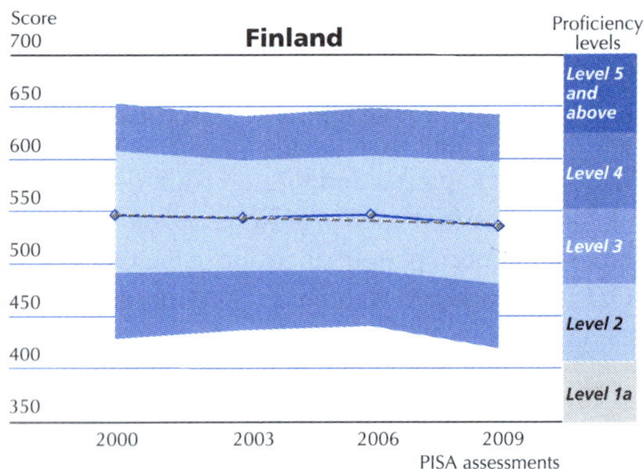

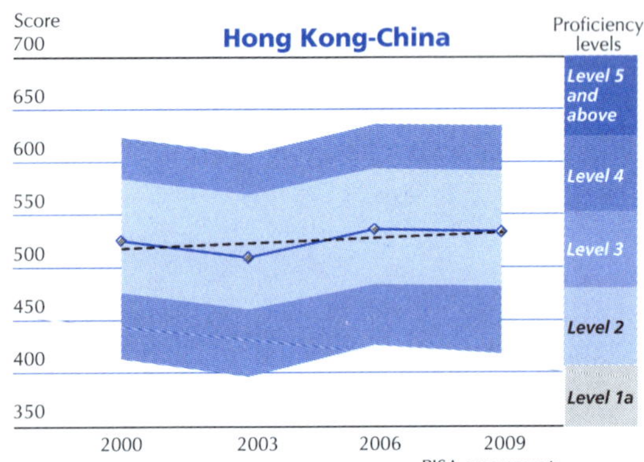

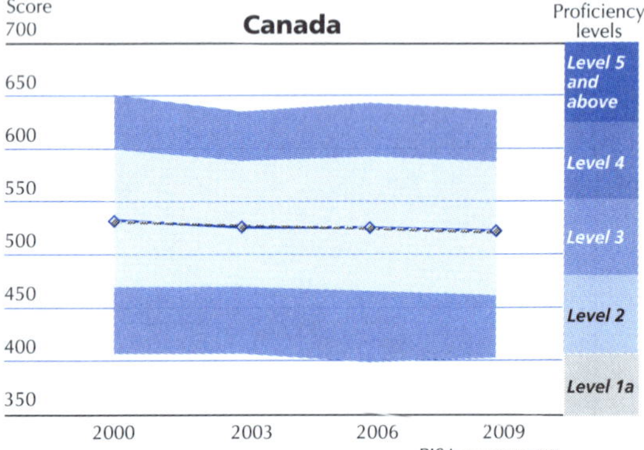

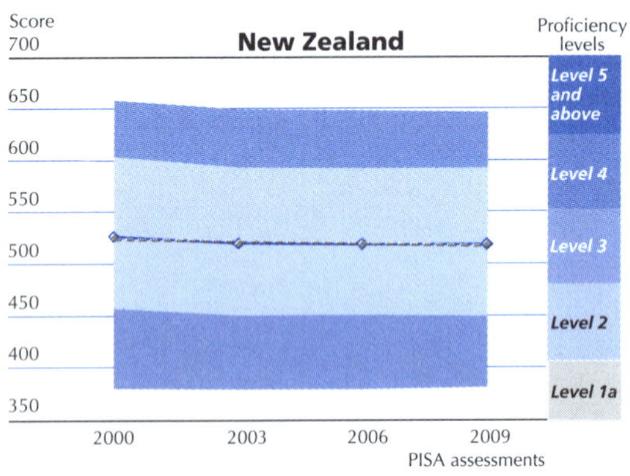

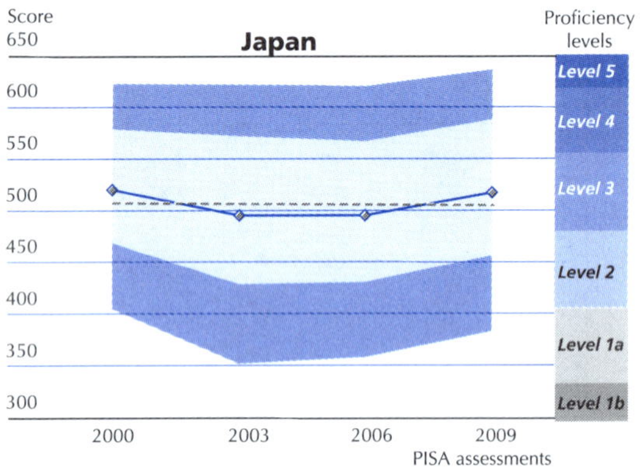

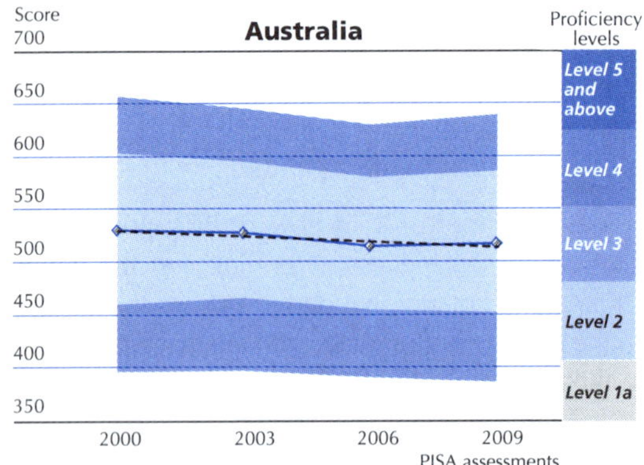

Source: OECD, *PISA 2000, 2003, 2006, 2009 Databases*

StatLink http://dx.doi.org/10.1787/888932359967

■ Figure V.2.11 [Part 2/2] ■

Trends in reading performance: countries above the OECD average

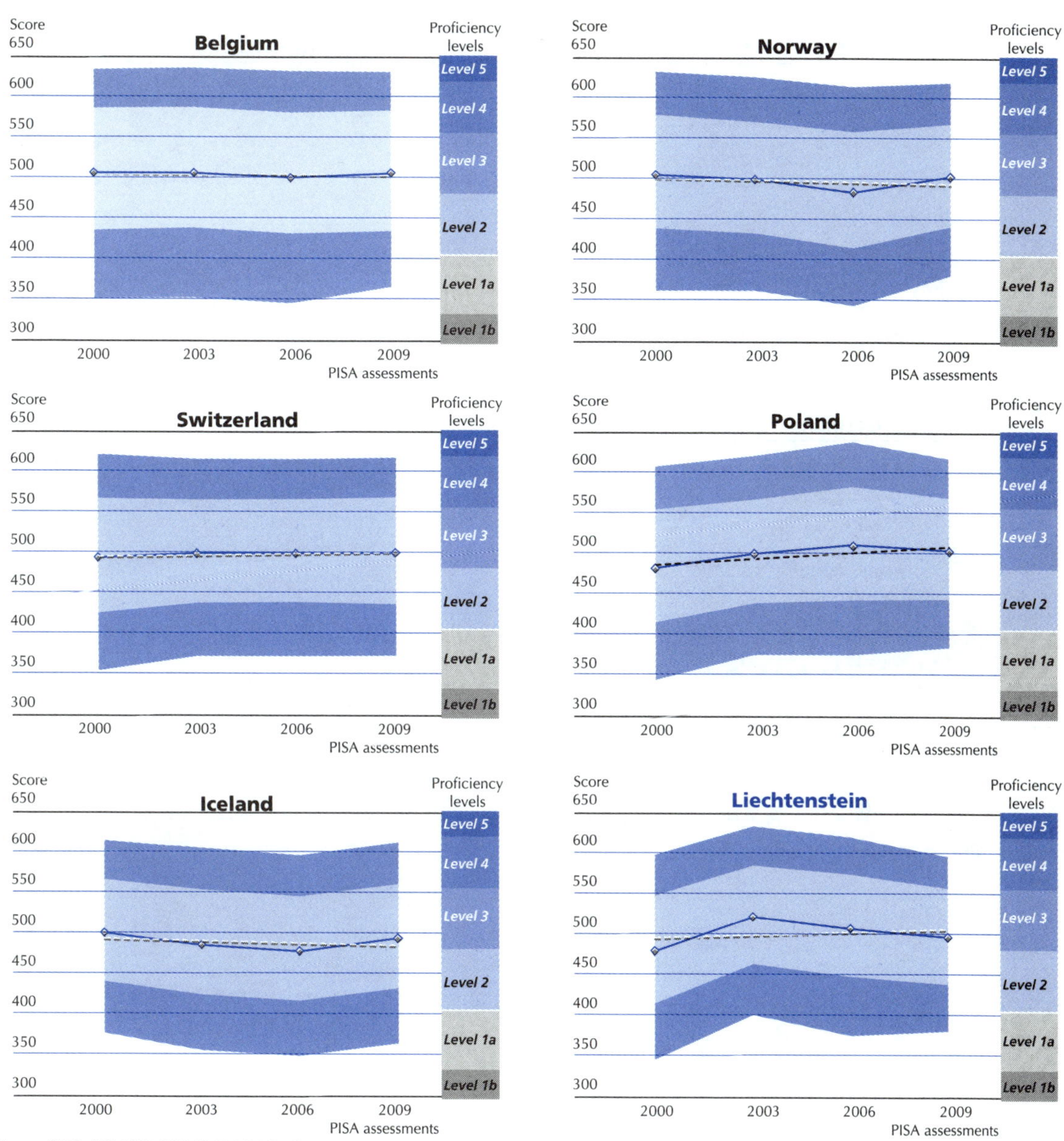

Source: OECD, *PISA 2000, 2003, 2006, 2009 Databases*

StatLink http://dx.doi.org/10.1787/888932359967

increased their scores and there was no significant change among the highest-achieving students. When comparing figures for these two countries, it is also clear that, although the gap between the highest- and the lowest-achieving students in Korea widened, the opposite was true in Poland, such that the resulting performance gaps in Korea are still smaller than those in Poland.

■ Figure V.2.12 ■

Trends in reading performance: countries at the OECD average

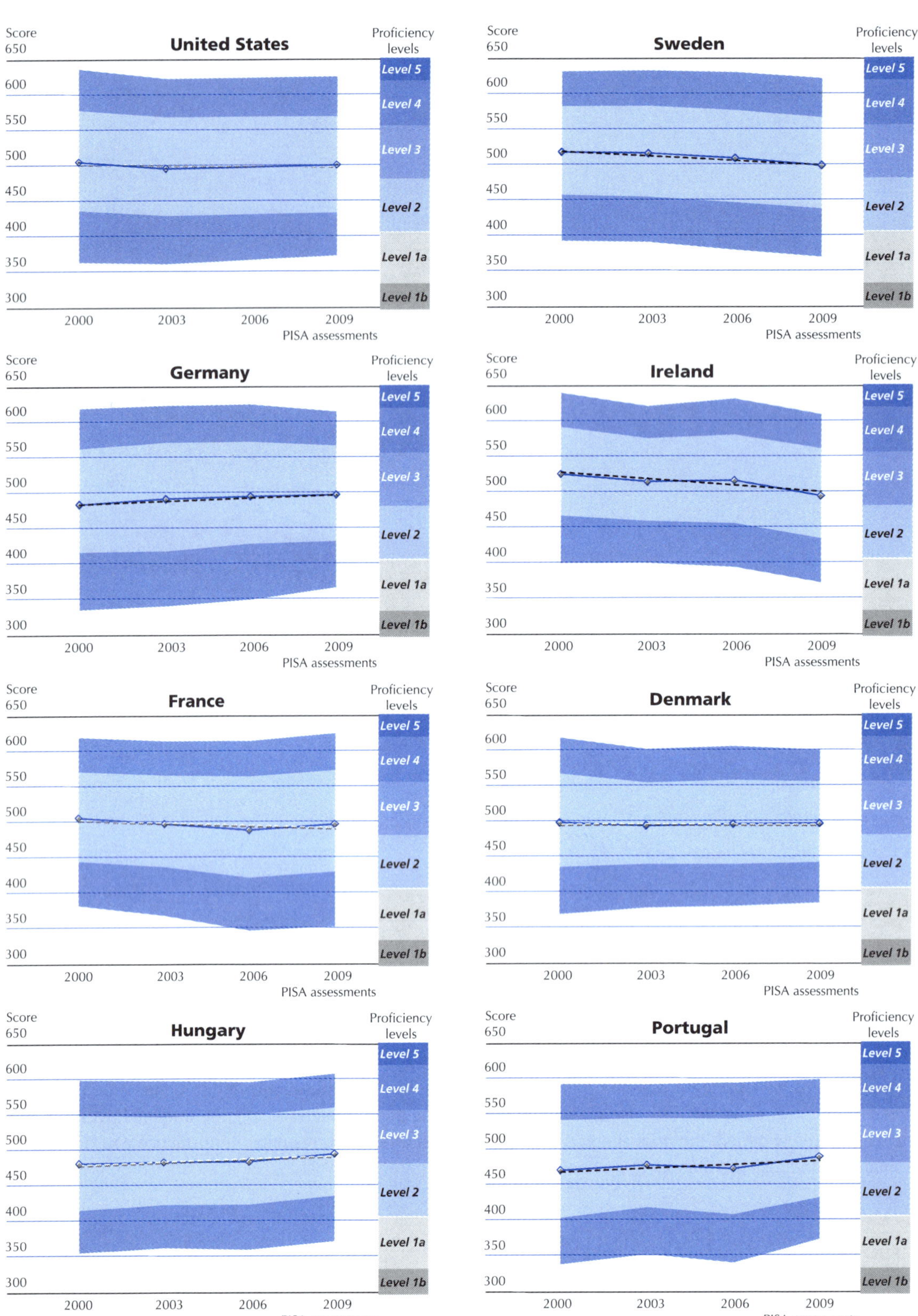

Source: OECD, *PISA 2000, 2003, 2006, 2009 Databases*.

StatLink http://dx.doi.org/10.1787/888932359967

■ Figure V.2.13 [Part 1/3] ■

Trends in reading performance: countries below the OECD average

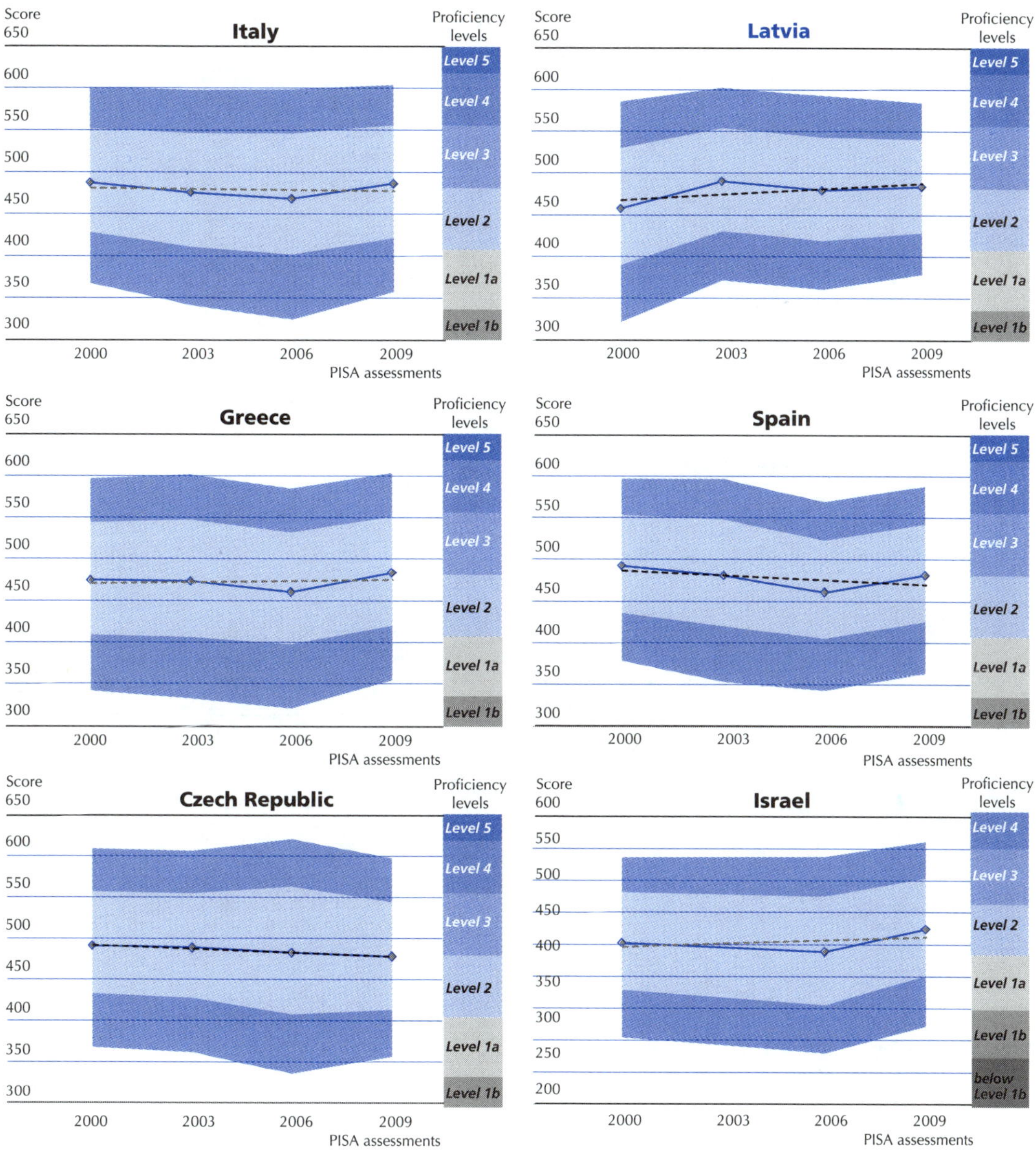

Source: OECD, *PISA 2000, 2003, 2006, 2009 Databases.*

StatLink http://dx.doi.org/10.1787/888932359967

■ Figure V.2.13 [Part 2/3] ■

Trends in reading performance: countries below the OECD average

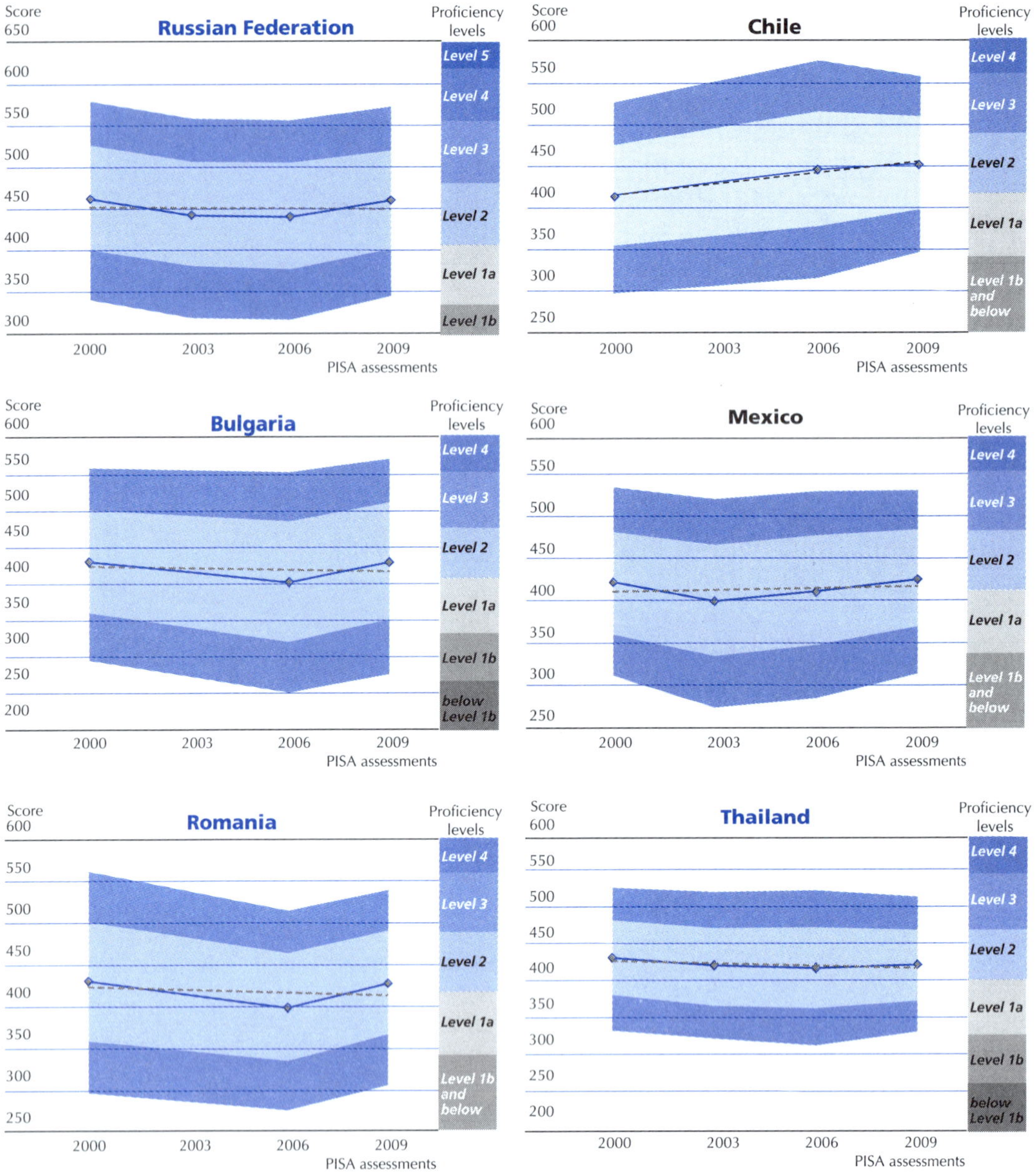

Russian Federation

Chile

Bulgaria

Mexico

Romania

Thailand

Source: OECD, *PISA 2000, 2003, 2006, 2009 Databases.*

StatLink http://dx.doi.org/10.1787/888932359967

■ Figure V.2.13 [Part 3/3] ■

Trends in reading performance: countries below the OECD average

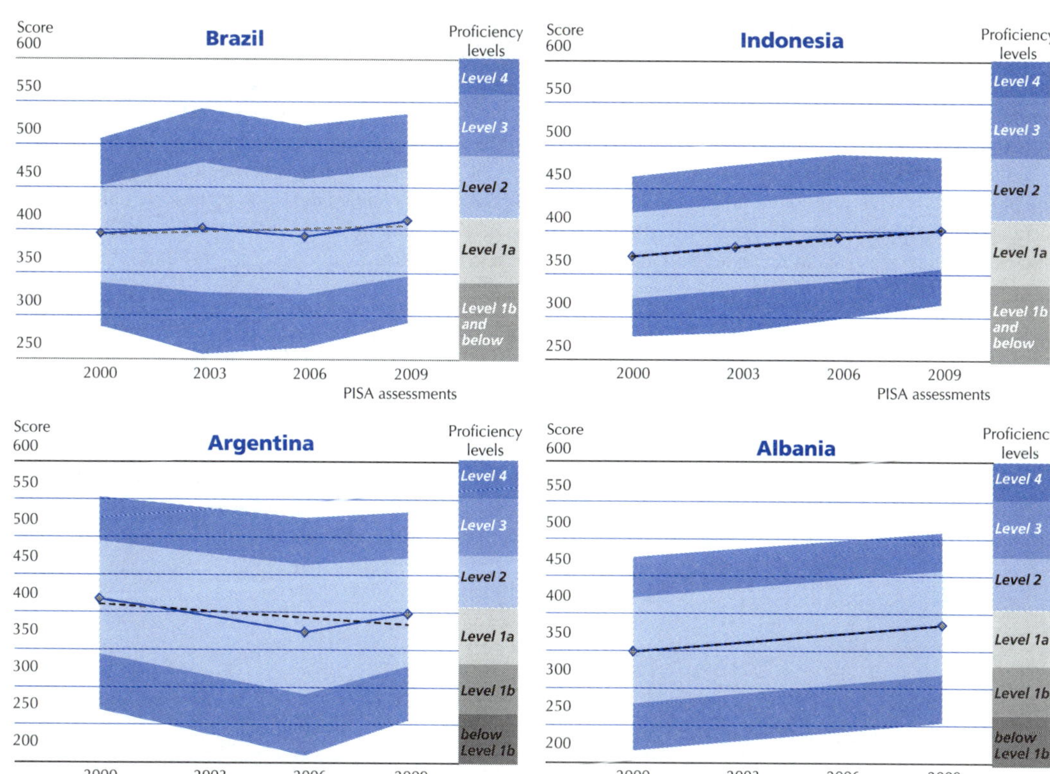

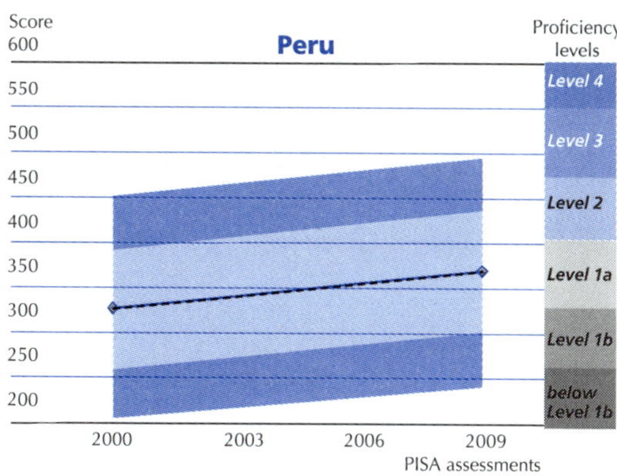

Source: OECD, *PISA 2000, 2003, 2006, 2009 Databases.*

StatLink http://dx.doi.org/10.1787/888932359967

Notes

1. The 2000 results for Luxembourg, the Netherlands and the United Kingdom are not considered here because of methodological problems that invalidate comparisons over time. Austrian data were corrected after publishing the PISA 2000 report; however, because of student boycotts, 2009 data were considered to be not comparable to those from previous assessments, so the trends for Austria are not discussed. Chile and Israel participated in PISA 2000. These countries joined the OECD recently, and for 2000 results reported in this volume are considered as OECD countries. The Slovak Republic and Turkey, which joined the OECD after 2000, did not participate in PISA 2000, so they are excluded from OECD averages for trends between 2000 and 2009. While the reading performance scale was not modified, it now has a mean of 496 and a standard deviation of 96 score points for the group of 26 countries that have comparable results from both the 2000 and 2009 assessments and that are now OECD members. More detailed explanations are given in Annex A5 and in the introduction to this volume.

2. Israel shows a seven percentage-point decline in the weighted percentage of girls assessed by PISA. Moreover, the socio-economic background of students in 2000 was more advantegous than in 2009. Overall, the adjusted 2000 results were lower than the original ones, which led to an increase in adjusted trends in comparison to observed ones. The sampling design for Israel in the PISA 2000 assessment did not account for the gender composition of schools, despite the different participation rates between boys and girls in Israel due to the fact that in some schools boys were not allowed to take part in the assessment. The gender distribution in the PISA 2000 data for Israel was subject to a relatively large sampling variance due to an inefficient sampling design. This section takes this into account by adjusting results for 2000 so that the gender distribution is comparable to the one observed in 2009. Nevertheless, trends in the socio-economic background of students and in the percentage of students with an immigrant background also played an important role in the observed performance changes for Israel.

3

Trends in Mathematics and Science

Changes in mathematics and science performance are smaller than those in reading, since performance in these two subjects is measured over a shorter period of time. This chapter describes trends in mathematics performance between 2003 and 2009, and trends in science performance between 2006 and 2009.

TRENDS IN MATHEMATICS

How student performance in mathematics has changed since 2003

Trends in performance in mathematics are derived by comparing results from PISA 2009 with those from the 2003 and 2006 assessments. Since trends in mathematics start in 2003, as opposed to trends in reading, which start in 2000, performance changes in mathematics since 2003 are expected to be smaller than performance changes in reading since 2000. PISA 2003 provides results in mathematics that were measured with more precision than in PISA 2006 and PISA 2009, since the latter two surveys devoted less assessment time to mathematics. Thus, trends in mathematics are not discussed in as much detail as the results for reading. The PISA 2003 mean score for mathematics for OECD countries was set at 500 and the standard deviation was set at 100, establishing the scale against which mathematics performance in PISA 2009 is compared. Most results in mathematics presented in this section discuss the difference between 2003 and 2009 assessments.

In terms of the OECD average, mathematics performance remained unchanged between 2003 and 2009 (Table V.3.1). However, several countries show marked changes in mathematics performance.

Students in 8 of the 39 countries with comparable results in both the 2003 and 2009 assessments show improvements in mathematics performance. This includes 6 out of the 28 OECD countries with valid data for both assessments. Students in Mexico improved their performance by 33 score points; students in Turkey, Greece and Portugal by more than 20 score points; and students in Italy and Germany by 17 and 10 score points, respectively. Among partner countries and economies, students in Brazil improved their performance by 30 score points, while students in Tunisia scored 13 score points higher (see Box V.G on Brazil).

In nine countries, mathematics performance in 2009 was significantly lower than in 2003. In the Czech Republic, students' scores decreased by 24 score points. In Ireland, Sweden, France, Belgium, the Netherlands and Denmark, students' scores in mathematics decreased by between 11 and 16 score points. In Australia student scores decreased by 10 score points, and in Iceland they decreased by 8 score points.

■ Figure V.3.1 ■

Change in mathematics performance between 2003 and 2009

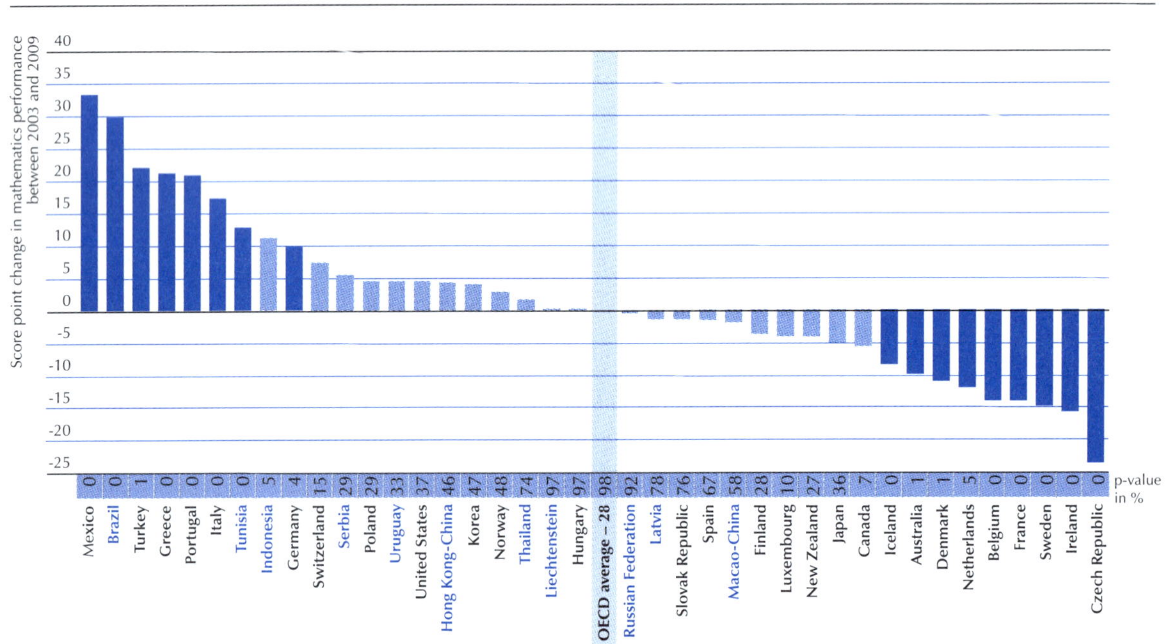

Note: Statistically significant score point changes are marked in a darker tone.
Countries are ranked in descending order of the score point change on the mathematical scale between 2003 and 2009.
Source: OECD, *PISA 2009 Database*, Table V.3.1
StatLink http://dx.doi.org/10.1787/888932359986

In 22 countries, performance in mathematics remained unchanged between 2003 and 2009, when considering a 95% confidence level. For those countries where the changes are not statistically significant, Figure V.3.1 provides the p-value, which allows the reader to interpret the score point differences.

Even countries that show improvements in mathematics performance can still perform below the OECD average, while those that show a decline in performance can continue to outperform others. Examined together, performance levels and trends provide a fuller picture of how student performance has evolved.

The relative standing of countries according to their mean performance in mathematics and the observed changes in mathematics performance are shown in Figure V.3.2. Countries towards the right side improved their performance since 2003, while those towards the left side showed a decrease in student scores. Countries towards the top end of the figure performed above the OECD average in 2009, while those towards the bottom end performed below the OECD average. A more detailed interpretation of this figure is given in Chapter 2 as it applies to Figure V.2.2.

None of the top-performing countries increased their scores in mathematics, and none of the lowest-performing countries saw a decline in their performance. In fact, seven out of the eight countries showing a significant improvement scored below the OECD average, both in 2003 and in 2009, while those showing a decline all started off with average or above-average mean scores.

Germany performed close to the OECD average in 2003, increased its performance by 10 score points between 2003 and 2009, and now performs above the OECD average. Portugal and Italy, which both scored 466 score points in 2003, increased their performance by 21 and 17 score points, respectively, and are now much closer to the OECD average (see Box V.D on policies implemented in Portugal).

■ Figure V.3.2 ■

How countries perform in mathematics and how mathematics performance has changed since 2003

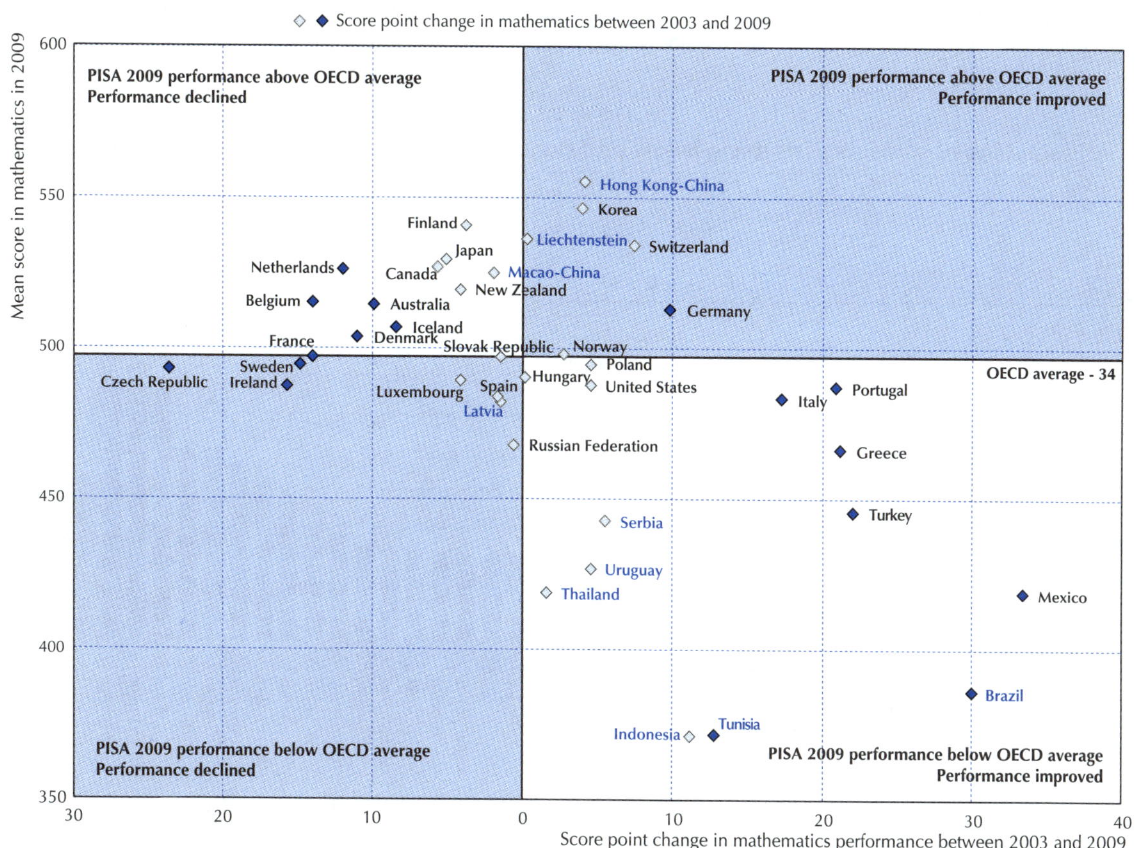

Note: Score point changes in mathematics between 2003 and 2009 that are statistically significant are marked in darker tone.
Source: OECD PISA 2009 database, Table V.3.1

StatLink http://dx.doi.org/10.1787/888932359986

The remaining five countries that performed below average in 2003 and improved their performance by 2009 showed a wide range in their mean scores. Mexico, the country with the largest improvement, increased student scores by 33 score points. While it now performs above 400 score points, it is still far below the OECD average. Turkey and Greece increased their performance by slightly more than 20 score points, now scoring at 445 and 466, respectively. Among partner countries, Brazil increased its performance in mathematics by 30 score points, and Tunisia by more than 10 score points. Yet both countries still perform below 400 score points.

A number of countries that score above the OECD average show a decline in mathematics performance but still outperform many others. In the Netherlands, student scores decreased by 12 score points, but the Netherlands is still among the top-performing countries in PISA. Student scores in Belgium, Denmark, Australia and Iceland decreased by around 10 score points, and these countries now score closer to the OECD average albeit above it.

Several countries that performed above the OECD average in mathematics now score at or below the average level. The Czech Republic scored above the OECD average in 2003, but because of a decrease of 24 score points, it now scores slightly below the OECD average. France and Sweden both declined in performance and moved from the group of countries performing above the OECD average to the OECD average.

Changes in mean mathematics achievement describe overall trends, but can mask changes among the lowest- and the highest-achieving students. These can be analysed by looking at changes in the proportion of students reaching certain proficiency levels. As described in Chapter 2 for reading, for the purpose of these analyses, students below Level 2 were combined into a single category of lowest performers, while those at Level 5 or above were combined into another category of top performers. Changes in percentages in both categories were compared between 2003 and 2009.

The proficiency levels used in the PISA 2009 mathematics assessment are the same as those established for mathematics when it was the major area of assessment in 2003. The process used to produce proficiency levels in mathematics is similar to that used to produce proficiency levels in reading, as described in detail in Volume I, *What Students Know and Can Do.*

On average across the 28 OECD countries with comparable data for the 2003 and 2009 assessments, the share of students below Level 2 remained broadly similar, with a minor decrease from 21.6% to 20.8% (Table V.3.2).

■ Figure V.3.3 ■

Percentage of students performing below proficiency Level 2 in mathematics in 2003 and 2009

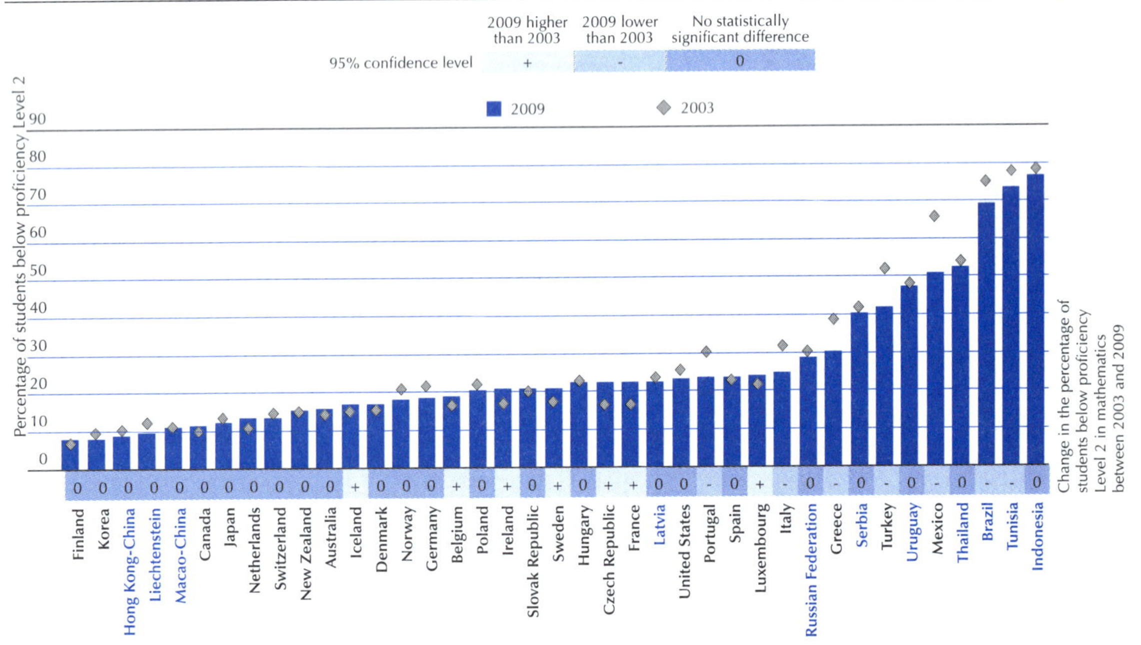

Countries are ranked in ascending order of the percentage of students below proficiency Level 2 in mathematics in 2009.
Source: OECD, *PISA 2009 Database*, Table V.3.2
StatLink http://dx.doi.org/10.1787/888932359986

Among the OECD countries in which more than half of students performed below Level 2 in 2003, this proportion decreased by 15 percentage points in Mexico, from 66% to 51%, while Turkey saw a 10 percentage point reduction, from 52% to 42% (see Box V.E on policies aimed at low-performing students in Turkey). In Greece, Italy and Portugal the percentage of lowest performers decreased by considerably less than in the countries mentioned above, but all these countries now all show 30% or less of these students. This percentage decreased in Greece from 39% to 30%, in Italy from 32% to 25%, and in Portugal from 30% to 24%. Two partner countries with a large share of lowest performers, Brazil and Tunisia, have seen a reduction in the proportion by four to six percentage points, but still show around 69% and 74% of students are not proficient at Level 2 in mathematics. None of the countries with a below-average share of lowest performers saw further reductions in this percentage.

The share of students performing below Level 2 increased in France, the Czech Republic, Ireland, Sweden, Belgium, Luxembourg and Iceland (Figure V.3.3).

On average across the 28 OECD countries with comparable data for the 2003 and 2009 assessments, the percentage of top performers decreased slightly from 14.7% in 2003 to 13.4% in 2009 (Table V.3.2).

Among countries where the percentage of students performing at Level 5 or above was below the average, Portugal saw an increase in this percentage by more than 4 percentage points to almost 10%, Italy by nearly 2 percentage points to 9%, and Greece by less than 2 percentage points to nearly 6%. This proportion increased by 0.3 percentage points in Mexico but remained at a low 0.7%. In 2003, Ireland and the partner country Latvia had shares of top performers below the OECD average. This proportion decreased in both countries: by nearly 5 percentage points in Ireland, to less than 7%, and by 2 percentage points in Latvia, to less than 6%.

Among countries that had an above-average share of top performers in mathematics in 2003, none saw a further increase in this share. The share decreased by almost seven percentage points in the Czech Republic, by six percentage points in Belgium and the Netherlands, by four percentage points in Denmark and Sweden, by three percentage points in Australia, by two percentage points in Canada, and by nearly two percentage points in Iceland (Figure V.3.4).

Mathematics performance can be annualised the same way that reading performance can. Those results can be compared with annualised results in reading or science to see how the magnitude of change differs across the three assessment areas. The annualised results are provided in Table V.3.3 together with additional comparisons of changes in mathematics performance between 2006 and 2009.

■ Figure V.3.4 ■

Percentage of top performers in mathematics in 2003 and 2009

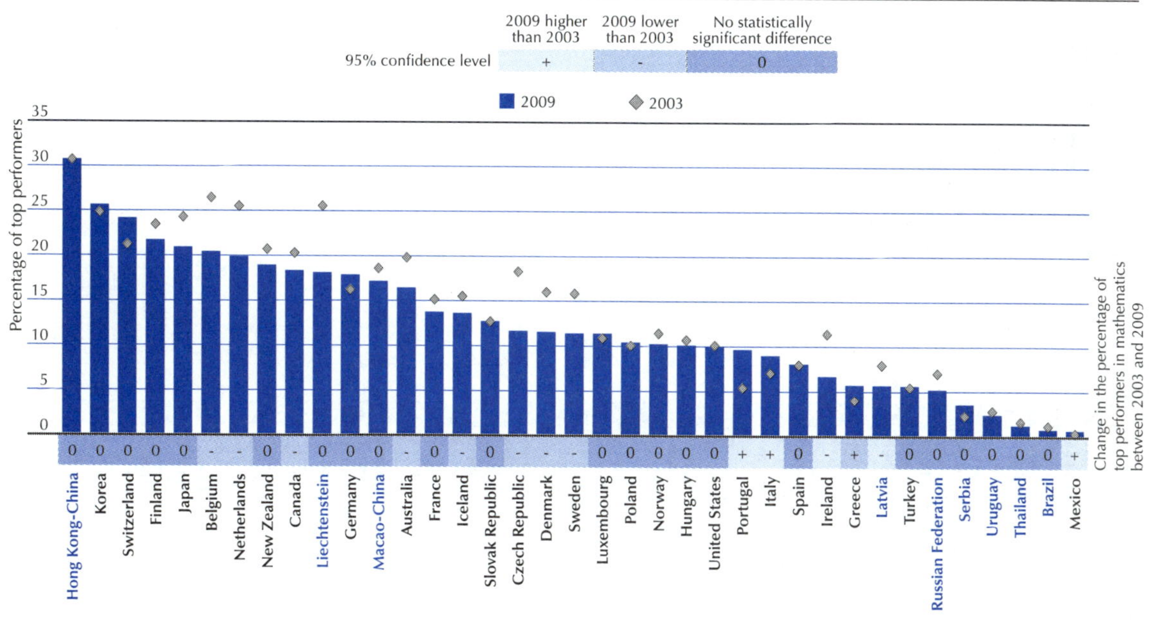

Countries are ranked in ascending order of the percentage of students at proficiency Level 5 or above in mathematics in 2009.
Source: OECD, *PISA 2009 Database*, Table V.3.2

StatLink http://dx.doi.org/10.1787/888932359986

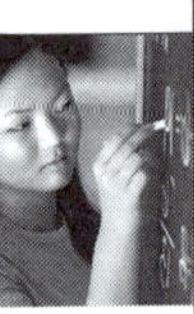

TRENDS IN SCIENCE

How student performance in science has changed since 2006

Trends in science performance are derived by comparing results from PISA 2009 with those from the PISA 2006 assessment. Since the trends in science start from 2006, as opposed to the trends in reading, which start from 2000, performance changes in science since 2006 are expected to be smaller than performance changes in reading since 2000, and smaller than performance changes in mathematics since 2003. The 56 participants in PISA 2006 also took part in PISA 2009, with comparable results, including 33 OECD countries. The PISA 2006 mean for OECD countries was set at 500 and the standard deviation was set at 100, establishing the scale against which science performance in PISA 2009 is compared.

The OECD average in science performance remained unchanged between 2006 and 2009. However, as shown in Figure V.3.5, several countries showed marked changes in science performance (Table V.3.4).

Eleven of the fifty-six countries that have comparable results in both 2006 and 2009 show increases in student performance. This includes 7 out of 33 OECD countries. In three years, Turkey increased its performance by 30 score points, by an average of nearly half a proficiency level (see Box V.E), and Portugal, Korea, Italy, Norway, the United States and Poland by between 10 and 19 score points. Among partner countries, Qatar increased its performance by 30 score points, and Tunisia, Brazil and Colombia by 14 or 15 score points (see Box V.G on Brazil).

In five countries, science performance in 2009 was significantly lower than in 2006. In the Czech Republic student scores decreased by 12 score points, and in Finland and Slovenia they dropped by 9 and 7 score points, respectively. Among partner countries and economies, student scores decreased by 12 score points in Chinese Taipei and by 11 score points in Montenegro.

Performance in science remained unchanged between 2006 and 2009 in 40 countries, when considering a 95% confidence level in PISA. For those countries for which the changes are not statistically significant, Figure V.3.5 provides the p-value which allows the reader to interpret the score point differences.

■ Figure V.3.5 ■

Change in science performance between 2006 and 2009

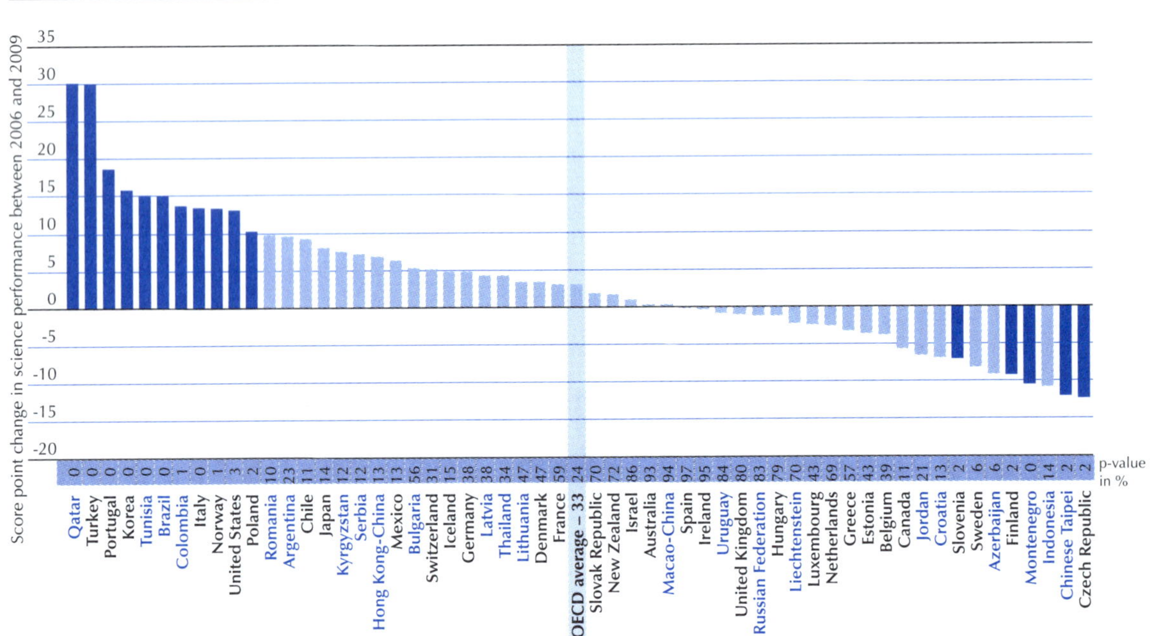

Note: Statistically significant score point changes are marked in a darker tone.
Countries are ranked in descending order of the score point change in science performance between 2006 and 2009.
Source: OECD, *PISA 2009 Database*, Table V.3.4

StatLink http://dx.doi.org/10.1787/888932359986

The relative standing of countries according to their mean performance in science is shown in Figure V.3.6 together with the observed changes in science performance. Countries towards the right side of the figure show improvements in science performance since 2006, while those towards the left show a decrease in student scores. Countries towards the top of the figure performed above the OECD average in science in 2009, while those at the bottom performed below the OECD average. This figure can be interpreted in the same way as Figures V.2.2 and V.3.2 (see Chapter 2).

This figure shows that countries with improvements or a decline in science performance tend to be more widely spread across mean performance levels than in mathematics or reading. Countries with improved science performance include Korea, which had performed well above the OECD average in 2006, Poland, which had performed around the OECD average, and Qatar, one of the lowest-performing countries in 2006 (see Boxes V.B on Korea and V.C on Poland). PISA science scores in 2009 were lower than in 2006 for Finland, a top-performing country, and Montenegro, a below-average performer. Although science performance declined in Finland, it still ranks second on the PISA science assessment. Chinese Taipei also performed very well in 2006. While student performance declined, Chinese Taipei still outperforms most of the PISA participants.

Four countries that performed below the OECD average in the PISA 2006 science assessment performed above or close to the average in 2009 because of improvements in learning outcomes. The United States and Norway both saw a performance increase of 13 score points and now they perform at the OECD average. Portugal and Italy saw performance increases of 19 and 13 score points, respectively, and now perform at slightly below the OECD average (see Box V.D on policies implemented in Portugal).

■ Figure V.3.6 ■

How countries perform in science and how science performance has changed since 2006

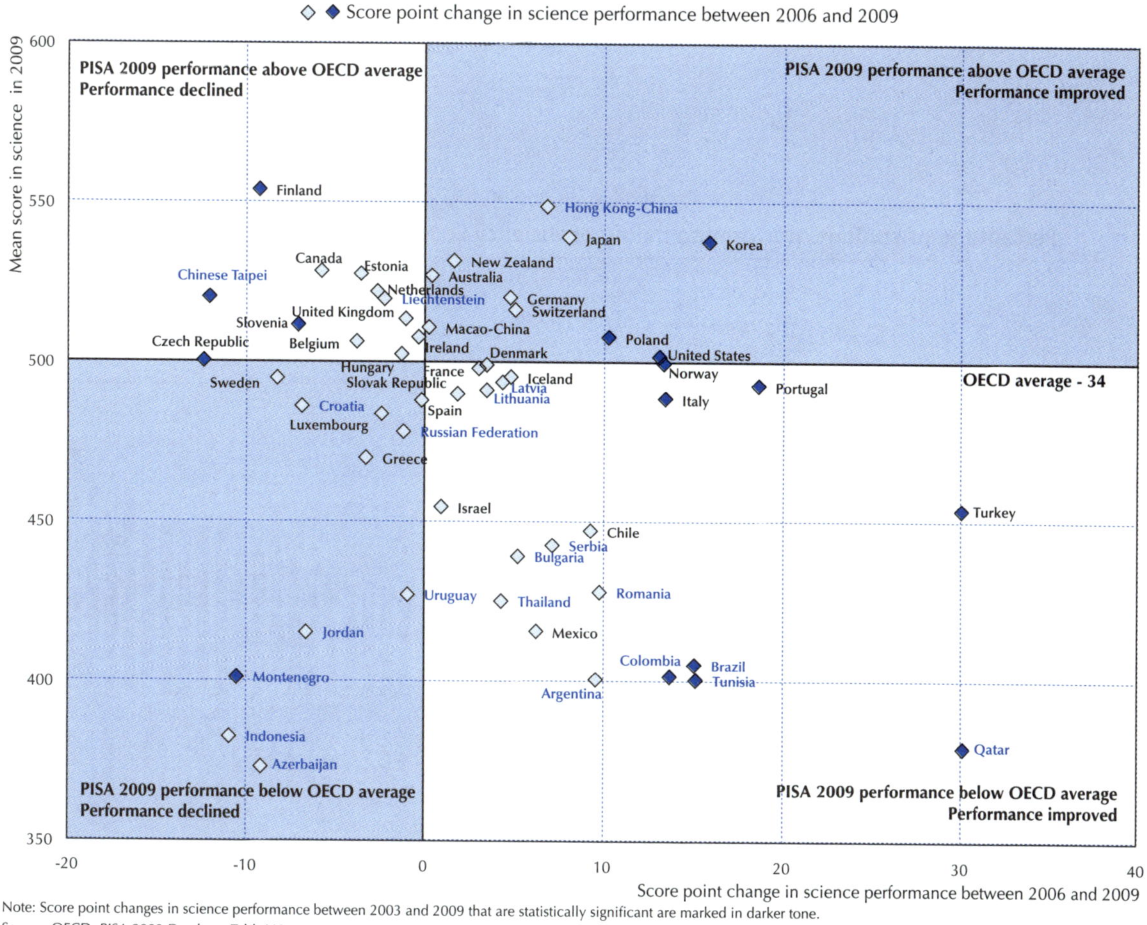

◇ ◆ Score point change in science performance between 2006 and 2009

PISA 2009 performance above OECD average
Performance declined

PISA 2009 performance above OECD average
Performance improved

PISA 2009 performance below OECD average
Performance declined

PISA 2009 performance below OECD average
Performance improved

OECD average - 34

Mean score in science in 2009

Score point change in science performance between 2006 and 2009

Note: Score point changes in science performance between 2003 and 2009 that are statistically significant are marked in darker tone.
Source: OECD, *PISA 2009 Database*, Table V.3.4

StatLink http://dx.doi.org/10.1787/888932359986

Slovenia and the Czech Republic performed above the average in 2006, but declined in performance in 2009. Although the performance in Slovenia decreased by 7 score points, Slovenia remains above the OECD average; but a decline of 12 score points in the Czech Republic leaves that country at the OECD average.

Five low-performing countries are among those that improved their science performance. Among these, Turkey now performs at 454 score points, 30 score points higher than in 2006. Other countries in this group continue to perform at much lower levels – close to 400 score points or below. Qatar increased its performance by 30 score points, but still scores below 400, while Brazil, Colombia and Tunisia increased their performance by around 15 score points and they all now score just above 400 score points. Among low-performing countries, Montenegro declined further in science performance by 11 score points. Other low-performing countries remain at 2006 levels.

In a number of countries, the share of the lowest performers decreased between 2006 and 2009 (Table V.3.5). Among countries that had the largest shares of students who did not reach the baseline Level 2, this share decreased in Qatar by 14 percentage points, even if almost two-thirds of students in Qatar still perform below Level 2. Kyrgyzstan saw a decrease of four percentage points, but the country still has the highest share of lowest performers in 2009. In Tunisia, Brazil and Colombia, the share decreased between 6 and 9 percentage points, although the share of students performing below Level 2 remains around 54% in these countries. Similarly, in Mexico the percentage of students below Level 2 decreased by 4 percentage points, but that proportion remains at a relatively high level of 47%, the highest among OECD countries.

In Turkey the proportion of students performing below Level 2 decreased by 17 percentage points, from 47% to 30%. This is the largest reduction among all countries. Chile saw a reduction in the percentage of lowest performers by 7 percentage points and now 32% of students in Chile perform below proficiency Level 2 in science (see Box V.F on Chile). Italy now shows 21% of students below Level 2, a 5 percentage point decrease since 2006. In the United States and Iceland, 18% of students now perform below Level 2, a decrease of 6 percentage points in the United States and 3 percentage points in Iceland. In the partner country Serbia, this percentage decreased by 4 percentage points to 34% (Figure V.3.7).

■ Figure V.3.7 ■

Percentage of students performing below proficiency Level 2 in science in 2006 and 2009

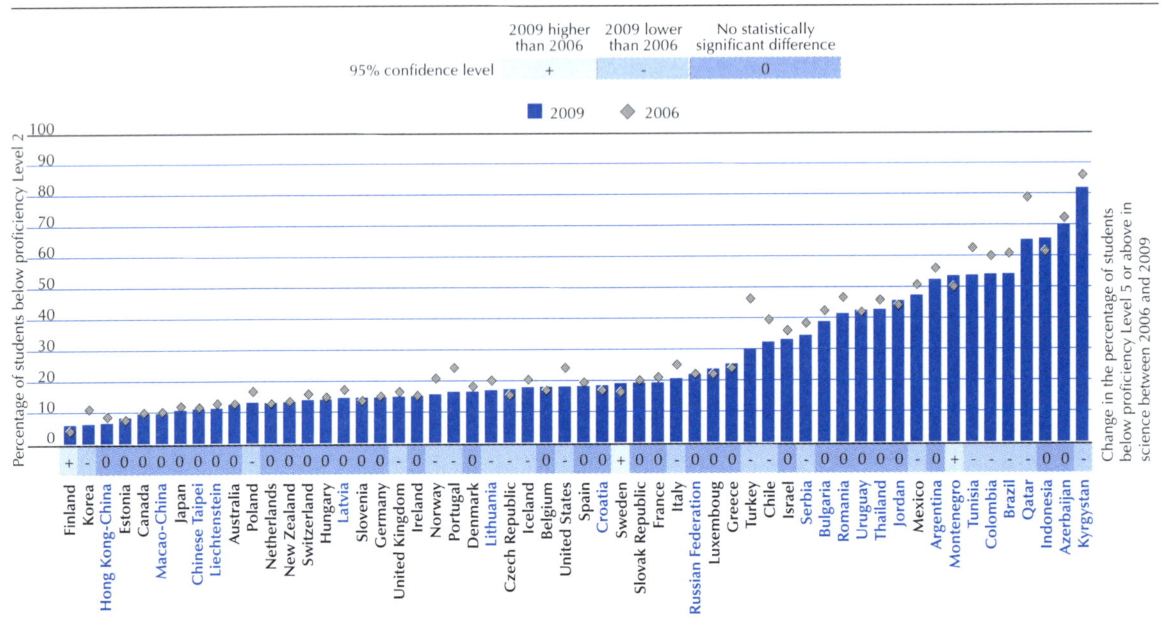

Countries are ranked in ascending order of the percentage of students below proficiency Level 2 in science in 2009.
Source: OECD, PISA 2009 Database, Table V.3.5
StatLink http://dx.doi.org/10.1787/888932359986

Among countries that had above-average proportions of students who performed below Level 2 in science, but now have below-average proportions of those students, Portugal reduced the share of those students by 8 percentage points to 17% and Norway reduced that share by 5 percentage points to 16%. The partner country Lithuania reduced this share of students by 3 percentage points to 17%.

Among countries that had below-average proportions of students who performed below Level 2 in science, only Poland and Korea reduced the proportion further, by 4 and 5 percentage points, respectively. Poland reduced the percentage of lowest performers from 17% to 13%, while Korea reduced it from 11% to 6%, very close to the lowest level among OECD countries.

The share of students performing below Level 2 increased in Sweden from 16% to 19%. In Finland, the percentage of students who perform below Level 2 rose from 4% to 6%, but this remains the lowest proportion across all countries taking part in 2009, as was the case in 2006. The share of students performing below Level 2 increased by 3 percentage points in the partner country Montenegro, where this share was about 50% in 2006.

The percentage of top performers in science increased in only two countries (Table V.3.5). In Italy, the percentage of students at proficiency Level 5 or 6 increased from 5% to 6%, while the partner country Qatar had barely any students at this level in 2006 and now has slightly more than 1%.

The percentage of students performing at Level 5 and above in science decreased only in countries that had above-average percentages of these students in 2006. In the Czech Republic and Slovenia, this share decreased by 3 percentage points, while in the United Kingdom and Canada, the proportion decreased by 2 percentage points. Some 8% of students in the Czech Republic now perform at Level 5 and above, close to the OECD average of 9%. In other countries, the percentage of top performers remained above average in Slovenia (around 10%), the United Kingdom (11%) and Canada (12%). Chile saw a slight reduction from an already low level, from 2% to 1%. The partner economy Chinese Taipei showed the largest reduction in the percentage of top performers in science: 6 percentage points, from 15% to 9%.

■ Figure V.3.8 ■

Percentage of top performers in science in 2006 and 2009

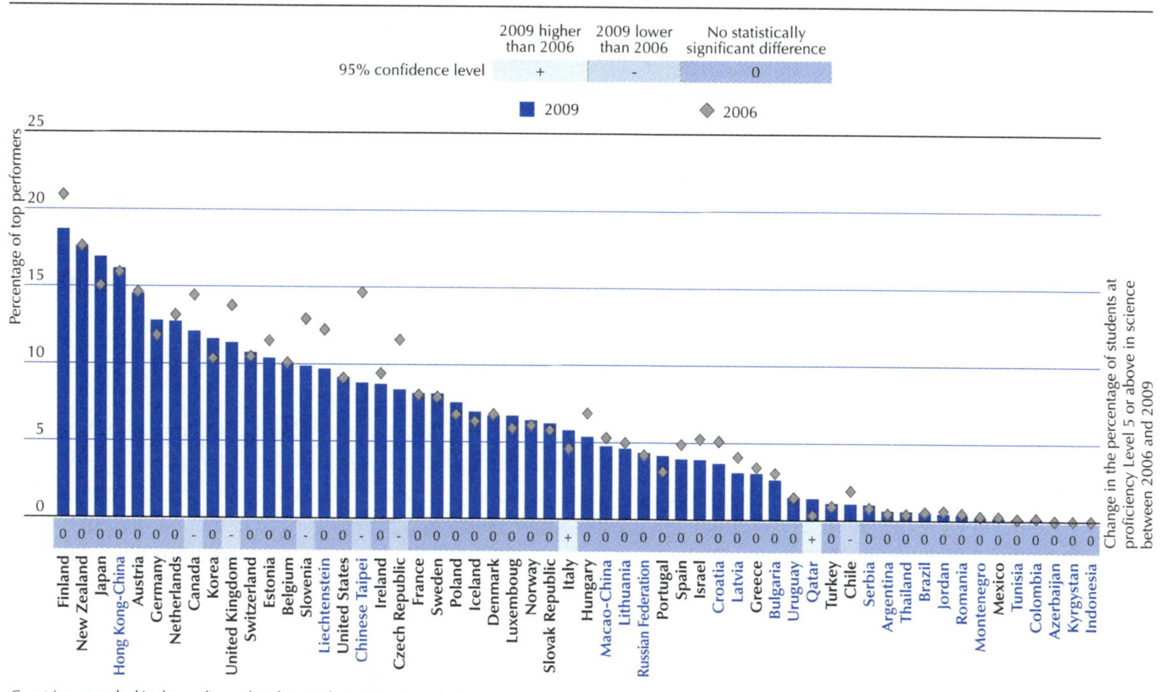

Countries are ranked in descending order of top performers in science in 2009.
Source: OECD, *PISA 2009 Database*, Table V.3.5
StatLink http://dx.doi.org/10.1787/888932359986

Box V.D **Portugal**

In 2000, the PISA reading performance in Portugal was one of the lowest among OECD countries and the proportion of students performing below baseline Level 2 was one of the highest. These results were widely debated in public, leading to a common view that too many Portuguese students lacked the knowledge and skills that were needed in a modern society and economy. In addition, high repetition rates were considered an obstacle to success among students from disadvantaged backgrounds.

The results from the PISA 2003 and 2006 assessments were discussed even more broadly in the context of proposed education reforms. The Minister of Education stressed the importance of the results and the lessons that could be learned from PISA's innovative approach to assessing the creative use of knowledge and skills. Since 2005, Portugal has put in place a vast set of policies designed to improve learning outcomes.

Many of these policies concentrated on reaching and improving the lives of people from disadvantaged backgrounds. Portugal has relatively large inequalities of wealth and one of the lowest shares of higher education among its working population. It is estimated that hourly productivity would be 14.4% higher if the working-age population in Portugal had the same level of education as that in the United States (OECD, 2010c). The reforms aimed to change this situation by improving learning opportunities for children and adults from relatively disadvantage backgrounds.

The Portuguese school system was highly selective with a large number of students repeating grades, many of whom eventually dropped out of school. Continual grade repetition was, and still is, to some extent, considered a trait of the Portuguese school system, and there is a high correlation between poor performance and low socio-economic status.

The concept underlying the policies implemented since 2005 is that improvements in the efficacy and quality of the education system depend on improving equity. The results from PISA have clearly indicated that equity does not have to be forsaken to quality.

Even though the Portuguese school system is almost entirely public, and compulsory education is free until 12th grade or when a student reaches the age of 18, the government has devoted more resources to supporting students from low-income families. Spending on laptops, meals, books, broadband Internet access, English teaching and other extra-curricular activities was subsidised by the government; depending on the family's economic status, additional support was provided to disadvantaged students. These measures were applied from the first year of primary school until the end of secondary school. Between 2005 and 2009, the number of beneficiaries of the School Social Action programme tripled.

Between 2004 and 2009 there was a dramatic decline in the repetition rate in 9th grade, from 21.5% to 12.8%. This, in itself, is a positive sign, given PISA's findings that grade repetition is generally associated with lower performance and a larger impact of socio-economic background on learning outcomes (see Chapter 2 in Volume IV, *What Makes a School Successful?*).This reduction also implied a higher enrolment of students in secondary education (10th to 12th grade) and a consequent decline in the number of students dropping out of school altogether. From 2007 on, the Ministry of Education considered 12th grade to be the minimum educational requirement for all Portuguese citizens. Legislation that extended compulsory education was approved and published in 2009.

In parallel, teachers were provided training, mostly in Portuguese language, mathematics and information technologies. In addition, a new system of evaluating teachers and schools was put in place to increase accountability. Although the original implementation plan was postponed because of opposition to the notion of strengthening accountability measures based on an assessment system, a shift towards more outcome-oriented accountability has already changed the ways teachers and schools perceive external assessments, including PISA. The efficiency of the school system was improved by reducing teacher absenteeism and replacing absent teachers, which helped avoid losing classroom hours.

Current policy also aims to change the management of schools. In 2006 and 2009, Portugal had one of the lowest mean values on the *index of school responsibility in resource allocation* and on the *index of school*

responsibility for curriculum and assessment among OECD countries (see Volume IV, *What Makes a School Successful?* and Tables IV.3.5 and IV.3.6). The policies that are now being implemented give greater autonomy to directors of "school clusters". A school cluster is an organisational unit comprising several schools from kindergarten to 9th or 12th grade, vertically structured under a unique educational project that is led by a director. The director is elected by a council of teachers, parents, students, municipal leaders, institution representatives, and relevant community members. The vast majority of school clusters are now led by an elected director who has much more autonomy to pursue a proposed educational project. This policy is also accompanied by major investments in the physical infrastructure that started in 2008.

As part of the reform, all students in 4th, 6th and 9th grades take part in annual national assessments in Portuguese language and mathematics. Although 4th and 6th grade assessments do not have a direct impact on students progressing through the grade system, these assessments are now applied universally in all schools and provide important evaluations for students, parents and teachers. In addition, secondary schools now offer vocational alternatives to students, and about half of students enrolled in 10th, 11th and 12th grades attend vocational courses. As a result, the number of students enrolled in basic and secondary schools has grown since 2005, ending the worrying decline in enrolment that had been observed since 1995.

Traditionally, mathematics was considered to be the most difficult subject for students in Portugal. In fact, 2003 PISA results in mathematics were even lower than in reading and almost one-third of students performed below Level 2 (see Figure V.3.3 and Table V.3.2). Following the PISA results and the 2005 results on mathematics examinations in 9th grade, the Ministry of Education promoted a broad debate on the subject. The Action Plan for Mathematics, which was launched in 2005 and involves some 78 000 teachers and 400 000 students, has six components: *i)* a mathematics plan in each school; *ii)* training for teachers in basic and secondary schools; *iii)* reinforcing mathematics in initial teacher training; *iv)* readjusting the mathematics curriculum throughout the compulsory education system; *v)* creating a resource bank specifically devoted to mathematics; and *(vi)* evaluating textbooks on mathematics. At the same time, more mathematics teachers were trained and hired.

The National Plan for Reading was launched in 2006 as a joint initiative involving the Ministry of Education, the Ministry of Culture and the Ministry of Parliament. This plan was devoted to improving reading proficiency among children and fostering good reading habits. More than one million children in all school clusters and secondary schools are involved in the programme.

The PISA 2009 results demonstrate that Portugal is making progress in achieving the goals set by the reformers. Among countries that are at or above the OECD average, Portugal was the only one that improved in all three PISA assessment areas, with most improvements occurring between 2006 and 2009 (see Figure V.1.2 and Tables V.2.1, V.3.1, V.3.3 and V.3.4). Reading performance has improved by 19 points since 2000; and over the same nine-year period, the changes for mathematics and science were of similar magnitude, although they were achieved over a shorter period of time.

In reading and science, these positive trends are mostly due to an improvement among the lowest-achieving students. In reading, Portugal reduced the share of low-performing students (below proficiency Level 2) by almost nine percentage points, while the share of top-performers (Level 5 or above) remained at a similar level (see Figures V.2.4 and V.2.5, and Table V.2.2). Similar results can be found in science (see Figures V.3.7 and V.3.8, and Table V.3.5). In mathematics, however, not only did the percentage of low-performers fall by six percentage points, but the share of top-performers also increased by around four percentage points (see Figures V.3.3 and V.3.4, and Table V.3.2).

Portugal is one of the six countries in PISA 2009 that both improved their overall reading performance and lowered variation in performance. This was mainly due to improvements among low achievers while high achievers remained at similar levels.

Box V.E **Turkey**

Turkey joined PISA in 2003. Results from that assessment showed that, with mean mathematics performance at around 425 score points and more than half of the students performing below baseline Level 2, Turkey's 15-year-olds were performing far below the OECD average. The picture was similar in 2006, although by that time, major reforms were already under way.

Turkey improved its mathematics performance by more than 20 score points between 2003 and 2009 (see Figure V.3.1 and Table V.3.1). That increase was accompanied by a 10-percentage-point reduction, from 52% to 42%, in the percentage of students performing below baseline Level 2. In science, Turkey's performance improved by 30 score points since 2006, the equivalent of almost a full school year, with the share of students below Level 2 declining by 17 percentage points from 47% to 30%. This is the largest reduction among the 56 countries with comparable results in the 2006 and 2009 PISA assessments.

Among several programmes that were implemented in Turkey, the Basic Education Programme (BEP) that started in 1998 had an impact on almost all students (OECD, 2007). The objectives of this programme, based on international educational standards, included expanding primary school education, improving the quality of education and overall student outcomes, closing the performance gap between boys and girls, providing equal opportunities, matching the performance indicators of the European Union, developing school libraries, increasing the efficiency of the education system, ensuring that qualified personnel were employed, integrating information and communication technologies into the education system and creating local learning centres, based in schools, that are open to everyone.

One of the major changes introduced with the BEP programme involved the compulsory education law. This change was first implemented in the 1997/1998 school year, and in 2003 the first students graduated from the eight-year compulsory education system. Since the launch of this programme, the attendance rate among students within the eight-year primary education system increased from around 85% to nearly 100%, while the attendance rate in pre-primary programmes increased from 10% to 25%. In addition, the system was expanded to include 3.5 million more pupils, average class size was reduced to roughly 30, all students learned at least one foreign language, computer laboratories were established in every primary school and overall conditions were improved in all 35 000 rural schools. Resources devoted to the programme exceeded the equivalent of USD 11 billion. This programme did not directly affect school participation for most of the 15-year-olds assessed by PISA, who are mainly in secondary schools where enrolment rates are close to 60%.

In line with those goals, and given Turkey's experiences with international assessments like PISA, new curricula were implemented in the 2006-2007 school year, starting from the 6th grade. The secondary school mathematics and language curricula were also revised and a new science curriculum was applied in the 9th grade for the 2008/2009 school year. PISA 2009 students had already been taught for one year using the new curriculum, although they still received their primary school education in the former system. The standards of the new curricula were intended to meet PISA goals: *"Increased importance has been placed on students' doing mathematics which means exploring mathematical ideas, solving problems, making connections among mathematical ideas, and applying them in real life situations (Talim ve Terbiye Kurulu [TTKB] [Board of Education], 2008).*

The curricular reform was designed not only to change the content of school education and encourage the introduction of innovative teaching methods, but above all to change the teaching philosophy and culture within schools. The new curricula and teaching materials emphasise "student-centred learning", giving students a more active role than before, when memorising information had been the dominant approach. They also reflect the assumption, on which PISA is based, that schools should equip students with the necessary skills and competencies that would ensure their success at school and in life, in general.

Several policies had sought to change the culture and management of schools. Schools were obliged to propose a plan of work, including development targets and strategic plans for reaching them. More democratic governance, parental involvement and teamwork were suggested. In 2004, a project aimed at teaching students democratic skills was started in all primary and secondary schools, with many responsibilities assigned to

student assemblies. This was accompanied by the development of new inspection tools that were more transparent and performance-oriented.

Private investments were also used to increase the capacity of the school system in Turkey. Throughout 2004 and 2005, private-sector investments funded 14 000 additional classrooms. Taxes were reduced for private businesses that invested in education. This was particularly helpful in provinces where there was large internal migration (OECD, 2006c).

Such major changes were accompanied by policies aimed directly at teachers. New arrangements were implemented to train teachers for upper-secondary education through five-year graduate studies. The arrangements also stipulated that graduates in other fields, such as science or literature, who wanted to teach would also have to attend a year-and-a-half of graduate training in education.

Several projects implemented in Turkey over the past decade have addressed equity issues. The Girls to Schools Now campaign that started in 2003 aimed to ensure that 100% of girls attended primary school (ages 6-14). Since 2003, textbooks for all primary-school students have been supplied free of charge by the Ministry of National Education. More recently, a Complementary Training Programme, begun in 2008, tries to ensure that 10 to 14-year-olds acquire a basic education even if they have never been enrolled in a school or if they had dropped out of school.

Whatever the relationship between these initiatives and the learning outcomes observed, with one of the largest improvements in both mathematics and science performance, Turkey is on its way to reaching the educational standards of other OECD countries.

4

Trends in Equity

This chapter examines trends in equity in learning opportunities and outcomes. It focuses on how variations in reading performance have changed between 2000 and 2009, and the extent to which the impact of socio-economic background and immigrant status on performance has also changed during the same period.

TRENDS IN THE VARIATION OF STUDENT PERFORMANCE

Although student mean performance shows how successful students are, on average, in each country, the extent to which student performance varies around the mean and the degree of variation in performance are also of interest to policy makers. Identifying countries where the variation in performance diminishes, especially those where this is accompanied by overall improvements in student performance, can provide important insights for policy.

Figure V.4.1 shows changes in the variation of reading performance that were observed between 2000 and 2009 (see also Table V.4.1). Countries are sorted by the variation of reading scores, as measured by the statistical variance in 2009, with dots representing the corresponding figures for 2000.

Across OECD countries, the average variation in student reading performance decreased by 3%; however, there were marked differences in this percentage across countries (Table V.4.1). Among those OECD countries where the variation in student performance was already at below-average levels, Chile, Canada and Hungary saw a further reduction, by 8% to 15%. Among OECD countries where reading performance varied around typical levels, Denmark, Poland, and Portugal observed a decline in this variation by more than 20%, while the Czech Republic saw a decrease by 8%. Among OECD countries with an above-average variation in student performance in 2000, Germany saw a reduction by 27%, Norway by 23% and Switzerland, the United States, New Zealand and Belgium by still sizeable degrees. Among the partner countries, Latvia, Liechtenstein and Romania observed a decline in performance variation to below-average levels by more than 20%. The partner countries Indonesia and Thailand saw a reduction of performance variation by 16% and 12%, respectively.

A number of countries have seen an increase in the variation of reading performance. While in Sweden, Italy, Iceland and Spain this increase was below 15%, it was larger in Japan and Korea where variation increased by 30% or more. Among the partner countries, variation increased considerably in Bulgaria and Brazil.

■ Figure V.4.1 ■

Comparison of the variation in student performance in reading between 2000 and 2009

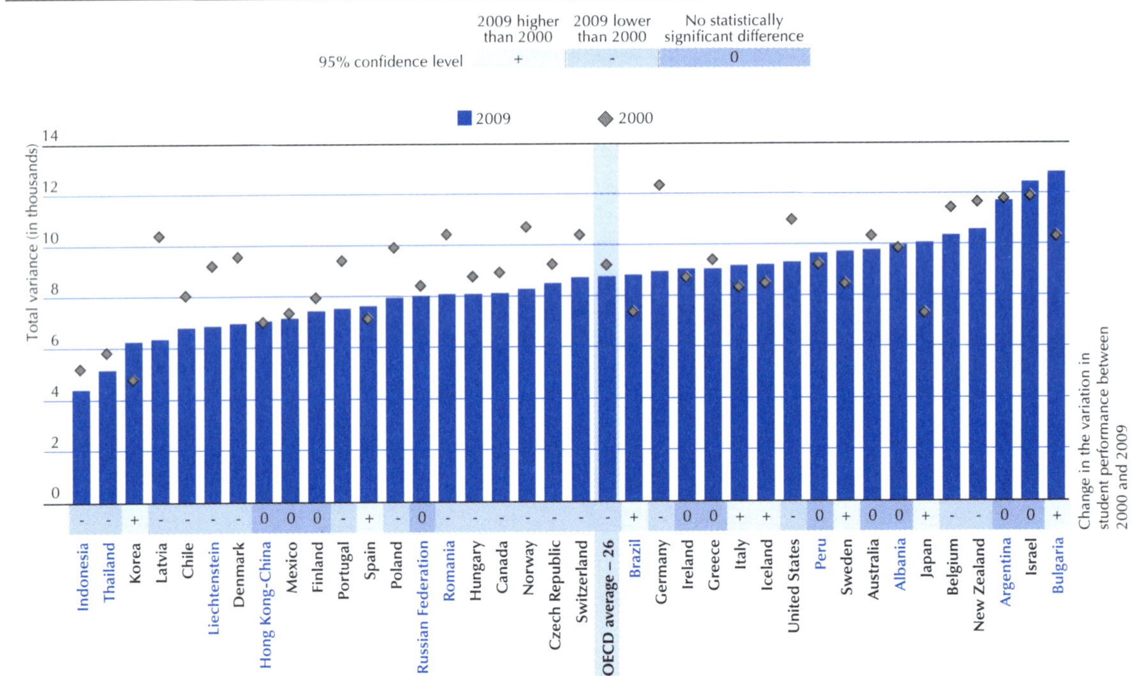

Note: Countries are ranked in ascending order of the total variance in student performance in 2009.
Source: OECD, *PISA Database 2009*, Table V.4.1.

StatLink http://dx.doi.org/10.1787/888932360005

These changes can be examined more closely by looking at the relative increases in reading performance among the lowest- and highest-performing students. For example, if low-achieving students improve while high-achieving students remain at the same level, then performance variation decreases. In contrast, when high-achievers improve while low-achievers do not, then overall variation increases. Results in Figure V.4.1 can thus be compared with those in Figure V.2.6, where changes at the 10th and 90th percentiles of reading performance are presented.

In countries where the variation in student performance decreased, scores among low-achieving students often improved (Table V.2.3). This was the case in Chile, Poland, Portugal, Germany, Switzerland, Norway and Denmark, where the increase among low-achieving students was 51 score points in Chile, 39 score points in Poland, 19 score points in Switzerland and Norway, and 16 score points in Denmark (see Boxes V.F on Chile and V.C on Poland, which discuss policies aimed at low-achieving students in these countries). The partner country Latvia shows the largest decrease in variation while also showing the largest improvement among low-achievers, by 57 score points, a small positive trend among average students, and no change among high-achievers. The partner countries Indonesia and Liechtenstein also saw a reduction in variation because of improvements among low-achievers. In all these countries, performance among high-achievers did not decline, and overall achievement improved, or at least remained the same. Interestingly, in two OECD countries, Denmark and Norway, large decreases in variation were not only the result of improvement among low-achievers but also due to a decline in performance among high-achievers or in the share of top performers, with the overall reading trend close to zero.

In Sweden, performance variation increased due to a decline in the performance of low-achieving students, while there was no change among high-achievers (Table V.2.3). In contrast, increases in variation in Korea and the partner country Brazil were the result of considerable improvements among high-achieving students, leading to an increase in overall performance in Korea and Brazil.

While it is useful to know how changes in variation are associated with trends among low- and high-achieving students, the relationship between changes in variation and overall performance is important for understanding how performance has evolved over successive PISA assessments. This relationship is presented in Figure V.4.2, where the vertical axis represents changes in variation and the horizontal axis indicates changes in mean performance. Countries towards the right saw increases in mean performance while those towards the left saw decreases in mean performance. Performance variation decreased across assessments in countries towards the bottom, but increased in countries towards the top. Countries that show statistically significant changes in both aspects are indicated by dark markers.

Interestingly, reductions in variation and rises in overall performance often go together, that is, countries showing the largest decreases in variation are often those in which mean scores increased noticeably. In Germany, Poland, Portugal, Chile and Hungary, and in the partner countries Liechtenstein and Indonesia, variation decreased while performance improved. The country with the largest reduction in performance variation, the partner country Latvia, also shows an increase of more than 20 score points in mean performance. In all these countries, the overall improvement in mean performance and the reduction in variation were the result of relatively larger improvements among low-achieving students. Performance variation decreased while overall performance declined in the Czech Republic.

There are exceptions to this pattern. Performance variation increased in Korea where the overall increase in student scores was largely the result of improvements among high-achieving students, while the percentage of low-performing students remained unchanged. Similarly, in the partner country Brazil, the overall improvement in reading performance was accompanied by an increase in performance variation, which was largely due to improvements among high-achieving students.

In Sweden, variation increased while overall performance declined, largely because of lower scores among low-achievers since 2000.

■ Figure V.4.2 ■

Change in variation and change in reading performance between 2000 and 2009

Note: Countries in which both the change in variation and score point change in reading are statistically significant are marked in a darker tone.
Source: OECD, *PISA 2009 Database*, Tables V.2.1 and V.4.1.
StatLink http://dx.doi.org/10.1787/888932360005

Figure V.4.3 shows the extent to which 15-year-olds' reading skills vary among schools and among students within schools, and how such variations have evolved over time (see also Table V.4.1).[1] The total length of both the dark and the light bars indicates the total variation in student performance on the PISA reading scale. For each country, the figure makes a distinction between the variation that can be attributed to differences in the average results attained by students in different schools (between-school variation, the dark part of the bar) and the part of the variation that can be attributed to the range of student results within schools (within-school variation, the light part of the bar).[2] The between-school variation is also used to sort countries in the figure. Longer dark segments indicate greater variation in the mean performance of different schools, while longer light segments indicate greater variation among students within schools. The diamonds in the figures represent the 2000 results for each country. The significance of changes between 2000 and 2009 is indicated by marks above country names, and is provided separately for the between- and within-school variations.

As shown in Figure V.4.3, all countries display considerable variation among students within schools, and many countries also show large variations in student performance between different schools. The percentage of the variation in student performance between schools can be interpreted as a measure of academic inclusion. Where there is substantial variation in performance between schools, but less variation among students within schools, students tend to be grouped in schools in which most students perform at similar levels. A school system's level of academic inclusion may reflect school choices made by families or according to where students live, and/or policies on school enrolment or according to how students are assigned different curricula in the form of tracking or streaming. For more details on academic inclusion, see Volume II, *Overcoming Social Background*.

Unlike the case of total variation, the relative share of between-school variation remained similar for most countries between 2000 and 2009. Two OECD countries, Poland and Switzerland, and three partner countries, Latvia, the

Russian Federation and Thailand, observed a decrease in the share of performance variation between schools. The largest decrease was in Poland, where from a relatively large level in 2000, between-school variation decreased by three-fourths to below average. While the decrease was smaller in magnitude, in Switzerland, the share of performance variation between schools was higher than the average in 2000. It is now below average. In Latvia and Thailand this variation decreased even further from already low levels, while in the Russian Federation it decreased by almost 40% from below-average levels.

In Italy and the partner country Argentina, between-school variation increased from already high levels. These countries show the largest differences among schools in 2009. There were no changes in any other country where between-school variation was large.

■ Figure V.4.3 ■

Variation in reading performance between and within schools in 2000 and 2009

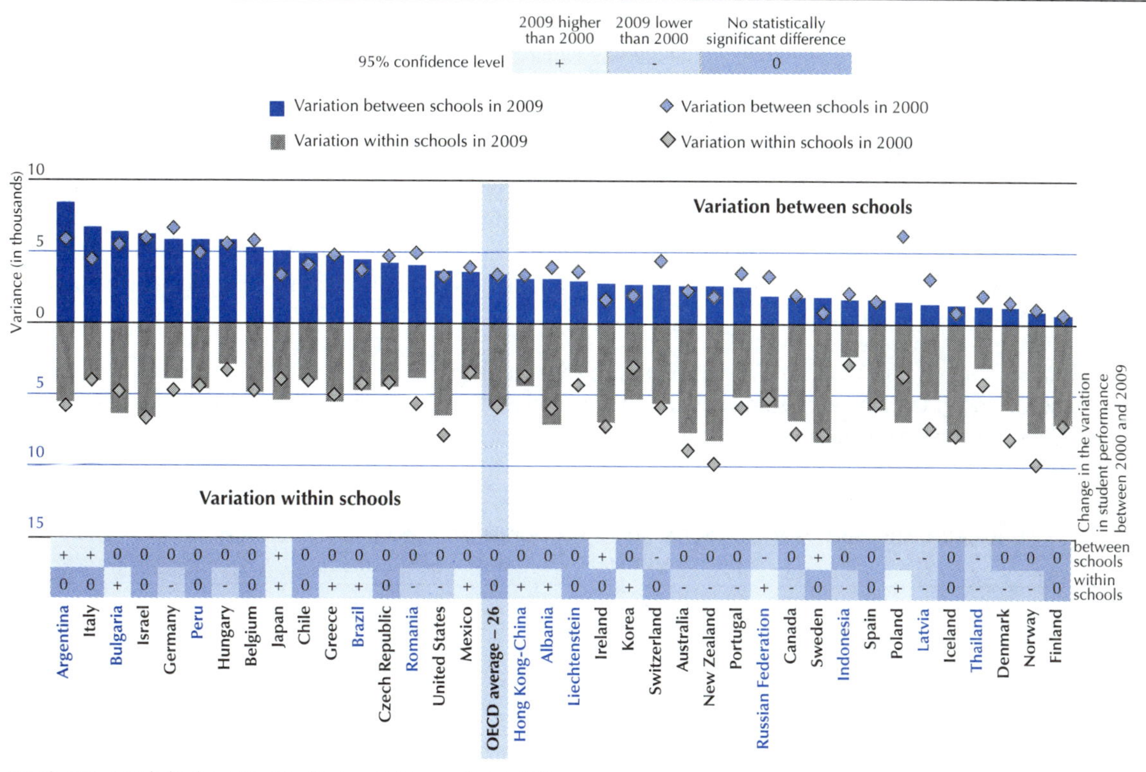

Note: Countries are ranked in descending order of the variance between schools in 2009.
Source: OECD, *PISA Database 2009*, Table V.4.1.

StatLink http://dx.doi.org/10.1787/888932360005

TRENDS IN STUDENT BACKGROUND FACTORS AND THEIR RELATION TO READING PERFORMANCE

Socio-economic status

Identifying the characteristics of those students, schools and education systems that perform well despite socio-economic disadvantages can help policy makers design effective policies to overcome inequalities in learning opportunities.

The way students are assigned to schools can lead to considerable variation in performance. Some countries have comprehensive school systems with no, or limited, differences among institutions. They seek to provide all students with similar opportunities for learning by requiring each school and teacher to provide for the full range of student abilities, interests and backgrounds. Other countries respond to diversity by grouping students through tracking or streaming, whether among schools or among classes within schools, with the aim of serving students according to their academic potential and/or interests in specific programmes. Many countries adopt a combination of these approaches (for details on how schol systems select and group students, see Volume IV, *What Makes a School Successful?*).

In all systems, there may be considerable variation in performance among schools due to the socio-economic and cultural characteristics of the communities they serve or due to geographical differences, such as among regions, provinces or states in federal systems, or between rural and urban areas. There may also be differences among individual schools that are more difficult to quantify, such as differences in the quality or effectiveness of the instruction that those schools provide. As a result, even in comprehensive systems, students' performance levels may still vary considerably across schools.

Differences in students' socio-economic background can also play an important role inside schools. Students can be separated into different learning programmes even in the same schools. Schools may struggle with disadvantaged students, while only the most privileged students may take additional courses to enhance their education. All these factors can reinforce the effect of students' socio-economic background on their performance, even within the same school.

Although the socio-economic background of students remains largely similar across PISA assessments, changes in some countries' economies and societies resulted in changes in student background between 2000 and 2009.[3] The largest decline in the socio-economic background of students was observed in the partner countries Albania and Bulgaria (see also Table V.4.2).

Volume II, *Overcoming Social Background*, analyses the relationships between family background and student performance in 2009. This section examines changes in these relationships. Figure V.4.4 shows how the relationship between socio-economic background and reading performance, which is used here as a measure of equity in the distribution of educational opportunities, changed from 2000 to 2009 (see also Table V.4.3). Dark bars indicate the slope of the socio-economic gradient in 2009, with countries sorted according to this value.[4] Markers indicate results for 2000 and additional information on the significance of the change between 2000 and 2009 is provided near country names.

Across OECD countries, the impact of socio-economic background on learning outcomes has remained unchanged between 2000 and 2009. However, some countries were able to improve equity in the distribution of educational opportunities. Among the countries where the impact of socio-economic background on performance was relatively

■ Figure V.4.4 ■

Relationship between students' socio-economic background and their reading performance in 2000 and 2009

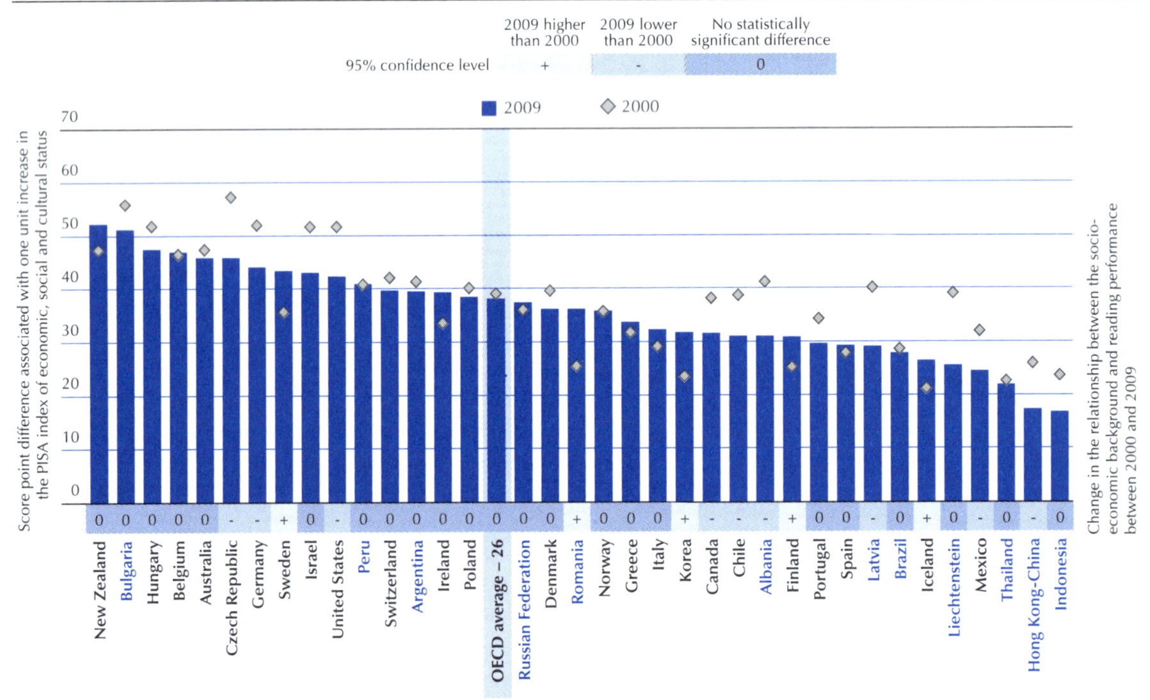

Note: Countries are ranked in descending order of the overall association of the socio-economic background in 2009.
Source: OECD, *PISA Database 2009*, Table V.4.3.
StatLink http://dx.doi.org/10.1787/888932360005

large, the Czech Republic, the United States and Germany were able to lower it so it is now closer to the average. In four countries that were close to the average, Chile, Canada and the partner countries Latvia and Albania, the impact of socio-economic background on performance was also weaker in 2009 than in 2000. In Mexico and the partner economy Hong Kong-China, the relationship between socio-economic background and performance was already relatively weak in 2000 and weakened further in 2009.

In contrast, the slope of the socio-economic gradient increased between 2000 and 2009 in five countries. Despite this increase, in Korea, Finland and Iceland the impact of socio-economic background on student performance is still below the average across OECD countries, while in the case of Sweden it is now stronger than the average level. The largest increase was observed in the partner country Romania where the slope of the socio-economic gradient increased to the average level.

In addressing socio-economic inequities, some policies aim to reduce the differences in the socio-economic composition of schools. Examples of these are changes in school systems in which differences in educational programmes across schools are narrowed. Other policies try to limit the impact of socio-economic background on student performance within schools by, for example, providing additional support to disadvantaged students.

Figure V.4.5 shows how the within- and between-school relationship between performance and the socio-economic background of students and schools has evolved over time (see also Table V.4.3). Dark bars on the top indicate the effect of socio-economic background between schools in 2009. Countries are sorted according to this value, with dots representing results in 2000. The between-school effect reflects the strength of the relationship between the average

■ Figure V.4.5 ■

Relationship between socio-economic background and reading performance between and within schools in 2000 and 2009

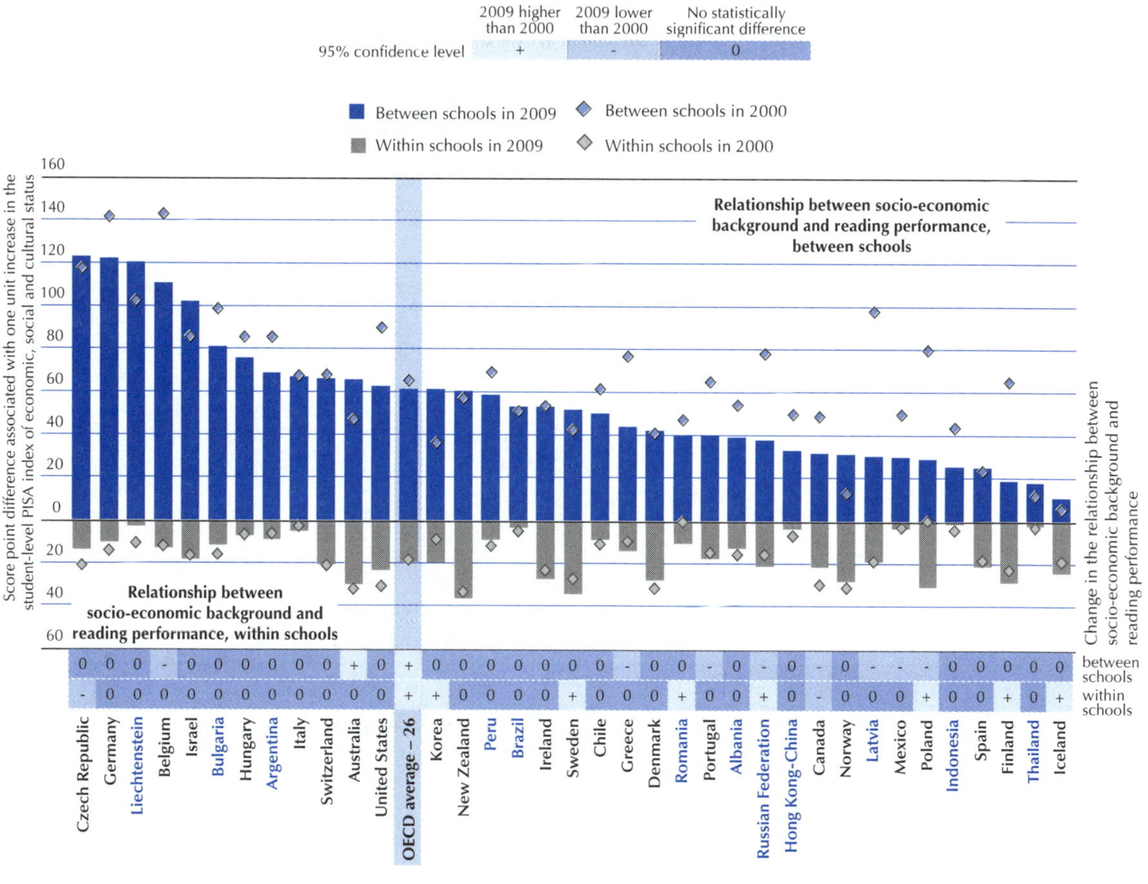

95% confidence level: + 2009 higher than 2000; - 2009 lower than 2000; 0 No statistically significant difference

Between schools in 2009 · Between schools in 2000 · Within schools in 2009 · Within schools in 2000

Score point difference associated with one unit increase in the student-level PISA index of economic, social and cultural status

Relationship between socio-economic background and reading performance, between schools

Relationship between socio-economic background and reading performance, within schools

Change in the relationship between socio-economic background and reading performance

Country	between schools	within schools
Czech Republic	0	-
Germany	0	0
Liechtenstein	0	0
Belgium	-	0
Israel	0	0
Bulgaria	0	0
Hungary	0	0
Argentina	0	0
Italy	0	0
Switzerland	0	0
Australia	+	0
United States	0	0
OECD average – 26	+	+
Korea	0	+
New Zealand	0	0
Peru	0	0
Brazil	0	0
Ireland	0	0
Sweden	0	+
Chile	0	0
Greece	-	0
Denmark	0	0
Romania	0	+
Portugal	-	0
Albania	0	0
Russian Federation	-	+
Hong Kong-China	0	0
Canada	-	-
Norway	0	0
Latvia	-	0
Mexico	-	0
Poland	-	+
Indonesia	0	0
Spain	0	0
Finland	0	+
Thailand	0	0
Iceland	0	+

Note: Countries are ranked in descending order of the association between socio-economic background and reading performance between schools in 2009.

Source: OECD, *PISA 2009 Database*, Table V.4.3.

StatLink http://dx.doi.org/10.1787/888932360005

socio-economic background of schools and the mean performance of schools. The lighter bars on the bottom represent the within-school effect, with dots showing its level in 2000. The within-school effect reflects the average relationship between students' socio-economic background and their performance inside schools. Additional information explaining statistically significant changes in both aspects is provided near the country names.

Across OECD countries, the association between socio-economic background and performance across schools decreased. The decrease was particularly pronounced in Poland and the partner country Latvia where, by 2009, the association was three times weaker in comparison with 2000. However, while the overall impact of socio-economic background on performance also decreased in Latvia, in Poland, the within-school effect increased, leaving the overall impact unchanged. This suggests that the school reform in Poland had the effect of distributing students from different backgrounds more evenly across schools, but made no difference in the extent to which students from more disadvantaged backgrounds fare overall (see Box V.C on the school reform in Poland). In Greece, Belgium, Portugal, Mexico, Canada and the partner country the Russian Federation, a decrease in the socio-economic disparities of schools was also observed, although only in Mexico and Canada was this accompanied by a weakening in the overall effect of student background on learning outcomes.

IMMIGRANT STATUS AND HOME LANGUAGE

Changes in the number of students with an immigrant background and the relationship with performance

Among OECD countries with comparable data,[5] on average, the percentage of students with an immigrant background increased by two percentage points between 2000 and 2009 (Table V.4.4). However, across all countries, the percentage of students with an immigrant background varies.

■ Figure V.4.6 ■

Percentage of students with an immigrant background in 2000 and 2009

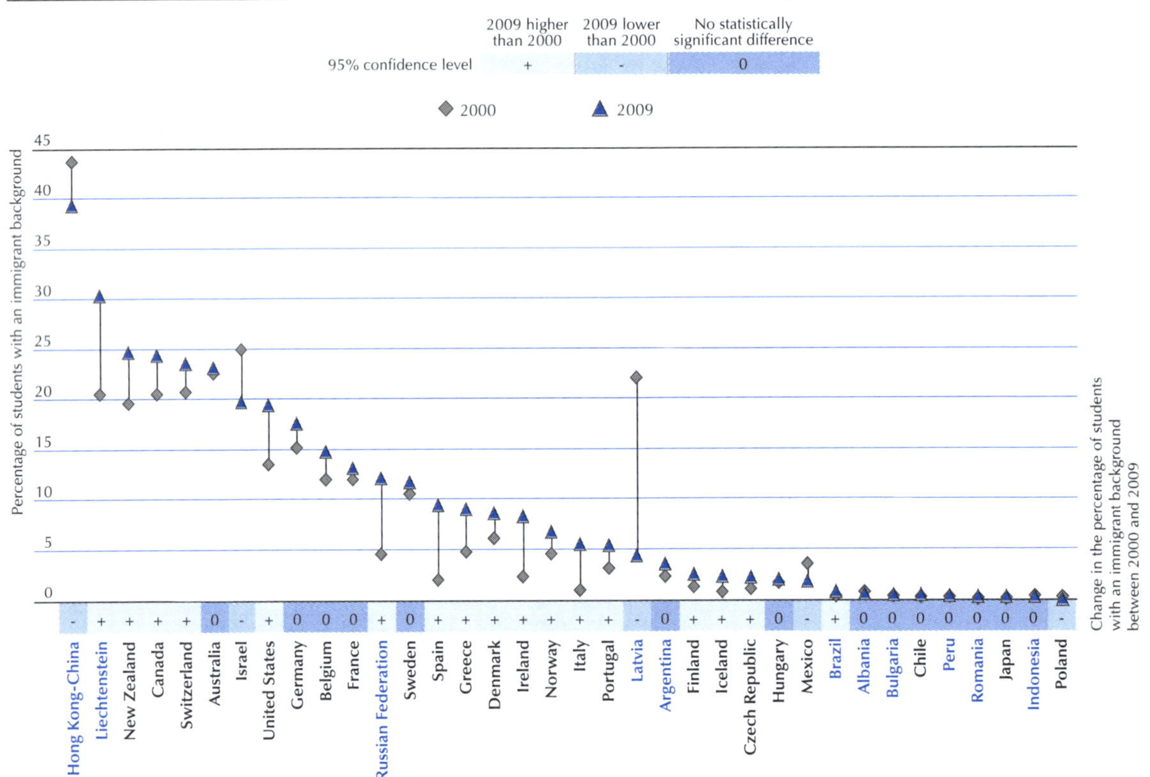

Note: Countries are ranked in descending order of percentage of students with an immigrant background in 2009.
Source: OECD, *PISA 2009 Database*, Table V.4.4.
StatLink http://dx.doi.org/10.1787/888932360005

In 13 countries, the percentage of students with an immigrant background increased by more than 2 percentage points, so that these students now constitute more than 5% of the student population. In Spain, Ireland, the United States, New Zealand and the partner countries Liechtenstein and the Russian Federation, the percentage of students with an immigrant background increased by five percentage points or more, and these students now represent from 8% to 30% of these countries' student population. In Italy, Greece and Canada, the percentage of students with an immigrant background increased by three to five percentage points.

In Israel and partner country and economy Latvia and Hong Kong-China, the percentage of students with an immigrant background decreased by 5, 18, and 4 percentage points, respectively. As a result, the proportion of students with an immigrant background dropped in Latvia to 4%, while these students still constitute 20% of the student population in Israel and 39% in Hong Kong-China.

Among OECD countries, the performance difference between students with and without an immigrant background remained broadly similar. Students without an immigrant background outperformed others by more than 40 score points in both 2000 and 2009 assessments (Table V.4.4).

In the countries showing the largest relative improvement among students with an immigrant background, the performance gap narrowed. Nevertheless, students without an immigrant background still perform better than students with an immigrant background in these countries. For example, in Belgium and Switzerland, the performance gap narrowed by nearly 40 score points, yet students without an immigrant background still outperform students with an immigrant background by 68 score points in Belgium and by 48 score points in Switzerland. Switzerland was able to close the performance gap despite the fact that the percentage of students with an immigrant background increased. Germany, New Zealand and the partner country Liechtenstein also show a narrowing gap between the performance of students with and without an immigrant background.

■ Figure V.4.7 ■

Immigrant background and reading performance in 2000 and 2009

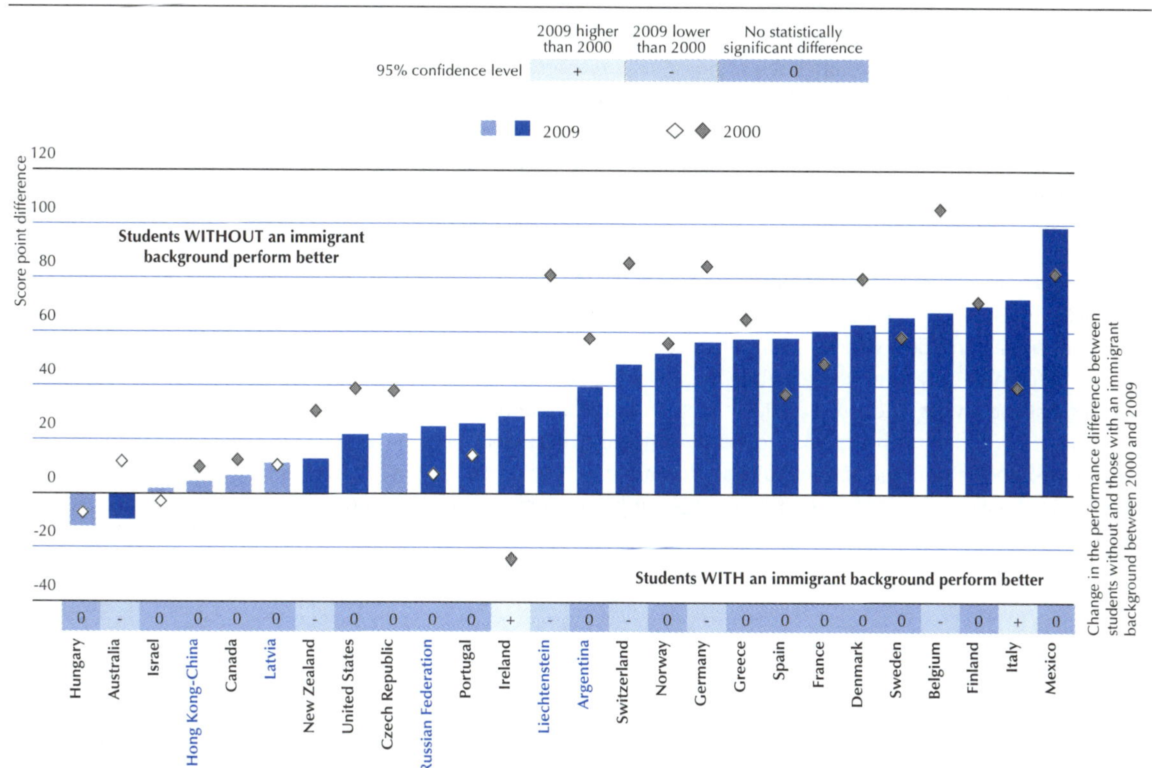

Note: Statistically significant score point differences are marked in a darker tone

Countries are ranked in ascending order of the performance difference between students without and those with an immigrant background in 2009.

Source: OECD, *PISA Database*, Table V.4.4.

StatLink http://dx.doi.org/10.1787/888932360005

Australia shows a decrease in the scores of students without an immigrant background and no change in the performance of students with an immigrant background, such that students with an immigrant background now outperform students without an immigrant background. This is the only country, among those for which trends can be calculated, in which, on average, students without an immigrant background now have lower scores than students with an immigrant background. Italy and Ireland are countries where the advantage of students without an immigrant background increased. In both countries, the percentage of students with an immigrant background increased by five to six percentage points from 2000 to 2009. In Italy, the performance of students without an immigrant background remained at the same level, but the performance of students with an immigrant background declined. In Ireland, the decline in the performance of students without an immigrant background was accompanied by an even larger decline in the performance of students with an immigrant background.

Changes in the number of students who speak another language at home and its relationship with performance

Among OECD countries, the percentage of students who speak a different language at home than the one in which the assessment was administered did not change between 2000 and 2009 (Table V.4.5).[6] However, this trend varies across countries.

In nine countries, the percentage of such students increased by one percentage point or more. As a result, in New Zealand, Canada, Germany and the partner country Bulgaria, the percentage of students who speak a different language at home is now 10% or more. In other countries that show a similar increase, the percentage is lower.

Among OECD countries with above the average percentage of students speaking a different language at home, this proportion decreased from 17% to 9% in Australia, from 18% to 14% in Italy, and from 19% to less than 16% in Switzerland.

Across the 32 countries among which reading performance can be compared between those students who speak the same language at home as the language of assessment and those who do not, 4 countries show a decrease in the performance advantage of those who speak the same language, while the reverse is true in 3 countries (Table V.4.5).

Germany, the United States, Switzerland and Canada saw a decline in the performance advantage among students who speak the same language at home as the assessment language. In Germany, the United States and Switzerland, this trend was largely due to improvements among students who speak a different language at home. In Canada, this change was the result of both a decline in performance among students who speak the same language at home and improvements among those who speak a different language at home. In all these countries, the performance advantage remained relatively high, above 30 score points, except in Canada, where it dropped from 35 to 18 score points.

Ireland, Belgium and the partner country Romania are the only countries where the advantage increased among students who speak the same language at home as the assessment language.[7] In Belgium, the considerable performance gap in 2000 widened further because of a noticeable decline in the performance of students who speak a different language at home. While the advantage of students speaking the language of assessment at home was not statistically significant in 2000 in Romania and Ireland, it is now relatively large. However, in Ireland, the number of students who speak a different language increased, and the 2000 results for these students were noticeably different from the 2009 results. In Romania, the performance of a relatively small percentage of students who do not speak in the language of assessment at home declined by 82 score points, while the performance of those who do remained almost unchanged.

■ Figure V.4.8 ■

Percentage of students who speak a language at home that is different from the language of assessment in 2000 and 2009

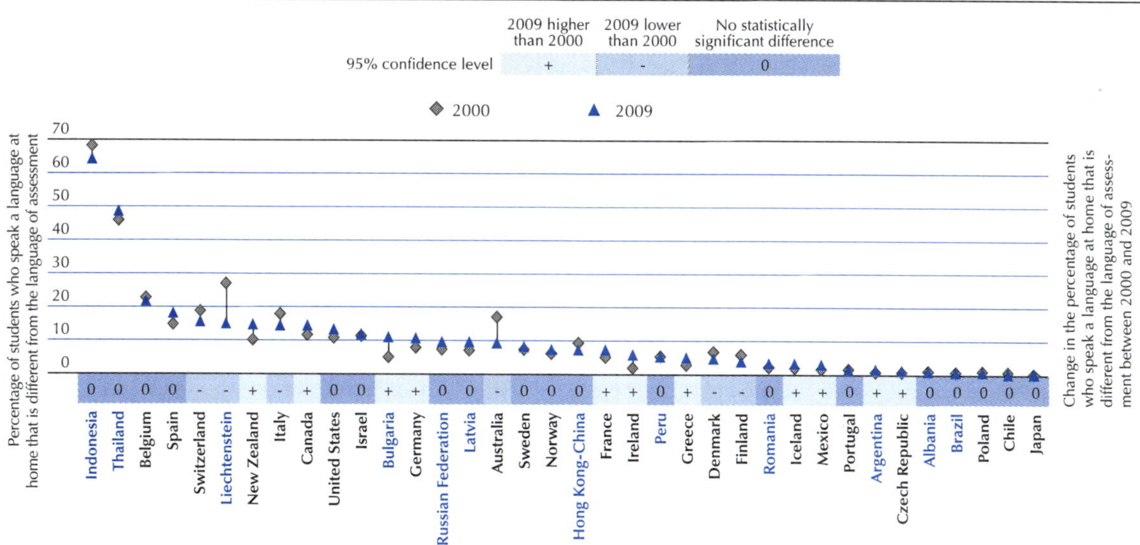

Note: Countries are ranked in descending order of percentage of students who speak at home a language that is different from the language of assessment in 2009.
Source: OECD, *PISA Database*, Table V.4.5.
StatLink http://dx.doi.org/10.1787/888932360005

■ Figure V.4.9 ■

Home language and reading performance in 2000 and 2009

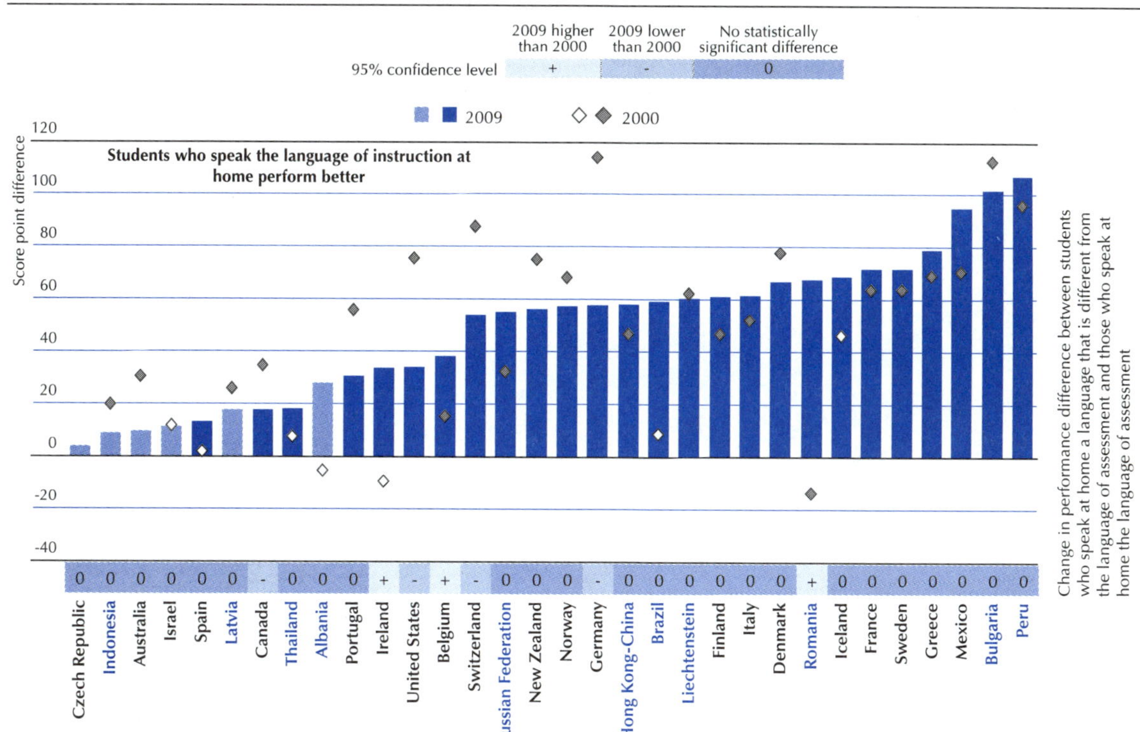

Note: Statistically significant score point differences are marked in a darker tone.
Countries are ranked in descending order of the performance difference between students who speak at home a language that is different from the language of assessment and those who speak at home the language of assessment in 2009.
Source: OECD, *PISA 2009 Database*, Table V.4.5.
StatLink http://dx.doi.org/10.1787/888932360005

Notes

1. The multilevel modelling method used in PISA has been updated since 2000, so the variance decomposition results reported in 2000, 2003 and 2006 reports are not directly comparable to those presented here. In this report, weights are used both at the student and school levels, while previously only the student weights were considered. The *PISA 2009 Technical Report* will give a full description of the weighting methods applied to 2009 data (OECD, forthcoming).

2. These results are affected by differences in how schools are defined and organised within countries and by the units that were chosen for sampling purposes. For example, in some countries, the schools in the PISA sample were defined as administrative units, even if they spanned several geographically separate institutions, as in Italy; in other countries, they were defined as those parts of larger educational institutions that serve 15-year-olds; in others, they were defined as physical school buildings; and yet in other countries, they were defined from a management perspective (*e.g.* entities having a principal). Annex A2 and the *PISA 2009 Technical Report* (OECD, forthcoming) provides an overview of how schools were defined. Note also that, because of the manner in which students were sampled, the within-school variance includes performance variation between classes as well as between students.

3. Various aspects of socio-economic background tend to be inter-related and are summarised in PISA in a single index–the *PISA index of the economic, social and cultural status* (ESCS). The index was constructed such that about two-thirds of students in OECD countries are between the values of -1 and 1, with an average score of 0 (*i.e.* the mean for the combined student population from participating OECD countries is set to 0 and the standard deviation is set to 1). Annex A1 provides details on how the ESCS index was equated across PISA assessments so that its values are comparable from 2000 to 2009.

4. The strength of the relationship is measured by a co-efficient in a linear regression of reading performance on the PISA *index of the economic, social and cultural status* of students.

5. Student performance is analysed only for countries where there are at least 30 students in five different schools who are compared with other students. This means that to be included in this analysis, a sample of students from a country has to include at least 30 students with an immigrant background and that these students must be dispersed among five different schools. Similarly, to make valid performance comparisons in the next section, the sample must include at least 30 students whose home language is different from the assessment language and who are from five different schools. This rule applies to data from each PISA assessment, so for comparisons of reading performance it must be applied in PISA 2000 and in PISA 2009.

6. Some countries administered PISA assessments in different languages.

7. Students in Ireland whose home language was different from the language of the assessment included students who spoke neither English nor Irish at home (3.7% of all students), those who spoke Irish at home but did the assessment in English (0.5%), and those who spoke English at home but did the assessment in Irish (1.8%).

Box V. F **Chile**

Chile's average reading performance increased by 40 score points from 2000 to 2009, the second largest improvement among PISA countries in this period (see Figure V.2.1 and Table V.2.1). While Chile's average performance still lies below the OECD average, this improvement from 2000 has lifted Chile's performance above that of Argentina, Bulgaria, Mexico, Romania and Thailand, all countries with similar or higher performance in 2000 (see Figure V.2.3).

Although improvements are observed throughout the performance distribution, these are strongest among low-achieving students. The performance of the lowest-achieving students has increased by 51 score points since 2000 and the percentage of students with a reading performance that falls below proficiency Level 2 has declined by 17.6 percentage points. In 2009, 30.6% of 15-year-old students were not proficient at Level 2, while in 2000 almost half of 15-year-olds lacked these basic reading skills. In contrast, changes at the top of the performance distribution have been smaller: the percentage of top-performing students, as measured by the proportion of students above proficiency Level 5, increased by only 0.8 percentage points (see Figures V.2.4 and V.2.5, and Table V.2.2).

As a result of this greater improvement among low-achieving students, the total variance in performance has decreased significantly in Chile, reducing the gap between high- and low-achieving students (see Figure V.4.1 and Table V.4.1). And because low-performing students are more likely to come from disadvantaged socio-economic backgrounds, Chile's equity levels have improved (see Figure V.4.4 and Table V.4.3). The score point difference associated with an increase of one unit in the *PISA index of economic, social and cultural status* decreased by eight score points.

In the 1980s, Chile had successfully expanded educational coverage to reach all students; in subsequent years, the challenge became to ensure educational quality for all students. Since the return to democracy in the 1990s, several policies and programmes have been adopted and implemented to raise educational quality and performance. Most of these policies target low-performing and disadvantaged schools which, as PISA 2000 revealed, require the largest improvements (see Cox [2003] for a review of educational policies in Chile).

Programmes that specifically target low-performing and disadvantaged students include the *P900 escuelas* in the early 1990s and the *Programa de Mejoramiento de la Educación con Calidad y Equidad* (MECE) programme a few years later. The P900 programme was oriented to the 10% lowest-performing primary schools, where instructors from the same community provided technical aid to teachers. These schools also received material help and educational resources. The MECE programme had a more thorough approach to helping schools: it sought to improve school infrastructure and resources, teacher training and school management, and to provide schools with the capacity to develop their own education programmes. This programme was implemented gradually throughout the educational system, starting from the lowest-performing schools and moving upwards. Also in the 1990s, classrooms in the early primary grades were equipped with books to become classroom libraries, and both public and government-dependent schools received textbooks to distribute to individual students. These textbooks were then owned by the students so that the most disadvantaged students could also have an initial set of books at home from which the entire family could benefit.

The Chilean government also substantially increased its level of investment in education from the 1990s onwards. Total expenditure on primary and secondary education more than doubled between 1995 and 2007 (see *Education at a Glance,* 2010, Table B1.5, p. 207) and teachers' salaries increased by more than 7.7% in real terms between 2000 and 2006 (see *Education at a Glance,* 2002, Table D6.1, p. 339; and *Education at a Glance, 2008*, Table D3.1, p. 452).

In addition, a curricular reform was implemented at the end of the 1990s. Following the results of PISA 2000, which showed low levels of functional reading skills among Chilean students, changes to the curriculum in language-of-instruction courses involved a shift from literature and grammar to a greater emphasis on reading comprehension and communication, abilities that are closer to the reading skills measured by PISA (Gysling 2003).

....

Other more general policies implemented to improve educational performance include an increase in school hours in 1997, moving from a two-shift day to whole-day schooling for all students. In 1998, the national assessment of educational performance (SIMCE) was improved significantly. Since 1995, school-level results from this assessment have been posted publicly and schools are provided with individual feedback. Teachers working in public schools undergo a thorough evaluation consisting of classroom observation, classroom planning and a portfolio analysis (*Docente Más*). Teachers that fail this assessment can opt for free teacher training. If a teacher fails three times, he or she is fired. Using student achievement data from SIMCE and other information, schools are classified in the *Sistema Nacional de Evaluación Docente* (SNED), which allocates additional resources to the highest-performing schools where it can be distributed directly to teachers. A second teacher-assessment programme, the *Asignación de Excelencia Pedagógica*, which is voluntary and open to all teachers, rewards teachers who have been recognised for pedagogical excellence with salary increases.

Students assessed by PISA in 2000 were affected by only a few of these programmes at the start of their school career. In contrast, students assessed by PISA in 2009 started school at the end of the 1990s and have benefitted from these programmes throughout their school career. Many of the programmes designed to improve educational and, more specifically, reading, performance focused on benefiting low-performing and disadvantaged students in early primary education.

The introduction of school vouchers in the early 1980s led to an increase in the number of private schools in the country and helped ensure that more children had access to education. Since the vouchers were introduced, enrolment in privately managed and government-subsidised schools has increased, drawing enrolment from public schools (Carnoy, 1998). As a result, enrolment in government-dependent schools has grown from 32.8% of enrolled 15-year-old students in 2000 (PISA 2000 Database) to 49.2% in 2009 (see Volume IV, *What Makes a School Successful?* and Table IV.3.9*)*, an increase of 16.4 percentage points.

While some research finds no impact of the vouchers on performance (Hsieh and Urquiola 2006), others see positive effects (Anand, Mizala and Repetto, 2006). These amount to roughly 0.14 standard deviations of improvement and are very small in comparison to the 40-point increase observed in Chile between 2000 and 2009 (see Figure V.2.1, Table V.2.1). The effect of voucher schools is seen more clearly in the socio-economic composition of schools, as the voucher programme has resulted in greater segregation of schools by academic performance and socio-economic background (see Hsieh and Urquiola, 2006; Belley, 2007; and Volume IV *What Makes a School Successful?*).

Despite Chile's great improvement in reading performance, PISA 2009 shows that the country still lags behind the OECD average, and three out of ten students still lack basic reading skills. Raising educational standards in Chile is high on both the public's and government's agenda. Policies and programmes are still being designed and implemented to improve educational quality, especially for disadvantaged and low-performing students. For example, the voucher programme has been reformed so that vouchers are weighed according to the socio-economic status of the student. Schools cannot select students based on socio-economic background or academic achievement during primary education, and schools cannot expel students unless they are first given the chance to repeat a grade. Incentives are offered to attract more qualified graduates to the teaching profession: pedagogical studies will receive public funding on the condition that students benefiting from this subsidy can teach in publicly funded schools for a given number of years once they have graduated.

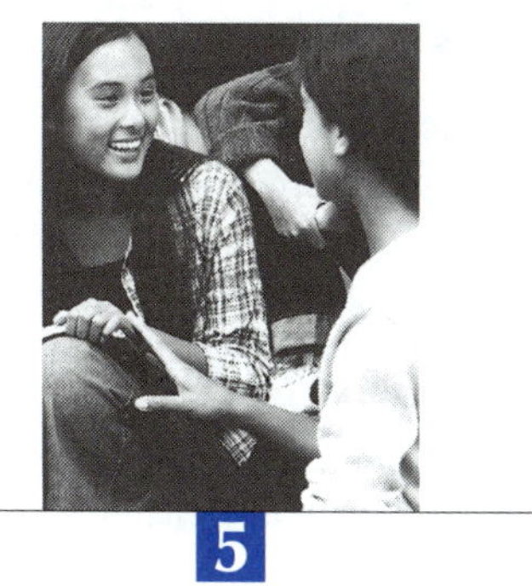

5

Trends in Attitudes and Student-School Relations

Have students' attitudes towards reading changed over the years? This chapter describes trends observed between 2000 and 2009 in whether and what students read for enjoyment, and how the gender gap in reading preferences and performance has evolved during that period. The chapter also discusses trends in teacher-student relations and disciplinary climate in the classroom.

TRENDS IN READING ENGAGEMENT

Changes in whether students read for enjoyment

Students who are highly engaged in a wide range of reading activities and who adopt particular learning strategies are more likely than other students to be effective learners and perform well at school. Research also documents a strong link between reading practices, motivation and proficiency among adults (OECD and Statistics Canada, 2000). Results presented in Volume III, *Learning to Learn*, indicate that reading for enjoyment is associated with reading proficiency. According to evidence presented in Volume III, a crucial difference between students who perform well in the PISA reading assessment and those who perform poorly lies in whether they read daily for enjoyment, rather than in how much time they spend reading.

In PISA 2009, students reported how much time they usually spent reading for enjoyment. Since they were asked the same question in PISA 2000, student responses can be compared between these two assessments. Students were classified into two categories: those who read for enjoyment and others.

Fifeteen-year-old students in 2009 tended to be less enthusiastic about reading than students were in 2000. On average across OECD countries, the percentage of students who reported reading for enjoyment daily decreased by five percentage points (Table V.5.1). In 2000, 69% of students reported reading for enjoyment daily, but in 2009, only 64% of students did so. As many as 22 countries saw a decrease in the percentage of students who read for enjoyment between 2000 and 2009. But not all countries did: Reading patterns have remained the same in 10 countries; and more students in Japan, Greece and Canada, and in the partner countries and economies Hong Kong-China, Bulgaria and Thailand read daily for enjoyment in 2009 than their counterparts did in 2000 (Figure V.5.1).

Some of the countries where the share of students who read for enjoyment decreased between 2000 and 2009 are countries with comparatively high levels of such readers. In Portugal, Finland and Mexico, and the partner country Latvia, the percentage of students reading for enjoyment decreased by more than 10 percentage points from relatively high levels (above 75% in 2000).

■ Figure V.5.1 ■

Percentage of students who read for enjoyment in 2000 and 2009

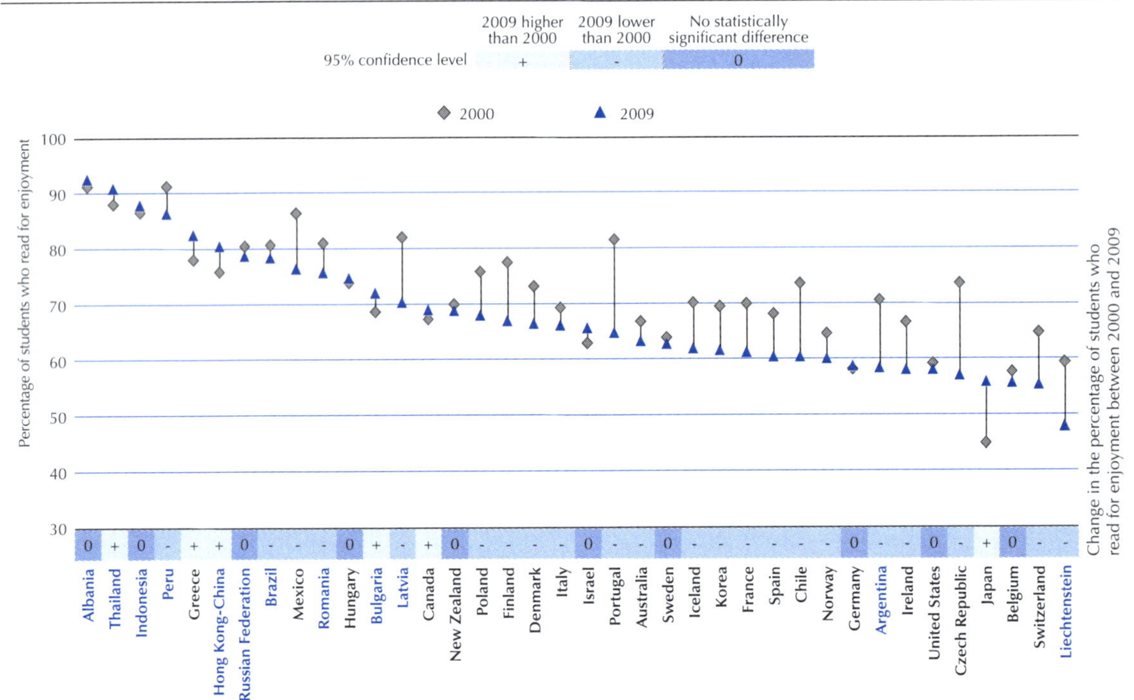

Note: Countries are ranked in descending order of percentage of students who read for enjoyment in 2009.
Source: OECD, *PISA 2009 Database*, Table V.5.1

StatLink http://dx.doi.org/10.1787/888932360024

Japan is the only country where fewer than two-thirds of students read for enjoyment daily in 2009 and where this proportion represented a large increase over levels observed in 2000. Because Japan was the country with the smallest share of students reading for enjoyment in 2000, even with an increase of 11 percentage points, this share remains lower than in most other countries.

Girls greatly outnumber boys among students who read for enjoyment. On average across OECD countries, 74% of girls read for enjoyment daily, while only 54% of boys do so – a gap of 20 percentage points (Table V.5.1). The gap between boys and girls widened between 2000 and 2009 by three percentage points across the OECD area: in 2000, 60% of boys and 77% of girls read for enjoyment; by 2009, these percentages had decreased to 54% and 74%, respectively. Interestingly, the widening of the gender gap was due to the fact that while, on average, a smaller percentage of boys and girls read for enjoyment in 2009 than in 2000, the decline is greater among boys than it is among girls. In other words, boys showed a greater decline in reading than girls did. The evolution of the gender gap in reading for enjoyment between 2000 and 2009 varies substantially across countries (see Figure V.5.2). While in most countries the proportion of boys who read for enjoyment decreased between 2000 and 2009, the trend among girls is less consistent.

Across all 38 countries with valid results in both the 2000 and 2009 reading assessments, only two countries show an increase in the proportion of boys who read for enjoyment. In Japan, the share of boys reading for enjoyment increased by nine percentage points, while in the partner economy Hong Kong-China it increased by five percentage points. In Japan, this increase was even greater among girls and was thus accompanied by a widening of the gender gap. In Hong Kong-China, boys and girls increased their reading habits similarly and therefore the gender gap remained stable at around eight percentage points. In 11 countries, including the OECD countries Belgium, Canada, Germany, Greece, Hungary, Israel and the United States, the proportion of boys who read for enjoyment did not change. In 25 countries, the proportion of boys who read for enjoyment has decreased since 2000. Portugal, the Czech Republic, Chile and the partner country Latvia are countries with the largest decrease. In these countries, the percentage of boys who read for enjoyment decreased by 15 percentage points or more, and now stands between 44% and 55%. Among other countries that saw a decrease in the percentage of boys reading for enjoyment, this

■ Figure V.5.2 ■

Changes in the percentage of boys and girls who read for enjoyment between 2000 and 2009

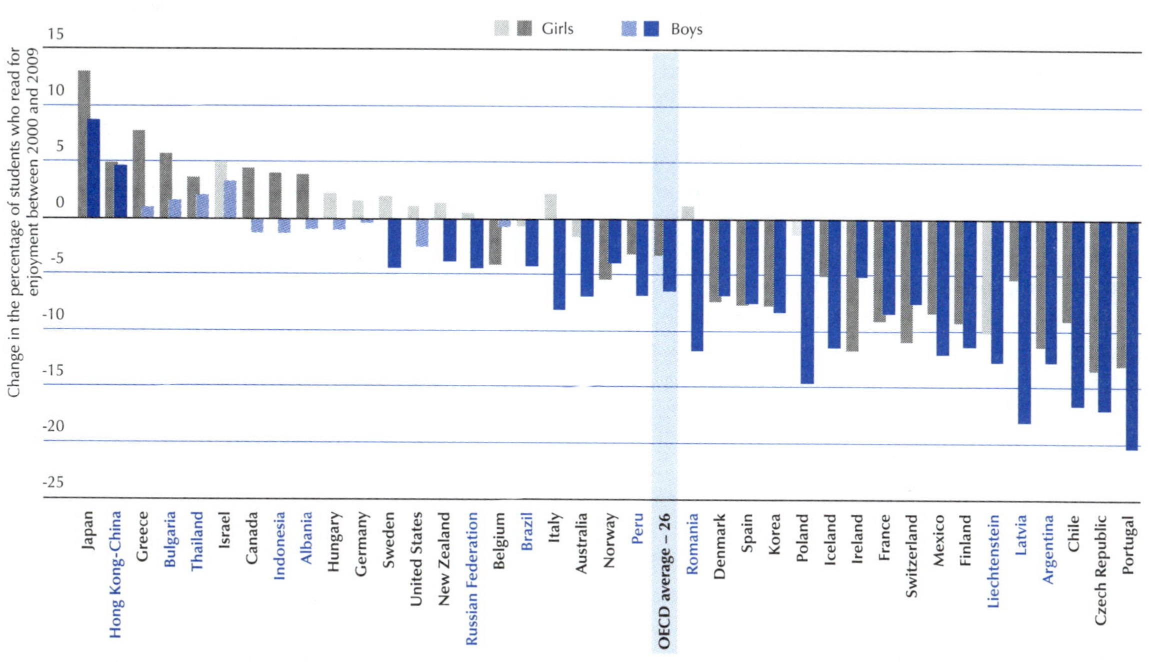

Note: Statistically significant score point changes are marked in a darker tone.
Countries are ranked in descending order of the change in percentage of all students who read for enjoyment between 2000 and 2009.
Source: OECD, *PISA 2009 Database*, Table V.5.1
StatLink http://dx.doi.org/10.1787/888932360024

percentage now stands at 50% or less in Switzerland and the partner countries Argentina and Liechtenstein, and at 55% or less in Iceland, Finland, France, Italy, Spain, Australia, Ireland, Sweden and Norway.

The percentage of girls who read for enjoyment decreased in 17 countries (see Figure V.5.2). In the Czech Republic, Portugal, Ireland, Switzerland, and the partner country Argentina, this proportion decreased by 11 to 13 percentage points and is now close to 70%, except in Portugal, when the overall percentage is close to 80% – well above the OECD average of 74%. In 12 other countries, the percentage of girls who read for enjoyment decreased by up to 10 percentage points. The share of girls reading for enjoyment remained unchanged in 13 OECD countries. In eight countries, the proportion of girls who reported reading for enjoyment increased. It is now above 80% in Greece and Canada, and the partner countries and economies Bulgaria, Hong Kong-China, Indonesia, Albania and Thailand, while despite the largest increase it is still below 60% in Japan.

Changes in how much students enjoy reading

Students' responses to statements describing their attitudes towards reading can be used to assess how much they enjoy reading. For example, students had to state whether they strongly disagreed, disagreed, agreed or strongly agreed with a statement like "I read only if I have to" or "I like talking about books with other people". Student responses to these questions can be summarised in an index on which the average student (e.g. the student with an average enjoyment of reading) is given an index value of zero, and about two-thirds of the OECD student population are between the values of minus one and one (i.e. the index has a standard deviation of one).

On average across OECD countries, the share of students reporting that they read only if they have to increase by about four percentage points between 2000 and 2009: in 2000, 36% of students in OECD countries reported reading only if they have to, while in 2009 this proportion reached 40%. The proportion of students who reported reading only if they have to increase in 21 countries, and the increase was particularly large, above 10 percentage points, in Mexico, Iceland, Korea and the Czech Republic, and in the partner countries Indonesia, Peru, Albania and Liechtenstein. In 2009, more than one in two students in Korea and Liechtenstein reported reading only when they have to. In Chile and the partner countries Thailand, Brazil and Romania, however, the percentage of students who reported reading only if they had to decrease by over 10 percentage points between 2000 and 2009 (Table V.5.3).

The general rise in students' reports of reading only when needed is matched by a large decline in the number of students reporting that they enjoy going to a bookstore or a library. In 2000, 49% of students reported enjoying going to a bookstore or a library, but in 2009, only 43% said they did – a six percentage point decrease. This drop was particularly pronounced in Mexico, the Czech Republic, Portugal, Chile, Denmark, Poland, Finland, Spain and Greece and the partner countries Peru and Romania. The proportion of students who enjoy going to bookstores or libraries increased only in Australia, Canada and in the partner economy Hong Kong-China.

Figure V.5.4 describes changes in the index of *enjoyment* of *reading* across countries participating in PISA 2000 and PISA 2009 (see also Table V.5.2). Unlike the section above, which looked at whether students read for enjoyment, this index summarises how much students enjoy reading. In general, across the 26 OECD countries for which data can be compared, enjoyment of reading decreased. In some countries students were more enthusiastic about reading in 2000 than in 2009, while in others the reverse was true. Enjoyment of reading increased in Germany, Canada, New Zealand, Japan and Korea and the partner countries and economies Thailand, Hong Kong-China, Albania and Brazil. In 15 countries, enjoyment of reading remained at similar levels, while it decreased in 14 other countries, with the Czech Republic, Mexico and Finland seeing the greatest decrease (one-fifth of the standard deviation of this index or more).

Gender differences in how much more – or less – boys and girls enjoy reading in 2009 compared to 2000 mirror findings described for gender differences over the same period in whether boys and girls read for enjoyment. On average, not only did boys enjoy reading less than girls in PISA 2009, but the gender gap is widening: boys are enjoying reading less and less, while the decline in enjoyment of reading is smaller among girls; and in some countries, girls enjoy reading more in 2009 than their counterparts did in 2000 (Table V.5.2). Although enjoyment of reading decreased more among boys than among girls in most countries, in Ireland in 2009, boys enjoyed reading as much as they did in 2000, while girls' enjoyment decreased over the same period. In the Czech Republic, Finland, Denmark both boys and girls reported less interest in reading, but the drop among girls was larger than that among boys (Figure V.5.5). In these countries, however, girls remain more enthusiastic readers than boys, despite the narrowing of the gender gap in reading enjoyment between 2000 and 2009.

■ Figure V.5.3 ■

Percentage of students who read only if they have to and percentage of students who enjoy going to a bookstore or a library in 2000 and 2009

Percentage of students who report «agree» or «strongly agree» on the following reading activities

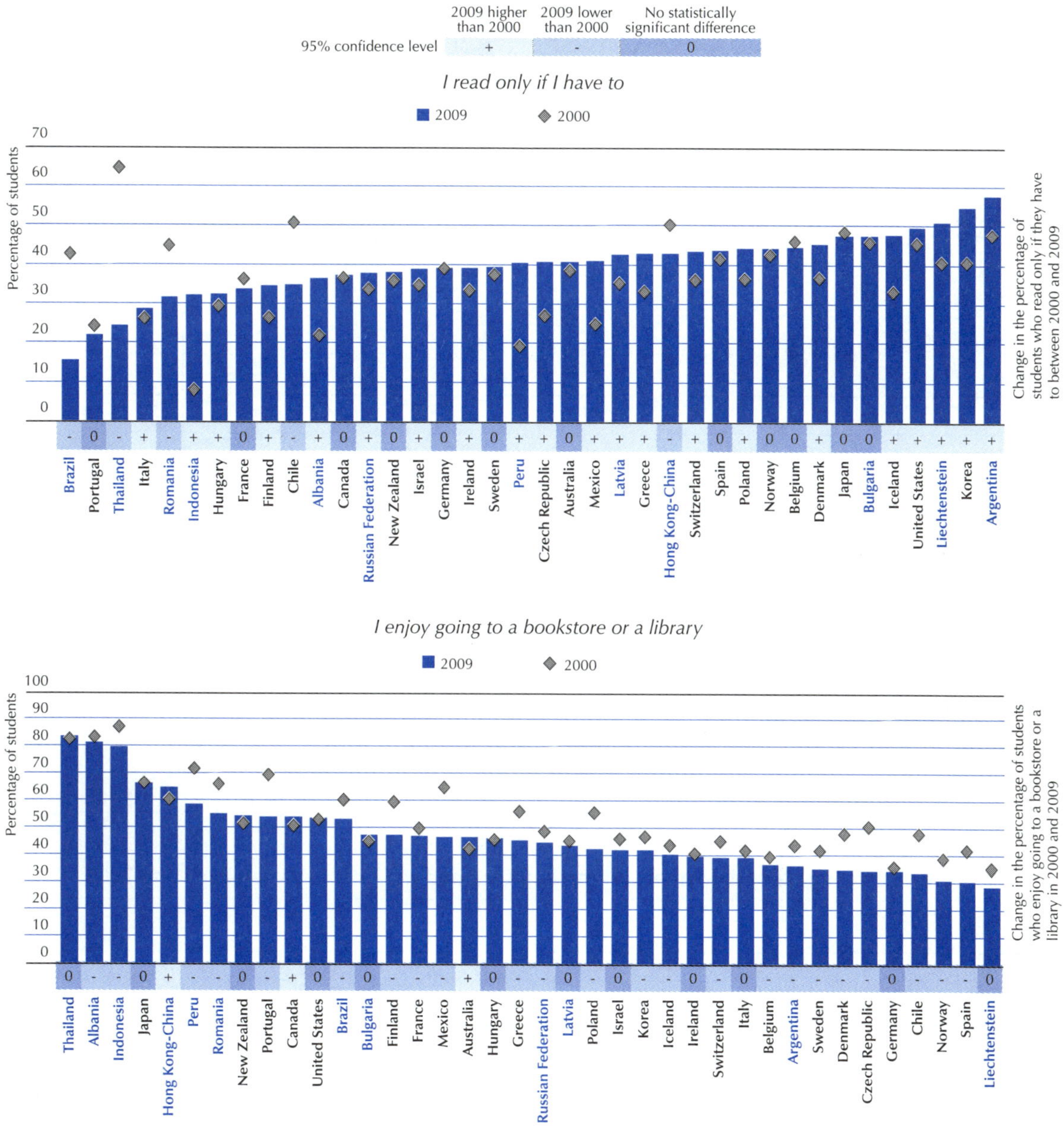

95% confidence level	2009 higher than 2000	2009 lower than 2000	No statistically significant difference
	+	-	0

I read only if I have to

■ 2009 ◆ 2000

Percentage of students (0–70)

Change in the percentage of students who read only if they have to between 2000 and 2009

Brazil	Portugal	Thailand	Italy	Romania	Indonesia	Hungary	France	Finland	Chile	Albania	Canada	Russian Federation	New Zealand	Israel	Germany	Ireland	Sweden	Peru
-	0	-	+	-	+	+	0	+	-	+	0	+	0	+	0	+	0	+

Czech Republic	Australia	Mexico	Latvia	Greece	Hong Kong-China	Switzerland	Spain	Poland	Norway	Belgium	Denmark	Japan	Bulgaria	Iceland	United States	Liechtenstein	Korea	Argentina
+	0	+	+	+	-	+	0	+	0	0	+	0	0	+	+	+	+	+

I enjoy going to a bookstore or a library

■ 2009 ◆ 2000

Percentage of students (0–100)

Change in the percentage of students who enjoy going to a bookstore or a library in 2000 and 2009

Thailand	Albania	Indonesia	Japan	Hong Kong-China	Peru	Romania	New Zealand	Portugal	Canada	United States	Brazil	Bulgaria	Finland	France	Mexico	Australia	Hungary	Greece
0	-	-	0	+	-	-	0	-	+	0	-	0	-	-	-	+	0	-

Russian Federation	Latvia	Poland	Israel	Korea	Iceland	Ireland	Switzerland	Italy	Belgium	Argentina	Sweden	Denmark	Czech Republic	Germany	Chile	Norway	Spain	Liechtenstein
-	0	-	0	-	-	0	-	0	-	-	-	-	-	0	-	-	-	0

Note: Countries are ranked in descending order of the percentage of students on these items in 2009.
Source: OECD, *PISA 2009 Database*, Table V.5.3.
StatLink http://dx.doi.org/10.1787/888932360024

In a large number of countries, the decrease in enjoyment of reading was much more pronounced among boys than among girls, leading to a widening of the gender gap. Poland and the partner country Albania saw the largest increase in the gender gap in enjoyment of reading. In Albania, girls' enjoyment of reading increased between 2000 and 2009, but on average in 2009, boys enjoyed reading as much as they did in 2000. In Poland, boys' enjoyment of reading decreased while girls' enjoyment increased.

Trends in the number of students who report that they read for enjoyment and in the levels of enjoyment of reading are highly related. In countries where students more often report that they read for enjoyment, students also more often report that they enjoy reading. As both aspects are also correlated at the individual student level in PISA 2009 (see Volume III,

■ Figure V.5.4 ■

Index of enjoyment of reading in 2000 and 2009

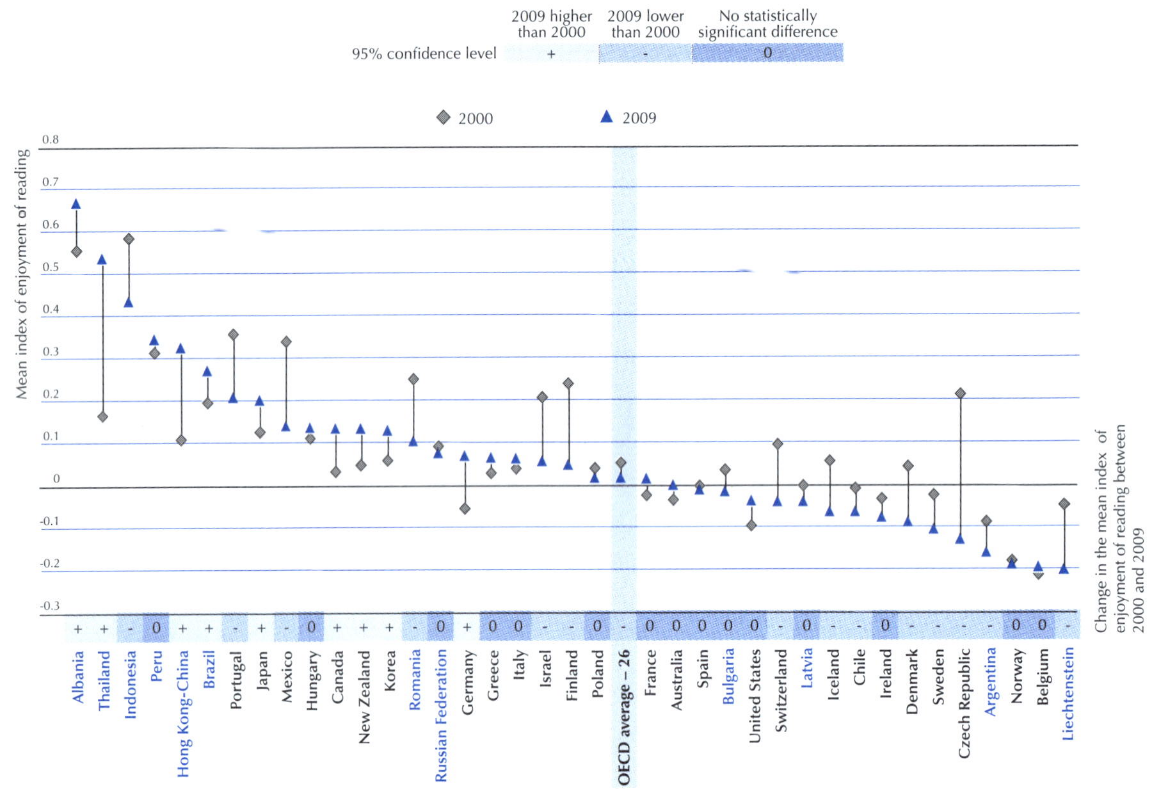

Note: Countries are ranked in descending order of the mean index of enjoyment of reading in 2009.
Source: OECD, *PISA 2009 Database*, Table V.5.2.
StatLink http://dx.doi.org/10.1787/888932360024

■ Figure V.5.5 ■

Change in the index of enjoyment of reading for boys and girls between 2000 and 2009

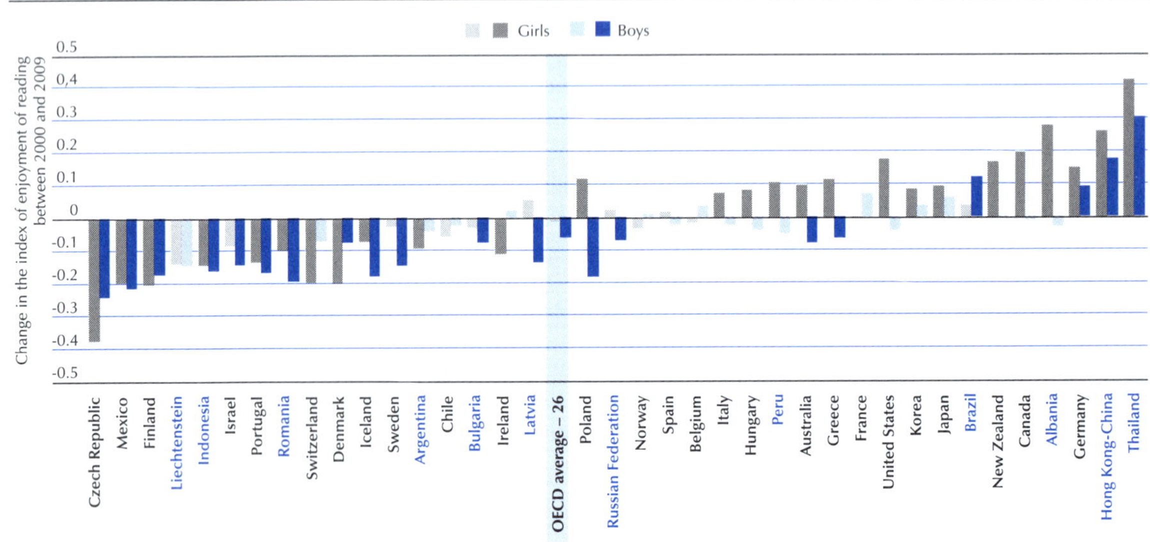

Note: Statistically significant score point changes are marked in a darker tone.
Countries are ranked in descending order of the change in the mean index of enjoyment of reading for all students between 2000 and 2009.
Source: OECD, *PISA 2009 Database*, Table V.5.2.
StatLink http://dx.doi.org/10.1787/888932360024

Learning to Learn), this demonstrates that students who read for enjoyment usually enjoy reading, and that an increase in whether students read for enjoyment is associated with an overall increase in how much students enjoy reading.

Figure V.5.6 shows the association between trends in whether students read for enjoyment and in how much they enjoy reading. Countries towards the right are those where more students reported reading for enjoyment in 2009 than in 2000, while countries towards the top are those where the average value of student enjoyment of reading increased. Clearly, similar trends can be observed in whether students read for enjoyment and in how much students enjoy reading. In Canada, Japan and the partner economy Hong Kong-China, both the percentage of students who read for enjoyment and how much students enjoy reading, on average, increased between 2000 and 2009. In 12 countries the percentage of students who read for enjoyment decreased, while these countries also saw a decrease in how much students enjoy reading. In only two countries, Korea and Brazil, the percentage of students who read for enjoyment decreased, while the average value of student enjoyment of reading increased.

■ Figure V.5.6 ■

Change in the index of enjoyment of reading and the proportion of students who read for enjoyment between 2000 and 2009

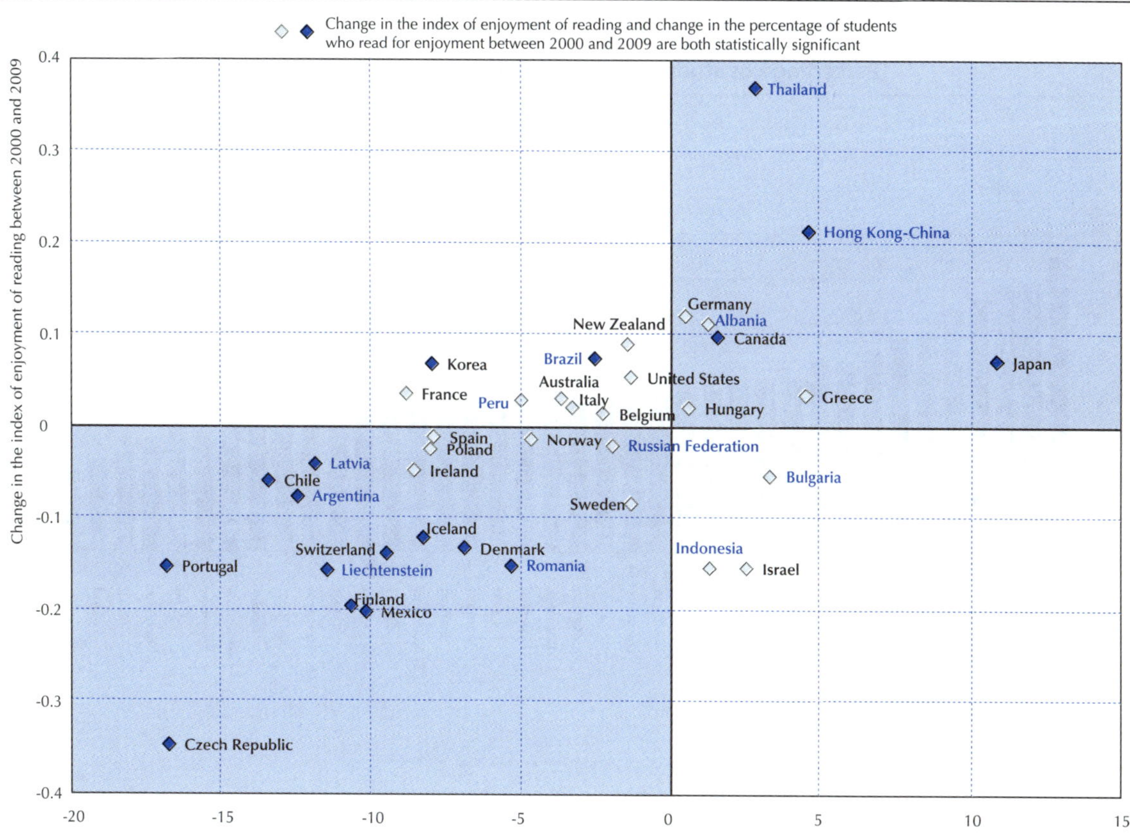

Note: Changes in the index of enjoyment of reading and changes in the percentage of students who read for enjoyment between 2000 and 2009 that are both statistically significant are marked in a darker tone.

Source: OECD, *PISA 2009 Database*, Tables V.5.1 and V.5.2.

StatLink http://dx.doi.org/10.1787/888932360024

Changes in what students read for enjoyment

Volume III, *Learning to Learn*, examines the reading habits of students in different countries and different groups of students within each country. PISA asked students to indicate the frequency with which they choose to read the following types of materials: magazines, comic books, fiction, non-fiction and newspapers. The categories for frequency ranged from "never", to "several times a week". Results presented in Figures V.5.7 and V.5.8 as well as Tables V.5.6, V.5.7, V.5.8 and V.5.9 focus on differences between students who report reading each type of material regularly, i.e. several times a month or several times a week. Results published in this Volume on changes in the materials students read for enjoyment between 2000 and 2009 should be interpreted in light of possible increases in the amount of time students spend reading online for enjoyment. Because the way in which PISA measures what students read online in 2000 and 2009 is not comparable, this Volume cannot examine potential substitutions between print and online materials.

Chapter 1 of Volume III identifies a particularly strong and positive association between reading performance and reading fiction regularly, and a negative association between reading performance and reading comic books regularly. Across OECD countries, the proportion of students who reported reading fiction regularly increased by three percentage points between 2000 and 2009. This average increase in the OECD area is a pattern that most countries share: fiction reading decreased in only three countries, while it increased in 19 countries and did not change in the remaining 16 countries. In the partner country Indonesia, the increase in reading fiction was particularly pronounced: while in 2000 only 37% of students there reported reading fiction regularly, in 2009 almost 60% of students did – a 23-percentage-point increase. In Japan, Korea, Canada and the partner countries and economies Indonesia, Thailand, Peru and Hong Kong-China, the proportion of students who reported reading fiction increased by more than 10 percentage points between 2000 and 2009. While in most of these countries only about one-third of students reported reading fiction regularly in 2000, nine years later, more than four in ten students in these countries did (see Figure V.5.7 and Table V.5.6).

■ Figure V.5.7 ■

Percentage of students who read fiction in 2000 and 2009

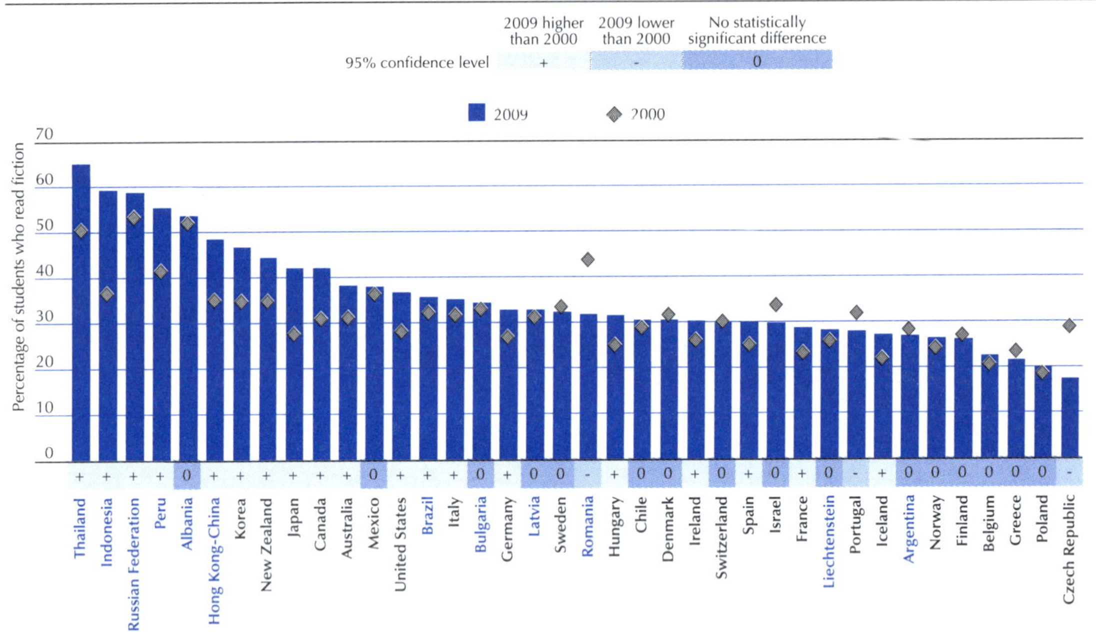

Note: Countries are ranked in descending order of the percentage of students on who read fiction for enjoyment in 2009.
Source: OECD, *PISA 2009 Database*, Table V.5.6.
StatLink http://dx.doi.org/10.1787/888932360024

Volume III, *Learning to Learn*, identifies substantial gender differences in the percentage of boys and girls who read fiction: in 2009, on average across OECD countries, girls were almost twice as likely to report reading fiction as boys. More boys and girls read fiction in 2009 than their counterparts did in 2000. On average across OECD countries, the percentage of boys who reported reading fiction increased by nearly three percentage points and that of girls increased by almost four percentage points. In most countries, however, the increase in the number of girls was larger than that of boys. A notable exception is the partner country the Russian Federation, where the percentage of boys reading fiction increased by almost eight percentage points while it grew by only three percentage points among girls; and Norway, where the proportion of boys reading fiction increased by four percentage points while it remained stable among girls. In Switzerland, the substantial gap between the percentage of boys and girls reading fiction narrowed considerably between 2000 and 2009. In 2009, almost one in five boys reported reading fiction regularly, an increase of more than four percentage points over 2000, while two in five girls reported the same in 2009, a decrease of four percentage points over 2000. The Czech Republic is one of the countries with the lowest

■ Figure V.5.8 ■

Percentage of students who read comic books in 2000 and 2009

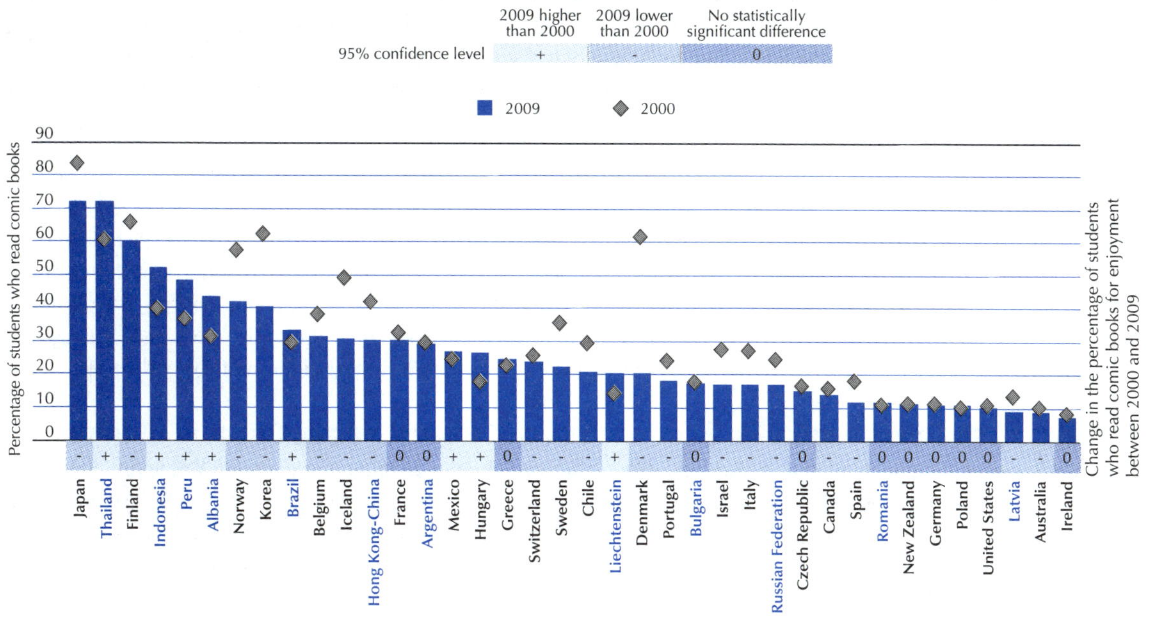

Note: Countries are ranked in descending order of the percentage of students on who read comic books for enjoyment in 2009.
Source: OECD, *PISA 2009 Database*, Table V.5.6.
StatLink http://dx.doi.org/10.1787/888932360024

number of both boys and girls who reported reading fiction regularly, and one where the decrease in reading fiction was particularly notable among girls. In 2000, almost 45% of girls reported reading fiction regularly, but in 2009, this percentage shrunk by 16 percentage points to 29% (Table V.5.7).

Students reported a declining interest in reading comic books regularly. On average, the percentage of students in OECD countries who reported reading comic books regularly decreased by almost seven percentage points between 2000 and 2009. The proportion of students who reported reading comic books regularly decreased in 19 countries, increased in eight countries and remained stable in the remaining 11 countries that participated in both PISA 2000 and PISA 2009. In general, the countries with the largest share of students who read comic books regularly are among those countries that saw the largest reduction in students' engagement with comic books. The only exception is Thailand, where the percentage of these students grew by almost 12 percentage points, from six in ten students in 2000, to seven in ten students in 2009. The drop in comic book reading was particularly steep in Denmark: while in 2000 almost three in five students there read comic books regularly, nine years later, only one in five did so – a drop of over 40 percentage points. The decline in the percentage of students who reported that they read comic books regularly is also above 15 percentage points in Korea, Iceland and Norway, all countries where relatively large numbers of students read comic books regularly in 2000 (see Figure V.5.8 and Table V.5.6).

In almost all countries taking part in both PISA 2000 and PISA 2009, a lower percentage of students reported reading newspapers and magazines in 2009 than in 2000. Across OECD countries, the number of students who reported reading magazines fell by ten percentage points, and all but nine countries saw a decline in this activity. Thailand, Peru and Indonesia are the only countries with an increase in the percentage of students who reported reading magazines regularly, and all three are among the countries where fewer than one in two students reported reading magazines regularly in 2000. Similarly, on average across OECD countries, the decline in the percentage of students who reported reading newspapers for enjoyment was relatively pronounced and equal to five percentage points. The percentage of students who reported reading newspapers regularly rose in seven countries, remained stable in ten countries and decreased in 21 countries (Table V.5.6). The decrease in the percentage of boys and girls who reported reading newspapers was similar and close to five percentage points (Table V.5.7).

Volume III illustrates that versatile readers – in other words, students who read not just one type of material but different kinds of materials – are more proficient readers than students with undiversified reading habits. Table V.5.10 compares differences in what students read between 2000 and 2009. Students became relatively more versative readers in seven countries, did not change in eight countries and became less versatile in 23 countries. Reading diversity increased in Hungary, Switzerland, Poland and the partner countries Indonesia, Peru, Thailand and Albania. The decrease was highest in Denmark, and close to one-third of a standard deviation of this index in Italy, Korea, Iceland, Sweden and the partner countries the Russian Federation and Bulgaria.

In almost all countries, girls are more versatile readers than boys, and this gap has widened as boys have become less versatile readers over time. However, countries differ in how reading diversity evolved from 2000. In Indonesia, for example, reading diversity increased equally among boys and girls by almost half a standard deviation, while in other countries, where diversity increased, girls became even more versatile readers. In none of the countries did reading diversity increase among boys while it remained the same or decreased among girls. In numerous countries, reading diversity decreased equally among boys and girls, while in Iceland, Sweden, Korea, Israel and Romania reading diversity decreased among boys more than among girls, further widening the gender gap.

Changes in socio-economically disadvantaged students' engagement in reading

It is often stated that students read less and less, especially boys. Evidence emerging from PISA supports the notion that not only do boys read less than girls, but in many countries, the percentage of students who read for enjoyment decreased, particularly among boys. There are also concerns that this negative trend is more prevalent among students from socio-economically disadvantaged backgrounds. Evidence from PISA 2009 confirms this, indicating that students from such backgrounds read less than others (see Volume III, *Learning to Learn,* for more detailed evidence). This section examines trends to determine how engagement in reading for boys and girls varies according to socio-economic background.

Table V.5.4 and Figure V.5.10 illustrate changes in the percentage of boys and girls from different socio-economic backgrounds who read for enjoyment. Table V.5.5 provides similar data with respect to changes in how much these groups of students enjoy reading between 2000 and 2009 assessments. The majority of students who read for enjoyment are socio-economically advantaged students (see Figure V.5.9).[1] These students are not only more likely to read for enjoyment than disadvantaged students, they also enjoy reading more than disadvantaged students. This is true both in 2000 and 2009.

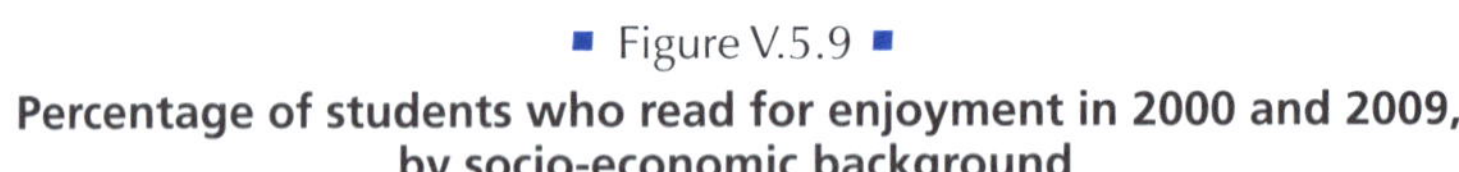

■ Figure V.5.9 ■

Percentage of students who read for enjoyment in 2000 and 2009, by socio-economic background

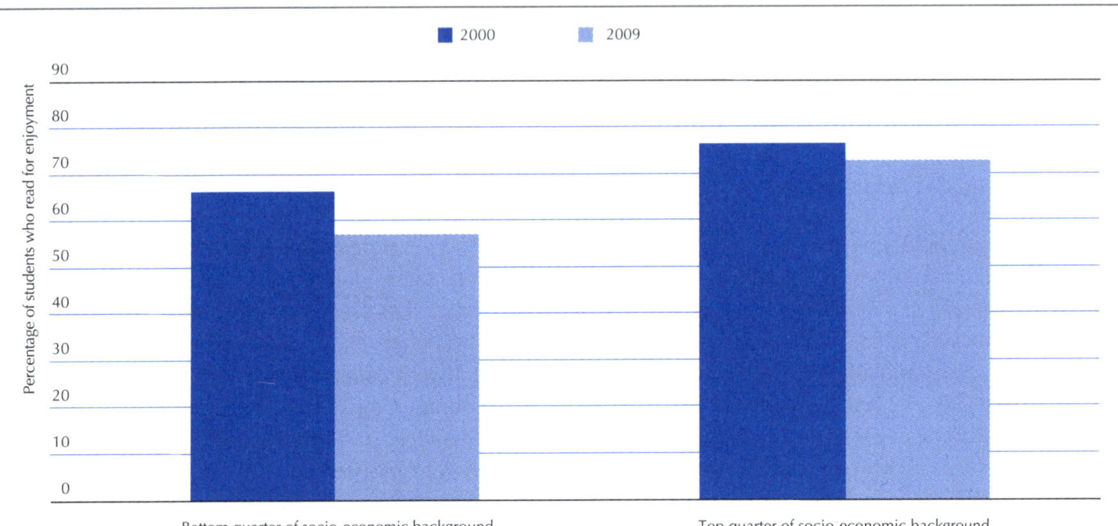

Source: OECD, *PISA 2009 Database*, Table V.5.4.

StatLink http://dx.doi.org/10.1787/888932360024

Socio-economically disadvantaged students reported disliking reading more in 2009 than they did in 2000 (see Figure V.5.9 and Table V.5.4). Across OECD coutnries, the proportion of disadvantaged students who read for enjoyment decreased by nine percentage points between 2000 and 2009, while the percentage among those students from a privileged background fell by three percentage points. The gap between these two groups widened from ten percentage points in 2000 to 16 percentage points in 2009. Similarly, the level of enjoyment of reading reported by disadvantaged students was, on average, lower than that reported by students from privileged backgrounds. In PISA 2000, the gap was 0.33 of the standard deviation, while it increased to 0.46 in PISA 2009 (Table V.5.5).

Relative changes in whether students reported reading for enjoyment and in how much they reported enjoying reading vary greatly among socio-economically disadvantaged and privileged students across countries (see Table V.5.4 and V.5.5). For example, in the partner country Hong Kong-China, the percentage of students who read for enjoyment increased among disadvantaged students, while it remained the same among privileged students. In Canada this percentage increased only among students from privileged socio-economic backgrounds. In contrast, in Ireland, the percentage of students who read for enjoyment remained the same among students from privileged backgrounds, but decreased by almost 18 percentage points among disadvantaged students. In Finland, the number

■ Figure V.5.10 ■

Change in the percentage of boys and girls who read for enjoyment between 2000 and 2009, by socio-economic background

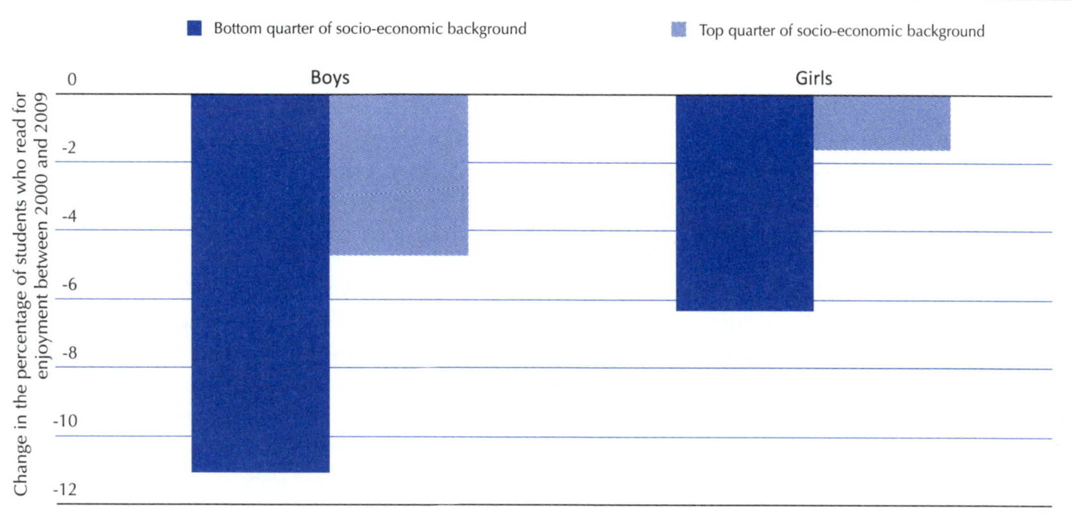

Source: OECD, *PISA 2009 Database*, Table V.5.4.
StatLink http://dx.doi.org/10.1787/888932360024

of students from disadvantaged backgrounds who reported reading for enjoyment decreased by 17 percentage points from 2000 to 2009. But unlike Ireland, in Finland, there was also a decrease by six percentage points in the percentage of advantaged students who reported reading for enjoyment.

Figure V.5.10 (see also Tables V.5.1 and V.5.4) shows the percentage of boys and girls from socio-economically disadvantaged and socio-economically advantaged backgrounds who read for enjoyment in PISA 2000 and PISA 2009. The Figure illustrates how this percentage decreased more among boys (six percentage points) than girls (three percentage points), irrespective of their socio-economic background. The percentage of girls from a disadvantaged background who read for enjoyment decreased by six percentage points while the same percentage decreased by 11 percentage points among boys from similar backgrounds. Among boys from privileged backgrounds, the percentage decreased by five percentage points while among girls from those backgrounds, it decreased by less than two percentage points. Socio-economically disadvantaged boys are the group of students who reads the least for enjoyment and are also the group that is growing the most disengaged from reading for enjoyment.

Changes in the reading performance of students who read fiction

Volume III, *Learning to Learn*, shows large performance gaps between students who read fiction regularly and students who do not. Table V.5.8 identifies changes between 2000 and 2009 in the reading performance of students

who reported that they read fiction. In 11 countries, the reading performance of students who reported reading fiction increased, in three countries it decreased, and no change was noted in 24 countries. In 15 countries, the "performance premium" that is associated with reading fiction increased, with a change of 20 score points or more in France, the Czech Republic, Italy, Poland, Greece, Portugal and Switzerland (Table V.5.8).

For girls, the advantage in reading performance that is associated with reading fiction increased in 12 countries between 2000 and 2009, remained stable in 22 countries and decreased in four countries: Korea, Mexico and the partner countries Latvia and Argentina (see Table V.5.9). For boys, the "performance premium" that is associated with reading fiction increased in eleven countries, decreased in Mexico and remained the same in other countries. The "performance premium" increased by 25 score points or more in the Czech Republic and France among girls, and in France, Poland, Belgium, Italy and the partner country Albania, among boys.

TRENDS IN STUDENT VIEWS ON SCHOOLS AND TEACHERS

Changes in teacher-student relations

Positive teacher-student relations are crucial for establishing an environment that is conducive to learning. Research finds that students, particularly socio-economically disadvantaged students, learn more and have fewer disciplinary problems when they feel that their teachers take them seriously (Gamoran, 1993) and when they have strong bonds with their teachers (Crosnoe, *et al.*, 2004). One explanation is that positive teacher-student relations help transmit social capital, create communal learning environments and promote and strengthen adherence to norms that are conducive to learning (Birch & Ladd, 1998).

PISA 2009 asked students to agree or disagree with several statements regarding their relationships with their teachers in school. These statements included whether they got along with their teachers, whether teachers were interested in their personal well-being, whether teachers took the students seriously, whether teachers were a source of support if the students needed extra help, and whether teachers treated the student fairly. Similar questions were asked in 2000, so teacher-student relations could be compared across time.

Results from PISA 2009 suggest that students in the OECD area are generally satisfied with the quality of teacher-student relations (see Chapter 2 of Volume IV, *What Makes a School Successful?*). The difference between responses in 2000 and 2009 suggests that the quality of teacher-student relations actually improved during the period (Figure V.5.11 and Table V.5.11). For example, across the 26 OECD countries with comparable data, 74% of students in 2000 agreed or strongly agreed with the statements, "If I need extra help, I will receive it from my teachers" or "Most of my teachers treat me fairly", while 79% of students agreed or strongly agreed with those statements in PISA 2009 – an increase of five percentage points. In 2000, 65% of students agreed or strongly agreed that "most of my teachers really listen to what I have to say" and by 2009 this proportion had increased to almost 68%, an increase of three percentage points.

The increase in the proportion of students reporting that their teachers "really listen to what I have to say" was above 10 percentage points in Germany, Korea, Japan, Iceland and the partner country Albania. The proportion of students agreeing that "If I need extra help, I will receive it from my teachers" also increased in many countries. This increase was most notable in Poland, Portugal, Germany and the partner countries Albania and Latvia, where it increased by more than 10 percentage points. The countries with the largest increases in the proportion of students feeling confident that they will receive help from their teachers are, in most instances, those where the lowest percentage of students expressed a high level of confidence in their teachers in 2000. The gap between countries in the percentage of students who believed "their teachers treat them fairly" also narrowed considerably, since the countries with the most marked increase were generally those, such as Italy and Poland, where a smaller share of students in 2000 reported that they thought their teachers treated them fairly.

■ Figure V.5.11 ■

Teacher-student relations in PISA 2000 and 2009

Percentage of students reporting that the following things happen «never or hardly ever» or «in some lessons»

Most of my teachers really listen to what I have to say

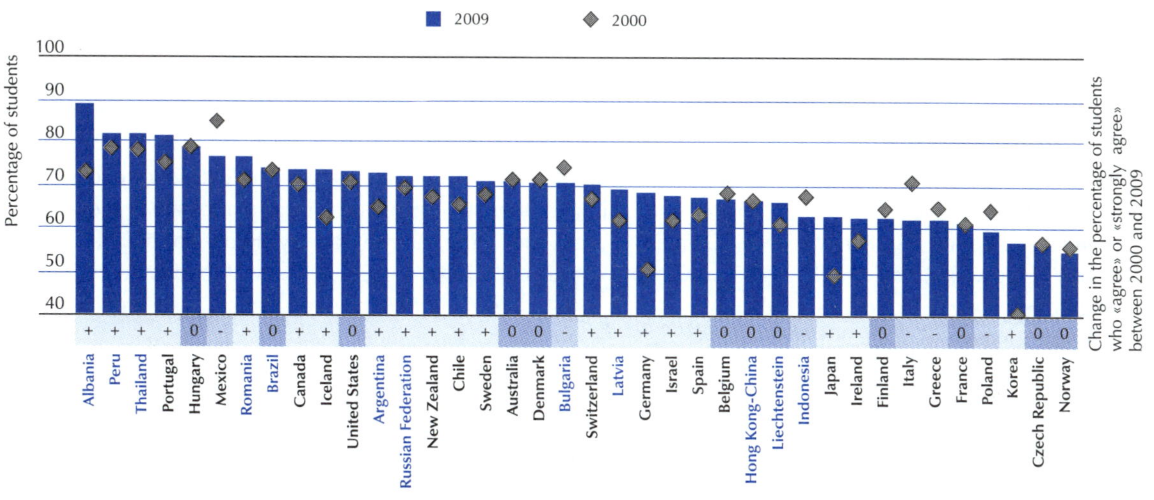

If I need extra help, I will receive it from my teachers

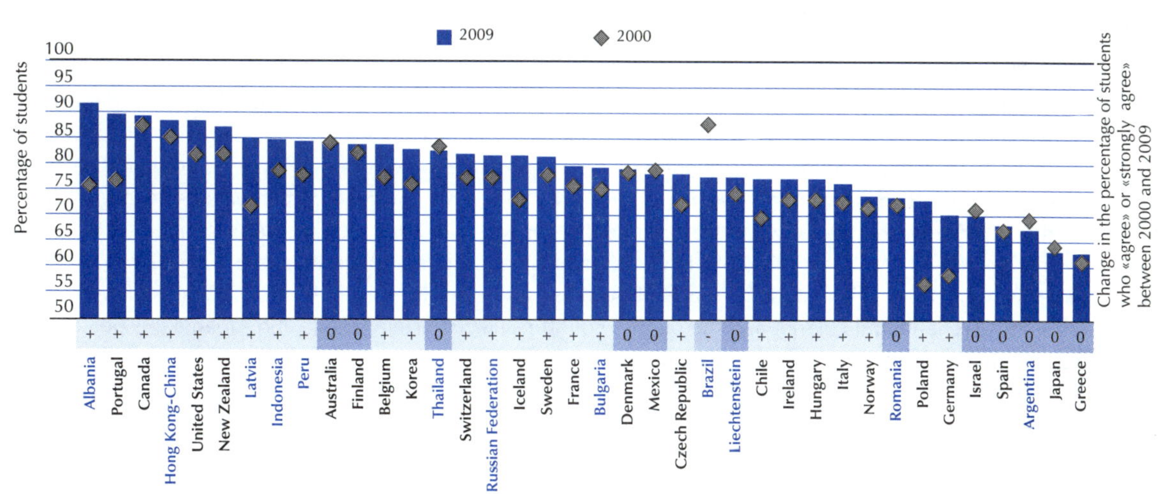

Note: Countries are ranked in descending order of the percentage of students on the items in 2009.
Source: OECD, *PISA 2009 Database*, Table V.5.11.
StatLink http://dx.doi.org/10.1787/888932360024

Changes in disciplinary climate

The disciplinary climate in the classroom and school can also affect learning. Classrooms and schools with more disciplinary problems are less conducive to learning, since teachers have to spend more time creating an orderly environment before instruction can begin (Gamoran and Nystrand in Newman, *et al.*, 1992). Interruptions in the classroom disrupt students' engagement and their ability to follow the lessons.

Students were asked to describe the disciplinary climate in their reading lessons. This includes how often – never, in some, most or all language-of-instruction lessons – students do not listen to what the teacher says, there is noise and disorder, the teacher has to wait a long time for students to quieten down, students cannot work well, and students do not start working for a long time after the lesson begins. Similar questions were asked in PISA 2000, so responses can be compared across time.

On average across OECD countries the percentage of students who reported that their teacher never or almost never has to wait a long time for them to quieten down increased by six percentage points – up to 73% in 2009 from 67% in 2000 (Table V.5.12). Improvements on this indicator of disciplinary climate occurred in 25 countries and in the remaining 13 countries there was no change. The increase in the percentage of students who reported that their teacher never or almost never has to wait a long time for them to quieten down was particularly large – above 10 percentage points – in Italy, Sweden, Germany, Spain, Israel, the partner country Indonesia and the partner economy Hong Kong-China. The largest improvements mostly occurred among countries with poorer conditions as, for example, in Italy or in Indonesia only half of the students in 2000 reported that their teacher did not need to wait a long time for them to quieten down.

Figure V.5.12 and Table V.5.12 illustrate how on average across OECD countries, three percentage points fewer students in 2009 responded "never" or "almost never" to the statement "students don't listen to what the teacher says"; but these proportions remain high: 75% in 2000 and 72% in 2009. In 18 countries, fewer students disagreed that "students don't listen to what the teacher says" in most or all lessons, signalling a worsening school climate. This proportion decreased by more than ten percentage points in Greece, Poland, Ireland, Australia, the Czech Republic and the partner country Liechtenstein. On the other hand, in ten countries, the share of students who did not agree with that statement increased. Korea and the partner economy Hong Kong-China witnessed the largest increases in this proportion, by more than ten percentage points. An increase between five and ten percentage points was observed in Japan, Germany, Israel and the partner countries Peru and Romania.

Table V.5.12 indicates that on average there was no change among OECD countries in the share of students who reported that there was noise and disorder, and an increase by two percentage points in the share of students who reported that "never"or "hardly ever" students cannot work well and that students do not start working for a long time after the lesson has begun. Some of the countries where almost one in two students reported noise and disorder in some lessons experienced large improvements: in 2000 only between 51% and 54% percent of students in Chile, Greece and Italy reported that there was never or almost never noise and disorder in some lessons. By 2009, this proportion had increased to 68% in Italy, 58% in Greece and 63% in Chile. At the same time many of the countries where more than eight out of ten students reported no noise and disorder in some lessons witnessed worsening conditions: in Switzerland and Poland, and the partner countries Liechtenstein, Latvia and Albania this percentage decreased by between four and nine percentage points.

■ Figure V.5.12 ■

Disciplinary climate in PISA 2000 and 2009

Percentage of students reporting that the following things happen «never or hardly ever» or «in some lessons»

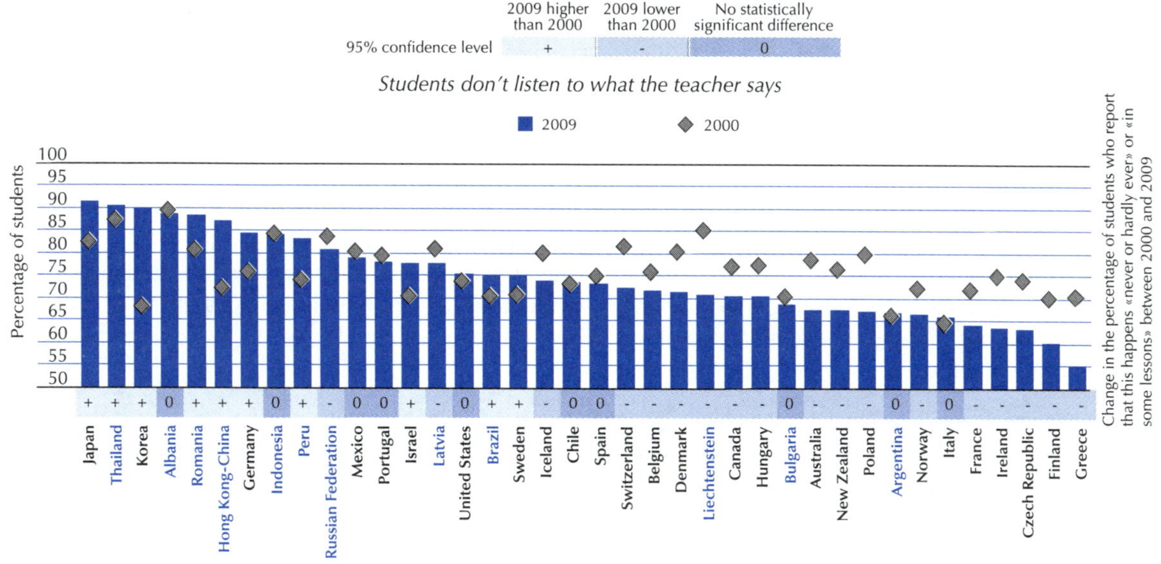

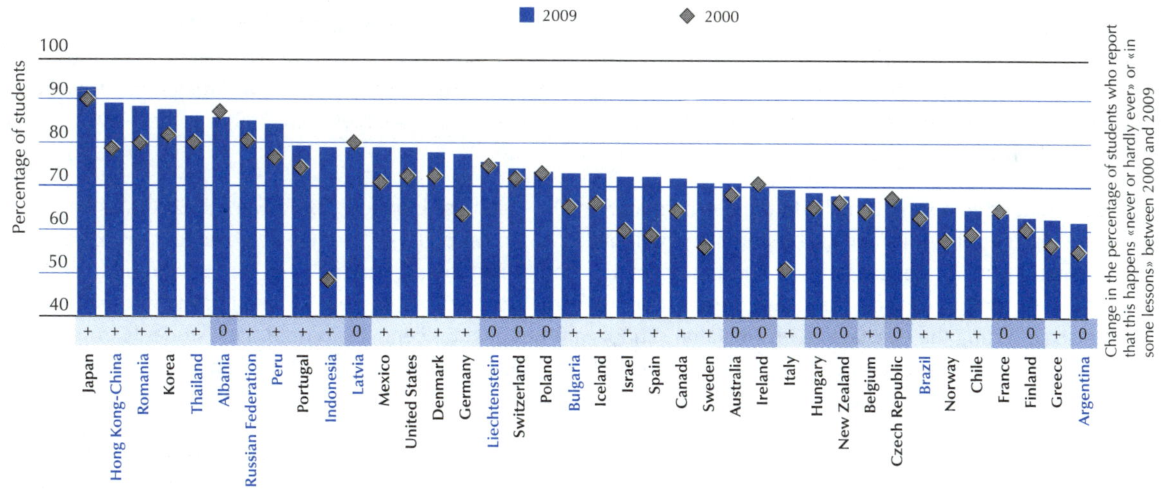

Note: Countries are ranked in descending order of the percentage of students on the items in 2009.
Source: OECD, *PISA 2009 Database*, Table V.5.12.
StatLink http://dx.doi.org/10.1787/888932360024

Notes

1. In this context, students with values in the bottom quarter of their country in the *PISA index of economic, social and cultural status* are considered to have a socio-economically disadavantged backgroundwhile students in the top quarter are considered to be socio-economically advantaged.

Box V.G **Brazil**

Brazil offers a good example of how low-performing countries can use international benchmarking to improve their education systems.

In the 1950s, 64% of the Brazilian population still lived in rural areas and more than 50% of those people were illiterate. Improving education gradually became a priority among the country's leaders, but convincing parents of the importance of more and better quality education for their children was a challenge when many parents had to send their children to work to help support the family.

Brazil's geography also made it difficult to improve access to education: the country's 193 million inhabitants are spread out over some 8.5 million square kilometres – an area slightly smaller than that of the United States. With around 83 000 rural schools, many with one or two teachers, scattered across the country, the quality of both the teachers and the education they provided was limited. And the school system's extensive use of grade repetition meant that the age of students in any given class could span two to six years, making teaching more difficult.

By 1995, 90% of students were in schools, but only half of them completed 8th grade. And those who made it that far took an average of 12 years to get there because of the poor quality of teaching and low student achievement that led to repeated grades. In 2000, 13.6% of Brazil's adult population was considered illiterate and 75% were functionally illiterate, meaning those people were not able to read long texts, follow subtitles, compare two texts, carry out inferences and syntheses, solve math problems, or work with maps and graphics. That year, Brazil was the lowest-scoring country in PISA: over 50% of students scored below Level 1 in reading proficiency while less than 1% scored at the top level.

But during the last decade, Brazil appears to have been able to produce measureable improvements in student achievement across different assessment areas (see Figure V.1.2 and Tables V.2.1, V.3.1 and V.3.4). The country has invested significantly more resources in education, raising spending on educational institutions from 4% of GDP in 2000 to 5.2% of GDP by 2009, and allocating more of those resources to raising teachers' salaries. It is also spending that money much more equitably than in the past. Federal funds are now directed towards the poorest of the country's 26 states, providing schools in those states with resources comparable to those available to schools in wealthier states.

In addition, educators in Brazil cite the Basic Education Development Index (IDEB), created in 2005, as key to improving school results across the country. The Index is based on both the average achievement on national examinations in Portuguese language and mathematics conducted in 4th, 8th and 11th grades, and on the rate of student promotion. The calculation creates a score from 1 to 10, with the levels linked to the international PISA scale. Using the two factors ensures that schools are not given incentives to hold back students from the tested grades or to encourage them to drop out of school. The explicit goal of the Brazilian government is to reach the average PISA score in 2021, the year before the two-hundredth anniversary of Brazil's independence.

The Index is set individually for each school in the country, creating a trajectory that begins at the school's 2005 level and ends where the school reaches average PISA performance in 2021. Educators have accepted the system because they believe it is fairer to compare a school's current performance to its past performance than to set an arbitrary score that all schools should reach. Unlike many other countries, Brazil includes both public and private schools in the assessment and for targeting purposes. Since the index was adopted, national performance in primary schools (1st to 4th grade) has risen from 3.8 in 2005 to 4.6 in 2009, outperforming the target of 4.2. In intermediate grades (5th to 8th grade), the index has gone from 3.5 in 2005 to 4.0 in 2009, outperforming the target of 3.7; and high school (9th to 11th grade) performance rose slightly from 3.4 to 3.6 during the same period.

PISA reading scores have also improved between 2000 and 2009. Brazil improved by 16 score points in reading performance (see Figure V.2.1 and Table V.2.1), reducing the proportion of students performing below proficiency Level 2 and slightly increasing the percentage of students at Level 5 or above (see Figures V.2.4 and V.2.5, and Table V.2.2).

....

The overall improvement in PISA reading performance was accompanied by an increase in performance variation. That was largely due to the fact that, in relative terms, Brazil raised the reading performance of its highest-achieving students while maintaining the performance level among the lowest-achieving students. Moreover, the positive trend in reading performance was driven mainly by greater improvements among girls relative to boys. An overall decrease in the share of low-performing students was mainly the result of improvements among girls, with nine percentage points fewer girls performing below Level 2 and three percentage points fewer boys performing below Level 2 (see Figure V.2.8 and Tables V.2.5 and V.2.6).

In mathematics, since 2003, students in Brazil have improved their PISA performance by 30 score points and the percentage of students below Level 2 has been reduced by four percentage points (see Figures V.3.1 and V.3.3, and Tables V.3.1 and V.3.2). In science, Brazil raised its performance by around 15 score points and decreased the share of students performing below Level 2 by seven percentage points since 2006 (see Figures V.3.5 and V.3.7, and Tables V.3.4 and V.3.5).

Despite these improvements, with 412 score points in reading, 386 score points in mathematics and 405 score points in science in the 2009 assessment, Brazil's mean scores remain well below the OECD average.

Changes in the evaluation system were accompanied by changes in teacher training. In return for additional resources, federal universities work with low-performing schools in their municipalities to assess the needs of individual schools and provide teacher training and assistance. The national Education Ministry also provides equipment and materials, transportation services, and technology to assist teacher training through the Open University at rural schools. These schools provide education to 13% of the country's students enrolled in basic education. Each state in Brazil is essentially a laboratory of innovation in education policies and practices.

Take the state of Acre. It is one of the smallest and least developed states in Brazil, located in the far northwest, in the Amazon forest. More than half of the population of 690 000 lives in two cities; the rest lives in small cities and isolated areas that depend on rivers as the only means of transportation. In 1999, Acre ranked last in the country in education outcomes, there were no school improvement plans, school buildings were dilapidated, only 14 out of the 22 municipalities offered high school education, and only 27% of teachers had a college education.

Improvements began with the teachers. Teachers' starting salaries were raised to 26% above the national minimum starting salary and a teacher training programme was developed with the federal university in Acre, making the teaching profession in Acre more attractive. Building standards were developed, and all students were guaranteed a high school education. The state decentralised supply budgets on a per-pupil basis and required school plans on how the funds would be spent. Acre worked in partnership with the Roberto Marinho Foundation on two special programmes to assist students in the 5th through 8th grades and high school students who had repeated grades several times. With these reforms, Acre has raised its IDEB index from 3.3 in 2005 to 4.5 in 2009.

São Paulo, Brazil's most populous and wealthiest state, has undergone a similar transformation in education. As in most states, the majority of upper-middle class students attend private schools, so the priority was to provide opportunities for all students to enrol in school. Then, the state created its own system of assessment and indicators that provided a biennial school-by-school target based on PISA and international standards. While the national goal is to attain the PISA average by 2021, the targets in São Paulo are more differentiated: they look at a school's performance by the proportion of students in each category: below basic, basic, adequate and advanced. This provides parents and the public with better information about the quality of school performance, but it also gives the districts and the state better information on where the school needs to improve.

The state's education secretary worked with teachers and university professors to develop a clearly defined common curriculum for every grade and subject and provided teacher training. Some 12 000 pedagogical assistants were hired so that each school would have a coach to work with teachers on improving their practice. Training on analysing data was a critical part of the programme. A school-wide incentive system was created to reward everyone at the schools that had met their improvement targets. The better a school's performance, the more autonomy the school was granted. Schools that did not reach their targets were given additional

....

technical assistance, infrastructure resources and professional development for teachers. In 2007, the 1 000 lowest-performing schools were identified and given technical assistance, targeting teacher development and additional learning resources. One year later, 95% had met their targets. Meanwhile, the state public schools of São Paulo have raised their IDEB index in 4th grade from 4.5 in 2005 to 5.4 in 2009; and in 8th grade, from 3.8 to 4.3 in the same period.

Conclusions and Policy Implications

The design of PISA does not just allow for a comparison of the relative standing of countries in terms of their learning outcomes; it also enables each country to monitor changes in those outcomes over time. Such changes indicate how successful education systems have been in developing the knowledge and skills of 15-year-olds. Indeed, some countries have seen impressive improvements in performance over the past decade, in some cases exceeding the equivalent of an average school year's progress for the entire student population. Some of these countries have been catching up from comparatively low performance levels while others have been advancing further from already high performance levels. All countries seeking to improve their results can draw encouragement — and learn lessons — from those that have succeeded in doing so in a relatively short period of time.

However, changes in student performance can also signal changes in demographic conditions and in the socio-economic composition of student populations. For example, in some countries, the growth of disadvantaged populations could translate into a general decline in learning outcomes, to the extent that socio-economic background and learning outcomes are related. These countries will need to focus on improving learning among disadvantaged students in order to avoid a long-term weakening of their performance.

PISA also shows important changes in the proportion of high- and low-performing students, the variability of student performance, performance differences between the genders, the relationship between performance and socio-economic background, and changes in the conditions that affect learning, such as students' attitudes and the disciplinary climate.

CHANGING CONDITIONS FOR LEARNING

The media often report that the conditions for teaching and learning are becoming more difficult, as schools have to compete with many different factors influencing young people's lives, some of which may detract from learning. PISA results show a mixed picture. On the one hand, enjoyment of reading tends to have deteriorated, especially among boys, signalling the challenge for schools to engage students in reading activities that 15-year-olds find relevant and interesting. On the other hand, changes in student-teacher relations and classroom climate have generally been favourable or, at least, they have not deteriorated as many would have expected. Generally, students have become more confident that they can get help from their teachers. Overall, aspects of classroom discipline have also improved, although in some countries where students were reportedly least likely to listen to what teachers say, this situation has deteriorated further. But there is no evidence to justify the notion that students are becoming progressively more disengaged from school.

PROGRESS TOWARDS RAISING PERFORMANCE AND LEVELLING THE PLAYING FIELD

The trends in student performance in each country are different, but the changes show that the profile of performance in reading is not set in stone. In both absolute and relative terms, educational results can improve, and they cannot be regarded either as part of fixed "cultural" differences between countries or as inevitably linked to each country's state of economic development. Overall, between 2000 and 2009:

- Average reading scores rose significantly in 13 countries and fell in 4 countries with comparable data.
- In many countries, improvements in results were largely driven by improvements at the bottom end of the performance distribution, signalling progress in improving equity. Among OECD countries, variation in student performance fell by 3%. On the other hand, gender differences widened or stayed the same rather than narrowing. In nine countries, the advantage of girls rose further. While the proportion of boys with low proficiency fell in seven countries, it rose in eight countries.
- Across OECD countries, the percentage of students with an immigrant background increased by an average of two percentage points between 2000 and 2009. However, the situation of students with an immigrant background improved in many countries. The reading performance gap between students without and with an immigrant background narrowed in six countries, while it widened in only two countries. Similarly, while the gap between students who speak the same language at home as the language of assessment and those who speak a different language narrowed in four countries, it grew in only three others. Despite these positive developments, in most countries students with an immigrant background — even second-generation students — still lag behind those students who are not from immigrant backgrounds.

To understand what has been achieved, it is useful to look more closely at the countries that have improved in terms of quality and/or equity.

Korea was able to raise its already-high reading performance even further by more than doubling the percentage of students reaching Level 5 or higher. Poland and the partner country Liechtenstein are countries that performed below the OECD average in 2000 but advanced to an above-average level of performance in 2009. Portugal, Hungary and Germany advanced from below-average to average. While Israel and the partner country Latvia still perform below the OECD average, they raised their scores substantially, bringing their performance closer to that of most OECD countries. Chile, which saw substantial improvements over the past nine years, is also now closer to the OECD average. Peru, Albania, Indonesia and Brazil also raised their reading performance, albeit from a low level.

Those countries that have improved the fastest — Chile and the partner countries Peru, Albania and Indonesia — have several key features in common. All had mean scores far below the OECD average in 2000. Each of these countries improved its average score by between 31 and 43 points – around half a proficiency level or roughly the equivalent of an average school year – by 2009, a significant improvement by any standard over a nine-year period. They achieved this partly by reducing the proportion of students at the lowest proficiency levels. In Chile, for example, the proportion of students performing below Level 2 fell from nearly half (48%) to below one-third (31%). In Albania, Indonesia and Peru the share of students performing at Level 2 and above fell by 14 to 15 percentage points. In all four countries, the performance of relatively high-achieving students also improved, although Chile was the only country that showed an increase in the share of students who attained Level 5 or 6. In addition, in Albania, Chile and Indonesia the relationship between socio-economic background and learning outcomes has weakened. This shows that improving outcomes among low achievers does not have to come at the expense of high achievers and can be accompanied by improvements in equity. In contrast, overall improvements in Peru did not lead to greater equity in education.

Poland and the partner country Liechtenstein, which advanced from below-average to above-average, Germany, Hungary and Portugal, which moved from below-average to average, and Latvia, which improved to just below the OECD average, have one important feature in common: in all six countries, the proportion of students performing below Level 2 decreased while the number of high-performing students at Level 5 or above remained unchanged. This is reflected in an overall decline in performance variation. In Portugal, the proportion of students performing below Level 2 declined from 26% to 18%, and in Latvia it declined from 30% to 18%. This represents a substantial improvement among low achievers in each of these countries. In addition, Latvia and Poland saw improvements in equity among schools, which can be associated with reforms that postponed the selection of students into academic or vocational programmes. The link between socio-economic background and student performance also weakened

in Germany. In response to the large inequities that the PISA 2000 assessment had revealed, German schools and states had invested heavily in disadvantaged students, including those from immigrant backgrounds.

In Korea and Brazil, and to some extent in Israel, the observed improvement in performance was largely due to better scores among top performers. In all three countries, the proportion of students performing at Level 5 or above doubled. Korea already showed high performance levels in 2000 and a very small number of low-performing students; but only a relatively small proportion of students demonstrated excellence in reading literacy. By more than doubling the proportion of high performers to 13%, Korea has caught up with the best-performing countries. Israel showed a significant increase in the proportion of high-performing students, although that share is still below the OECD average. Improvement in Brazil has been led by its high-achieving students, even though the proportion of high performers in Brazil is small compared with that in OECD countries.

These overall changes mask significant differences between improvements among boys and girls. Since 2000, boys' reading performance has improved in only five countries, while performance among girls has improved in 13 countries. As noted earlier, girls continue to outperform boys in reading in all countries, as they had in 2000, but in 2009, they do so by an even wider margin. In eight countries the percentage of boys who do not attain baseline Level 2 in reading increased, while it decreased in seven countries. Boys, especially those from socio-economically disadvantaged backgrounds, are also more apt not to read for enjoyment or report negative attitudes towards reading. While the need to raise the level of engagement in reading among boys, particularly those from disadvantaged backgrounds, was recognised in 2000, the latest PISA results suggest that little progress has been made on this front.

PISA also makes it possible to compare student performance in mathematics and science over time, although these are observed over a shorter periods. In mathematics, students in Mexico, Turkey, Greece, Portugal, Italy, Germany and the partner countries Brazil and Tunisia improved their scores considerably since 2003. Mexico reduced the share of students performing below the baseline Level 2 in mathematics by 15 percentage points since 2003, from 66% to 51%, and Turkey from 52% to 42% over the same period. Greece, Italy, Portugal and the partner countries Brazil and Tunisia also reduced the share of students performing below Level 2 in mathematics. In Portugal, the percentage of students performing at Level 5 or above in mathematics increased by four percentage points, while the share of these top performers increased by almost two percentage points in Italy and Greece.

In science, 11 of the 56 countries that have comparable results in the 2006 and 2009 assessments show improvements in student performance. Turkey, for example, saw a 30-score-point increase, nearly half a proficiency level, in just three years. Science performance also improved in the OECD countries Portugal, Korea, Italy, Norway, the United States and Poland, and in partner countries Qatar, Tunisia, Brazil and Colombia. Turkey, Portugal, Chile, the United States, Norway, Korea and Italy all saw reductions in the share of their lowest performers in science by around five percentage points or more, as did the partner countries Qatar, Tunisia, Brazil and Colombia. Turkey reduced this share from 47% to 30%. In the partner country Qatar, the share of students who did not reach Level 2 decreased by 14 percentage points, even if almost two-thirds of students in Qatar still perform below proficiency Level 2 in science.

Several countries improved across different assessment areas. Korea attained very high levels not only in reading, but also in science. Poland also improved both in reading and in science. Germany improved in reading and mathematics. Portugal improved across all assessment areas. Several countries that still perform below the OECD average in reading saw improvements in other assessment areas.

Overall, the message is that countries from a variety of starting points have shown the potential to improve performance, both raising average levels of reading proficiency and reducing inequities in outcomes without seeing a deterioration among the most able students. In some, but not all, cases these improvements have also had a positive effect on social equity. However, the gender gap in reading performance remains large and presents a growing challenge for most countries, including those with very high performance levels.

References

Anand, P., A. Mizala and **A. Repetto** (2006), "Using School Scholarships to Estimate the Effect of Government Subsidized Private Education on Academic Achievement in Chile", *Documentos de Trabajo*, No. 220, Universidad de Chile, Santiago.

Belley, C. (2007), "Expansión de la educación privada y mejoramiento de la educación en Chile. Evaluación a partir de la evidencia" (Expansion of Private Education and Improvement of Education in Chile. Evidence-based evaluation), *Revista Pensamiento Educativo*, Vol. 40, No. 1, pp. 1-21.

Birch, S.H., and **G.W. Ladd** (1998), "Children's interpersonal behaviors and teacher-child relationships", *Developmental Psychology*, Vol. 34, pp. 934-946.

Carnoy, M. (1998), "National Voucher Plans in Chile and Sweden: Did Privatization Make for Better Education?", *Comparative Education Review*, Vol. 42, No. 3, pp. 309-337.

Crosnoe, R., G.H. Elder, and **M. Johnson** (2004), "Intergenerational Bonding in School: The Behavioral and Contextual Correlates of Student-Teacher Relationships", *Sociology of Education,* Vol. 77, No. 1, pp. 60-81.

Gamoran, A. (1993), "Alternative uses of ability grouping in secondary schools: Can we bring high-quality instruction to low-ability classes?", *American Journal of Education,* Vol. 102, No. 1, pp. 1-22.

Gamoran, A. and M. Nystrand (1992), "Taking students seriously" in F.M. Newman (ed.), *Student engagement and achievement in American secondary schools*, Teachers College Press, New York.

Ganzeboom, H.B.G., P.M. De Graaf and **D.J. Treiman** (1992), "A Standard International Socio-economic Index of Occupational Status", *Social Science Research 21.1*, pp. 1-56.

Gebhardt, E. and **R.J. Adams** (2007), "The influence of equating methodology on reported trends in PISA", *Journal of Applied Measurement,* Vol. 8, No. 3, pp. 305-322.

GUS (2009), Kształcenie dorosłych, Warsaw.

Gysling, J. (2003), *Reforma Curricular: Itinerario de una transformación cultural* (Curricular Reform: Itinerary of a Cultural Transformation), in C.Cox (ed.), *Políticas Educacionales en el cambio de siglo. La reforma del sistema escolar de Chile*, Editorial Universitaria, Santiago.

Hsieh, C. and **M. Urquiola** (2006), "The Effects of Generalized School Choice on Achievement and Stratification: Evidence from Chile's Voucher Program", *Journal of Public Economics*, Vol. 90, pp. 1477-1503.

ILO (International Labour Organization) (1990), *International Standard Classification of Occupations*, ISCO-88, Geneva.

Jakubowski, M., H. Patrinos, E. Porta, J. Wisniewski (2010), "The Impact of the 1999 Education Reform in Poland", *OECD Education Working Papers*, No. 49.

Ministry of Education and Human Resources Development (MEHRD) (2007), *3-1 Mathematics textbook* (in Korean), Seoul.

Neuwirth, E. (2006), "PISA 2000: Sample Weight Problems in Austria", *OECD Education Working Papers*, No. 5.

Matthews, P., E. Klaver, J. Lannert, G. Ó Conluain and **A. Ventura** (2008), *Policy measures implemented in the first cycle of compulsory education in Portugal (International evaluation)*, OECD Publishing.

Pinto Ferreira, C. and **A. Serrão** (2008), "Literacy competences of the Portuguese students: cross-national comparison among some Mediterranean countries", a presentation from a conference, *PISA 2006: The performance of educational systems in countries and regions*, Trento, Italy.

OECD (1999), *Classifying Educational Programmes: Manual for ISCED-97 Implementation in OECD Countries,* OECD Publishing.

OECD (2001), *Knowledge and Skills for Life: First Results from PISA 2000*, OECD Publishing.

OECD (2002a), *PISA 2000 Technical Report,* OECD Publishing.

OECD (2002b), *Education at a Glance 2002: OECD Indicators*, OECD Publishing.

OECD (2005), *PISA 2003 Technical Report*, OECD Publishing.

OECD (2006a), *Economic Survey of Poland: 2006*, OECD Publishing.

OECD (2006b), *Assessing Scientific, Reading and Mathematical Literacy: A Framework for PISA 2006,* OECD Publishing.

OECD (2006c), *Economic Survey of Turkey: 2006,* OECD Publishing.

OECD (2007), *Reviews of National Policies for Education: Basic Education in Turkey*, OECD Publishing.

OECD (2008), *PISA 2006 Technical Report*, OECD Publishing.

OECD (2010a), *Pathways to Success: How knowledge and skills at age 15 shape future lives in Canada,* OECD Publishing.

OECD (2010b), *Education at a Glance 2010: OECD Indicators*, OECD Publishing.

OECD (2010c), *Economic Survey of Portugal: 2010,* OECD Publishing.

OECD (2010d), *Quality time for students. Learning in and out of school,* OECD Publishing

OECD (forthcoming), *PISA 2009 Technical Report, OECD Publishing.*

OECD and **Statistics Canada** (2000), *Literacy in the Information Age: Final Report of the International Adult Literacy Survey*, OECD Publishing.

Royston, P. (2004), "Multiple imputation of missing values", *Stata Journal,* Vol. 4, No.3, pp. 227-241.

Rubin, D.B. (1987), "Multiple imputation for non-response in surveys", John Wiley & Sons, New York.

Santiago, P., D. Roseveare, G. van Amelsvoort, J. Manzi and **P. Matthews** (2009), *OECD Review of Teacher Evaluation in Portugal,* OECD Publishing.

Talim ve Terbiye Kurulu (TTKB) (2008). İlkögretim Matematik Dersi 6–8 Sınıflar Öğretim Programı ve Kılavuzu (Teaching Syllabus and Curriculum Guidebook for Elementary school mathematics course: Grades 6 to 8), Ankara, Milli Eğitim Bakanlığı.

Warm, T.A. (1985), "Weighted Maximum Likelihood Estimation of Ability Item Response Theory with Tests of Finite Length", *Technical Report CGI-TR-85-08,* U.S. Coast Guard Institute, Oklahoma City.

Annex A

TECHNICAL BACKGROUND

All tables in Annex A are available on line

ANNEX A1

CONSTRUCTION OF READING SCALES AND INDICES FROM THE STUDENT CONTEXT QUESTIONNAIRES

How the PISA 2009 reading assessments were designed, analysed and scaled

The development of the PISA 2009 reading tasks was co-ordinated by an international consortium of educational research institutions contracted by the OECD, under the guidance of a group of reading experts from participating countries. Participating countries contributed stimulus material and questions, which were reviewed, tried out and refined iteratively over the three years leading up to the administration of the assessment in 2009. The development process involved provisions for several rounds of commentary from participating countries, as well as small-scale piloting and a formal field trial in which samples of 15-year-olds from all participating countries took part. The reading expert group recommended the final selection of tasks, which included material submitted by 21 of the participating countries. The selection was made with regard to both their technical quality, assessed on the basis of their performance in the field trial, and their cultural appropriateness and interest level for 15-year-olds, as judged by the participating countries. Another essential criterion for selecting the set of material as a whole was its fit to the framework described in *Volume 1, What Students Know and Can Do*, to maintain the balance across various categories of text, aspect and situation. Finally, it was carefully ensured that the set of questions covered a range of difficulty, allowing good measurement and description of the reading literacy of all 15-year-old students, from the least proficient to the highly able.

More than 130 print reading questions were used in PISA 2009, but each student in the sample only saw a fraction of the total pool because different sets of questions were given to different students. The reading questions selected for inclusion in PISA 2009 were organised into half-hour clusters. These, along with clusters of mathematics and science questions, were assembled into booklets containing four clusters each. Each participating student was then given a two-hour assessment. As reading was the focus of the PISA 2009 assessment, every booklet included at least one cluster of reading material. The clusters were rotated so that each cluster appeared in each of the four possible positions in the booklets, and each pair of clusters appeared in at least one of the 13 booklets that were used.

This design, similar to those used in previous PISA assessments, makes it possible to construct a single scale of reading proficiency, in which each question is associated with a particular point on the scale that indicates its difficulty, whereby each student's performance is associated with a particular point on the same scale that indicates his or her estimated proficiency. A description of the modelling technique used to construct this scale can be found in the *PISA 2009 Technical Report* (OECD, forthcoming).

The relative difficulty of tasks in a test is estimated by considering the proportion of test takers who answer each question correctly. The relative proficiency of students taking a particular test can be estimated by considering the proportion of test questions they answer correctly. A single continuous scale shows the relationship between the difficulty of questions and the proficiency of students. By constructing a scale that shows the difficulty of each question, it is possible to locate the level of reading literacy that the question represents. By showing the proficiency of each student on the same scale, it is possible to describe the level of reading literacy that the student possesses.

The location of student proficiency on this scale is set in relation to the particular group of questions used in the assessment. However, just as the sample of students taking PISA in 2009 is drawn to represent all the 15-year-olds in the participating countries, so the individual questions used in the assessment are designed to represent the definition of reading literacy adequately. Estimates of student proficiency reflect the kinds of tasks they would be expected to perform successfully. This means that students are likely to be able to complete questions successfully at or below the difficulty level associated with their own position on the scale (but they may not always do so). Conversely, they are unlikely to be able to successfully complete questions above the difficulty level associated with their position on the scale (but they may sometimes do so).

The further a student's proficiency is located above a given question, the more likely he or she is to successfully complete the question (and other questions of similar difficulty); the further the student's proficiency is located below a given question, the lower the probability that the student will be able to successfully complete the question, and other questions of similar difficulty.

How the PISA 2009 reading scales were aligned with PISA 2000, 2003 and 2006 reading scales

The reading performance scale used in the 2000, 2003, 2006 and 2009 assessments is the same, which means that score points on this scale are directly comparable over time. This is due to the use of link items that are common across assessments and can be used in the equating procedure to align performance scales.

A two-step equating approach was used to report PISA 2009 reading results on the PISA 2000 reading scale. In the first step, a shift to align items was computed. Although 28 out of the 101 items were link items that had been used in each previous PISA

assessment, only 26 link items were finally considered since the performance of two of the items was deemed unsatisfactory for linking purposes. The average item difficulty of the 26 link items was computed for 2009 and 2006 assessments and the difference was then applied to shift 2009 performance to align with the 2006 scale. The 2006 reading performance scale was already aligned to 2003, and 2003 was previously aligned to 2000, meaning that the 2009 performance scale was thus aligned with the one constructed for the first time in 2000.

In the second step, a shift to align the scale made up of link items and the scale made up of link items and new items (the so-called combined items scale) was computed using the following procedure. The PISA 2009 dataset was scaled twice, once using all the items and once using only link items. The difference between the OECD means of these two scalings was calculated and this shift was applied to align the link items only scale with the combined items scale. After applying this shift, the scores derived from the Item Response Theory (IRT) models were transformed to the PISA scale, which was done separately by gender.

As the equating procedure introduces random error related to performance changes on the link items, standard errors for performance trend estimates were adjusted. These more conservative standard errors reflect not only the measurement precision and sampling variation as for the usual PISA results, but also the linking error.

It should be noted that in addition to the 26 link items that were included in the three consecutive PISA cycles 2000, 2003 and 2006, an additional 11 items from PISA 2000 were included in the PISA 2009 assessment. The 39 items common to the two assessments were used to estimate the linking error between the PISA 2000 and 2009 reading scales while 28 items were used for the computation of the linking error for other cycles. Linking errors were added to all respective results whenever performance is compared across assessments. These linking errors are provided in Table A1.1.

Table A1.1 Link Error Estimates

	Link Error on PISA Scale
PISA Reading scale 2000 to 2003	5.307
PISA Reading scale 2000 to 2006	4.976
PISA Reading scale 2000 to 2009	4.936
PISA Reading scale 2003 to 2006	4.474
PISA Reading scale 2003 to 2009	4.088
PISA Reading scale 2006 to 2009	4.069
PISA Mathematics scale 2003 to 2009	1.990
PISA Mathematics scale 2006 to 2009	1.333
PISA Mathematics scale 2003 to 2006	1.382
PISA Science scale 2006 to 2009	2.566

How reading proficiency levels are defined in PISA 2009

PISA 2009 provides an overall reading literacy scale for the reading texts, drawing on all the questions in the reading assessment, as well as scales for three aspects and two text formats. The metric for the overall reading scale is based on a mean for OECD countries set at 500 in PISA 2000, with a standard deviation of 100. To help interpret what students' scores mean in substantive terms, the scale is divided into levels, based on a set of statistical principles, and then descriptions are generated, based on the tasks that are located within each level, to describe the kinds of skills and knowledge needed to successfully complete those tasks.

For PISA 2009, the range of difficulty of tasks allows for the description of seven levels of reading proficiency: Level 1b is the lowest described level, then Level 1a, Level 2, Level 3 and so on up to Level 6.

Students with a proficiency within the range of Level 1b are likely to be able to successfully complete Level 1b tasks (and others like them), but are unlikely to be able to complete tasks at higher levels. Level 6 reflects tasks that present the greatest challenge in terms of reading skills and knowledge. Students with scores in this range are likely to be able to complete reading tasks located at that level successfully, as well as all the other reading tasks in PISA.

PISA applies a standard methodology for constructing proficiency scales. Based on a student's performance on the tasks in the test, his or her score is generated and located in a specific part of the scale, thus allowing the score to be associated with a defined proficiency level. The level at which the student's score is located is the highest level for which he or she would be expected to answer correctly, most of a random selection of questions within the same level. Thus, for example, in an assessment composed of

tasks spread uniformly across Level 3, students with a score located within Level 3 would be expected to complete at least 50% of the tasks successfully. Because a level covers a range of difficulty and proficiency, success rates across the band vary. Students near the bottom of the level would be likely to succeed on just over 50% of the tasks spread uniformly across the level, while students at the top of the level would be likely to succeed on well over 70% of the same tasks.

Figure I.2.12 in Volume I provides details of the nature of reading skills, knowledge and understanding required at each level of the reading scale.

Explanation of indices

This section explains the indices derived from the student, school and parent context questionnaires used in PISA 2009. Parent questionnaire indices are only available for the 14 countries that chose to administer the optional parent questionnaire.

Several PISA measures reflect indices that summarise responses from students, their parents or school representatives (typically principals) to a series of related questions. The questions were selected from a larger pool of questions on the basis of theoretical considerations and previous research. Structural equation modelling was used to confirm the theoretically expected behaviour of the indices and to validate their comparability across countries. For this purpose, a model was estimated separately for each country and collectively for all OECD countries.

For a detailed description of other PISA indices and details on the methods, see the *PISA 2000 Technical Report* (OECD, 2002a), the *PISA 2003 Technical Report* (OECD, 2005), the *PISA 2006 Technical Report* (OECD, 2008) and the *PISA 2009 Technical Report* (OECD, forthcoming).

There are two types of indices: simple indices and scale indices.

Simple indices are the variables that are constructed through the arithmetic transformation or recoding of one or more items, in exactly the same way across assessments. Here, item responses are used to calculate meaningful variables, such as the recoding of the four-digit ISCO-88 codes into "Highest parents' socio-economic index (HISEI)" or, teacher-student ratio based on information from the school questionnaire.

Scale indices are the variables constructed through the scaling of multiple items. Unless otherwise indicated, the index was scaled using a weighted maximum likelihood estimate (WLE) (Warm, 1985), using a one-parameter item response model (a partial credit model was used in the case of items with more than two categories). Analogous to the reading performance scales, the indices derived from a student questionnaire have to be equated. This has been done by estimating item parameters using response data from all cycles, in which a trends index appears. This is known as the concurrent estimation of item parameters. Any items which were missing in a certain assessment were treated as structurally missing data in the estimation procedure.

The scaling was done in three stages:

- The item parameters were estimated from equal-sized subsamples of students from each OECD country and from each PISA assessment.
- The estimates were computed for all students and all schools by anchoring the item parameters obtained in the preceding step.
- The indices were then standardised for 2009 data so that the mean of the index value for the OECD student population was 0 and the standard deviation was 1 in 2009 (countries being given equal weight in the standardisation process).

Sequential codes were assigned to the different response categories of the questions in the sequence in which the latter appeared in the student, school or parent questionnaires. Where indicated in this section, these codes were inverted for the purpose of constructing indices or scales. It is important to note that negative values for an index do not necessarily imply that students responded negatively to the underlying questions. A negative value merely indicates that the respondents answered less positively than all respondents did on average across OECD countries. Likewise, a positive value on an index indicates that the respondents answered more favourably, or more positively, than respondents did, on average, in OECD countries.

As noted above, for the re-estimated indices the mean of the index value for the OECD student population in 2009 is 0 and the standard deviation is 1. However, means and standard deviations for previous assessments can depart from that. Indices re-estimated for trends analysis do not have to match values reported in previous reports. While country means and other statistics should be close to those reported previously, they could often differ slightly because in previous assessments indices were standardised in relation to the data from the earlier assessment and not with regard to 2009 results.

In addition to simple and scaled indices described in this annex, there are a number of variables from the questionnaires that correspond to single items not used to construct indices. These non-recoded variables have prefix of "ST" for the questionnaire items in the student questionnaire, "SC" for the items in the school questionnaire, and "PA" for the items in the parent questionnaire. All the context questionnaires as well as the PISA international database, including all variables, are available through *www.pisa.oecd.org*.

Student-level simple indices

Age

The variable AGE is calculated for trends differently than for 2009 results, because information on the actual month of testing, which was used to construct AGE index for the analysis of 2009 data, is not available for 2000. Thus, for the analysis of trends, the information on the middle month of the testing period was used instead. Results from all assessments were recomputed as the difference between the middle month and the year in which students were assessed and their month and year of birth, expressed in years and months.

Occupational status of parents

Occupational data for both a student's father and a student's mother were obtained by asking open-ended questions in the student questionnaire (ST9a, ST9b, ST12, ST13a, ST13b and ST16). The responses were coded to four-digit ISCO codes (ILO, 1990) and then mapped to Ganzeboom et al's SEI index (1992). Higher scores of SEI indicate higher levels of occupational status. The following three indices are obtained:

- Mother's occupational status (BMMJ).
- Father's occupational status (BFMJ).
- The highest occupational level of parents (HISEI) corresponds to the higher SEI score of either parent or to the only available parent's SEI score.

Educational level of parents

The educational level of parents is classified using ISCED (OECD, 1999) based on students' responses in the student questionnaire (ST10, ST11, ST14 and ST15). Please note that the question format for school education in PISA 2009 differs from the one used in PISA 2000, 2003 and 2006 but the method used to compute parental education is the same.

As in PISA 2000, 2003 and 2006, indices were constructed by selecting the highest level for each parent and then assigning them to the following categories: (0) None, (1) ISCED 1 (primary education), (2) ISCED 2 (lower secondary), (3) ISCED Level 3B or 3C (vocational/pre-vocational upper secondary), (4) ISCED 3A (upper secondary) and/or ISCED 4 (non-tertiary post-secondary), (5) ISCED 5B (vocational tertiary), (6) ISCED 5A, 6 (theoretically oriented tertiary and post-graduate). The following three indices with these categories are developed:

- Mother's educational level (MISCED).
- Father's educational level (FISCED).
- Highest educational level of parents (HISCED) corresponds to the higher ISCED level of either parent.

Highest educational level of parents was also converted into the number of years of schooling (PARED). For the conversion of level of education into years of schooling, see Table A1.2.

Relative grade

Data on the student's grade are obtained both from the student questionnaire (ST01) and from the student tracking form. As with all variables that are on both the tracking form and the questionnaire, inconsistencies between the two sources are reviewed and resolved during data-cleaning. In order to capture between-country variation, the relative grade index (GRADE) indicates whether students are at the modal grade in a country (value of 0), or whether they are below or above the modal grade level (+ x grades, - x grades).

The relationship between the grade and student performance was estimated through a multilevel model accounting for the following background variables: *i)* the ***PISA index of economic, social and cultural status***; *ii)* the ***PISA index of economic, social and cultural status*** squared; *iii)* the school mean of the ***PISA index of economic, social and cultural status***; *iv)* an indicator as to whether students were foreign born first-generation students; *v)* the percentage of first-generation students in the school; and *vi)* students' gender.

Table A1.3 presents the results of the multilevel model. Column 1 in Table A1.3 estimates the score point difference that is associated with one grade level (or school year). This difference can be estimated for the 32 OECD countries in which a sizeable number of 15-year-olds in the PISA samples were enrolled in at least two different grades. Since 15-year-olds cannot be assumed to be distributed at random across the grade levels, adjustments had to be made for the above-mentioned contextual factors that may relate to the assignment of students to the different grade levels. These adjustments are documented in columns 2 to 7 of the table. While it is possible to estimate the typical performance difference among students in two adjacent grades net of the effects of selection and contextual factors, this difference cannot automatically be equated with the progress that students have made over the last school year but should be interpreted as a lower boundary of the progress achieved. This is not only because different students were assessed but also because the content of the PISA assessment was not expressly designed to match what students had learned in the preceding school year but more broadly to assess the cumulative outcome of learning in school up to age 15. For

[Part 1/1]
Table A1.2 **Levels of parental education converted into years of schooling**

		Did not go to school	Completed ISCED Level 1 (primary education)	Completed ISCED Level 2 (lower secondary education)	Completed ISCED Levels3B or 3C (upper secondary education providing direct access to the labor market or to ISCED 5B programmes)	Completed ISCED Level 3A (upper secondary education providing access to ISCED 5A and 5B programmes) and/or ISCED Level 4 (non-tertiary post-secondary)	Completed ISCED Level 5A (university level tertiary education) or ISCED Level 6 (advanced research programmes)	Completed ISCED Level 5B (non-university tertiary education)
OECD	Australia	0.0	6.0	10.0	11.0	12.0	15.0	14.0
	Austria	0.0	4.0	9.0	12.0	12.5	17.0	15.0
	Belgium	0.0	6.0	9.0	12.0	12.0	17.0	14.5
	Canada	0.0	6.0	9.0	12.0	12.0	17.0	15.0
	Chile	0.0	6.0	8.0	12.0	12.0	17.0	16.0
	Czech Republic	0.0	5.0	9.0	11.0	13.0	16.0	16.0
	Denmark	0.0	6.0	9.0	12.0	12.0	17.0	15.0
	Estonia	0.0	4.0	9.0	12.0	12.0	16.0	15.0
	Finland	0.0	6.0	9.0	12.0	12.0	16.5	14.5
	France	0.0	5.0	9.0	12.0	12.0	15.0	14.0
	Germany	0.0	4.0	10.0	13.0	13.0	18.0	15.0
	Greece	0.0	6.0	9.0	11.5	12.0	17.0	15.0
	Hungary	0.0	4.0	8.0	10.5	12.0	16.5	13.5
	Iceland	0.0	7.0	10.0	13.0	14.0	18.0	16.0
	Ireland	0.0	6.0	9.0	12.0	12.0	16.0	14.0
	Israel	0.0	6.0	9.0	12.0	12.0	15.0	15.0
	Italy	0.0	5.0	8.0	12.0	13.0	17.0	16.0
	Japan	0.0	6.0	9.0	12.0	12.0	16.0	14.0
	Korea	0.0	6.0	9.0	12.0	12.0	16.0	14.0
	Luxembourg	0.0	6.0	9.0	12.0	13.0	17.0	16.0
	Mexico	0.0	6.0	9.0	12.0	12.0	16.0	14.0
	Netherlands	0.0	6.0	10.0	a	12.0	16.0	a
	New Zealand	0.0	5.5	10.0	11.0	12.0	15.0	14.0
	Norway	0.0	6.0	9.0	12.0	12.0	16.0	14.0
	Poland	0.0	a	8.0	11.0	12.0	16.0	15.0
	Portugal	0.0	6.0	9.0	12.0	12.0	17.0	15.0
	Scotland	0.0	7.0	11.0	13.0	13.0	16.0	16.0
	Slovak Republic	0.0	4.5	8.5	12.0	12.0	17.5	13.5
	Slovenia	0.0	4.0	8.0	11.0	12.0	16.0	15.0
	Spain	0.0	5.0	8.0	10.0	12.0	16.5	13.0
	Sweden	0.0	6.0	9.0	11.5	12.0	15.5	14.0
	Switzerland	0.0	6.0	9.0	12.5	12.5	17.5	14.5
	Turkey	0.0	5.0	8.0	11.0	11.0	15.0	13.0
	United Kingdom	0.0	6.0	9.0	12.0	13.0	16.0	15.0
	United States	0.0	6.0	9.0	a	12.0	16.0	14.0
Partners	Albania	0.0	6.0	9.0	12.0	12.0	16.0	16.0
	Argentina	0.0	6.0	10.0	12.0	12.0	17.0	14.5
	Azerbaijan	0.0	4.0	9.0	11.0	11.0	17.0	14.0
	Brazil	0.0	4.0	8.0	11.0	11.0	16.0	14.5
	Bulgaria	0.0	4.0	8.0	12.0	12.0	17.5	15.0
	Colombia	0.0	5.0	9.0	11.0	11.0	15.5	14.0
	Croatia	0.0	4.0	8.0	11.0	12.0	17.0	15.0
	Dubai (UAE)	0.0	5.0	9.0	12.0	12.0	16.0	15.0
	Hong Kong- China	0.0	6.0	9.0	11.0	13.0	16.0	14.0
	Indonesia	0.0	6.0	9.0	12.0	12.0	15.0	14.0
	Jordan	0.0	6.0	10.0	12.0	12.0	16.0	14.5
	Kazakhstan	0.0	4.0	9.0	11.5	12.5	15.0	14.0
	Kyrgyzstan	0.0	4.0	8.0	11.0	10.0	15.0	13.0
	Latvia	0.0	3.0	8.0	11.0	11.0	16.0	16.0
	Liechtenstein	0.0	5.0	9.0	11.0	13.0	17.0	14.0
	Lithuania	0.0	3.0	8.0	11.0	11.0	16.0	15.0
	Macao-China	0.0	6.0	9.0	11.0	12.0	16.0	15.0
	Montenegro	0.0	4.0	8.0	11.0	12.0	16.0	15.0
	Panama	0.0	6.0	9.0	12.0	12.0	16.0	a
	Peru	0.0	6.0	9.0	11.0	11.0	17.0	14.0
	Qatar	0.0	6.0	9.0	12.0	12.0	16.0	15.0
	Romania	0.0	4.0	8.0	11.5	12.5	16.0	14.0
	Russian Federation	0.0	4.0	9.0	11.5	12.0	15.0	a
	Serbia	0.0	4.0	8.0	11.0	12.0	17.0	14.5
	Shanghai-China	0.0	6.0	9.0	12.0	12.0	16.0	15.0
	Singapore	0.0	6.0	8.0	10.5	10.5	12.5	12.5
	Chinese Taipei	0.0	6.0	9.0	12.0	12.0	16.0	14.0
	Thailand	0.0	6.0	9.0	12.0	12.0	16.0	14.0
	Trinidad and Tobago	0.0	5.0	9.0	12.0	12.0	16.0	15.0
	Tunisia	0.0	6.0	9.0	12.0	13.0	17.0	16.0
	Uruguay	0.0	6.0	9.0	12.0	12.0	17.0	15.0

StatLink http://dx.doi.org/10.1787/888932343171

[Part 1/1]

Table A1.3 A multilevel model to estimate grade effects in reading, accounting for some background variables

		Grade		Index of economic, social and cultural status		Index of economic, social and cultural status squared		School mean index of economic, social and cultural status		First generation students		School percentage of first generation students		Gender – student is a female		Intercept	
		Coeff	S.E.	Coeff	S.E.	Coeff	S.E.	Coeff	S.E.	Coeff	S.E.	Coeff	S.E.	Coeff	S.E.	Coeff	S.E.
OECD	Australia	33.2	(1.95)	30.0	(1.36)	-3.8	(1.05)	66.4	(1.87)	-7.4	(2.82)	0.1	(0.07)	32.9	(1.91)	466.0	(1.39)
	Austria	35.3	(2.18)	11.4	(1.66)	-0.5	(1.00)	89.7	(3.86)	-33.1	(6.11)	1.4	(0.13)	19.9	(2.67)	467.9	(2.45)
	Belgium	48.9	(1.98)	10.0	(1.12)	-0.1	(0.63)	79.9	(1.73)	-3.2	(5.18)	0.3	(0.11)	11.3	(1.81)	507.0	(1.70)
	Canada	45.0	(2.14)	19.4	(1.52)	1.5	(0.91)	33.9	(2.28)	-13.7	(3.18)	0.3	(0.04)	30.4	(1.60)	483.4	(1.76)
	Chile	35.5	(1.55)	8.6	(1.52)	0.3	(0.63)	37.4	(1.61)	c	c	c	c	13.8	(2.33)	478.6	(1.60)
	Czech Republic	44.6	(3.39)	13.4	(1.89)	-2.3	(1.47)	111.5	(3.12)	-8.9	(12.29)	0.4	(0.33)	32.3	(2.84)	460.7	(2.39)
	Denmark	36.1	(3.02)	27.9	(1.51)	-2.8	(1.10)	35.1	(2.91)	-37.5	(5.97)	0.0	(0.14)	25.5	(2.59)	474.0	(1.95)
	Estonia	44.4	(2.74)	14.1	(1.80)	1.6	(1.43)	52.1	(4.52)	-18.7	(14.08)	-3.3	(0.44)	36.7	(2.45)	485.8	(2.02)
	Finland	37.3	(3.60)	27.7	(1.66)	-2.5	(1.30)	10.4	(3.28)	-56.0	(13.09)	-0.1	(0.29)	51.5	(2.26)	500.6	(2.02)
	France	47.1	(5.14)	12.5	(1.70)	-1.9	(1.12)	81.6	(4.04)	-11.6	(9.24)	0.2	(0.15)	25.9	(2.67)	516.5	(2.35)
	Germany	34.4	(1.74)	9.2	(1.23)	-1.6	(0.74)	109.1	(2.16)	-13.2	(4.80)	0.2	(0.12)	27.2	(1.92)	458.0	(1.46)
	Greece	22.6	(10.86)	15.9	(1.46)	1.5	(1.07)	41.2	(2.84)	-15.0	(7.82)	0.0	(0.18)	36.2	(2.55)	469.0	(2.04)
	Hungary	25.6	(2.19)	8.3	(1.39)	0.9	(0.87)	74.8	(2.09)	2.8	(7.92)	0.0	(0.27)	21.4	(2.22)	494.1	(1.65)
	Iceland	c	c	29.8	(2.56)	-5.1	(1.56)	-3.8	(5.12)	-52.2	(11.45)	-1.3	(0.40)	44.9	(2.59)	469.1	(4.23)
	Ireland	18.2	(1.99)	29.7	(1.78)	-3.5	(1.44)	43.6	(2.68)	-32.8	(6.52)	-0.1	(0.20)	33.9	(3.62)	474.8	(2.77)
	Israel	36.6	(3.85)	19.9	(1.90)	3.4	(1.04)	104.7	(2.10)	-11.0	(6.13)	1.5	(0.08)	29.4	(2.81)	460.1	(2.13)
	Italy	36.1	(1.67)	4.5	(0.69)	-1.4	(0.42)	76.4	(1.07)	-29.7	(3.36)	0.2	(0.08)	24.0	(1.29)	491.4	(0.85)
	Japan	a	a	4.1	(1.51)	0.1	(1.47)	144.2	(2.40)	c	c	c	c	27.9	(2.43)	508.6	(1.58)
	Korea	31.2	(9.77)	12.9	(1.42)	1.9	(1.18)	64.9	(2.24)	a	a	a	a	30.6	(3.21)	537.7	(2.08)
	Luxembourg	45.3	(1.95)	16.6	(1.31)	-2.6	(1.08)	62.0	(2.89)	-10.4	(5.11)	-0.2	(0.10)	33.0	(2.22)	435.7	(2.40)
	Mexico	32.6	(1.59)	7.5	(0.92)	0.8	(0.34)	27.8	(0.80)	-41.9	(6.36)	-1.8	(0.15)	17.9	(1.03)	473.7	(1.02)
	Netherlands	26.6	(2.04)	6.0	(1.52)	-1.2	(1.02)	106.7	(2.32)	-11.6	(5.72)	1.7	(0.14)	15.3	(1.85)	484.5	(2.33)
	New Zealand	44.2	(4.15)	38.9	(1.82)	-1.7	(1.44)	56.3	(3.35)	-12.2	(3.84)	0.0	(0.10)	44.8	(2.62)	496.5	(2.44)
	Norway	37.6	(18.19)	34.2	(2.00)	-3.4	(1.62)	31.1	(4.32)	-33.4	(7.52)	0.4	(0.25)	48.3	(2.56)	453.2	(2.87)
	Poland	73.8	(4.44)	29.4	(1.59)	-1.8	(1.21)	19.4	(2.99)	c	c	c	c	44.2	(2.41)	498.9	(1.89)
	Portugal	48.9	(1.71)	12.0	(0.94)	1.0	(0.64)	21.3	(1.33)	-5.3	(5.75)	0.0	(0.23)	22.9	(1.84)	518.6	(1.92)
	Slovak Republic	34.2	(3.85)	14.7	(1.44)	-3.2	(0.98)	64.3	(6.30)	c	c	c	c	39.1	(2.58)	483.2	(2.33)
	Slovenia	22.8	(3.41)	4.8	(1.28)	0.0	(1.25)	100.2	(2.74)	-23.4	(7.48)	-0.2	(0.24)	27.7	(2.16)	452.4	(1.63)
	Spain	61.7	(1.22)	9.8	(0.83)	0.4	(0.64)	22.7	(1.25)	-29.7	(2.86)	0.4	(0.04)	18.0	(1.42)	511.3	(1.07)
	Sweden	63.8	(6.69)	31.4	(1.82)	-1.3	(1.04)	49.0	(6.55)	-38.8	(8.53)	0.3	(0.34)	43.2	(2.41)	454.4	(3.62)
	Switzerland	45.5	(2.75)	18.2	(1.27)	-1.0	(1.23)	59.5	(2.95)	-25.1	(3.99)	-0.7	(0.11)	27.0	(2.00)	488.8	(1.50)
	Turkey	33.7	(1.96)	7.7	(1.50)	0.3	(0.61)	46.3	(1.70)	c	c	c	c	27.9	(1.74)	524.0	(1.59)
	United Kingdom	35.9	(6.21)	27.7	(2.01)	-0.3	(1.51)	65.7	(2.49)	-13.6	(8.49)	-0.3	(0.13)	23.1	(2.48)	468.7	(1.73)
	United States	36.3	(2.17)	23.5	(1.70)	4.4	(1.15)	50.4	(2.56)	-5.6	(5.57)	0.8	(0.14)	25.4	(2.36)	463.5	(2.01)
Partners	Albania	11.9	(5.07)	20.8	(3.04)	3.2	(1.35)	43.0	(2.47)	c	c	c	c	56.5	(3.40)	421.5	(3.44)
	Argentina	33.6	(2.50)	11.2	(1.96)	0.9	(0.87)	52.6	(2.03)	-27.0	(10.55)	0.5	(0.20)	24.0	(2.38)	439.7	(2.32)
	Azerbaijan	13.2	(1.78)	10.5	(1.67)	1.3	(0.90)	36.4	(2.00)	-9.8	(12.34)	-0.3	(0.49)	22.6	(2.16)	390.9	(2.12)
	Brazil	36.1	(1.23)	7.7	(1.54)	1.3	(0.57)	38.3	(1.25)	-71.7	(17.16)	-0.9	(0.47)	20.2	(1.63)	445.5	(1.33)
	Bulgaria	27.8	(5.08)	15.7	(1.93)	0.2	(1.29)	75.7	(3.99)	c	c	c	c	42.1	(3.51)	423.7	(2.61)
	Colombia	33.2	(1.12)	6.9	(2.01)	0.9	(0.72)	39.4	(1.53)	c	c	c	c	3.2	(2.17)	477.7	(1.83)
	Croatia	31.8	(2.33)	10.3	(1.36)	-4.0	(0.99)	75.3	(2.01)	-13.0	(5.71)	-0.1	(0.22)	31.4	(2.56)	472.8	(1.69)
	Dubai (UAE)	34.6	(1.56)	15.2	(1.52)	3.2	(1.03)	25.9	(3.13)	21.5	(3.25)	1.1	(0.05)	28.2	(3.94)	362.4	(2.92)
	Hong Kong-China	33.6	(2.03)	-0.9	(1.70)	-1.0	(0.76)	41.9	(1.64)	23.4	(3.70)	-0.4	(0.06)	21.9	(2.42)	575.8	(1.83)
	Indonesia	14.4	(2.00)	4.7	(2.44)	0.9	(0.62)	29.1	(1.83)	c	c	c	c	28.0	(1.48)	430.8	(2.46)
	Jordan	47.6	(6.38)	17.7	(1.52)	0.7	(0.81)	26.9	(1.55)	-11.5	(7.50)	-0.2	(0.20)	48.1	(2.73)	415.5	(2.04)
	Kazakhstan	22.2	(2.42)	16.2	(2.12)	-1.7	(1.31)	55.7	(2.70)	-12.2	(6.78)	0.0	(0.10)	38.1	(2.23)	411.1	(1.57)
	Kyrgyzstan	20.8	(2.92)	18.3	(2.23)	1.7	(1.10)	75.2	(2.03)	-23.4	(21.78)	3.3	(0.50)	46.0	(2.45)	345.7	(1.83)
	Latvia	43.8	(3.07)	16.2	(1.89)	-0.8	(1.35)	37.0	(2.77)	c	c	c	c	38.9	(2.36)	479.6	(1.77)
	Liechtenstein	23.8	(7.40)	2.1	(4.18)	-5.3	(3.07)	112.5	(12.17)	-12.6	(10.22)	-0.7	(0.44)	20.3	(6.86)	499.8	(8.42)
	Lithuania	27.4	(2.87)	18.1	(1.56)	0.2	(1.04)	44.0	(2.45)	c	c	c	c	51.1	(2.34)	447.6	(1.87)
	Macao-China	36.7	(1.01)	1.8	(1.61)	-1.1	(0.78)	1.0	(4.75)	16.7	(2.17)	-0.1	(0.23)	14.1	(1.51)	511.0	(3.47)
	Montenegro	22.9	(3.44)	12.1	(1.38)	-0.3	(1.05)	64.2	(6.54)	-1.8	(6.69)	-1.2	(0.32)	39.3	(2.63)	409.5	(2.58)
	Panama	32.6	(3.41)	7.9	(2.42)	1.2	(0.79)	45.8	(2.60)	-3.4	(10.77)	-1.4	(0.16)	15.8	(4.48)	431.3	(3.22)
	Peru	27.5	(1.23)	10.5	(2.05)	0.9	(0.64)	47.2	(1.46)	c	c	c	c	8.3	(2.17)	445.6	(1.59)
	Qatar	30.7	(1.70)	5.3	(0.98)	0.4	(0.85)	12.7	(2.91)	31.5	(2.98)	1.7	(0.07)	31.4	(3.71)	302.5	(2.94)
	Romania	19.6	(4.19)	10.7	(1.63)	-0.3	(0.79)	63.9	(2.34)	c	c	c	c	13.7	(2.56)	446.4	(1.70)
	Russian Federation	31.0	(2.01)	18.2	(1.93)	-1.6	(1.40)	38.8	(3.32)	-9.1	(5.88)	-0.4	(0.22)	38.7	(2.28)	452.9	(1.89)
	Serbia	21.3	(4.48)	9.2	(1.25)	-0.8	(0.74)	55.1	(3.42)	1.2	(5.65)	0.3	(0.13)	27.1	(2.22)	425.1	(1.60)
	Shanghai-China	21.8	(3.34)	4.6	(1.41)	0.1	(0.85)	57.3	(1.48)	c	c	c	c	29.3	(1.98)	583.5	(2.04)
	Singapore	28.9	(2.09)	22.2	(2.19)	-2.8	(1.14)	104.7	(2.86)	0.4	(4.21)	-1.0	(0.13)	24.6	(2.57)	590.2	(2.76)
	Chinese Taipei	15.4	(4.12)	15.5	(1.50)	-1.2	(1.05)	82.8	(3.06)	c	c	c	c	36.8	(2.25)	515.6	(2.03)
	Thailand	22.1	(2.05)	10.4	(1.54)	2.4	(0.66)	28.8	(1.31)	a	a	a	a	31.3	(1.78)	454.6	(1.67)
	Trinidad and Tobago	35.3	(1.60)	-0.6	(2.00)	-0.2	(0.91)	123.2	(3.42)	-9.2	(13.59)	-0.7	(0.28)	40.4	(2.90)	484.9	(2.77)
	Tunisia	49.7	(1.57)	3.7	(1.76)	0.7	(0.56)	17.8	(1.25)	c	c	c	c	14.4	(1.84)	449.6	(1.63)
	Uruguay	41.4	(1.49)	12.4	(1.58)	0.5	(0.75)	29.7	(1.58)	c	c	c	c	30.1	(2.48)	464.2	(2.29)

StatLink http://dx.doi.org/10.1787/888932343171

example, if the curriculum of the grades in which 15-year-olds are enrolled mainly includes material other than that assessed by PISA (which, in turn, may have been included in earlier school years) then the observed performance difference will underestimate student progress.

Immigration and language background

Information on the country of birth of students and their parents (ST17) is collected in a similar manner as in PISA 2000, PISA 2003 and PISA 2006 by using nationally specific ISO coded variables. The ISO codes of the country of birth for students and their parents are available in the PISA international database (COBN_S, COBN_M, and COBN_F).

For trends analysis, a dichotomous index was constructed that has the following categories: (1) native students (those students born in the country of assessment, or those with at least one parent born in that country; students who were born abroad with at least one parent born in the country of assessment are also classified as 'native' students), (2) second- and first-generation students (those born in the country of assessment but whose parents were born in another country and those born outside the country of assessment and whose parents were also born in another country). Students with missing responses for either the student or for both parents, or for all three questions have been given missing values for this variable.

Students indicate the language they usually speak at home. The data are captured in nationally-specific language codes, which were recoded into variable ST19Q01 with the following two values: (1) language at home is the same as the language of assessment, and (2) language at home is a different language than the language of assessment. Similar recoding was used in 2003 and 2006. In 2000 students directly provided information on whether they speak the language of assessment or another language at home. These responses were dichotomised and compared to recoded values for 2003, 2006 and 2009.

Student-level scale indices

Four indices were created based on possessions at home, namely, WEALTH, CULTPOSS, HEDRES and HOMEPOS. These are described in more detail below. These indices were estimated in two steps. As international item parameters were not deemed suitable to estimate scales for possessions at home, a two step procedure was adopted. In step 1 a concurrent estimation was done to compute these indices using national item parameters (*i.e.* item parameters were estimated within countries.) This made it possible to see within country trends in the possessions indices. However, in order to enable comparisons across countries for these scales, the relative positions of the countries were estimated on a joint scale. The resulting differences in the means of the possessions indices were imposed on the weighted maximum likelihood estimates (from step 1) using a linear transformation.

Family wealth

The *index of family wealth* (WEALTH) is based on the students' responses on whether they had the following at home: a room of their own, a link to the Internet, a dishwasher (treated as a country-specific item), a DVD player, and three other country-specific items (some items in ST20); and their responses on the number of cellular phones, televisions, computers, cars and the rooms with a bath or shower (ST21).

Home educational resources

The *index of home educational resources* (HEDRES) is based on the items measuring the existence of educational resources at home including a desk and a quiet place to study, a computer that students can use for schoolwork, educational software, books to help with students' school work, technical reference books and a dictionary (some items in ST20).

Cultural possessions

The *index of cultural possessions* (CULTPOSS) is based on the students' responses to whether they had the following at home: classic literature, books of poetry and works of art (some items in ST20).

Economic, social and cultural status

The *PISA index of economic, social and cultural status* (ESCS) was derived from the following three indices: highest occupational status of parents (HISEI), highest educational level of parents in years of education according to ISCED (PARED), and home possessions (HOMEPOS). The index of home possessions (HOMEPOS) comprises all items on the indices of WEALTH, CULTPOSS and HEDRES, as well as books in the home recoded into a four-level categorical variable (0-10 books, 11-25 or 26-100 books, 101-200 or 201-500 books, more than 500 books). In order to facilitate a trends study similar ISCED levels to PARED mappings were used for each cycle and the *index on home possessions* (HOMEPOS) was also estimated concurrently across cycles.

The *PISA index of economic, social and cultural status* (ESCS) was derived from a principal component analysis of standardised variables (each variable has an OECD mean of 0 and a standard deviation of 1), taking the factor scores for the first principal component as measures of the index of economic, social and cultural status.

Principal component analysis was also performed for each participating country to determine to what extent the components of

the index operate in similar ways across countries. The analysis revealed that patterns of factor loading were very similar across countries, with all three components contributing to a similar extent to the index. For the occupational component, the average factor loading was 0.80, ranging from 0.66 to 0.87 across countries. For the educational component, the average factor loading was 0.79, ranging from 0.69 to 0.87 across countries. For the home possession component, the average factor loading was 0.73, ranging from 0.60 to 0.84 across countries. The reliability of the index ranged from 0.41 to 0.81. These results support the cross-national validity of the *PISA index of economic, social and cultural status*.

The imputation of components for students missing data on one component was done on the basis of a regression on the other two variables, with an additional random error component. The final values on the *PISA index of economic, social and cultural status* (ESCS) have an OECD mean of 0 and a standard deviation of 1.

Enjoyment of reading activities

The *index of enjoyment of reading activities* (ENJOY) was derived from students' level of agreement with the following statements (ST24 in 2009 and ST35 in 2000): i) I read only if I have to; ii) reading is one of my favourite hobbies; iii) I like talking about books with other people; iv) I find it hard to finish books; v) I feel happy if I receive a book as a present; vi) for me, reading is a waste of time; vii) I enjoy going to a bookstore or a library; viii) I read only to get information that I need; ix) I cannot sit still and read for more than a few minutes; (x) I like to express my opinions about books I have read; and (xi) I like to exchange books with my friends.

As all items that are negatively phrased (items i, iv, vi, viii and ix) are inverted for scaling, the higher values on this index indicate higher levels of enjoyment of reading.

Diversity of reading materials

The *index of diversity of reading materials* (DIVREAD) was derived from the frequency with which students read the following materials because they want to (ST25 in 2009 and ST36 in 2000): magazines, comic books, fiction, non-fiction books and newspapers. The higher values on this index indicate higher diversity in reading.

ANNEX A2
THE PISA TARGET POPULATION, THE PISA SAMPLES AND THE DEFINITION OF SCHOOLS

Definition of the PISA target population

PISA 2009 provides an assessment of the cumulative yield of education and learning at a point at which most young adults are still enrolled in initial education.

A major challenge for an international survey is to ensure that international comparability of national target populations is guaranteed in such a venture.

Differences between countries in the nature and extent of pre-primary education and care, the age of entry into formal schooling and the institutional structure of educational systems do not allow the definition of internationally comparable grade levels of schooling. Consequently, international comparisons of educational performance typically define their populations with reference to a target age group. Some previous international assessments have defined their target population on the basis of the grade level that provides maximum coverage of a particular age cohort. A disadvantage of this approach is that slight variations in the age distribution of students across grade levels often lead to the selection of different target grades in different countries, or between education systems within countries, raising serious questions about the comparability of results across, and at times within, countries. In addition, because not all students of the desired age are usually represented in grade-based samples, there may be a more serious potential bias in the results if the unrepresented students are typically enrolled in the next higher grade in some countries and the next lower grade in others. This would exclude students with potentially higher levels of performance in the former countries and students with potentially lower levels of performance in the latter.

In order to address this problem, PISA uses an age-based definition for its target population, *i.e.* a definition that is not tied to the institutional structures of national education systems. PISA assesses students who were aged between 15 years and 3 (complete) months and 16 years and 2 (complete) months at the beginning of the assessment period, plus or minus a 1 month allowable variation, and who were enrolled in an educational institution with Grade 7 or higher, regardless of the grade levels or type of institution in which they were enrolled, and regardless of whether they were in full-time or part-time education. Educational institutions are generally referred to as schools in this publication, although some educational institutions (in particular, some types of vocational education establishments) may not be termed schools in certain countries. As expected from this definition, the average age of students across OECD countries was 15 years and 9 months. The range in country means was 2 months and 5 days (0.18 years), from the minimum country mean of 15 years and 8 months to the maximum country mean of 15 years and 10 months.

Given this definition of population, PISA makes statements about the knowledge and skills of a group of individuals who were born within a comparable reference period, but who may have undergone different educational experiences both in and outside of schools. In PISA, these knowledge and skills are referred to as the yield of education at an age that is common across countries. Depending on countries' policies on school entry, selection and promotion, these students may be distributed over a narrower or a wider range of grades across different education systems, tracks or streams. It is important to consider these differences when comparing PISA results across countries, as observed differences between students at age 15 may no longer appear as students' educational experiences converge later on.

If a country's scale scores in reading, scientific or mathematical literacy are significantly higher than those in another country, it cannot automatically be inferred that the schools or particular parts of the education system in the first country are more effective than those in the second. However, one can legitimately conclude that the cumulative impact of learning experiences in the first country, starting in early childhood and up to the age of 15, and embracing experiences both in school, home and beyond, have resulted in higher outcomes in the literacy domains that PISA measures.

The PISA target population did not include residents attending schools in a foreign country. It does, however, include foreign nationals attending schools in the country of assessment.

To accommodate countries that desired grade-based results for the purpose of national analyses, PISA 2009 provided a sampling option to supplement age-based sampling with grade-based sampling.

Population coverage

All countries attempted to maximise the coverage of 15-year-olds enrolled in education in their national samples, including students enrolled in special educational institutions. As a result, PISA 2009 reached standards of population coverage that are unprecedented in international surveys of this kind.

The sampling standards used in PISA permitted countries to exclude up to a total of 5% of the relevant population either by excluding schools or by excluding students within schools. All but 5 countries, Denmark (8.17%), Luxembourg (8.15%), Canada (6.00%), Norway (5.93%) and the United States (5.16%), achieved this standard, and in 36 countries and economies, the overall exclusion rate was less than 2%. When language exclusions were accounted for (*i.e.* removed from the overall exclusion rate), the United States no longer had an exclusion rate greater than 5%. For details, see *www.pisa.oecd.org*.

Exclusions within the above limits include:

- *At the school level: i)* schools that were geographically inaccessible or where the administration of the PISA assessment was not considered feasible; and *ii)* schools that provided teaching only for students in the categories defined under "within-school exclusions", such as schools for the blind. The percentage of 15-year-olds enrolled in such schools had to be less than 2.5% of the nationally desired target population [0.5% maximum for *i)* and 2% maximum for *ii)*]. The magnitude, nature and justification of school-level exclusions are documented in the *PISA 2009 Technical Report* (OECD, forthcoming).
- *At the student level: i)* students with an intellectual disability; *ii)* students with a functional disability; *iii)* students with limited assessment language proficiency; *iv)* other – a category defined by the national centres and approved by the international centre; and *v)* students taught in a language of instruction for the main domain for which no materials were available. Students could not be excluded solely because of low proficiency or common discipline problems. The percentage of 15-year-olds excluded within schools had to be less than 2.5% of the nationally desired target population.

Table A2.1 describes the target population of the countries participating in PISA 2009. Further information on the target population and the implementation of PISA sampling standards can be found in the *PISA 2009 Technical Report* (OECD, forthcoming).

- ***Column 1*** shows the **total number of 15-year-olds** according to the most recent available information, which in most countries meant the year 2008 as the year before the assessment.
- ***Column 2*** shows the number of 15-year-olds enrolled in schools in Grade 7 or above (as defined above), which is referred to as the **eligible population**.
- ***Column 3*** shows the **national desired target population**. Countries were allowed to exclude up to 0.5% of students *a priori* from the eligible population, essentially for practical reasons. The following *a priori* exclusions exceed this limit but were agreed with the PISA Consortium: Canada excluded 1.1% of its population from Territories and Aboriginal reserves; France excluded 1.7% of its students in its *territoires d'outre-mer* and other institutions; Indonesia excluded 4.7% of its students from four provinces because of security reasons; Kyrgyzstan excluded 2.3% of its population in remote, inaccessible schools; and Serbia excluded 2% of its students taught in Serbian in Kosovo.
- ***Column 4*** shows the **number of students enrolled in schools that were excluded from the national desired target population** either from the sampling frame or later in the field during data collection.
- ***Column 5*** shows the **size of the national desired target population after subtracting the students enrolled in excluded schools**. This is obtained by subtracting Column 4 from Column 3.
- ***Column 6*** shows the **percentage of students enrolled in excluded schools**. This is obtained by dividing Column 4 by Column 3 and multiplying by 100.
- ***Column 7*** shows the **number of students participating in PISA 2009**. Note that in some cases this number does not account for 15-year-olds assessed as part of additional national options.
- ***Column 8*** shows the **weighted number of participating students**, *i.e.* the number of students in the nationally defined target population that the PISA sample represents.
- Each country attempted to maximise the coverage of PISA's target population within the sampled schools. In the case of each sampled school, all eligible students, namely those 15 years of age, regardless of grade, were first listed. Sampled students who were to be excluded had still to be included in the sampling documentation, and a list drawn up stating the reason for their exclusion. ***Column 9*** indicates the **total number of excluded students,** which is further described and classified into specific categories in Table A2.2. ***Column 10*** indicates the **weighted number of excluded students,** *i.e.* the overall number of students in the nationally defined target population represented by the number of students excluded from the sample, which is also described and classified by exclusion categories in Table A2.2. Excluded students were excluded based on five categories: *i)* students with an intellectual disability – the student has a mental or emotional disability and is cognitively delayed such that he/she cannot perform in the PISA testing situation; *ii)* students with a functional disability – the student has a moderate to severe permanent physical disability such that he/she cannot perform in the PISA testing situation; *iii)* students with a limited assessment language proficiency – the student is unable to read or speak any of the languages of the assessment in the country and would be unable to overcome the language barrier in the testing situation (typically a student who has received less than one year of instruction in the languages of the assessment may be excluded); *iv)* other – a category defined by the national centres and approved by the international centre; and *v)* students taught in a language of instruction for the main domain for which no materials were available.
- ***Column 11*** shows the **percentage of students excluded within schools**. This is calculated as the weighted number of excluded students (Column 10), divided by the weighted number of excluded and participating students (Column 8 plus Column 10), then multiplied by 100.

[Part 1/2]

Table A2.1 **PISA target populations and samples**

		Population and sample information							
		Total population of 15-year-olds	Total enrolled population of 15-year-olds at Grade 7 or above	Total in national desired target population	Total school-level exclusions	Total in national desired target population after all school exclusions and before within-school exclusions	School-level exclusion rate (%)	Number of participating students	Weighted number of participating students
		(1)	(2)	(3)	(4)	(5)	(6)	(7)	(8)
OECD	Australia	286 334	269 669	269 669	7 057	262 612	2.62	14 251	240 851
	Austria	99 818	94 192	94 192	115	94 077	0.12	6 590	87 326
	Belgium	126 377	126 335	126 335	2 474	123 861	1.96	8 501	119 140
	Canada	430 791	426 590	422 052	2 370	419 682	0.56	23 207	360 286
	Chile	290 056	265 542	265 463	2 594	262 869	0.98	5 669	247 270
	Czech Republic	122 027	116 153	116 153	1 619	114 534	1.39	6 064	113 951
	Denmark	70 522	68 897	68 897	3 082	65 815	4.47	5 924	60 855
	Estonia	14 248	14 106	14 106	436	13 670	3.09	4 727	12 978
	Finland	66 198	66 198	66 198	1 507	64 691	2.28	5 810	61 463
	France	749 808	732 825	720 187	18 841	701 346	2.62	4 298	677 620
	Germany	852 044	852 044	852 044	7 138	844 906	0.84	4 979	766 993
	Greece	102 229	105 664	105 664	696	104 968	0.66	4 969	93 088
	Hungary	121 155	118 387	118 387	3 322	115 065	2.81	4 605	105 611
	Iceland	4 738	4 738	4 738	20	4 718	0.42	3 646	4 410
	Ireland	56 635	55 464	55 446	276	55 170	0.50	3 937	52 794
	Israel	122 701	112 254	112 254	1 570	110 684	1.40	5 761	103 184
	Italy	586 904	573 542	573 542	2 694	570 848	0.47	30 905	506 733
	Japan	1 211 642	1 189 263	1 189 263	22 955	1 166 308	1.93	6 088	1 113 403
	Korea	717 164	700 226	700 226	2 927	697 299	0.42	4 989	630 030
	Luxembourg	5 864	5 623	5 623	186	5 437	3.31	4 622	5 124
	Mexico	2 151 771	1 425 397	1 425 397	5 825	1 419 572	0.41	38 250	1 305 461
	Netherlands	199 000	198 334	198 334	6 179	192 155	3.12	4 760	183 546
	New Zealand	63 460	60 083	60 083	645	59 438	1.07	4 643	55 129
	Norway	63 352	62 948	62 948	1 400	61 548	2.22	4 660	57 367
	Poland	482 500	473 700	473 700	7 650	466 050	1.61	4 917	448 866
	Portugal	115 669	107 583	107 583	0	107 583	0.00	6 298	96 820
	Slovak Republic	72 826	72 454	72 454	1 803	70 651	2.49	4 555	69 274
	Slovenia	20 314	19 571	19 571	174	19 397	0.89	6 155	18 773
	Spain	433 224	425 336	425 336	3 133	422 203	0.74	25 887	387 054
	Sweden	121 486	121 216	121 216	2 323	118 893	1.92	4 567	113 054
	Switzerland	90 623	89 423	89 423	1 747	87 676	1.95	11 812	80 839
	Turkey	1 336 842	859 172	859 172	8 569	850 603	1.00	4 996	757 298
	United Kingdom	786 626	786 825	786 825	17 593	769 232	2.24	12 179	683 380
	United States	4 103 738	4 210 475	4 210 475	15 199	4 195 276	0.36	5 233	3 373 264
Partners	Albania	55 587	42 767	42 767	372	42 395	0.87	4 596	34 134
	Argentina	688 434	636 713	636 713	2 238	634 475	0.35	4 774	472 106
	Azerbaijan	185 481	184 980	184 980	1 886	183 094	1.02	4 727	105 886
	Brazil	3 292 022	2 654 489	2 654 489	15 571	2 638 918	0.59	20 127	2 080 159
	Bulgaria	80 226	70 688	70 688	1 369	69 319	1.94	4 507	57 833
	Colombia	893 057	582 640	582 640	412	582 228	0.07	7 921	522 388
	Croatia	48 491	46 256	46 256	535	45 721	1.16	4 994	43 065
	Dubai (UAE)	10 564	10 327	10 327	167	10 160	1.62	5 620	9 179
	Hong Kong-China	85 000	78 224	78 224	809	77 415	1.03	4 837	75 548
	Indonesia	4 267 801	3 158 173	3 010 214	10 458	2 999 756	0.35	5 136	2 259 118
	Jordan	117 732	107 254	107 254	0	107 254	0.00	6 486	104 056
	Kazakhstan	281 659	263 206	263 206	7 210	255 996	2.74	5 412	250 657
	Kyrgyzstan	116 795	93 989	91 793	1 149	90 644	1.25	4 986	78 493
	Latvia	28 749	28 149	28 149	943	27 206	3.35	4 502	23 362
	Liechtenstein	399	360	360	5	355	1.39	329	355
	Lithuania	51 822	43 967	43 967	522	43 445	1.19	4 528	40 530
	Macao-China	7 500	5 969	5 969	3	5 966	0.05	5 952	5 978
	Montenegro	8 500	8 493	8 493	10	8 483	0.12	4 825	7 728
	Panama	57 919	43 623	43 623	501	43 122	1.15	3 969	30 510
	Peru	585 567	491 514	490 840	984	489 856	0.20	5 985	427 607
	Qatar	10 974	10 665	10 665	114	10 551	1.07	9 078	9 806
	Romania	152 084	152 084	152 084	679	151 405	0.45	4 776	151 130
	Russian Federation	1 673 085	1 667 460	1 667 460	25 012	1 642 448	1.50	5 308	1 290 047
	Serbia	85 121	75 128	73 628	1 580	72 048	2.15	5 523	70 796
	Shanghai-China	112 000	100 592	100 592	1 287	99 305	1.28	5 115	97 045
	Singapore	54 982	54 212	54 212	633	53 579	1.17	5 283	51 874
	Chinese Taipei	329 249	329 189	329 189	1 778	327 411	0.54	5 831	297 203
	Thailand	949 891	763 679	763 679	8 438	755 241	1.10	6 225	691 916
	Trinidad and Tobago	19 260	17 768	17 768	0	17 768	0.00	4 778	14 938
	Tunisia	153 914	153 914	153 914	0	153 914	0.00	4 955	136 545
	Uruguay	53 801	43 281	43 281	30	43 251	0.07	5 957	33 971

Note: For a full explanation of the details in this table, please refer to the *PISA 2009 Technical Report* (OECD, forthcoming). The figure for total national population of 15-year-olds enrolled in Column 1 may occasionally be larger than the total number of 15-year-olds in Column 2 due to differing data sources. In Greece, Column 1 does not include immigrants but Column 2 does include immigrants.

StatLink http://dx.doi.org/10.1787/888932343190

[Part 2/2]
Table A2.1 PISA target populations and samples

		Population and sample information				Coverage indices		
		Number of excluded students	Weighted number of excluded students	Within-school exclusion rate (%)	Overall exclusion rate (%)	Coverage index 1: Coverage of national desired population	Coverage index 2: Coverage of national enrolled population	Coverage index 3: Coverage of 15-year-old population
		(9)	(10)	(11)	(12)	(13)	(14)	(15)
OECD	Australia	313	4 389	1.79	4.36	0.956	0.956	0.841
	Austria	45	607	0.69	0.81	0.992	0.992	0.875
	Belgium	30	292	0.24	2.20	0.978	0.978	0.943
	Canada	1 607	20 837	5.47	6.00	0.940	0.930	0.836
	Chile	15	620	0.25	1.22	0.988	0.987	0.852
	Czech Republic	24	423	0.37	1.76	0.982	0.982	0.934
	Denmark	296	2 448	3.87	8.17	0.918	0.918	0.863
	Estonia	32	97	0.74	3.81	0.962	0.962	0.911
	Finland	77	717	1.15	3.40	0.966	0.966	0.928
	France	1	304	0.04	2.66	0.973	0.957	0.904
	Germany	28	3 591	0.47	1.30	0.987	0.987	0.900
	Greece	142	2 977	3.10	3.74	0.963	0.963	0.911
	Hungary	10	361	0.34	3.14	0.969	0.969	0.872
	Iceland	187	189	4.10	4.50	0.955	0.955	0.931
	Ireland	136	1 492	2.75	3.23	0.968	0.967	0.932
	Israel	86	1 359	1.30	2.68	0.973	0.973	0.841
	Italy	561	10 663	2.06	2.52	0.975	0.975	0.863
	Japan	0	0	0.00	1.93	0.981	0.981	0.919
	Korea	16	1 748	0.28	0.69	0.993	0.993	0.879
	Luxembourg	196	270	5.01	8.15	0.919	0.919	0.874
	Mexico	52	1 951	0.15	0.56	0.994	0.994	0.607
	Netherlands	19	648	0.35	3.46	0.965	0.965	0.922
	New Zealand	184	1 793	3.15	4.19	0.958	0.958	0.869
	Norway	207	2 260	3.79	5.93	0.941	0.941	0.906
	Poland	15	1 230	0.27	1.88	0.981	0.981	0.930
	Portugal	115	1 544	1.57	1.57	0.984	0.984	0.837
	Slovak Republic	106	1 516	2.14	4.58	0.954	0.954	0.951
	Slovenia	43	138	0.73	1.61	0.984	0.984	0.924
	Spain	775	12 673	3.17	3.88	0.961	0.961	0.893
	Sweden	146	3 360	2.89	4.75	0.953	0.953	0.931
	Switzerland	209	940	1.15	3.08	0.969	0.969	0.892
	Turkey	11	1 497	0.20	1.19	0.988	0.988	0.566
	United Kingdom	318	17 094	2.44	4.62	0.954	0.954	0.869
	United States	315	170 542	4.81	5.16	0.948	0.948	0.822
Partners	Albania	0	0	0.00	0.87	0.991	0.991	0.614
	Argentina	14	1 225	0.26	0.61	0.994	0.994	0.686
	Azerbaijan	0	0	0.00	1.02	0.990	0.990	0.571
	Brazil	24	2 692	0.13	0.72	0.993	0.993	0.632
	Bulgaria	0	0	0.00	1.94	0.981	0.981	0.721
	Colombia	11	490	0.09	0.16	0.998	0.998	0.585
	Croatia	34	273	0.63	1.78	0.982	0.982	0.888
	Dubai (UAE)	5	7	0.07	1.69	0.983	0.983	0.869
	Hong Kong-China	9	119	0.16	1.19	0.988	0.988	0.889
	Indonesia	0	0	0.00	0.35	0.997	0.950	0.529
	Jordan	24	443	0.42	0.42	0.996	0.996	0.884
	Kazakhstan	82	3 844	1.51	4.21	0.958	0.958	0.890
	Kyrgyzstan	86	1 384	1.73	2.96	0.970	0.948	0.672
	Latvia	19	102	0.43	3.77	0.962	0.962	0.813
	Liechtenstein	0	0	0.00	1.39	0.986	0.986	0.890
	Lithuania	74	632	1.53	2.70	0.973	0.973	0.782
	Macao-China	0	0	0.00	0.05	0.999	0.999	0.797
	Montenegro	0	0	0.00	0.12	0.999	0.999	0.909
	Panama	0	0	0.00	1.15	0.989	0.989	0.527
	Peru	9	558	0.13	0.33	0.997	0.995	0.730
	Qatar	28	28	0.28	1.35	0.986	0.986	0.894
	Romania	0	0	0.00	0.45	0.996	0.996	0.994
	Russian Federation	59	15 247	1.17	2.65	0.973	0.973	0.771
	Serbia	10	133	0.19	2.33	0.977	0.957	0.832
	Shanghai-China	7	130	0.13	1.41	0.986	0.986	0.866
	Singapore	48	417	0.80	1.96	0.980	0.980	0.943
	Chinese Taipei	32	1 662	0.56	1.09	0.989	0.989	0.903
	Thailand	6	458	0.07	1.17	0.988	0.988	0.728
	Trinidad and Tobago	11	36	0.24	0.24	0.998	0.998	0.776
	Tunisia	7	184	0.13	0.13	0.999	0.999	0.887
	Uruguay	14	67	0.20	0.26	0.997	0.997	0.631

Note: For a full explanation of the details in this table please refer to the *PISA 2009 Technical Report* (OECD, forthcoming). The figure for total national population of 15-year-olds enrolled in Column 1 may occasionally be larger than the total number of 15-year-olds in Column 2 due to differing data sources. In Greece, Column 1 does not include immigrants but Column 2 does include immigrants.

StatLink http://dx.doi.org/10.1787/888932343190

[Part 1/1]

Table A2.2 **Exclusions**

		Student exclusions (unweighted)						Student exclusion (weighted)					
		Number of excluded students with a disability (Code 1)	Number of excluded students with a disability (Code 2)	Number of excluded students because of language (Code 3)	Number of excluded students for other reasons (Code 4)	Number of excluded students because of no materials available in the language of instruction (Code 5)	Total number of excluded students	Weighted number of excluded students with a disability (Code 1)	Weighted number of excluded students with a disability (Code 2)	Weighted number of excluded students because of language (Code 3)	Weighted number of excluded students for other reasons (Code 4)	Number of excluded students because of no materials available in the language of instruction (Code 5)	Total weighted number of excluded students
		(1)	(2)	(3)	(4)	(5)	(6)	(7)	(8)	(9)	(10)	(11)	(12)
OECD	Australia	24	210	79	0	0	313	272	2 834	1 283	0	0	4 389
	Austria	0	26	19	0	0	45	0	317	290	0	0	607
	Belgium	3	17	10	0	0	30	26	171	95	0	0	292
	Canada	49	1 458	100	0	0	1 607	428	19 082	1 326	0	0	20 837
	Chile	5	10	0	0	0	15	177	443	0	0	0	620
	Czech Republic	8	7	9	0	0	24	117	144	162	0	0	423
	Denmark	13	182	35	66	0	296	165	1 432	196	656	0	2 448
	Estonia	3	28	1	0	0	32	8	87	2	0	0	97
	Finland	4	48	12	11	2	77	38	447	110	99	23	717
	France	1	0	0	0	0	1	304	0	0	0	0	304
	Germany	6	20	2	0	0	28	864	2 443	285	0	0	3 591
	Greece	7	11	7	117	0	142	172	352	195	2 257	0	2 977
	Hungary	0	1	0	9	0	10	0	48	0	313	0	361
	Iceland	3	78	64	38	1	187	3	78	65	39	1	189
	Ireland	4	72	25	35	0	136	51	783	262	396	0	1 492
	Israel	10	69	7	0	0	86	194	1 049	116	0	0	1 359
	Italy	45	348	168	0	0	561	748	6 241	3 674	0	0	10 663
	Japan	0	0	0	0	0	0	0	0	0	0	0	0
	Korea	7	9	0	0	0	16	994	753	0	0	0	1 748
	Luxembourg	2	132	62	0	0	196	2	206	62	0	0	270
	Mexico	25	25	2	0	0	52	1 010	905	36	0	0	1 951
	Netherlands	6	13	0	0	0	19	178	470	0	0	0	648
	New Zealand	19	84	78	0	3	184	191	824	749	0	29	1 793
	Norway	8	160	39	0	0	207	90	1 756	414	0	0	2 260
	Poland	2	13	0	0	0	15	169	1 061	0	0	0	1 230
	Portugal	2	100	13	0	0	115	25	1 322	197	0	0	1 544
	Slovak Republic	12	37	1	56	0	106	171	558	19	768	0	1 516
	Slovenia	6	10	27	0	0	43	40	32	66	0	0	138
	Spain	45	441	289	0	0	775	1 007	7 141	4 525	0	0	12 673
	Sweden	115	0	31	0	0	146	2 628	0	732	0	0	3 360
	Switzerland	11	106	92	0	0	209	64	344	532	0	0	940
	Turkey	3	3	5	0	0	11	338	495	665	0	0	1 497
	United Kingdom	40	247	31	0	0	318	2 438	13 482	1 174	0	0	17 094
	United States	29	236	40	10	0	315	15 367	127 486	21 718	5 971	0	170 542
Partners	Albania	0	0	0	0	0	0	0	0	0	0	0	0
	Argentina	4	10	0	0	0	14	288	937	0	0	0	1 225
	Azerbaijan	0	0	0	0	0	0	0	0	0	0	0	0
	Brazil	21	3	0	0	0	24	2 495	197	0	0	0	2 692
	Bulgaria	0	0	0	0	0	0	0	0	0	0	0	0
	Colombia	7	2	2	0	0	11	200	48	242	0	0	490
	Croatia	4	30	0	0	0	34	34	239	0	0	0	273
	Dubai (UAE)	1	1	3	0	0	5	2	2	3	0	0	7
	Hong Kong-China	0	9	0	0	0	9	0	119	0	0	0	119
	Indonesia	0	0	0	0	0	0	0	0	0	0	0	0
	Jordan	11	7	6	0	0	24	166	149	127	0	0	443
	Kazakhstan	10	17	0	0	55	82	429	828	0	0	2 587	3 844
	Kyrgyzstan	68	13	5	0	0	86	1 093	211	80	0	0	1 384
	Latvia	6	8	5	0	0	19	25	44	33	0	0	102
	Liechtenstein	0	0	0	0	0	0	0	0	0	0	0	0
	Lithuania	4	69	1	0	0	74	33	590	9	0	0	632
	Macao-China	0	0	0	0	0	0	0	0	0	0	0	0
	Montenegro	0	0	0	0	0	0	0	0	0	0	0	0
	Panama	0	0	0	0	0	0	0	0	0	0	0	0
	Peru	4	5	0	0	0	9	245	313	0	0	0	558
	Qatar	9	18	1	0	0	28	9	18	1	0	0	28
	Romania	0	0	0	0	0	0	0	0	0	0	0	0
	Russian Federation	11	47	1	0	0	59	2 081	13 010	157	0	0	15 247
	Serbia	4	5	0	0	1	10	66	53	0	0	13	133
	Shanghai-China	1	6	0	0	0	7	19	111	0	0	0	130
	Singapore	2	22	24	0	0	48	17	217	182	0	0	417
	Chinese Taipei	13	19	0	0	0	32	684	977	0	0	0	1 662
	Thailand	0	5	1	0	0	6	0	260	198	0	0	458
	Trinidad and Tobago	1	10	0	0	0	11	3	33	0	0	0	36
	Tunisia	4	1	2	0	0	7	104	21	58	0	0	184
	Uruguay	2	9	3	0	0	14	14	34	18	0	0	67

Exclusion codes:

Code 1 Functional disability – student has a moderate to severe permanent physical disability.

Code 2 Intellectual disability – student has a mental or emotional disability and has either been tested as cognitively delayed or is considered in the professional opinion of qualified staff to be cognitively delayed.

Code 3 Limited assessment language proficiency – student is not a native speaker of any of the languages of the assessment in the country and has been resident in the country for less than one year.

Code 4 Other defined by the national centres and approved by the international centre.

Code 5 No materials available in the language of instruction.

Note: For a full explanation of other details in this table, please refer to the *PISA 2009 Technical Report* (OECD, forthcoming).

StatLink http://dx.doi.org/10.1787/888932343190

- ***Column 12*** shows the **overall exclusion rate**, which represents the weighted percentage of the national desired target population excluded from PISA either through school-level exclusions or through the exclusion of students within schools. It is calculated as the school-level exclusion rate (Column 6 divided by 100) plus within-school exclusion rate (Column 11 divided by 100) multiplied by 1 minus the school-level exclusion rate (Column 6 divided by 100). This result is then multiplied by 100. Five countries, Denmark, Luxembourg, Canada, Norway and the United States, had exclusion rates higher than 5%. When language exclusions were accounted for (*i.e.* removed from the overall exclusion rate), the United States no longer had an exclusion rate greater than 5%.
- ***Column 13*** presents an **index of the extent to which the national desired target population is covered by the PISA sample**. Denmark, Luxembourg, Canada, Norway and the United States were the only countries where the coverage is below 95%.
- ***Column 14*** presents an **index of the extent to which 15-year-olds enrolled in schools are covered by the PISA sample**. The index measures the overall proportion of the national enrolled population that is covered by the non-excluded portion of the student sample. The index takes into account both school-level and student-level exclusions. Values close to 100 indicate that the PISA sample represents the entire education system as defined for PISA 2009. The index is the weighted number of participating students (Column 8) divided by the weighted number of participating and excluded students (Column 8 plus Column 10), times the nationally defined target population (Column 5) divided by the eligible population (Column 2) (times 100).
- ***Column 15*** presents an **index of the coverage of the 15-year-old population**. This index is the weighted number of participating students (Column 8) divided by the total population of 15-year-old students (Column 1).

This high level of coverage contributes to the comparability of the assessment results. For example, even assuming that the excluded students would have systematically scored worse than those who participated, and that this relationship is moderately strong, an exclusion rate in the order of 5% would likely lead to an overestimation of national mean scores of less than 5 score points (on a scale with an international mean of 500 score points and a standard deviation of 100 score points). This assessment is based on the following calculations: if the correlation between the propensity of exclusions and student performance is 0.3, resulting mean scores would likely be overestimated by 1 score point if the exclusion rate is 1%, by 3 score points if the exclusion rate is 5%, and by 6 score points if the exclusion rate is 10%. If the correlation between the propensity of exclusions and student performance is 0.5, resulting mean scores would be overestimated by 1 score point if the exclusion rate is 1%, by 5 score points if the exclusion rate is 5%, and by 10 score points if the exclusion rate is 10%. For this calculation, a model was employed that assumes a bivariate normal distribution for performance and the propensity to participate. For details, see the *PISA 2009 Technical Report* (OECD, forthcoming).

Sampling procedures and response rates

The accuracy of any survey results depends on the quality of the information on which national samples are based as well as on the sampling procedures. Quality standards, procedures, instruments and verification mechanisms were developed for PISA that ensured that national samples yielded comparable data and that the results could be compared with confidence.

Most PISA samples were designed as two-stage stratified samples (where countries applied different sampling designs, these are documented in the *PISA 2009 Technical Report* [OECD, forthcoming]). The first stage consisted of sampling individual schools in which 15-year-old students could be enrolled. Schools were sampled systematically with probabilities proportional to size, the measure of size being a function of the estimated number of eligible (15-year-old) students enrolled. A minimum of 150 schools were selected in each country (where this number existed), although the requirements for national analyses often required a somewhat larger sample. As the schools were sampled, replacement schools were simultaneously identified, in case a sampled school chose not to participate in PISA 2009.

In the case of Iceland, Liechtenstein, Luxembourg, Macao-China and Qatar, all schools and all eligible students within schools were included in the sample.

Experts from the PISA Consortium performed the sample selection process for most participating countries and monitored it closely in those countries that selected their own samples. The second stage of the selection process sampled students within sampled schools. Once schools were selected, a list of each sampled school's 15-year-old students was prepared. From this list, 35 students were then selected with equal probability (all 15-year-old students were selected if fewer than 35 were enrolled). The number of students to be sampled per school could deviate from 35, but could not be less than 20.

Data-quality standards in PISA required minimum participation rates for schools as well as for students. These standards were established to minimise the potential for response biases. In the case of countries meeting these standards, it was likely that any bias resulting from non-response would be negligible, *i.e.* typically smaller than the sampling error.

A minimum response rate of 85% was required for the schools initially selected. Where the initial response rate of schools was between 65 and 85%, however, an acceptable school response rate could still be achieved through the use of replacement schools. This procedure brought with it a risk of increased response bias. Participating countries were, therefore, encouraged to persuade as many of the schools in the original sample as possible to participate. Schools with a student participation rate between 25% and 50% were not regarded as participating schools, but data from these schools were included in the database and contributed to the various estimations. Data from schools with a student participation rate of less than 25% were excluded from the database.

[Part 1/2]
Table A2.3 **Response rates**

	Initial sample – before school replacement					Final sample – after school replacement		
	Weighted school participation rate before replacement (%)	Weighted number of responding schools (weighted also by enrolment)	Weighted number of schools sampled (responding and non-responding) (weighted also by enrolment)	Number of responding schools (unweighted)	Number of responding and non-responding schools (unweighted)	Weighted school participation rate after replacement (%)	Weighted number of responding schools (weighted also by enrolment)	Weighted number of schools sampled (responding and non-responding) (weighted also by enrolment)
	(1)	(2)	(3)	(4)	(5)	(6)	(7)	(8)
OECD								
Australia	97.78	265 659	271 696	342	357	98.85	268 780	271 918
Austria	93.94	88 551	94 261	280	291	93.94	88 551	94 261
Belgium	88.76	112 594	126 851	255	292	95.58	121 291	126 899
Canada	88.04	362 152	411 343	893	1 001	89.64	368 708	411 343
Chile	94.34	245 583	260 331	189	201	99.04	257 594	260 099
Czech Republic	83.09	94 696	113 961	226	270	97.40	111 091	114 062
Denmark	83.94	55 375	65 967	264	325	90.75	59 860	65 964
Estonia	100.00	13 230	13 230	175	175	100.00	13 230	13 230
Finland	98.65	62 892	63 751	201	204	100.00	63 748	63 751
France	94.14	658 769	699 776	166	177	94.14	658 769	699 776
Germany	98.61	826 579	838 259	223	226	100.00	838 259	838 259
Greece	98.19	98 710	100 529	181	184	99.40	99 925	100 529
Hungary	98.21	101 523	103 378	184	190	99.47	103 067	103 618
Iceland	98.46	4 488	4 558	129	141	98.46	4 488	4 558
Ireland	87.18	48 821	55 997	139	160	88.44	49 526	55 997
Israel	92.03	103 141	112 069	170	186	95.40	106 918	112 069
Italy	94.27	532 432	564 811	1 054	1 108	99.08	559 546	564 768
Japan	87.77	999 408	1 138 694	171	196	94.99	1 081 662	1 138 694
Korea	100.00	683 793	683 793	157	157	100.00	683 793	683 793
Luxembourg	100.00	5 437	5 437	39	39	100.00	5 437	5 437
Mexico	95.62	1 338 291	1 399 638	1 512	1 560	97.71	1 367 668	1 399 730
Netherlands	80.40	154 471	192 140	155	194	95.54	183 555	192 118
New Zealand	84.11	49 917	59 344	148	179	91.00	54 130	59 485
Norway	89.61	55 484	61 920	183	207	96.53	59 759	61 909
Poland	88.16	409 513	464 535	159	187	97.70	453 855	464 535
Portugal	93.61	102 225	109 205	201	216	98.43	107 535	109 251
Slovak Republic	93.33	67 284	72 092	180	191	99.01	71 388	72 105
Slovenia	98.36	19 798	20 127	337	352	98.36	19 798	20 127
Spain	99.53	422 692	424 705	888	892	99.53	422 692	424 705
Sweden	99.91	120 693	120 802	189	191	99.91	120 693	120 802
Switzerland	94.25	81 005	85 952	413	429	98.71	84 896	86 006
Turkey	100.00	849 830	849 830	170	170	100.00	849 830	849 830
United Kingdom	71.06	523 271	736 341	418	549	87.35	643 027	736 178
United States	67.83	2 673 852	3 941 908	140	208	77.50	3 065 651	3 955 606
Partners								
Albania	97.29	39 168	40 259	177	182	99.37	39 999	40 253
Argentina	97.18	590 215	607 344	194	199	99.42	603 817	607 344
Azerbaijan	99.86	168 646	168 890	161	162	100.00	168 890	168 890
Brazil	93.13	2 435 250	2 614 824	899	976	94.75	2 477 518	2 614 806
Bulgaria	98.16	56 922	57 991	173	178	99.10	57 823	58 346
Colombia	90.21	507 649	562 728	260	285	94.90	533 899	562 587
Croatia	99.19	44 561	44 926	157	159	99.86	44 862	44 926
Dubai (UAE)	100.00	10 144	10 144	190	190	100.00	10 144	10 144
Hong Kong-China	69.19	53 800	77 758	108	156	96.75	75 232	77 758
Indonesia	94.54	2 337 438	2 472 502	172	183	100.00	2 473 528	2 473 528
Jordan	100.00	105 906	105 906	210	210	100.00	105 906	105 906
Kazakhstan	100.00	257 427	257 427	199	199	100.00	257 427	257 427
Kyrgyzstan	98.53	88 412	89 733	171	174	99.47	89 260	89 733
Latvia	97.46	26 986	27 689	180	185	99.39	27 544	27 713
Liechtenstein	100.00	356	356	12	12	100.00	356	356
Lithuania	98.13	41 759	42 555	192	197	99.91	42 526	42 564
Macao-China	100.00	5 966	5 966	45	45	100.00	5 966	5 966
Montenegro	100.00	8 527	8 527	52	52	100.00	8 527	8 527
Panama	82.58	33 384	40 426	180	220	83.76	33 779	40 329
Peru	100.00	480 640	480 640	240	240	100.00	480 640	480 640
Qatar	97.30	10 223	10 507	149	154	97.30	10 223	10 507
Romania	100.00	150 114	150 114	159	159	100.00	150 114	150 114
Russian Federation	100.00	1 392 765	1 392 765	213	213	100.00	1 392 765	1 392 765
Serbia	99.21	70 960	71 524	189	191	99.97	71 504	71 524
Shanghai-China	99.32	98 841	99 514	151	152	100.00	99 514	99 514
Singapore	96.19	51 552	53 592	168	175	97.88	52 454	53 592
Chinese Taipei	99.34	322 005	324 141	157	158	100.00	324 141	324 141
Thailand	98.01	737 225	752 193	225	230	100.00	752 392	752 392
Trinidad and Tobago	97.21	17 180	17 673	155	160	97.21	17 180	17 673
Tunisia	100.00	153 198	153 198	165	165	100.00	153 198	153 198
Uruguay	98.66	42 820	43 400	229	233	98.66	42 820	43 400

StatLink http://dx.doi.org/10.1787/888932343190

[Part 2/2]
Table A2.3 **Response rates**

		Final sample – after school replacement		Final sample – students within schools after school replacement				
		Number of responding schools (unweighted)	Number of responding and non-responding schools (unweighted)	Weighted student participation rate after replacement (%)	Number of students assessed (weighted)	Number of students sampled (assessed and absent) (weighted)	Number of students assessed (unweighted)	Number of students sampled (assessed and absent) (unweighted)
		(9)	(10)	(11)	(12)	(13)	(14)	(15)
OECD	Australia	345	357	86.05	205 234	238 498	14 060	16 903
	Austria	280	291	88.63	72 793	82 135	6 568	7 587
	Belgium	275	292	91.38	104 263	114 097	8 477	9 245
	Canada	908	1 001	79.52	257 905	324 342	22 383	27 603
	Chile	199	201	92.88	227 541	244 995	5 663	6 097
	Czech Republic	260	270	90.75	100 685	110 953	6 049	6 656
	Denmark	285	325	89.29	49 236	55 139	5 924	6 827
	Estonia	175	175	94.06	12 208	12 978	4 727	5 023
	Finland	203	204	92.27	56 709	61 460	5 810	6 309
	France	166	177	87.12	556 054	638 284	4 272	4 900
	Germany	226	226	93.93	720 447	766 993	4 979	5 309
	Greece	183	184	95.95	88 875	92 631	4 957	5 165
	Hungary	187	190	93.25	97 923	105 015	4 605	4 956
	Iceland	129	141	83.91	3 635	4 332	3 635	4 332
	Ireland	141	160	83.81	39 248	46 830	3 896	4 654
	Israel	176	186	89.45	88 480	98 918	5 761	6 440
	Italy	1 095	1 108	92.13	462 655	502 190	30 876	33 390
	Japan	185	196	95.32	1 010 801	1 060 382	6 077	6 377
	Korea	157	157	98.76	622 187	630 030	4 989	5 057
	Luxembourg	39	39	95.57	4 897	5 124	4 622	4 833
	Mexico	1 531	1 560	95.13	1 214 827	1 276 982	38 213	40 125
	Netherlands	185	194	89.78	157 912	175 897	4 747	5 286
	New Zealand	161	179	84.65	42 452	50 149	4 606	5 476
	Norway	197	207	89.92	49 785	55 366	4 660	5 194
	Poland	179	187	85.87	376 767	438 739	4 855	5 674
	Portugal	212	216	87.11	83 094	95 386	6 263	7 169
	Slovak Republic	189	191	93.03	63 854	68 634	4 555	4 898
	Slovenia	337	352	90.92	16 777	18 453	6 135	6 735
	Spain	888	892	89.60	345 122	385 164	25 871	28 280
	Sweden	189	191	92.97	105 026	112 972	4 567	4 912
	Switzerland	425	429	93.58	74 712	79 836	11 810	12 551
	Turkey	170	170	97.85	741 029	757 298	4 996	5 108
	United Kingdom	481	549	86.96	520 121	598 110	12 168	14 046
	United States	160	208	86.99	2 298 889	2 642 598	5 165	5 951
Partners	Albania	181	182	95.39	32 347	33 911	4 596	4 831
	Argentina	198	199	88.25	414 166	469 285	4 762	5 423
	Azerbaijan	162	162	99.14	105 095	106 007	4 691	4 727
	Brazil	926	976	89.04	1 767 872	1 985 479	19 901	22 715
	Bulgaria	176	178	97.34	56 096	57 630	4 499	4 617
	Colombia	274	285	92.83	462 602	498 331	7 910	8 483
	Croatia	158	159	93.76	40 321	43 006	4 994	5 326
	Dubai (UAE)	190	190	90.39	8 297	9 179	5 620	6 218
	Hong Kong-China	151	156	93.19	68 142	73 125	4 837	5 195
	Indonesia	183	183	96.91	2 189 287	2 259 118	5 136	5 313
	Jordan	210	210	95.85	99 734	104 056	6 486	6 777
	Kazakhstan	199	199	98.49	246 872	250 657	5 412	5 489
	Kyrgyzstan	173	174	98.04	76 523	78 054	4 986	5 086
	Latvia	184	185	91.27	21 241	23 273	4 502	4 930
	Liechtenstein	12	12	92.68	329	355	329	355
	Lithuania	196	197	93.36	37 808	40 495	4 528	4 854
	Macao-China	45	45	99.57	5 952	5 978	5 952	5 978
	Montenegro	52	52	95.43	7 375	7 728	4 825	5 062
	Panama	183	220	88.67	22 666	25 562	3 913	4 449
	Peru	240	240	96.35	412 011	427 607	5 985	6 216
	Qatar	149	154	93.63	8 990	9 602	8 990	9 602
	Romania	159	159	99.47	150 331	151 130	4 776	4 803
	Russian Federation	213	213	96.77	1 248 353	1 290 047	5 308	5 502
	Serbia	190	191	95.37	67 496	70 775	5 522	5 804
	Shanghai-China	152	152	98.89	95 966	97 045	5 115	5 175
	Singapore	171	175	91.04	46 224	50 775	5 283	5 809
	Chinese Taipei	158	158	95.30	283 239	297 203	5 831	6 108
	Thailand	230	230	97.37	673 688	691 916	6 225	6 396
	Trinidad and Tobago	155	160	85.92	12 275	14 287	4 731	5 518
	Tunisia	165	165	96.93	132 354	136 545	4 955	5 113
	Uruguay	229	233	87.03	29 193	33 541	5 924	6 815

StatLink http://dx.doi.org/10.1787/888932343190

PISA 2009 also required a minimum participation rate of 80% of students within participating schools. This minimum participation rate had to be met at the national level, not necessarily by each participating school. Follow-up sessions were required in schools in which too few students had participated in the original assessment sessions. Student participation rates were calculated over all original schools, and also over all schools, whether original sample or replacement schools, and from the participation of students in both the original assessment and any follow-up sessions. A student who participated in the original or follow-up cognitive sessions was regarded as a participant. Those who attended only the questionnaire session were included in the international database and contributed to the statistics presented in this publication if they provided at least a description of their father's or mother's occupation.

Table A2.3 shows the response rates for students and schools, before and after replacement.

- ***Column 1*** shows the **weighted participation rate of schools before replacement**. This is obtained by dividing Column 2 by Column 3.
- ***Column 2*** shows the **weighted number of responding schools before school replacement** (weighted by student enrolment).
- ***Column 3*** shows the **weighted number of sampled schools before school replacement** (including both responding and non-responding schools, weighted by student enrolment).
- ***Column 4*** shows the unweighted number **of responding schools before school replacement**.
- ***Column 5*** shows the unweighted **number of responding and non-responding schools before school replacement**.
- ***Column 6*** shows the **weighted participation rate of schools after replacement**. This is obtained by dividing Column 7 by Column 8.
- ***Column 7*** shows the **weighted number of responding schools after school replacement** (weighted by student enrolment).
- ***Column 8*** shows the **weighted number of schools sampled after school replacement** (including both responding and non-responding schools, weighted by student enrolment).
- ***Column 9*** shows the unweighted number of responding schools after school replacement.
- ***Column 10*** shows the unweighted number of responding and non-responding schools after school replacement.
- ***Column 11*** shows the **weighted student participation rate after replacement**. This is obtained by dividing Column 12 by Column 13.
- ***Column 12*** shows the **weighted number of students assessed**.
- ***Column 13*** shows the **weighted number of students sampled** (including both students who were assessed and students who were absent on the day of the assessment).
- ***Column 14*** shows the **unweighted number of students assessed.** Note that any students in schools with student-response rates less than 50% were not included in these rates (both weighted and unweighted).
- ***Column 15*** shows the **unweighted number of students sampled** (including both students that were assessed and students who were absent on the day of the assessment). Note that any students in schools where fewer than half of the eligible students were assessed were not included in these rates (neither weighted nor unweighted).

Definition of schools

In some countries, sub-units within schools were sampled instead of schools and this may affect the estimation of the between-school variance components. In Austria, the Czech Republic, Germany, Hungary, Japan, Romania and Slovenia, schools with more than one study programme were split into the units delivering these programmes. In the Netherlands, for schools with both lower and upper secondary programmes, schools were split into units delivering each programme level. In the Flemish Community of Belgium, in the case of multi-campus schools, implantations (campuses) were sampled, whereas in the French Community, in the case of multi-campus schools, the larger administrative units were sampled. In Australia, for schools with more than one campus, the individual campuses were listed for sampling. In Argentina, Croatia and Dubai (UAE), schools that had more than one campus had the locations listed for sampling. In Spain, the schools in the Basque region with multi-linguistic models were split into linguistic models for sampling.

Grade levels

Students assessed in PISA 2009 are at various grade levels. The percentage of students at each grade level is presented by country in Table A2.4a and by gender within each country in Table A2.4b.

[Part 1/1]

Table A2.4a Percentage of students at each grade level

		Grade level											
		7th grade		8th grade		9th grade		10th grade		11th grade		12th grade	
		%	S.E.	%	S.E.	%	S.E.	%	S.E.	%	S.E.	%	S.E.
OECD	Australia	0.0	(0.0)	0.1	(0.0)	10.4	(0.6)	70.8	(0.6)	18.6	(0.6)	0.1	(0.0)
	Austria	0.7	(0.2)	6.2	(1.0)	42.4	(0.9)	50.7	(1.0)	0.0	(0.0)	0.0	c
	Belgium	0.4	(0.2)	5.5	(0.5)	32.0	(0.6)	60.8	(0.7)	1.2	(0.1)	0.0	(0.0)
	Canada	0.0	(0.0)	1.2	(0.2)	13.6	(0.5)	84.1	(0.5)	1.1	(0.1)	0.0	(0.0)
	Chile	1.0	(0.2)	3.9	(0.5)	20.5	(0.8)	69.4	(1.0)	5.2	(0.3)	0.0	(0.0)
	Czech Republic	0.5	(0.2)	3.8	(0.3)	48.9	(1.0)	46.7	(1.1)	0.0	c	0.0	c
	Denmark	0.1	(0.0)	14.7	(0.6)	83.5	(0.8)	1.7	(0.5)	0.0	c	0.0	c
	Estonia	1.6	(0.3)	24.0	(0.7)	72.4	(0.9)	1.8	(0.3)	0.1	(0.1)	0.0	c
	Finland	0.5	(0.1)	11.8	(0.5)	87.3	(0.5)	0.0	c	0.4	(0.1)	0.0	c
	France	1.3	(0.9)	3.6	(0.7)	34.4	(1.2)	56.6	(1.5)	4.0	(0.7)	0.1	(0.0)
	Germany	1.2	(0.2)	11.0	(0.5)	54.8	(0.8)	32.5	(0.8)	0.4	(0.1)	0.0	(0.0)
	Greece	0.4	(0.2)	1.4	(0.5)	5.5	(0.8)	92.7	(1.0)	0.0	c	0.0	c
	Hungary	2.8	(0.6)	7.6	(1.1)	67.1	(1.4)	22.4	(0.9)	0.1	(0.1)	0.0	(0.0)
	Iceland	0.0	c	0.0	c	0.0	(0.0)	98.3	(0.1)	1.7	(0.1)	0.0	c
	Ireland	0.1	(0.0)	2.4	(0.3)	59.1	(1.0)	24.0	(1.4)	14.4	(1.1)	0.0	c
	Israel	0.0	c	0.3	(0.1)	17.9	(1.0)	81.3	(1.0)	0.5	(0.2)	0.0	(0.0)
	Italy	0.1	(0.1)	1.4	(0.3)	16.9	(0.4)	78.4	(0.6)	3.2	(0.3)	0.0	c
	Japan	0.0	c	0.0	c	0.0	c	100.0	(0.0)	0.0	c	0.0	c
	Korea	0.0	c	0.0	(0.0)	4.2	(0.9)	95.1	(0.9)	0.7	(0.1)	0.0	c
	Luxembourg	0.6	(0.1)	11.6	(0.2)	51.6	(0.3)	36.0	(0.2)	0.3	(0.0)	0.0	c
	Mexico	1.7	(0.1)	7.4	(0.3)	34.5	(0.8)	55.6	(0.9)	0.7	(0.2)	0.0	(0.0)
	Netherlands	0.2	(0.2)	2.7	(0.3)	46.2	(1.1)	50.5	(1.1)	0.5	(0.1)	0.0	c
	New Zealand	0.0	c	0.0	c	0.0	(0.0)	5.9	(0.4)	88.8	(0.5)	5.3	(0.3)
	Norway	0.0	c	0.0	c	0.5	(0.1)	99.3	(0.2)	0.2	(0.1)	0.0	c
	Poland	1.0	(0.2)	4.5	(0.4)	93.6	(0.6)	0.9	(0.3)	0.0	c	0.0	c
	Portugal	2.3	(0.3)	9.0	(0.8)	27.9	(1.6)	60.4	(2.2)	0.4	(0.1)	0.0	c
	Slovak Republic	1.0	(0.2)	2.6	(0.3)	35.7	(1.4)	56.9	(1.6)	3.8	(0.8)	0.0	(0.0)
	Slovenia	0.0	c	0.1	(0.1)	3.0	(0.7)	90.7	(0.7)	6.2	(0.2)	0.0	c
	Spain	0.1	(0.0)	9.9	(0.4)	26.5	(0.6)	63.4	(0.7)	0.0	(0.0)	0.0	c
	Sweden	0.1	(0.1)	3.2	(0.3)	95.1	(0.6)	1.6	(0.5)	0.0	c	0.0	c
	Switzerland	0.6	(0.1)	15.5	(0.9)	61.7	(1.3)	21.0	(1.1)	1.2	(0.5)	0.0	(0.0)
	Turkey	0.7	(0.1)	3.5	(0.8)	25.2	(1.3)	66.6	(1.5)	3.8	(0.3)	0.2	(0.1)
	United Kingdom	0.0	c	0.0	c	0.0	c	1.2	(0.1)	98.0	(0.1)	0.8	(0.0)
	United States	0.0	c	0.1	(0.1)	10.9	(0.8)	68.5	(1.0)	20.3	(0.7)	0.1	(0.1)
	OECD average	0.8	(0.1)	5.8	(0.1)	37.0	(0.2)	52.9	(0.2)	9.9	(0.1)	0.5	(0.0)
Partners	Albania	0.4	(0.1)	2.2	(0.3)	50.9	(2.0)	46.4	(2.0)	0.1	(0.0)	0.0	c
	Argentina	4.7	(0.9)	12.9	(1.3)	20.4	(1.2)	57.8	(2.1)	4.3	(0.5)	0.0	c
	Azerbaijan	0.6	(0.2)	5.3	(0.5)	49.4	(1.3)	44.3	(1.3)	0.4	(0.1)	0.0	c
	Brazil	6.8	(0.4)	18.0	(0.7)	37.5	(0.8)	35.7	(0.8)	2.1	(0.1)	0.0	c
	Bulgaria	1.5	(0.3)	6.1	(0.6)	88.7	(0.9)	3.8	(0.6)	0.0	c	0.0	c
	Colombia	4.4	(0.5)	10.3	(0.7)	22.1	(0.8)	42.3	(1.0)	21.0	(1.0)	0.0	c
	Croatia	0.0	c	0.2	(0.2)	77.5	(0.4)	22.3	(0.4)	0.0	c	0.0	c
	Dubai (UAE)	1.1	(0.1)	3.4	(0.1)	14.8	(0.4)	56.9	(0.5)	22.9	(0.4)	0.9	(0.1)
	Hong Kong-China	1.7	(0.2)	7.2	(0.5)	25.2	(0.5)	65.9	(0.9)	0.1	(0.0)	0.0	c
	Indonesia	1.5	(0.5)	6.5	(0.8)	46.0	(3.1)	40.5	(3.2)	5.0	(0.8)	0.5	(0.4)
	Jordan	0.1	(0.1)	1.3	(0.2)	7.0	(0.5)	91.6	(0.6)	0.0	c	0.0	c
	Kazakhstan	0.4	(0.1)	6.4	(0.4)	73.3	(1.9)	19.7	(2.0)	0.1	(0.0)	0.0	c
	Kyrgyzstan	0.2	(0.1)	7.9	(0.5)	71.4	(1.3)	19.8	(1.4)	0.7	(0.1)	0.0	c
	Latvia	2.7	(0.5)	15.5	(0.7)	79.4	(0.9)	2.4	(0.3)	0.1	(0.1)	0.0	(0.0)
	Liechtenstein	0.8	(0.5)	17.5	(1.1)	71.3	(0.8)	10.4	(1.0)	0.0	c	0.0	c
	Lithuania	0.5	(0.1)	10.2	(0.9)	80.9	(0.8)	8.4	(0.6)	0.0	(0.0)	0.0	c
	Macao-China	6.7	(0.1)	19.2	(0.2)	34.9	(0.1)	38.7	(0.1)	0.5	(0.1)	0.0	c
	Montenegro	0.0	c	2.5	(1.7)	82.7	(1.5)	14.8	(0.3)	0.0	c	0.0	c
	Panama	2.9	(0.8)	10.6	(1.6)	30.6	(3.3)	49.8	(4.5)	6.1	(1.4)	0.0	c
	Peru	4.0	(0.4)	8.9	(0.6)	17.1	(0.7)	44.6	(1.1)	25.4	(0.8)	0.0	c
	Qatar	1.7	(0.1)	3.6	(0.1)	13.5	(0.2)	62.6	(0.2)	18.2	(0.2)	0.4	(0.1)
	Romania	0.0	c	7.2	(1.0)	88.6	(1.1)	4.3	(0.6)	0.0	c	0.0	c
	Russian Federation	0.9	(0.2)	10.0	(0.7)	60.1	(1.8)	28.1	(1.6)	0.9	(0.2)	0.0	c
	Serbia	0.2	(0.1)	2.1	(0.5)	96.0	(0.6)	1.7	(0.2)	0.0	c	0.0	c
	Shanghai-China	1.0	(0.2)	4.1	(0.4)	37.4	(0.8)	57.1	(0.9)	0.4	(0.2)	0.0	(0.0)
	Singapore	1.0	(0.2)	2.6	(0.2)	34.7	(0.4)	61.6	(0.3)	0.0	c	0.0	(0.0)
	Chinese Taipei	0.0	c	0.1	(0.0)	34.4	(0.9)	65.5	(0.9)	0.0	(0.0)	0.0	c
	Thailand	0.1	(0.0)	0.5	(0.1)	23.2	(1.1)	73.5	(1.1)	2.7	(0.4)	0.0	c
	Trinidad and Tobago	2.1	(0.2)	8.8	(0.4)	25.3	(0.4)	56.1	(0.4)	7.7	(0.3)	0.0	c
	Tunisia	6.4	(0.4)	13.4	(0.6)	23.9	(0.9)	50.9	(1.4)	5.4	(0.4)	0.0	c
	Uruguay	7.1	(0.8)	10.6	(0.6)	21.5	(0.8)	56.2	(1.1)	4.6	(0.4)	0.0	c

StatLink http://dx.doi.org/10.1787/888932343190

[Part 1/2]

Table A2.4b Percentage of students at each grade level, by gender

		Boys – Grade level											
		7th grade		8th grade		9th grade		10th grade		11th grade		12th grade	
		%	S.E.	%	S.E.	%	S.E.	%	S.E.	%	S.E.	%	S.E.
OECD	Australia	0.0	c	0.1	(0.0)	13.1	(0.9)	69.6	(1.1)	17.1	(0.8)	0.1	(0.0)
	Austria	0.7	(0.2)	7.4	(1.2)	42.6	(1.3)	49.3	(1.3)	0.0	(0.0)	0.0	c
	Belgium	0.6	(0.2)	6.4	(0.7)	34.6	(0.9)	57.3	(1.0)	1.1	(0.2)	0.0	(0.0)
	Canada	0.0	(0.0)	1.4	(0.3)	14.6	(0.6)	82.9	(0.6)	1.1	(0.1)	0.0	(0.0)
	Chile	1.3	(0.3)	4.9	(0.6)	23.2	(1.0)	65.9	(1.3)	4.7	(0.3)	0.0	c
	Czech Republic	0.7	(0.2)	4.5	(0.5)	52.5	(2.2)	42.3	(2.4)	0.0	c	0.0	c
	Denmark	0.1	(0.0)	19.5	(0.9)	79.5	(1.0)	0.8	(0.3)	0.0	c	0.0	c
	Estonia	2.4	(0.5)	27.0	(1.0)	69.6	(1.1)	1.0	(0.3)	0.0	c	0.0	c
	Finland	0.6	(0.2)	14.0	(0.8)	85.2	(0.8)	0.0	c	0.2	(0.1)	0.0	c
	France	1.3	(0.9)	4.0	(0.6)	39.6	(1.5)	51.4	(1.9)	3.6	(0.8)	0.0	(0.0)
	Germany	1.4	(0.3)	13.1	(0.7)	56.1	(1.0)	28.8	(0.9)	0.6	(0.1)	0.0	c
	Greece	0.5	(0.2)	1.9	(0.5)	6.2	(1.2)	91.4	(1.5)	0.0	c	0.0	c
	Hungary	3.2	(0.8)	9.3	(1.3)	68.8	(1.6)	18.7	(0.9)	0.0	(0.0)	0.0	(0.0)
	Iceland	0.0	c	0.0	c	0.0	c	98.7	(0.2)	1.3	(0.2)	0.0	c
	Ireland	0.1	(0.0)	2.8	(0.5)	60.9	(1.3)	22.4	(1.5)	13.8	(1.4)	0.0	c
	Israel	0.0	c	0.5	(0.2)	19.9	(1.1)	78.7	(1.2)	1.0	(0.4)	0.0	c
	Italy	0.1	(0.1)	1.7	(0.4)	20.1	(0.6)	75.7	(0.7)	2.5	(0.3)	0.0	c
	Japan	0.0	c	0.0	c	0.0	c	100.0	(0.0)	0.0	c	0.0	c
	Korea	0.0	c	0.1	(0.1)	4.7	(1.3)	94.5	(1.4)	0.7	(0.2)	0.0	c
	Luxembourg	0.8	(0.2)	12.5	(0.4)	52.4	(0.5)	34.0	(0.4)	0.3	(0.1)	0.0	c
	Mexico	2.0	(0.2)	8.8	(0.5)	37.6	(0.9)	51.0	(0.9)	0.5	(0.2)	0.0	c
	Netherlands	0.4	(0.3)	3.0	(0.4)	48.9	(1.3)	47.3	(1.3)	0.3	(0.1)	0.0	c
	New Zealand	0.0	c	0.0	c	0.0	c	6.9	(0.5)	87.9	(0.6)	5.2	(0.5)
	Norway	0.0	c	0.0	c	0.5	(0.1)	99.2	(0.2)	0.3	(0.2)	0.0	c
	Poland	1.5	(0.3)	6.5	(0.6)	91.6	(0.7)	0.5	(0.2)	0.0	c	0.0	c
	Portugal	3.4	(0.5)	10.5	(0.9)	30.9	(2.0)	54.9	(2.6)	0.4	(0.1)	0.0	c
	Slovak Republic	1.4	(0.3)	3.7	(0.5)	40.1	(1.9)	51.6	(2.1)	3.3	(0.7)	0.0	c
	Slovenia	0.0	c	0.1	(0.1)	4.0	(1.2)	91.1	(1.2)	4.7	(0.4)	0.0	c
	Spain	0.1	(0.0)	12.2	(0.6)	28.7	(0.8)	58.9	(0.9)	0.0	(0.0)	0.0	c
	Sweden	0.0	(0.0)	4.1	(0.4)	94.7	(0.6)	1.1	(0.3)	0.0	c	0.0	c
	Switzerland	0.8	(0.2)	18.0	(1.2)	60.7	(1.8)	19.4	(1.8)	1.0	(0.4)	0.1	(0.1)
	Turkey	1.0	(0.2)	4.0	(0.9)	30.2	(1.4)	61.3	(1.7)	3.2	(0.3)	0.2	(0.1)
	United Kingdom	0.0	c	0.0	c	0.0	c	1.3	(0.2)	98.0	(0.2)	0.7	(0.1)
	United States	0.0	c	0.1	(0.0)	13.2	(1.0)	68.6	(1.4)	17.9	(0.9)	0.1	(0.1)
	OECD average	1.0	(0.1)	7.0	(0.1)	40.8	(0.2)	50.8	(0.2)	9.8	(0.1)	0.7	(0.0)
Partners	Albania	0.5	(0.2)	2.6	(0.4)	54.0	(2.0)	42.9	(2.1)	0.0	(0.0)	0.0	c
	Argentina	5.9	(1.1)	15.4	(1.4)	22.7	(1.5)	52.5	(2.4)	3.5	(0.5)	0.0	c
	Azerbaijan	0.6	(0.2)	4.7	(0.5)	47.8	(1.4)	46.5	(1.5)	0.3	(0.1)	0.0	c
	Brazil	8.4	(0.6)	21.0	(0.9)	37.8	(0.8)	31.1	(0.9)	1.7	(0.2)	0.0	c
	Bulgaria	2.0	(0.4)	7.4	(0.9)	86.9	(1.2)	3.7	(0.6)	0.0	c	0.0	c
	Colombia	5.5	(0.9)	11.5	(0.9)	21.9	(1.1)	42.4	(1.4)	18.7	(1.2)	0.0	c
	Croatia	0.0	c	0.1	(0.1)	79.1	(0.6)	20.7	(0.6)	0.0	c	0.0	c
	Dubai (UAE)	1.6	(0.2)	4.5	(0.3)	16.0	(0.6)	53.6	(0.7)	23.1	(0.6)	1.1	(0.2)
	Hong Kong-China	1.9	(0.3)	7.3	(0.6)	26.6	(0.7)	64.1	(1.0)	0.1	(0.1)	0.0	c
	Indonesia	1.8	(0.7)	8.2	(1.0)	49.3	(3.4)	36.2	(3.6)	4.0	(0.9)	0.5	(0.3)
	Jordan	0.1	(0.1)	1.2	(0.4)	7.5	(0.8)	91.2	(0.9)	0.0	c	0.0	c
	Kazakhstan	0.5	(0.1)	7.1	(0.6)	75.2	(2.2)	17.2	(2.3)	0.1	(0.0)	0.0	c
	Kyrgyzstan	0.2	(0.1)	8.9	(0.7)	72.9	(1.6)	17.4	(1.6)	0.5	(0.2)	0.0	c
	Latvia	3.6	(0.9)	19.9	(1.1)	74.7	(1.4)	1.6	(0.4)	0.1	(0.1)	0.0	(0.0)
	Liechtenstein	1.1	(0.7)	19.7	(1.6)	68.9	(1.2)	10.3	(1.2)	0.0	c	0.0	c
	Lithuania	0.6	(0.2)	12.3	(1.2)	80.0	(1.2)	7.2	(0.7)	0.0	c	0.0	c
	Macao-China	8.9	(0.2)	22.0	(0.2)	34.9	(0.2)	33.6	(0.2)	0.5	(0.1)	0.0	c
	Montenegro	0.0	c	3.0	(2.0)	85.0	(1.8)	12.0	(0.4)	0.0	c	0.0	c
	Panama	3.4	(1.1)	13.6	(2.5)	32.6	(4.4)	45.7	(5.5)	4.7	(1.8)	0.0	c
	Peru	4.9	(0.5)	11.2	(0.8)	18.8	(1.0)	42.3	(1.4)	22.9	(0.9)	0.0	c
	Qatar	1.9	(0.1)	4.3	(0.2)	14.8	(0.3)	60.4	(0.3)	18.2	(0.2)	0.4	(0.1)
	Romania	0.0	c	6.3	(1.1)	89.9	(1.3)	3.9	(0.7)	0.0	c	0.0	c
	Russian Federation	1.4	(0.3)	10.4	(0.9)	61.2	(1.9)	26.3	(1.9)	0.8	(0.2)	0.0	c
	Serbia	0.3	(0.1)	2.7	(0.7)	95.6	(0.8)	1.4	(0.2)	0.0	c	0.0	c
	Shanghai-China	1.2	(0.3)	5.1	(0.6)	38.8	(1.2)	54.7	(1.4)	0.2	(0.1)	0.0	c
	Singapore	0.8	(0.2)	2.9	(0.3)	35.7	(0.6)	60.6	(0.5)	0.0	c	0.0	c
	Chinese Taipei	0.0	c	0.2	(0.1)	35.2	(1.5)	64.7	(1.5)	0.0	c	0.0	c
	Thailand	0.2	(0.1)	0.8	(0.2)	26.3	(1.4)	70.5	(1.4)	2.2	(0.5)	0.0	c
	Trinidad and Tobago	2.7	(0.3)	10.7	(0.5)	28.4	(0.6)	51.0	(0.5)	7.1	(0.4)	0.0	c
	Tunisia	8.9	(0.6)	16.8	(0.9)	24.4	(1.1)	45.3	(1.5)	4.7	(0.5)	0.0	c
	Uruguay	9.1	(1.0)	12.0	(0.8)	24.9	(0.8)	50.4	(1.3)	3.6	(0.4)	0.0	c

StatLink http://dx.doi.org/10.1787/888932343190

[Part 2/2]

Table A2.4b Percentage of students at each grade level, by gender

		Girls – Grade level											
		7th grade		8th grade		9th grade		10th grade		11th grade		12th grade	
		%	S.E.	%	S.E.	%	S.E.	%	S.E.	%	S.E.	%	S.E.
OECD	Australia	0.0	(0.0)	0.1	(0.0)	7.9	(0.5)	72.0	(0.8)	20.0	(0.8)	0.1	(0.0)
	Austria	0.6	(0.4)	5.0	(1.2)	42.2	(1.4)	52.1	(1.5)	0.0	(0.0)	0.0	c
	Belgium	0.3	(0.1)	4.5	(0.5)	29.3	(1.1)	64.5	(1.1)	1.3	(0.2)	0.0	(0.0)
	Canada	0.0	(0.0)	1.0	(0.2)	12.5	(0.5)	85.3	(0.5)	1.1	(0.1)	0.0	(0.0)
	Chile	0.7	(0.1)	2.9	(0.5)	17.7	(0.9)	73.0	(1.1)	5.6	(0.4)	0.0	(0.0)
	Czech Republic	0.3	(0.2)	3.1	(0.4)	44.8	(1.9)	51.8	(1.9)	0.0	c	0.0	c
	Denmark	0.1	(0.0)	10.0	(0.7)	87.3	(0.9)	2.5	(0.8)	0.0	c	0.0	c
	Estonia	0.9	(0.3)	20.8	(0.9)	75.4	(1.1)	2.7	(0.5)	0.2	(0.2)	0.0	c
	Finland	0.4	(0.1)	9.6	(0.6)	89.4	(0.6)	0.0	c	0.6	(0.2)	0.0	c
	France	1.3	(0.9)	3.2	(0.9)	29.4	(1.5)	61.6	(1.7)	4.4	(0.8)	0.1	(0.1)
	Germany	1.1	(0.2)	8.8	(0.6)	53.4	(1.1)	36.4	(1.1)	0.3	(0.1)	0.0	(0.0)
	Greece	0.2	(0.2)	0.9	(0.5)	4.9	(0.7)	94.0	(0.9)	0.0	c	0.0	c
	Hungary	2.3	(0.7)	5.9	(1.1)	65.4	(1.6)	26.2	(1.2)	0.2	(0.1)	0.0	c
	Iceland	0.0	c	0.0	c	0.0	(0.1)	97.9	(0.2)	2.1	(0.2)	0.0	c
	Ireland	0.1	(0.1)	2.0	(0.4)	57.3	(1.5)	25.7	(2.0)	15.1	(1.5)	0.0	c
	Israel	0.0	c	0.1	(0.1)	15.9	(1.0)	83.8	(1.1)	0.2	(0.1)	0.0	(0.0)
	Italy	0.2	(0.1)	1.0	(0.2)	13.5	(0.6)	81.4	(0.7)	3.9	(0.3)	0.0	c
	Japan	0.0	c	0.0	c	0.0	c	100.0	(0.0)	0.0	c	0.0	c
	Korea	0.0	c	0.0	c	3.6	(1.0)	95.6	(1.0)	0.8	(0.1)	0.0	c
	Luxembourg	0.4	(0.1)	10.6	(0.3)	50.8	(0.4)	38.0	(0.3)	0.2	(0.1)	0.0	c
	Mexico	1.5	(0.2)	6.1	(0.4)	31.5	(0.9)	60.1	(1.0)	0.8	(0.3)	0.0	(0.0)
	Netherlands	0.1	(0.1)	2.3	(0.4)	43.4	(1.4)	53.5	(1.3)	0.7	(0.2)	0.0	c
	New Zealand	0.0	c	0.0	c	0.1	(0.1)	4.8	(0.5)	89.8	(0.6)	5.4	(0.5)
	Norway	0.0	c	0.0	c	0.4	(0.1)	99.4	(0.2)	0.1	(0.1)	0.0	c
	Poland	0.6	(0.2)	2.5	(0.3)	95.6	(0.7)	1.3	(0.6)	0.0	c	0.0	c
	Portugal	1.4	(0.2)	7.7	(0.8)	25.1	(1.4)	65.4	(1.9)	0.4	(0.1)	0.0	c
	Slovak Republic	0.7	(0.2)	1.5	(0.3)	31.4	(1.8)	62.1	(2.1)	4.3	(0.9)	0.0	(0.0)
	Slovenia	0.0	c	0.0	c	1.9	(0.7)	90.3	(0.8)	7.8	(0.5)	0.0	c
	Spain	0.1	(0.1)	7.6	(0.4)	24.2	(0.7)	68.0	(0.8)	0.0	(0.0)	0.0	c
	Sweden	0.1	(0.1)	2.3	(0.3)	95.4	(0.7)	2.2	(0.7)	0.0	c	0.0	c
	Switzerland	0.4	(0.1)	12.9	(0.9)	62.6	(1.8)	22.7	(2.0)	1.4	(0.6)	0.0	c
	Turkey	0.4	(0.2)	2.9	(0.8)	19.8	(1.3)	72.3	(1.6)	4.4	(0.4)	0.2	(0.1)
	United Kingdom	0.0	c	0.0	c	0.0	c	1.0	(0.1)	98.1	(0.1)	0.9	(0.1)
	United States	0.0	c	0.2	(0.2)	8.5	(0.7)	68.4	(1.1)	22.8	(1.0)	0.1	(0.1)
	OECD average	0.6	(0.1)	5.0	(0.1)	35.6	(0.2)	55.0	(0.2)	10.2	(0.1)	0.5	(0.0)
Partners	Albania	0.2	(0.1)	1.8	(0.4)	47.6	(2.3)	50.2	(2.3)	0.2	(0.1)	0.0	c
	Argentina	3.6	(0.9)	10.7	(1.5)	18.4	(1.2)	62.3	(2.2)	4.9	(0.6)	0.0	c
	Azerbaijan	0.6	(0.3)	5.8	(0.6)	51.0	(1.5)	42.1	(1.4)	0.4	(0.1)	0.0	c
	Brazil	5.4	(0.4)	15.3	(0.6)	37.1	(0.9)	39.7	(0.9)	2.5	(0.2)	0.0	c
	Bulgaria	0.9	(0.3)	4.6	(0.7)	90.6	(1.0)	3.9	(0.7)	0.0	c	0.0	c
	Colombia	3.3	(0.4)	9.1	(0.8)	22.4	(1.0)	42.2	(1.1)	23.0	(1.1)	0.0	c
	Croatia	0.0	c	0.2	(0.2)	75.8	(0.6)	24.1	(0.5)	0.0	c	0.0	c
	Dubai (UAE)	0.6	(0.1)	2.2	(0.2)	13.5	(0.5)	60.4	(0.6)	22.7	(0.7)	0.6	(0.1)
	Hong Kong-China	1.5	(0.2)	7.1	(0.6)	23.5	(0.6)	67.9	(1.0)	0.0	c	0.0	c
	Indonesia	1.2	(0.3)	4.9	(0.8)	42.7	(3.7)	44.6	(3.8)	6.0	(1.1)	0.6	(0.5)
	Jordan	0.1	(0.0)	1.3	(0.3)	6.5	(0.7)	92.1	(0.9)	0.0	c	0.0	c
	Kazakhstan	0.4	(0.1)	5.7	(0.5)	71.5	(2.0)	22.3	(2.1)	0.2	(0.1)	0.0	c
	Kyrgyzstan	0.1	(0.1)	7.1	(0.6)	69.9	(1.5)	22.0	(1.6)	0.9	(0.2)	0.0	c
	Latvia	1.7	(0.4)	11.2	(0.6)	83.9	(0.8)	3.1	(0.4)	0.1	(0.1)	0.0	c
	Liechtenstein	0.6	(0.6)	15.0	(1.5)	74.0	(1.2)	10.4	(1.6)	0.0	c	0.0	c
	Lithuania	0.3	(0.1)	8.1	(0.8)	81.9	(0.9)	9.6	(0.7)	0.0	(0.0)	0.0	c
	Macao-China	4.4	(0.1)	16.3	(0.2)	34.9	(0.2)	43.9	(0.2)	0.5	(0.1)	0.0	c
	Montenegro	0.0	c	2.0	(1.4)	80.3	(1.3)	17.8	(0.4)	0.0	c	0.0	c
	Panama	2.4	(0.6)	7.7	(1.1)	28.7	(3.0)	53.8	(4.0)	7.5	(1.6)	0.0	c
	Peru	3.2	(0.4)	6.5	(0.6)	15.4	(0.8)	47.0	(1.2)	27.9	(1.2)	0.0	c
	Qatar	1.4	(0.1)	3.0	(0.1)	12.1	(0.2)	64.9	(0.2)	18.1	(0.2)	0.5	(0.1)
	Romania	0.0	c	8.1	(1.5)	87.3	(1.5)	4.7	(0.6)	0.0	c	0.0	c
	Russian Federation	0.5	(0.1)	9.7	(0.8)	59.0	(2.0)	29.8	(1.8)	1.0	(0.2)	0.0	c
	Serbia	0.1	(0.1)	1.4	(0.5)	96.4	(0.6)	2.0	(0.2)	0.0	c	0.0	c
	Shanghai-China	0.8	(0.2)	3.0	(0.4)	36.1	(1.0)	59.5	(1.0)	0.6	(0.2)	0.0	(0.0)
	Singapore	1.2	(0.2)	2.3	(0.3)	33.7	(0.5)	62.7	(0.4)	0.0	c	0.0	(0.0)
	Chinese Taipei	0.0	c	0.0	(0.0)	33.7	(1.5)	66.3	(1.5)	0.0	(0.0)	0.0	c
	Thailand	0.0	c	0.3	(0.1)	20.9	(1.4)	75.8	(1.4)	3.0	(0.4)	0.0	c
	Trinidad and Tobago	1.5	(0.3)	6.9	(0.5)	22.3	(0.6)	61.0	(0.6)	8.3	(0.4)	0.0	c
	Tunisia	4.2	(0.4)	10.3	(0.5)	23.4	(1.0)	56.1	(1.4)	6.0	(0.5)	0.0	c
	Uruguay	5.4	(0.6)	9.4	(0.5)	18.5	(0.9)	61.4	(1.2)	5.4	(0.6)	0.0	c

StatLink http://dx.doi.org/10.1787/888932343190

Students in or out of the regular education system in Argentina

The low performance of 15-year-old students in Argentina is, to some extent, influenced by a fairly large proportion of 15-year-olds enrolled in programmes outside the regular education system. Table A2.5 shows the proportion of students inside and outside the regular education system, alongside their performance in PISA 2009.

Table A2.5 Percentage of students and mean scores in reading, mathematics and science, according to whether students are in or out of the regular education system in Argentina

	Percentage of students		Mean performance					
			Reading		Mathematics		Science	
	%	S.E.	Mean	S.E.	Mean	S.E.	Mean	S.E.
Students in the regular educational system[1]	60.9	2.2	439	5.1	421	4.8	439	4.9
Students out of the regular educational system[2]	39.1	2.2	335	8.0	337	6.7	341	8.3

1. Students who are not in grade 10 or 11 and in programme 3, 4, 5, 6, 7 or 8.
2. Students who are in grade 10 or 11 and in programme 3, 4, 5, 6, 7 or 8.
StatLink http://dx.doi.org/10.1787/888932343190

ANNEX A3

STANDARD ERRORS, SIGNIFICANCE TESTS AND SUBGROUP COMPARISONS

The statistics in this report represent estimates of national performance based on samples of students, rather than values that could be calculated if every student in every country had answered every question. Consequently, it is important to measure the degree of uncertainty of the estimates. In PISA, each estimate has an associated degree of uncertainty, which is expressed through a standard error. The use of confidence intervals provides a way to make inferences about the population means and proportions in a manner that reflects the uncertainty associated with the sample estimates. From an observed sample statistic and assuming a normal distribution, it can be inferred that the corresponding population result would lie within the confidence interval in 95 out of 100 replications of the measurement on different samples drawn from the same population.

In many cases, readers are primarily interested in whether a given value in a particular country is different from a second value in the same or another country, e.g. whether females in a country perform better than males in the same country. In the tables and charts used in this report, differences are labelled as statistically significant when a difference of that size, smaller or larger, would be observed less than 5% of the time, if there were actually no difference in corresponding population values. Similarly, the risk of reporting a correlation as significant if there is, in fact, no correlation between two measures, is contained at 5%.

Throughout the report, significance tests were undertaken to assess the statistical significance of the comparisons made.

Gender differences

Gender differences in student performance or other indices were tested for statistical significance. Positive differences indicate higher scores for males while negative differences indicate higher scores for females. Generally, differences marked in bold in the tables in this volume are statistically significant at the 95% confidence level.

Performance differences between the top and bottom quartiles of PISA indices and scales

Differences in average performance between the top and bottom quarters of the PISA indices and scales were tested for statistical significance. Figures marked in bold indicate that performance between the top and bottom quarters of students on the respective index is statistically significantly different at the 95% confidence level.

Change in the performance per unit of the index

For many tables, the difference in student performance per unit of the index shown was calculated. Figures in bold indicate that the differences are statistically significantly different from zero at the 95% confidence level.

Difference in reading performance between native students and students with an immigrant background

Differences in performance between native and non-native students were tested for statistical significance. For this purpose, first-generation and second-generation students were jointly considered as students with an immigrant background. Positive differences represent higher scores for native students, while negative differences represent higher scores for first-generation and second-generation students. Figures in bold in data tables presented in this volume indicate statistically significantly different scores at the 95% confidence level.

ANNEX A4
QUALITY ASSURANCE

Quality assurance procedures were implemented in all parts of PISA 2009, as was done for all previous PISA surveys.

The consistent quality and linguistic equivalence of the PISA 2009 assessment instruments were facilitated by providing countries with equivalent source versions of the assessment instruments in English and French, and requiring countries (other than those assessing students in English and French) to prepare and consolidate two independent translations using both source versions. Precise translation and adaptation guidelines were supplied, also including instructions for selecting and training the translators. For each country, the translation and format of the assessment instruments (including test materials, marking guides, questionnaires and manuals) were verified by expert translators appointed by the PISA Consortium before they were used in the PISA 2009 Field Trial and Main Study. These translators' mother tongue was the language of instruction in the country concerned and they were knowledgeable about education systems. For further information on the PISA translation procedures, see the *PISA 2009 Technical Report* (OECD, forthcoming).

The survey was implemented through standardised procedures. The PISA Consortium provided comprehensive manuals that explained the implementation of the survey, including precise instructions for the work of School Co-ordinators and scripts for Test Administrators to use during the assessment sessions. Proposed adaptations to survey procedures, or proposed modifications to the assessment session script, were submitted to the PISA Consortium for approval prior to verification. The PISA Consortium then verified the national translation and adaptation of these manuals.

To establish the credibility of PISA as valid and unbiased, and to encourage uniformity in administering the assessment sessions, Test Administrators in participating countries were selected using the following criteria: it was required that the Test Administrator not be the reading, mathematics or science instructor of any students in the sessions he or she would administer for PISA; it was recommended that the Test Administrator not be a member of the staff of any school where he or she would administer for PISA; and it was considered preferable that the Test Administrator not be a member of the staff of any school in the PISA sample. Participating countries organised an in-person training session for Test Administrators.

Participating countries were required to ensure that: Test Administrators worked with the School Co-ordinator to prepare the assessment session, including updating student tracking forms and identifying excluded students; no extra time was given for the cognitive items (while it was permissible to give extra time for the student questionnaire); no instrument was administered before the two one-hour parts of the cognitive session; Test Administrators recorded the student participation status on the student tracking forms and filled in a Session Report Form; no cognitive instrument was permitted to be photocopied; no cognitive instrument could be viewed by school staff before the assessment session; and Test Administrators returned the material to the National Centre immediately after the assessment sessions.

National Project Managers were encouraged to organise a follow-up session when more than 15% of the PISA sample was not able to attend the original assessment session.

National Quality Monitors from the PISA Consortium visited all National Centres to review data-collection procedures. Finally, School Quality Monitors from the PISA Consortium visited a sample of 15 schools during the assessment. For further information on the field operations, see the *PISA 2009 Technical Report* (OECD, forthcoming).

Marking procedures were designed to ensure consistent and accurate application of the marking guides outlined in the PISA Operations Manuals. National Project Managers were required to submit proposed modifications to these procedures to the Consortium for approval. Reliability studies to analyse the consistency of marking were implemented, these are discussed in more detail below.

Software specially designed for PISA facilitated data entry, detected common errors during data entry, and facilitated the process of data cleaning. Training sessions familiarised National Project Managers with these procedures.

For a description of the quality assurance procedures applied in PISA and in the results, see the *PISA 2009 Technical Report* (OECD, forthcoming).

The results of data adjudication show that the PISA Technical Standards were fully met in all countries and economies that participated in PISA 2009, though for one country, some serious doubts were raised. Analysis of the data for Azerbaijan suggest that the PISA Technical Standards may not have been fully met for the following four main reasons: *i)* the order of difficulty of the clusters is inconsistent with previous experience and the ordering varies across booklets; *ii)* the percentage correct on some items is higher than that of the highest scoring countries; *iii)* the difficulty of the clusters varies widely across booklets; and *iv)* the coding of items in Azerbaijan is at an extremely high level of agreement between independent coders, and was judged, on some items, to be too lenient. However, further investigation of the survey instruments, the procedures for test implementation and coding of student responses at the national level did not provide sufficient evidence of systematic errors or violations of the PISA Technical Standards. Azerbaijan's data are, therefore, included in the PISA 2009 international dataset.

For the PISA 2009 assessment in Austria, a dispute between teacher unions and the education minister has led to the announcement of a boycott of PISA which was withdrawn after the first week of testing. The boycott required the OECD to remove identifiable cases from the dataset. Although the Austrian dataset met the PISA 2009 technical standards after the removal of these cases, the negative atmosphere in regard to educational assessment has affected the conditions under which the assessment was administered and could have adversely affected student motivation to respond to the PISA tasks. The comparability of the 2009 data with data from earlier PISA assessments can therefore not be ensured and data for Austria have therefore been excluded from trend comparisons.

ANNEX A5
PARTICIPATION OF COUNTRIES ACROSS PISA ASSESSMENTS

Not all the OECD members participated in every PISA assessment and the list of participating partner countries and economies has widened substantially since 2000. As explained in Chapter 1, reading performance trends are reported for all countries that have comparable results in both the 2000 and 2009 assessments, because PISA 2000 focused on reading and established a performance scale that was comparable across all future assessments. Since PISA 2003 focused on mathematics and established a performance scale that became the baseline for subsequent mathematics assessments, trends in mathematics are reported only for countries that have comparable results in both the 2003 and 2009 assessments. For science, only 2006 and 2009 assessments provide comparable results since PISA 2006 focused on science and established a baseline scale for science.

As a consequence, the countries for which trends are reported differ between assessment areas (Table A5.1). Moreover, the group of OECD countries for which the OECD average can be compared across time also differs between assessment areas.

As explained in Chapter 1, for methodological reasons, some countries have not been included in comparisons between 2000, 2003, 2006 and 2009. The PISA 2000 sample for the Netherlands did not meet the PISA response-rate standards. Therefore, the mean scores for the Netherlands were not reported for 2000. In Luxembourg, the assessment conditions were changed substantially between the 2000 and 2003 PISA surveys. Therefore, results are only comparable between 2003, 2006 and 2009. The PISA 2000 and PISA 2003 samples for the United Kingdom did not meet the PISA response-rate standards, so data from the United Kingdom are not comparable to the other countries. For the United States, no reading results are available for 2006. The sampling weights for the PISA 2000 assessment in Austria have been adjusted to allow for comparisons with subsequent PISA assessments. However, due to a boycott of PISA in some Austrian schools it was not possible to ensure the comparability of the 2009 data with those from earlier assessments. Therefore, data for Austria have been excluded from trend comparisons. Details of this are given in the main text and in the endnotes to Chapter 1.

For comparing trends in reading, this volume considers the 38 countries that have comparable results in both the 2000 and 2009 assessments. This includes the 26 OECD countries. Among the 34 current OECD members, Estonia, the Slovak Republic, Slovenia and Turkey did not participate in PISA 2000, while 2000 data for Luxembourg, the Netherlands and the United Kingdom, and 2009 data for Austria, are deemed not sufficiently comparable with those from other PISA assessments and were excluded from the analysis. The OECD 26 average is reported for most comparisons in this volume, namely, whenever 2009 results are compared to those from 2000. However, three other OECD countries do not have valid results for the 2003 or 2006 assessments. Chile and Israel did not participate in 2003, while no data on reading for the United States were available for 2006. Thus, across the four reading assessments, only the OECD 23 average can be calculated. The OECD 23 average is reported in tables where data for 2000 and 2009 are reported together with results for 2003 and 2006.

For comparing trends in mathematics, results are discussed for the 39 countries that have comparable results for the 2003 and 2009 assessments. These include 28 OECD countries. Chile, Estonia, Israel and Slovenia did not participate in PISA 2003, while data for the United Kingdom were deemed not comparable for 2003 and data for Austria were deemed not comparable for 2009.

For comparing trends in science, 56 countries that participated in the 2006 and 2009 assessments are compared, including 33 OECD countries. Data for Austria were deemed not comparable for 2009.

Thus, several different OECD averages are reported in this volume. The OECD 26 average is reported for all comparisons between 2000 and 2009. For comparisons of reading performance across all four PISA assessments, the OECD 23 average is reported in Tables V.2.1, V.2.3 and V.2.7. In Table V.2.9, the OECD 28 average is reported for comparisons between 2003 and 2009 and the OECD 32 average is reported for comparisons between 2006 and 2009. For mathematics, the OECD 28 average is used to compare results. For science the OECD average for 33 OECD members is presented.

As a result, the OECD averages for cross-sectional comparisons reported in other volumes of this report differ from the ones reported in Volume V for comparing student performance and other measures over time.

The OECD average is calculated separately for each assessment and includes all the OECD countries that have valid results in this assessment. In some cases, the results for one or two OECD countries are not reported due to small sample size, which is denoted by "c", missing data ("m") or because results were withdrawn ("w"). In such cases, the OECD average for one assessment can be calculated for a smaller number of countries than for the other assessment. The change in the OECD average includes only countries that have valid results in both assessments. Therefore, in some rare cases, the difference between OECD averages calculated separately for two assessments do not equal the change in the OECD average. For example, because socio-economic data were not collected in PISA 2000 in Japan, the OECD average reported in Table V.4.3 for 2000 does not include Japan. Similarly, the change in the OECD average is calculated without Japan. However, the 2009 average does include Japan. Similarly, averages reported in Tables V.4.4 and V.4.5 are calculated for countries that have sufficient number of observations to report performance gaps between various groups of students. OECD averages in Tables V.4.1 and V.4.3 include France; however, the data for France were withdrawn from the tables.

[Part 1/1]

Table A5.1 **Participation of countries in different PISA assessments**

		PISA 2000	PISA 2003	PISA 2006	PISA 2009
OECD	Australia	yes	yes	yes	yes
	Austria	yes	yes	yes	not comparable
	Belgium	yes	yes	yes	yes
	Canada	yes	yes	yes	yes
	Chile	yes	no	yes	yes
	Czech Republic	yes	yes	yes	yes
	Denmark	yes	yes	yes	yes
	Estonia	no	no	yes	yes
	Finland	yes	yes	yes	yes
	France	yes	yes	yes	yes
	Germany	yes	yes	yes	yes
	Greece	yes	yes	yes	yes
	Hungary	yes	yes	yes	yes
	Iceland	yes	yes	yes	yes
	Ireland	yes	yes	yes	yes
	Israel	yes	no	yes	yes
	Italy	yes	yes	yes	yes
	Japan	yes	yes	yes	yes
	Korea	yes	yes	yes	yes
	Luxembourg	not comparable	yes	yes	yes
	Mexico	yes	yes	yes	yes
	Netherlands	not comparable	yes	yes	yes
	New Zealand	yes	yes	yes	yes
	Norway	yes	yes	yes	yes
	Poland	yes	yes	yes	yes
	Portugal	yes	yes	yes	yes
	Slovak Republic	no	yes	yes	yes
	Slovenia	no	no	yes	yes
	Spain	yes	yes	yes	yes
	Sweden	yes	yes	yes	yes
	Switzerland	yes	yes	yes	yes
	Turkey	no	yes	yes	yes
	United Kingdom	not comparable	not comparable	yes	yes
	United States	yes	yes	reading results not available	yes
	Number of OECD countries that have valid data in:				
	reading	27	29	33	33
	mathematics	not comparable	29	34	33
	science	not comparable	not comparable	34	33
Partners	Albania	yes	no	no	yes
	Argentina	yes	no	yes	yes
	Azerbaijan	no	no	yes	yes
	Brazil	yes	yes	yes	yes
	Bulgaria	yes	no	yes	yes
	Chinese Taipei	no	no	yes	yes
	Colombia	no	no	yes	yes
	Croatia	no	no	yes	yes
	Dubai (UAE)	no	no	no	yes
	Hong Kong-China	yes	yes	yes	yes
	Indonesia	yes	yes	yes	yes
	Jordan	no	no	yes	yes
	Kazakhstan	no	no	no	yes
	Kyrgyzstan	no	no	yes	yes
	Latvia	yes	yes	yes	yes
	Liechtenstein	yes	yes	yes	yes
	Lithuania	no	no	yes	yes
	Macao-China	no	yes	yes	yes
	Montenegro	no	no	yes	yes
	Panama	no	no	no	yes
	Peru	yes	no	no	yes
	Qatar	no	no	yes	yes
	Romania	yes	no	yes	yes
	Russian Federation	yes	yes	yes	yes
	Serbia	no	yes	yes	yes
	Shanghai-China	no	no	no	yes
	Singapore	no	no	no	yes
	Thailand	yes	yes	yes	yes
	Trinidad and Tobago	no	no	no	yes
	Tunisia	no	yes	yes	yes
	Uruguay	no	yes	yes	yes

ANNEX A6
LINEAR AND ADJUSTED TRENDS

Survey results can vary between assessments due to sampling and measurement errors, even if the true proficiency level of students does not change. The precision of the results can be increased by using information from all assessments. This provides an opportunity to look at trends more robustly than is possible by using just two observations. This annex describes how a linear regression model was fitted to results from the four PISA assessments to estimate linear trends.

Moreover, when reviewing and interpreting the changes in country-level PISA results it is important to account for the potential influence of changes in factors such as demography and sampling methodology on the results. This was highlighted by Gebhardt and Adams (2007) who illustrated how changes over time in factors such as the estimated distribution of socio-economic background and the estimated percentage of male and female students can have a material effect on the trend results.

Gebhardt and Adams (2007) referred to trends that were unadjusted for such changes as marginal trends and trends that were adjusted as conditional trends. They found that a more complete understanding of country trend results could be obtained if both the marginal and conditional trends were reviewed. This report refers to these two sets of results as unadjusted and adjusted trends, respectively.

As the results presented in Chapter 2 and in this Annex demonstrate, these adjustments do not alter the main conclusions regarding trends in different countries. Chapter 2 of this volume discusses those cases when such adjustments do lead to different conclusions.

Linear trends

Trends cannot be assessed fully when only looking at the difference in performance between two points in time. In some countries, the average performance varies across assessments with year-to-year changes in different directions. To see whether performance in a particular country varies around similar levels or consistently increases or declines over time, the following method of combining information from successive PISA assessments was used.

Chapter 2 summarises reading performance from all assessments in one indicator. This indicator is obtained from a linear regression, which was applied at country level, to the results from all available PISA assessments. Although the same method is applied for countries with results from two, three or four assessments, the linear trends indicator is more precise for countries with valid results from all four PISA reading assessments. In cases where countries have data from just two assessments, the linear trends are identical to the annualised difference between these two assessments.

In all cases, linear trends are expressed in performance changes by one year, so that the results can be compared between countries even if they participated in different assessments covering different time periods. Thus, linear trends are represented on a similar scale to annualised trends that are also discussed in Chapter 2. However, linear trends do account for data from several assessments, if they are available, while the annualised trend is equal to a difference between two assessments divided by the number of years between them.

Some countries administered the PISA 2000 assessment one or two years later (see endnote 6 in Chapter 1). This is taken into account when estimating linear trends.

As for all statistics presented in this report, the precision of trend estimates needs to be estimated. For linear trends, the standard errors have to account for two sources of random variation: (i) those related to sampling variation and (ii) those related to the link error associated with comparing results across successive assessments (see Annex A1 for details on link error).

The link error reflects the precision with which student performance scores are aligned across assessments. For changes in performance between two assessments link errors were estimated and incorporated in the presented results (see Annex A1 for details). For linear trends, the Monte Carlo approach was used to estimate the standard errors of regression parameters (*i.e.* the linear trend). Under the Monte Carlo approach, 500 sets of possible means were drawn for each country. These means were drawn assuming that the uncertainty associated with each national mean was independent over time and was normally distributed around the estimated mean with a variance that was

estimated by combining the sampling and link errors. Linear regressions were run for each of the 500 replications and standard errors were estimated via the standard deviations of the 500 estimated regression coefficients.

Adjusted trends

PISA maintains its technical standards over time. Although this means that trends can be calculated over comparable populations, in some countries small departures in sampling methods were observed. Furthermore, the demographic characteristics and socio-economic background of 15-year-old populations can also be subject to change. To draw reliable conclusions from trends results, it is important to check if those reported without any corrections were sustained after adjusting for the demographic and socio-economic background of students.

Linear regression can be used to adjust performance results for differences in student background. The regression model used for this report includes the background characteristics that were to be accounted for and allows the relationship between them and student performance to vary across assessments. In this way, three kinds of results were calculated separately for each country: (i) the adjusted performance results from each assessment (ii) the adjusted difference between two assessments, and (iii) the adjusted linear trend from several assessments.

The adjusted reading performance results reported in Chapter 2 use the 2009 PISA sample as a reference. Thus, the results from previous assessments were adjusted to be comparable to the 2009 results. This was achieved by centring background characteristics on the 2009 average values for each country and then carrying out a regression with centred background characteristics to obtain adjusted trends. In other words, results for 2000, 2003 and 2006 were adjusted to match the 2009 data.

Table A6.1 provides means for background variables, with the following measures used for the adjustment: the student gender and age, as well as indicators for students whose language spoken at home is different from the language of assessment, whether the student was born in another country, whether the student's mother was born in another country and whether the student's father was born in another country. The last columns show changes in these characteristics. The results were also adjusted for changes in the socio-economic background as measured by *the PISA index of economic, social and cultural status* (variable ESCS). As explained in Annex A1, the ESCS index was re-estimated for 2000, 2003 and 2006 assessments to be comparable with 2009 results. Mean values, the standard deviation and changes in these statistics for the re-estimated ESCS index are reported in Table V.4.3. These statistics could differ from those reported in 2000, 2003 and 2006 reports, since the re-estimated values of the ESCS index that are comparable with 2009 results can differ slightly from those reported in previous assessments. In both tables, changes that are in bold print suggest that mean values on the respective measure changed between assessments. In this case, the difference between unadjusted and adjusted trends reflects this change with adjusted trends accounting for it.

Unadjusted performance results are averaged across all students participating in PISA assessments. Thus, adjusted results should be also calculated over all participants in each country. That is not always possible, as in some cases, information on student background characteristics is missing due to non-response or invalid responses. Imputation of missing values was needed prior to the adjustments to sustain sample sizes and comparisons with unadjusted results. This was achieved using multiple imputation models that maintained the relationships between performance and background characteristics when imputing missing information (Rubin, 1987; Royston, 2004). The imputation model was carried out once for each plausible value and included all student background characteristics that were listed in the previous paragraph. After the imputation, all calculations were carried out five times, once for each imputed dataset containing one of five plausible values of the performance measures. Final results were obtained by averaging regression outcomes obtained from each imputed dataset and by accounting for imputation error using so-called Rubin's combination rules (Rubin, 1987). The results after imputation differ negligibly from those without the imputation given that for most countries and assessments the number of missing observations was relatively low.

Adjusting trends for changes in the age and gender of students

The population of students assessed by PISA are 15-year-olds enrolled in education. However, in some countries, the testing window may have moved slightly between PISA assessments, which can affect trends. For example, if, during one assessment, students were two months younger than the average student tested in PISA, comparisons with other countries would not be affected, as a two-month age difference is negligible. However, if students were two months older in another assessment, the average age in the two samples could differ by four months, which is more substantial. If these differences are then related to other discrepancies between student samples across time,

the comparability of trends can suffer, producing higher values for countries where the mean age difference between two assessments is larger. In fact, however, age differences between PISA assessments are minor, with a maximum of one month difference among countries.

Another common criterion in sampling populations is gender representation. Because girls' reading performance is usually higher than that of boys, gender imbalances among samples from different PISA assessments can affect the reliability of trend estimates. For example, if girls show higher achievement and girls were more numerous in PISA 2000 than in PISA 2009, there would be a downward change in achievement, as the composition of PISA 2000 sample was more favourable. Gender imbalance is very rare in PISA assessments, but PISA reviewed whether small changes in the percentage of boys and girls have affected trends.

Results for trends adjusted for age and gender sampling differences are compared to unadjusted trend estimates in Figure A6.1 (see also Table A6.2 with adjusted trends and adjusted results for 2000, 2003 and 2006). The trends are very similar. This shows that PISA sampling procedures are consistent and assure comparability of results between and within countries over time. Chapter 2 discusses results for further adjustments, accounting for changes in the demographic and socio-economic background of students.

■ Figure A6.1 ■

Observed score change and score point change adjusted for sampling differences between 2000 and 2009

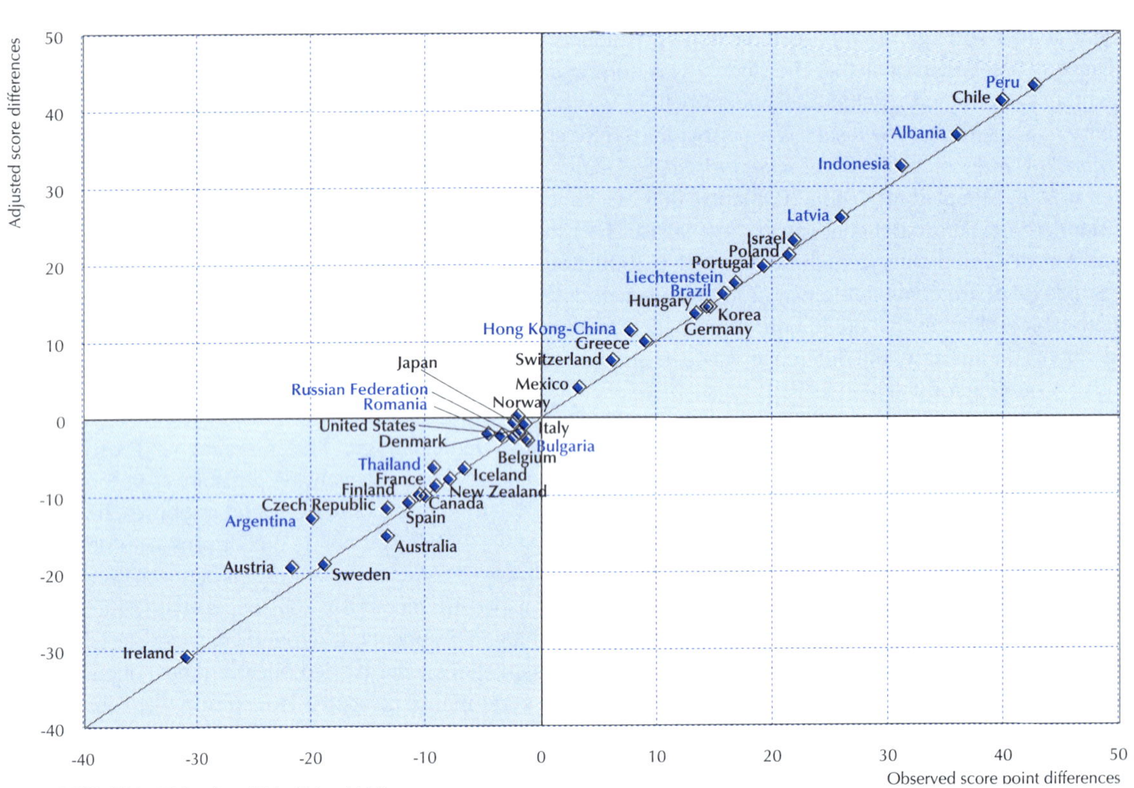

Source: OECD, *PISA 2009 Database*, Table A6.1 and A6.2

[Part 1/3]
Table A6.1 **Student background characteristics in PISA 2000 and 2009**

		PISA 2000									
		Percentage of girls		Age		Student born in another country		Student's mother born in another country		Student's father born in another country	
		%	S.E.	Mean	S.E.	%	S.E.	%	S.E.	%	S.E.
OECD	Australia	47.5	(2.2)	15.7	(0.0)	13.0	(1.2)	31.5	(1.6)	33.0	(1.7)
	Austria	48.8	(2.3)	15.8	(0.0)	8.1	(0.7)	14.1	(1.0)	13.7	(0.9)
	Belgium	47.9	(1.7)	15.7	(0.0)	5.8	(0.5)	16.9	(1.1)	18.6	(1.2)
	Canada	50.1	(0.5)	15.8	(0.0)	10.7	(0.6)	24.9	(1.0)	26.8	(1.1)
	Chile	53.0	(1.8)	15.8	(0.0)	1.5	(0.2)	0.9	(0.2)	1.1	(0.2)
	Czech Republic	51.7	(1.8)	15.8	(0.0)	1.0	(0.1)	4.5	(0.3)	4.8	(0.3)
	Denmark	49.7	(0.9)	15.7	(0.0)	6.3	(0.5)	9.5	(0.6)	10.0	(0.7)
	Finland	51.4	(0.8)	15.7	(0.0)	2.5	(0.3)	2.1	(0.3)	2.6	(0.3)
	France	51.3	(1.3)	15.9	(0.0)	3.5	(0.3)	17.2	(1.0)	19.6	(1.0)
	Germany	49.7	(1.5)	15.8	(0.0)	11.3	(0.6)	18.0	(0.9)	19.0	(0.9)
	Greece	49.8	(1.3)	15.8	(0.0)	6.6	(1.0)	8.6	(1.0)	6.8	(1.0)
	Hungary	49.6	(2.1)	15.7	(0.0)	2.2	(0.2)	2.7	(0.3)	2.8	(0.3)
	Iceland	50.4	(0.8)	15.7	(0.0)	5.9	(0.4)	3.2	(0.4)	3.8	(0.4)
	Ireland	50.4	(1.8)	15.7	(0.0)	4.2	(0.4)	7.9	(0.5)	6.0	(0.5)
	Israel	58.2	(2.7)	15.7	(0.0)	10.9	(1.2)	34.2	(1.9)	36.3	(2.1)
	Italy	49.3	(2.7)	15.7	(0.0)	2.2	(0.3)	3.7	(0.3)	2.2	(0.3)
	Japan	50.5	(2.4)	15.8	(0.0)	0.2	(0.1)	0.4	(0.1)	0.3	(0.1)
	Korea	44.1	(3.5)	15.7	(0.0)	m	m	m	m	m	m
	Luxembourg	m	m	m	m	m	m	m	m	m	m
	Mexico	50.0	(1.2)	15.8	(0.0)	3.2	(0.4)	4.5	(0.4)	4.7	(0.4)
	Netherlands	m	m	m	m	m	m	m	m	m	m
	New Zealand	49.7	(2.4)	15.7	(0.0)	16.7	(0.9)	27.3	(1.1)	29.4	(1.2)
	Norway	49.0	(0.9)	15.8	(0.0)	5.5	(0.4)	7.6	(0.5)	7.9	(0.5)
	Poland	49.1	(2.6)	15.7	(0.0)	1.0	(0.2)	0.7	(0.2)	1.5	(0.3)
	Portugal	52.0	(0.9)	15.7	(0.0)	6.0	(0.5)	6.9	(0.4)	6.1	(0.4)
	Spain	50.8	(1.3)	15.8	(0.0)	2.5	(0.4)	4.3	(0.4)	3.6	(0.4)
	Sweden	49.2	(0.9)	15.7	(0.0)	8.3	(0.6)	15.7	(0.9)	16.1	(1.1)
	Switzerland	49.8	(1.0)	15.9	(0.0)	14.1	(0.7)	28.3	(0.9)	28.9	(1.0)
	United Kingdom	m	m	m	m	m	m	m	m	m	m
	United States	51.6	(1.0)	15.8	(0.0)	7.3	(1.0)	15.8	(2.3)	17.2	(2.5)
	OECD average - 23	49.7	(0.4)	15.8	(0.0)	6.0	(0.1)	11.2	(0.2)	11.6	(0.2)
	OECD average - 26	50.2	(0.3)	15.8	(0.0)	6.1	(0.1)	11.9	(0.2)	12.4	(0.2)
Partners	Albania	51.0	(1.2)	15.7	(0.0)	0.5	(0.1)	1.2	(0.2)	1.3	(0.2)
	Argentina	56.4	(2.5)	15.9	(0.0)	0.8	(0.2)	5.1	(0.8)	5.5	(0.4)
	Brazil	54.0	(1.2)	15.8	(0.0)	0.2	(0.1)	0.8	(0.2)	1.1	(0.2)
	Bulgaria	48.5	(1.9)	15.7	(0.0)	1.1	(0.2)	2.3	(0.3)	1.6	(0.3)
	Hong Kong-China	49.8	(2.1)	15.8	(0.0)	20.7	(0.9)	52.3	(1.0)	54.2	(1.2)
	Indonesia	51.1	(1.8)	15.7	(0.0)	0.3	(0.1)	0.5	(0.1)	0.6	(0.1)
	Latvia	51.3	(1.6)	15.7	(0.0)	30.5	(3.4)	30.8	(2.6)	30.9	(2.5)
	Liechtenstein	49.7	(2.9)	15.7	(0.0)	12.9	(1.8)	35.4	(2.6)	30.4	(2.6)
	Peru	49.9	(2.2)	15.9	(0.0)	0.6	(0.1)	0.7	(0.2)	1.1	(0.2)
	Romania	52.7	(1.1)	15.8	(0.0)	0.2	(0.1)	0.5	(0.2)	0.6	(0.2)
	Russian Federation	50.1	(0.9)	15.8	(0.0)	5.4	(0.5)	8.1	(0.7)	9.6	(0.8)
	Thailand	58.8	(2.0)	15.8	(0.0)	0.1	(0.0)	0.9	(0.5)	1.1	(0.5)

Note: Values that are statistically significant are indicated in bold (see Annex A3).
StatLink http://dx.doi.org/10.1787/888932360100

[Part 2/3]

Table A6.1 Student background characteristics in PISA 2000 and 2009

		PISA 2009									
		Percentage of girls		Age		Student born in another country		Student's mother born in another country		Student's father born in another country	
		%	S.E.	Mean	S.E.	%	S.E.	%	S.E.	%	S.E.
OECD	Australia	51.1	(1.3)	15.7	(0.0)	12.8	(0.6)	32.6	(1.1)	33.1	(1.1)
	Austria	m	m	m	m	m	m	m	m	m	m
	Belgium	48.9	(1.2)	15.8	(0.0)	9.2	(0.7)	20.5	(1.2)	21.7	(1.1)
	Canada	49.7	(0.5)	15.8	(0.0)	12.3	(0.7)	29.4	(1.3)	30.3	(1.3)
	Chile	49.0	(1.1)	15.8	(0.0)	1.1	(0.1)	1.1	(0.2)	1.4	(0.2)
	Czech Republic	46.8	(1.8)	15.8	(0.0)	1.4	(0.2)	4.8	(0.3)	6.2	(0.4)
	Denmark	50.5	(0.7)	15.7	(0.0)	4.7	(0.3)	12.2	(0.5)	13.1	(0.5)
	Finland	49.9	(0.5)	15.7	(0.0)	2.7	(0.3)	4.7	(0.4)	5.0	(0.5)
	France	51.3	(1.2)	15.9	(0.0)	5.0	(0.6)	18.5	(1.4)	20.3	(1.6)
	Germany	48.9	(1.0)	15.8	(0.0)	7.2	(0.4)	21.3	(1.1)	22.0	(1.0)
	Greece	50.9	(1.1)	15.7	(0.0)	9.0	(0.8)	15.6	(0.9)	11.2	(0.9)
	Hungary	49.6	(1.5)	15.7	(0.0)	2.0	(0.3)	3.8	(0.3)	3.3	(0.3)
	Iceland	50.3	(0.3)	15.7	(0.0)	6.3	(0.4)	6.6	(0.4)	5.5	(0.4)
	Ireland	49.4	(1.1)	15.7	(0.0)	14.9	(0.7)	17.0	(0.8)	16.4	(0.7)
	Israel	50.9	(0.9)	15.7	(0.0)	9.2	(0.8)	26.8	(1.1)	27.3	(1.1)
	Italy	48.6	(0.9)	15.7	(0.0)	5.8	(0.2)	9.7	(0.3)	7.6	(0.3)
	Japan	48.4	(1.8)	15.7	(0.0)	0.4	(0.1)	0.9	(0.1)	0.5	(0.1)
	Korea	47.3	(1.8)	15.7	(0.0)	0.4	(0.1)	0.3	(0.1)	m	m
	Luxembourg	49.3	(0.2)	15.8	(0.0)	19.3	(0.5)	48.0	(0.6)	49.2	(0.7)
	Mexico	50.6	(0.4)	15.7	(0.0)	2.4	(0.1)	2.9	(0.2)	3.0	(0.2)
	Netherlands	50.3	(0.7)	15.7	(0.0)	4.8	(0.5)	16.0	(1.6)	16.7	(1.6)
	New Zealand	49.0	(1.2)	15.7	(0.0)	20.8	(0.7)	32.5	(1.2)	32.8	(1.2)
	Norway	48.9	(0.5)	15.7	(0.0)	5.4	(0.4)	11.0	(0.6)	10.9	(0.7)
	Poland	50.0	(0.5)	15.7	(0.0)	0.4	(0.1)	0.1	(0.1)	0.5	(0.1)
	Portugal	51.1	(0.6)	15.7	(0.0)	7.4	(0.5)	13.0	(0.6)	11.2	(0.6)
	Spain	49.2	(0.6)	15.8	(0.0)	10.0	(0.5)	13.1	(0.5)	11.8	(0.5)
	Sweden	49.2	(0.5)	15.7	(0.0)	5.8	(0.5)	16.6	(1.3)	18.0	(1.3)
	Switzerland	49.2	(1.1)	15.8	(0.0)	10.9	(0.6)	33.7	(0.9)	32.2	(1.0)
	United Kingdom	50.9	(1.6)	15.7	(0.0)	6.8	(0.5)	14.2	(1.0)	15.8	(1.2)
	United States	48.7	(0.8)	15.7	(0.0)	7.4	(0.5)	23.3	(1.4)	23.6	(1.5)
	OECD average - 23	49.5	(0.2)	15.7	(0.0)	6.8	(0.1)	13.9	(0.2)	14.4	(0.2)
	OECD average - 26	49.5	(0.2)	15.7	(0.0)	6.7	(0.1)	14.3	(0.2)	14.8	(0.2)
Partners	Albania	48.7	(0.9)	15.8	(0.0)	1.5	(0.2)	0.8	(0.2)	0.8	(0.2)
	Argentina	53.7	(1.1)	15.7	(0.0)	1.9	(0.3)	6.3	(0.7)	6.3	(0.7)
	Brazil	53.1	(0.4)	15.9	(0.0)	0.5	(0.1)	1.1	(0.2)	1.7	(0.2)
	Bulgaria	48.1	(2.2)	15.8	(0.0)	1.3	(0.2)	1.9	(0.3)	1.3	(0.2)
	Hong Kong-China	47.1	(1.8)	15.7	(0.0)	22.8	(1.0)	53.0	(1.4)	45.8	(1.4)
	Indonesia	50.5	(1.9)	15.7	(0.0)	0.6	(0.1)	0.3	(0.1)	0.5	(0.2)
	Latvia	50.7	(0.9)	15.7	(0.0)	1.6	(0.3)	11.3	(0.9)	12.7	(1.0)
	Liechtenstein	47.0	(1.2)	15.7	(0.0)	26.1	(2.3)	54.2	(2.7)	48.1	(2.8)
	Peru	49.5	(1.2)	15.8	(0.0)	0.7	(0.1)	0.9	(0.1)	0.9	(0.1)
	Romania	50.9	(1.4)	15.7	(0.0)	0.6	(0.1)	0.5	(0.1)	0.6	(0.1)
	Russian Federation	50.4	(0.7)	15.8	(0.0)	6.9	(0.5)	16.7	(0.8)	17.2	(0.8)
	Thailand	56.7	(1.5)	15.7	(0.0)	0.1	(0.0)	0.0	(0.0)	0.1	(0.1)

Note: Values that are statistically significant are indicated in bold (see Annex A3).
StatLink http://dx.doi.org/10.1787/888932360100

[Part 3/3]
Table A6.1 Student background characteristics in PISA 2000 and 2009

		Change between 2000 and 2009 (PISA 2009 – PISA 2000)									
		Percentage of girls		Age		Student born in another country		Student's mother born in another country		Student's father born in another country	
		% dif.	S.E.	Dif.	S.E.	% dif.	S.E.	% dif.	S.E.	% dif.	S.E.
OECD	Australia	3.6	(2.5)	0.02	(0.01)	-0.1	(1.4)	1.1	(2.0)	0.1	(2.0)
	Austria	m	m	m	m	m	m	m	m	m	m
	Belgium	1.1	(2.1)	**0.09**	(0.00)	**3.3**	(0.9)	**3.6**	(1.7)	3.1	(1.7)
	Canada	-0.4	(0.7)	**0.01**	(0.00)	1.6	(1.0)	**4.5**	(1.6)	**3.5**	(1.7)
	Chile	-4.0	(2.1)	**-0.02**	(0.01)	-0.4	(0.3)	0.3	(0.2)	0.2	(0.2)
	Czech Republic	-4.9	(2.5)	-0.00	(0.01)	0.4	(0.2)	0.3	(0.4)	**1.4**	(0.5)
	Denmark	0.8	(1.2)	-0.01	(0.01)	**-1.5**	(0.6)	**2.8**	(0.8)	**3.1**	(0.9)
	Finland	-1.5	(0.9)	0.01	(0.01)	0.1	(0.4)	**2.6**	(0.5)	**2.4**	(0.5)
	France	-0.1	(1.8)	**-0.01**	(0.01)	**1.5**	(0.6)	1.2	(1.7)	0.6	(1.9)
	Germany	-0.7	(1.8)	0.00	(0.01)	**-4.1**	(0.7)	**3.3**	(1.4)	**3.0**	(1.3)
	Greece	1.1	(1.7)	**-0.08**	(0.01)	2.3	(1.3)	**7.0**	(1.3)	**4.5**	(1.3)
	Hungary	-0.0	(2.6)	-0.01	(0.01)	-0.2	(0.4)	**1.1**	(0.4)	0.5	(0.4)
	Iceland	-0.2	(0.9)	0.00	(0.01)	0.4	(0.5)	**3.4**	(0.6)	**1.7**	(0.5)
	Ireland	-1.1	(2.1)	0.01	(0.01)	**10.7**	(0.8)	**9.1**	(1.0)	**10.4**	(0.9)
	Israel	**-7.3**	(2.8)	**0.02**	(0.01)	-1.7	(1.4)	**-7.4**	(2.2)	**-9.0**	(2.3)
	Italy	-0.7	(2.9)	**-0.02**	(0.00)	**3.6**	(0.4)	**6.0**	(0.4)	**5.4**	(0.4)
	Japan	-2.1	(2.9)	**-0.09**	(0.01)	0.2	(0.1)	**0.6**	(0.1)	0.2	(0.1)
	Korea	3.1	(4.0)	**-0.04**	(0.01)	m	m	m	m	m	m
	Luxembourg	m	m	m	m	m	m	m	m	m	m
	Mexico	0.6	(1.3)	**-0.07**	(0.01)	-0.7	(0.4)	**-1.6**	(0.5)	**-1.7**	(0.4)
	Netherlands	m	m	m	m	m	m	m	m	m	m
	New Zealand	-0.8	(2.7)	**0.01**	(0.01)	**4.0**	(1.2)	**5.2**	(1.6)	**3.4**	(1.6)
	Norway	-0.1	(1.0)	**-0.09**	(0.01)	-0.1	(0.6)	**3.4**	(0.8)	**3.1**	(0.8)
	Poland	0.8	(2.7)	-0.00	(0.01)	**-0.6**	(0.3)	**-0.6**	(0.2)	**-1.1**	(0.3)
	Portugal	-0.8	(1.1)	-0.01	(0.01)	1.3	(0.7)	**6.1**	(0.7)	**5.1**	(0.7)
	Spain	-1.6	(1.5)	**-0.01**	(0.00)	**7.6**	(0.7)	**8.8**	(0.7)	**8.2**	(0.7)
	Sweden	-0.0	(1.0)	0.00	(0.01)	**-2.5**	(0.8)	0.9	(1.6)	1.9	(1.7)
	Switzerland	-0.6	(1.5)	**-0.07**	(0.01)	**-3.2**	(0.9)	**5.3**	(1.3)	**3.4**	(1.4)
	United Kingdom	m	m	m	m	m	m	m	m	m	m
	United States	**-2.9**	(1.2)	**-0.06**	(0.01)	0.1	(1.1)	**7.5**	(2.7)	**6.4**	(3.0)
	OECD average - 23	-0.2	(0.4)	-0.0	(0.0)	**1.1**	(0.2)	**3.2**	(0.2)	**2.8**	(0.2)
	OECD average - 26	-0.7	(0.4)	-0.0	(0.0)	**0.9**	(0.2)	**2.9**	(0.2)	**2.4**	(0.3)
Partners	Albania	-2.3	(1.5)	**0.03**	(0.01)	**1.0**	(0.3)	-0.3	(0.3)	-0.5	(0.3)
	Argentina	-2.7	(2.7)	**-0.16**	(0.01)	**1.1**	(0.3)	1.2	(1.1)	0.8	(0.8)
	Brazil	-0.9	(1.2)	**0.07**	(0.01)	**0.3**	(0.2)	0.3	(0.2)	**0.6**	(0.3)
	Bulgaria	-0.4	(2.9)	**0.09**	(0.01)	0.1	(0.3)	-0.4	(0.4)	-0.3	(0.3)
	Hong Kong-China	-2.8	(2.7)	**-0.11**	(0.01)	2.1	(1.4)	0.7	(1.8)	**-8.4**	(1.8)
	Indonesia	-0.7	(2.7)	**-0.07**	(0.01)	0.3	(0.2)	-0.2	(0.2)	-0.1	(0.2)
	Latvia	-0.7	(1.8)	0.02	(0.01)	**-28.9**	(3.4)	**-19.5**	(2.7)	**-18.2**	(2.7)
	Liechtenstein	-2.7	(3.1)	0.01	(0.02)	**13.2**	(3.0)	**18.8**	(3.7)	**17.7**	(3.8)
	Peru	-0.4	(2.5)	**-0.07**	(0.01)	0.2	(0.2)	0.2	(0.2)	-0.2	(0.2)
	Romania	-1.8	(1.8)	**-0.04**	(0.01)	**0.4**	(0.1)	0.0	(0.2)	0.0	(0.2)
	Russian Federation	0.4	(1.1)	-0.01	(0.01)	**1.5**	(0.7)	**8.6**	(1.1)	**7.6**	(1.1)
	Thailand	-2.1	(2.6)	**-0.14**	(0.01)	-0.0	(0.1)	-0.9	(0.5)	-0.9	(0.5)

Note: Values that are statistically significant are indicated in bold (see Annex A3).
StatLink http://dx.doi.org/10.1787/888932360100

[Part 1/1]

Table A6.2 Trends adjusted for sampling differences

		Adjusted PISA 2000 results		Adjusted PISA 2003 results		Adjusted PISA 2006 results		Original PISA 2009 results		Change between 2000 and 2009 (PISA 2009 - PISA 2000)	
		Mean score	S.E.	Mean score	S.E.	Mean score	S.E.	Mean score	S.E.	Score dif.	S.E.
OECD	Australia	530	(3.4)	526	(2.0)	514	(1.9)	515	(2.3)	**-15.3**	(6.5)
	Austria	490	(2.5)	490	(3.5)	491	(4.3)	m	m	m	m
	Belgium	509	(3.6)	507	(2.5)	502	(3.0)	506	(2.3)	-3.0	(6.5)
	Canada	534	(1.6)	528	(1.8)	527	(2.4)	524	(1.5)	-10.0	(5.4)
	Chile	408	(3.5)	m	m	443	(4.9)	449	(3.1)	**41.1**	(6.8)
	Czech Republic	490	(2.5)	488	(3.5)	484	(4.2)	478	(2.9)	-11.6	(6.3)
	Denmark	497	(2.4)	492	(2.8)	495	(3.2)	495	(2.1)	-2.0	(5.9)
	Estonia	m	m	m	m	501	(2.9)	501	(2.6)	m	m
	Finland	546	(2.6)	543	(1.6)	548	(2.1)	536	(2.3)	-9.9	(6.0)
	France	504	(2.6)	496	(2.7)	490	(4.1)	496	(3.4)	-8.8	(6.6)
	Germany	484	(2.4)	493	(3.5)	495	(4.4)	497	(2.7)	**13.5**	(6.1)
	Greece	473	(4.9)	472	(4.1)	460	(3.8)	483	(4.3)	10.0	(8.2)
	Hungary	480	(3.9)	483	(2.5)	483	(3.2)	494	(3.2)	**14.4**	(7.1)
	Iceland	507	(1.4)	493	(1.5)	485	(1.9)	500	(1.4)	-6.5	(5.3)
	Ireland	527	(3.2)	515	(2.6)	517	(3.4)	496	(3.0)	**-30.9**	(6.6)
	Israel	451	(8.6)	m	m	438	(4.5)	474	(3.6)	**23.0**	(10.6)
	Italy	487	(2.8)	474	(3.1)	468	(2.4)	486	(1.6)	-0.8	(5.9)
	Japan	520	(5.2)	495	(4.1)	497	(3.7)	520	(3.5)	-0.6	(8.0)
	Korea	525	(2.2)	535	(2.8)	554	(3.5)	539	(3.5)	**14.4**	(6.4)
	Luxembourg	m	m	481	(1.5)	479	(1.3)	472	(1.3)	m	m
	Mexico	421	(3.3)	399	(4.1)	410	(3.0)	425	(2.0)	4.0	(6.2)
	Netherlands	m	m	513	(2.8)	507	(2.9)	508	(5.1)	m	m
	New Zealand	529	(2.5)	521	(2.3)	520	(2.7)	521	(2.4)	-7.9	(6.0)
	Norway	503	(2.7)	499	(2.9)	485	(3.2)	503	(2.6)	0.3	(6.2)
	Poland	479	(4.6)	497	(2.8)	508	(2.7)	500	(2.6)	**21.1**	(7.2)
	Portugal	470	(4.4)	475	(3.9)	472	(3.5)	489	(3.1)	**19.7**	(7.3)
	Slovak Republic	m	m	470	(3.0)	467	(3.0)	477	(2.5)	m	m
	Slovenia	m	m	m	m	494	(1.0)	483	(1.0)	m	m
	Spain	492	(2.7)	479	(2.7)	461	(2.2)	481	(2.0)	-10.9	(6.0)
	Sweden	516	(2.2)	514	(2.4)	507	(3.4)	497	(2.9)	**-18.9**	(6.1)
	Switzerland	493	(4.1)	500	(3.0)	500	(3.0)	501	(2.4)	7.5	(6.9)
	Turkey	m	m	441	(5.7)	447	(4.2)	464	(3.5)	m	m
	United Kingdom	m	m	m	m	495	(2.2)	494	(2.3)	m	m
	United States	502	(7.2)	494	(3.2)	m	m	500	(3.7)	-2.1	(9.5)
	OECD average - 23	501	(0.7)	497	(0.6)	495	(0.7)	499	(0.6)	-1	(1.4)
	OECD average - 26	495	(0.8)	497	(0.6)	490	(0.7)	496	(0.5)	1	(1.3)
Partners	Albania	348	(2.9)	m	m	m	m	385	(4.0)	**36.6**	(7.0)
	Argentina	411	(8.6)	m	m	374	(6.9)	398	(4.6)	-12.9	(10.9)
	Azerbaijan	m	m	m	m	353	(3.4)	362	(3.3)	m	m
	Brazil	396	(3.0)	405	(4.6)	393	(4.0)	412	(2.7)	**16.1**	(6.4)
	Bulgaria	432	(4.8)	m	m	404	(6.5)	429	(6.7)	-2.6	(9.6)
	Colombia	m	m	m	m	385	(4.9)	413	(3.7)	m	m
	Croatia	m	m	m	m	476	(2.7)	476	(2.9)	m	m
	Hong Kong-China	522	(3.1)	509	(3.6)	533	(2.4)	533	(2.1)	11.4	(6.2)
	Indonesia	369	(3.9)	381	(3.3)	391	(5.8)	402	(3.7)	**32.6**	(7.3)
	Jordan	m	m	m	m	400	(3.3)	405	(3.3)	m	m
	Kyrgyzstan	m	m	m	m	284	(3.4)	314	(3.2)	m	m
	Latvia	458	(4.9)	489	(3.5)	479	(3.6)	484	(3.0)	**25.9**	(7.5)
	Liechtenstein	482	(4.0)	525	(3.7)	507	(4.0)	499	(2.8)	**17.5**	(7.0)
	Lithuania	m	m	m	m	470	(3.0)	468	(2.4)	m	m
	Macao-China	m	m	497	(2.2)	492	(1.1)	487	(0.9)	m	m
	Montenegro	m	m	m	m	392	(1.2)	408	(1.7)	m	m
	Peru	327	(4.6)	m	m	m	m	370	(4.0)	**43.0**	(7.8)
	Qatar	m	m	m	m	312	(1.2)	372	(0.8)	m	m
	Romania	427	(3.5)	m	m	396	(4.5)	424	(4.1)	-2.3	(7.3)
	Russian Federation	462	(4.1)	442	(3.8)	439	(4.2)	459	(3.3)	-2.5	(7.2)
	Serbia	m	m	411	(3.2)	401	(3.2)	442	(2.4)	m	m
	Chinese Taipei	m	m	m	m	507	(4.1)	495	(2.6)	m	m
	Thailand	428	(3.0)	421	(2.7)	418	(2.5)	421	(2.6)	-6.4	(6.3)
	Tunisia	m	m	375	(2.8)	380	(3.9)	404	(2.9)	m	m
	Uruguay	m	m	436	(3.4)	413	(3.3)	426	(2.6)	m	m

Note: Values that are statistically significant are indicated in bold (see Annex A3).

StatLink http://dx.doi.org/10.1787/888932360100

Annex B

TABLES OF RESULTS

All tables in Annex B are available on line

Annex B1: Results for countries and economies

Annex B2: Results for regions within countries

Adjudicated regions
Data for which adherence to the PISA sampling standards and international comparability was internationally adjudicated.

Non-adjudicated regions
Data for which adherence to the PISA sampling standards at subnational levels was assessed by the countries concerned.

In these countries, adherence to the PISA sampling standards and international comparability was internationally adjudicated only for the combined set of all subnational entities.

Note: Unless otherwise specified, all the data contained in the following tables are drawn from the OECD PISA Database.

ANNEX B1
RESULTS FOR COUNTRIES AND ECONOMIES

[Part 1/1]
Table V.2.1 **Mean reading performance in PISA 2000, 2003, 2006 and 2009**

		PISA 2000		PISA 2003		PISA 2006		PISA 2009		Change between 2000 and 2009 (PISA 2009 – PISA 2000)		
		Mean score	S.E.	Mean score	S.E.	Mean score	S.E.	Mean score	S.E.	Score dif.	S.E.	p-value
OECD	Australia	528	(3.5)	525	(2.1)	513	(2.1)	515	(2.3)	**-13**	(6.5)	0.04
	Austria	492	(2.7)	491	(3.8)	490	(4.1)	m	m	m	m	m
	Belgium	507	(3.6)	507	(2.6)	501	(3.0)	506	(2.3)	-1	(6.5)	0.86
	Canada	534	(1.6)	528	(1.7)	527	(2.4)	524	(1.5)	-10	(5.4)	0.06
	Chile	410	(3.6)	m	m	442	(5.0)	449	(3.1)	**40**	(6.9)	0.00
	Czech Republic	492	(2.4)	489	(3.5)	483	(4.2)	478	(2.9)	**-13**	(6.2)	0.03
	Denmark	497	(2.4)	492	(2.8)	494	(3.2)	495	(2.1)	-2	(5.8)	0.74
	Estonia	m	m	m	m	501	(2.9)	501	(2.6)	m	m	m
	Finland	546	(2.6)	543	(1.6)	547	(2.1)	536	(2.3)	-11	(6.0)	0.08
	France	505	(2.7)	496	(2.7)	488	(4.1)	496	(3.4)	-9	(6.6)	0.17
	Germany	484	(2.5)	491	(3.4)	495	(4.4)	497	(2.7)	**13**	(6.1)	0.03
	Greece	474	(5.0)	472	(4.1)	460	(4.0)	483	(4.3)	9	(8.2)	0.28
	Hungary	480	(4.0)	482	(2.5)	482	(3.3)	494	(3.2)	**14**	(7.1)	0.04
	Iceland	507	(1.5)	492	(1.6)	484	(1.9)	500	(1.4)	-7	(5.3)	0.21
	Ireland	527	(3.2)	515	(2.6)	517	(3.5)	496	(3.0)	**-31**	(6.6)	0.00
	Israel	452	(8.5)	m	m	439	(4.6)	474	(3.6)	**22**	(10.5)	0.04
	Italy	487	(2.9)	476	(3.0)	469	(2.4)	486	(1.6)	-1	(5.9)	0.81
	Japan	522	(5.2)	498	(3.9)	498	(3.6)	520	(3.5)	-2	(8.0)	0.77
	Korea	525	(2.4)	534	(3.1)	556	(3.8)	539	(3.5)	**15**	(6.5)	0.03
	Luxembourg	m	m	479	(1.5)	479	(1.3)	472	(1.3)	m	m	m
	Mexico	422	(3.3)	400	(4.1)	410	(3.1)	425	(2.0)	3	(6.3)	0.60
	Netherlands	m	m	513	(2.9)	507	(2.9)	508	(5.1)	m	m	m
	New Zealand	529	(2.8)	522	(2.5)	521	(3.0)	521	(2.4)	-8	(6.1)	0.20
	Norway	505	(2.8)	500	(2.8)	484	(3.2)	503	(2.6)	-2	(6.2)	0.74
	Poland	479	(4.5)	497	(2.9)	508	(2.8)	500	(2.6)	**21**	(7.1)	0.00
	Portugal	470	(4.5)	478	(3.7)	472	(3.6)	489	(3.1)	**19**	(7.4)	0.01
	Slovak Republic	m	m	469	(3.1)	466	(3.1)	477	(2.5)	m	m	m
	Slovenia	m	m	m	m	494	(1.0)	483	(1.0)	m	m	m
	Spain	493	(2.7)	481	(2.6)	461	(2.2)	481	(2.0)	-12	(6.0)	0.05
	Sweden	516	(2.2)	514	(2.4)	507	(3.4)	497	(2.9)	**-19**	(6.1)	0.00
	Switzerland	494	(4.2)	499	(3.3)	499	(3.1)	501	(2.4)	6	(7.0)	0.38
	Turkey	m	m	441	(5.8)	447	(4.2)	464	(3.5)	m	m	m
	United Kingdom	m	m	m	m	495	(2.3)	494	(2.3)	m	m	m
	United States	504	(7.0)	495	(3.2)	m	m	500	(3.7)	-5	(9.3)	0.62
	OECD average-23	501	(0.7)	497	(0.6)	495	(0.7)	499	(0.6)	-2	(5.0)	0.73
	OECD average-26	496	(0.8)	m	m	m	m	496	(0.5)	1	(5.0)	0.90
Partners	Albania	349	(3.3)	m	m	m	m	385	(4.0)	**36**	(7.2)	0.00
	Argentina	418	(9.9)	m	m	374	(7.2)	398	(4.6)	-20	(12.0)	0.09
	Azerbaijan	m	m	m	m	353	(3.1)	362	(3.3)	m	m	m
	Brazil	396	(3.1)	403	(4.6)	393	(3.7)	412	(2.7)	**16**	(6.4)	0.01
	Bulgaria	430	(4.9)	m	m	402	(6.9)	429	(6.7)	-1	(9.6)	0.89
	Colombia	m	m	m	m	385	(5.1)	413	(3.7)	m	m	m
	Croatia	m	m	m	m	477	(2.8)	476	(2.9)	m	m	m
	Hong Kong-China	525	(2.9)	510	(3.7)	536	(2.4)	533	(2.1)	8	(6.1)	0.21
	Indonesia	371	(4.0)	382	(3.4)	393	(5.9)	402	(3.7)	**31**	(7.4)	0.00
	Jordan	m	m	m	m	401	(3.3)	405	(3.3)	m	m	m
	Kyrgyzstan	m	m	m	m	285	(3.5)	314	(3.2)	m	m	m
	Latvia	458	(5.3)	491	(3.7)	479	(3.7)	484	(3.0)	**26**	(7.8)	0.00
	Liechtenstein	483	(4.1)	525	(3.6)	510	(3.9)	499	(2.8)	**17**	(7.0)	0.02
	Lithuania	m	m	m	m	470	(3.0)	468	(2.4)	m	m	m
	Macao-China	m	m	498	(2.2)	492	(1.1)	487	(0.9)	m	m	m
	Montenegro	m	m	m	m	392	(1.2)	408	(1.7)	m	m	m
	Peru	327	(4.4)	m	m	m	m	370	(4.0)	**43**	(7.7)	0.00
	Qatar	m	m	m	m	312	(1.2)	372	(0.8)	m	m	m
	Romania	428	(3.5)	m	m	396	(4.7)	424	(4.1)	-3	(7.3)	0.63
	Russian Federation	462	(4.2)	442	(3.9)	440	(4.3)	459	(3.3)	-2	(7.3)	0.74
	Serbia	m	m	412	(3.6)	401	(3.5)	442	(2.4)	m	m	m
	Chinese Taipei	m	m	m	m	496	(3.4)	495	(2.6)	m	m	m
	Thailand	431	(3.2)	420	(2.8)	417	(2.6)	421	(2.6)	-9	(6.5)	0.15
	Tunisia	m	m	375	(2.8)	380	(4.0)	404	(2.9)	m	m	m
	Uruguay	m	m	434	(3.4)	413	(3.4)	426	(2.6)	m	m	m

Note: Values that are statistically significant are indicated in bold (see Annex A3).
StatLink http://dx.doi.org/10.1787/888932343285

[Part 1/1]

Table V.2.2 **Percentage of students below Level 2 and at Level 5 or above on the reading scale in PISA 2000 and 2009**

		Proficiency levels in PISA 2000				Proficiency levels in PISA 2009				Change between 2000 and 2009 (PISA 2009 – PISA 2000)			
		Below Level 2 (less than 407 score points)		Level 5 or above (above 626 score points)		Below Level 2 (less than 407 score points)		Level 5 or above (above 626 score points)		Below Level 2 (less than 407 score points)		Level 5 or above (above 626 score points)	
		%	S.E.	%	S.E.	%	S.E.	%	S.E.	% dif.	S.E.	% dif.	S.E.
OECD	Australia	12.5	(0.9)	17.6	(1.2)	14.2	(0.6)	12.8	(0.8)	1.8	(1.0)	**-4.9**	(1.4)
	Austria	19.3	(0.9)	7.5	(0.7)	m	m	m	m	m	m	m	m
	Belgium	19.0	(1.3)	12.0	(0.7)	17.7	(0.9)	11.2	(0.6)	-1.2	(1.6)	-0.8	(0.9)
	Canada	9.6	(0.4)	16.8	(0.5)	10.3	(0.5)	12.8	(0.5)	0.7	(0.6)	**-4.0**	(0.7)
	Chile	48.2	(1.9)	0.5	(0.1)	30.6	(1.5)	1.3	(0.3)	**-17.6**	(2.4)	**0.8**	(0.3)
	Czech Republic	17.5	(0.8)	7.0	(0.6)	23.1	(1.3)	5.1	(0.5)	**5.6**	(1.5)	**-1.9**	(0.7)
	Denmark	17.9	(0.9)	8.1	(0.5)	15.2	(0.9)	4.7	(0.5)	**-2.7**	(1.3)	**-3.4**	(0.7)
	Finland	7.0	(0.7)	18.5	(0.9)	8.1	(0.5)	14.5	(0.8)	1.2	(0.8)	**-4.0**	(1.2)
	France	15.2	(1.1)	8.5	(0.5)	19.8	(1.2)	9.6	(1.0)	**4.6**	(1.6)	1.1	(1.1)
	Germany	22.6	(1.0)	8.8	(0.5)	18.5	(1.1)	7.6	(0.6)	**-4.2**	(1.4)	-1.2	(0.8)
	Greece	24.4	(2.1)	5.0	(0.7)	21.3	(1.8)	5.6	(0.5)	-3.1	(2.8)	0.6	(0.8)
	Hungary	22.7	(1.5)	5.1	(0.8)	17.6	(1.4)	6.1	(0.7)	**-5.1**	(2.1)	1.0	(1.0)
	Iceland	14.5	(0.7)	9.1	(0.7)	16.8	(0.6)	8.5	(0.6)	**2.3**	(0.9)	-0.5	(0.9)
	Ireland	11.0	(1.0)	14.2	(0.8)	17.2	(1.0)	7.0	(0.5)	**6.2**	(1.4)	**-7.3**	(1.0)
	Israel	33.2	(3.2)	4.2	(0.8)	26.5	(1.2)	7.4	(0.6)	-6.7	(3.4)	**3.3**	(1.0)
	Italy	18.9	(1.1)	5.3	(0.5)	21.0	(0.6)	5.8	(0.3)	2.1	(1.3)	0.5	(0.6)
	Japan	10.1	(1.5)	9.9	(1.1)	13.6	(1.1)	13.4	(0.9)	3.5	(1.9)	**3.6**	(1.4)
	Korea	5.8	(0.7)	5.7	(0.6)	5.8	(0.8)	12.9	(1.1)	0.0	(1.1)	**7.2**	(1.2)
	Luxembourg	m	m	m	m	26.0	(0.6)	5.7	(0.5)	m	m	m	m
	Mexico	44.1	(1.7)	0.9	(0.2)	40.1	(1.0)	0.4	(0.1)	**-4.0**	(2.0)	-0.5	(0.2)
	Netherlands	m	m	m	m	14.3	(1.5)	9.8	(1.1)	m	m	m	m
	New Zealand	13.7	(0.8)	18.7	(1.0)	14.3	(0.7)	15.7	(0.8)	0.6	(1.1)	**-3.0**	(1.3)
	Norway	17.5	(1.1)	11.2	(0.7)	15.0	(0.8)	8.4	(0.9)	-2.5	(1.3)	**-2.8**	(1.1)
	Poland	23.2	(1.4)	5.9	(0.9)	15.0	(0.8)	7.2	(0.6)	**-8.2**	(1.7)	1.3	(1.1)
	Portugal	26.3	(1.9)	4.2	(0.5)	17.6	(1.2)	4.8	(0.5)	**-8.6**	(2.2)	0.6	(0.8)
	Spain	16.3	(1.1)	4.2	(0.5)	19.6	(0.9)	3.3	(0.3)	**3.3**	(1.4)	-0.9	(0.6)
	Sweden	12.6	(0.7)	11.2	(0.7)	17.4	(0.9)	9.0	(0.7)	**4.9**	(1.2)	**-2.2**	(1.0)
	Switzerland	20.4	(1.3)	9.2	(1.0)	16.8	(0.9)	8.1	(0.7)	**-3.6**	(1.6)	-1.1	(1.3)
	United Kingdom	m	m	m	m	18.4	(0.8)	8.0	(0.5)	m	m	m	m
	United States	17.9	(2.2)	12.2	(1.4)	17.6	(1.1)	9.9	(0.9)	-0.3	(2.4)	-2.4	(1.6)
	OECD average-26	19.3	(0.3)	9.0	(0.2)	18.1	(0.2)	8.2	(0.1)	**-1.2**	(0.3)	**-0.8**	(0.2)
Partners	Albania	70.4	(1.1)	0.1	(0.1)	56.7	(1.9)	0.2	(0.1)	**-13.7**	(2.2)	0.1	(0.1)
	Argentina	43.9	(4.5)	1.7	(0.5)	51.6	(1.9)	1.0	(0.2)	7.7	(4.9)	-0.7	(0.5)
	Brazil	55.8	(1.7)	0.6	(0.2)	49.6	(1.3)	1.3	(0.2)	**-6.2**	(2.1)	**0.8**	(0.3)
	Bulgaria	40.3	(2.1)	2.2	(0.6)	41.0	(2.6)	2.8	(0.5)	0.7	(3.3)	0.6	(0.8)
	Hong Kong-China	9.1	(1.0)	9.5	(0.8)	8.3	(0.7)	12.4	(0.8)	-0.8	(1.2)	**2.9**	(1.1)
	Indonesia	68.7	(2.5)	0.0	c	53.4	(2.3)	0.0	c	**-15.2**	(3.4)	c	c
	Latvia	30.1	(2.0)	4.2	(0.6)	17.6	(1.2)	2.9	(0.4)	**-12.5**	(2.4)	-1.2	(0.8)
	Liechtenstein	22.1	(2.1)	5.1	(1.6)	15.7	(1.8)	4.6	(1.4)	**-6.4**	(2.7)	-0.4	(2.1)
	Peru	79.5	(1.5)	0.1	(0.1)	64.8	(1.7)	0.5	(0.2)	**-14.8**	(2.2)	0.4	(0.2)
	Romania	41.3	(1.5)	2.2	(0.3)	40.4	(2.0)	0.7	(0.2)	-0.9	(2.5)	**-1.5**	(0.3)
	Russian Federation	27.4	(1.7)	3.2	(0.5)	27.4	(1.3)	3.2	(0.5)	-0.1	(2.2)	0.0	(0.7)
	Thailand	37.1	(1.7)	0.5	(0.2)	42.9	(1.5)	0.3	(0.2)	**5.8**	(2.3)	-0.2	(0.2)

Note: Values that are statistically significant are indicated in bold (see Annex A3).
StatLink http://dx.doi.org/10.1787/888932343285

[Part 1/2]

Table V.2.3 Percentiles on the reading scale in PISA 2000 and 2009

		PISA 2000								PISA 2003								PISA 2006							
		10th percentile		25th percentile		75th percentile		90th percentile		10th percentile		25th percentile		75th percentile		90th percentile		10th percentile		25th percentile		75th percentile		90th percentile	
		Score	S.E.	Score	S.E.	Score	S.E.	Score	S.E.	Score	S.E.	Score	S.E.	Score	S.E.	Score	S.E.	Score	S.E.	Score	S.E.	Score	S.E.	Score	S.E.
OECD	Australia	394	(4.4)	458	(4.4)	602	(4.6)	656	(4.2)	395	(3.6)	464	(3.0)	594	(2.5)	644	(2.7)	388	(3.4)	453	(2.4)	579	(2.3)	628	(2.9)
	Austria	359	(5.8)	428	(3.4)	563	(3.4)	614	(3.8)	354	(6.3)	423	(4.9)	565	(4.2)	617	(3.7)	348	(9.4)	421	(5.5)	568	(3.7)	621	(3.1)
	Belgium	354	(8.9)	437	(6.6)	587	(2.3)	634	(2.5)	355	(6.6)	440	(4.2)	587	(2.1)	635	(2.1)	347	(8.3)	433	(4.7)	581	(2.3)	631	(2.2)
	Canada	410	(2.4)	472	(2.0)	600	(1.5)	652	(1.9)	410	(3.1)	472	(2.3)	590	(2.1)	636	(2.1)	402	(3.9)	468	(3.0)	593	(2.6)	644	(2.7)
	Chile	291	(5.3)	350	(4.4)	472	(3.9)	524	(3.8)	m	m	m	m	m	m	m	m	310	(5.8)	373	(5.4)	513	(6.4)	575	(6.7)
	Czech Republic	368	(4.9)	433	(2.7)	557	(2.8)	610	(3.2)	362	(6.9)	428	(4.7)	555	(4.0)	607	(3.8)	335	(7.0)	408	(6.2)	564	(3.8)	621	(4.2)
	Denmark	367	(5.0)	434	(3.3)	566	(2.7)	617	(2.9)	376	(4.6)	438	(4.0)	553	(3.0)	600	(2.7)	378	(5.0)	437	(3.9)	557	(2.9)	604	(3.7)
	Estonia	m	m	m	m	m	m	m	m	m	m	m	m	m	m	m	m	389	(5.4)	448	(3.8)	560	(2.8)	606	(3.2)
	Finland	429	(5.1)	492	(2.9)	608	(2.6)	654	(2.8)	437	(3.1)	494	(2.4)	599	(1.7)	641	(2.2)	441	(3.8)	494	(2.9)	603	(2.2)	649	(2.5)
	France	381	(5.2)	444	(4.5)	570	(2.4)	619	(2.9)	367	(7.0)	436	(4.0)	565	(2.8)	614	(2.7)	346	(7.5)	421	(6.1)	564	(3.8)	614	(4.0)
	Germany	335	(6.3)	417	(4.6)	563	(3.1)	619	(2.8)	341	(6.8)	419	(5.6)	572	(3.4)	624	(3.2)	350	(8.0)	429	(5.9)	573	(3.4)	625	(3.7)
	Greece	342	(8.4)	409	(7.4)	543	(4.5)	595	(5.1)	333	(6.2)	406	(5.2)	546	(4.4)	599	(4.4)	321	(8.5)	398	(5.2)	531	(3.8)	583	(4.2)
	Hungary	354	(5.5)	414	(5.3)	549	(4.5)	598	(4.4)	361	(4.2)	422	(3.3)	546	(3.3)	597	(3.4)	359	(5.0)	422	(4.8)	549	(3.6)	595	(4.4)
	Iceland	383	(3.6)	447	(3.1)	573	(2.1)	621	(3.5)	362	(4.8)	431	(2.3)	560	(2.2)	612	(2.8)	356	(4.1)	423	(3.0)	552	(2.8)	603	(3.2)
	Ireland	401	(6.4)	468	(4.3)	593	(3.6)	641	(4.0)	401	(4.6)	460	(3.8)	577	(2.8)	622	(3.0)	395	(5.5)	457	(4.7)	582	(3.9)	633	(3.5)
	Israel	305	(13.0)	379	(11.1)	532	(8.1)	587	(7.1)	m	m	m	m	m	m	m	m	280	(8.0)	356	(6.2)	526	(4.8)	588	(4.9)
	Italy	368	(5.8)	429	(4.1)	552	(3.2)	601	(2.7)	341	(6.8)	411	(4.4)	547	(2.5)	598	(2.1)	325	(4.8)	402	(3.6)	546	(2.3)	599	(2.9)
	Japan	407	(9.8)	471	(7.0)	582	(4.4)	625	(4.5)	355	(6.5)	431	(5.4)	574	(3.7)	624	(4.8)	361	(6.6)	433	(6.1)	569	(3.4)	623	(3.5)
	Korea	433	(4.4)	481	(2.9)	574	(2.6)	608	(2.9)	428	(5.2)	484	(4.1)	590	(2.8)	634	(4.1)	440	(7.9)	503	(4.8)	617	(3.4)	663	(4.3)
	Luxembourg	m	m	m	m	m	m	m	m	344	(2.9)	416	(2.8)	551	(1.9)	601	(2.1)	344	(3.3)	415	(2.3)	552	(1.8)	602	(2.5)
	Mexico	311	(3.4)	360	(3.6)	482	(4.8)	535	(5.5)	274	(5.5)	335	(4.9)	467	(4.3)	521	(6.1)	285	(6.2)	348	(4.2)	478	(2.8)	530	(3.1)
	Netherlands	m	m	m	m	m	m	m	m	400	(5.2)	454	(4.5)	576	(3.2)	621	(2.9)	379	(6.4)	446	(4.3)	578	(2.5)	622	(2.4)
	New Zealand	382	(5.2)	459	(4.0)	606	(3.0)	661	(4.4)	381	(4.4)	453	(3.5)	596	(2.8)	652	(2.9)	381	(4.6)	453	(4.5)	595	(2.9)	651	(2.8)
	Norway	364	(5.5)	440	(4.5)	579	(2.7)	631	(3.1)	364	(4.7)	434	(3.8)	571	(3.6)	625	(3.9)	346	(5.5)	416	(4.6)	558	(3.0)	613	(4.1)
	Poland	343	(6.8)	414	(5.8)	551	(6.0)	603	(6.6)	374	(5.0)	436	(3.6)	563	(3.1)	616	(3.4)	374	(4.6)	441	(3.5)	579	(3.2)	633	(3.4)
	Portugal	337	(6.2)	403	(6.4)	541	(4.5)	592	(4.2)	351	(7.1)	418	(5.2)	544	(3.5)	592	(3.5)	339	(6.3)	408	(5.3)	543	(3.6)	594	(3.7)
	Slovak Republic	m	m	m	m	m	m	m	m	348	(5.8)	408	(4.6)	535	(3.2)	587	(3.0)	326	(6.6)	398	(4.3)	542	(3.4)	597	(3.8)
	Slovenia	m	m	m	m	m	m	m	m	m	m	m	m	m	m	m	m	377	(2.6)	437	(1.8)	558	(2.2)	603	(2.1)
	Spain	379	(5.0)	436	(4.6)	553	(2.6)	597	(2.6)	354	(4.9)	421	(3.4)	548	(2.8)	597	(2.8)	343	(4.1)	405	(2.9)	523	(2.3)	569	(2.7)
	Sweden	392	(4.0)	456	(3.1)	581	(3.1)	630	(2.9)	390	(4.3)	453	(3.4)	582	(2.9)	631	(2.9)	378	(5.6)	445	(3.8)	575	(3.3)	629	(4.0)
	Switzerland	355	(5.8)	426	(5.5)	567	(4.6)	621	(5.5)	373	(5.6)	439	(4.5)	565	(3.7)	615	(3.9)	373	(5.1)	440	(3.5)	566	(3.1)	615	(3.6)
	Turkey	m	m	m	m	m	m	m	m	324	(5.3)	377	(5.7)	500	(6.6)	562	(11.4)	330	(6.4)	388	(4.4)	510	(5.2)	564	(6.5)
	United Kingdom	m	m	m	m	m	m	m	m	m	m	m	m	m	m	m	m	359	(4.0)	431	(2.8)	566	(2.5)	621	(3.1)
	United States	363	(11.4)	436	(8.8)	577	(6.8)	636	(6.5)	361	(5.2)	429	(4.1)	568	(3.6)	622	(3.5)	m	m	m	m	m	m	m	m
	OECD average-23	373	(1.2)	439	(1.0)	569	(0.7)	618	(0.8)	369	(1.1)	436	(0.8)	565	(0.6)	615	(0.7)	364	(1.2)	432	(0.9)	564	(0.7)	615	(0.7)
	OECD average-26	367	(1.3)	433	(1.0)	564	(0.8)	614	(0.8)	m	m	m	m	m	m	m	m	m	m	m	m	m	m	m	m
Partners	Albania	216	(6.4)	279	(4.9)	421	(3.2)	476	(2.9)	m	m	m	m	m	m	m	m	m	m	m	m	m	m	m	m
	Argentina	270	(11.5)	344	(13.2)	495	(8.8)	554	(9.6)	m	m	m	m	m	m	m	m	209	(10.7)	291	(9.0)	464	(7.1)	527	(7.0)
	Azerbaijan	m	m	m	m	m	m	m	m	m	m	m	m	m	m	m	m	266	(3.9)	305	(3.6)	397	(3.7)	441	(5.0)
	Brazil	288	(4.5)	339	(3.4)	452	(3.4)	507	(4.2)	256	(7.5)	328	(5.5)	479	(5.1)	542	(5.2)	264	(6.0)	326	(4.2)	460	(4.0)	523	(5.3)
	Bulgaria	295	(6.6)	361	(5.8)	502	(6.6)	560	(7.4)	m	m	m	m	m	m	m	m	251	(9.0)	321	(8.5)	486	(7.6)	554	(7.8)
	Colombia	m	m	m	m	m	m	m	m	m	m	m	m	m	m	m	m	243	(7.0)	316	(7.2)	462	(5.6)	518	(5.2)
	Croatia	m	m	m	m	m	m	m	m	m	m	m	m	m	m	m	m	359	(5.4)	418	(4.1)	540	(3.0)	589	(3.4)
	Hong Kong-China	413	(7.3)	477	(3.8)	584	(2.7)	624	(2.9)	397	(6.7)	461	(5.1)	569	(2.8)	608	(2.9)	426	(5.8)	484	(3.7)	594	(2.4)	636	(2.9)
	Indonesia	277	(4.0)	321	(4.3)	422	(5.7)	464	(6.9)	282	(4.9)	332	(3.7)	433	(4.0)	478	(4.6)	298	(5.0)	342	(5.3)	444	(8.4)	490	(8.6)
	Jordan	m	m	m	m	m	m	m	m	m	m	m	m	m	m	m	m	277	(6.1)	342	(3.7)	467	(3.8)	514	(4.5)
	Kyrgyzstan	m	m	m	m	m	m	m	m	m	m	m	m	m	m	m	m	159	(5.3)	216	(3.8)	349	(4.1)	419	(5.9)
	Latvia	322	(8.2)	390	(6.9)	530	(5.2)	586	(5.8)	372	(5.3)	431	(4.9)	554	(3.5)	603	(4.6)	361	(5.4)	419	(4.9)	543	(4.2)	593	(4.0)
	Liechtenstein	350	(11.8)	419	(9.4)	551	(5.7)	601	(7.1)	405	(11.7)	467	(9.1)	588	(5.7)	636	(11.8)	379	(10.6)	452	(9.9)	578	(6.5)	623	(10.5)
	Lithuania	m	m	m	m	m	m	m	m	m	m	m	m	m	m	m	m	343	(3.9)	405	(4.0)	538	(3.9)	591	(3.9)
	Macao-China	m	m	m	m	m	m	m	m	409	(5.1)	455	(3.5)	544	(4.4)	583	(3.7)	394	(2.5)	445	(1.9)	545	(1.6)	587	(1.8)
	Montenegro	m	m	m	m	m	m	m	m	m	m	m	m	m	m	m	m	276	(3.2)	331	(2.1)	454	(1.9)	506	(2.6)
	Peru	205	(4.9)	259	(5.2)	392	(5.5)	452	(5.6)	m	m	m	m	m	m	m	m	m	m	m	m	m	m	m	m
	Qatar	m	m	m	m	m	m	m	m	m	m	m	m	m	m	m	m	181	(2.7)	237	(1.8)	380	(1.9)	456	(3.6)
	Romania	295	(6.1)	357	(7.1)	499	(3.4)	559	(3.5)	m	m	m	m	m	m	m	m	274	(7.2)	333	(7.3)	461	(5.2)	512	(5.6)
	Russian Federation	340	(5.4)	400	(5.1)	526	(4.5)	579	(4.4)	319	(6.1)	381	(5.4)	506	(3.9)	558	(4.4)	316	(6.0)	377	(5.7)	505	(4.2)	556	(3.6)
	Serbia	m	m	m	m	m	m	m	m	306	(4.6)	358	(4.0)	467	(4.0)	516	(4.8)	282	(4.6)	339	(4.5)	466	(3.9)	518	(3.7)
	Chinese Taipei	m	m	m	m	m	m	m	m	m	m	m	m	m	m	m	m	381	(5.9)	442	(4.9)	556	(3.0)	598	(3.0)
	Thailand	333	(4.8)	381	(4.0)	482	(3.3)	526	(4.6)	322	(3.4)	366	(3.1)	472	(3.6)	520	(4.5)	312	(3.9)	363	(3.3)	472	(2.9)	522	(3.7)
	Tunisia	m	m	m	m	m	m	m	m	251	(3.8)	310	(3.2)	441	(3.5)	497	(4.3)	252	(5.3)	315	(4.4)	450	(5.0)	502	(5.3)
	Uruguay	m	m	m	m	m	m	m	m	272	(6.0)	355	(4.4)	518	(4.4)	587	(4.5)	253	(5.8)	333	(5.0)	497	(3.8)	565	(4.3)

Note: Values that are statistically significant are indicated in bold (see Annex A3).
StatLink http://dx.doi.org/10.1787/888932343285

[Part 2/2]
Table V.2.3 Percentiles on the reading scale in PISA 2000 and 2009

		PISA 2009								Change in percentiles between 2009 and 2000							
		10th percentile		25th percentile		75th percentile		90th percentile		10th percentile		25th percentile		75th percentile		90th percentile	
		Score	S.E.	Score	S.E.	Score	S.E.	Score	S.E.	Score dif.	S.E.	Score dif.	S.E.	Score dif.	S.E.	Score dif.	S.E.
OECD	Australia	384	(3.1)	450	(2.9)	584	(2.7)	638	(3.2)	-10	(7.3)	-8	(7.2)	**-18**	(7.3)	**-18**	(7.2)
	Austria	m	m	m	m	m	m	m	m	m	m	m	m	m	m	m	m
	Belgium	368	(4.3)	436	(3.8)	583	(2.2)	631	(2.7)	14	(11.0)	-1	(9.1)	-4	(5.9)	-3	(6.2)
	Canada	406	(2.7)	464	(1.9)	588	(1.7)	637	(1.9)	-4	(6.1)	-8	(5.7)	**-12**	(5.4)	**-15**	(5.6)
	Chile	342	(5.0)	393	(4.1)	506	(3.3)	556	(3.6)	**51**	(8.8)	**44**	(7.8)	**35**	(7.1)	**32**	(7.2)
	Czech Republic	357	(4.9)	413	(4.2)	545	(3.3)	598	(3.2)	-11	(8.5)	**-20**	(7.0)	-13	(6.6)	-12	(6.7)
	Denmark	383	(3.7)	440	(2.9)	554	(2.8)	599	(3.0)	**16**	(8.0)	6	(6.6)	-12	(6.3)	**-18**	(6.4)
	Estonia	392	(4.4)	446	(3.3)	559	(2.8)	605	(3.6)	m	m	m	m	m	m	m	m
	Finland	419	(3.6)	481	(2.7)	597	(2.2)	642	(2.6)	-10	(8.0)	-11	(6.3)	-11	(6.0)	-11	(6.2)
	France	352	(7.0)	429	(4.7)	572	(4.0)	624	(3.9)	**-29**	(10.0)	-15	(8.2)	2	(6.8)	6	(6.9)
	Germany	367	(5.1)	432	(4.5)	567	(2.8)	615	(3.2)	**31**	(9.5)	15	(8.1)	5	(6.4)	-5	(6.5)
	Greece	355	(8.0)	420	(6.3)	550	(3.1)	601	(3.7)	13	(12.6)	11	(10.9)	7	(7.4)	7	(8.0)
	Hungary	371	(6.9)	435	(4.3)	559	(3.6)	607	(3.5)	17	(10.1)	**20**	(8.4)	11	(7.6)	9	(7.5)
	Iceland	371	(4.1)	439	(2.9)	567	(2.0)	619	(2.6)	-12	(7.4)	-8	(6.5)	-5	(5.7)	-2	(6.6)
	Ireland	373	(4.7)	435	(3.9)	562	(2.8)	611	(2.8)	**-28**	(9.3)	**-32**	(7.6)	**-31**	(6.7)	**-31**	(7.0)
	Israel	322	(7.8)	401	(4.4)	554	(3.4)	611	(4.0)	17	(15.9)	22	(12.9)	**22**	(10.1)	**25**	(9.5)
	Italy	358	(2.6)	422	(2.3)	556	(1.7)	604	(1.7)	-10	(8.0)	-7	(6.8)	4	(6.1)	3	(5.9)
	Japan	386	(7.1)	459	(4.8)	590	(3.0)	639	(3.6)	-22	(13.0)	-12	(9.8)	9	(7.2)	14	(7.6)
	Korea	435	(5.9)	490	(4.1)	595	(3.4)	635	(3.0)	2	(8.9)	9	(7.0)	**22**	(6.6)	**27**	(6.5)
	Luxembourg	332	(3.6)	403	(2.4)	547	(1.7)	600	(2.0)	m	m	m	m	m	m	m	m
	Mexico	314	(2.9)	370	(2.4)	485	(1.9)	531	(2.2)	3	(6.6)	9	(6.6)	3	(7.1)	-4	(7.7)
	Netherlands	390	(5.0)	442	(6.1)	575	(5.4)	625	(4.6)	m	m	m	m	m	m	m	m
	New Zealand	383	(4.5)	452	(3.1)	595	(2.8)	649	(2.7)	1	(8.5)	-8	(7.1)	-11	(6.4)	-12	(7.2)
	Norway	382	(4.0)	443	(3.6)	568	(2.9)	619	(3.9)	**19**	(8.4)	3	(7.6)	-11	(6.3)	-13	(7.0)
	Poland	382	(4.2)	441	(3.4)	565	(3.2)	613	(3.3)	**39**	(9.4)	**27**	(8.3)	14	(8.4)	9	(8.8)
	Portugal	373	(4.9)	432	(4.4)	551	(3.4)	599	(3.5)	**35**	(9.3)	**29**	(9.2)	10	(7.4)	7	(7.3)
	Slovak Republic	358	(5.2)	416	(4.1)	543	(2.7)	594	(3.2)	m	m	m	m	m	m	m	m
	Slovenia	359	(2.1)	421	(1.9)	550	(1.7)	598	(2.9)	m	m	m	m	m	m	m	m
	Spain	364	(3.5)	426	(3.3)	543	(2.0)	588	(2.0)	-15	(7.8)	-11	(7.5)	-11	(5.9)	-9	(5.9)
	Sweden	368	(5.5)	437	(3.3)	565	(3.2)	620	(3.7)	**-23**	(8.4)	**-20**	(6.7)	**-16**	(6.6)	-10	(6.8)
	Switzerland	374	(4.0)	437	(3.6)	569	(3.0)	617	(3.3)	**19**	(8.6)	11	(8.2)	2	(7.4)	-4	(8.1)
	Turkey	356	(4.3)	409	(3.8)	522	(4.5)	569	(5.2)	m	m	m	m	m	m	m	m
	United Kingdom	370	(3.1)	430	(2.8)	561	(3.2)	616	(2.6)	m	m	m	m	m	m	m	m
	United States	372	(3.9)	433	(4.0)	569	(4.6)	625	(5.0)	9	(13.1)	-3	(10.8)	-8	(9.6)	-11	(9.6)
	OECD average-23	375	(1.0)	438	(0.8)	566	(0.6)	615	(0.6)	1	(5.2)	-1	(5.1)	-3	(5.0)	-4	(5.0)
	OECD average-26	372	(1.0)	435	(0.7)	563	(0.6)	613	(0.6)	4	(5.2)	2	(5.1)	-1	(5.0)	-1	(5.0)
Partners	Albania	254	(5.4)	319	(4.9)	458	(4.8)	509	(4.9)	**38**	(9.7)	**39**	(8.5)	**36**	(7.6)	**33**	(7.5)
	Argentina	257	(8.3)	329	(5.8)	473	(6.3)	535	(7.1)	-14	(15.0)	-15	(15.2)	-22	(11.9)	-19	(12.9)
	Azerbaijan	263	(4.8)	311	(4.3)	413	(4.0)	458	(4.4)	m	m	m	m	m	m	m	m
	Brazil	293	(3.2)	348	(2.7)	474	(3.9)	537	(4.2)	5	(7.4)	9	(6.6)	**22**	(7.2)	**30**	(7.7)
	Bulgaria	276	(7.8)	351	(8.6)	512	(6.5)	572	(7.3)	-19	(11.4)	-9	(11.4)	10	(10.4)	12	(11.5)
	Colombia	302	(5.2)	355	(4.4)	473	(3.9)	524	(4.1)	m	m	m	m	m	m	m	m
	Croatia	359	(3.6)	416	(4.5)	539	(3.1)	586	(3.5)	m	m	m	m	m	m	m	m
	Hong Kong-China	418	(4.5)	482	(3.0)	592	(2.5)	634	(2.9)	5	(9.9)	6	(6.9)	8	(6.2)	11	(6.4)
	Indonesia	315	(5.0)	357	(4.1)	447	(4.6)	487	(5.0)	**38**	(8.1)	**36**	(7.7)	**25**	(8.8)	**24**	(9.8)
	Jordan	284	(5.0)	350	(4.1)	468	(3.5)	515	(3.9)	m	m	m	m	m	m	m	m
	Kyrgyzstan	190	(4.7)	249	(4.1)	377	(4.2)	441	(6.4)	m	m	m	m	m	m	m	m
	Latvia	379	(4.2)	429	(3.8)	541	(3.3)	584	(3.2)	**57**	(10.4)	**39**	(9.3)	11	(7.9)	-2	(8.3)
	Liechtenstein	385	(10.6)	442	(6.5)	560	(4.7)	599	(7.9)	**36**	(16.6)	24	(12.4)	9	(8.9)	-2	(11.7)
	Lithuania	353	(4.2)	409	(3.3)	530	(3.1)	580	(3.4)	m	m	m	m	m	m	m	m
	Macao-China	388	(1.9)	437	(1.4)	540	(1.4)	582	(1.8)	m	m	m	m	m	m	m	m
	Montenegro	288	(3.8)	345	(2.6)	473	(2.4)	526	(2.7)	m	m	m	m	m	m	m	m
	Peru	241	(3.9)	302	(4.3)	437	(5.2)	496	(6.4)	**36**	(8.0)	**43**	(8.4)	**45**	(9.0)	**43**	(9.8)
	Qatar	228	(2.2)	288	(1.4)	450	(1.4)	529	(2.1)	m	m	m	m	m	m	m	m
	Romania	304	(5.7)	365	(6.0)	488	(4.7)	537	(4.0)	9	(9.7)	8	(10.6)	-11	(7.6)	**-22**	(7.3)
	Russian Federation	344	(5.5)	401	(3.6)	519	(3.2)	572	(4.5)	4	(9.2)	1	(7.9)	-7	(7.4)	-7	(8.0)
	Serbia	331	(3.8)	388	(3.2)	501	(2.5)	547	(2.7)	m	m	m	m	m	m	m	m
	Chinese Taipei	380	(3.9)	439	(3.2)	555	(2.9)	600	(4.6)	m	m	m	m	m	m	m	m
	Thailand	331	(3.8)	373	(3.2)	469	(2.6)	514	(4.0)	-2	(7.9)	-8	(7.1)	**-13**	(6.5)	-13	(7.9)
	Tunisia	293	(3.8)	348	(3.4)	462	(3.4)	510	(4.8)	m	m	m	m	m	m	m	m
	Uruguay	297	(4.2)	359	(3.5)	495	(3.1)	552	(3.3)	m	m	m	m	m	m	m	m

Note: Values that are statistically significant are indicated in bold (see Annex A3).
StatLink http://dx.doi.org/10.1787/888932343285

[Part 1/1]

Table V.2.4 Gender differences in reading performance in PISA 2000 and 2009

		PISA 2000						PISA 2009						Change between 2000 and 2009 (PISA 2009 – PISA 2000)					
		Boys		Girls		Difference (B – G)		Boys		Girls		Difference (B – G)		Boys		Girls		Difference (B – G)	
		Mean score	S.E.	Mean score	S.E.	Score dif.	S.E.	Mean score	S.E.	Mean score	S.E.	Score dif.	S.E.	Score dif.	S.E.	Score dif.	S.E.	Score dif.	S.E.
OECD	Australia	513	(4.0)	546	(4.7)	**-34**	(5.4)	496	(2.9)	533	(2.6)	**-37**	(3.1)	**-17**	(7.0)	-13	(7.3)	-3	(6.2)
	Austria	476	(3.6)	509	(4.0)	**-33**	(5.7)	m	m	m	m	m	m	m	m	m	m	m	m
	Belgium	492	(4.2)	525	(4.9)	**-33**	(6.0)	493	(3.4)	520	(2.9)	**-27**	(4.4)	0	(7.3)	-5	(7.6)	6	(7.4)
	Canada	519	(1.8)	551	(1.7)	**-32**	(1.6)	507	(1.8)	542	(1.7)	**-34**	(1.9)	**-12**	(5.5)	-10	(5.5)	-2	(2.5)
	Chile	396	(4.3)	421	(4.6)	**-25**	(5.6)	439	(3.9)	461	(3.6)	**-22**	(4.1)	**42**	(7.6)	**40**	(7.6)	3	(6.9)
	Czech Republic	473	(4.1)	510	(2.5)	**-37**	(4.7)	456	(3.7)	504	(3.0)	**-48**	(4.1)	**-17**	(7.4)	-6	(6.3)	-11	(6.2)
	Denmark	485	(3.0)	510	(2.9)	**-25**	(3.3)	480	(2.5)	509	(2.5)	**-29**	(2.9)	-5	(6.3)	-1	(6.2)	-4	(4.4)
	Finland	520	(3.0)	571	(2.8)	**-51**	(2.6)	508	(2.6)	563	(2.4)	**-55**	(2.3)	-12	(6.3)	-8	(6.2)	-4	(3.5)
	France	490	(3.5)	519	(2.7)	**-29**	(3.4)	475	(4.3)	515	(3.4)	**-40**	(3.7)	**-15**	(7.4)	-4	(6.6)	**-11**	(5.0)
	Germany	468	(3.2)	502	(3.9)	**-35**	(5.2)	478	(3.6)	518	(2.9)	**-40**	(3.9)	10	(6.9)	**15**	(6.9)	-5	(6.5)
	Greece	456	(6.1)	493	(4.6)	**-37**	(5.0)	459	(5.5)	506	(3.5)	**-47**	(4.3)	3	(9.6)	13	(7.6)	-10	(6.6)
	Hungary	465	(5.3)	496	(4.3)	**-32**	(5.7)	475	(3.9)	513	(3.6)	**-38**	(4.0)	11	(8.3)	**17**	(7.5)	-6	(7.0)
	Iceland	488	(2.1)	528	(2.1)	**-40**	(3.1)	478	(2.1)	522	(1.9)	**-44**	(2.8)	-10	(5.8)	-6	(5.7)	-4	(4.2)
	Ireland	513	(4.2)	542	(3.6)	**-29**	(4.6)	476	(4.2)	515	(3.1)	**-39**	(4.7)	**-37**	(7.7)	**-26**	(6.8)	-11	(6.6)
	Israel	444	(10.9)	459	(8.1)	-16	(9.1)	452	(5.2)	495	(3.4)	**-42**	(5.2)	9	(13.1)	**35**	(10.1)	**-27**	(10.5)
	Italy	469	(5.1)	507	(3.6)	**-38**	(7.0)	464	(2.3)	510	(1.9)	**-46**	(2.8)	-5	(7.5)	2	(6.4)	-8	(7.6)
	Japan	507	(6.7)	537	(5.4)	**-30**	(6.4)	501	(5.6)	540	(3.7)	**-39**	(6.8)	-6	(10.0)	3	(8.2)	-9	(9.3)
	Korea	519	(3.8)	533	(3.7)	**-14**	(6.0)	523	(4.9)	558	(3.8)	**-35**	(5.9)	4	(7.9)	**25**	(7.3)	**-21**	(8.4)
	Luxembourg	m	m	m	m	m	m	453	(1.9)	492	(1.5)	**-39**	(2.3)	m	m	m	m	m	m
	Mexico	411	(4.2)	432	(3.8)	**-20**	(4.3)	413	(2.1)	438	(2.1)	**-25**	(1.6)	1	(6.8)	6	(6.6)	-5	(4.6)
	Netherlands	m	m	m	m	m	m	496	(5.1)	521	(5.3)	**-24**	(2.4)	m	m	m	m	m	m
	New Zealand	507	(4.2)	553	(3.8)	**-46**	(6.3)	499	(3.6)	544	(2.6)	**-46**	(4.3)	-8	(7.4)	-8	(6.8)	0	(7.6)
	Norway	486	(3.8)	529	(2.9)	**-43**	(4.0)	480	(3.0)	527	(2.9)	**-47**	(2.9)	-5	(6.9)	-1	(6.4)	-4	(5.0)
	Poland	461	(6.0)	497	(5.5)	**-36**	(7.0)	476	(2.8)	525	(2.9)	**-50**	(2.5)	14	(8.2)	**28**	(8.0)	-14	(7.4)
	Portugal	458	(5.0)	482	(4.6)	**-25**	(3.8)	470	(3.5)	508	(2.9)	**-38**	(2.4)	12	(7.8)	**26**	(7.4)	**-13**	(4.5)
	Spain	481	(3.4)	505	(2.8)	**-24**	(3.2)	467	(2.2)	496	(2.2)	**-29**	(2.0)	**-14**	(6.4)	-10	(6.1)	-5	(3.8)
	Sweden	499	(2.6)	536	(2.5)	**-37**	(2.7)	475	(3.2)	521	(3.1)	**-46**	(2.7)	**-24**	(6.4)	**-15**	(6.3)	**-9**	(3.8)
	Switzerland	480	(4.9)	510	(4.5)	**-30**	(4.2)	481	(2.9)	520	(2.7)	**-39**	(2.5)	1	(7.5)	10	(7.2)	-9	(4.9)
	United Kingdom	m	m	m	m	m	m	481	(3.5)	507	(2.9)	**-25**	(4.5)	m	m	m	m	m	m
	United States	490	(8.4)	518	(6.2)	**-29**	(4.1)	488	(4.2)	513	(3.8)	**-25**	(3.4)	-2	(10.6)	-6	(8.8)	4	(5.3)
	OECD average-26	480	(1.0)	512	(0.8)	**-32**	(1.0)	477	(0.7)	516	(0.6)	**-39**	(0.7)	-3	(5.1)	4	(5.0)	**-7**	(1.2)
Partners	Albania	319	(4.2)	378	(2.7)	**-58**	(3.8)	355	(5.1)	417	(3.9)	**-62**	(4.4)	**35**	(8.3)	**39**	(6.9)	-4	(5.8)
	Argentina	393	(7.7)	437	(12.3)	**-44**	(10.7)	379	(5.1)	415	(4.9)	**-37**	(3.8)	-15	(10.5)	-22	(14.1)	8	(11.3)
	Brazil	388	(3.9)	404	(3.4)	**-17**	(4.0)	397	(2.9)	425	(2.8)	**-29**	(1.7)	9	(6.9)	**21**	(6.6)	**-12**	(4.3)
	Bulgaria	407	(4.9)	455	(6.3)	**-47**	(5.6)	400	(7.3)	461	(5.8)	**-61**	(4.7)	-8	(10.1)	6	(9.9)	-14	(7.3)
	Hong Kong-China	518	(4.8)	533	(3.6)	**-16**	(6.1)	518	(3.3)	550	(2.8)	**-33**	(4.4)	0	(7.6)	**17**	(6.7)	**-17**	(7.5)
	Indonesia	360	(3.7)	380	(4.6)	**-20**	(3.4)	383	(3.8)	420	(3.9)	**-37**	(3.3)	**23**	(7.2)	**39**	(7.8)	**-16**	(4.7)
	Latvia	432	(5.5)	485	(5.4)	**-53**	(4.2)	460	(3.4)	507	(3.1)	**-47**	(3.2)	**28**	(8.2)	**23**	(7.9)	5	(5.3)
	Liechtenstein	468	(7.3)	500	(6.8)	**-31**	(11.5)	484	(4.5)	516	(4.5)	**-32**	(7.1)	16	(9.9)	17	(9.5)	-1	(13.5)
	Peru	324	(6.3)	330	(5.3)	-7	(7.5)	359	(4.2)	381	(4.9)	**-22**	(4.7)	**35**	(9.0)	**50**	(8.8)	-16	(8.9)
	Romania	421	(4.3)	434	(4.2)	**-14**	(4.9)	403	(4.6)	445	(4.3)	**-43**	(4.4)	**-18**	(8.0)	11	(7.8)	**-29**	(6.5)
	Russian Federation	443	(4.5)	481	(4.1)	**-38**	(2.9)	437	(3.6)	482	(3.4)	**-45**	(2.7)	-6	(7.6)	1	(7.3)	-6	(4.0)
	Thailand	406	(3.9)	448	(3.1)	**-41**	(3.8)	400	(3.3)	438	(3.1)	**-38**	(3.8)	-6	(7.1)	-10	(6.6)	4	(5.3)

Note: Values that are statistically significant are indicated in bold (see Annex A3).
StatLink http://dx.doi.org/10.1787/888932343285

[Part 1/1]

Table V.2.5 **Percentage of boys below Level 2 and at Level 5 or above on the reading scale in PISA 2000 and 2009**

		Boys – Proficiency levels in PISA 2000				Boys – Proficiency levels in PISA 2009				Change between 2000 and 2009 (PISA 2009 – PISA 2000)			
		Below Level 2 (less than 407 score points)		Level 5 or above (above 626 score points)		Below Level 2 (less than 407 score points)		Level 5 or above (above 626 score points)		Below Level 2 (less than 407 score points)		Level 5 or above (above 626 score points)	
		%	S.E.	%	S.E.	%	S.E.	%	S.E.	% dif.	S.E.	% dif.	S.E.
OECD	Australia	16.0	(1.3)	14.2	(1.1)	19.7	(0.8)	9.8	(0.8)	**3.7**	(1.6)	**-4.4**	(1.3)
	Austria	23.8	(1.5)	5.1	(0.7)	m	m	m	m	m	m	m	m
	Belgium	22.8	(1.4)	9.9	(0.9)	21.5	(1.3)	9.4	(0.8)	-1.3	(1.9)	-0.5	(1.2)
	Canada	12.7	(0.6)	12.8	(0.6)	14.5	(0.7)	9.4	(0.5)	1.8	(0.9)	**-3.5**	(0.8)
	Chile	53.6	(2.2)	0.4	(0.2)	36.1	(2.0)	1.0	(0.4)	**-17.5**	(3.0)	0.7	(0.4)
	Czech Republic	23.6	(1.6)	5.3	(0.7)	30.8	(1.9)	2.8	(0.4)	**7.2**	(2.5)	**-2.6**	(0.8)
	Denmark	21.8	(1.3)	6.8	(0.7)	19.0	(1.3)	3.2	(0.5)	-2.7	(1.8)	**-3.6**	(0.9)
	Finland	11.0	(0.9)	11.0	(0.9)	13.0	(0.9)	8.1	(0.8)	2.0	(1.3)	**-2.9**	(1.2)
	France	19.9	(1.5)	6.4	(0.7)	25.7	(1.7)	6.9	(0.8)	**5.7**	(2.3)	0.5	(1.1)
	Germany	26.6	(1.2)	6.7	(0.8)	24.0	(1.5)	4.4	(0.5)	-2.6	(1.9)	**-2.3**	(0.9)
	Greece	30.9	(2.7)	3.6	(0.7)	29.7	(2.4)	3.4	(0.6)	-1.1	(3.6)	-0.2	(1.0)
	Hungary	27.2	(2.2)	3.5	(0.8)	23.6	(1.8)	3.9	(0.7)	-3.6	(2.9)	0.3	(1.0)
	Iceland	20.1	(1.1)	6.4	(0.9)	23.8	(1.0)	5.6	(0.6)	**3.8**	(1.5)	-0.8	(1.1)
	Ireland	13.5	(1.3)	11.2	(1.1)	23.1	(1.7)	4.5	(0.6)	**9.6**	(2.1)	**-6.7**	(1.3)
	Israel	36.5	(4.0)	4.2	(1.1)	34.1	(1.6)	6.3	(0.9)	-2.4	(4.4)	2.2	(1.4)
	Italy	24.6	(2.1)	3.7	(0.6)	28.9	(0.9)	3.9	(0.3)	4.3	(2.3)	0.1	(0.7)
	Japan	14.2	(2.3)	7.5	(1.3)	18.9	(1.8)	10.1	(1.1)	4.6	(3.0)	2.6	(1.6)
	Korea	7.3	(1.1)	4.4	(0.6)	8.8	(1.4)	9.3	(1.2)	1.5	(1.7)	**4.9**	(1.4)
	Luxembourg	m	m	m	m	32.8	(1.1)	3.7	(0.5)	m	m	m	m
	Mexico	49.8	(2.0)	0.8	(0.3)	46.2	(1.1)	0.3	(0.1)	-3.6	(2.3)	-0.5	(0.3)
	Netherlands	m	m	m	m	17.9	(1.9)	7.8	(1.0)	m	m	m	m
	New Zealand	18.5	(1.4)	13.7	(1.2)	20.6	(1.2)	11.9	(1.1)	2.2	(1.8)	-1.8	(1.6)
	Norway	23.2	(1.6)	8.1	(0.8)	21.4	(1.2)	5.0	(0.8)	-1.8	(2.0)	**-3.1**	(1.2)
	Poland	30.3	(2.5)	4.1	(0.8)	22.6	(1.2)	4.3	(0.6)	**-7.7**	(2.8)	0.2	(1.0)
	Portugal	31.3	(2.2)	3.8	(0.6)	24.7	(1.6)	3.3	(0.5)	**-6.6**	(2.7)	-0.5	(0.7)
	Spain	20.4	(1.4)	3.6	(0.7)	24.4	(1.0)	2.4	(0.3)	**4.0**	(1.7)	-1.2	(0.8)
	Sweden	16.8	(1.0)	7.4	(0.8)	24.2	(1.3)	6.0	(0.6)	**7.3**	(1.7)	-1.4	(1.1)
	Switzerland	24.6	(1.8)	7.3	(0.9)	22.0	(1.2)	5.1	(0.6)	-2.6	(2.1)	-2.1	(1.1)
	United Kingdom	m	m	m	m	23.1	(1.2)	6.9	(0.7)	m	m	m	m
	United States	23.0	(3.0)	11.0	(1.6)	21.4	(1.4)	8.2	(1.0)	-1.6	(3.3)	-2.8	(1.9)
	OECD average-26	23.8	(0.4)	6.8	(0.2)	24.0	(0.3)	5.7	(0.1)	0.1	(0.5)	**-1.1**	(0.2)
Partners	Albania	80.6	(1.2)	0.1	(0.1)	69.0	(2.4)	0.0	c	**-11.6**	(2.7)	c	c
	Argentina	53.3	(3.4)	0.9	(0.4)	58.8	(2.1)	0.7	(0.2)	5.6	(4.0)	-0.2	(0.4)
	Brazil	59.5	(1.9)	0.4	(0.2)	56.5	(1.4)	1.0	(0.2)	-3.0	(2.4)	0.5	(0.3)
	Bulgaria	50.3	(2.4)	1.2	(0.4)	52.0	(3.0)	1.5	(0.5)	1.7	(3.8)	0.2	(0.6)
	Hong Kong-China	11.9	(1.5)	9.0	(1.1)	11.3	(1.2)	8.9	(1.0)	-0.6	(1.9)	-0.1	(1.5)
	Indonesia	74.5	(2.4)	0.0	c	65.5	(2.3)	0.0	c	**-9.0**	(3.3)	c	c
	Latvia	40.3	(2.5)	2.5	(0.5)	26.6	(1.8)	1.6	(0.4)	**-13.7**	(3.1)	-0.9	(0.7)
	Liechtenstein	27.1	(3.9)	3.9	(1.9)	21.2	(3.3)	3.1	(1.5)	-5.9	(5.1)	-0.8	(2.4)
	Peru	80.7	(2.3)	0.1	(0.2)	69.7	(1.8)	0.6	(0.3)	**-11.0**	(2.9)	0.4	(0.3)
	Romania	44.2	(2.2)	2.0	(0.4)	50.7	(2.5)	0.3	(0.2)	**6.5**	(3.3)	**-1.7**	(0.4)
	Russian Federation	35.1	(1.9)	2.3	(0.5)	36.3	(1.8)	1.7	(0.4)	1.2	(2.7)	-0.6	(0.6)
	Thailand	51.1	(2.1)	0.3	(0.2)	55.5	(1.9)	0.1	(0.1)	4.4	(2.9)	-0.2	(0.2)

Note: Values that are statistically significant are indicated in bold (see Annex A3).
StatLink http://dx.doi.org/10.1787/888932343285

[Part 1/1]

Table V.2.6 Percentage of girls below Level 2 and at Level 5 or above on the reading scale in PISA 2000 and 2009

		Girls – Proficiency levels in PISA 2000				Girls – Proficiency levels in PISA 2009				Change between 2000 and 2009 (PISA 2009 – PISA 2000)			
		Below Level 2 (less than 407 score points)		Level 5 or above (above 626 score points)		Below Level 2 (less than 407 score points)		Level 5 or above (above 626 score points)		Below Level 2 (less than 407 score points)		Level 5 or above (above 626 score points)	
		%	S.E.	%	S.E.	%	S.E.	%	S.E.	% dif.	S.E.	% dif.	S.E.
OECD	Australia	8.4	(0.9)	21.6	(2.0)	9.1	(0.6)	15.6	(0.9)	0.7	(1.1)	**-6.0**	(2.2)
	Austria	14.6	(1.0)	10.0	(1.1)	m	m	m	m	m	m	m	m
	Belgium	14.1	(1.7)	14.5	(1.0)	13.8	(1.0)	13.0	(0.8)	-0.3	(2.0)	-1.5	(1.3)
	Canada	6.0	(0.4)	21.0	(0.7)	6.0	(0.4)	16.2	(0.7)	0.0	(0.6)	**-4.8**	(1.0)
	Chile	43.4	(2.3)	0.6	(0.2)	24.8	(1.5)	1.6	(0.4)	**-18.6**	(2.7)	**0.9**	(0.4)
	Czech Republic	11.5	(0.8)	8.6	(0.7)	14.3	(1.2)	7.8	(0.8)	2.8	(1.4)	-0.8	(1.1)
	Denmark	13.3	(1.0)	9.6	(0.9)	11.5	(0.9)	6.2	(0.6)	-1.9	(1.4)	**-3.4**	(1.1)
	Finland	3.2	(0.7)	25.5	(1.4)	3.2	(0.5)	20.9	(1.1)	0.0	(0.8)	**-4.6**	(1.7)
	France	10.5	(1.1)	10.5	(0.8)	14.1	(1.0)	12.1	(1.3)	**3.6**	(1.5)	1.6	(1.5)
	Germany	18.2	(1.4)	11.1	(0.8)	12.7	(1.1)	11.0	(1.0)	**-5.5**	(1.8)	-0.1	(1.3)
	Greece	17.7	(2.0)	6.4	(0.9)	13.2	(1.4)	7.7	(0.9)	-4.5	(2.5)	1.3	(1.2)
	Hungary	17.9	(1.7)	6.7	(1.0)	11.4	(1.5)	8.3	(1.0)	**-6.6**	(2.3)	1.6	(1.4)
	Iceland	8.0	(0.8)	11.9	(0.9)	9.9	(0.8)	11.4	(0.9)	1.9	(1.1)	-0.5	(1.3)
	Ireland	8.3	(1.1)	17.4	(1.2)	11.2	(1.0)	9.5	(0.9)	3.0	(1.5)	**-7.9**	(1.5)
	Israel	30.6	(3.1)	4.2	(1.0)	19.3	(1.3)	8.5	(0.8)	**-11.3**	(3.4)	**4.3**	(1.3)
	Italy	12.6	(1.4)	7.0	(0.7)	12.7	(0.7)	7.9	(0.5)	0.1	(1.5)	0.8	(0.8)
	Japan	6.0	(1.2)	12.1	(1.4)	8.0	(1.0)	16.9	(1.4)	2.0	(1.5)	**4.8**	(2.0)
	Korea	3.7	(0.7)	7.4	(1.0)	2.4	(0.5)	16.9	(1.6)	-1.3	(0.9)	**9.5**	(1.9)
	Luxembourg	m	m	m	m	19.1	(0.9)	7.7	(0.7)	m	m	m	m
	Mexico	38.9	(2.1)	0.9	(0.3)	34.1	(1.1)	0.5	(0.1)	**-4.8**	(2.3)	-0.4	(0.3)
	Netherlands	m	m	m	m	10.8	(1.4)	11.8	(1.3)	m	m	m	m
	New Zealand	8.3	(0.7)	24.0	(1.5)	7.8	(0.7)	19.7	(1.1)	-0.5	(1.0)	**-4.3**	(1.9)
	Norway	10.4	(1.0)	14.7	(1.0)	8.3	(0.8)	12.0	(1.3)	-2.1	(1.3)	-2.8	(1.6)
	Poland	15.9	(1.7)	7.7	(1.3)	7.4	(0.8)	10.1	(0.9)	**-8.4**	(1.9)	2.4	(1.6)
	Portugal	21.2	(1.9)	4.6	(0.7)	10.8	(1.1)	6.2	(0.8)	**-10.4**	(2.2)	1.6	(1.1)
	Spain	11.5	(1.1)	4.9	(0.5)	14.6	(0.9)	4.3	(0.3)	**3.1**	(1.5)	-0.6	(0.6)
	Sweden	7.8	(0.8)	15.1	(1.1)	10.5	(1.0)	12.2	(1.0)	**2.7**	(1.2)	**-2.9**	(1.5)
	Switzerland	15.7	(1.3)	11.3	(1.4)	11.4	(0.8)	11.2	(1.1)	**-4.3**	(1.5)	-0.1	(1.8)
	United Kingdom	m	m	m	m	14.0	(0.9)	9.1	(0.8)	m	m	m	m
	United States	13.1	(1.7)	13.4	(1.6)	13.6	(1.1)	11.6	(1.2)	0.5	(2.0)	-1.8	(2.0)
	OECD average-26	14.5	(0.3)	11.3	(0.2)	12.2	(0.2)	10.7	(0.2)	**-2.3**	(0.3)	-0.5	(0.3)
Partners	Albania	60.4	(1.4)	0.1	(0.1)	43.6	(2.2)	0.3	(0.2)	**-16.8**	(2.6)	0.3	(0.2)
	Argentina	36.7	(5.6)	2.3	(0.8)	45.3	(2.1)	1.2	(0.4)	8.6	(6.0)	-1.1	(0.9)
	Brazil	52.1	(2.0)	0.7	(0.3)	43.4	(1.3)	1.6	(0.3)	**-8.7**	(2.4)	**0.9**	(0.4)
	Bulgaria	29.8	(2.3)	3.3	(1.0)	29.2	(2.2)	4.2	(0.7)	-0.6	(3.2)	0.9	(1.2)
	Hong Kong-China	6.3	(1.0)	10.1	(1.2)	4.9	(0.7)	16.4	(1.0)	-1.4	(1.2)	**6.3**	(1.6)
	Indonesia	63.1	(2.9)	0.0	c	41.6	(2.6)	0.0	c	**-21.5**	(3.9)	c	c
	Latvia	19.7	(1.8)	5.8	(1.0)	8.8	(1.2)	4.3	(0.6)	**-10.9**	(2.1)	-1.6	(1.2)
	Liechtenstein	15.8	(3.2)	6.4	(2.6)	9.4	(2.0)	6.4	(2.3)	-6.4	(3.8)	0.0	(3.4)
	Peru	78.3	(2.0)	0.1	(0.1)	59.8	(2.2)	0.4	(0.2)	**-18.5**	(3.0)	0.3	(0.2)
	Romania	38.6	(1.9)	2.4	(0.4)	30.4	(2.2)	1.1	(0.3)	**-8.2**	(2.8)	**-1.3**	(0.5)
	Russian Federation	19.6	(1.6)	4.1	(0.6)	18.6	(1.3)	4.6	(0.8)	-1.0	(2.1)	0.5	(1.0)
	Thailand	27.3	(1.6)	0.6	(0.2)	33.3	(1.9)	0.4	(0.2)	**6.0**	(2.5)	-0.2	(0.3)

Note: Values that are statistically significant are indicated in bold (see Annex A3).
StatLink http://dx.doi.org/10.1787/888932343285

[Part 1/1]

Table V.2.7 Trends in reading performance adjusted for demographic changes

		Adjusted PISA 2000 results		Adjusted PISA 2003 results		Adjusted PISA 2006 results		Original PISA 2009 results		Change between 2000 and 2009 (PISA 2009 – PISA 2000)		
		Mean score	S.E.	Mean score	S.E.	Mean score	S.E.	Mean score	S.E.	Score dif.	S.E.	p-value
OECD	Australia	535	(2.7)	526	(1.6)	511	(1.6)	515	(2.3)	**-20.2**	(6.1)	0.00
	Austria	491	(2.4)	488	(2.9)	486	(3.9)	m	m	m	m	m
	Belgium	508	(3.4)	506	(2.0)	501	(2.7)	506	(2.3)	-1.8	(6.4)	0.78
	Canada	529	(1.4)	530	(1.5)	527	(2.1)	524	(1.5)	-4.6	(5.3)	0.39
	Chile	410	(2.6)	m	m	447	(3.5)	449	(3.1)	**39.4**	(6.4)	0.00
	Czech Republic	489	(2.0)	482	(3.1)	483	(3.7)	478	(2.9)	-10.6	(6.0)	0.08
	Denmark	498	(1.9)	496	(2.2)	494	(2.8)	495	(2.1)	-3.4	(5.7)	0.55
	Estonia	m	m	m	m	504	(2.8)	501	(2.6)	m	m	m
	Finland	555	(2.2)	546	(1.5)	550	(2.0)	536	(2.3)	**-18.9**	(5.8)	0.00
	France	504	(2.1)	491	(2.2)	488	(3.7)	496	(3.4)	-8.7	(6.4)	0.17
	Germany	480	(2.4)	491	(2.8)	489	(3.5)	497	(2.7)	**17.6**	(6.1)	0.00
	Greece	473	(4.4)	475	(3.2)	462	(3.2)	483	(4.3)	9.8	(7.9)	0.22
	Hungary	484	(2.6)	481	(1.9)	481	(2.7)	494	(3.2)	10.6	(6.4)	0.10
	Iceland	510	(1.4)	495	(1.5)	486	(2.0)	500	(1.4)	-10.0	(5.3)	0.06
	Ireland	530	(2.9)	516	(2.0)	516	(2.9)	496	(3.0)	**-34.6**	(6.5)	0.00
	Israel	445	(8.1)	m	m	430	(4.4)	474	(3.6)	**29.3**	(10.2)	0.00
	Italy	483	(2.7)	474	(3.0)	467	(2.2)	486	(1.6)	2.7	(5.8)	0.65
	Japan	521	(5.1)	493	(3.6)	495	(3.5)	520	(3.5)	-0.7	(7.9)	0.93
	Korea	530	(2.0)	538	(2.6)	553	(3.2)	539	(3.5)	9.8	(6.3)	0.12
	Luxembourg	m	m	479	(1.6)	479	(1.4)	472	(1.3)	m	m	m
	Mexico	422	(2.3)	399	(2.5)	410	(2.1)	425	(2.0)	3.6	(5.8)	0.53
	Netherlands	m	m	515	(2.4)	505	(2.5)	508	(5.1)	m	m	m
	New Zealand	525	(2.1)	518	(2.0)	515	(2.5)	521	(2.4)	-4.6	(5.9)	0.43
	Norway	506	(2.4)	499	(2.6)	486	(2.9)	503	(2.6)	-3.2	(6.1)	0.60
	Poland	478	(4.0)	494	(2.4)	509	(2.4)	500	(2.6)	**22.6**	(6.8)	0.00
	Portugal	471	(3.3)	479	(3.0)	480	(2.6)	489	(3.1)	**18.6**	(6.7)	0.01
	Slovak Republic	m	m	466	(2.0)	469	(2.7)	477	(2.5)	m	m	m
	Slovenia	m	m	m	m	494	(1.0)	483	(1.0)	m	m	m
	Spain	495	(2.0)	479	(2.2)	462	(1.7)	481	(2.0)	**-14.4**	(5.7)	0.01
	Sweden	516	(1.7)	517	(1.8)	507	(3.2)	497	(2.9)	**-18.4**	(6.0)	0.00
	Switzerland	495	(3.2)	502	(2.3)	501	(2.6)	501	(2.4)	5.3	(6.4)	0.40
	Turkey	m	m	433	(3.6)	449	(3.5)	464	(3.5)	m	m	m
	United Kingdom	m	m	m	m	492	(2.0)	494	(2.3)	m	m	m
	United States	497	(4.5)	486	(2.6)	m	m	500	(3.7)	2.9	(7.6)	0.71
	OECD average-23	502	(0.6)	497	(0.5)	494	(0.6)	499	(0.6)	-2.3	(5.0)	0.64
	OECD average-26	496	(0.6)	m	m	m	m	496	(0.5)	0.7	(5.0)	0.89
Partners	Albania	336	(2.8)	m	m	m	m	385	(4.0)	**48.3**	(7.0)	0.00
	Argentina	411	(7.1)	m	m	374	(5.1)	398	(4.6)	-12.6	(9.8)	0.20
	Azerbaijan	m	m	m	m	352	(3.4)	362	(3.3)	m	m	m
	Brazil	393	(2.6)	399	(3.9)	395	(3.5)	412	(2.7)	**18.3**	(6.2)	0.00
	Bulgaria	416	(3.2)	m	m	407	(4.7)	429	(6.7)	12.6	(8.9)	0.16
	Colombia	m	m	m	m	384	(4.1)	413	(3.7)	m	m	m
	Croatia	m	m	m	m	476	(2.6)	476	(2.9)	m	m	m
	Hong Kong-China	523	(2.9)	510	(3.2)	534	(2.3)	533	(2.1)	10.6	(6.1)	0.08
	Indonesia	369	(3.2)	377	(2.8)	392	(5.1)	402	(3.7)	**32.7**	(7.0)	0.00
	Jordan	m	m	m	m	398	(2.8)	405	(3.3)	m	m	m
	Kyrgyzstan	m	m	m	m	289	(3.1)	314	(3.2)	m	m	m
	Latvia	452	(5.4)	487	(3.3)	479	(3.2)	484	(3.0)	**31.5**	(7.9)	0.00
	Liechtenstein	477	(7.2)	522	(6.9)	509	(4.3)	499	(2.8)	**22.4**	(9.2)	0.01
	Lithuania	m	m	m	m	469	(2.6)	468	(2.4)	m	m	m
	Macao-China	m	m	499	(2.1)	482	(7.8)	487	(0.9)	m	m	m
	Montenegro	m	m	m	m	395	(1.9)	408	(1.7)	m	m	m
	Peru	323	(3.2)	m	m	m	m	370	(4.0)	**47.0**	(7.1)	0.00
	Qatar	m	m	m	m	319	(1.2)	372	(0.8)	m	m	m
	Romania	434	(4.0)	m	m	397	(3.8)	424	(4.1)	-9.7	(7.5)	0.20
	Russian Federation	472	(3.1)	441	(3.3)	440	(3.2)	459	(3.3)	-12.1	(6.7)	0.07
	Serbia	m	m	414	(2.6)	402	(2.7)	442	(2.4)	m	m	m
	Chinese Taipei	m	m	m	m	505	(3.5)	495	(2.6)	m	m	m
	Thailand	435	(2.9)	421	(2.4)	420	(2.2)	421	(2.6)	**-13.7**	(6.3)	0.03
	Tunisia	m	m	357	(9.0)	377	(3.1)	404	(2.9)	m	m	m
	Uruguay	m	m	418	(3.2)	406	(3.2)	426	(2.6)	m	m	m

Note: Values that are statistically significant are indicated in bold (see Annex A3).
StatLink http://dx.doi.org/10.1787/888932343285

[Part 1/1]

Table V.2.8 Linear trends and annual changes in reading performance across all PISA assessments

		Number of years for which PISA results are available	Score change associated with one year[1]					
			Observed linear trend		Annualised observed change between 2000 and 2009, 2003 and 2009 or 2006 and 2009		Annualised observed change between 2000 and 2009, 2003 and 2009 or 2006 and 2009 adjusted for demographic differences	
			Score dif.	S.E.	Score dif.	S.E.	Score dif.	S.E.
OECD	Australia	9	**-1.8**	(0.7)	**-1.5**	(0.7)	**-2.2**	(0.7)
	Austria	6	m	m	m	m	m	m
	Belgium	9	-0.3	(0.7)	-0.1	(0.7)	-0.2	(0.7)
	Canada	9	-1.0	(0.6)	-1.1	(0.6)	-0.5	(0.6)
	Chile	8	**5.1**	(0.8)	**5.0**	(0.9)	**4.9**	(0.8)
	Czech Republic	9	**-1.5**	(0.7)	**-1.5**	(0.7)	-1.2	(0.7)
	Denmark	9	-0.1	(0.6)	-0.2	(0.6)	-0.4	(0.6)
	Estonia	3	0.1	(2.7)	0.1	(1.9)	-0.9	(1.9)
	Finland	9	-0.9	(0.6)	-1.2	(0.7)	**-2.1**	(0.6)
	France	9	-1.2	(0.7)	-1.0	(0.7)	-1.0	(0.7)
	Germany	9	**1.5**	(0.7)	**1.5**	(0.7)	**2.0**	(0.7)
	Greece	9	0.5	(0.9)	1.0	(0.9)	1.1	(0.9)
	Hungary	9	1.4	(0.7)	**1.6**	(0.8)	1.2	(0.7)
	Iceland	9	-0.9	(0.6)	-0.7	(0.6)	-1.1	(0.6)
	Ireland	9	**-3.0**	(0.7)	**-3.4**	(0.7)	**-3.8**	(0.7)
	Israel	8	2.2	(1.4)	**2.7**	(1.3)	**3.7**	(1.3)
	Italy	9	-0.4	(0.7)	-0.2	(0.7)	0.3	(0.6)
	Japan	9	-0.2	(0.9)	-0.3	(0.9)	-0.1	(0.9)
	Korea	9	**2.2**	(0.7)	**1.6**	(0.7)	1.1	(0.7)
	Luxembourg	6	-1.2	(1.2)	-1.2	(0.8)	-1.1	(0.8)
	Mexico	9	0.7	(0.8)	0.4	(0.7)	0.4	(0.6)
	Netherlands	6	-0.8	(1.6)	-0.8	(1.2)	-1.0	(1.2)
	New Zealand	9	-0.8	(0.7)	-0.9	(0.7)	-0.5	(0.7)
	Norway	9	-0.7	(0.5)	-0.2	(0.7)	-0.4	(0.7)
	Poland	9	**2.5**	(0.7)	**2.4**	(0.8)	**2.5**	(0.8)
	Portugal	9	**1.7**	(0.8)	**2.1**	(0.8)	**2.1**	(0.7)
	Slovak Republic	6	1.4	(1.4)	1.4	(1.0)	**1.9**	(0.9)
	Slovenia	3	-3.8	(2.4)	**-3.8**	(1.4)	**-3.8**	(1.4)
	Spain	9	**-1.8**	(0.7)	-1.3	(0.7)	**-1.6**	(0.6)
	Sweden	9	**-2.1**	(0.7)	**-2.1**	(0.7)	**-2.0**	(0.7)
	Switzerland	9	0.6	(0.8)	0.7	(0.8)	0.6	(0.7)
	Turkey	6	**3.9**	(1.7)	**3.9**	(1.3)	**5.3**	(1.1)
	United Kingdom	3	-0.3	(2.5)	-0.3	(1.7)	0.8	(1.7)
	United States	9	-0.3	(1.0)	-0.5	(1.0)	0.3	(0.8)
	OECD average-26	9	0.0	(0.6)	0.1	(0.6)	0.1	(0.6)
	OECD average-33	9	0.0	(0.6)	0.1	(0.6)	0.1	(0.6)
Partners	Albania	8	**4.5**	(0.9)	**4.5**	(0.9)	**6.0**	(0.9)
	Argentina	8	**-3.2**	(1.5)	-2.5	(1.5)	-1.6	(1.2)
	Azerbaijan	3	2.9	(2.8)	2.9	(2.0)	3.0	(2.1)
	Brazil	9	1.2	(0.7)	**1.7**	(0.7)	**2.0**	(0.7)
	Bulgaria	8	-0.7	(1.1)	-0.2	(1.2)	1.6	(1.1)
	Colombia	3	**9.3**	(3.1)	**9.3**	(2.5)	**9.6**	(2.3)
	Croatia	3	-0.5	(2.7)	-0.5	(1.9)	0.0	(1.9)
	Hong Kong-China	8	**2.0**	(0.8)	1.0	(0.8)	1.3	(0.8)
	Indonesia	8	**3.8**	(0.9)	**3.9**	(0.9)	**4.1**	(0.9)
	Jordan	3	1.5	(2.8)	1.5	(2.1)	2.2	(2.0)
	Kyrgyzstan	3	**9.8**	(2.9)	**9.8**	(2.1)	**8.3**	(2.0)
	Latvia	9	**2.2**	(0.9)	**2.9**	(0.9)	**3.5**	(0.9)
	Liechtenstein	9	1.2	(0.8)	**1.9**	(0.8)	**2.5**	(1.0)
	Lithuania	3	-0.5	(2.7)	-0.5	(1.9)	-0.1	(1.8)
	Macao-China	6	-1.8	(1.3)	**-1.8**	(0.8)	**-2.0**	(0.8)
	Montenegro	3	**5.2**	(2.4)	**5.2**	(1.5)	**4.1**	(1.6)
	Peru	8	**5.3**	(1.0)	**5.3**	(1.0)	**5.9**	(0.9)
	Qatar	3	**19.8**	(2.4)	**19.8**	(1.4)	**17.6**	(1.4)
	Romania	7	-0.9	(1.0)	-0.5	(1.0)	-1.4	(1.1)
	Russian Federation	9	-0.3	(0.8)	-0.3	(0.8)	-1.3	(0.7)
	Serbia	6	**5.0**	(1.4)	**5.0**	(1.0)	**4.6**	(0.9)
	Chinese Taipei	3	-0.3	(2.4)	-0.3	(2.0)	-3.3	(2.0)
	Thailand	8	-1.0	(0.8)	-1.2	(0.8)	**-1.7**	(0.8)
	Tunisia	6	**4.8**	(1.4)	**4.8**	(1.0)	**7.8**	(1.7)
	Uruguay	6	-1.4	(1.4)	-1.4	(1.0)	1.3	(1.0)

Note: Values that are statistically significant are indicated in bold (see Annex A3).

1. Linear trends are estimated using linear regression applied to data from all PISA cycles. Annualised changes are calculated by dividing the performance difference by the number of years between two assessments. The results reflect the average score change associated with one calendar year.

StatLink http://dx.doi.org/10.1787/888932343285

[Part 1/1]

Table V.2.9 Mean reading score change between 2003 and 2009 and between 2006 and 2009

		Change between PISA 2009 and PISA 2003		Change between PISA 2009 and PISA 2006	
		Score dif.	S.E.	Score dif.	S.E.
OECD	Australia	**-11**	(5.2)	2	(5.1)
	Austria	m	m	m	m
	Belgium	-1	(5.4)	5	(5.6)
	Canada	-4	(4.7)	-3	(5.0)
	Chile	m	m	7	(7.2)
	Czech Republic	-10	(6.1)	-5	(6.5)
	Denmark	3	(5.4)	0	(5.6)
	Estonia	m	m	0	(5.7)
	Finland	-8	(5.0)	**-11**	(5.1)
	France	-1	(6.0)	8	(6.7)
	Germany	6	(5.9)	2	(6.6)
	Greece	11	(7.2)	**23**	(7.2)
	Hungary	**12**	(5.7)	12	(6.1)
	Iceland	9	(4.6)	**16**	(4.7)
	Ireland	**-20**	(5.7)	**-22**	(6.2)
	Israel	m	m	**35**	(7.1)
	Italy	10	(5.3)	**18**	(5.0)
	Japan	**22**	(6.6)	**22**	(6.5)
	Korea	5	(6.2)	**-17**	(6.6)
	Luxembourg	-7	(4.5)	-7	(4.4)
	Mexico	**26**	(6.1)	**15**	(5.5)
	Netherlands	-5	(7.2)	2	(7.2)
	New Zealand	-1	(5.3)	0	(5.6)
	Norway	3	(5.6)	**19**	(5.8)
	Poland	4	(5.6)	-7	(5.6)
	Portugal	12	(6.3)	**17**	(6.2)
	Slovak Republic	8	(5.7)	11	(5.7)
	Slovenia	m	m	**-11**	(4.3)
	Spain	1	(5.3)	**20**	(5.1)
	Sweden	**-17**	(5.6)	-10	(6.1)
	Switzerland	1	(5.8)	1	(5.6)
	Turkey	**23**	(7.9)	**17**	(6.8)
	United Kingdom	m	m	-1	(5.2)
	United States	5	(6.4)	m	m
	OECD average-28	3	(4.2)	m	m
	OECD average-32	m	m	5	(4.1)
Partners	Argentina	m	m	**25**	(9.5)
	Azerbaijan	m	m	9	(6.1)
	Brazil	9	(6.7)	**19**	(6.2)
	Bulgaria	m	m	**27**	(10.4)
	Colombia	m	m	**28**	(7.5)
	Croatia	m	m	-2	(5.7)
	Hong Kong-China	**24**	(5.9)	-3	(5.2)
	Indonesia	**20**	(6.5)	9	(8.1)
	Jordan	m	m	4	(6.2)
	Kyrgyzstan	m	m	**29**	(6.2)
	Latvia	-7	(6.2)	4	(6.3)
	Liechtenstein	**-26**	(6.1)	-11	(6.3)
	Lithuania	m	m	-2	(5.6)
	Macao-China	**-11**	(4.7)	-6	(4.3)
	Montenegro	m	m	**16**	(4.6)
	Qatar	m	m	**60**	(4.3)
	Romania	m	m	**29**	(7.4)
	Russian Federation	**17**	(6.6)	**20**	(6.8)
	Serbia	**30**	(5.9)	**41**	(5.9)
	Chinese Taipei	m	m	-1	(5.9)
	Thailand	1	(5.6)	5	(5.5)
	Tunisia	**29**	(5.7)	**23**	(6.4)
	Uruguay	-8	(5.9)	**13**	(5.9)

Note: Values that are statistically significant are indicated in bold (see Annex A3).
StatLink http://dx.doi.org/10.1787/888932343285

[Part 1/1]
Table V.3.1 **Mean mathematics performance in PISA 2003, 2006 and 2009**

		PISA 2003		PISA 2006		PISA 2009		Change between 2003 and 2009 (PISA 2009 – PISA 2003)		
		Mean score	S.E.	Mean score	S.E.	Mean score	S.E.	Score dif.	S.E.	p-value
OECD	Australia	524	(2.1)	520	(2.2)	514	(2.5)	**-10**	(3.9)	0.01
	Austria	506	(3.3)	505	(3.7)	m	m	m	m	m
	Belgium	529	(2.3)	520	(3.0)	515	(2.3)	**-14**	(3.8)	0.00
	Canada	532	(1.8)	527	(2.0)	527	(1.6)	-6	(3.1)	0.07
	Chile	m	m	411	(4.6)	421	(3.1)	m	m	m
	Czech Republic	516	(3.5)	510	(3.6)	493	(2.8)	**-24**	(5.0)	0.00
	Denmark	514	(2.7)	513	(2.6)	503	(2.6)	**-11**	(4.3)	0.01
	Estonia	m	m	515	(2.7)	512	(2.6)	m	m	m
	Finland	544	(1.9)	548	(2.3)	541	(2.2)	-4	(3.5)	0.28
	France	511	(2.5)	496	(3.2)	497	(3.1)	**-14**	(4.4)	0.00
	Germany	503	(3.3)	504	(3.9)	513	(2.9)	**10**	(4.8)	0.04
	Greece	445	(3.9)	459	(3.0)	466	(3.9)	**21**	(5.9)	0.00
	Hungary	490	(2.8)	491	(2.9)	490	(3.5)	0	(4.9)	0.97
	Iceland	515	(1.4)	506	(1.8)	507	(1.4)	**-8**	(2.8)	0.00
	Ireland	503	(2.4)	501	(2.8)	487	(2.5)	**-16**	(4.1)	0.00
	Israel	m	m	442	(4.3)	447	(3.3)	m	m	m
	Italy	466	(3.1)	462	(2.3)	483	(1.9)	**17**	(4.1)	0.00
	Japan	534	(4.0)	523	(3.3)	529	(3.3)	-5	(5.6)	0.36
	Korea	542	(3.2)	547	(3.8)	546	(4.0)	4	(5.5)	0.47
	Luxembourg	493	(1.0)	490	(1.1)	489	(1.2)	-4	(2.5)	0.10
	Mexico	385	(3.6)	406	(2.9)	419	(1.8)	**33**	(4.5)	0.00
	Netherlands	538	(3.1)	531	(2.6)	526	(4.7)	**-12**	(6.0)	0.05
	New Zealand	523	(2.3)	522	(2.4)	519	(2.3)	-4	(3.8)	0.27
	Norway	495	(2.4)	490	(2.6)	498	(2.4)	3	(3.9)	0.48
	Poland	490	(2.5)	495	(2.4)	495	(2.8)	5	(4.3)	0.29
	Portugal	466	(3.4)	466	(3.1)	487	(2.9)	**21**	(4.9)	0.00
	Slovak Republic	498	(3.3)	492	(2.8)	497	(3.1)	-2	(5.0)	0.76
	Slovenia	m	m	504	(1.0)	501	(1.2)	m	m	m
	Spain	485	(2.4)	480	(2.3)	483	(2.1)	-2	(3.8)	0.67
	Sweden	509	(2.6)	502	(2.4)	494	(2.9)	**-15**	(4.3)	0.00
	Switzerland	527	(3.4)	530	(3.2)	534	(3.3)	7	(5.1)	0.15
	Turkey	423	(6.7)	424	(4.9)	445	(4.4)	**22**	(8.3)	0.01
	United Kingdom	m	m	495	(2.1)	492	(2.4)	m	m	m
	United States	483	(2.9)	474	(4.0)	487	(3.6)	5	(5.0)	0.37
	OECD average-28	500	(0.6)	497	(0.6)	499	(0.6)	0	(2.1)	0.98
Partners	Argentina	m	m	381	(6.2)	388	(4.1)	m	m	m
	Azerbaijan	m	m	476	(2.3)	431	(2.8)	m	m	m
	Brazil	356	(4.8)	370	(2.9)	386	(2.4)	**30**	(5.7)	0.00
	Bulgaria	m	m	413	(6.1)	428	(5.9)	m	m	m
	Colombia	m	m	370	(3.8)	381	(3.2)	m	m	m
	Croatia	m	m	467	(2.4)	460	(3.1)	m	m	m
	Hong Kong-China	550	(4.5)	547	(2.7)	555	(2.7)	4	(5.7)	0.46
	Indonesia	360	(3.9)	391	(5.6)	371	(3.7)	11	(5.8)	0.05
	Jordan	m	m	384	(3.3)	387	(3.7)	m	m	m
	Kyrgyzstan	m	m	311	(3.4)	331	(2.9)	m	m	m
	Latvia	483	(3.7)	486	(3.0)	482	(3.1)	-1	(5.2)	0.78
	Liechtenstein	536	(4.1)	525	(4.2)	536	(4.1)	0	(6.1)	0.97
	Lithuania	m	m	486	(2.9)	477	(2.6)	m	m	m
	Macao-China	527	(2.9)	525	(1.3)	525	(0.9)	-2	(3.6)	0.58
	Montenegro	m	m	399	(1.4)	403	(2.0)	m	m	m
	Qatar	m	m	318	(1.0)	368	(0.7)	m	m	m
	Romania	m	m	415	(4.2)	427	(3.4)	m	m	m
	Russian Federation	468	(4.2)	476	(3.9)	468	(3.3)	-1	(5.7)	0.92
	Serbia	437	(3.8)	435	(3.5)	442	(2.9)	6	(5.2)	0.29
	Chinese Taipei	m	m	549	(4.1)	543	(3.4)	m	m	m
	Thailand	417	(3.0)	417	(2.3)	419	(3.2)	2	(4.8)	0.74
	Tunisia	359	(2.5)	365	(4.0)	371	(3.0)	**13**	(4.4)	0.00
	Uruguay	422	(3.3)	427	(2.6)	427	(2.6)	5	(4.6)	0.33

Note: Values that are statistically significant are indicated in bold (see Annex A3).
StatLink http://dx.doi.org/10.1787/888932343285

[Part 1/1]

Table V.3.2 **Percentage of students below Level 2 and at Level 5 or above on the mathematics scale in PISA 2003 and 2009**

		Proficiency levels in PISA 2003				Change between 2003 and 2009 (PISA 2009 – PISA 2003)			
		Below Level 2 (less than 420 score points)		Level 5 or above (above 607 score points)		Below Level 2 (less than 420 score points)		Level 5 or above (above 607 score points)	
		%	S.E.	%	S.E.	% dif.	S.E.	% dif.	S.E.
OECD	Australia	14.3	(0.7)	19.8	(0.8)	1.5	(1.0)	**-3.3**	(1.2)
	Austria	18.8	(1.2)	14.3	(1.0)	m	m	m	m
	Belgium	16.5	(0.8)	26.4	(0.8)	**2.6**	(1.1)	**-6.1**	(1.1)
	Canada	10.1	(0.5)	20.3	(0.7)	1.4	(0.7)	**-2.0**	(0.9)
	Czech Republic	16.6	(1.3)	18.3	(1.2)	**5.8**	(1.7)	**-6.6**	(1.5)
	Denmark	15.4	(0.8)	15.9	(0.9)	1.6	(1.2)	**-4.4**	(1.2)
	Finland	6.8	(0.5)	23.4	(0.8)	1.1	(0.7)	-1.7	(1.2)
	France	16.6	(1.1)	15.1	(0.9)	**5.9**	(1.7)	-1.4	(1.3)
	Germany	21.6	(1.2)	16.2	(0.9)	-3.0	(1.6)	1.6	(1.3)
	Greece	38.9	(1.9)	4.0	(0.6)	**-8.6**	(2.6)	**1.7**	(0.8)
	Hungary	23.0	(1.0)	10.7	(0.9)	-0.7	(1.8)	-0.6	(1.4)
	Iceland	15.0	(0.7)	15.5	(0.7)	**2.0**	(0.9)	**-1.9**	(0.9)
	Ireland	16.8	(1.0)	11.4	(0.8)	**4.0**	(1.4)	**-4.7**	(1.0)
	Italy	31.9	(1.5)	7.0	(0.5)	**-7.0**	(1.6)	**1.9**	(0.7)
	Japan	13.3	(1.2)	24.3	(1.5)	-0.8	(1.6)	-3.4	(2.0)
	Korea	9.5	(0.8)	24.8	(1.4)	-1.4	(1.3)	0.8	(2.1)
	Luxembourg	21.7	(0.6)	10.8	(0.6)	**2.2**	(0.9)	0.5	(0.9)
	Mexico	65.9	(1.7)	0.4	(0.1)	**-15.1**	(2.0)	**0.3**	(0.2)
	Netherlands	10.9	(1.1)	25.5	(1.3)	2.5	(1.8)	**-5.6**	(2.0)
	New Zealand	15.1	(0.8)	20.7	(0.7)	0.3	(1.2)	-1.8	(1.1)
	Norway	20.8	(1.0)	11.4	(0.6)	-2.7	(1.4)	-1.2	(1.0)
	Poland	22.0	(1.1)	10.1	(0.6)	-1.6	(1.5)	0.3	(1.0)
	Portugal	30.1	(1.7)	5.4	(0.5)	**-6.4**	(2.1)	**4.3**	(1.0)
	Slovak Republic	19.9	(1.4)	12.7	(0.9)	1.1	(1.8)	0.0	(1.3)
	Spain	23.0	(1.0)	7.9	(0.7)	0.8	(1.3)	0.1	(0.8)
	Sweden	17.3	(0.9)	15.8	(0.8)	**3.8**	(1.4)	**-4.4**	(1.2)
	Switzerland	14.5	(0.8)	21.2	(1.5)	-1.1	(1.2)	2.9	(2.0)
	Turkey	52.2	(2.6)	5.5	(1.6)	**-10.1**	(3.1)	0.2	(2.0)
	United Kingdom	m	m	m	m	m	m	m	m
	United States	25.7	(1.2)	10.1	(0.7)	-2.3	(1.8)	-0.2	(1.2)
	OECD average-28	21.6	(0.2)	14.7	(0.2)	**-0.9**	(0.3)	**-1.2**	(0.2)
Partners	Brazil	75.2	(1.7)	1.2	(0.4)	**-6.0**	(2.1)	-0.4	(0.5)
	Hong Kong-China	10.4	(1.2)	30.7	(1.5)	-1.6	(1.4)	0.0	(1.9)
	Indonesia	78.1	(1.7)	0.2	(0.1)	-1.5	(2.6)	-0.2	(0.1)
	Latvia	23.7	(1.4)	8.0	(0.8)	-1.2	(2.0)	**-2.3**	(1.0)
	Liechtenstein	12.3	(1.7)	25.6	(3.4)	-2.8	(2.5)	-7.6	(4.2)
	Macao-China	11.2	(1.2)	18.7	(1.4)	-0.2	(1.3)	-1.5	(1.5)
	Russian Federation	30.2	(1.8)	7.0	(0.8)	-1.6	(2.4)	-1.8	(1.1)
	Serbia	42.1	(1.9)	2.3	(0.4)	-1.5	(2.4)	1.2	(0.7)
	Thailand	54.0	(1.7)	1.6	(0.4)	-1.4	(2.3)	-0.4	(0.6)
	Tunisia	78.0	(1.2)	0.2	(0.1)	**-4.4**	(1.9)	0.0	(0.2)
	Uruguay	48.1	(1.5)	2.8	(0.4)	-0.5	(2.0)	-0.4	(0.6)

Note: Values that are statistically significant are indicated in bold (see Annex A3).
StatLink http://dx.doi.org/10.1787/888932343285

[Part 1/1]

Table V.3.3 Annualised changes in mathematics since 2003

		Annualised change between 2003 and 2009[1] (PISA 2009 – PISA 2003)		Change between 2006 and 2009 (PISA 2009 – PISA 2006)		Annualised change between 2006 and 2009[1] (PISA 2009 – PISA 2006)	
		Score dif.	S.E.	Score dif.	S.E.	Score dif.	S.E.
OECD	Australia	**-1.7**	(0.6)	-6	(3.6)	-1.9	(1.2)
	Austria	m	m	m	m	m	m
	Belgium	**-2.3**	(0.6)	-5	(3.9)	-1.7	(1.3)
	Canada	-0.9	(0.5)	0	(2.9)	-0.1	(1.0)
	Chile	m	m	10	(5.7)	3.2	(1.9)
	Czech Republic	**-3.9**	(0.8)	**-17**	(4.7)	**-5.7**	(1.6)
	Denmark	**-1.8**	(0.7)	**-10**	(3.9)	**-3.2**	(1.3)
	Estonia	m	m	-2	(4.0)	-0.8	(1.3)
	Finland	-0.6	(0.6)	**-8**	(3.4)	**-2.6**	(1.1)
	France	**-2.3**	(0.7)	1	(4.6)	0.4	(1.5)
	Germany	**1.6**	(0.8)	9	(5.0)	3.0	(1.7)
	Greece	**3.5**	(1.0)	7	(5.1)	2.3	(1.7)
	Hungary	0.0	(0.8)	-1	(4.7)	-0.3	(1.6)
	Iceland	**-1.4**	(0.5)	1	(2.6)	0.4	(0.9)
	Ireland	**-2.6**	(0.7)	**-14**	(4.0)	**-4.8**	(1.3)
	Israel	m	m	5	(5.6)	1.7	(1.9)
	Italy	**2.9**	(0.7)	**21**	(3.2)	**7.1**	(1.1)
	Japan	-0.9	(0.9)	6	(4.9)	2.0	(1.6)
	Korea	0.7	(0.9)	-1	(5.7)	-0.4	(1.9)
	Luxembourg	-0.7	(0.4)	-1	(2.1)	-0.3	(0.7)
	Mexico	**5.5**	(0.8)	**13**	(3.7)	**4.3**	(1.2)
	Netherlands	**-2.0**	(1.0)	-5	(5.6)	-1.6	(1.9)
	New Zealand	-0.7	(0.6)	-3	(3.6)	-0.9	(1.2)
	Norway	0.5	(0.7)	**8**	(3.8)	**2.7**	(1.3)
	Poland	0.8	(0.7)	-1	(4.0)	-0.2	(1.3)
	Portugal	**3.5**	(0.8)	**21**	(4.4)	**6.9**	(1.5)
	Slovak Republic	-0.3	(0.8)	5	(4.4)	1.5	(1.5)
	Slovenia	m	m	-3	(2.1)	-1.0	(0.7)
	Spain	-0.3	(0.6)	4	(3.4)	1.2	(1.1)
	Sweden	**-2.5**	(0.7)	**-8**	(4.0)	**-2.7**	(1.3)
	Switzerland	1.2	(0.9)	4	(4.8)	1.4	(1.6)
	Turkey	**3.7**	(1.4)	**22**	(6.7)	**7.2**	(2.2)
	United Kingdom	m	m	-3	(3.5)	-1.0	(1.2)
	United States	0.8	(0.8)	**13**	(5.5)	**4.3**	(1.8)
	OECD average-28	0.0	(0.4)	2	(1.5)	0.7	(0.5)
Partners	Argentina	m	m	7	(7.6)	2.3	(2.5)
	Azerbaijan	m	m	**-45**	(3.8)	**-15.0**	(1.3)
	Brazil	**5.0**	(1.0)	**16**	(4.0)	**5.4**	(1.3)
	Bulgaria	m	m	15	(8.6)	4.9	(2.9)
	Colombia	m	m	**11**	(5.2)	**3.6**	(1.7)
	Croatia	m	m	-7	(4.1)	-2.4	(1.4)
	Hong Kong-China	0.7	(0.9)	7	(4.0)	2.4	(1.3)
	Indonesia	1.9	(1.0)	**-20**	(6.9)	**-6.6**	(2.3)
	Jordan	m	m	3	(5.1)	0.9	(1.7)
	Kyrgyzstan	m	m	**21**	(4.7)	**6.9**	(1.6)
	Latvia	-0.2	(0.9)	-4	(4.5)	-1.4	(1.5)
	Liechtenstein	0.0	(1.0)	11	(6.0)	3.7	(2.0)
	Lithuania	m	m	**-10**	(4.1)	**-3.3**	(1.4)
	Macao-China	-0.3	(0.6)	0	(2.1)	0.1	(0.7)
	Montenegro	m	m	3	(2.8)	1.1	(0.9)
	Qatar	m	m	**50**	(1.8)	**16.7**	(0.6)
	Romania	m	m	**12**	(5.6)	**4.1**	(1.9)
	Russian Federation	-0.1	(0.9)	-8	(5.3)	-2.6	(1.8)
	Serbia	0.9	(0.9)	7	(4.8)	2.3	(1.6)
	Chinese Taipei	m	m	-6	(5.5)	-2.1	(1.8)
	Thailand	0.3	(0.8)	2	(4.2)	0.5	(1.4)
	Tunisia	**2.1**	(0.7)	6	(5.1)	2.0	(1.7)
	Uruguay	0.8	(0.8)	0	(3.9)	0.0	(1.3)

Note: Values that are statistically significant are indicated in bold (see Annex A3).
1. Annualised changes are calculated by dividing the performance difference by the number of years between two assessments. The results reflect a score change associated with one calendar year.

StatLink http://dx.doi.org/10.1787/888932343285

[Part 1/1]
Table V.3.4 Mean science performance in PISA 2006 and 2009

		PISA 2006		PISA 2009		Change between 2006 and 2009 (PISA 2009 – PISA 2006)		
		Mean score	S.E.	Mean score	S.E.	Score dif.	S.E.	p-value
OECD	Australia	527	(2.3)	527	(2.5)	0	(4.3)	0.93
	Austria	511	(3.9)	m	m	m	m	m
	Belgium	510	(2.5)	507	(2.5)	-4	(4.4)	0.39
	Canada	534	(2.0)	529	(1.6)	-6	(3.7)	0.11
	Chile	438	(4.3)	447	(2.9)	9	(5.8)	0.11
	Czech Republic	513	(3.5)	500	(3.0)	**-12**	(5.2)	0.02
	Denmark	496	(3.1)	499	(2.5)	3	(4.7)	0.47
	Estonia	531	(2.5)	528	(2.7)	-4	(4.5)	0.43
	Finland	563	(2.0)	554	(2.3)	**-9**	(4.0)	0.02
	France	495	(3.4)	498	(3.6)	3	(5.6)	0.59
	Germany	516	(3.8)	520	(2.8)	5	(5.4)	0.38
	Greece	473	(3.2)	470	(4.0)	-3	(5.8)	0.57
	Hungary	504	(2.7)	503	(3.1)	-1	(4.9)	0.79
	Iceland	491	(1.6)	496	(1.4)	5	(3.4)	0.15
	Ireland	508	(3.2)	508	(3.3)	0	(5.2)	0.95
	Israel	454	(3.7)	455	(3.1)	1	(5.5)	0.86
	Italy	475	(2.0)	489	(1.8)	**13**	(3.7)	0.00
	Japan	531	(3.4)	539	(3.4)	8	(5.4)	0.14
	Korea	522	(3.4)	538	(3.4)	**16**	(5.5)	0.00
	Luxembourg	486	(1.1)	484	(1.2)	-2	(3.0)	0.43
	Mexico	410	(2.7)	416	(1.8)	6	(4.1)	0.13
	Netherlands	525	(2.7)	522	(5.4)	-3	(6.6)	0.69
	New Zealand	530	(2.7)	532	(2.6)	2	(4.5)	0.72
	Norway	487	(3.1)	500	(2.6)	**13**	(4.8)	0.01
	Poland	498	(2.3)	508	(2.4)	**10**	(4.2)	0.02
	Portugal	474	(3.0)	493	(2.9)	**19**	(4.9)	0.00
	Slovak Republic	488	(2.6)	490	(3.0)	2	(4.7)	0.70
	Slovenia	519	(1.1)	512	(1.1)	-7	(3.0)	0.02
	Spain	488	(2.6)	488	(2.1)	0	(4.2)	0.97
	Sweden	503	(2.4)	495	(2.7)	-8	(4.4)	0.06
	Switzerland	512	(3.2)	517	(2.8)	5	(5.0)	0.31
	Turkey	424	(3.8)	454	(3.6)	**30**	(5.9)	0.00
	United Kingdom	515	(2.3)	514	(2.5)	-1	(4.3)	0.80
	United States	489	(4.2)	502	(3.6)	**13**	(6.1)	0.03
	OECD average -33	498	(0.5)	501	(0.5)	3	(2.7)	0.24
Partners	Argentina	391	(6.1)	401	(4.6)	10	(8.0)	0.23
	Azerbaijan	382	(2.8)	373	(3.1)	-9	(4.8)	0.06
	Brazil	390	(2.8)	405	(2.4)	**15**	(4.5)	0.00
	Bulgaria	434	(6.1)	439	(5.9)	5	(8.9)	0.56
	Colombia	388	(3.4)	402	(3.6)	**14**	(5.6)	0.01
	Croatia	493	(2.4)	486	(2.8)	-7	(4.5)	0.13
	Hong Kong-China	542	(2.5)	549	(2.8)	7	(4.5)	0.13
	Indonesia	393	(5.7)	383	(3.8)	-11	(7.3)	0.14
	Jordan	422	(2.8)	415	(3.5)	-7	(5.2)	0.21
	Kyrgyzstan	322	(2.9)	330	(2.9)	8	(4.9)	0.12
	Latvia	490	(3.0)	494	(3.1)	4	(5.0)	0.38
	Liechtenstein	522	(4.1)	520	(3.4)	-2	(5.9)	0.70
	Lithuania	488	(2.8)	491	(2.9)	3	(4.8)	0.47
	Macao-China	511	(1.1)	511	(1.0)	0	(3.0)	0.94
	Montenegro	412	(1.1)	401	(2.0)	**-11**	(3.4)	0.00
	Qatar	349	(0.9)	379	(0.9)	**30**	(2.9)	0.00
	Romania	418	(4.2)	428	(3.4)	10	(6.0)	0.10
	Russian Federation	479	(3.7)	478	(3.3)	-1	(5.6)	0.83
	Serbia	436	(3.0)	443	(2.4)	7	(4.6)	0.12
	Chinese Taipei	532	(3.6)	520	(2.6)	**-12**	(5.1)	0.02
	Thailand	421	(2.1)	425	(3.0)	4	(4.5)	0.34
	Tunisia	386	(3.0)	401	(2.7)	**15**	(4.8)	0.00
	Uruguay	428	(2.7)	427	(2.6)	-1	(4.6)	0.84

Note: Values that are statistically significant are indicated in bold (see Annex A3).
StatLink http://dx.doi.org/10.1787/888932343285

[Part 1/1]

Table V.3.5 **Percentage of students below Level 2 and at Level 5 or above on the science scale in PISA 2006 and 2009**

		Proficiency levels in PISA 2006				Proficiency levels in PISA 2009				Change between 2006 and 2009 (PISA 2009 – PISA 2006)			
		Below Level 2 (less than 410 score points)		Level 5 or above (above 633 score points)		Below Level 2 (less than 410 score points)		Level 5 or above (above 633 score points)		Below Level 2 (less than 410 score points)		Level 5 or above (above 633 score points)	
		%	S.E.	%	S.E.	%	S.E.	%	S.E.	% dif.	S.E.	% dif.	S.E.
OECD	Australia	12.9	(0.6)	14.6	(0.7)	12.6	(0.6)	14.5	(0.8)	-0.3	(0.9)	-0.1	(1.1)
	Austria	16.3	(1.4)	10.0	(0.8)	m	m	m	m	m	m	m	m
	Belgium	17.0	(1.0)	10.1	(0.5)	18.0	(0.8)	10.1	(0.7)	1.0	(1.3)	0.0	(0.9)
	Canada	10.0	(0.6)	14.4	(0.5)	9.6	(0.5)	12.1	(0.5)	-0.5	(0.7)	**-2.3**	(0.7)
	Chile	39.7	(2.1)	1.9	(0.3)	32.3	(1.4)	1.1	(0.2)	**-7.4**	(2.5)	**-0.8**	(0.4)
	Czech Republic	15.5	(1.2)	11.6	(0.9)	17.3	(1.2)	8.4	(0.7)	1.8	(1.6)	**-3.2**	(1.2)
	Denmark	18.4	(1.1)	6.8	(0.7)	16.6	(0.8)	6.7	(0.6)	-1.9	(1.4)	-0.1	(0.9)
	Estonia	7.7	(0.6)	11.5	(0.8)	8.3	(0.8)	10.4	(0.8)	0.7	(1.0)	-1.1	(1.1)
	Finland	4.1	(0.5)	20.9	(0.8)	6.0	(0.5)	18.7	(0.9)	**1.9**	(0.7)	-2.2	(1.2)
	France	21.2	(1.4)	8.0	(0.7)	19.3	(1.3)	8.1	(0.8)	-1.9	(1.9)	0.1	(1.0)
	Germany	15.4	(1.3)	11.8	(0.7)	14.8	(1.0)	12.8	(0.8)	-0.6	(1.7)	1.0	(1.0)
	Greece	24.0	(1.3)	3.4	(0.4)	25.3	(1.6)	3.1	(0.4)	1.2	(2.1)	-0.4	(0.5)
	Hungary	15.0	(1.0)	6.9	(0.6)	14.1	(1.4)	5.4	(0.6)	-0.9	(1.7)	-1.5	(0.9)
	Iceland	20.6	(0.8)	6.3	(0.5)	17.9	(0.7)	7.0	(0.4)	**-2.6**	(1.1)	0.6	(0.6)
	Ireland	15.5	(1.1)	9.4	(0.7)	15.2	(1.1)	8.7	(0.8)	-0.3	(1.5)	-0.7	(1.0)
	Israel	36.1	(1.4)	5.2	(0.6)	33.1	(1.2)	3.9	(0.4)	-3.0	(1.9)	-1.3	(0.7)
	Italy	25.3	(0.9)	4.6	(0.3)	20.6	(0.6)	5.8	(0.3)	**-4.6**	(1.1)	**1.2**	(0.5)
	Japan	12.0	(1.0)	15.1	(0.8)	10.7	(1.0)	16.9	(0.9)	-1.4	(1.5)	1.9	(1.2)
	Korea	11.2	(1.1)	10.3	(1.1)	6.3	(0.8)	11.6	(1.1)	**-4.9**	(1.4)	1.3	(1.5)
	Luxembourg	22.1	(0.5)	5.9	(0.4)	23.7	(0.8)	6.7	(0.5)	1.6	(1.0)	0.8	(0.6)
	Mexico	50.9	(1.4)	0.3	(0.1)	47.4	(1.0)	0.2	(0.0)	**-3.6**	(1.7)	-0.1	(0.1)
	Netherlands	13.0	(1.0)	13.1	(0.9)	13.2	(1.6)	12.7	(1.2)	0.2	(1.9)	-0.4	(1.5)
	New Zealand	13.7	(0.7)	17.6	(0.8)	13.4	(0.7)	17.6	(0.8)	-0.3	(1.0)	0.0	(1.1)
	Norway	21.1	(1.3)	6.1	(0.5)	15.8	(0.9)	6.4	(0.6)	**-5.3**	(1.6)	0.3	(0.8)
	Poland	17.0	(0.8)	6.8	(0.5)	13.1	(0.8)	7.5	(0.5)	**-3.8**	(1.2)	0.8	(0.7)
	Portugal	24.5	(1.4)	3.1	(0.4)	16.5	(1.1)	4.2	(0.5)	**-8.0**	(1.7)	1.0	(0.6)
	Slovak Republic	20.2	(1.0)	5.8	(0.5)	19.3	(1.2)	6.2	(0.6)	-0.9	(1.5)	0.5	(0.8)
	Slovenia	13.9	(0.6)	12.9	(0.6)	14.8	(0.5)	9.9	(0.6)	0.9	(0.8)	**-3.0**	(0.9)
	Spain	19.6	(0.9)	4.9	(0.4)	18.2	(0.9)	4.0	(0.3)	-1.4	(1.3)	-0.9	(0.5)
	Sweden	16.4	(0.8)	7.9	(0.5)	19.1	(1.0)	8.1	(0.6)	**2.8**	(1.3)	0.2	(0.8)
	Switzerland	16.1	(0.9)	10.5	(0.8)	14.0	(0.8)	10.7	(0.9)	-2.0	(1.2)	0.3	(1.2)
	Turkey	46.6	(1.6)	0.9	(0.3)	30.0	(1.5)	1.1	(0.3)	**-16.6**	(2.2)	0.2	(0.5)
	United Kingdom	16.7	(0.8)	13.7	(0.6)	15.0	(0.8)	11.4	(0.7)	-1.7	(1.1)	**-2.4**	(0.9)
	United States	24.4	(1.6)	9.1	(0.7)	18.1	(1.1)	9.2	(1.0)	**-6.3**	(1.9)	0.1	(1.2)
	OECD average-33	19.9	(0.2)	8.8	(0.1)	17.9	(0.2)	8.5	(0.1)	**-2.1**	(0.3)	**-0.3**	(0.2)
Partners	Argentina	56.3	(2.5)	0.4	(0.1)	52.4	(1.9)	0.7	(0.2)	-3.8	(3.2)	0.2	(0.2)
	Azerbaijan	72.5	(1.9)	0.0	c	70.0	(1.5)	0.0	(0.0)	-2.5	(2.4)	c	c
	Brazil	61.0	(1.4)	0.6	(0.2)	54.2	(1.3)	0.6	(0.1)	**-6.8**	(1.9)	0.0	(0.2)
	Bulgaria	42.6	(2.4)	3.1	(0.6)	38.8	(2.5)	2.6	(0.5)	-3.8	(3.5)	-0.4	(0.8)
	Colombia	60.2	(1.8)	0.2	(0.1)	54.1	(1.9)	0.1	(0.1)	**-6.1**	(2.6)	0.0	(0.1)
	Croatia	17.0	(0.9)	5.1	(0.5)	18.5	(1.1)	3.7	(0.6)	1.5	(1.4)	-1.4	(0.8)
	Hong Kong-China	8.7	(0.8)	15.9	(0.9)	6.6	(0.7)	16.2	(1.0)	-2.1	(1.1)	0.3	(1.4)
	Indonesia	61.6	(3.4)	0.0	c	65.6	(2.3)	0.0	c	4.0	(4.1)	c	c
	Jordan	44.3	(1.2)	0.6	(0.2)	45.6	(1.7)	0.5	(0.2)	1.3	(2.1)	-0.2	(0.3)
	Kyrgyzstan	86.3	(1.0)	0.0	c	82.0	(1.1)	0.0	(0.0)	**-4.4**	(1.5)	c	c
	Latvia	17.4	(1.2)	4.1	(0.4)	14.7	(1.2)	3.1	(0.5)	-2.7	(1.7)	-1.0	(0.6)
	Liechtenstein	12.9	(2.2)	12.2	(1.7)	11.3	(1.9)	9.7	(1.8)	-1.6	(2.9)	-2.5	(2.5)
	Lithuania	20.3	(1.0)	5.0	(0.7)	17.0	(1.1)	4.6	(0.5)	**-3.3**	(1.5)	-0.4	(0.8)
	Macao-China	10.3	(0.5)	5.3	(0.4)	9.6	(0.4)	4.8	(0.5)	-0.7	(0.7)	-0.5	(0.6)
	Montenegro	50.2	(0.9)	0.3	(0.1)	53.6	(1.0)	0.2	(0.1)	**3.3**	(1.4)	0.0	(0.2)
	Qatar	79.1	(0.4)	0.3	(0.1)	65.2	(0.6)	1.4	(0.1)	**-13.9**	(0.7)	**1.1**	(0.2)
	Romania	46.9	(2.4)	0.5	(0.1)	41.4	(2.1)	0.4	(0.1)	-5.5	(3.2)	-0.1	(0.2)
	Russian Federation	22.2	(1.4)	4.2	(0.5)	22.0	(1.4)	4.4	(0.5)	-0.2	(2.0)	0.2	(0.7)
	Serbia	38.5	(1.6)	0.8	(0.2)	34.4	(1.3)	1.0	(0.2)	**-4.1**	(2.0)	0.2	(0.3)
	Chinese Taipei	11.6	(1.0)	14.6	(0.9)	11.1	(0.7)	8.8	(0.9)	-0.6	(1.2)	**-5.8**	(1.2)
	Thailand	46.1	(1.2)	0.4	(0.1)	42.8	(1.6)	0.6	(0.3)	-3.3	(2.0)	0.2	(0.3)
	Tunisia	62.8	(1.4)	0.1	(0.1)	53.7	(1.4)	0.2	(0.1)	**-9.0**	(2.0)	0.0	(0.1)
	Uruguay	42.1	(1.4)	1.4	(0.2)	42.6	(1.1)	1.5	(0.2)	0.4	(1.8)	0.1	(0.3)

Note: Values that are statistically significant are indicated in bold (see Annex A3).

StatLink http://dx.doi.org/10.1787/888932343285

[Part 1/1]
Table V.4.1 Between- and within-school variance in reading performance in PISA 2000 and 2009

		PISA 2000			PISA 2009			Change between 2000 and 2009 (PISA 2009 – PISA 2000)						Change between 2000 and 2009 as a percentage of 2000 variance (PISA 2009 – PISA 2000) / PISA 2000		
								Total variance		Between-school variance		Within-school variance		Total variance	Between-school variance	Within-school variance
		Total variance	Between-school variance	Within-school variance	Total variance	Between-school variance	Within-school variance	Dif.	S.E.	Dif.	S.E.	Dif.	S.E.	Change as %	Change as %	Change as %
OECD	Australia	10 357	2 221	8 850	9 783	2 692	7 631	-574	(297)	471	(490)	**-1 219**	(288)	-5.5	21.2	**-13.8**
	Austria	9 703	6 046	4 408	m	m	m	m	m	m	m	m	m	m	m	m
	Belgium	11 454	5 797	4 702	10 360	5 343	4 833	**-1 094**	(305)	-453	(604)	132	(222)	**-9.6**	-7.8	2.8
	Canada	8 954	1 934	7 632	8 163	1 877	6 780	**-791**	(163)	-57	(242)	**-853**	(158)	**-8.8**	-2.9	**-11.2**
	Chile	8 074	4 081	3 981	6 833	4 893	4 005	**-1 241**	(239)	813	(729)	24	(154)	**-15.4**	19.9	0.6
	Czech Republic	9 277	4 651	4 152	8 516	4 249	4 428	**-761**	(361)	-402	(725)	276	(204)	**-8.2**	-8.6	6.7
	Denmark	9 615	1 472	8 068	6 987	1 134	6 012	**-2 628**	(306)	-338	(430)	**-2 056**	(274)	**-27.3**	-22.9	**-25.5**
	Finland	7 994	591	7 117	7 467	665	6 993	-526	(327)	74	(198)	-124	(279)	-6.6	12.5	-1.7
	France	w	w	w	w	w	w	w	w	w	w	w	w	w	w	w
	Germany	12 367	6 667	4 717	8 978	5 890	3 890	**-3 389**	(485)	-777	(950)	**-827**	(197)	**-27.4**	-11.7	**-17.5**
	Greece	9 436	4 762	4 984	9 054	4 745	5 558	-383	(355)	-17	(924)	**574**	(239)	-4.1	-0.4	**11.5**
	Hungary	8 810	5 571	3 275	8 133	5 846	2 923	**-678**	(344)	275	(749)	**-352**	(129)	**-7.7**	4.9	**-10.8**
	Iceland	8 529	732	7 805	9 211	1 348	8 186	**682**	(340)	616	(429)	381	(365)	**8.0**	84.1	4.9
	Ireland	8 756	1 593	7 181	9 053	2 805	6 966	297	(340)	**1 211**	(587)	-215	(324)	3.4	**76.0**	-3.0
	Israel	11 909	5 923	6 634	12 438	6 250	6 615	529	(467)	327	(1 463)	-19	(388)	4.4	5.5	-0.3
	Italy	8 355	4 453	4 001	9 193	6 695	4 085	**838**	(282)	**2 242**	(1 011)	84	(145)	**10.0**	**50.3**	2.1
	Japan	7 359	3 378	3 907	10 072	5 087	5 386	**2 713**	(317)	**1 709**	(833)	**1 480**	(240)	**36.9**	**50.6**	**37.9**
	Korea	4 834	1 937	3 087	6 271	2 741	5 283	**1 437**	(209)	804	(724)	**2 196**	(530)	**29.7**	41.5	**71.1**
	Luxembourg	m	m	m	10 759	5 335	6 906	m	m	m	m	m	m	m	m	m
	Mexico	7 371	3 907	3 484	7 158	3 583	3 869	-213	(235)	-324	(504)	**385**	(142)	-2.9	-8.3	**11.1**
	Netherlands	m	m	m	7 857	5 107	2 795	m	m	m	m	m	m	m	m	m
	New Zealand	11 700	1 867	9 765	10 575	2 622	8 228	**-1 124**	(428)	755	(576)	**-1 537**	(441)	**-9.6**	40.4	**-15.7**
	Norway	10 743	1 040	9 753	8 310	874	7 598	**-2 433**	(351)	-167	(276)	**-2 155**	(373)	**-22.6**	-16.0	**-22.1**
	Poland	9 958	6 125	3 712	7 950	1 585	6 869	**-2 008**	(376)	**-4 540**	(710)	**3 157**	(261)	**-20.2**	**-74.1**	**85.1**
	Portugal	9 436	3 536	5 855	7 534	2 565	5 191	**-1 902**	(278)	-971	(527)	**-664**	(270)	**-20.2**	-27.4	**-11.3**
	Spain	7 180	1 533	5 662	7 658	1 690	6 048	**478**	(231)	158	(212)	385	(209)	**6.7**	10.3	6.8
	Sweden	8 495	786	7 729	9 729	1 877	8 290	**1 234**	(311)	**1 090**	(398)	561	(309)	**14.5**	**138.6**	7.3
	Switzerland	10 409	4 340	5 867	8 735	2 740	5 652	**-1 674**	(286)	**-1 600**	(521)	-215	(264)	**-16.1**	**-36.9**	-3.7
	United Kingdom	m	m	m	9 096	2 775	6 684	m	m	m	m	m	m	m	m	m
	United States	10 979	3 306	7 846	9 330	3 638	6 476	**-1 649**	(386)	332	(1 130)	**-1 370**	(345)	**-15.0**	10.0	**-17.5**
	OECD average-26	9 260	3 324	5 922	8 793	3 420	5 875	**-467**	(64)	96	(140)	-47	(56)	**-3.1**	14.6	4.3
Partners	Albania	9 882	3 915	5 946	9 969	3 127	7 105	87	(370)	-788	(654)	**1 159**	(336)	0.9	-20.1	**19.5**
	Argentina	11 800	5 885	5 763	11 714	8 456	5 523	-85	(558)	**2 572**	(1 258)	-240	(300)	-0.7	**43.7**	-4.2
	Brazil	7 427	3 651	4 206	8 838	4 417	4 702	**1 410**	(255)	766	(520)	**496**	(162)	**19.0**	21.0	**11.8**
	Bulgaria	10 332	5 435	4 795	12 823	6 418	6 439	**2 491**	(407)	983	(945)	**1 644**	(273)	**24.1**	18.1	**34.3**
	Hong Kong-China	7 050	3 357	3 646	7 058	3 143	4 360	8	(275)	-214	(556)	**714**	(224)	0.1	-6.4	**19.6**
	Indonesia	5 246	2 117	2 785	4 418	1 749	2 298	**-828**	(172)	-368	(300)	**-487**	(97)	**-15.8**	-17.4	**-17.5**
	Latvia	10 434	3 121	7 297	6 394	1 391	5 200	**-4 041**	(348)	**-1 730**	(498)	**-2 096**	(306)	**-38.7**	**-55.4**	**-28.7**
	Liechtenstein	9 254	3 581	4 293	6 896	2 944	3 453	**-2 357**	(981)	-637	(1 625)	-840	(631)	**-25.5**	-17.8	-19.6
	Peru	9 243	4 906	4 368	9 670	5 886	4 623	426	(328)	980	(1 067)	254	(192)	4.6	20.0	5.8
	Romania	10 438	4 922	5 624	8 105	4 057	3 832	**-2 333**	(484)	-865	(851)	**-1 792**	(239)	**-22.4**	-17.6	**-31.9**
	Russian Federation	8 465	3 238	5 221	8 050	1 965	5 826	-416	(277)	**-1 273**	(472)	**605**	(241)	-4.9	**-39.3**	**11.6**
	Thailand	5 871	1 918	4 212	5 164	1 231	3 052	**-707**	(193)	**-687**	(328)	**-1 161**	(176)	**-12.0**	**-35.8**	**-27.6**

Note: Values that are statistically significant are indicated in bold (see Annex A3).
StatLink http://dx.doi.org/10.1787/888932343285

[Part 1/1]

Table V.4.2 Socio-economic background of students in PISA 2000 and 2009

Results based on students' self-reports

		PISA 2000				PISA 2009				Change between 2000 and 2009 (PISA 2009 – PISA 2000)	
		PISA index of economic, social and cultural status (ESCS)		Variability in ESCS		PISA index of economic, social and cultural status (ESCS)		Variability in ESCS		PISA index of economic, social and cultural status (ESCS)	
		Mean index	S.E.	S.D.	S.E.	Mean index	S.E.	S.D.	S.E.	Dif.	S.E.
OECD	Australia	0.28	(0.03)	0.80	(0.01)	0.34	(0.01)	0.75	(0.01)	**0.07**	(0.03)
	Austria	-0.01	(0.02)	0.86	(0.01)	m	m	m	m	m	m
	Belgium	0.15	(0.02)	0.88	(0.01)	0.20	(0.02)	0.93	(0.01)	0.05	(0.03)
	Canada	0.62	(0.01)	0.79	(0.01)	0.50	(0.02)	0.83	(0.01)	**-0.12**	(0.02)
	Chile	-0.62	(0.04)	1.11	(0.02)	-0.57	(0.04)	1.14	(0.02)	0.06	(0.05)
	Czech Republic	-0.07	(0.02)	0.74	(0.01)	-0.09	(0.01)	0.71	(0.01)	-0.01	(0.02)
	Denmark	0.28	(0.03)	0.92	(0.01)	0.30	(0.02)	0.87	(0.01)	0.02	(0.04)
	Finland	0.04	(0.02)	0.94	(0.01)	0.37	(0.02)	0.78	(0.01)	**0.33**	(0.03)
	France	-0.15	(0.02)	0.84	(0.01)	-0.13	(0.03)	0.84	(0.02)	0.01	(0.04)
	Germany	0.21	(0.02)	0.92	(0.01)	0.18	(0.02)	0.90	(0.01)	-0.03	(0.03)
	Greece	-0.11	(0.04)	1.04	(0.02)	-0.02	(0.03)	0.99	(0.01)	0.09	(0.05)
	Hungary	-0.27	(0.03)	0.89	(0.01)	-0.20	(0.03)	0.97	(0.02)	0.08	(0.04)
	Iceland	0.53	(0.02)	0.91	(0.01)	0.72	(0.01)	0.89	(0.01)	**0.19**	(0.02)
	Ireland	-0.03	(0.03)	0.86	(0.01)	0.05	(0.03)	0.85	(0.01)	0.08	(0.04)
	Israel	0.15	(0.05)	0.84	(0.02)	-0.02	(0.03)	0.89	(0.02)	**-0.17**	(0.05)
	Italy	0.03	(0.02)	0.95	(0.01)	-0.12	(0.01)	1.02	(0.01)	**-0.16**	(0.02)
	Japan	m	m	m	m	-0.01	(0.01)	0.72	(0.01)	m	m
	Korea	-0.39	(0.03)	0.85	(0.02)	-0.15	(0.03)	0.82	(0.01)	**0.24**	(0.04)
	Luxembourg	m	m	m	m	0.19	(0.01)	1.10	(0.01)	m	m
	Mexico	-1.23	(0.06)	1.21	(0.04)	-1.22	(0.03)	1.30	(0.01)	0.01	(0.06)
	Netherlands	m	m	m	m	0.27	(0.03)	0.86	(0.02)	m	m
	New Zealand	0.10	(0.02)	0.81	(0.01)	0.09	(0.02)	0.79	(0.01)	-0.02	(0.03)
	Norway	0.37	(0.02)	0.83	(0.01)	0.47	(0.02)	0.74	(0.01)	**0.10**	(0.03)
	Poland	-0.22	(0.03)	0.87	(0.01)	-0.28	(0.02)	0.88	(0.01)	-0.06	(0.04)
	Portugal	-0.38	(0.05)	1.13	(0.02)	-0.32	(0.04)	1.18	(0.02)	0.06	(0.06)
	Spain	-0.56	(0.05)	1.12	(0.02)	-0.31	(0.03)	1.09	(0.01)	**0.25**	(0.06)
	Sweden	0.35	(0.02)	0.79	(0.01)	0.33	(0.02)	0.81	(0.01)	-0.02	(0.03)
	Switzerland	0.06	(0.03)	0.93	(0.02)	0.08	(0.02)	0.88	(0.01)	0.02	(0.04)
	United Kingdom	m	m	m	m	0.20	(0.02)	0.79	(0.01)	m	m
	United States	0.35	(0.06)	0.84	(0.03)	0.17	(0.04)	0.93	(0.02)	**-0.18**	(0.07)
	OECD average-26	-0.02	(0.01)	0.91	(0.00)	0.01	(0.00)	0.90	(0.00)	**0.03**	(0.01)
Partners	Albania	-0.65	(0.02)	0.92	(0.01)	-0.95	(0.04)	1.04	(0.02)	**-0.30**	(0.04)
	Argentina	-0.60	(0.08)	1.14	(0.03)	-0.62	(0.05)	1.19	(0.03)	-0.01	(0.09)
	Brazil	-1.10	(0.04)	1.17	(0.02)	-1.16	(0.03)	1.21	(0.01)	-0.07	(0.05)
	Bulgaria	0.12	(0.04)	0.81	(0.02)	-0.11	(0.04)	0.98	(0.02)	**-0.23**	(0.05)
	Hong Kong-China	-0.82	(0.03)	0.88	(0.02)	-0.80	(0.04)	1.02	(0.02)	0.02	(0.05)
	Indonesia	-1.57	(0.04)	0.96	(0.02)	-1.55	(0.06)	1.10	(0.02)	0.02	(0.07)
	Latvia	-0.03	(0.03)	0.76	(0.01)	-0.13	(0.03)	0.88	(0.01)	**-0.10**	(0.04)
	Liechtenstein	-0.08	(0.05)	0.90	(0.04)	0.09	(0.05)	0.94	(0.03)	**0.16**	(0.07)
	Peru	-1.22	(0.04)	1.11	(0.02)	-1.31	(0.05)	1.25	(0.03)	-0.09	(0.06)
	Romania	-0.67	(0.04)	1.12	(0.02)	-0.34	(0.03)	0.92	(0.03)	**0.32**	(0.06)
	Russian Federation	-0.52	(0.03)	0.78	(0.01)	-0.21	(0.02)	0.80	(0.01)	**0.31**	(0.04)
	Thailand	-1.59	(0.04)	0.99	(0.03)	-1.31	(0.04)	1.19	(0.02)	**0.28**	(0.06)

Note: Values that are statistically significant are indicated in bold (see Annex A3).

StatLink http://dx.doi.org/10.1787/888932343285

[Part 1/1]

Table V.4.3 Relationship between reading performance and the PISA index of economic, social, and cultural status (ESCS) in PISA 2000 and 2009

Results based on students' self-reports

		PISA 2000						PISA 2009						Change between 2000 and 2009 (PISA 2009 – PISA 2000)					
		Overall effect of ESCS[1]		Within-school effect of ESCS[2]		Between-school effect of ESCS[3]		Overall effect of ESCS[1]		Within-school effect of ESCS[2]		Between-school effect of ESCS[3]		Overall effect of ESCS[1]		Within-school effect of ESCS[2]		Between-school effect of ESCS[3]	
		Student-level score point difference associated with one unit increase in the ESCS	S.E.	Student-level score point difference associated with one unit increase in the student-level ESCS	S.E.	School-level score point difference associated with one unit increase in the school mean ESCS	S.E.	Student-level score point difference associated with one unit increase in the ESCS	S.E.	Student-level score point difference associated with one unit increase in the student-level ESCS	S.E.	School-level score point difference associated with one unit increase in the school mean ESCS	S.E.	Student-level score point difference associated with one unit increase in the ESCS	S.E.	Student-level score point difference associated with one unit increase in the student-level ESCS	S.E.	School-level score point difference associated with one unit increase in the school mean ESCS	S.E.
OECD	Australia	47	(2.7)	32	(3.1)	47	(7.0)	46	(1.8)	30	(1.9)	66	(6.2)	-1	(3.2)	-2	(3.6)	**19**	(9.4)
	Austria	43	(2.5)	8	(1.8)	109	(7.9)	m	m	m	m	m	m	m	m	m	m	m	m
	Belgium	46	(2.3)	12	(1.9)	143	(10.6)	47	(1.5)	13	(1.4)	111	(6.1)	1	(2.7)	1	(2.4)	**-32**	(12.2)
	Canada	38	(1.3)	29	(0.7)	49	(3.4)	32	(1.4)	21	(1.4)	32	(6.7)	**-6**	(1.9)	**-8**	(1.6)	**-18**	(7.5)
	Chile	39	(1.7)	11	(2.1)	62	(6.0)	31	(1.5)	8	(1.8)	50	(4.3)	**-8**	(2.3)	-2	(2.7)	-11	(7.4)
	Czech Republic	57	(2.8)	21	(2.0)	118	(11.9)	46	(2.3)	14	(2.0)	123	(7.7)	**-11**	(3.6)	**-7**	(2.9)	6	(14.1)
	Denmark	40	(1.9)	31	(1.9)	41	(9.7)	36	(1.4)	28	(1.7)	42	(5.9)	-3	(2.4)	-4	(2.5)	1	(11.4)
	Finland	25	(2.3)	22	(1.7)	65	(55.3)	31	(1.7)	28	(2.0)	19	(10.3)	**6**	(2.8)	**6**	(2.6)	-46	(56.2)
	France	w	w	w	w	w	w	w	w	w	w	w	w	w	w	w	w	w	w
	Germany	52	(2.6)	14	(2.3)	142	(17.7)	44	(1.9)	10	(1.6)	122	(8.4)	**-8**	(3.2)	-4	(2.8)	-19	(19.6)
	Greece	32	(2.7)	9	(1.7)	77	(8.0)	34	(2.4)	14	(1.8)	44	(10.7)	2	(3.7)	5	(2.5)	**-33**	(13.4)
	Hungary	52	(2.6)	6	(1.6)	86	(9.3)	48	(2.2)	7	(1.7)	76	(7.3)	-4	(3.4)	0	(2.3)	-10	(11.8)
	Iceland	21	(1.6)	18	(2.0)	6	(7.5)	27	(1.8)	24	(1.8)	11	(11.3)	**5**	(2.4)	**5**	(2.7)	5	(13.6)
	Ireland	34	(2.2)	23	(2.0)	54	(7.1)	39	(2.0)	27	(2.2)	53	(7.7)	6	(3.0)	4	(3.0)	-1	(10.5)
	Israel	52	(4.7)	16	(3.1)	86	(12.3)	43	(2.4)	18	(2.3)	102	(14.1)	-8	(5.3)	2	(3.9)	16	(18.7)
	Italy	29	(2.0)	2	(1.7)	68	(26.3)	32	(1.3)	5	(0.8)	67	(11.1)	3	(2.4)	3	(1.9)	-1	(28.6)
	Japan	m	m	m	m	m	m	40	(2.8)	5	(2.7)	137	(15.5)	m	m	m	m	m	m
	Korea	23	(2.4)	8	(2.6)	36	(13.0)	32	(2.5)	20	(2.9)	62	(8.7)	**8**	(3.5)	**11**	(3.9)	25	(15.6)
	Luxembourg	m	m	m	m	m	m	40	(1.3)	21	(3.0)	65	(9.6)	m	m	m	m	m	m
	Mexico	32	(1.9)	3	(1.3)	50	(4.1)	25	(1.0)	3	(0.9)	30	(3.3)	**-7**	(2.1)	1	(1.6)	**-20**	(5.3)
	Netherlands	m	m	m	m	m	m	37	(1.9)	5	(1.5)	93	(16.2)	m	m	m	m	m	m
	New Zealand	47	(2.7)	33	(2.9)	57	(10.4)	52	(1.9)	36	(2.9)	61	(9.3)	5	(3.3)	4	(4.1)	4	(13.9)
	Norway	36	(2.2)	31	(2.7)	13	(12.7)	36	(2.1)	28	(2.8)	31	(14.7)	0	(3.1)	-3	(3.8)	18	(19.4)
	Poland	40	(3.3)	-1	(2.3)	80	(17.8)	39	(1.9)	31	(2.2)	29	(5.7)	-2	(3.8)	**31**	(3.2)	**-51**	(18.7)
	Portugal	34	(2.0)	15	(2.0)	65	(7.5)	30	(1.6)	17	(1.3)	40	(5.7)	-5	(2.6)	3	(2.4)	**-25**	(9.4)
	Spain	28	(1.4)	18	(1.1)	23	(3.7)	29	(1.5)	21	(1.0)	25	(3.9)	1	(2.0)	3	(1.5)	2	(5.4)
	Sweden	36	(1.8)	27	(2.2)	43	(9.6)	43	(2.2)	34	(2.2)	52	(10.1)	**8**	(2.8)	**7**	(3.1)	9	(13.9)
	Switzerland	42	(2.1)	21	(1.9)	68	(14.5)	40	(2.1)	20	(1.6)	66	(11.6)	-2	(3.0)	0	(2.5)	-2	(18.6)
	United Kingdom	m	m	m	m	m	m	44	(1.9)	27	(2.0)	69	(7.0)	m	m	m	m	m	m
	United States	52	(3.0)	30	(4.6)	90	(10.9)	42	(2.3)	23	(2.9)	63	(12.1)	**-9**	(3.8)	-7	(5.5)	-27	(16.3)
	OECD average-26	39	(0.5)	18	(0.5)	66	(3.2)	38	(0.4)	19	(0.4)	61	(1.9)	-1	(0.6)	**2**	(0.6)	**-7**	(3.7)
Partners	Albania	41	(2.2)	15	(2.7)	54	(17.6)	31	(2.6)	13	(2.6)	39	(7.4)	**-10**	(3.4)	-3	(3.7)	-15	(19.1)
	Argentina	41	(2.9)	6	(3.0)	86	(7.8)	40	(2.3)	9	(1.7)	69	(5.5)	-2	(3.7)	3	(3.4)	-17	(9.6)
	Brazil	29	(1.8)	5	(1.5)	51	(3.4)	28	(1.4)	3	(1.2)	53	(3.8)	-1	(2.2)	-2	(1.9)	2	(5.1)
	Bulgaria	56	(4.3)	16	(3.1)	99	(20.2)	51	(2.8)	11	(2.3)	81	(7.7)	-4	(5.1)	-4	(3.9)	-18	(21.6)
	Hong Kong-China	26	(2.7)	6	(1.6)	50	(26.3)	17	(2.2)	3	(1.5)	33	(15.0)	**-9**	(3.5)	-3	(2.2)	-17	(30.3)
	Indonesia	24	(2.9)	4	(1.6)	44	(8.4)	17	(2.4)	1	(1.1)	25	(5.2)	-7	(3.8)	-3	(2.0)	-18	(9.9)
	Latvia	40	(3.8)	18	(3.0)	98	(15.0)	29	(2.6)	19	(2.6)	30	(8.5)	**-11**	(4.6)	0	(4.0)	**-68**	(17.2)
	Liechtenstein	39	(6.0)	10	(5.4)	102	(42.1)	26	(5.0)	3	(2.9)	121	(22.0)	-13	(7.8)	-8	(6.1)	18	(47.5)
	Peru	41	(2.1)	12	(2.3)	70	(6.2)	41	(2.0)	8	(1.6)	59	(4.0)	0	(2.9)	-3	(2.8)	-11	(7.4)
	Romania	26	(2.4)	0	(2.7)	47	(10.6)	36	(2.8)	10	(2.0)	40	(10.0)	**11**	(3.7)	**10**	(3.4)	-7	(14.6)
	Russian Federation	36	(2.8)	15	(1.8)	78	(10.8)	37	(2.5)	21	(2.2)	38	(7.6)	1	(3.8)	**6**	(2.8)	**-40**	(13.2)
	Thailand	23	(2.6)	3	(3.0)	12	(9.9)	22	(1.8)	2	(1.6)	18	(7.3)	-1	(3.2)	-1	(3.4)	6	(12.4)

Note: Values that are statistically significant are indicated in bold (see Annex A3).
1. Single-level bivariate regression of reading performance on the ESCS: the slope is the regression coefficient for the ESCS.
2. Two-level regression of reading performance on student ESCS and school mean ESCS: within-school slope for ESCS at the student level.
3. Two-level regression of reading performance on student ESCS and school mean ESCS: between-school slope for ESCS at the school level.
StatLink http://dx.doi.org/10.1787/888932343285

[Part 1/1]

Table V.4.4 Percentage of students and reading performance by immigrant status in PISA 2000 and 2009

Results based on students' self-reports

	PISA 2000								PISA 2009								Change between 2000 and 2009 (PISA 2009 – PISA 2000)			
	Percentage of students with an immigrant background		Performance of native students		Performance of students with an immigrant background		Difference in performance between native students and students with an immigrant background		Percentage of students with an immigrant background		Performance of native students		Performance of students with an immigrant background		Difference in performance between native students and students with an immigrant background		Change in the percentage of students with an immigrant background		Change in the performance difference between native students and students with an immigrant background	
	%	S.E.	Mean score	S.E.	Mean score	S.E.	Score dif.	S.E.	%	S.E.	Mean score	S.E.	Mean score	S.E.	Score dif.	S.E.	% dif.	S.E.	Score dif.	S.E.
OECD																				
Australia	22.6	(1.8)	532	(3.6)	520	(6.7)	12	(6.6)	23.2	(1.1)	515	(2.1)	524	(5.8)	**-10**	(5.8)	0.6	(2.1)	**-22**	(8.8)
Austria	11.0	(0.9)	502	(2.8)	409	(7.2)	**93**	(7.9)	m	m	m	m	m	m	m	m	m	m	m	m
Belgium	12.0	(1.1)	522	(3.8)	417	(7.6)	**106**	(8.2)	14.8	(1.1)	519	(2.2)	451	(6.4)	**68**	(6.3)	2.8	(1.6)	**-38**	(10.3)
Canada	20.5	(1.0)	538	(1.5)	526	(3.2)	**12**	(3.2)	24.4	(1.3)	528	(1.5)	521	(3.4)	7	(3.6)	**3.8**	(1.7)	-6	(4.8)
Chile	0.3	(0.1)	411	(3.6)	c	c	c	c	0.5	(0.1)	452	(3.0)	c	c	c	c	0.2	(0.1)	c	c
Czech Republic	1.1	(0.2)	501	(2.1)	463	(15.1)	**38**	(14.9)	2.3	(0.2)	479	(2.8)	457	(13.7)	22	(13.2)	**1.2**	(0.3)	-16	(19.9)
Denmark	6.2	(0.6)	504	(2.2)	424	(7.6)	**80**	(7.6)	8.6	(0.4)	502	(2.2)	438	(3.8)	**63**	(3.9)	**2.5**	(0.7)	-17	(8.5)
Finland	1.3	(0.2)	548	(2.6)	476	(12.8)	**71**	(12.8)	2.6	(0.3)	538	(2.2)	468	(12.8)	**70**	(12.7)	**1.3**	(0.4)	-2	(18.0)
France	12.0	(0.9)	512	(2.8)	464	(6.2)	**48**	(6.5)	13.1	(1.4)	505	(3.8)	444	(8.5)	**60**	(9.2)	1.1	(1.6)	12	(11.3)
Germany	15.2	(0.8)	507	(2.3)	423	(6.1)	**84**	(6.2)	17.6	(1.0)	511	(2.6)	455	(4.7)	**56**	(4.8)	2.4	(1.3)	**-28**	(7.8)
Greece	4.8	(0.9)	478	(4.7)	413	(16.3)	**65**	(15.9)	9.0	(0.8)	489	(4.2)	432	(11.5)	**57**	(11.1)	**4.2**	(1.2)	-7	(19.4)
Hungary	1.7	(0.2)	482	(4.0)	489	(11.2)	-7	(11.0)	2.1	(0.3)	495	(3.1)	507	(8.3)	-12	(8.4)	0.4	(0.3)	-5	(13.9)
Iceland	0.8	(0.2)	509	(1.5)	c	c	c	c	2.4	(0.2)	504	(1.4)	423	(11.7)	**81**	(11.7)	**1.6**	(0.3)	c	c
Ireland	2.3	(0.3)	528	(3.2)	552	(11.0)	**-24**	(10.7)	8.3	(0.6)	502	(3.0)	473	(7.1)	**29**	(7.3)	**5.9**	(0.7)	**53**	(12.9)
Israel	25.0	(1.7)	456	(9.6)	459	(9.9)	-3	(9.6)	19.7	(1.1)	480	(3.3)	478	(6.4)	2	(6.1)	**-5.2**	(2.0)	5	(11.4)
Italy	0.9	(0.2)	489	(2.9)	450	(13.3)	**39**	(13.8)	5.5	(0.3)	491	(1.6)	418	(4.2)	**72**	(4.4)	**4.6**	(0.3)	**33**	(14.5)
Japan	0.1	(0.1)	525	(5.1)	c	c	c	c	0.3	(0.1)	521	(3.4)	c	c	c	c	0.1	(0.1)	c	c
Korea	m	m	m	m	m	m	m	m	0.0	(0.0)	540	(3.4)	c	c	c	c	m	m	m	m
Luxembourg	m	m	m	m	m	m	m	m	40.2	(0.7)	495	(1.9)	442	(2.1)	**52**	(3.0)	m	m	m	m
Mexico	3.6	(0.4)	427	(3.3)	345	(8.1)	**82**	(8.3)	1.9	(0.2)	430	(1.8)	331	(7.9)	**99**	(7.5)	**-1.7**	(0.4)	17	(11.2)
Netherlands	m	m	m	m	m	m	m	m	12.1	(1.4)	515	(5.2)	470	(7.8)	**46**	(8.0)	m	m	m	m
New Zealand	19.6	(1.1)	538	(2.7)	507	(7.1)	**30**	(7.1)	24.7	(1.0)	526	(2.6)	513	(4.7)	**13**	(5.3)	**5.0**	(1.5)	**-18**	(8.9)
Norway	4.6	(0.4)	510	(2.7)	454	(6.7)	**56**	(6.3)	6.8	(0.6)	508	(2.6)	456	(5.9)	**52**	(5.7)	**2.2**	(0.7)	-4	(8.5)
Poland	0.3	(0.1)	482	(4.4)	c	c	c	c	0.0	(0.0)	502	(2.6)	c	c	c	c	**-0.2**	(0.1)	c	c
Portugal	3.1	(0.3)	472	(4.5)	457	(12.1)	14	(11.8)	5.5	(0.5)	492	(3.1)	466	(6.9)	**26**	(7.0)	**2.3**	(0.5)	12	(13.7)
Spain	2.0	(0.4)	494	(2.6)	457	(13.1)	**37**	(12.9)	9.5	(0.5)	488	(2.0)	430	(4.0)	**58**	(3.9)	**7.5**	(0.6)	21	(13.5)
Sweden	10.5	(0.9)	523	(2.1)	465	(5.4)	**58**	(5.7)	11.7	(1.2)	507	(2.7)	442	(6.9)	**66**	(7.2)	1.2	(1.5)	8	(9.2)
Switzerland	20.7	(0.9)	514	(4.0)	428	(4.8)	**86**	(4.4)	23.5	(0.9)	513	(2.2)	465	(4.1)	**48**	(3.5)	**2.8**	(1.3)	**-38**	(5.6)
United Kingdom	m	m	m	m	m	m	m	m	10.6	(1.0)	499	(2.2)	476	(7.5)	**23**	(7.6)	m	m	m	m
United States	13.6	(2.1)	511	(6.5)	472	(14.1)	**39**	(11.7)	19.5	(1.3)	506	(3.8)	484	(5.8)	**22**	(5.5)	**5.9**	(2.5)	-17	(12.9)
OECD average-26	8.2	(0.2)	500	(0.8)	460	(2.2)	**44**	(2.2)	9.9	(0.2)	502	(0.5)	458	(1.6)	**43**	(1.6)	**2.1**	(0.2)	-3	(2.7)
Partners																				
Albania	0.8	(0.2)	351	(3.3)	296	(18.0)	**-55**	(18.7)	0.6	(0.2)	389	(4.0)	c	c	c	c	-0.1	(0.3)	c	c
Argentina	2.3	(0.5)	422	(9.2)	364	(22.6)	**58**	(19.0)	3.6	(0.5)	401	(4.6)	362	(15.2)	**40**	(15.6)	1.3	(0.7)	-18	(24.6)
Brazil	0.4	(0.1)	398	(3.0)	c	c	c	c	0.8	(0.1)	416	(2.7)	317	(13.5)	**99**	(13.8)	**0.4**	(0.2)	c	c
Bulgaria	0.4	(0.1)	434	(4.9)	c	c	c	c	0.5	(0.1)	433	(6.7)	c	c	c	c	0.1	(0.2)	c	c
Hong Kong-China	43.8	(1.0)	531	(3.3)	521	(3.2)	**10**	(3.2)	39.4	(1.5)	535	(2.7)	531	(3.4)	4	(4.3)	**-4.4**	(1.8)	-5	(5.3)
Indonesia	0.4	(0.1)	372	(3.7)	294	(16.4)	**78**	(16.2)	0.3	(0.1)	403	(3.7)	c	c	c	c	-0.1	(0.1)	c	c
Latvia	22.1	(2.4)	462	(6.0)	452	(6.9)	11	(8.0)	4.5	(0.5)	485	(2.9)	474	(9.0)	11	(8.4)	**-17.6**	(2.4)	1	(11.6)
Liechtenstein	20.6	(2.1)	500	(5.0)	419	(13.7)	**81**	(15.7)	30.3	(2.5)	510	(4.3)	479	(7.4)	**31**	(10.3)	**9.8**	(3.3)	**-50**	(18.7)
Peru	0.3	(0.1)	331	(4.3)	c	c	c	c	0.4	(0.1)	374	(3.9)	c	c	c	c	0.2	(0.1)	c	c
Romania	0.2	(0.1)	428	(3.5)	c	c	c	c	0.3	(0.1)	426	(4.0)	c	c	c	c	0.2	(0.1)	c	c
Russian Federation	4.6	(0.6)	463	(4.3)	456	(6.1)	7	(6.6)	12.1	(0.7)	464	(3.2)	439	(7.0)	**25**	(6.8)	**7.5**	(1.0)	18	(9.5)
Thailand	0.7	(0.5)	432	(3.2)	c	c	c	c	0.0	c	421	(2.6)	c	c	c	c	c	c	c	c

Note: Values that are statistically significant are indicated in bold (see Annex A3).

StatLink http://dx.doi.org/10.1787/888932343285

[Part 1/1]

Table V.4.5 Language spoken at home and reading performance in PISA 2000 and 2009

Results based on students' self-reports

		PISA 2000								PISA 2009								Change between 2000 and 2009 (PISA 2009 – PISA 2000)			
		Percentage of students whose language spoken at home most of the time is DIFFERENT from the language of assessment		Performance of students whose language spoken at home most of the time is the SAME as the language of assessment		Performance of students whose language spoken at home most of the time is DIFFERENT from the language of assessment		Difference in the performance of students whose language spoken at home is the SAME and those whose language spoken at home is DIFFERENT from the language of assessment		Percentage of students whose language spoken at home most of the time is DIFFERENT from the language of assessment		Performance of students whose language spoken at home most of the time is the SAME as the language of assessment		Performance of students whose language spoken at home most of the time is DIFFERENT from the language of assessment		Difference in the performance of students whose language spoken at home is the SAME and those whose language spoken at home is DIFFERENT from the language of assessment		Change in the percentage of students whose language spoken at home most of the time is DIFFERENT from the language of assessment		Change in the performance difference between students whose language spoken at home is the SAME and those whose language spoken at home is DIFFERENT from the language of assessment	
		%	S.E.	Mean score	S.E.	Mean score	S.E.	Score dif.	S.E.	%	S.E.	Mean score	S.E.	Mean score	S.E.	Score dif.	S.E.	% dif.	S.E.	Score dif.	S.E.
OECD	Australia	17.2	(1.6)	535	(3.6)	504	(7.5)	**31**	(7.4)	9.2	(0.7)	518	(2.0)	509	(8.9)	10	(8.3)	**-8.0**	(1.8)	-21	(11.1)
	Austria	7.8	(0.7)	502	(2.8)	410	(7.9)	**92**	(8.5)	m	m	m	m	m	m	m	m	m	m	m	m
	Belgium	22.9	(1.0)	516	(3.9)	500	(4.7)	**15**	(5.6)	21.6	(1.1)	518	(2.4)	480	(5.6)	**38**	(5.6)	-1.2	(1.5)	**23**	(7.9)
	Canada	11.5	(0.6)	540	(1.5)	505	(3.2)	**35**	(3.0)	14.2	(0.8)	530	(1.5)	512	(3.9)	**18**	(4.1)	**2.7**	(1.0)	**-17**	(5.1)
	Chile	0.7	(0.1)	410	(3.6)	364	(18.5)	**47**	(18.6)	0.5	(0.1)	451	(3.0)	c	c	c	c	-0.2	(0.2)	c	c
	Czech Republic	0.8	(0.2)	494	(2.2)	432	(39.6)	62	(39.0)	1.3	(0.2)	481	(2.8)	477	(16.5)	4	(16.1)	**0.5**	(0.2)	-58	(42.2)
	Denmark	6.7	(0.4)	503	(2.2)	425	(8.1)	**78**	(7.7)	4.5	(0.3)	501	(2.1)	434	(5.3)	**67**	(5.2)	**-2.1**	(0.5)	-11	(9.3)
	Finland	5.8	(0.3)	549	(2.6)	502	(10.2)	**47**	(10.3)	3.7	(0.3)	538	(2.2)	477	(7.8)	**61**	(7.5)	**-2.2**	(0.4)	14	(12.8)
	France	5.1	(0.5)	510	(2.6)	446	(7.5)	**64**	(7.7)	7.0	(0.6)	505	(3.6)	433	(9.2)	**72**	(9.7)	**2.0**	(0.8)	8	(12.4)
	Germany	7.9	(0.8)	500	(2.9)	386	(13.9)	**114**	(15.5)	10.5	(0.8)	510	(2.5)	452	(6.4)	**58**	(6.4)	**2.5**	(1.1)	**-57**	(16.8)
	Greece	2.8	(0.6)	477	(4.8)	407	(18.3)	**69**	(17.6)	4.8	(0.6)	488	(4.4)	408	(14.8)	**79**	(14.6)	**2.0**	(0.9)	10	(22.9)
	Hungary	m	m	m	m	m	m	m	m	1.0	(0.3)	496	(3.1)	403	(35.0)	**93**	(35.0)	m	m	m	m
	Iceland	1.9	(0.3)	509	(1.5)	463	(13.4)	**46**	(13.5)	3.1	(0.3)	504	(1.4)	435	(10.7)	**69**	(10.8)	**1.2**	(0.4)	22	(17.3)
	Ireland	2.0	(0.5)	527	(3.1)	537	(18.0)	-9	(17.1)	5.8	(0.9)	500	(3.0)	467	(13.9)	**34**	(13.7)	**3.9**	(1.0)	**43**	(21.9)
	Israel	11.3	(1.2)	459	(8.9)	447	(12.6)	12	(9.5)	11.8	(1.1)	482	(3.4)	470	(11.5)	11	(11.9)	0.5	(1.6)	-1	(15.2)
	Italy	18.0	(1.1)	500	(2.9)	448	(6.8)	**52**	(7.0)	14.3	(0.4)	503	(1.4)	441	(3.0)	**62**	(3.2)	**-3.7**	(1.2)	10	(7.7)
	Japan	0.3	(0.1)	525	(5.2)	c	c	c	c	0.2	(0.1)	522	(3.4)	c	c	c	c	0.0	(0.1)	c	c
	Korea	m	m	m	m	m	m	m	m	0.1	(0.0)	540	(3.4)	c	c	c	c	m	m	m	m
	Luxembourg	m	m	m	m	m	m	m	m	88.9	(0.4)	519	(4.8)	479	(1.5)	**40**	(4.9)	m	m	m	m
	Mexico	1.7	(0.5)	423	(3.4)	352	(12.9)	**71**	(13.2)	2.8	(0.3)	429	(1.8)	334	(8.0)	**95**	(8.0)	**1.1**	(0.6)	24	(15.5)
	Netherlands	m	m	m	m	m	m	m	m	6.4	(0.8)	513	(5.1)	474	(11.4)	**39**	(10.8)	m	m	m	m
	New Zealand	10.3	(0.6)	542	(2.6)	467	(9.1)	**75**	(8.6)	14.5	(0.7)	530	(2.4)	474	(5.5)	**56**	(5.7)	**4.2**	(0.9)	-19	(10.3)
	Norway	6.3	(0.5)	512	(2.8)	444	(7.8)	**68**	(7.5)	7.3	(0.5)	508	(2.6)	451	(5.6)	**58**	(5.3)	0.9	(0.7)	-11	(9.2)
	Poland	1.0	(0.2)	483	(4.4)	417	(23.6)	**65**	(23.1)	0.6	(0.1)	502	(2.6)	c	c	c	c	-0.4	(0.3)	c	c
	Portugal	1.5	(0.2)	471	(4.6)	416	(13.8)	**56**	(14.7)	1.6	(0.2)	491	(3.1)	460	(9.4)	**31**	(9.3)	0.1	(0.3)	-25	(17.4)
	Spain	14.6	(1.5)	495	(2.8)	493	(5.9)	2	(6.1)	18.1	(1.0)	484	(1.9)	471	(3.8)	**13**	(3.6)	3.4	(1.8)	11	(7.0)
	Sweden	7.4	(0.6)	523	(2.0)	459	(6.6)	**64**	(6.8)	8.1	(0.9)	507	(2.7)	435	(7.7)	**72**	(7.7)	0.6	(1.1)	8	(10.3)
	Switzerland	18.9	(0.8)	512	(4.1)	425	(5.6)	**88**	(4.7)	15.5	(0.7)	514	(2.2)	460	(3.6)	**54**	(3.2)	**-3.4**	(1.1)	**-33**	(5.7)
	United Kingdom	m	m	m	m	m	m	m	m	6.2	(0.6)	499	(2.2)	453	(8.3)	**46**	(8.4)	m	m	m	m
	United States	10.8	(2.4)	514	(5.8)	438	(13.1)	**76**	(11.4)	13.1	(1.0)	506	(3.7)	471	(5.8)	**34**	(5.9)	2.3	(2.6)	**-41**	(12.8)
	OECD average-26	7.8	(0.2)	501	(0.8)	447	(3.0)	**53**	(3.0)	7.5	(0.1)	502	(0.5)	453	(2.4)	**50**	(2.4)	0.3	(0.2)	-6	(3.5)
Partners	Albania	1.2	(0.2)	351	(3.2)	356	(12.6)	-5	(12.3)	1.0	(0.2)	386	(4.1)	358	(18.9)	28	(18.9)	-0.1	(0.3)	33	(22.5)
	Argentina	0.7	(0.2)	420	(9.5)	c	c	c	c	1.4	(0.2)	403	(4.6)	320	(18.2)	**82**	(17.8)	**0.6**	(0.3)	c	c
	Brazil	0.8	(0.2)	397	(3.0)	388	(28.2)	9	(27.5)	0.7	(0.1)	413	(2.8)	354	(11.2)	**59**	(11.3)	-0.2	(0.2)	50	(29.7)
	Bulgaria	5.0	(0.8)	439	(4.8)	326	(13.4)	**113**	(14.4)	10.9	(1.7)	444	(6.5)	342	(9.7)	**102**	(10.1)	**5.9**	(1.9)	-11	(17.6)
	Hong Kong-China	9.3	(0.8)	531	(2.8)	484	(11.1)	**47**	(10.7)	7.2	(1.1)	538	(2.1)	480	(8.8)	**58**	(9.0)	-2.1	(1.3)	11	(14.0)
	Indonesia	68.3	(2.4)	386	(7.5)	366	(3.7)	**20**	(7.8)	64.4	(2.1)	408	(6.5)	399	(3.6)	9	(6.4)	-3.9	(3.2)	-11	(10.1)
	Latvia	7.0	(0.9)	462	(5.2)	436	(13.1)	**26**	(11.9)	9.4	(1.3)	487	(3.0)	469	(9.4)	18	(9.7)	2.4	(1.6)	-8	(15.4)
	Liechtenstein	26.9	(2.4)	500	(5.4)	438	(11.7)	**62**	(13.8)	15.0	(2.2)	512	(3.8)	451	(11.7)	**60**	(13.4)	**-11.9**	(3.3)	-2	(19.2)
	Peru	5.3	(1.2)	334	(4.0)	238	(6.3)	**96**	(7.2)	5.3	(0.9)	378	(4.0)	270	(7.0)	**107**	(7.8)	0.0	(1.5)	11	(10.6)
	Romania	2.2	(0.5)	428	(3.5)	442	(17.2)	-14	(17.0)	3.2	(0.6)	427	(4.1)	359	(12.8)	**68**	(12.7)	1.1	(0.7)	**81**	(21.3)
	Russian Federation	7.3	(2.1)	465	(4.3)	432	(9.3)	**33**	(10.5)	9.6	(1.5)	465	(3.3)	410	(8.3)	**55**	(8.7)	2.3	(2.6)	22	(13.6)
	Thailand	46.0	(2.3)	437	(4.8)	429	(3.1)	8	(5.2)	48.6	(1.6)	431	(3.3)	413	(3.5)	**18**	(4.3)	2.6	(2.9)	10	(6.7)

Note: Values that are statistically significant are indicated in bold (see Annex A3).

StatLink http://dx.doi.org/10.1787/888932343285

[Part 1/1]

Table V.5.1 **Percentage of students reading for enjoyment in PISA 2000 and 2009, by gender**
Results based on students' self-reports

		PISA 2000						PISA 2009						Change between 2000 and 2009 (PISA 2009 – PISA 2000)					
		All students		Girls		Boys		All students		Girls		Boys		All students		Girls		Boys	
		%	S.E.	%	S.E.	%	S.E.	%	S.E.	%	S.E.	%	S.E.	% dif.	S.E.	% dif.	S.E.	% dif.	S.E.
OECD	Australia	66.9	(1.2)	74.6	(1.5)	59.9	(1.7)	63.3	(0.6)	73.1	(0.8)	53.0	(0.8)	**-3.6**	(1.3)	-1.5	(1.6)	**-6.9**	(1.9)
	Austria	56.5	(1.2)	68.6	(1.1)	44.9	(1.3)	m	m	m	m	m	m	m	m	m	m	m	m
	Belgium	57.8	(0.9)	69.4	(0.7)	46.9	(1.4)	55.6	(0.8)	65.4	(1.0)	46.2	(1.0)	-2.2	(1.2)	**-4.1**	(1.2)	-0.7	(1.7)
	Canada	67.3	(0.4)	77.0	(0.5)	57.4	(0.7)	68.9	(0.5)	81.6	(0.5)	56.2	(0.8)	**1.6**	(0.7)	**4.5**	(0.7)	-1.3	(1.0)
	Chile	73.7	(0.8)	79.3	(1.0)	67.3	(1.1)	60.3	(0.8)	70.3	(0.9)	50.7	(1.0)	**-13.4**	(1.1)	**-9.0**	(1.3)	**-16.6**	(1.5)
	Czech Republic	73.8	(0.8)	84.9	(0.7)	61.3	(1.4)	57.0	(0.8)	71.5	(1.2)	44.3	(1.0)	**-16.7**	(1.2)	**-13.4**	(1.4)	**-17.0**	(1.7)
	Denmark	73.3	(0.8)	82.6	(1.0)	64.2	(1.3)	66.4	(0.9)	75.3	(1.1)	57.3	(1.1)	**-6.9**	(1.2)	**-7.3**	(1.5)	**-6.8**	(1.7)
	Finland	77.6	(0.7)	89.7	(0.6)	64.7	(1.1)	67.0	(0.8)	80.6	(1.0)	53.3	(1.1)	**-10.7**	(1.0)	**-9.2**	(1.2)	**-11.4**	(1.6)
	France	70.0	(0.8)	78.8	(0.9)	60.5	(1.1)	61.2	(1.0)	69.8	(1.3)	52.1	(1.3)	**-8.8**	(1.3)	**-9.0**	(1.6)	**-8.4**	(1.7)
	Germany	58.2	(0.9)	70.9	(0.9)	45.5	(1.2)	58.7	(0.9)	72.5	(1.1)	45.1	(1.1)	0.5	(1.2)	1.6	(1.4)	-0.4	(1.6)
	Greece	78.0	(0.8)	80.6	(0.9)	75.4	(1.4)	82.5	(0.8)	88.4	(0.9)	76.4	(1.1)	**4.5**	(1.1)	**7.8**	(1.3)	1.0	(1.8)
	Hungary	73.9	(0.9)	81.2	(1.0)	66.7	(1.2)	74.5	(0.8)	83.5	(0.9)	65.7	(1.2)	0.6	(1.2)	2.3	(1.4)	-1.0	(1.7)
	Iceland	70.2	(0.7)	77.3	(1.0)	63.0	(1.0)	62.0	(0.8)	72.3	(1.0)	51.5	(1.3)	**-8.2**	(1.0)	**-5.0**	(1.5)	**-11.5**	(1.7)
	Ireland	66.6	(0.9)	75.5	(1.0)	57.6	(1.4)	58.1	(1.0)	63.8	(1.3)	52.5	(1.4)	**-8.5**	(1.3)	**-11.7**	(1.6)	**-5.1**	(1.9)
	Israel	63.0	(2.4)	70.1	(2.9)	51.9	(2.0)	65.5	(0.9)	75.1	(1.0)	55.2	(1.5)	2.5	(2.6)	5.0	(3.0)	3.3	(2.5)
	Italy	69.4	(1.1)	76.7	(1.1)	62.0	(1.3)	66.1	(0.6)	79.0	(0.6)	53.9	(0.8)	**-3.3**	(1.2)	2.3	(1.3)	**-8.1**	(1.5)
	Japan	45.0	(1.2)	45.1	(1.5)	44.8	(1.6)	55.8	(0.9)	58.2	(1.3)	53.6	(1.1)	**10.9**	(1.6)	**13.1**	(2.0)	**8.8**	(1.9)
	Korea	69.4	(0.8)	70.3	(1.4)	68.8	(1.2)	61.5	(0.8)	62.6	(1.4)	60.5	(1.0)	**-8.0**	(1.2)	**-7.7**	(2.0)	**-8.3**	(1.5)
	Luxembourg	m	m	m	m	m	m	51.8	(0.8)	64.2	(1.0)	39.6	(1.1)	m	m	m	m	m	m
	Mexico	86.4	(0.7)	91.1	(0.8)	81.6	(1.1)	76.2	(0.4)	82.8	(0.4)	69.5	(0.7)	**-10.2**	(0.8)	**-8.3**	(0.9)	**-12.1**	(1.3)
	Netherlands	m	m	m	m	m	m	51.4	(1.3)	66.8	(1.4)	35.8	(1.5)	m	m	m	m	m	m
	New Zealand	70.1	(0.9)	76.9	(1.0)	63.2	(1.3)	68.7	(0.8)	78.3	(1.0)	59.4	(1.1)	-1.4	(1.2)	1.4	(1.4)	**-3.8**	(1.7)
	Norway	64.6	(0.8)	75.3	(1.1)	54.4	(1.3)	60.0	(0.9)	70.0	(1.1)	50.4	(1.1)	**-4.6**	(1.2)	**-5.3**	(1.6)	**-4.0**	(1.7)
	Poland	75.8	(1.1)	83.9	(1.0)	67.8	(1.8)	67.8	(0.8)	82.5	(0.9)	53.1	(1.3)	**-8.0**	(1.4)	-1.3	(1.3)	**-14.6**	(2.2)
	Portugal	81.6	(0.8)	91.7	(0.6)	70.6	(1.3)	64.8	(0.7)	78.7	(0.8)	50.2	(1.0)	**-16.8**	(1.1)	**-13.0**	(1.0)	**-20.4**	(1.7)
	Spain	68.2	(0.9)	77.6	(1.1)	58.5	(1.2)	60.4	(0.7)	70.0	(0.8)	51.0	(0.9)	**-7.9**	(1.1)	**-7.6**	(1.4)	**-7.5**	(1.5)
	Sweden	64.0	(1.0)	73.0	(1.3)	55.1	(1.2)	62.7	(0.9)	75.0	(1.0)	50.7	(1.1)	-1.3	(1.3)	2.0	(1.7)	**-4.5**	(1.6)
	Switzerland	64.9	(1.1)	78.5	(1.1)	51.1	(1.6)	55.4	(0.9)	67.6	(1.0)	43.6	(1.1)	**-9.5**	(1.4)	**-10.9**	(1.5)	**-7.6**	(1.9)
	United Kingdom	m	m	m	m	m	m	60.4	(0.9)	69.7	(1.1)	50.7	(1.0)	m	m	m	m	m	m
	United States	59.3	(1.3)	68.0	(1.5)	49.9	(1.8)	58.0	(1.0)	69.2	(1.3)	47.4	(1.2)	-1.3	(1.7)	1.2	(2.0)	-2.5	(2.2)
	OECD average-26	68.8	(0.2)	76.9	(0.2)	60.4	(0.3)	63.8	(0.2)	73.7	(0.2)	54.0	(0.2)	**-5.0**	(0.3)	**-3.2**	(0.3)	**-6.4**	(0.3)
Partners	Albania	91.4	(0.6)	93.4	(0.6)	88.9	(1.1)	92.6	(0.5)	97.4	(0.4)	88.0	(0.8)	1.2	(0.8)	**4.0**	(0.7)	-0.9	(1.4)
	Argentina	70.7	(0.9)	77.1	(1.2)	62.2	(1.3)	58.3	(1.0)	65.8	(1.3)	49.4	(1.2)	**-12.4**	(1.3)	**-11.3**	(1.8)	**-12.8**	(1.8)
	Brazil	80.7	(1.0)	87.2	(0.9)	72.9	(1.4)	78.2	(0.6)	86.6	(0.5)	68.7	(1.0)	**-2.5**	(1.1)	-0.6	(1.1)	**-4.2**	(1.7)
	Bulgaria	68.7	(1.0)	76.9	(1.3)	60.2	(1.2)	72.0	(1.3)	82.7	(1.1)	61.9	(1.6)	**3.3**	(1.7)	**5.8**	(1.7)	1.7	(2.0)
	Hong Kong-China	75.9	(0.9)	80.0	(0.9)	71.8	(1.3)	80.5	(0.6)	84.9	(0.9)	76.5	(0.8)	**4.6**	(1.1)	**5.0**	(1.3)	**4.7**	(1.5)
	Indonesia	86.5	(1.1)	88.1	(1.5)	84.7	(1.1)	87.9	(0.6)	92.2	(0.6)	83.4	(0.9)	1.3	(1.2)	**4.1**	(1.6)	-1.3	(1.4)
	Latvia	82.1	(1.1)	90.5	(0.9)	73.2	(1.6)	70.3	(0.9)	85.2	(0.9)	55.1	(1.5)	**-11.8**	(1.4)	**-5.3**	(1.3)	**-18.2**	(2.2)
	Liechtenstein	59.5	(2.7)	68.5	(3.9)	51.5	(3.9)	48.0	(2.4)	58.4	(3.7)	38.8	(3.4)	**-11.5**	(3.7)	-10.1	(5.4)	**-12.7**	(5.2)
	Peru	91.3	(0.6)	92.2	(0.7)	90.4	(0.9)	86.3	(0.5)	89.1	(0.6)	83.5	(0.8)	**-5.0**	(0.8)	**-3.1**	(0.9)	**-6.8**	(1.2)
	Romania	81.0	(0.8)	83.4	(1.0)	78.2	(1.3)	75.7	(0.9)	84.6	(1.0)	66.4	(1.3)	**-5.3**	(1.2)	1.2	(1.4)	**-11.8**	(1.8)
	Russian Federation	80.6	(0.7)	86.1	(0.7)	75.0	(0.9)	78.6	(0.8)	86.6	(0.9)	70.6	(1.2)	-1.9	(1.1)	0.5	(1.1)	**-4.4**	(1.5)
	Thailand	88.1	(0.9)	91.4	(0.8)	83.0	(1.7)	90.8	(0.5)	95.1	(0.4)	85.1	(0.9)	**2.8**	(1.0)	**3.7**	(0.9)	2.1	(2.0)

Note: Values that are statistically significant are indicated in bold (see Annex A3).
StatLink http://dx.doi.org/10.1787/888932343285

[Part 1/1]
Table V.5.2 Index of enjoyment of reading in PISA 2000 and 2009, by gender
Results based on students' self-reports

		PISA 2000						PISA 2009						Change between 2000 and 2009 (PISA 2009 – PISA 2000)					
		All students		Girls		Boys		All students		Girls		Boys		All students		Girls		Boys	
		Mean index	S.E.	Mean index	S.E.	Mean index	S.E.	Mean index	S.E.	Mean index	S.E.	Mean index	S.E.	Dif.	S.E.	Dif.	S.E.	Dif.	S.E.
OECD	Australia	-0.03	(0.03)	0.21	(0.03)	-0.25	(0.03)	0.00	(0.02)	0.31	(0.02)	-0.33	(0.02)	0.03	(0.03)	**0.10**	(0.04)	**-0.08**	(0.03)
	Austria	-0.09	(0.03)	0.34	(0.03)	-0.51	(0.03)	m	m	m	m	m	m	m	m	m	m	m	m
	Belgium	-0.21	(0.02)	0.09	(0.02)	-0.49	(0.02)	-0.20	(0.02)	0.07	(0.02)	-0.45	(0.02)	0.01	(0.02)	-0.01	(0.03)	0.03	(0.03)
	Canada	0.04	(0.01)	0.34	(0.02)	-0.27	(0.01)	0.13	(0.01)	0.55	(0.02)	-0.28	(0.02)	**0.10**	(0.02)	**0.20**	(0.02)	-0.01	(0.02)
	Chile	-0.01	(0.02)	0.22	(0.02)	-0.26	(0.02)	-0.06	(0.01)	0.16	(0.02)	-0.28	(0.02)	**-0.06**	(0.02)	-0.06	(0.03)	-0.02	(0.03)
	Czech Republic	0.22	(0.02)	0.59	(0.02)	-0.20	(0.03)	-0.13	(0.02)	0.22	(0.02)	-0.44	(0.02)	**-0.35**	(0.03)	**-0.37**	(0.04)	**-0.24**	(0.03)
	Denmark	0.04	(0.02)	0.37	(0.03)	-0.27	(0.02)	-0.09	(0.02)	0.17	(0.02)	-0.35	(0.02)	**-0.13**	(0.02)	**-0.20**	(0.03)	**-0.08**	(0.03)
	Finland	0.24	(0.02)	0.69	(0.02)	-0.24	(0.02)	0.05	(0.02)	0.50	(0.02)	-0.41	(0.02)	**-0.20**	(0.03)	**-0.20**	(0.03)	**-0.17**	(0.03)
	France	-0.02	(0.02)	0.24	(0.02)	-0.30	(0.02)	0.01	(0.03)	0.24	(0.03)	-0.23	(0.03)	0.04	(0.03)	0.00	(0.04)	0.07	(0.04)
	Germany	-0.05	(0.03)	0.36	(0.03)	-0.47	(0.03)	0.07	(0.02)	0.52	(0.03)	-0.38	(0.02)	**0.12**	(0.03)	**0.16**	(0.04)	**0.09**	(0.04)
	Greece	0.03	(0.02)	0.24	(0.02)	-0.18	(0.02)	0.07	(0.02)	0.36	(0.02)	-0.24	(0.02)	0.03	(0.03)	**0.12**	(0.03)	**-0.06**	(0.03)
	Hungary	0.11	(0.02)	0.34	(0.03)	-0.11	(0.03)	0.14	(0.02)	0.43	(0.02)	-0.15	(0.03)	0.02	(0.03)	**0.09**	(0.04)	-0.04	(0.04)
	Iceland	0.06	(0.02)	0.32	(0.02)	-0.20	(0.02)	-0.06	(0.02)	0.25	(0.02)	-0.38	(0.02)	**-0.12**	(0.02)	**-0.07**	(0.03)	**-0.18**	(0.03)
	Ireland	-0.03	(0.02)	0.25	(0.03)	-0.32	(0.03)	-0.08	(0.02)	0.15	(0.03)	-0.30	(0.03)	-0.05	(0.03)	**-0.11**	(0.04)	0.02	(0.04)
	Israel	0.21	(0.06)	0.43	(0.08)	-0.11	(0.04)	0.06	(0.02)	0.35	(0.03)	-0.26	(0.03)	**-0.15**	(0.07)	-0.08	(0.08)	**-0.14**	(0.06)
	Italy	0.04	(0.03)	0.33	(0.03)	-0.24	(0.02)	0.06	(0.01)	0.41	(0.01)	-0.27	(0.01)	0.02	(0.03)	**0.08**	(0.03)	-0.03	(0.03)
	Japan	0.13	(0.03)	0.28	(0.04)	-0.03	(0.03)	0.20	(0.02)	0.38	(0.02)	0.02	(0.03)	**0.07**	(0.03)	**0.10**	(0.04)	0.06	(0.04)
	Korea	0.06	(0.02)	0.18	(0.04)	-0.04	(0.02)	0.13	(0.02)	0.27	(0.02)	0.00	(0.02)	**0.07**	(0.03)	**0.09**	(0.04)	0.04	(0.03)
	Luxembourg	m	m	m	m	m	m	-0.16	(0.02)	0.20	(0.03)	-0.51	(0.02)	m	m	m	m	m	m
	Mexico	0.34	(0.02)	0.51	(0.02)	0.18	(0.02)	0.14	(0.01)	0.32	(0.01)	-0.04	(0.01)	**-0.20**	(0.02)	**-0.19**	(0.02)	**-0.21**	(0.02)
	Netherlands	m	m	m	m	m	m	-0.32	(0.03)	0.02	(0.03)	-0.66	(0.03)	m	m	m	m	m	m
	New Zealand	0.05	(0.02)	0.27	(0.02)	-0.17	(0.02)	0.13	(0.02)	0.44	(0.02)	-0.17	(0.02)	**0.08**	(0.03)	**0.17**	(0.03)	0.00	(0.03)
	Norway	-0.18	(0.02)	0.16	(0.03)	-0.50	(0.02)	-0.19	(0.02)	0.13	(0.03)	-0.50	(0.02)	-0.01	(0.03)	-0.03	(0.04)	0.01	(0.03)
	Poland	0.04	(0.03)	0.27	(0.03)	-0.18	(0.03)	0.02	(0.02)	0.39	(0.03)	-0.36	(0.02)	-0.02	(0.03)	**0.12**	(0.04)	**-0.18**	(0.04)
	Portugal	0.36	(0.02)	0.68	(0.02)	0.02	(0.02)	0.21	(0.02)	0.54	(0.02)	-0.15	(0.02)	**-0.15**	(0.03)	**-0.13**	(0.03)	**-0.17**	(0.03)
	Spain	0.00	(0.02)	0.24	(0.03)	-0.26	(0.02)	-0.01	(0.01)	0.26	(0.01)	-0.28	(0.02)	-0.01	(0.02)	0.02	(0.03)	-0.02	(0.03)
	Sweden	-0.02	(0.02)	0.28	(0.03)	-0.32	(0.03)	-0.11	(0.02)	0.26	(0.03)	-0.47	(0.02)	**-0.08**	(0.03)	-0.02	(0.04)	**-0.15**	(0.03)
	Switzerland	0.10	(0.03)	0.56	(0.03)	-0.37	(0.03)	-0.04	(0.02)	0.37	(0.03)	-0.44	(0.02)	**-0.14**	(0.04)	**-0.19**	(0.04)	-0.07	(0.04)
	United Kingdom	m	m	m	m	m	m	-0.12	(0.02)	0.13	(0.02)	-0.37	(0.02)	m	m	m	m	m	m
	United States	-0.09	(0.03)	0.10	(0.04)	-0.30	(0.04)	-0.04	(0.03)	0.28	(0.03)	-0.35	(0.03)	0.05	(0.04)	**0.18**	(0.05)	-0.04	(0.05)
	OECD average-26	0.05	(0.00)	0.33	(0.01)	-0.23	(0.01)	0.02	(0.00)	0.32	(0.00)	-0.29	(0.00)	**-0.04**	(0.01)	-0.01	(0.01)	**-0.06**	(0.01)
Partners	Albania	0.56	(0.01)	0.70	(0.02)	0.39	(0.02)	0.67	(0.02)	0.99	(0.02)	0.36	(0.02)	**0.11**	(0.02)	**0.28**	(0.03)	-0.03	(0.03)
	Argentina	-0.08	(0.03)	0.09	(0.04)	-0.30	(0.04)	-0.16	(0.02)	-0.01	(0.02)	-0.34	(0.02)	**-0.08**	(0.03)	**-0.09**	(0.04)	-0.04	(0.04)
	Brazil	0.20	(0.02)	0.43	(0.02)	-0.08	(0.02)	0.27	(0.01)	0.47	(0.01)	0.05	(0.01)	**0.07**	(0.02)	0.04	(0.03)	**0.12**	(0.02)
	Bulgaria	0.04	(0.03)	0.26	(0.03)	-0.18	(0.02)	-0.02	(0.03)	0.23	(0.03)	-0.25	(0.03)	-0.05	(0.04)	-0.03	(0.05)	**-0.08**	(0.03)
	Hong Kong-China	0.11	(0.01)	0.24	(0.02)	-0.02	(0.02)	0.32	(0.01)	0.51	(0.02)	0.16	(0.02)	**0.21**	(0.02)	**0.27**	(0.03)	**0.18**	(0.03)
	Indonesia	0.59	(0.01)	0.69	(0.02)	0.48	(0.02)	0.43	(0.01)	0.55	(0.01)	0.32	(0.01)	**-0.15**	(0.02)	**-0.14**	(0.02)	**-0.16**	(0.02)
	Latvia	0.00	(0.02)	0.24	(0.03)	-0.25	(0.03)	-0.04	(0.02)	0.30	(0.02)	-0.39	(0.02)	-0.04	(0.03)	0.06	(0.03)	**-0.14**	(0.03)
	Liechtenstein	-0.04	(0.06)	0.35	(0.09)	-0.43	(0.07)	-0.20	(0.05)	0.21	(0.08)	-0.57	(0.07)	**-0.16**	(0.08)	-0.14	(0.12)	-0.15	(0.10)
	Peru	0.32	(0.02)	0.37	(0.02)	0.26	(0.02)	0.35	(0.01)	0.48	(0.02)	0.21	(0.02)	0.03	(0.02)	**0.11**	(0.03)	-0.05	(0.03)
	Romania	0.25	(0.02)	0.42	(0.03)	0.07	(0.02)	0.10	(0.02)	0.32	(0.03)	-0.13	(0.02)	**-0.15**	(0.03)	**-0.10**	(0.04)	**-0.19**	(0.03)
	Russian Federation	0.09	(0.01)	0.27	(0.02)	-0.08	(0.02)	0.07	(0.01)	0.29	(0.02)	-0.15	(0.02)	-0.02	(0.02)	0.02	(0.03)	**-0.07**	(0.02)
	Thailand	0.17	(0.01)	0.25	(0.01)	0.05	(0.01)	0.54	(0.01)	0.67	(0.01)	0.36	(0.02)	**0.37**	(0.02)	**0.42**	(0.02)	**0.31**	(0.02)

Note: Values that are statistically significant are indicated in bold (see Annex A3).
StatLink http://dx.doi.org/10.1787/888932343285

[Part 1/3]

Percentage of students for several items in the index of enjoyment of reading in PISA 2000 and 2009[1]

Table V.5.3 *Percentage of students who report "agree" or "strongly agree" on the following reading activities*

		PISA 2000																	
		I read only if I have to		Reading is one of my favourite hobbies		I like talking about books with other people		I find it hard to finish books		I feel happy if I receive a book as a present		For me, reading is a waste of time		I enjoy going to a bookstore or a library		I read only to get information that I need		I cannot sit still and read for more than a few minutes	
		%	S.E.	%	S.E.	%	S.E.	%	S.E.	%	S.E.	%	S.E.	%	S.E.	%	S.E.	%	S.E.
OECD	Australia	38.6	(1.2)	31.4	(1.1)	29.6	(1.2)	32.8	(0.9)	45.1	(1.3)	23.7	(0.8)	42.4	(1.1)	44.9	(1.3)	21.0	(0.8)
	Austria	42.9	(1.1)	28.6	(1.2)	24.5	(1.0)	33.6	(0.9)	45.4	(1.3)	30.0	(1.1)	30.1	(1.0)	55.1	(1.3)	22.0	(0.9)
	Belgium	45.9	(0.8)	26.4	(0.8)	29.0	(0.8)	33.8	(0.7)	36.5	(0.7)	33.6	(0.7)	39.8	(0.8)	50.6	(0.7)	29.4	(0.7)
	Canada	36.7	(0.5)	33.7	(0.5)	32.8	(0.6)	30.7	(0.4)	46.4	(0.5)	23.4	(0.4)	50.7	(0.5)	43.3	(0.5)	24.8	(0.4)
	Chile	50.8	(1.0)	36.7	(0.9)	57.4	(1.0)	45.9	(0.8)	45.0	(0.9)	18.8	(0.8)	48.1	(1.0)	57.4	(1.0)	37.2	(1.0)
	Czech Republic	27.0	(0.9)	51.6	(0.9)	48.6	(0.9)	32.3	(0.8)	58.6	(0.9)	21.1	(0.8)	50.7	(0.8)	44.4	(1.0)	23.3	(0.7)
	Denmark	36.6	(0.8)	31.0	(0.7)	35.8	(0.9)	28.3	(0.8)	47.6	(1.0)	24.3	(0.8)	48.3	(0.9)	43.8	(0.9)	21.3	(0.7)
	Finland	26.4	(0.7)	41.0	(0.9)	33.3	(0.8)	24.8	(0.7)	54.7	(1.0)	23.2	(0.8)	59.6	(0.8)	34.7	(0.8)	13.8	(0.6)
	France	36.5	(0.9)	32.7	(0.8)	38.7	(0.9)	33.6	(0.8)	42.1	(1.0)	22.6	(0.8)	50.2	(0.9)	47.0	(0.8)	30.0	(0.8)
	Germany	39.1	(0.8)	29.1	(0.7)	25.6	(0.9)	33.1	(0.9)	45.9	(1.1)	30.7	(0.9)	35.7	(0.9)	52.4	(1.1)	20.1	(0.7)
	Greece	33.1	(1.2)	37.3	(1.0)	49.2	(1.3)	35.8	(0.9)	44.9	(1.5)	15.5	(0.9)	56.4	(1.2)	46.8	(1.2)	35.3	(1.1)
	Hungary	29.3	(1.0)	29.1	(0.9)	36.8	(0.9)	24.7	(0.7)	56.5	(1.2)	15.8	(0.7)	46.0	(0.9)	47.1	(1.1)	23.5	(0.9)
	Iceland	33.1	(0.8)	27.0	(0.8)	25.8	(0.8)	22.3	(0.6)	59.7	(0.9)	20.5	(0.7)	43.8	(0.8)	37.4	(0.9)	24.0	(0.7)
	Ireland	33.5	(0.9)	35.7	(1.0)	27.8	(0.9)	41.7	(0.9)	47.7	(1.0)	19.3	(0.7)	40.9	(1.2)	45.7	(1.1)	29.8	(0.8)
	Israel	34.8	(1.7)	38.4	(2.5)	41.9	(2.4)	22.6	(1.4)	52.0	(1.9)	21.3	(1.2)	46.4	(2.3)	41.3	(2.2)	21.3	(1.4)
	Italy	26.1	(1.0)	44.8	(1.0)	43.2	(1.0)	40.0	(0.7)	46.1	(1.1)	17.8	(0.6)	41.8	(1.4)	50.6	(1.0)	31.6	(0.9)
	Japan	48.3	(1.0)	36.4	(1.0)	36.5	(0.9)	40.6	(0.8)	40.9	(1.0)	19.7	(0.8)	66.8	(1.1)	30.3	(0.7)	27.4	(1.0)
	Korea	40.8	(0.9)	34.5	(0.9)	30.5	(0.9)	42.6	(0.7)	49.0	(1.2)	12.7	(0.6)	47.1	(1.1)	40.4	(1.0)	18.1	(0.7)
	Luxembourg	m	m	m	m	m	m	m	m	m	m	m	m	m	m	m	m	m	m
	Mexico	24.9	(0.9)	61.6	(1.3)	65.2	(1.1)	41.8	(0.8)	72.7	(1.1)	9.2	(0.5)	65.3	(1.3)	52.6	(0.9)	20.7	(0.8)
	Netherlands	m	m	m	m	m	m	m	m	m	m	m	m	m	m	m	m	m	m
	New Zealand	36.0	(1.0)	33.1	(0.9)	33.2	(1.1)	36.7	(1.0)	50.6	(0.9)	19.3	(0.8)	51.5	(1.2)	43.5	(1.0)	21.1	(0.8)
	Norway	42.6	(0.8)	24.1	(0.8)	21.9	(0.7)	29.2	(0.7)	39.0	(0.9)	30.4	(0.9)	39.0	(0.9)	49.1	(0.9)	24.1	(1.0)
	Poland	36.3	(1.4)	38.6	(1.1)	38.3	(1.0)	36.3	(1.1)	47.9	(1.2)	24.9	(1.1)	56.0	(1.1)	53.6	(1.4)	21.2	(1.0)
	Portugal	24.3	(1.1)	54.3	(0.9)	57.3	(0.9)	27.8	(0.8)	64.7	(0.9)	13.2	(0.8)	69.6	(1.0)	35.2	(0.9)	24.6	(1.0)
	Spain	41.3	(1.1)	35.4	(0.9)	41.5	(1.1)	42.3	(0.7)	37.7	(0.9)	15.7	(0.7)	42.1	(1.0)	46.0	(1.1)	19.9	(0.8)
	Sweden	37.4	(1.0)	29.4	(0.7)	30.0	(0.8)	25.7	(0.7)	38.0	(0.8)	28.9	(0.9)	42.0	(1.0)	43.4	(0.9)	21.9	(0.7)
	Switzerland	36.1	(0.9)	34.9	(1.1)	31.8	(1.0)	30.6	(0.8)	53.4	(1.1)	25.5	(0.9)	45.6	(1.1)	45.6	(1.1)	22.3	(0.7)
	United Kingdom	m	m	m	m	m	m	m	m	m	m	m	m	m	m	m	m	m	m
	United States	45.4	(1.5)	29.8	(1.0)	34.7	(1.5)	35.8	(1.0)	39.9	(1.4)	26.0	(1.4)	53.0	(1.5)	47.5	(1.7)	30.6	(1.4)
	OECD average-26	36.2	(0.2)	36.1	(0.2)	37.6	(0.2)	33.5	(0.2)	48.6	(0.2)	21.4	(0.2)	49.2	(0.2)	45.2	(0.2)	24.6	(0.2)
Partners	Albania	22.0	(0.8)	64.1	(1.0)	78.3	(0.8)	23.1	(0.8)	84.9	(0.6)	11.5	(0.8)	83.6	(0.7)	33.0	(1.1)	17.5	(0.9)
	Argentina	47.7	(1.7)	39.7	(1.1)	42.3	(1.6)	49.5	(1.5)	42.3	(1.7)	19.5	(1.1)	43.8	(1.3)	58.7	(1.7)	34.2	(1.4)
	Brazil	42.8	(1.1)	48.6	(1.1)	52.5	(1.2)	35.0	(1.0)	63.0	(1.2)	10.2	(0.5)	60.3	(1.2)	54.1	(1.3)	26.5	(1.0)
	Bulgaria	45.7	(1.2)	45.8	(1.4)	43.6	(1.7)	27.0	(0.9)	48.5	(1.1)	18.9	(0.7)	45.2	(1.1)	55.9	(1.1)	27.8	(1.0)
	Hong Kong-China	50.4	(0.9)	53.0	(0.9)	56.7	(0.7)	34.6	(0.9)	45.7	(0.9)	12.6	(0.5)	60.4	(0.9)	49.1	(0.9)	24.6	(0.7)
	Indonesia	7.9	(0.5)	89.8	(0.9)	85.0	(0.6)	29.2	(0.8)	89.0	(0.7)	6.8	(0.5)	87.7	(0.8)	50.6	(1.1)	27.4	(0.9)
	Latvia	35.2	(1.3)	37.5	(1.0)	37.5	(1.2)	35.4	(1.2)	48.1	(1.6)	23.5	(1.0)	45.3	(1.1)	55.8	(1.3)	20.1	(1.1)
	Liechtenstein	40.8	(2.9)	31.0	(2.4)	24.4	(2.2)	30.6	(2.6)	49.6	(2.8)	28.1	(2.4)	35.4	(2.7)	50.5	(2.7)	19.2	(2.1)
	Peru	19.2	(0.9)	65.4	(1.0)	70.0	(1.1)	55.8	(0.8)	69.0	(1.1)	16.6	(0.6)	72.1	(1.2)	49.5	(0.9)	47.2	(1.0)
	Romania	45.0	(1.0)	59.8	(1.1)	57.8	(1.0)	37.8	(1.1)	70.9	(0.8)	19.8	(1.0)	66.1	(0.8)	49.8	(1.0)	29.8	(1.1)
	Russian Federation	33.6	(0.8)	42.6	(1.1)	43.7	(1.0)	31.6	(0.6)	47.5	(1.0)	16.6	(0.7)	49.1	(0.8)	59.6	(0.8)	12.7	(0.5)
	Thailand	64.9	(0.8)	81.0	(0.8)	71.8	(1.0)	44.9	(1.0)	71.9	(1.0)	20.6	(1.1)	82.9	(0.9)	56.1	(1.2)	27.6	(1.1)

Note: Values that are statistically significant are indicated in bold (see Annex A3).

1. Items "I like to express my opinions about books I have read" and "I like to exchange books with my friends" were not used in PISA 2000 and cannot be compared with PISA 2009.

StatLink http://dx.doi.org/10.1787/888932343285

[Part 2/3]
Percentage of students for several items in the index of enjoyment of reading in PISA 2000 and 2009[1]
Table V.5.3 *Percentage of students who report "agree" or "strongly agree" on the following reading activities*

		PISA 2009																	
		I read only if I have to		Reading is one of my favourite hobbies		I like talking about books with other people		I find it hard to finish books		I feel happy if I receive a book as a present		For me, reading is a waste of time		I enjoy going to a bookstore or a library		I read only to get information that I need		I cannot sit still and read for more than a few minutes	
		%	S.E.	%	S.E.	%	S.E.	%	S.E.	%	S.E.	%	S.E.	%	S.E.	%	S.E.	%	S.E.
OECD	Australia	40.9	(0.6)	35.5	(0.8)	38.8	(0.7)	32.7	(0.5)	50.6	(0.6)	25.9	(0.5)	46.6	(0.7)	42.3	(0.8)	23.6	(0.5)
	Austria	m	m	m	m	m	m	m	m	m	m	m	m	m	m	m	m	m	m
	Belgium	44.5	(0.7)	24.1	(0.6)	28.9	(0.7)	34.5	(0.8)	36.9	(0.7)	34.6	(0.8)	36.7	(0.7)	47.3	(0.7)	28.3	(0.7)
	Canada	37.3	(0.5)	38.6	(0.5)	43.2	(0.5)	27.4	(0.5)	49.6	(0.7)	22.1	(0.5)	54.0	(0.6)	38.7	(0.6)	22.2	(0.5)
	Chile	34.8	(0.8)	32.1	(0.6)	47.4	(0.8)	46.5	(0.8)	38.3	(0.9)	17.8	(0.6)	33.7	(0.8)	64.8	(0.8)	33.0	(0.8)
	Czech Republic	40.8	(0.8)	33.4	(0.7)	34.9	(0.9)	34.3	(0.7)	43.8	(0.9)	32.5	(0.8)	34.5	(0.8)	51.8	(0.9)	32.5	(0.8)
	Denmark	45.4	(1.0)	24.2	(0.7)	36.7	(1.0)	25.2	(0.8)	42.8	(1.0)	25.9	(0.9)	34.7	(0.9)	47.5	(0.9)	19.6	(0.7)
	Finland	34.7	(0.8)	34.0	(0.8)	34.1	(0.9)	27.7	(0.7)	52.1	(0.8)	27.3	(0.8)	47.6	(0.9)	36.3	(0.8)	14.5	(0.6)
	France	33.9	(1.0)	31.2	(1.0)	42.6	(1.2)	39.2	(1.0)	41.5	(1.0)	25.8	(1.0)	47.2	(1.1)	43.5	(1.2)	26.5	(0.9)
	Germany	39.1	(0.8)	32.6	(0.8)	32.2	(0.8)	27.5	(0.7)	48.5	(0.8)	29.5	(0.7)	34.5	(0.8)	44.6	(0.8)	17.0	(0.5)
	Greece	42.8	(1.1)	29.1	(0.8)	37.7	(1.0)	38.6	(0.9)	42.7	(1.0)	13.0	(0.6)	45.5	(1.1)	39.2	(1.2)	30.9	(0.8)
	Hungary	32.5	(1.1)	34.8	(1.0)	38.8	(1.0)	20.9	(0.7)	55.4	(1.1)	22.2	(0.8)	46.5	(1.0)	47.4	(0.9)	19.5	(0.9)
	Iceland	47.8	(0.9)	24.0	(0.8)	33.0	(0.8)	29.8	(0.8)	60.8	(0.8)	25.0	(0.7)	40.5	(0.8)	41.6	(0.8)	25.7	(0.7)
	Ireland	39.2	(1.0)	31.7	(0.9)	34.7	(1.1)	40.4	(1.0)	45.8	(0.9)	24.1	(0.9)	40.0	(0.9)	44.9	(1.1)	31.6	(0.9)
	Israel	38.8	(0.9)	40.7	(1.0)	41.0	(0.9)	31.4	(0.7)	47.0	(1.0)	23.6	(0.8)	42.2	(1.0)	47.0	(1.0)	25.9	(0.8)
	Italy	28.8	(0.5)	39.8	(0.5)	44.2	(0.5)	38.4	(0.4)	48.8	(0.5)	21.5	(0.5)	39.4	(0.6)	47.8	(0.5)	30.4	(0.5)
	Japan	47.5	(0.8)	42.0	(0.9)	43.6	(0.8)	28.4	(0.7)	45.6	(0.8)	15.2	(0.6)	66.5	(0.7)	24.2	(0.7)	20.6	(0.6)
	Korea	54.8	(0.9)	39.1	(0.8)	38.5	(0.8)	32.4	(0.8)	55.2	(1.0)	9.5	(0.5)	42.2	(1.0)	31.0	(0.8)	15.9	(0.6)
	Luxembourg	47.7	(0.8)	26.2	(0.8)	25.6	(0.7)	29.9	(0.8)	36.9	(0.7)	33.4	(0.8)	29.4	(0.7)	49.0	(0.7)	25.9	(0.6)
	Mexico	41.1	(0.6)	49.3	(0.5)	48.2	(0.4)	39.2	(0.4)	57.3	(0.5)	12.2	(0.3)	46.9	(0.5)	55.4	(0.5)	23.9	(0.4)
	Netherlands	52.7	(1.4)	19.1	(1.0)	18.9	(0.9)	25.6	(0.8)	40.4	(1.2)	33.9	(1.3)	28.6	(0.9)	49.3	(1.4)	26.7	(1.1)
	New Zealand	38.0	(0.8)	37.5	(0.8)	42.7	(0.9)	30.6	(0.7)	56.5	(0.8)	18.1	(0.7)	54.4	(0.9)	39.7	(0.9)	18.3	(0.7)
	Norway	44.4	(0.9)	22.0	(0.7)	28.1	(0.8)	28.8	(0.7)	40.4	(0.9)	29.9	(0.8)	31.2	(0.7)	50.3	(0.9)	24.9	(0.7)
	Poland	44.2	(0.8)	37.1	(0.9)	38.9	(0.7)	34.5	(0.7)	41.1	(0.9)	26.8	(0.8)	42.7	(1.0)	53.6	(0.7)	29.9	(0.8)
	Portugal	22.0	(0.6)	35.6	(0.8)	48.6	(0.8)	29.4	(0.7)	52.9	(0.6)	18.8	(0.5)	54.0	(0.8)	42.9	(0.9)	31.3	(0.7)
	Spain	43.7	(0.7)	33.7	(0.5)	42.4	(0.7)	44.2	(0.6)	35.3	(0.5)	17.7	(0.6)	30.4	(0.6)	46.2	(0.7)	22.8	(0.5)
	Sweden	39.4	(0.7)	27.2	(0.7)	33.6	(0.9)	23.9	(0.7)	35.6	(0.9)	27.7	(0.7)	35.2	(0.9)	41.6	(0.9)	20.6	(0.7)
	Switzerland	43.4	(1.0)	29.5	(0.6)	31.2	(0.8)	31.7	(0.7)	45.0	(0.8)	31.3	(0.8)	39.6	(0.9)	45.8	(0.8)	21.6	(0.6)
	United Kingdom	41.8	(0.8)	27.1	(0.6)	35.0	(0.9)	37.1	(0.8)	49.1	(0.7)	23.4	(0.7)	34.2	(0.8)	48.2	(0.8)	28.0	(0.7)
	United States	49.7	(1.0)	30.5	(1.1)	40.9	(1.0)	31.0	(1.0)	37.9	(1.0)	25.8	(0.9)	53.8	(1.0)	47.1	(1.1)	28.3	(0.9)
	OECD average-26	40.4	(0.2)	33.4	(0.2)	38.6	(0.2)	32.6	(0.1)	46.4	(0.2)	23.2	(0.1)	43.1	(0.2)	44.7	(0.2)	24.6	(0.1)
Partners	Albania	36.5	(1.0)	67.7	(0.9)	72.6	(0.8)	22.4	(0.8)	84.8	(0.7)	6.3	(0.5)	81.3	(0.7)	37.4	(1.1)	21.5	(0.7)
	Argentina	57.7	(1.0)	32.2	(0.9)	38.8	(1.0)	55.1	(1.0)	46.3	(1.1)	19.6	(0.8)	36.2	(1.0)	66.4	(1.0)	35.1	(1.0)
	Brazil	15.6	(0.5)	48.1	(0.8)	51.3	(0.7)	35.3	(0.6)	51.4	(0.6)	7.6	(0.3)	53.4	(0.6)	40.7	(0.8)	30.4	(0.6)
	Bulgaria	47.6	(1.3)	36.3	(1.3)	36.3	(1.4)	31.0	(0.8)	43.0	(1.4)	21.6	(1.2)	47.6	(1.3)	56.8	(1.4)	30.9	(1.0)
	Hong Kong-China	42.9	(0.9)	64.9	(0.8)	60.6	(0.8)	23.2	(0.6)	58.5	(1.0)	9.2	(0.4)	64.8	(0.8)	37.7	(0.8)	16.4	(0.5)
	Indonesia	32.4	(1.0)	77.3	(0.9)	73.6	(0.9)	38.2	(0.9)	85.4	(0.7)	4.3	(0.4)	80.1	(0.9)	52.8	(1.0)	28.4	(0.7)
	Latvia	42.7	(1.0)	29.4	(0.9)	38.9	(1.1)	31.3	(0.8)	41.1	(1.1)	26.6	(1.0)	43.6	(1.2)	54.6	(1.1)	23.3	(0.8)
	Liechtenstein	51.0	(2.4)	21.2	(2.2)	21.1	(2.1)	29.3	(2.1)	40.4	(2.6)	38.9	(2.6)	28.8	(2.2)	51.6	(2.6)	21.2	(2.3)
	Peru	40.5	(0.8)	62.2	(0.9)	64.0	(0.9)	38.1	(0.8)	70.6	(0.9)	9.7	(0.5)	58.9	(0.9)	50.1	(0.9)	23.8	(0.7)
	Romania	31.8	(1.1)	40.2	(1.1)	47.7	(1.0)	39.6	(1.1)	65.0	(1.1)	23.3	(0.8)	55.3	(1.2)	60.6	(1.2)	28.1	(0.8)
	Russian Federation	38.0	(0.9)	37.9	(1.0)	41.3	(1.0)	28.8	(0.7)	43.0	(1.0)	18.1	(0.7)	44.9	(1.0)	59.5	(0.9)	13.6	(0.6)
	Thailand	24.3	(0.7)	82.0	(0.6)	66.9	(0.6)	31.5	(0.8)	73.4	(0.7)	9.3	(0.5)	83.8	(0.6)	33.3	(0.8)	20.2	(0.6)

Note: Values that are statistically significant are indicated in bold (see Annex A3).
1. Items "I like to express my opinions about books I have read" and "I like to exchange books with my friends" were not used in PISA 2000 and cannot be compared with PISA 2009.
StatLink http://dx.doi.org/10.1787/888932343285

[Part 3/3]

Percentage of students for several items in the index of enjoyment of reading in PISA 2000 and 2009[1]

Table V.5.3 *Percentage of students who report "agree" or "strongly agree" on the following reading activities*

		Change between 2000 and 2009 (PISA 2009 – PISA 2000)																	
		I read only if I have to		Reading is one of my favourite hobbies		I like talking about books with other people		I find it hard to finish books		I feel happy if I receive a book as a present		For me, reading is a waste of time		I enjoy going to a bookstore or a library		I read only to get information that I need		I cannot sit still and read for more than a few minutes	
		% dif.	S.E.	% dif.	S.E.	% dif.	S.E.	% dif.	S.E.	% dif.	S.E.	% dif.	S.E.	% dif.	S.E.	% dif.	S.E.	% dif.	S.E.
OECD	Australia	2.3	(1.3)	**4.1**	(1.3)	**9.3**	(1.4)	-0.1	(1.1)	**5.6**	(1.4)	**2.2**	(1.0)	**4.2**	(1.4)	-2.6	(1.5)	**2.6**	(1.0)
	Austria	m	m	m	m	m	m	m	m	m	m	m	m	m	m	m	m	m	m
	Belgium	-1.5	(1.1)	**-2.3**	(0.9)	-0.1	(1.1)	0.7	(1.1)	0.4	(1.0)	1.0	(1.1)	**-3.1**	(1.1)	**-3.4**	(1.0)	-1.1	(1.0)
	Canada	0.6	(0.7)	**4.9**	(0.7)	**10.4**	(0.8)	**-3.3**	(0.7)	**3.2**	(0.8)	**-1.4**	(0.6)	**3.3**	(0.8)	**-4.6**	(0.8)	**-2.6**	(0.6)
	Chile	**-16.1**	(1.3)	**-4.6**	(1.1)	**-10.0**	(1.3)	0.6	(1.1)	**-6.7**	(1.3)	-1.0	(1.0)	**-14.4**	(1.3)	**7.4**	(1.2)	**-4.2**	(1.3)
	Czech Republic	**13.8**	(1.2)	**-18.2**	(1.1)	**-13.7**	(1.3)	1.9	(1.1)	**-14.8**	(1.3)	**11.4**	(1.1)	**-16.2**	(1.1)	**7.4**	(1.3)	**9.2**	(1.0)
	Denmark	**8.8**	(1.3)	**-6.8**	(1.0)	0.8	(1.3)	**-3.1**	(1.1)	**-4.8**	(1.4)	1.7	(1.2)	**-13.6**	(1.3)	**3.7**	(1.3)	-1.7	(1.0)
	Finland	**8.2**	(1.1)	**-7.0**	(1.2)	0.7	(1.2)	**2.9**	(1.0)	**-2.7**	(1.3)	**4.1**	(1.1)	**-12.0**	(1.2)	1.6	(1.1)	0.7	(0.9)
	France	-2.6	(1.4)	-1.5	(1.2)	**3.9**	(1.5)	**5.6**	(1.3)	-0.6	(1.4)	**3.2**	(1.3)	**-2.9**	(1.5)	**-3.5**	(1.5)	**-3.5**	(1.2)
	Germany	0.0	(1.1)	**3.4**	(1.0)	**6.5**	(1.2)	**-5.6**	(1.2)	2.7	(1.4)	-1.2	(1.1)	-1.2	(1.2)	**-7.9**	(1.3)	**-3.1**	(0.8)
	Greece	**9.7**	(1.6)	**-8.2**	(1.3)	**-11.5**	(1.6)	**2.8**	(1.2)	-2.2	(1.8)	**-2.5**	(1.1)	**-10.9**	(1.6)	**-7.7**	(1.7)	**-4.4**	(1.4)
	Hungary	**3.1**	(1.4)	**5.7**	(1.4)	1.9	(1.4)	**-3.8**	(1.0)	-1.1	(1.6)	**6.5**	(1.0)	0.5	(1.4)	0.4	(1.4)	**-3.9**	(1.2)
	Iceland	**14.7**	(1.2)	**-3.0**	(1.1)	**7.2**	(1.2)	**7.5**	(1.0)	1.1	(1.2)	**4.5**	(1.0)	**-3.3**	(1.1)	**4.2**	(1.1)	1.8	(1.0)
	Ireland	**5.6**	(1.4)	**-4.0**	(1.4)	**6.9**	(1.4)	-1.3	(1.4)	-1.9	(1.4)	**4.7**	(1.1)	-1.0	(1.5)	-0.8	(1.5)	1.7	(1.2)
	Israel	**4.1**	(2.0)	2.3	(2.7)	-0.9	(2.6)	**8.8**	(1.6)	**-5.0**	(2.1)	2.3	(1.5)	-4.2	(2.5)	**5.6**	(2.4)	**4.6**	(1.6)
	Italy	**2.7**	(1.1)	**-5.1**	(1.1)	1.0	(1.2)	-1.6	(0.9)	**2.6**	(1.2)	**3.8**	(0.8)	-2.4	(1.5)	**-2.8**	(1.1)	-1.2	(1.0)
	Japan	-0.8	(1.3)	**5.5**	(1.3)	**7.1**	(1.2)	**-12.2**	(1.1)	**4.7**	(1.3)	**-4.5**	(1.0)	-0.3	(1.3)	**-6.2**	(1.0)	**-6.7**	(1.1)
	Korea	**14.0**	(1.3)	**4.6**	(1.2)	**7.9**	(1.2)	**-10.2**	(1.1)	**6.2**	(1.5)	**-3.2**	(0.8)	**-4.9**	(1.4)	**-9.5**	(1.3)	**-2.2**	(0.9)
	Luxembourg	m	m	m	m	m	m	m	m	m	m	m	m	m	m	m	m	m	m
	Mexico	**16.2**	(1.0)	**-12.3**	(1.4)	**-17.0**	(1.2)	**-2.6**	(0.9)	**-15.5**	(1.2)	**3.0**	(0.6)	**-18.4**	(1.4)	**2.8**	(1.0)	**3.2**	(0.9)
	Netherlands	m	m	m	m	m	m	m	m	m	m	m	m	m	m	m	m	m	m
	New Zealand	2.0	(1.3)	**4.4**	(1.2)	**9.5**	(1.4)	**-6.0**	(1.2)	**5.9**	(1.2)	-1.2	(1.1)	2.9	(1.5)	**-3.9**	(1.4)	**-2.9**	(1.0)
	Norway	1.8	(1.2)	**-2.1**	(1.1)	**6.3**	(1.1)	-0.4	(1.0)	1.4	(1.3)	-0.6	(1.2)	**-7.8**	(1.2)	1.2	(1.3)	0.7	(1.2)
	Poland	**7.9**	(1.6)	-1.5	(1.4)	0.5	(1.3)	-1.9	(1.3)	**-6.8**	(1.5)	2.0	(1.3)	**-13.3**	(1.5)	0.0	(1.6)	**8.7**	(1.2)
	Portugal	-2.3	(1.2)	**-18.8**	(1.2)	**-8.7**	(1.3)	1.6	(1.0)	**-11.8**	(1.1)	**5.6**	(0.9)	**-15.5**	(1.3)	**7.7**	(1.3)	**6.7**	(1.2)
	Spain	2.3	(1.3)	-1.7	(1.1)	0.9	(1.3)	1.9	(1.0)	**-2.4**	(1.1)	**2.0**	(0.9)	**-11.7**	(1.1)	0.2	(1.3)	**2.9**	(0.9)
	Sweden	2.0	(1.2)	**-2.2**	(1.0)	**3.6**	(1.2)	-1.8	(1.0)	-2.4	(1.2)	-1.2	(1.1)	**-6.9**	(1.3)	-1.8	(1.3)	-1.3	(1.0)
	Switzerland	**7.3**	(1.3)	**-5.5**	(1.3)	-0.6	(1.2)	1.1	(1.1)	**-8.4**	(1.4)	**5.8**	(1.2)	**-5.9**	(1.4)	0.1	(1.4)	-0.7	(0.9)
	United Kingdom	m	m	m	m	m	m	m	m	m	m	m	m	m	m	m	m	m	m
	United States	**4.3**	(1.8)	0.7	(1.5)	**6.2**	(1.8)	**-4.8**	(1.4)	-2.1	(1.7)	-0.2	(1.7)	0.8	(1.8)	-0.4	(2.0)	-2.3	(1.7)
	OECD average-26	**4.2**	(0.3)	**-2.7**	(0.3)	**1.1**	(0.3)	**-0.9**	(0.2)	**-2.1**	(0.3)	**1.8**	(0.2)	**-6.1**	(0.3)	-0.5	(0.3)	0.0	(0.2)
Partners	Albania	**14.5**	(1.3)	**3.7**	(1.4)	**-5.7**	(1.2)	-0.7	(1.1)	-0.1	(0.9)	**-5.2**	(0.9)	**-2.3**	(1.0)	**4.4**	(1.5)	**4.0**	(1.1)
	Argentina	**9.9**	(2.0)	**-7.5**	(1.4)	-3.6	(1.9)	**5.5**	(1.8)	**4.0**	(2.0)	0.0	(1.4)	**-7.6**	(1.6)	**7.7**	(1.9)	1.0	(1.7)
	Brazil	**-27.2**	(1.2)	-0.5	(1.3)	-1.2	(1.4)	0.4	(1.2)	**-11.5**	(1.3)	**-2.7**	(0.6)	**-6.9**	(1.4)	**-13.4**	(1.5)	**3.9**	(1.2)
	Bulgaria	1.9	(1.8)	**-9.5**	(1.9)	**-7.3**	(2.2)	**4.0**	(1.3)	**-5.5**	(1.8)	2.7	(1.4)	2.4	(1.7)	1.0	(1.8)	**3.0**	(1.4)
	Hong Kong-China	**-7.5**	(1.3)	**11.9**	(1.2)	**3.9**	(1.1)	**-11.4**	(1.1)	**12.8**	(1.4)	**-3.4**	(0.7)	**4.4**	(1.2)	**-11.4**	(1.2)	**-8.2**	(0.9)
	Indonesia	**24.4**	(1.2)	**-12.5**	(1.3)	**-11.5**	(1.0)	**9.0**	(1.2)	**-3.6**	(1.0)	**-2.5**	(0.7)	**-7.5**	(1.2)	2.2	(1.5)	1.1	(1.2)
	Latvia	**7.5**	(1.6)	**-8.1**	(1.4)	1.4	(1.6)	**-4.2**	(1.5)	**-7.0**	(1.9)	**3.1**	(1.4)	-1.7	(1.6)	-1.2	(1.7)	**3.1**	(1.3)
	Liechtenstein	**10.3**	(3.8)	**-9.8**	(3.2)	-3.2	(3.0)	-1.3	(3.4)	**-9.2**	(3.8)	**10.8**	(3.5)	-6.6	(3.5)	1.1	(3.7)	2.0	(3.1)
	Peru	**21.3**	(1.2)	**-3.2**	(1.4)	**-6.0**	(1.4)	**-17.7**	(1.2)	1.6	(1.4)	**-6.9**	(0.8)	**-13.2**	(1.5)	0.6	(1.3)	**-23.4**	(1.2)
	Romania	**-13.2**	(1.5)	**-19.6**	(1.5)	**-10.1**	(1.4)	1.8	(1.6)	**-5.9**	(1.4)	**3.6**	(1.3)	**-10.8**	(1.5)	**10.8**	(1.6)	-1.7	(1.4)
	Russian Federation	**4.4**	(1.2)	**-4.7**	(1.5)	-2.4	(1.4)	**-2.8**	(1.0)	**-4.5**	(1.4)	1.4	(0.9)	**-4.2**	(1.3)	-0.1	(1.2)	0.9	(0.7)
	Thailand	**-40.5**	(1.1)	1.0	(1.0)	**-4.9**	(1.2)	**-13.4**	(1.3)	1.5	(1.2)	**-11.3**	(1.3)	0.9	(1.1)	**-22.8**	(1.4)	**-7.4**	(1.3)

Note: Values that are statistically significant are indicated in bold (see Annex A3).

1. Items "I like to express my opinions about books I have read" and "I like to exchange books with my friends" were not used in PISA 2000 and cannot be compared with PISA 2009.

StatLink http://dx.doi.org/10.1787/888932343285

[Part 1/3]

Table V.5.4 **Percentage of students reading for enjoyment in PISA 2000 and 2009, by socio-economic background and gender**
Results based on students' self-reports

		PISA 2000											
		All students				Boys				Girls			
		Bottom quarter of ESCS		Top quarter of ESCS		Bottom quarter of ESCS		Top quarter of ESCS		Bottom quarter of ESCS		Top quarter of ESCS	
		%	S.E.	%	S.E.	%	S.E.	%	S.E.	%	S.E.	%	S.E.
OECD	Australia	58.5	(2.1)	78.2	(1.8)	49.0	(2.7)	74.4	(2.3)	68.2	(2.6)	82.6	(2.6)
	Austria	53.0	(1.8)	66.1	(1.8)	43.6	(2.3)	53.8	(2.0)	62.6	(2.3)	79.4	(1.9)
	Belgium	55.6	(2.1)	67.8	(1.3)	46.7	(2.9)	59.8	(2.1)	64.6	(1.9)	77.5	(1.4)
	Canada	61.4	(0.7)	75.1	(0.7)	49.0	(0.9)	68.2	(1.2)	72.8	(0.9)	82.4	(0.8)
	Chile	73.9	(1.5)	77.0	(1.2)	69.0	(2.2)	69.0	(1.7)	78.1	(1.8)	83.5	(1.5)
	Czech Republic	69.7	(1.4)	80.7	(1.1)	58.9	(2.3)	71.3	(2.0)	79.5	(1.3)	90.4	(1.2)
	Denmark	69.2	(1.4)	80.7	(1.5)	55.9	(2.3)	74.4	(2.1)	79.8	(1.7)	88.2	(1.5)
	Finland	75.9	(1.2)	81.7	(1.3)	63.5	(2.0)	71.7	(2.0)	86.3	(1.3)	92.1	(1.1)
	France	65.6	(1.4)	78.3	(1.5)	56.9	(2.0)	71.7	(2.0)	73.5	(1.9)	85.0	(1.5)
	Germany	56.3	(1.6)	70.8	(1.5)	47.6	(3.6)	58.6	(2.4)	64.5	(2.1)	84.7	(1.5)
	Greece	74.8	(1.5)	80.1	(1.4)	70.6	(2.6)	79.2	(2.1)	78.7	(1.8)	81.1	(1.5)
	Hungary	70.4	(2.2)	82.4	(1.1)	63.9	(2.9)	76.7	(1.8)	76.6	(2.4)	88.7	(1.6)
	Iceland	67.6	(1.5)	75.8	(1.4)	59.6	(2.4)	70.0	(2.0)	74.6	(1.9)	81.9	(1.9)
	Ireland	62.1	(1.6)	73.7	(1.6)	54.2	(2.6)	64.6	(2.3)	69.0	(1.9)	83.1	(1.9)
	Israel	64.8	(4.1)	63.3	(2.8)	56.1	(4.9)	54.2	(3.1)	69.2	(4.3)	71.5	(3.5)
	Italy	65.8	(1.8)	76.7	(1.4)	58.1	(2.7)	70.8	(1.8)	72.8	(2.0)	82.7	(1.8)
	Japan	m	m	m	m	m	m	m	m	m	m	m	m
	Korea	61.3	(1.5)	77.9	(1.3)	59.1	(1.9)	76.9	(1.7)	63.7	(2.5)	79.3	(2.5)
	Luxembourg	m	m	m	m	m	m	m	m	m	m	m	m
	Mexico	89.4	(1.1)	83.1	(2.0)	85.4	(1.6)	77.5	(2.7)	93.6	(1.1)	89.0	(1.9)
	Netherlands	m	m	m	m	m	m	m	m	m	m	m	m
	New Zealand	67.8	(1.7)	76.6	(1.5)	62.9	(2.0)	70.7	(2.1)	72.6	(2.3)	82.8	(2.0)
	Norway	62.9	(1.7)	72.5	(1.5)	50.7	(2.7)	64.0	(1.8)	73.6	(2.0)	83.2	(2.0)
	Poland	72.0	(1.9)	81.5	(1.7)	61.0	(2.9)	77.5	(2.2)	81.6	(1.9)	86.0	(2.3)
	Portugal	79.7	(1.5)	87.7	(1.0)	68.5	(2.4)	80.2	(1.7)	88.4	(1.4)	94.8	(1.0)
	Spain	61.6	(2.1)	76.8	(1.5)	51.0	(2.7)	70.3	(1.9)	69.7	(2.8)	84.0	(1.8)
	Sweden	60.1	(1.8)	69.6	(1.6)	47.5	(2.4)	63.2	(2.0)	71.4	(2.0)	77.5	(2.2)
	Switzerland	58.6	(1.9)	74.8	(1.4)	42.8	(2.8)	66.0	(1.8)	75.3	(1.9)	85.2	(1.5)
	United Kingdom	m	m	m	m	m	m	m	m	m	m	m	m
	United States	56.7	(2.0)	67.9	(1.5)	47.4	(3.5)	62.9	(2.3)	65.1	(2.8)	73.4	(2.0)
	OECD average-26	66.5	(0.4)	76.4	(0.3)	57.4	(0.5)	69.7	(0.4)	74.5	(0.4)	83.6	(0.4)
Partners	Albania	93.1	(1.3)	92.1	(0.8)	92.6	(2.2)	88.5	(1.4)	93.6	(1.1)	95.3	(1.0)
	Argentina	70.0	(2.7)	73.0	(1.8)	63.8	(3.3)	64.3	(2.7)	75.1	(3.9)	80.8	(2.1)
	Brazil	80.4	(1.6)	81.9	(1.7)	72.5	(2.9)	74.6	(2.8)	86.2	(1.5)	89.3	(1.8)
	Bulgaria	65.1	(1.9)	74.9	(1.5)	57.4	(2.4)	65.4	(2.0)	72.8	(2.3)	85.4	(1.6)
	Hong Kong-China	67.3	(1.7)	85.6	(1.1)	58.3	(2.4)	83.0	(1.7)	77.1	(1.9)	88.1	(1.4)
	Indonesia	92.4	(0.8)	92.7	(0.8)	91.6	(1.1)	90.8	(1.4)	93.1	(1.1)	94.5	(1.1)
	Latvia	79.5	(1.6)	84.6	(2.1)	69.1	(2.8)	75.3	(3.7)	88.7	(1.8)	94.1	(1.0)
	Liechtenstein	49.9	(5.6)	71.8	(5.1)	36.1	(6.9)	79.7	(6.5)	71.9	(8.0)	65.6	(7.9)
	Peru	92.6	(0.9)	89.6	(1.1)	91.7	(1.5)	87.6	(1.6)	93.5	(1.2)	91.4	(1.2)
	Romania	79.4	(1.8)	86.1	(1.1)	78.7	(3.0)	82.7	(2.1)	80.0	(2.3)	89.4	(1.2)
	Russian Federation	76.8	(1.1)	84.6	(1.2)	69.7	(1.7)	78.8	(1.5)	82.9	(1.4)	90.9	(1.6)
	Thailand	86.9	(1.2)	90.6	(1.2)	80.5	(2.1)	89.7	(1.9)	91.0	(2.2)	91.4	(1.1)

Note: Values that are statistically significant are indicated in bold (see Annex A3).
StatLink http://dx.doi.org/10.1787/888932343285

[Part 2/3]
Percentage of students reading for enjoyment in PISA 2000 and 2009, by socio-economic background and gender
Table V.5.4 *Results based on students' self-reports*

		PISA 2009												
		All students				Boys				Girls				
		Bottom quarter of ESCS		Top quarter of ESCS		Bottom quarter of ESCS		Top quarter of ESCS		Bottom quarter of ESCS		Top quarter of ESCS		
		%	S.E.	%	S.E.	%	S.E.	%	S.E.	%	S.E.	%	S.E.
OECD	Australia	52.9	(1.1)	75.2	(0.9)	40.3	(1.6)	68.2	(1.4)	64.5	(1.3)	82.1	(1.1)
	Austria	m	m	m	m	m	m	m	m	m	m	m	m
	Belgium	45.3	(1.3)	68.5	(1.0)	34.5	(1.6)	60.9	(1.5)	55.6	(1.9)	76.7	(1.2)
	Canada	61.3	(1.0)	78.4	(0.8)	46.1	(1.5)	68.8	(1.3)	76.2	(1.2)	88.4	(0.7)
	Chile	62.3	(1.4)	62.6	(1.4)	55.5	(2.0)	52.8	(1.8)	69.0	(1.9)	72.4	(1.8)
	Czech Republic	49.1	(1.6)	67.5	(1.4)	37.4	(2.5)	55.4	(1.9)	61.1	(2.6)	81.4	(1.3)
	Denmark	60.1	(1.5)	77.7	(1.3)	48.9	(2.0)	72.6	(1.8)	69.7	(1.9)	82.7	(1.6)
	Finland	59.4	(1.6)	75.5	(1.4)	44.8	(2.1)	64.2	(2.3)	75.1	(2.0)	87.0	(1.4)
	France	48.9	(1.9)	74.2	(1.6)	38.0	(2.5)	65.9	(2.2)	58.6	(2.6)	82.5	(1.8)
	Germany	45.6	(1.8)	73.6	(1.4)	31.9	(2.2)	63.5	(2.0)	58.6	(2.1)	84.8	(1.5)
	Greece	79.3	(1.8)	86.3	(1.2)	73.2	(2.5)	80.1	(1.7)	85.1	(1.6)	93.2	(1.1)
	Hungary	67.9	(1.8)	84.6	(1.2)	57.5	(2.8)	77.2	(2.0)	76.9	(2.0)	92.9	(1.2)
	Iceland	57.8	(1.7)	69.9	(1.5)	42.4	(2.7)	62.5	(2.5)	71.3	(2.3)	77.7	(2.2)
	Ireland	44.3	(2.0)	74.1	(1.5)	40.7	(2.7)	70.5	(2.2)	47.9	(2.5)	78.0	(1.8)
	Israel	65.6	(1.7)	68.5	(1.3)	51.9	(2.7)	62.2	(1.9)	76.1	(1.7)	76.0	(1.9)
	Italy	58.5	(1.0)	74.2	(0.8)	45.1	(1.4)	63.6	(1.0)	71.6	(1.3)	85.9	(0.8)
	Japan	48.8	(1.4)	65.0	(1.6)	46.7	(2.1)	60.6	(1.6)	51.3	(2.0)	69.4	(2.6)
	Korea	51.7	(1.5)	73.1	(1.3)	51.3	(2.0)	72.2	(1.7)	52.2	(2.6)	74.0	(1.8)
	Luxembourg	41.8	(1.5)	65.2	(1.5)	26.2	(1.9)	52.8	(2.0)	55.4	(2.0)	79.3	(1.8)
	Mexico	83.4	(0.6)	72.4	(0.9)	78.9	(1.1)	64.4	(1.3)	87.2	(0.8)	81.1	(0.7)
	Netherlands	44.7	(2.2)	63.4	(1.8)	27.9	(2.4)	49.7	(2.3)	60.0	(2.7)	77.6	(2.2)
	New Zealand	60.4	(1.7)	78.7	(1.3)	47.6	(2.4)	73.0	(1.7)	72.3	(1.9)	84.6	(1.9)
	Norway	54.6	(1.6)	69.0	(1.7)	42.4	(2.0)	62.1	(2.2)	65.9	(2.2)	76.6	(2.0)
	Poland	63.6	(1.3)	77.5	(1.4)	44.5	(2.5)	66.4	(2.2)	80.3	(1.4)	88.4	(1.6)
	Portugal	61.4	(1.5)	71.1	(1.5)	46.5	(2.0)	59.6	(1.9)	73.6	(1.7)	83.2	(1.9)
	Spain	52.2	(1.6)	68.9	(1.1)	42.8	(2.0)	59.8	(1.6)	61.8	(2.1)	78.7	(1.3)
	Sweden	56.4	(1.8)	71.4	(1.4)	45.5	(2.2)	58.9	(2.1)	67.9	(2.2)	84.7	(1.6)
	Switzerland	47.1	(1.9)	69.0	(1.5)	32.6	(1.8)	60.3	(2.1)	61.4	(2.8)	78.0	(1.6)
	United Kingdom	53.8	(1.8)	71.9	(1.3)	44.7	(2.1)	63.1	(1.7)	62.1	(2.2)	81.1	(1.4)
	United States	51.5	(1.6)	69.4	(1.5)	38.6	(1.8)	60.2	(1.6)	65.1	(2.3)	80.0	(2.2)
	OECD average-26	57.3	(0.3)	72.9	(0.3)	46.4	(0.4)	64.8	(0.4)	67.6	(0.4)	81.6	(0.3)
Partners	Albania	92.2	(1.2)	93.3	(0.8)	88.4	(1.8)	89.2	(1.3)	95.7	(1.2)	97.6	(0.6)
	Argentina	63.3	(1.6)	58.5	(1.7)	55.4	(2.3)	50.6	(2.3)	69.7	(2.1)	66.3	(2.4)
	Brazil	80.7	(1.1)	78.4	(1.1)	73.0	(1.7)	68.9	(1.8)	85.8	(1.2)	88.1	(1.1)
	Bulgaria	65.6	(2.4)	78.9	(1.6)	56.2	(2.9)	68.3	(2.5)	75.7	(2.5)	90.3	(1.3)
	Hong Kong-China	74.3	(1.3)	85.2	(1.2)	69.1	(1.9)	81.4	(1.5)	80.3	(1.8)	89.8	(1.4)
	Indonesia	85.2	(1.2)	91.6	(0.8)	78.2	(1.9)	88.9	(1.2)	91.8	(1.2)	94.6	(0.8)
	Latvia	64.4	(1.7)	78.8	(1.4)	44.5	(2.9)	66.2	(2.5)	80.2	(2.4)	91.5	(1.3)
	Liechtenstein	41.1	(5.2)	58.2	(5.3)	26.7	(7.0)	54.0	(6.2)	54.5	(7.5)	63.2	(8.2)
	Peru	90.3	(0.9)	83.3	(1.1)	89.3	(1.3)	79.9	(1.6)	91.4	(1.1)	86.6	(1.3)
	Romania	75.1	(1.6)	75.4	(1.4)	67.4	(1.8)	65.7	(2.1)	82.3	(2.1)	85.7	(1.6)
	Russian Federation	76.1	(1.4)	83.2	(1.0)	65.5	(2.3)	77.0	(1.6)	86.2	(1.6)	89.6	(1.3)
	Thailand	90.5	(1.0)	92.8	(0.9)	84.0	(1.8)	88.3	(1.6)	94.7	(0.9)	96.8	(0.8)

Note: Values that are statistically significant are indicated in bold (see Annex A3).
StatLink http://dx.doi.org/10.1787/888932343285

[Part 3/3]

Table V.5.4 Percentage of students reading for enjoyment in PISA 2000 and 2009, by socio-economic background and gender

Results based on students' self-reports

		Change between 2000 and 2009 (PISA 2009 – PISA 2000)											
		All students				Boys				Girls			
		Bottom quarter of ESCS		Top quarter of ESCS		Bottom quarter of ESCS		Top quarter of ESCS		Bottom quarter of ESCS		Top quarter of ESCS	
		% dif.	S.E.	% dif.	S.E.	% dif.	S.E.	% dif.	S.E.	% dif.	S.E.	% dif.	S.E.
OECD	Australia	**-5.6**	(2.3)	-3.0	(2.0)	**-8.7**	(3.2)	**-6.2**	(2.7)	-3.7	(2.9)	-0.5	(2.8)
	Austria	m	m	m	m	m	m	m	m	m	m	m	m
	Belgium	**-10.3**	(2.4)	0.7	(1.6)	**-12.1**	(3.3)	1.2	(2.6)	**-8.9**	(2.7)	-0.8	(1.9)
	Canada	-0.1	(1.2)	**3.3**	(1.1)	-3.0	(1.7)	0.6	(1.8)	**3.3**	(1.5)	**6.0**	(1.0)
	Chile	**-11.7**	(2.1)	**-14.5**	(1.9)	**-13.5**	(3.0)	**-16.2**	(2.5)	**-9.1**	(2.7)	**-11.1**	(2.4)
	Czech Republic	**-20.6**	(2.1)	**-13.2**	(1.8)	**-21.5**	(3.3)	**-16.0**	(2.8)	**-18.3**	(2.9)	**-8.9**	(1.8)
	Denmark	**-9.1**	(2.0)	-3.1	(2.0)	**-7.0**	(3.1)	-1.8	(2.7)	**-10.1**	(2.6)	**-5.5**	(2.2)
	Finland	**-16.5**	(2.0)	**-6.2**	(1.9)	**-18.8**	(2.9)	**-7.5**	(3.0)	**-11.2**	(2.4)	**-5.1**	(1.8)
	France	**-16.7**	(2.3)	-4.1	(2.2)	**-18.9**	(3.2)	-5.8	(3.0)	**-14.8**	(3.3)	-2.5	(2.4)
	Germany	**-10.7**	(2.4)	2.8	(2.0)	**-15.7**	(4.2)	4.9	(3.1)	-5.8	(3.0)	0.1	(2.2)
	Greece	4.5	(2.4)	**6.2**	(1.8)	2.7	(3.6)	0.9	(2.7)	**6.4**	(2.4)	**12.1**	(1.9)
	Hungary	-2.6	(2.9)	2.2	(1.6)	-6.3	(4.0)	0.6	(2.7)	0.4	(3.1)	**4.2**	(2.0)
	Iceland	**-9.8**	(2.2)	**-5.9**	(2.0)	**-17.3**	(3.6)	**-7.5**	(3.1)	-3.4	(3.0)	-4.2	(2.9)
	Ireland	**-17.8**	(2.6)	0.4	(2.1)	**-13.5**	(3.7)	5.9	(3.1)	**-21.1**	(3.2)	-5.1	(2.6)
	Israel	0.8	(4.4)	5.3	(3.1)	-4.1	(5.6)	**8.0**	(3.7)	6.9	(4.6)	4.4	(4.0)
	Italy	**-7.3**	(2.0)	-2.5	(1.6)	**-13.0**	(3.0)	**-7.2**	(2.1)	-1.2	(2.4)	3.2	(1.9)
	Japan	m	m	m	m	m	m	m	m	m	m	m	m
	Korea	**-9.5**	(2.2)	**-4.8**	(1.8)	**-7.8**	(2.7)	**-4.7**	(2.4)	**-11.4**	(3.6)	-5.3	(3.1)
	Luxembourg	m	m	m	m	m	m	m	m	m	m	m	m
	Mexico	**-6.0**	(1.2)	**-10.7**	(2.2)	**-6.5**	(2.0)	**-13.1**	(3.0)	**-6.4**	(1.3)	**-7.9**	(2.0)
	Netherlands	m	m	m	m	m	m	m	m	m	m	m	m
	New Zealand	**-7.5**	(2.4)	2.2	(2.0)	**-15.3**	(3.2)	2.4	(2.7)	-0.3	(3.0)	1.8	(2.7)
	Norway	**-8.3**	(2.3)	-3.5	(2.2)	**-8.2**	(3.3)	-1.9	(2.9)	**-7.7**	(3.0)	**-6.6**	(2.8)
	Poland	**-8.4**	(2.3)	-4.0	(2.2)	**-16.5**	(3.8)	**-11.1**	(3.1)	-1.4	(2.4)	2.4	(2.8)
	Portugal	**-18.3**	(2.1)	**-16.7**	(1.8)	**-22.0**	(3.1)	**-20.6**	(2.5)	**-14.8**	(2.2)	**-11.6**	(2.1)
	Spain	**-9.4**	(2.6)	**-7.9**	(1.9)	**-8.2**	(3.3)	**-10.5**	(2.5)	**-7.9**	(3.5)	**-5.3**	(2.2)
	Sweden	-3.7	(2.5)	1.7	(2.1)	-2.1	(3.2)	-4.3	(2.9)	-3.4	(3.0)	**7.2**	(2.7)
	Switzerland	**-11.5**	(2.7)	**-5.8**	(2.0)	**-10.1**	(3.3)	**-5.7**	(2.8)	**-13.9**	(3.4)	**-7.2**	(2.2)
	United Kingdom	m	m	m	m	m	m	m	m	m	m	m	m
	United States	**-5.3**	(2.6)	1.5	(2.1)	**-8.8**	(4.0)	-2.6	(2.8)	0.0	(3.6)	**6.7**	(3.0)
	OECD average-26	**-8.9**	(0.5)	**-3.2**	(0.4)	**-11.1**	(0.7)	**-4.7**	(0.6)	**-6.3**	(0.6)	**-1.6**	(0.5)
Partners	Albania	-0.9	(1.8)	1.2	(1.1)	-4.2	(2.9)	0.8	(1.9)	2.1	(1.6)	**2.3**	(1.1)
	Argentina	**-6.6**	(3.1)	**-14.5**	(2.5)	**-8.3**	(4.0)	**-13.7**	(3.6)	-5.4	(4.5)	**-14.5**	(3.2)
	Brazil	0.3	(1.9)	-3.5	(2.0)	0.5	(3.3)	-5.7	(3.3)	-0.4	(1.9)	-1.2	(2.1)
	Bulgaria	0.6	(3.0)	3.9	(2.1)	-1.2	(3.8)	2.9	(3.2)	2.9	(3.4)	**4.9**	(2.1)
	Hong Kong-China	**7.0**	(2.1)	-0.4	(1.6)	**10.7**	(3.0)	-1.7	(2.3)	3.2	(2.6)	1.8	(2.0)
	Indonesia	**-7.1**	(1.5)	-1.1	(1.1)	**-13.4**	(2.2)	-1.9	(1.8)	-1.3	(1.6)	0.1	(1.3)
	Latvia	**-15.1**	(2.4)	**-5.7**	(2.5)	**-24.6**	(4.0)	**-9.2**	(4.5)	**-8.5**	(3.0)	-2.5	(1.6)
	Liechtenstein	-8.8	(7.6)	-13.6	(7.3)	-9.3	(9.8)	**-25.7**	(9.0)	-17.4	(11.0)	-2.4	(11.3)
	Peru	-2.3	(1.3)	**-6.3**	(1.6)	-2.5	(2.0)	**-7.7**	(2.3)	-2.1	(1.6)	**-4.9**	(1.7)
	Romania	-4.3	(2.5)	**-10.8**	(1.8)	**-11.3**	(3.5)	**-17.1**	(2.9)	2.2	(3.1)	-3.7	(2.0)
	Russian Federation	-0.6	(1.8)	-1.4	(1.6)	-4.2	(2.8)	-1.7	(2.2)	3.3	(2.1)	-1.3	(2.1)
	Thailand	**3.5**	(1.6)	2.1	(1.5)	3.5	(2.7)	-1.4	(2.5)	3.7	(2.4)	**5.4**	(1.4)

Note: Values that are statistically significant are indicated in bold (see Annex A3).

StatLink http://dx.doi.org/10.1787/888932343285

[Part 1/3]

Table V.5.5 Index of enjoyment of reading in PISA 2000 and 2009, by socio-economic background and gender

Results based on students' self-reports

		PISA 2000											
		All students				Boys				Girls			
		Bottom quarter of ESCS		Top quarter of ESCS		Bottom quarter of ESCS		Top quarter of ESCS		Bottom quarter of ESCS		Top quarter of ESCS	
		Mean index	S.E.	Mean index	S.E.	Mean index	S.E.	Mean index	S.E.	Mean index	S.E.	Mean index	S.E.
OECD	Australia	-0.25	(0.04)	0.28	(0.05)	-0.47	(0.04)	0.09	(0.05)	-0.03	(0.05)	0.50	(0.08)
	Austria	-0.29	(0.04)	0.24	(0.05)	-0.68	(0.04)	-0.22	(0.04)	0.11	(0.05)	0.75	(0.07)
	Belgium	-0.37	(0.03)	-0.03	(0.03)	-0.58	(0.04)	-0.30	(0.04)	-0.17	(0.04)	0.29	(0.04)
	Canada	-0.16	(0.01)	0.29	(0.02)	-0.49	(0.02)	0.01	(0.03)	0.15	(0.02)	0.59	(0.03)
	Chile	-0.08	(0.03)	0.15	(0.04)	-0.31	(0.05)	-0.21	(0.04)	0.12	(0.04)	0.43	(0.05)
	Czech Republic	0.03	(0.03)	0.39	(0.03)	-0.39	(0.04)	0.01	(0.05)	0.37	(0.04)	0.78	(0.04)
	Denmark	-0.12	(0.03)	0.29	(0.03)	-0.45	(0.05)	-0.01	(0.04)	0.14	(0.05)	0.66	(0.04)
	Finland	0.13	(0.03)	0.43	(0.04)	-0.43	(0.04)	0.00	(0.04)	0.59	(0.04)	0.87	(0.05)
	France	-0.21	(0.03)	0.20	(0.04)	-0.44	(0.04)	-0.09	(0.05)	0.01	(0.04)	0.49	(0.05)
	Germany	-0.28	(0.03)	0.29	(0.04)	-0.67	(0.05)	-0.16	(0.06)	0.06	(0.05)	0.80	(0.05)
	Greece	-0.05	(0.03)	0.09	(0.04)	-0.24	(0.03)	-0.16	(0.05)	0.14	(0.03)	0.37	(0.04)
	Hungary	-0.08	(0.03)	0.35	(0.04)	-0.26	(0.05)	0.11	(0.05)	0.08	(0.04)	0.62	(0.04)
	Iceland	-0.03	(0.03)	0.21	(0.03)	-0.31	(0.04)	-0.06	(0.04)	0.21	(0.04)	0.49	(0.04)
	Ireland	-0.20	(0.04)	0.20	(0.04)	-0.50	(0.05)	-0.10	(0.06)	0.05	(0.05)	0.50	(0.05)
	Israel	0.12	(0.08)	0.23	(0.06)	-0.15	(0.09)	-0.03	(0.07)	0.26	(0.09)	0.45	(0.09)
	Italy	-0.06	(0.03)	0.25	(0.04)	-0.26	(0.05)	-0.07	(0.05)	0.13	(0.04)	0.57	(0.04)
	Japan	m	m	m	m	m	m	m	m	m	m	m	m
	Korea	-0.14	(0.03)	0.29	(0.04)	-0.24	(0.03)	0.20	(0.05)	-0.03	(0.04)	0.42	(0.07)
	Luxembourg	m	m	m	m	m	m	m	m	m	m	m	m
	Mexico	0.39	(0.03)	0.25	(0.04)	0.28	(0.03)	0.07	(0.05)	0.51	(0.04)	0.44	(0.05)
	Netherlands	m	m	m	m	m	m	m	m	m	m	m	m
	New Zealand	-0.14	(0.03)	0.26	(0.05)	-0.30	(0.04)	-0.01	(0.05)	0.02	(0.04)	0.55	(0.05)
	Norway	-0.25	(0.03)	0.00	(0.03)	-0.65	(0.04)	-0.29	(0.04)	0.10	(0.04)	0.36	(0.05)
	Poland	-0.02	(0.04)	0.16	(0.06)	-0.23	(0.04)	-0.09	(0.05)	0.16	(0.05)	0.45	(0.06)
	Portugal	0.30	(0.03)	0.55	(0.03)	-0.04	(0.04)	0.20	(0.04)	0.56	(0.03)	0.88	(0.05)
	Spain	-0.19	(0.04)	0.21	(0.03)	-0.44	(0.04)	-0.03	(0.04)	0.00	(0.06)	0.46	(0.05)
	Sweden	-0.15	(0.04)	0.21	(0.03)	-0.54	(0.05)	-0.07	(0.05)	0.20	(0.05)	0.54	(0.04)
	Switzerland	-0.15	(0.04)	0.39	(0.05)	-0.62	(0.05)	0.02	(0.05)	0.35	(0.04)	0.81	(0.06)
	United Kingdom	m	m	m	m	m	m	m	m	m	m	m	m
	United States	-0.28	(0.04)	0.09	(0.05)	-0.42	(0.05)	-0.12	(0.07)	-0.15	(0.06)	0.31	(0.07)
	OECD average-26	-0.09	(0.01)	0.24	(0.01)	-0.37	(0.01)	-0.04	(0.01)	0.15	(0.01)	0.55	(0.01)
Partners	Albania	0.52	(0.03)	0.59	(0.02)	0.38	(0.05)	0.40	(0.04)	0.67	(0.04)	0.75	(0.03)
	Argentina	-0.18	(0.05)	0.00	(0.05)	-0.34	(0.07)	-0.25	(0.06)	-0.04	(0.07)	0.22	(0.05)
	Brazil	0.16	(0.03)	0.21	(0.05)	-0.09	(0.04)	-0.08	(0.04)	0.34	(0.03)	0.51	(0.06)
	Bulgaria	-0.08	(0.03)	0.20	(0.05)	-0.24	(0.04)	-0.06	(0.05)	0.09	(0.04)	0.48	(0.06)
	Hong Kong-China	-0.02	(0.02)	0.30	(0.03)	-0.16	(0.02)	0.20	(0.05)	0.13	(0.03)	0.40	(0.03)
	Indonesia	0.59	(0.02)	0.57	(0.02)	0.48	(0.03)	0.43	(0.02)	0.69	(0.03)	0.70	(0.04)
	Latvia	-0.04	(0.04)	0.03	(0.03)	-0.28	(0.07)	-0.26	(0.04)	0.18	(0.04)	0.33	(0.03)
	Liechtenstein	-0.25	(0.11)	0.19	(0.13)	-0.73	(0.11)	0.03	(0.14)	0.40	(0.17)	0.40	(0.23)
	Peru	0.35	(0.03)	0.28	(0.04)	0.30	(0.04)	0.22	(0.05)	0.40	(0.04)	0.33	(0.05)
	Romania	0.17	(0.04)	0.26	(0.04)	0.02	(0.04)	0.02	(0.05)	0.30	(0.05)	0.50	(0.04)
	Russian Federation	0.02	(0.03)	0.23	(0.03)	-0.15	(0.03)	0.02	(0.03)	0.18	(0.03)	0.46	(0.04)
	Thailand	0.14	(0.02)	0.20	(0.02)	0.00	(0.02)	0.12	(0.02)	0.23	(0.02)	0.25	(0.03)

Note: Values that are statistically significant are indicated in bold (see Annex A3).

StatLink http://dx.doi.org/10.1787/888932343285

[Part 2/3]

Table V.5.5 Index of enjoyment of reading in PISA 2000 and 2009, by socio-economic background and gender

Results based on students' self-reports

		PISA 2009											
		All students				Boys				Girls			
		Bottom quarter of ESCS		Top quarter of ESCS		Bottom quarter of ESCS		Top quarter of ESCS		Bottom quarter of ESCS		Top quarter of ESCS	
		Mean index	S.E.	Mean index	S.E.	Mean index	S.E.	Mean index	S.E.	Mean index	S.E.	Mean index	S.E.
OECD	Australia	-0.29	(0.02)	0.34	(0.03)	-0.64	(0.02)	0.03	(0.03)	0.02	(0.04)	0.65	(0.04)
	Austria	m	m	m	m	m	m	m	m	m	m	m	m
	Belgium	-0.44	(0.03)	0.13	(0.02)	-0.69	(0.03)	-0.13	(0.03)	-0.21	(0.03)	0.42	(0.03)
	Canada	-0.07	(0.02)	0.39	(0.03)	-0.50	(0.03)	-0.02	(0.03)	0.34	(0.03)	0.80	(0.03)
	Chile	-0.11	(0.02)	0.07	(0.03)	-0.28	(0.03)	-0.19	(0.04)	0.06	(0.03)	0.33	(0.05)
	Czech Republic	-0.29	(0.03)	0.08	(0.03)	-0.55	(0.03)	-0.25	(0.03)	-0.02	(0.04)	0.47	(0.04)
	Denmark	-0.35	(0.02)	0.22	(0.02)	-0.62	(0.03)	-0.03	(0.03)	-0.11	(0.03)	0.47	(0.03)
	Finland	-0.19	(0.03)	0.27	(0.03)	-0.66	(0.04)	-0.16	(0.04)	0.30	(0.04)	0.69	(0.04)
	France	-0.24	(0.04)	0.36	(0.03)	-0.47	(0.06)	0.11	(0.05)	-0.03	(0.05)	0.61	(0.04)
	Germany	-0.28	(0.03)	0.44	(0.04)	-0.70	(0.04)	0.01	(0.04)	0.11	(0.04)	0.91	(0.05)
	Greece	-0.10	(0.03)	0.27	(0.03)	-0.35	(0.04)	-0.07	(0.04)	0.13	(0.04)	0.64	(0.04)
	Hungary	-0.09	(0.03)	0.48	(0.03)	-0.34	(0.04)	0.16	(0.05)	0.13	(0.04)	0.84	(0.04)
	Iceland	-0.25	(0.03)	0.13	(0.03)	-0.58	(0.05)	-0.17	(0.05)	0.03	(0.04)	0.43	(0.05)
	Ireland	-0.42	(0.04)	0.26	(0.04)	-0.59	(0.05)	-0.01	(0.05)	-0.25	(0.05)	0.55	(0.04)
	Israel	-0.04	(0.03)	0.21	(0.04)	-0.41	(0.04)	-0.04	(0.05)	0.25	(0.04)	0.49	(0.05)
	Italy	-0.15	(0.02)	0.29	(0.02)	-0.46	(0.02)	-0.04	(0.02)	0.15	(0.02)	0.66	(0.02)
	Japan	0.01	(0.03)	0.44	(0.03)	-0.19	(0.04)	0.25	(0.05)	0.24	(0.04)	0.62	(0.05)
	Korea	-0.07	(0.03)	0.36	(0.03)	-0.16	(0.03)	0.25	(0.03)	0.05	(0.04)	0.47	(0.04)
	Luxembourg	-0.40	(0.03)	0.16	(0.03)	-0.80	(0.04)	-0.24	(0.04)	-0.06	(0.05)	0.59	(0.05)
	Mexico	0.20	(0.02)	0.18	(0.02)	0.05	(0.02)	-0.05	(0.02)	0.32	(0.02)	0.42	(0.02)
	Netherlands	-0.49	(0.04)	-0.06	(0.04)	-0.81	(0.04)	-0.43	(0.05)	-0.19	(0.05)	0.32	(0.05)
	New Zealand	-0.11	(0.03)	0.47	(0.04)	-0.42	(0.04)	0.15	(0.04)	0.17	(0.04)	0.80	(0.05)
	Norway	-0.36	(0.03)	0.05	(0.04)	-0.71	(0.04)	-0.26	(0.04)	-0.04	(0.04)	0.39	(0.05)
	Poland	-0.15	(0.02)	0.39	(0.04)	-0.52	(0.04)	-0.05	(0.04)	0.16	(0.04)	0.81	(0.06)
	Portugal	0.08	(0.02)	0.38	(0.03)	-0.26	(0.03)	0.05	(0.03)	0.35	(0.03)	0.72	(0.04)
	Spain	-0.25	(0.03)	0.21	(0.02)	-0.45	(0.03)	-0.09	(0.03)	-0.04	(0.04)	0.54	(0.02)
	Sweden	-0.30	(0.03)	0.14	(0.03)	-0.61	(0.04)	-0.26	(0.04)	0.02	(0.04)	0.55	(0.05)
	Switzerland	-0.32	(0.05)	0.36	(0.03)	-0.74	(0.03)	-0.03	(0.04)	0.09	(0.07)	0.75	(0.05)
	United Kingdom	-0.35	(0.03)	0.20	(0.03)	-0.57	(0.04)	-0.06	(0.04)	-0.15	(0.04)	0.47	(0.04)
	United States	-0.24	(0.03)	0.28	(0.04)	-0.56	(0.03)	-0.05	(0.04)	0.09	(0.04)	0.65	(0.05)
	OECD average-26	-0.19	(0.01)	0.28	(0.01)	-0.48	(0.01)	-0.04	(0.01)	0.09	(0.01)	0.60	(0.01)
Partners	Albania	0.62	(0.03)	0.76	(0.02)	0.29	(0.04)	0.43	(0.03)	0.92	(0.03)	1.11	(0.03)
	Argentina	-0.14	(0.03)	-0.12	(0.03)	-0.32	(0.04)	-0.30	(0.04)	0.01	(0.04)	0.06	(0.04)
	Brazil	0.27	(0.02)	0.35	(0.03)	0.08	(0.02)	0.07	(0.04)	0.39	(0.02)	0.63	(0.03)
	Bulgaria	-0.16	(0.03)	0.24	(0.04)	-0.36	(0.04)	-0.08	(0.05)	0.04	(0.04)	0.57	(0.05)
	Hong Kong-China	0.17	(0.02)	0.48	(0.03)	0.00	(0.02)	0.32	(0.04)	0.36	(0.03)	0.67	(0.04)
	Indonesia	0.41	(0.02)	0.43	(0.02)	0.31	(0.02)	0.30	(0.03)	0.51	(0.02)	0.58	(0.03)
	Latvia	-0.17	(0.03)	0.14	(0.03)	-0.57	(0.03)	-0.23	(0.04)	0.14	(0.04)	0.52	(0.03)
	Liechtenstein	-0.42	(0.11)	-0.04	(0.13)	-0.76	(0.15)	-0.44	(0.15)	-0.11	(0.17)	0.43	(0.19)
	Peru	0.36	(0.02)	0.32	(0.02)	0.30	(0.03)	0.11	(0.03)	0.43	(0.03)	0.53	(0.03)
	Romania	0.06	(0.03)	0.16	(0.03)	-0.13	(0.03)	-0.09	(0.03)	0.24	(0.04)	0.42	(0.04)
	Russian Federation	-0.03	(0.02)	0.24	(0.03)	-0.26	(0.03)	-0.04	(0.04)	0.19	(0.03)	0.52	(0.03)
	Thailand	0.55	(0.02)	0.55	(0.03)	0.38	(0.02)	0.37	(0.04)	0.66	(0.03)	0.71	(0.03)

Note: Values that are statistically significant are indicated in bold (see Annex A3).
StatLink http://dx.doi.org/10.1787/888932343285

[Part 3/3]
Table V.5.5 Index of enjoyment of reading in PISA 2000 and 2009, by socio-economic background and gender
Results based on students' self-reports

		Change between 2000 and 2009 (PISA 2009 – PISA 2000)											
		All students				Boys				Girls			
		Bottom quarter of ESCS		Top quarter of ESCS		Bottom quarter of ESCS		Top quarter of ESCS		Bottom quarter of ESCS		Top quarter of ESCS	
		Dif.	S.E.	Dif.	S.E.	Dif.	S.E.	Dif.	S.E.	Dif.	S.E.	Dif.	S.E.
OECD	Australia	-0.04	(0.04)	0.07	(0.06)	**-0.16**	(0.05)	-0.05	(0.06)	0.06	(0.06)	0.15	(0.09)
	Austria	m	m	m	m	m	m	m	m	m	m	m	m
	Belgium	-0.07	(0.04)	**0.17**	(0.04)	**-0.11**	(0.05)	**0.17**	(0.05)	-0.04	(0.05)	**0.13**	(0.05)
	Canada	**0.09**	(0.03)	**0.10**	(0.04)	-0.01	(0.03)	-0.03	(0.04)	**0.19**	(0.04)	**0.21**	(0.04)
	Chile	-0.03	(0.04)	-0.07	(0.05)	0.03	(0.05)	0.02	(0.06)	-0.06	(0.05)	-0.10	(0.07)
	Czech Republic	**-0.32**	(0.04)	**-0.31**	(0.04)	**-0.16**	(0.05)	**-0.26**	(0.06)	**-0.39**	(0.06)	**-0.32**	(0.06)
	Denmark	**-0.22**	(0.04)	-0.07	(0.04)	**-0.17**	(0.06)	-0.01	(0.05)	**-0.25**	(0.06)	**-0.19**	(0.06)
	Finland	**-0.32**	(0.05)	**-0.16**	(0.05)	**-0.23**	(0.06)	**-0.16**	(0.06)	**-0.29**	(0.06)	**-0.17**	(0.06)
	France	-0.03	(0.05)	**0.16**	(0.05)	-0.03	(0.07)	**0.20**	(0.07)	-0.03	(0.06)	0.12	(0.06)
	Germany	-0.01	(0.05)	**0.15**	(0.06)	-0.03	(0.06)	**0.16**	(0.07)	0.05	(0.06)	0.11	(0.08)
	Greece	-0.06	(0.04)	**0.18**	(0.05)	**-0.10**	(0.05)	0.09	(0.06)	-0.01	(0.05)	**0.28**	(0.05)
	Hungary	-0.01	(0.04)	**0.13**	(0.05)	-0.08	(0.06)	0.04	(0.07)	0.05	(0.05)	**0.22**	(0.06)
	Iceland	**-0.22**	(0.05)	-0.08	(0.05)	**-0.27**	(0.06)	-0.11	(0.06)	**-0.18**	(0.06)	-0.06	(0.07)
	Ireland	**-0.22**	(0.05)	0.06	(0.05)	-0.09	(0.07)	0.09	(0.07)	**-0.31**	(0.07)	0.05	(0.06)
	Israel	-0.15	(0.09)	-0.02	(0.08)	**-0.27**	(0.10)	-0.01	(0.09)	-0.02	(0.10)	0.03	(0.10)
	Italy	**-0.09**	(0.04)	0.05	(0.04)	**-0.19**	(0.06)	0.02	(0.05)	0.01	(0.04)	0.09	(0.05)
	Japan	m	m	m	m	m	m	m	m	m	m	m	m
	Korea	0.07	(0.04)	0.07	(0.05)	0.07	(0.05)	0.05	(0.06)	0.08	(0.06)	0.04	(0.08)
	Luxembourg	m	m	m	m	m	m	m	m	m	m	m	m
	Mexico	**-0.20**	(0.03)	-0.07	(0.04)	**-0.23**	(0.04)	**-0.12**	(0.05)	**-0.19**	(0.04)	-0.02	(0.05)
	Netherlands	m	m	m	m	m	m	m	m	m	m	m	m
	New Zealand	0.03	(0.04)	**0.21**	(0.06)	**-0.12**	(0.06)	**0.16**	(0.06)	**0.15**	(0.06)	**0.25**	(0.07)
	Norway	**-0.12**	(0.05)	0.05	(0.05)	-0.05	(0.06)	0.03	(0.06)	**-0.14**	(0.06)	0.04	(0.07)
	Poland	**-0.13**	(0.05)	**0.23**	(0.07)	**-0.29**	(0.06)	0.05	(0.07)	0.00	(0.06)	**0.36**	(0.09)
	Portugal	**-0.22**	(0.04)	**-0.18**	(0.04)	**-0.22**	(0.05)	**-0.15**	(0.05)	**-0.21**	(0.05)	**-0.17**	(0.06)
	Spain	-0.06	(0.05)	0.01	(0.04)	-0.01	(0.05)	-0.07	(0.05)	-0.04	(0.07)	0.08	(0.06)
	Sweden	**-0.15**	(0.05)	-0.07	(0.05)	-0.08	(0.06)	**-0.19**	(0.07)	**-0.18**	(0.06)	0.01	(0.06)
	Switzerland	**-0.17**	(0.06)	-0.03	(0.06)	**-0.12**	(0.06)	-0.05	(0.06)	**-0.25**	(0.08)	-0.06	(0.07)
	United Kingdom	m	m	m	m	m	m	m	m	m	m	m	m
	United States	0.03	(0.05)	**0.19**	(0.06)	**-0.14**	(0.06)	0.07	(0.08)	**0.24**	(0.07)	**0.35**	(0.08)
	OECD average-26	**-0.10**	(0.01)	**0.03**	(0.01)	**-0.12**	(0.01)	0.00	(0.01)	**-0.07**	(0.01)	**0.06**	(0.01)
Partners	Albania	**0.10**	(0.04)	**0.17**	(0.04)	-0.09	(0.06)	0.04	(0.05)	**0.25**	(0.05)	**0.37**	(0.05)
	Argentina	0.04	(0.06)	**-0.12**	(0.06)	0.02	(0.09)	-0.05	(0.07)	0.05	(0.08)	**-0.16**	(0.07)
	Brazil	**0.11**	(0.03)	**0.14**	(0.05)	**0.17**	(0.04)	**0.15**	(0.06)	0.05	(0.04)	0.12	(0.06)
	Bulgaria	-0.08	(0.05)	0.04	(0.07)	**-0.12**	(0.05)	-0.03	(0.07)	-0.05	(0.06)	0.10	(0.08)
	Hong Kong-China	**0.19**	(0.03)	**0.18**	(0.04)	**0.15**	(0.03)	0.12	(0.07)	**0.23**	(0.04)	**0.27**	(0.05)
	Indonesia	**-0.18**	(0.03)	**-0.14**	(0.03)	**-0.17**	(0.03)	**-0.13**	(0.04)	**-0.19**	(0.04)	**-0.11**	(0.05)
	Latvia	**-0.14**	(0.05)	**0.11**	(0.04)	**-0.29**	(0.07)	0.03	(0.05)	-0.04	(0.06)	**0.19**	(0.04)
	Liechtenstein	-0.17	(0.16)	-0.23	(0.19)	-0.03	(0.19)	**-0.47**	(0.20)	**-0.51**	(0.24)	0.03	(0.30)
	Peru	0.01	(0.04)	0.05	(0.04)	0.00	(0.05)	**-0.12**	(0.06)	0.03	(0.05)	**0.21**	(0.06)
	Romania	**-0.11**	(0.05)	**-0.11**	(0.05)	**-0.15**	(0.05)	-0.11	(0.06)	-0.06	(0.07)	-0.08	(0.06)
	Russian Federation	-0.05	(0.03)	0.01	(0.04)	**-0.11**	(0.04)	-0.06	(0.05)	0.01	(0.04)	0.06	(0.05)
	Thailand	**0.42**	(0.03)	**0.35**	(0.03)	**0.39**	(0.03)	**0.25**	(0.04)	**0.44**	(0.04)	**0.45**	(0.04)

Note: Values that are statistically significant are indicated in bold (see Annex A3).
StatLink http://dx.doi.org/10.1787/888932343285

[Part 1/2]

Table V.5.6 Percentage of students who read diverse materials in PISA 2000 and 2009

Percentage of students who reported that they read the following materials because they want to "several times a month" or "several times a week"

		PISA 2000										PISA 2009									
		Magazines		Comic books		Fiction (novels, narratives, stories)		Non-fiction books		Newspapers		Magazines		Comic books		Fiction (novels, narratives, stories)		Non-fiction books		Newspapers	
		%	S.E.	%	S.E.	%	S.E.	%	S.E.	%	S.E.	%	S.E.	%	S.E.	%	S.E.	%	S.E.	%	S.E.
OECD	Australia	63.2	(0.9)	10.4	(0.6)	31.3	(1.2)	19.6	(0.9)	65.9	(1.2)	50.0	(0.6)	9.0	(0.4)	38.3	(0.6)	20.0	(0.4)	53.7	(0.7)
	Austria	71.0	(0.7)	16.5	(0.6)	24.1	(0.9)	18.6	(0.7)	72.0	(1.0)	m	m	m	m	m	m	m	m	m	m
	Belgium	68.1	(0.9)	38.3	(0.8)	20.8	(0.8)	16.2	(0.6)	46.2	(0.6)	65.8	(0.7)	31.8	(0.7)	22.5	(0.7)	13.7	(0.6)	50.4	(0.9)
	Canada	67.0	(0.4)	16.3	(0.4)	30.9	(0.5)	16.7	(0.3)	57.6	(0.5)	48.1	(0.5)	14.4	(0.4)	42.0	(0.6)	20.0	(0.4)	47.9	(0.8)
	Chile	55.6	(0.8)	29.8	(0.8)	28.8	(0.9)	24.8	(0.7)	58.0	(1.0)	49.6	(0.8)	20.9	(0.6)	30.6	(0.8)	16.4	(0.6)	58.5	(0.9)
	Czech Republic	79.3	(0.6)	17.0	(0.7)	29.0	(0.8)	13.2	(0.6)	62.1	(0.9)	68.3	(0.8)	15.4	(0.6)	17.5	(0.8)	12.0	(0.6)	66.0	(0.8)
	Denmark	74.1	(0.8)	61.8	(1.0)	31.9	(0.9)	27.8	(1.0)	64.3	(1.0)	65.5	(0.8)	20.6	(0.7)	30.5	(0.8)	27.1	(0.7)	51.7	(0.9)
	Finland	75.1	(0.7)	65.9	(0.9)	27.2	(0.7)	14.5	(0.6)	85.1	(0.7)	64.9	(0.8)	60.1	(0.9)	26.1	(0.8)	15.5	(0.5)	75.4	(0.8)
	France	62.3	(0.9)	32.6	(0.9)	23.4	(0.7)	20.6	(0.6)	47.3	(1.0)	62.5	(0.8)	30.4	(0.8)	28.9	(1.0)	12.0	(0.5)	46.7	(1.1)
	Germany	65.7	(1.0)	11.8	(0.5)	26.8	(0.7)	16.8	(0.6)	62.9	(1.0)	54.9	(0.8)	11.3	(0.5)	32.8	(0.8)	17.2	(0.8)	61.8	(1.0)
	Greece	60.8	(0.9)	23.1	(0.8)	23.6	(0.8)	26.4	(1.0)	46.2	(0.9)	60.5	(0.9)	24.7	(0.7)	21.5	(0.7)	7.2	(0.4)	42.8	(0.9)
	Hungary	71.8	(0.9)	18.0	(0.7)	25.1	(1.1)	31.6	(0.8)	60.8	(1.2)	60.7	(1.0)	26.6	(0.8)	31.5	(1.0)	34.9	(0.8)	71.8	(0.9)
	Iceland	79.1	(0.6)	49.5	(0.7)	22.0	(0.7)	18.0	(0.6)	89.2	(0.6)	58.2	(0.9)	30.9	(0.8)	27.3	(0.7)	17.1	(0.7)	82.0	(0.7)
	Ireland	61.5	(0.9)	8.6	(0.6)	26.2	(0.9)	14.8	(0.7)	75.2	(0.8)	57.1	(0.9)	7.5	(0.5)	30.3	(1.0)	16.0	(0.7)	67.5	(0.9)
	Israel	48.9	(1.2)	28.1	(1.5)	33.9	(2.1)	26.5	(1.8)	79.6	(1.0)	38.8	(0.9)	17.5	(0.6)	29.7	(0.7)	26.5	(1.0)	74.7	(0.8)
	Italy	66.1	(0.9)	27.7	(0.9)	31.7	(0.9)	14.1	(0.6)	61.1	(0.8)	48.8	(0.5)	17.4	(0.3)	35.0	(0.5)	4.9	(0.2)	53.4	(0.5)
	Japan	81.8	(0.7)	83.8	(0.7)	27.5	(0.8)	9.8	(0.5)	69.9	(1.1)	64.5	(0.8)	72.4	(0.8)	42.0	(1.1)	11.1	(0.4)	57.6	(0.9)
	Korea	39.3	(0.8)	62.7	(1.2)	34.9	(0.8)	23.1	(0.6)	69.7	(0.9)	21.2	(0.6)	40.5	(1.0)	46.6	(0.8)	30.0	(0.9)	45.1	(1.2)
	Luxembourg	m	m	m	m	m	m	m	m	m	m	68.7	(0.8)	20.3	(0.7)	28.8	(0.7)	19.3	(0.5)	70.7	(0.6)
	Mexico	46.3	(1.3)	24.8	(0.8)	36.4	(0.9)	22.2	(0.7)	46.1	(1.6)	46.9	(0.5)	27.1	(0.4)	37.9	(0.4)	18.7	(0.3)	47.8	(0.5)
	Netherlands	m	m	m	m	m	m	m	m	m	m	57.2	(1.4)	23.1	(0.9)	21.5	(1.0)	12.6	(0.6)	48.5	(1.5)
	New Zealand	70.3	(0.8)	11.6	(0.6)	34.8	(0.8)	25.2	(0.8)	66.4	(0.9)	53.1	(1.0)	11.6	(0.5)	44.3	(0.8)	25.4	(0.7)	53.1	(0.9)
	Norway	69.2	(0.9)	57.7	(0.9)	24.3	(0.8)	21.2	(0.6)	84.4	(0.7)	60.6	(0.9)	42.2	(0.9)	26.3	(0.8)	27.2	(0.8)	73.4	(0.8)
	Poland	70.8	(1.0)	10.7	(0.7)	18.7	(1.0)	17.2	(0.7)	74.2	(1.0)	65.8	(0.7)	11.3	(0.5)	20.1	(0.7)	20.8	(0.8)	79.1	(0.6)
	Portugal	71.5	(0.9)	24.4	(0.7)	32.0	(0.7)	13.1	(0.7)	52.8	(1.0)	63.8	(0.7)	18.6	(0.5)	28.0	(0.6)	14.2	(0.5)	51.5	(0.7)
	Spain	61.3	(0.7)	18.7	(0.7)	25.1	(0.7)	23.0	(0.8)	46.4	(1.1)	51.3	(0.7)	12.0	(0.4)	30.1	(0.5)	18.3	(0.4)	45.1	(0.7)
	Sweden	68.3	(0.8)	35.9	(0.8)	33.6	(0.8)	12.7	(0.6)	82.6	(0.6)	58.2	(0.9)	22.5	(0.7)	32.4	(0.9)	9.9	(0.6)	71.6	(0.9)
	Switzerland	66.5	(0.7)	26.2	(0.8)	30.3	(0.9)	16.8	(0.6)	66.1	(1.0)	66.8	(0.7)	24.1	(0.6)	30.1	(0.7)	15.0	(0.5)	79.5	(0.8)
	United Kingdom	m	m	m	m	m	m	m	m	m	m	59.6	(0.8)	7.8	(0.4)	31.5	(0.7)	19.5	(0.5)	61.2	(0.8)
	United States	68.1	(1.4)	11.4	(1.1)	28.2	(1.1)	18.4	(1.0)	56.0	(1.4)	46.8	(0.7)	10.4	(0.6)	36.6	(1.1)	20.5	(0.8)	37.0	(1.0)
	OECD average-26	65.8	(0.2)	31.0	(0.2)	28.4	(0.2)	19.4	(0.2)	64.5	(0.2)	55.9	(0.2)	24.3	(0.1)	31.5	(0.2)	18.1	(0.1)	59.4	(0.2)
Partners	Albania	54.2	(1.2)	31.9	(1.4)	51.9	(1.1)	18.4	(0.7)	52.7	(0.9)	44.6	(1.1)	43.7	(1.2)	53.7	(1.1)	22.1	(0.8)	60.2	(1.2)
	Argentina	62.5	(2.0)	29.9	(1.6)	28.5	(1.3)	27.3	(1.7)	58.9	(1.9)	52.6	(0.9)	29.3	(0.9)	26.9	(0.9)	28.5	(0.9)	49.0	(1.1)
	Brazil	60.0	(0.9)	29.9	(1.1)	32.3	(1.0)	36.3	(1.0)	50.8	(1.4)	48.9	(0.6)	33.5	(0.7)	35.7	(0.6)	15.1	(0.4)	44.3	(0.8)
	Bulgaria	70.5	(1.0)	18.3	(0.8)	32.9	(1.0)	34.4	(0.9)	82.8	(0.9)	61.8	(1.1)	17.7	(0.8)	34.3	(1.5)	29.6	(1.0)	57.2	(1.1)
	Hong Kong-China	68.7	(0.6)	42.2	(1.0)	35.1	(1.0)	36.3	(0.8)	88.0	(0.6)	48.5	(0.9)	30.4	(0.8)	48.5	(0.8)	35.0	(0.9)	84.1	(0.7)
	Indonesia	49.3	(1.2)	40.0	(1.2)	36.6	(1.1)	21.9	(0.9)	67.1	(1.0)	55.2	(1.2)	52.3	(0.9)	59.3	(1.0)	36.1	(1.2)	65.4	(1.1)
	Latvia	76.4	(0.9)	14.0	(0.9)	31.3	(1.0)	18.1	(1.5)	76.5	(1.0)	71.1	(1.1)	9.5	(0.6)	32.8	(1.1)	25.9	(0.8)	65.2	(1.0)
	Liechtenstein	70.5	(2.5)	14.9	(2.1)	25.9	(2.5)	15.2	(2.0)	67.3	(2.7)	64.8	(2.6)	20.9	(2.1)	28.3	(2.3)	14.9	(2.0)	72.1	(2.4)
	Peru	38.2	(1.2)	36.8	(1.0)	41.5	(0.9)	39.2	(0.9)	64.0	(1.0)	47.9	(0.9)	48.6	(0.7)	55.4	(0.9)	39.9	(0.8)	73.9	(1.0)
	Romania	63.0	(1.2)	11.5	(0.6)	43.9	(0.9)	27.4	(1.0)	52.0	(1.0)	62.7	(1.0)	11.9	(0.5)	31.8	(1.0)	22.8	(0.6)	50.3	(1.4)
	Russian Federation	74.8	(0.8)	24.8	(1.3)	53.4	(1.0)	48.6	(0.8)	76.1	(0.9)	67.3	(0.9)	17.3	(0.9)	58.7	(1.0)	26.3	(0.7)	64.1	(1.1)
	Thailand	37.9	(1.0)	60.6	(1.1)	50.5	(1.0)	46.3	(1.1)	73.5	(1.4)	53.1	(1.0)	72.2	(0.8)	65.1	(0.8)	50.5	(0.7)	72.0	(0.9)

Note: Values that are statistically significant are indicated in bold (see Annex A3).

StatLink http://dx.doi.org/10.1787/888932343285

[Part 2/2]

Table V.5.6 Percentage of students who read diverse materials in PISA 2000 and 2009

Percentage of students who reported that they read the following materials because they want to "several times a month" or "several times a week"

		Change between 2000 and 2009 (PISA 2009 – PISA 2000)									
		Magazines		Comic books		Fiction (novels, narratives, stories)		Non-fiction books		Newspapers	
		% dif.	S.E.	% dif.	S.E.	% dif.	S.E.	% dif.	S.E.	% dif.	S.E.
OECD	Australia	**-13.2**	(1.1)	**-1.4**	(0.7)	**7.0**	(1.4)	0.4	(0.9)	**-12.1**	(1.3)
	Austria	m	m	m	m	m	m	m	m	m	m
	Belgium	**-2.3**	(1.1)	**-6.6**	(1.1)	1.7	(1.1)	**-2.5**	(0.9)	**4.2**	(1.1)
	Canada	**-18.9**	(0.6)	**-1.9**	(0.6)	**11.1**	(0.8)	**3.2**	(0.6)	**-9.7**	(0.9)
	Chile	**-5.9**	(1.1)	**-8.8**	(1.0)	1.8	(1.2)	**-8.5**	(0.9)	0.5	(1.4)
	Czech Republic	**-11.0**	(1.0)	-1.6	(0.9)	**-11.5**	(1.1)	-1.2	(0.8)	**3.9**	(1.2)
	Denmark	**-8.5**	(1.1)	**-41.2**	(1.2)	-1.3	(1.2)	-0.7	(1.2)	**-12.5**	(1.4)
	Finland	**-10.2**	(1.1)	**-5.8**	(1.3)	-1.1	(1.1)	1.0	(0.8)	**-9.7**	(1.0)
	France	0.2	(1.2)	-2.2	(1.2)	**5.5**	(1.2)	**-8.6**	(0.8)	-0.6	(1.5)
	Germany	**-10.8**	(1.3)	-0.5	(0.7)	**6.0**	(1.1)	0.3	(1.0)	-1.1	(1.4)
	Greece	-0.3	(1.2)	1.6	(1.1)	-2.1	(1.1)	**-19.3**	(1.0)	**-3.4**	(1.3)
	Hungary	**-11.1**	(1.3)	**8.6**	(1.0)	**6.3**	(1.5)	**3.3**	(1.2)	**10.9**	(1.5)
	Iceland	**-20.9**	(1.1)	**-18.5**	(1.1)	**5.3**	(1.0)	-0.9	(0.9)	**-7.3**	(0.9)
	Ireland	**-4.4**	(1.2)	-1.1	(0.7)	**4.1**	(1.4)	1.2	(1.0)	**-7.8**	(1.2)
	Israel	**-10.2**	(1.5)	**-10.6**	(1.6)	-4.2	(2.2)	0.0	(2.0)	**-4.8**	(1.2)
	Italy	**-17.2**	(1.0)	**-10.3**	(0.9)	**3.3**	(1.1)	**-9.1**	(0.6)	**-7.7**	(1.0)
	Japan	**-17.3**	(1.0)	**-11.5**	(1.0)	**14.5**	(1.3)	**1.3**	(0.7)	**-12.3**	(1.4)
	Korea	**-18.1**	(1.0)	**-22.2**	(1.5)	**11.8**	(1.1)	**6.9**	(1.1)	**-24.6**	(1.5)
	Luxembourg	m	m	m	m	m	m	m	m	m	m
	Mexico	0.6	(1.3)	**2.3**	(0.9)	1.5	(0.9)	**-3.5**	(0.8)	1.7	(1.7)
	Netherlands	m	m	m	m	m	m	m	m	m	m
	New Zealand	**-17.2**	(1.3)	0.0	(0.8)	**9.4**	(1.2)	0.2	(1.1)	**-13.3**	(1.3)
	Norway	**-8.7**	(1.3)	**-15.6**	(1.3)	2.1	(1.1)	**6.0**	(1.0)	**-11.0**	(1.1)
	Poland	**-5.0**	(1.2)	0.5	(0.9)	1.4	(1.3)	**3.6**	(1.1)	**4.9**	(1.1)
	Portugal	**-7.7**	(1.2)	**-5.8**	(0.9)	**-3.9**	(1.0)	1.1	(0.8)	-1.3	(1.2)
	Spain	**-9.9**	(1.0)	**-6.6**	(0.8)	**5.0**	(0.8)	**-4.7**	(0.9)	-1.3	(1.3)
	Sweden	**-10.1**	(1.2)	**-13.5**	(1.1)	-1.2	(1.2)	**-2.7**	(0.8)	**-11.0**	(1.1)
	Switzerland	0.3	(1.0)	**-2.1**	(1.0)	-0.2	(1.2)	**-1.8**	(0.7)	**13.4**	(1.3)
	United Kingdom	m	m	m	m	m	m	m	m	m	m
	United States	**-21.4**	(1.6)	-1.0	(1.3)	**8.4**	(1.6)	2.1	(1.2)	**-19.0**	(1.8)
	OECD average-26	**-10.0**	(0.2)	**-6.8**	(0.2)	**3.1**	(0.2)	**-1.3**	(0.2)	**-5.0**	(0.3)
Partners	Albania	**-9.5**	(1.6)	**11.8**	(1.8)	1.7	(1.6)	**3.7**	(1.1)	**7.4**	(1.5)
	Argentina	**-10.0**	(2.2)	-0.6	(1.9)	-1.6	(1.6)	1.2	(1.9)	**-9.9**	(2.2)
	Brazil	**-11.0**	(1.1)	**3.6**	(1.3)	**3.4**	(1.2)	**-21.2**	(1.1)	**-6.5**	(1.6)
	Bulgaria	**-8.7**	(1.4)	-0.6	(1.1)	1.3	(1.8)	**-4.8**	(1.3)	**-25.6**	(1.4)
	Hong Kong-China	**-20.2**	(1.1)	**-11.8**	(1.3)	**13.4**	(1.3)	-1.3	(1.2)	**-3.9**	(1.0)
	Indonesia	**5.9**	(1.7)	**12.3**	(1.5)	**22.7**	(1.5)	**14.2**	(1.5)	-1.6	(1.5)
	Latvia	**-5.4**	(1.4)	**-4.5**	(1.1)	1.5	(1.6)	**7.8**	(1.7)	**-11.3**	(1.4)
	Liechtenstein	-5.7	(3.6)	**6.0**	(3.0)	2.4	(3.4)	-0.4	(2.8)	4.8	(3.6)
	Peru	**9.6**	(1.5)	**11.8**	(1.2)	**13.9**	(1.3)	0.8	(1.2)	**10.0**	(1.4)
	Romania	-0.3	(1.6)	0.4	(0.8)	**-12.1**	(1.4)	**-4.6**	(1.2)	-1.7	(1.8)
	Russian Federation	**-7.5**	(1.2)	**-7.5**	(1.6)	**5.3**	(1.5)	**-22.3**	(1.0)	**-12.0**	(1.5)
	Thailand	**15.1**	(1.4)	**11.5**	(1.4)	**14.6**	(1.3)	**4.3**	(1.3)	-1.6	(1.7)

Note: Values that are statistically significant are indicated in bold (see Annex A3).

StatLink http://dx.doi.org/10.1787/888932343285

[Part 1/4]
Table V.5.7 Percentage of students who read diverse materials in PISA 2000 and 2009, by gender
Percentage of boys and girls who reported that they read the following materials because they want to "several times a month" or "several times a week"

		Boys																			
		PISA 2000										PISA 2009									
		Magazines		Comic books		Fiction		Non-fiction books		Newspapers		Magazines		Comic books		Fiction		Non-fiction books		Newspapers	
		%	S.E.	%	S.E.	%	S.E.	%	S.E.	%	S.E.	%	S.E.	%	S.E.	%	S.E.	%	S.E.	%	S.E.
OECD	Australia	64.0	(1.2)	15.1	(0.9)	23.2	(1.2)	19.4	(1.1)	68.3	(1.5)	47.1	(0.8)	11.6	(0.4)	28.3	(0.8)	18.9	(0.6)	58.1	(0.9)
	Austria	72.6	(1.0)	22.6	(1.0)	11.2	(0.8)	23.4	(0.9)	72.2	(1.3)	m	m	m	m	m	m	m	m	m	m
	Belgium	64.1	(1.1)	43.3	(1.0)	13.5	(1.1)	14.6	(0.8)	50.5	(0.8)	57.4	(1.0)	39.7	(0.9)	15.2	(0.6)	13.9	(0.7)	57.8	(1.2)
	Canada	62.2	(0.6)	19.9	(0.5)	23.0	(0.6)	14.9	(0.4)	60.4	(0.7)	39.7	(0.7)	18.2	(0.6)	29.5	(0.8)	18.6	(0.6)	52.2	(1.0)
	Chile	48.7	(1.2)	31.5	(1.3)	20.9	(1.1)	21.6	(1.1)	55.0	(1.5)	39.2	(1.1)	22.9	(0.8)	22.0	(0.8)	12.7	(0.7)	58.3	(1.4)
	Czech Republic	75.4	(0.9)	21.2	(1.1)	11.5	(0.7)	14.7	(0.8)	69.9	(1.0)	63.1	(1.0)	18.3	(1.0)	7.7	(0.6)	11.4	(0.8)	68.4	(1.2)
	Denmark	69.1	(1.1)	65.9	(1.1)	20.9	(1.0)	29.3	(1.3)	68.7	(1.2)	55.0	(1.1)	27.9	(1.2)	22.8	(1.0)	27.7	(0.9)	57.6	(1.1)
	Finland	66.8	(1.0)	75.2	(1.1)	12.2	(0.7)	17.9	(0.9)	84.8	(0.9)	53.8	(1.3)	70.0	(1.1)	13.0	(0.7)	19.3	(0.7)	76.0	(1.1)
	France	63.0	(1.2)	42.8	(1.3)	17.7	(0.9)	21.8	(0.9)	48.6	(1.3)	56.5	(1.2)	40.6	(1.3)	21.1	(1.1)	15.0	(0.8)	51.4	(1.4)
	Germany	63.2	(1.4)	17.2	(1.0)	13.8	(0.8)	18.6	(1.0)	65.6	(1.4)	53.4	(1.2)	16.2	(0.7)	20.4	(1.0)	21.9	(1.1)	67.3	(1.2)
	Greece	60.8	(1.2)	27.4	(1.1)	15.6	(1.0)	26.1	(1.2)	62.2	(1.3)	55.2	(1.1)	30.5	(1.0)	12.6	(0.8)	6.0	(0.5)	58.7	(1.2)
	Hungary	67.8	(1.3)	19.0	(1.0)	15.0	(1.2)	35.4	(1.3)	61.5	(1.7)	56.0	(1.2)	28.3	(1.0)	24.1	(1.3)	35.7	(1.2)	66.7	(1.2)
	Iceland	76.5	(1.0)	55.1	(1.2)	13.9	(0.8)	13.8	(0.7)	89.9	(0.8)	48.8	(1.3)	35.1	(1.2)	18.9	(0.8)	13.0	(0.8)	80.9	(1.0)
	Ireland	58.0	(1.3)	10.8	(0.8)	18.2	(1.3)	11.6	(0.9)	78.1	(1.0)	45.6	(1.2)	10.2	(0.8)	24.4	(1.4)	15.0	(1.0)	73.4	(1.2)
	Israel	41.2	(1.4)	25.7	(1.7)	26.0	(1.9)	22.8	(1.7)	79.2	(1.6)	29.6	(1.3)	14.0	(0.8)	19.2	(1.1)	25.1	(1.4)	71.4	(1.0)
	Italy	59.5	(1.3)	32.8	(1.2)	23.4	(0.8)	15.1	(0.8)	66.0	(1.2)	42.2	(0.6)	23.1	(0.5)	24.9	(0.6)	4.3	(0.2)	58.1	(0.7)
	Japan	82.7	(0.9)	88.2	(0.8)	24.9	(1.0)	9.7	(0.6)	74.0	(1.2)	60.8	(1.1)	81.4	(0.7)	36.7	(1.2)	10.6	(0.6)	61.9	(1.1)
	Korea	40.8	(1.1)	71.0	(1.3)	35.8	(1.0)	22.4	(0.8)	73.4	(1.2)	17.2	(0.8)	49.8	(1.4)	40.8	(1.1)	27.4	(1.3)	46.6	(1.5)
	Luxembourg	m	m	m	m	m	m	m	m	m	m	64.2	(1.2)	26.3	(1.1)	16.8	(0.8)	24.9	(0.8)	73.5	(0.8)
	Mexico	43.8	(1.5)	30.5	(1.1)	32.9	(1.1)	23.2	(1.1)	47.7	(1.8)	42.8	(0.7)	31.8	(0.6)	31.1	(0.7)	18.4	(0.5)	51.6	(0.7)
	Netherlands	m	m	m	m	m	m	m	m	m	m	46.2	(1.8)	31.6	(1.4)	10.1	(0.7)	8.2	(0.7)	54.7	(1.9)
	New Zealand	70.5	(1.2)	16.5	(1.0)	26.8	(1.0)	25.7	(1.1)	68.0	(1.2)	47.6	(1.2)	14.9	(0.8)	34.8	(1.1)	24.1	(1.0)	54.3	(1.2)
	Norway	61.4	(1.3)	67.7	(1.3)	12.6	(0.8)	24.4	(1.0)	85.8	(0.9)	49.6	(1.2)	50.5	(1.3)	16.9	(0.8)	28.0	(1.1)	75.6	(1.0)
	Poland	67.0	(1.5)	13.5	(0.9)	10.6	(0.9)	17.0	(1.0)	69.7	(1.3)	56.9	(1.1)	14.1	(0.8)	11.5	(0.7)	17.9	(1.0)	76.1	(0.8)
	Portugal	64.4	(1.5)	26.9	(1.1)	19.5	(1.1)	7.4	(0.6)	67.9	(1.5)	56.1	(0.9)	23.7	(0.8)	16.4	(0.8)	10.4	(0.5)	66.2	(1.0)
	Spain	56.1	(1.3)	26.4	(1.1)	18.2	(0.8)	20.7	(1.2)	56.1	(1.2)	46.0	(0.8)	16.7	(0.6)	21.4	(0.7)	13.4	(0.6)	58.1	(0.9)
	Sweden	61.5	(1.1)	46.5	(1.1)	22.5	(1.2)	13.9	(0.8)	83.2	(0.9)	49.7	(1.2)	28.7	(1.1)	20.1	(0.9)	9.3	(0.7)	71.4	(1.1)
	Switzerland	64.2	(1.2)	33.3	(1.2)	15.0	(1.0)	18.8	(0.8)	71.0	(1.1)	61.0	(1.0)	30.8	(0.9)	19.1	(0.8)	19.6	(0.8)	81.1	(1.0)
	United Kingdom	m	m	m	m	m	m	m	m	m	m	48.1	(0.9)	10.5	(0.6)	23.8	(1.0)	18.8	(0.9)	67.7	(1.1)
	United States	62.5	(2.0)	15.7	(1.5)	22.0	(1.4)	16.0	(1.3)	56.4	(1.9)	44.3	(1.2)	12.7	(0.9)	27.8	(1.2)	18.5	(1.0)	41.2	(1.1)
	OECD average-26	62.1	(0.2)	36.1	(0.2)	19.6	(0.2)	19.1	(0.2)	67.8	(0.3)	49.0	(0.2)	29.3	(0.2)	22.3	(0.2)	17.5	(0.2)	63.1	(0.2)
Partners	Albania	48.0	(1.9)	30.6	(1.6)	41.5	(1.7)	18.7	(1.3)	58.7	(1.4)	37.3	(1.3)	47.0	(1.6)	40.5	(1.5)	20.1	(1.1)	61.4	(1.3)
	Argentina	55.6	(2.1)	30.1	(1.8)	20.8	(1.6)	21.9	(1.6)	58.2	(2.1)	41.6	(1.2)	28.0	(1.3)	19.4	(1.0)	22.4	(1.3)	53.4	(1.5)
	Brazil	46.3	(1.3)	31.1	(1.5)	16.5	(0.9)	33.9	(1.4)	50.7	(1.6)	36.7	(0.8)	35.5	(0.9)	21.2	(0.6)	13.3	(0.6)	46.2	(1.2)
	Bulgaria	64.4	(1.4)	19.2	(1.0)	22.5	(1.0)	29.5	(1.2)	79.2	(1.1)	49.1	(1.3)	19.7	(1.2)	25.1	(1.5)	29.3	(1.5)	54.7	(1.7)
	Hong Kong-China	66.3	(0.9)	54.8	(1.3)	27.8	(1.3)	35.1	(1.2)	86.8	(0.8)	46.9	(1.2)	37.6	(1.2)	41.9	(1.0)	36.3	(1.2)	84.0	(1.0)
	Indonesia	43.9	(1.3)	38.1	(1.5)	31.1	(1.1)	20.5	(1.2)	68.6	(1.3)	51.4	(1.3)	51.3	(1.1)	51.6	(1.3)	31.1	(1.3)	67.7	(1.4)
	Latvia	67.9	(1.4)	15.8	(1.0)	21.1	(1.3)	18.0	(2.0)	73.1	(1.5)	61.9	(1.3)	12.0	(0.9)	23.3	(1.3)	20.5	(0.9)	63.5	(1.3)
	Liechtenstein	70.4	(3.6)	21.0	(3.1)	16.1	(3.4)	13.4	(3.0)	77.0	(3.6)	57.7	(3.7)	26.2	(3.2)	20.1	(2.8)	17.7	(2.8)	75.0	(3.3)
	Peru	40.3	(1.5)	38.7	(1.3)	38.7	(1.1)	39.1	(1.5)	65.8	(1.3)	44.6	(1.2)	48.1	(1.1)	48.3	(1.3)	37.9	(1.0)	74.7	(1.1)
	Romania	58.8	(1.7)	12.8	(0.8)	36.7	(1.6)	28.0	(1.4)	54.2	(1.5)	52.5	(1.4)	11.7	(0.7)	22.7	(1.0)	22.1	(0.9)	54.1	(1.5)
	Russian Federation	67.3	(1.2)	24.5	(1.5)	42.2	(1.3)	43.2	(1.2)	73.8	(1.1)	58.6	(1.3)	18.7	(1.2)	49.7	(1.6)	25.8	(0.8)	62.6	(1.1)
	Thailand	29.7	(1.3)	57.8	(1.9)	43.6	(1.4)	40.7	(1.9)	66.3	(2.1)	41.0	(1.2)	67.2	(1.2)	53.5	(1.2)	45.5	(1.1)	70.4	(1.1)

Note: Values that are statistically significant are indicated in bold (see Annex A3).
StatLink http://dx.doi.org/10.1787/888932343285

[Part 2/4]

Table V.5.7 Percentage of students who read diverse materials in PISA 2000 and 2009, by gender

Percentage of boys and girls who reported that they read the following materials because they want to "several times a month" or "several times a week"

		Boys									
		Change between 2000 and 2009 (PISA 2009 – PISA 2000)									
		Magazines		Comic books		Fiction		Non-fiction books		Newspapers	
		% dif.	S.E.	% dif.	S.E.	% dif.	S.E.	% dif.	S.E.	% dif.	S.E.
OECD	Australia	**-16.9**	(1.5)	**-3.5**	(1.0)	**5.1**	(1.4)	-0.6	(1.3)	**-10.1**	(1.8)
	Austria	m	m	m	m	m	m	m	m	m	m
	Belgium	**-6.8**	(1.4)	**-3.6**	(1.3)	1.8	(1.3)	-0.7	(1.1)	**7.3**	(1.5)
	Canada	**-22.5**	(1.0)	**-1.7**	(0.8)	**6.5**	(1.0)	**3.7**	(0.7)	**-8.2**	(1.2)
	Chile	**-9.6**	(1.6)	**-8.7**	(1.5)	1.1	(1.3)	**-8.8**	(1.3)	3.3	(2.1)
	Czech Republic	**-12.3**	(1.3)	-2.9	(1.5)	**-3.8**	(0.9)	**-3.4**	(1.1)	-1.5	(1.6)
	Denmark	**-14.2**	(1.5)	**-38.0**	(1.7)	2.0	(1.4)	-1.6	(1.6)	**-11.1**	(1.7)
	Finland	**-13.0**	(1.6)	**-5.2**	(1.6)	0.8	(1.0)	1.4	(1.1)	**-8.8**	(1.4)
	France	**-6.6**	(1.7)	-2.1	(1.8)	**3.4**	(1.4)	**-6.8**	(1.2)	2.8	(2.0)
	Germany	**-9.7**	(1.9)	-1.0	(1.3)	**6.7**	(1.2)	**3.4**	(1.5)	1.7	(1.8)
	Greece	**-5.6**	(1.6)	**3.1**	(1.5)	**-2.9**	(1.2)	**-20.2**	(1.3)	**-3.5**	(1.8)
	Hungary	**-11.8**	(1.8)	**9.3**	(1.5)	**9.2**	(1.8)	0.3	(1.8)	**5.2**	(2.1)
	Iceland	**-27.7**	(1.6)	**-20.0**	(1.7)	**4.9**	(1.2)	-0.8	(1.0)	**-8.9**	(1.3)
	Ireland	**-12.4**	(1.8)	-0.6	(1.1)	**6.2**	(1.9)	**3.3**	(1.3)	**-4.6**	(1.6)
	Israel	**-11.6**	(1.9)	**-11.7**	(1.9)	**-6.8**	(2.2)	2.3	(2.2)	**-7.8**	(1.9)
	Italy	**-17.4**	(1.4)	**-9.7**	(1.3)	1.5	(1.0)	**-10.8**	(0.8)	**-7.9**	(1.4)
	Japan	**-21.9**	(1.5)	**-6.7**	(1.1)	**11.8**	(1.6)	0.9	(0.9)	**-12.1**	(1.6)
	Korea	**-23.6**	(1.4)	**-21.2**	(1.9)	**5.0**	(1.5)	**5.0**	(1.5)	**-26.8**	(1.9)
	Luxembourg	m	m	m	m	m	m	m	m	m	m
	Mexico	-0.9	(1.7)	1.3	(1.3)	-1.8	(1.3)	**-4.8**	(1.2)	**3.9**	(2.0)
	Netherlands	m	m	m	m	m	m	m	m	m	m
	New Zealand	**-22.9**	(1.7)	-1.6	(1.3)	**8.0**	(1.5)	-1.6	(1.5)	**-13.7**	(1.7)
	Norway	**-11.7**	(1.8)	**-17.1**	(1.8)	**4.3**	(1.1)	**3.6**	(1.4)	**-10.2**	(1.3)
	Poland	**-10.1**	(1.9)	0.7	(1.2)	0.9	(1.2)	0.9	(1.4)	**6.4**	(1.6)
	Portugal	**-8.3**	(1.7)	**-3.2**	(1.4)	**-3.1**	(1.3)	**3.0**	(0.8)	-1.8	(1.8)
	Spain	**-10.1**	(1.5)	**-9.7**	(1.2)	**3.2**	(1.1)	**-7.3**	(1.3)	2.0	(1.5)
	Sweden	**-11.9**	(1.6)	**-17.8**	(1.6)	-2.3	(1.5)	**-4.6**	(1.1)	**-11.9**	(1.4)
	Switzerland	**-3.2**	(1.5)	-2.5	(1.5)	**4.1**	(1.3)	0.9	(1.1)	**10.1**	(1.5)
	United Kingdom	m	m	m	m	m	m	m	m	m	m
	United States	**-18.2**	(2.3)	-3.1	(1.7)	**5.8**	(1.9)	2.4	(1.6)	**-15.2**	(2.2)
	OECD average-26	**-13.1**	(0.3)	**-6.8**	(0.3)	**2.8**	(0.3)	**-1.6**	(0.3)	**-4.7**	(0.3)
Partners	Albania	**-10.7**	(2.3)	**16.5**	(2.3)	-0.9	(2.3)	1.4	(1.7)	2.8	(1.9)
	Argentina	**-14.1**	(2.4)	-2.2	(2.2)	-1.4	(1.9)	0.5	(2.1)	-4.8	(2.6)
	Brazil	**-9.7**	(1.5)	**4.4**	(1.7)	**4.6**	(1.1)	**-20.6**	(1.5)	**-4.5**	(2.0)
	Bulgaria	**-15.3**	(2.0)	0.4	(1.5)	2.6	(1.8)	-0.2	(1.9)	**-24.5**	(2.0)
	Hong Kong-China	**-19.4**	(1.5)	**-17.2**	(1.8)	**14.1**	(1.7)	1.1	(1.7)	**-2.8**	(1.2)
	Indonesia	**7.5**	(1.8)	**13.1**	(1.9)	**20.5**	(1.7)	**10.6**	(1.7)	-0.9	(1.9)
	Latvia	**-6.0**	(1.9)	**-3.8**	(1.4)	2.3	(1.8)	2.5	(2.2)	**-9.6**	(2.0)
	Liechtenstein	**-12.7**	(5.2)	5.2	(4.5)	4.1	(4.4)	4.3	(4.1)	-2.0	(4.9)
	Peru	**4.3**	(1.9)	**9.5**	(1.6)	**9.7**	(1.7)	-1.2	(1.8)	**8.9**	(1.7)
	Romania	**-6.3**	(2.2)	-1.0	(1.1)	**-14.0**	(1.9)	**-6.0**	(1.7)	-0.1	(2.2)
	Russian Federation	**-8.7**	(1.7)	**-5.9**	(1.9)	**7.5**	(2.0)	**-17.5**	(1.4)	**-11.2**	(1.5)
	Thailand	**11.2**	(1.7)	**9.4**	(2.2)	**10.0**	(1.8)	**4.8**	(2.2)	4.1	(2.4)

Note: Values that are statistically significant are indicated in bold (see Annex A3).

StatLink http://dx.doi.org/10.1787/888932343285

[Part 3/4]

Table V.5.7 Percentage of students who read diverse materials in PISA 2000 and 2009, by gender

Percentage of boys and girls who reported that they read the following materials because they want to "several times a month" or "several times a week"

		Girls																			
		PISA 2000										PISA 2009									
		Magazines		Comic books		Fiction		Non-fiction books		Newspapers		Magazines		Comic books		Fiction		Non-fiction books		Newspapers	
		%	S.E.	%	S.E.	%	S.E.	%	S.E.	%	S.E.	%	S.E.	%	S.E.	%	S.E.	%	S.E.	%	S.E.
OECD	Australia	62.2	(1.2)	5.3	(0.6)	40.2	(1.6)	19.7	(1.1)	63.2	(1.3)	52.7	(0.7)	6.6	(0.5)	47.8	(0.8)	21.1	(0.5)	49.5	(0.9)
	Austria	69.3	(1.1)	10.1	(0.6)	37.6	(1.1)	13.5	(0.7)	71.7	(1.3)	m	m	m	m	m	m	m	m	m	m
	Belgium	72.3	(1.2)	33.0	(1.0)	28.8	(1.0)	17.8	(0.8)	41.4	(1.0)	74.4	(0.8)	23.7	(0.9)	29.9	(1.0)	13.5	(0.7)	42.8	(1.0)
	Canada	71.8	(0.6)	12.7	(0.5)	38.8	(0.7)	18.5	(0.5)	54.8	(0.6)	56.5	(0.8)	10.6	(0.5)	54.5	(0.8)	21.3	(0.6)	43.7	(0.9)
	Chile	61.5	(1.0)	28.2	(0.9)	35.8	(1.1)	27.7	(0.9)	60.7	(1.3)	60.4	(0.9)	18.9	(0.7)	39.6	(1.1)	20.1	(0.9)	58.7	(1.0)
	Czech Republic	82.8	(0.8)	13.3	(0.7)	44.6	(1.3)	11.8	(0.7)	55.3	(1.1)	74.2	(1.0)	12.2	(0.7)	28.5	(1.2)	12.7	(0.7)	63.4	(1.0)
	Denmark	79.1	(1.1)	57.8	(1.2)	43.0	(1.3)	26.2	(1.2)	59.7	(1.4)	75.9	(1.0)	13.5	(0.8)	38.1	(1.1)	26.6	(1.0)	45.9	(1.2)
	Finland	83.0	(0.8)	57.2	(1.0)	41.2	(1.1)	11.2	(0.7)	85.3	(0.8)	76.0	(0.9)	50.3	(1.2)	39.2	(1.2)	11.7	(0.6)	74.8	(0.9)
	France	61.5	(1.1)	23.1	(0.9)	28.7	(0.9)	19.5	(0.8)	46.1	(1.3)	68.2	(1.1)	20.7	(0.9)	36.2	(1.3)	9.1	(0.7)	42.3	(1.3)
	Germany	68.3	(1.2)	6.7	(0.6)	39.7	(1.1)	15.3	(0.7)	60.3	(1.1)	56.3	(1.1)	6.5	(0.5)	45.1	(1.1)	12.4	(0.8)	56.3	(1.3)
	Greece	60.8	(1.4)	18.8	(1.0)	31.6	(1.1)	26.7	(1.2)	30.2	(1.3)	65.6	(1.1)	19.1	(0.9)	30.1	(0.9)	8.3	(0.7)	27.6	(1.3)
	Hungary	75.9	(1.1)	16.9	(1.0)	35.4	(1.5)	27.7	(1.0)	60.4	(1.4)	65.4	(1.3)	24.9	(1.1)	38.9	(1.3)	34.1	(1.1)	76.9	(1.2)
	Iceland	81.5	(1.0)	43.9	(1.0)	29.9	(1.0)	21.9	(0.9)	88.6	(0.8)	67.5	(1.1)	26.8	(1.1)	35.7	(1.2)	21.2	(1.1)	83.0	(0.8)
	Ireland	64.9	(1.1)	6.6	(0.7)	34.0	(1.1)	17.9	(1.0)	72.5	(1.1)	68.8	(1.3)	4.8	(0.5)	36.3	(1.3)	17.1	(0.8)	61.4	(1.3)
	Israel	54.4	(1.7)	29.7	(1.8)	39.3	(2.4)	29.0	(2.1)	79.8	(1.5)	47.4	(1.2)	20.8	(0.9)	39.5	(1.0)	27.8	(1.2)	77.8	(1.0)
	Italy	72.5	(0.9)	22.6	(0.9)	40.1	(1.2)	13.1	(0.8)	56.2	(1.4)	55.8	(0.6)	11.3	(0.3)	45.7	(0.6)	5.7	(0.3)	48.5	(0.7)
	Japan	81.0	(0.9)	79.7	(1.0)	30.1	(1.2)	9.9	(0.6)	65.9	(1.4)	68.5	(0.8)	62.7	(1.1)	47.8	(1.2)	11.7	(0.6)	53.0	(1.2)
	Korea	37.4	(1.0)	52.1	(1.4)	33.8	(1.5)	23.9	(1.0)	65.0	(1.5)	25.6	(1.0)	30.2	(1.0)	53.2	(1.2)	33.0	(1.2)	43.4	(1.8)
	Luxembourg	m	m	m	m	m	m	m	m	m	m	73.2	(1.0)	14.2	(0.8)	41.0	(1.1)	13.6	(0.7)	67.8	(1.0)
	Mexico	48.9	(1.5)	19.1	(0.9)	39.9	(1.0)	21.2	(1.0)	44.5	(1.9)	50.9	(0.5)	22.5	(0.5)	44.4	(0.5)	18.9	(0.5)	44.1	(0.6)
	Netherlands	m	m	m	m	m	m	m	m	m	m	67.9	(1.4)	14.9	(1.1)	32.7	(1.5)	16.8	(1.1)	42.4	(1.6)
	New Zealand	70.1	(1.1)	6.7	(0.7)	42.7	(1.1)	24.6	(1.2)	65.0	(1.3)	58.8	(1.4)	8.2	(0.6)	53.9	(1.0)	26.7	(1.0)	51.9	(1.4)
	Norway	77.6	(1.1)	47.6	(1.3)	36.3	(1.2)	17.9	(0.9)	83.1	(1.0)	72.0	(1.2)	33.4	(1.1)	36.2	(1.4)	26.5	(1.1)	71.1	(1.2)
	Poland	74.7	(1.3)	8.0	(0.9)	26.8	(1.5)	17.3	(1.0)	78.8	(1.1)	74.7	(0.9)	8.4	(0.6)	28.6	(1.1)	23.6	(0.9)	82.1	(0.7)
	Portugal	78.1	(0.8)	22.0	(1.0)	43.4	(0.9)	18.3	(1.1)	38.9	(1.2)	71.3	(1.0)	13.7	(0.8)	39.2	(1.1)	17.8	(0.7)	37.5	(1.0)
	Spain	66.5	(1.1)	11.2	(0.7)	31.7	(1.1)	25.2	(0.9)	37.1	(1.4)	56.8	(0.9)	7.2	(0.5)	39.0	(0.7)	23.3	(0.7)	31.8	(0.9)
	Sweden	75.4	(1.0)	25.2	(1.0)	45.1	(1.1)	11.5	(0.9)	82.0	(0.9)	66.9	(1.1)	16.1	(0.9)	45.1	(1.3)	10.6	(0.8)	71.8	(1.0)
	Switzerland	68.7	(1.0)	19.3	(0.8)	45.6	(1.2)	14.8	(0.7)	61.4	(1.3)	72.8	(0.9)	17.3	(0.8)	41.5	(1.1)	10.3	(0.5)	77.9	(0.9)
	United Kingdom	m	m	m	m	m	m	m	m	m	m	70.7	(1.0)	5.2	(0.4)	38.9	(1.0)	20.1	(0.6)	54.9	(0.9)
	United States	73.3	(1.5)	7.4	(1.1)	33.9	(1.5)	20.7	(1.3)	55.6	(1.8)	49.3	(1.0)	7.9	(0.6)	45.8	(1.3)	22.7	(1.1)	32.6	(1.5)
	OECD average-26	69.4	(0.2)	25.9	(0.2)	36.9	(0.2)	19.6	(0.2)	61.2	(0.2)	62.8	(0.2)	19.2	(0.2)	40.8	(0.2)	18.8	(0.2)	55.8	(0.2)
Partners	Albania	59.7	(1.2)	33.0	(1.5)	61.1	(1.4)	18.2	(0.8)	47.5	(1.4)	52.3	(1.4)	40.2	(1.3)	67.1	(1.5)	24.3	(1.1)	58.9	(1.6)
	Argentina	67.9	(2.0)	29.7	(2.2)	34.6	(1.6)	31.5	(2.5)	59.4	(2.2)	61.8	(1.1)	30.4	(1.2)	33.4	(1.3)	33.6	(1.2)	45.3	(1.3)
	Brazil	71.5	(1.1)	28.9	(1.5)	45.7	(1.4)	38.3	(1.2)	50.9	(1.7)	59.7	(0.9)	31.7	(0.8)	48.4	(0.9)	16.6	(0.6)	42.6	(1.0)
	Bulgaria	76.8	(1.2)	17.3	(0.9)	43.5	(1.2)	39.4	(1.2)	86.5	(0.9)	75.3	(1.2)	15.6	(1.0)	43.9	(1.7)	29.9	(1.2)	59.7	(1.1)
	Hong Kong-China	71.2	(0.9)	29.6	(1.0)	42.4	(1.3)	37.5	(1.2)	89.3	(0.9)	50.3	(1.2)	22.4	(1.0)	55.8	(1.2)	33.6	(1.0)	84.3	(0.9)
	Indonesia	54.4	(1.6)	41.8	(1.5)	41.8	(1.5)	23.7	(1.1)	65.6	(1.3)	59.0	(1.6)	53.3	(1.2)	66.8	(1.3)	41.0	(1.4)	63.2	(1.3)
	Latvia	84.5	(1.0)	12.3	(1.4)	41.0	(1.5)	18.2	(1.5)	79.7	(1.1)	80.0	(1.2)	7.1	(0.8)	42.0	(1.7)	31.2	(1.3)	66.8	(1.3)
	Liechtenstein	71.9	(3.1)	8.5	(2.4)	36.1	(3.6)	17.3	(2.8)	58.8	(4.4)	72.7	(3.4)	15.0	(2.8)	37.2	(3.9)	11.7	(2.4)	68.8	(3.4)
	Peru	36.1	(1.7)	34.9	(1.3)	44.3	(1.3)	39.3	(1.2)	62.1	(1.5)	51.2	(1.2)	49.0	(1.2)	62.5	(1.0)	42.1	(1.2)	73.2	(1.3)
	Romania	66.7	(1.5)	10.4	(0.8)	50.3	(1.3)	26.8	(1.4)	50.0	(1.2)	72.4	(1.2)	12.1	(0.7)	40.5	(1.4)	23.5	(1.0)	46.7	(1.7)
	Russian Federation	82.1	(0.8)	25.1	(1.4)	64.3	(1.0)	53.9	(0.8)	78.4	(1.1)	75.8	(0.9)	16.0	(1.0)	67.5	(1.0)	26.8	(1.0)	65.6	(1.5)
	Thailand	43.6	(1.3)	62.6	(1.2)	55.3	(1.1)	50.1	(1.2)	78.5	(1.3)	62.2	(1.0)	75.9	(0.7)	73.9	(0.8)	54.4	(1.0)	73.1	(1.1)

Note: Values that are statistically significant are indicated in bold (see Annex A3).
StatLink http://dx.doi.org/10.1787/888932343285

[Part 4/4]

Percentage of students who read diverse materials in PISA 2000 and 2009, by gender

Table V.5.7 *Percentage of boys and girls who reported that they read the following materials because they want to "several times a month" or "several times a week"*

		Girls									
		Change between 2000 and 2009 (PISA 2009 – PISA 2000)									
		Magazines		Comic books		Fiction		Non-fiction books		Newspapers	
		% dif.	S.E.	% dif.	S.E.	% dif.	S.E.	% dif.	S.E.	% dif.	S.E.
OECD	Australia	**-9.5**	(1.4)	1.3	(0.8)	**7.6**	(1.8)	1.4	(1.2)	**-13.7**	(1.6)
	Austria	m	m	m	m	m	m	m	m	m	m
	Belgium	2.1	(1.4)	**-9.3**	(1.3)	1.1	(1.4)	**-4.3**	(1.0)	1.4	(1.5)
	Canada	**-15.3**	(1.0)	**-2.1**	(0.7)	**15.7**	(1.1)	**2.7**	(0.8)	**-11.1**	(1.0)
	Chile	-1.1	(1.3)	**-9.3**	(1.2)	**3.8**	(1.5)	**-7.6**	(1.2)	-2.0	(1.6)
	Czech Republic	**-8.6**	(1.2)	-1.0	(1.0)	**-16.1**	(1.7)	0.9	(1.0)	**8.1**	(1.5)
	Denmark	**-3.2**	(1.4)	**-44.2**	(1.5)	**-4.9**	(1.7)	0.4	(1.5)	**-13.8**	(1.9)
	Finland	**-7.0**	(1.2)	**-6.9**	(1.6)	-2.1	(1.6)	0.5	(1.0)	**-10.5**	(1.2)
	France	**6.6**	(1.5)	-2.4	(1.3)	**7.5**	(1.6)	**-10.4**	(1.1)	**-3.8**	(1.8)
	Germany	**-11.9**	(1.6)	-0.1	(0.8)	**5.4**	(1.6)	**-2.9**	(1.1)	**-4.0**	(1.7)
	Greece	**4.8**	(1.7)	0.2	(1.4)	-1.5	(1.5)	**-18.4**	(1.4)	-2.6	(1.8)
	Hungary	**-10.5**	(1.7)	**8.0**	(1.5)	3.6	(2.0)	**6.4**	(1.4)	**16.5**	(1.8)
	Iceland	**-14.1**	(1.5)	**-17.1**	(1.5)	**5.8**	(1.6)	-0.7	(1.4)	**-5.6**	(1.1)
	Ireland	**3.9**	(1.7)	**-1.8**	(0.8)	2.3	(1.7)	-0.8	(1.3)	**-11.1**	(1.7)
	Israel	**-7.0**	(2.1)	**-9.0**	(2.0)	0.2	(2.6)	-1.2	(2.4)	-2.0	(1.8)
	Italy	**-16.8**	(1.1)	**-11.3**	(1.0)	**5.6**	(1.3)	**-7.4**	(0.9)	**-7.7**	(1.5)
	Japan	**-12.4**	(1.2)	**-17.0**	(1.5)	**17.7**	(1.7)	**1.8**	(0.9)	**-13.0**	(1.9)
	Korea	**-11.8**	(1.4)	**-22.0**	(1.8)	**19.4**	(1.9)	**9.0**	(1.6)	**-21.6**	(2.4)
	Luxembourg	m	m	m	m	m	m	m	m	m	m
	Mexico	2.0	(1.6)	**3.4**	(1.0)	**4.6**	(1.2)	**-2.3**	(1.1)	-0.4	(2.0)
	Netherlands	m	m	m	m	m	m	m	m	m	m
	New Zealand	**-11.3**	(1.8)	1.5	(0.9)	**11.3**	(1.5)	2.1	(1.5)	**-13.0**	(1.9)
	Norway	**-5.6**	(1.6)	**-14.2**	(1.7)	-0.1	(1.8)	**8.6**	(1.4)	**-11.9**	(1.6)
	Poland	0.0	(1.6)	0.5	(1.1)	1.7	(1.9)	**6.3**	(1.3)	**3.2**	(1.4)
	Portugal	**-6.8**	(1.3)	**-8.2**	(1.2)	**-4.2**	(1.4)	-0.5	(1.3)	-1.4	(1.5)
	Spain	**-9.7**	(1.4)	**-4.1**	(0.8)	**7.2**	(1.3)	-1.9	(1.1)	**-5.4**	(1.7)
	Sweden	**-8.5**	(1.5)	**-9.1**	(1.4)	0.0	(1.7)	-0.9	(1.1)	**-10.2**	(1.4)
	Switzerland	**4.1**	(1.3)	-1.9	(1.1)	**-4.1**	(1.6)	**-4.5**	(0.9)	**16.5**	(1.6)
	United Kingdom	m	m	m	m	m	m	m	m	m	m
	United States	**-23.9**	(1.8)	0.5	(1.3)	**12.0**	(2.0)	2.1	(1.7)	**-23.0**	(2.3)
	OECD average-26	**-6.6**	(0.3)	**-6.7**	(0.3)	**3.8**	(0.3)	**-0.8**	(0.3)	**-5.5**	(0.3)
Partners	Albania	**-7.4**	(1.9)	**7.2**	(2.0)	**6.0**	(2.0)	**6.0**	(1.4)	**11.5**	(2.1)
	Argentina	**-6.0**	(2.3)	0.8	(2.5)	-1.3	(2.1)	2.1	(2.8)	**-14.1**	(2.6)
	Brazil	**-11.8**	(1.4)	2.8	(1.7)	2.8	(1.7)	**-21.7**	(1.3)	**-8.3**	(2.0)
	Bulgaria	-1.4	(1.7)	-1.7	(1.4)	0.4	(2.1)	**-9.5**	(1.7)	**-26.7**	(1.5)
	Hong Kong-China	**-20.8**	(1.5)	**-7.2**	(1.5)	**13.4**	(1.8)	**-3.9**	(1.6)	**-5.0**	(1.3)
	Indonesia	**4.6**	(2.2)	**11.5**	(1.9)	**25.0**	(2.0)	**17.7**	(1.8)	-2.5	(1.8)
	Latvia	**-4.5**	(1.6)	**-5.2**	(1.6)	1.0	(2.3)	**13.0**	(2.0)	**-12.8**	(1.7)
	Liechtenstein	0.8	(4.6)	6.6	(3.7)	1.2	(5.3)	-5.6	(3.7)	10.0	(5.6)
	Peru	**15.0**	(2.1)	**14.1**	(1.8)	**18.2**	(1.6)	2.7	(1.7)	**11.1**	(2.0)
	Romania	**5.7**	(1.9)	1.7	(1.0)	**-9.8**	(1.9)	-3.3	(1.7)	-3.4	(2.1)
	Russian Federation	**-6.4**	(1.2)	**-9.1**	(1.7)	**3.2**	(1.4)	**-27.1**	(1.3)	**-12.8**	(1.9)
	Thailand	**18.6**	(1.6)	**13.3**	(1.4)	**18.6**	(1.4)	**4.2**	(1.5)	**-5.4**	(1.7)

Note: Values that are statistically significant are indicated in bold (see Annex A3).
StatLink http://dx.doi.org/10.1787/888932343285

[Part 1/1]

Table V.5.8 **Reading performance of students who read fiction in PISA 2000 and 2009**
Results based on students' self-reports

		PISA 2000						PISA 2009						Change between 2000 and 2009 (PISA 2009 – PISA 2000)					
		Students who read fiction		Students who do not read fiction		Difference (F-NF)		Students who read fiction		Students who do not read fiction		Difference (F-NF)		Students who read fiction		Students who do not read fiction		Difference (F-NF)	
		Mean score	S.E.	Mean score	S.E.	Score dif.	S.E.	Mean score	S.E.	Mean score	S.E.	Score dif.	S.E.	Score dif.	S.E.	Score dif.	S.E.	Score dif.	S.E.
OECD	Australia	573	(4.7)	510	(3.2)	**63**	(4.3)	564	(2.8)	488	(2.0)	**75**	(2.3)	-10	(7.3)	**-22**	(6.2)	**12**	(4.9)
	Austria	532	(4.2)	482	(2.5)	**50**	(4.2)	m	m	m	m	m	m	m	m	m	m	m	m
	Belgium	551	(7.9)	503	(3.3)	**48**	(7.3)	561	(3.1)	499	(2.4)	**62**	(3.5)	10	(9.8)	-4	(6.4)	15	(8.1)
	Canada	572	(2.0)	519	(1.6)	**53**	(2.0)	558	(1.7)	502	(1.6)	**56**	(1.8)	**-14**	(5.6)	**-17**	(5.4)	3	(2.7)
	Chile	422	(4.7)	408	(3.5)	**14**	(3.6)	462	(3.8)	446	(3.1)	**16**	(2.7)	**40**	(7.8)	**38**	(6.8)	2	(4.6)
	Czech Republic	532	(3.1)	490	(2.4)	**43**	(3.2)	541	(4.1)	470	(2.9)	**71**	(4.1)	9	(7.1)	**-19**	(6.2)	**28**	(5.2)
	Denmark	535	(3.1)	484	(2.5)	**52**	(3.4)	525	(2.7)	483	(2.3)	**42**	(2.8)	-10	(6.4)	0	(6.0)	**-10**	(4.4)
	Finland	595	(2.7)	530	(2.9)	**66**	(3.3)	590	(2.8)	517	(2.2)	**73**	(2.9)	-5	(6.3)	**-12**	(6.2)	7	(4.4)
	France	536	(3.3)	502	(2.8)	**34**	(3.4)	549	(3.9)	477	(3.6)	**72**	(4.8)	13	(7.1)	**-25**	(6.7)	**38**	(5.9)
	Germany	539	(3.2)	479	(2.5)	**60**	(3.1)	551	(2.9)	483	(3.0)	**69**	(3.3)	12	(6.6)	3	(6.3)	**9**	(4.5)
	Greece	499	(6.0)	470	(4.9)	**29**	(4.5)	523	(3.5)	472	(4.9)	**50**	(4.7)	**23**	(8.5)	2	(8.5)	**21**	(6.5)
	Hungary	514	(5.2)	471	(3.9)	**43**	(4.9)	519	(4.6)	484	(3.1)	**35**	(4.2)	5	(8.5)	12	(7.0)	-8	(6.5)
	Iceland	553	(3.5)	497	(1.7)	**56**	(4.1)	549	(2.8)	484	(1.7)	**65**	(3.3)	-4	(6.7)	**-13**	(5.5)	9	(5.2)
	Ireland	567	(4.1)	515	(3.2)	**52**	(4.1)	542	(3.5)	480	(3.1)	**62**	(3.6)	**-25**	(7.3)	**-35**	(6.6)	10	(5.4)
	Israel	474	(10.2)	455	(9.1)	**19**	(7.1)	500	(4.2)	471	(3.6)	**30**	(4.3)	**26**	(12.1)	15	(11.0)	11	(8.3)
	Italy	505	(3.1)	482	(3.1)	**23**	(3.1)	517	(1.9)	471	(1.8)	**47**	(2.3)	**12**	(6.1)	-12	(6.1)	**24**	(3.9)
	Japan	550	(5.4)	515	(5.1)	**36**	(3.0)	548	(3.3)	501	(4.0)	**47**	(3.8)	-2	(8.0)	-14	(8.2)	**12**	(4.8)
	Korea	545	(2.5)	514	(2.7)	**31**	(2.3)	556	(3.1)	526	(4.0)	**30**	(2.8)	11	(6.4)	11	(6.9)	0	(3.6)
	Luxembourg	m	m	m	m	m	m	527	(2.6)	452	(1.4)	**75**	(3.1)	m	m	m	m	m	m
	Mexico	430	(3.9)	419	(3.6)	**11**	(3.1)	424	(2.2)	429	(2.0)	**-5**	(1.6)	-7	(6.7)	10	(6.4)	**-16**	(3.5)
	Netherlands	m	m	m	m	m	m	552	(5.1)	501	(5.5)	**52**	(4.8)	m	m	m	m	m	m
	New Zealand	565	(3.8)	516	(2.8)	**48**	(3.8)	559	(3.0)	494	(2.6)	**65**	(3.6)	-6	(6.9)	**-22**	(6.3)	**16**	(5.2)
	Norway	557	(3.3)	494	(3.2)	**63**	(4.0)	551	(3.4)	487	(2.5)	**63**	(3.3)	-7	(6.8)	-6	(6.4)	0	(5.2)
	Poland	509	(7.4)	479	(4.3)	**30**	(6.6)	544	(4.0)	491	(2.5)	**53**	(3.7)	**35**	(9.7)	12	(7.0)	**23**	(7.5)
	Portugal	485	(5.8)	467	(4.4)	**19**	(4.2)	518	(3.8)	479	(3.0)	**39**	(3.1)	**33**	(8.5)	12	(7.3)	**21**	(5.2)
	Spain	521	(3.2)	486	(2.9)	**35**	(3.5)	519	(2.2)	466	(2.1)	**54**	(2.0)	-2	(6.3)	**-20**	(6.1)	**18**	(4.0)
	Sweden	557	(3.1)	497	(2.3)	**60**	(3.2)	549	(3.3)	475	(2.7)	**74**	(3.1)	-7	(6.7)	**-22**	(6.0)	**15**	(4.5)
	Switzerland	532	(5.8)	483	(3.6)	**49**	(4.5)	550	(3.3)	480	(2.4)	**70**	(2.9)	**18**	(8.3)	-2	(6.6)	**20**	(5.4)
	United Kingdom	m	m	m	m	m	m	542	(3.0)	475	(2.3)	**67**	(3.1)	m	m	m	m	m	m
	United States	539	(7.2)	498	(7.0)	**41**	(4.7)	532	(4.8)	483	(3.1)	**50**	(3.6)	-7	(9.9)	-15	(9.1)	8	(6.0)
	OECD average-26	529	(1.0)	488	(0.8)	**41**	(0.8)	535	(0.7)	482	(0.6)	**53**	(0.7)	5	(5.1)	-6	(5.0)	**11**	(1.1)
Partners	Albania	361	(4.2)	353	(3.4)	**8**	(4.2)	400	(4.2)	375	(4.7)	**25**	(4.3)	**39**	(7.7)	**22**	(7.6)	**17**	(6.0)
	Argentina	443	(11.2)	421	(8.3)	**22**	(5.2)	406	(5.8)	402	(4.7)	4	(4.8)	**-37**	(13.6)	-18	(10.7)	**-19**	(7.1)
	Brazil	402	(3.5)	399	(3.5)	3	(3.6)	416	(3.5)	414	(2.8)	1	(2.8)	**14**	(7.0)	**15**	(6.7)	-1	(4.6)
	Bulgaria	466	(5.9)	425	(4.7)	**41**	(4.4)	461	(8.2)	420	(6.0)	**41**	(6.2)	-4	(11.2)	-4	(9.0)	0	(7.5)
	Hong Kong-China	551	(3.5)	513	(3.0)	**38**	(3.6)	552	(2.5)	516	(2.4)	**36**	(2.5)	1	(6.5)	3	(6.2)	-2	(4.4)
	Indonesia	377	(4.8)	371	(3.8)	6	(3.6)	408	(3.9)	394	(4.0)	**14**	(2.5)	**31**	(7.9)	**23**	(7.4)	8	(4.4)
	Latvia	491	(5.8)	448	(5.7)	**43**	(4.8)	500	(4.0)	477	(3.0)	**23**	(3.5)	9	(8.6)	**29**	(8.1)	**-20**	(5.9)
	Liechtenstein	527	(10.8)	471	(5.7)	**56**	(13.6)	543	(7.5)	484	(4.0)	**59**	(9.6)	16	(14.0)	13	(8.5)	3	(16.7)
	Peru	338	(4.8)	333	(4.6)	5	(3.9)	372	(3.6)	372	(5.0)	0	(3.5)	**34**	(7.7)	**39**	(8.4)	-5	(5.2)
	Romania	432	(3.5)	428	(4.7)	3	(4.6)	437	(4.7)	421	(4.2)	**16**	(3.8)	6	(7.6)	-8	(8.0)	**13**	(6.0)
	Russian Federation	482	(4.1)	445	(4.5)	**38**	(2.6)	477	(3.3)	439	(3.9)	**38**	(3.4)	-5	(7.2)	-5	(7.7)	0	(4.3)
	Thailand	440	(3.5)	422	(3.3)	**18**	(2.7)	428	(2.8)	410	(2.9)	**18**	(2.4)	-12	(6.7)	-12	(6.6)	0	(3.6)

Note: Values that are statistically significant are indicated in bold (see Annex A3).
StatLink http://dx.doi.org/10.1787/888932343285

[Part 1/2]

Table V.5.9 Performance of students who read fiction in PISA 2000 and 2009, by gender

Results based on students' self-reports

		Boys																	
		PISA 2000						PISA 2009						Change between 2000 and 2009 (PISA 2009 – PISA 2000)					
		Students who read fiction		Students who do not read fiction		Difference (F-NF)		Students who read fiction		Students who do not read fiction		Difference (F-NF)		Students who read fiction		Students who do not read fiction		Difference (F-NF)	
		Mean score	S.E.	Mean score	S.E.	Score dif.	S.E.	Mean score	S.E.	Mean score	S.E.	Score dif.	S.E.	Mean score	S.E.	Mean score	S.E.	Score dif.	S.E.
OECD	Australia	569	(5.2)	498	(4.0)	**71**	(5.9)	554	(3.8)	477	(2.6)	**77**	(3.6)	-15	(8.1)	**-21**	(6.9)	6	(6.9)
	Austria	533	(6.8)	471	(3.5)	**62**	(6.5)	m	m	m	m	m	m	m	m	m	m	m	m
	Belgium	531	(14.5)	492	(3.8)	**39**	(13.6)	559	(4.9)	491	(3.2)	**68**	(5.4)	28	(16.1)	-1	(7.0)	**29**	(14.6)
	Canada	563	(2.7)	507	(1.7)	**56**	(2.8)	546	(2.5)	494	(2.0)	**52**	(2.9)	**-17**	(6.2)	**-13**	(5.6)	-4	(4.0)
	Chile	409	(8.1)	397	(4.1)	12	(7.3)	448	(5.4)	438	(3.7)	**10**	(4.2)	**39**	(10.9)	**41**	(7.4)	-2	(8.4)
	Czech Republic	558	(5.5)	477	(3.5)	**80**	(6.1)	534	(8.0)	454	(3.7)	**80**	(7.9)	**-24**	(10.9)	**-23**	(7.1)	0	(9.9)
	Denmark	528	(5.2)	477	(3.4)	**51**	(6.3)	513	(3.4)	473	(3.0)	**41**	(4.4)	-15	(7.9)	-5	(6.7)	-11	(7.7)
	Finland	582	(6.1)	513	(2.9)	**69**	(6.1)	572	(5.4)	500	(2.5)	**72**	(5.4)	-10	(9.6)	**-13**	(6.3)	3	(8.1)
	France	517	(5.6)	491	(3.8)	**26**	(5.9)	536	(5.6)	462	(4.5)	**74**	(7.0)	**19**	(9.3)	**-29**	(7.6)	**48**	(9.2)
	Germany	547	(5.8)	472	(3.0)	**74**	(5.9)	544	(4.7)	472	(3.7)	**72**	(5.0)	-3	(8.9)	-1	(6.9)	-2	(7.7)
	Greece	481	(8.0)	456	(6.1)	**26**	(7.1)	500	(6.5)	454	(5.9)	**46**	(7.3)	18	(11.4)	-2	(9.8)	**20**	(10.2)
	Hungary	498	(12.2)	463	(4.9)	**35**	(11.3)	502	(6.8)	468	(3.8)	**35**	(6.8)	4	(14.9)	5	(7.9)	-1	(13.2)
	Iceland	535	(7.4)	483	(2.3)	**52**	(8.0)	530	(5.5)	468	(2.1)	**62**	(5.8)	-5	(10.4)	**-15**	(5.9)	10	(9.9)
	Ireland	558	(6.5)	505	(3.9)	**53**	(6.4)	517	(6.4)	468	(4.3)	**49**	(6.3)	**-41**	(10.3)	**-37**	(7.6)	-3	(8.9)
	Israel	471	(13.2)	450	(11.2)	**21**	(10.3)	478	(8.4)	456	(4.8)	**22**	(8.3)	6	(16.4)	6	(13.1)	0	(13.2)
	Italy	481	(5.4)	468	(5.2)	**13**	(4.2)	494	(2.8)	455	(2.5)	**38**	(3.0)	13	(7.8)	-13	(7.6)	**25**	(5.2)
	Japan	533	(8.0)	503	(6.6)	**30**	(4.6)	535	(4.8)	483	(5.9)	**52**	(3.9)	2	(10.6)	-20	(10.1)	**22**	(6.0)
	Korea	539	(3.5)	508	(4.2)	**31**	(3.1)	545	(4.3)	508	(5.4)	**38**	(3.6)	6	(7.4)	0	(8.4)	6	(4.7)
	Luxembourg	m	m	m	m	m	m	520	(5.6)	442	(2.1)	**78**	(6.1)	m	m	m	m	m	m
	Mexico	418	(5.3)	410	(4.6)	7	(5.0)	407	(2.7)	418	(2.4)	**-11**	(3.0)	-11	(7.7)	8	(7.2)	**-19**	(5.8)
	Netherlands	m	m	m	m	m	m	560	(8.2)	493	(5.3)	**66**	(7.2)	m	m	m	m	m	m
	New Zealand	545	(7.2)	499	(3.7)	**46**	(6.5)	543	(5.0)	479	(3.5)	**64**	(5.1)	-2	(10.1)	**-20**	(7.1)	**18**	(8.2)
	Norway	547	(7.6)	482	(4.0)	**65**	(7.9)	535	(4.8)	470	(3.0)	**64**	(5.4)	-12	(10.2)	-11	(7.0)	-1	(9.6)
	Poland	480	(11.2)	467	(6.0)	14	(10.4)	517	(7.3)	472	(2.7)	**44**	(7.4)	**36**	(14.3)	6	(8.2)	**30**	(12.8)
	Portugal	476	(9.8)	457	(4.9)	**18**	(8.9)	502	(6.6)	465	(3.5)	**37**	(6.1)	**26**	(12.8)	8	(7.8)	18	(10.8)
	Spain	515	(4.5)	476	(3.7)	**39**	(5.1)	509	(3.1)	457	(2.2)	**52**	(3.0)	-6	(7.4)	**-19**	(6.6)	**13**	(6.0)
	Sweden	554	(4.8)	484	(2.7)	**70**	(5.0)	535	(4.8)	463	(3.2)	**72**	(5.1)	**-19**	(8.4)	**-21**	(6.4)	1	(7.1)
	Switzerland	532	(9.2)	475	(4.4)	**57**	(8.3)	545	(4.2)	468	(2.9)	**77**	(4.1)	13	(11.3)	-7	(7.2)	**20**	(9.3)
	United Kingdom	m	m	m	m	m	m	532	(4.7)	469	(3.4)	**63**	(4.7)	m	m	m	m	m	m
	United States	537	(12.3)	484	(8.0)	**52**	(10.2)	524	(5.9)	475	(3.8)	**49**	(4.8)	-12	(14.5)	-9	(10.2)	-3	(11.3)
	OECD average-26	519	(1.6)	477	(1.0)	**43**	(1.5)	520	(1.1)	469	(0.7)	**51**	(1.1)	1	(5.3)	-8	(5.1)	**9**	(1.8)
Partners	Albania	321	(6.2)	336	(4.3)	**-15**	(6.4)	367	(6.4)	355	(5.4)	12	(6.6)	**47**	(10.2)	**19**	(8.5)	**27**	(9.2)
	Argentina	415	(10.4)	402	(7.6)	12	(8.7)	389	(8.8)	383	(5.2)	6	(8.7)	-26	(14.5)	-19	(10.5)	-6	(12.3)
	Brazil	389	(6.8)	393	(4.0)	-4	(6.3)	396	(4.6)	401	(2.9)	-5	(3.8)	8	(9.6)	9	(7.0)	-1	(7.4)
	Bulgaria	438	(6.4)	410	(4.6)	**27**	(4.8)	428	(9.7)	399	(6.6)	**28**	(7.0)	-10	(12.6)	-11	(9.4)	1	(8.5)
	Hong Kong-China	548	(5.3)	508	(4.9)	**40**	(5.5)	536	(3.8)	505	(3.6)	**31**	(3.5)	-11	(8.2)	-3	(7.8)	-9	(6.5)
	Indonesia	360	(4.4)	365	(4.1)	-5	(4.7)	387	(4.2)	380	(4.2)	7	(3.5)	**27**	(7.9)	**15**	(7.6)	**12**	(5.8)
	Latvia	462	(9.0)	427	(6.4)	**35**	(10.8)	470	(5.6)	457	(3.5)	**13**	(5.2)	8	(11.7)	**30**	(8.8)	-22	(12.0)
	Liechtenstein	520	(22.8)	463	(8.1)	**57**	(24.9)	544	(12.7)	471	(5.5)	**73**	(14.7)	23	(26.5)	7	(11.0)	16	(28.9)
	Peru	334	(7.1)	330	(6.9)	4	(5.8)	356	(4.2)	365	(5.3)	-9	(5.0)	**23**	(9.6)	**35**	(10.0)	-13	(7.7)
	Romania	424	(5.5)	422	(6.6)	3	(9.0)	407	(5.6)	404	(4.6)	3	(4.9)	-17	(9.3)	-18	(9.4)	1	(10.2)
	Russian Federation	466	(4.6)	432	(4.7)	**34**	(3.7)	457	(3.9)	422	(4.2)	**34**	(4.4)	-10	(7.7)	-10	(8.0)	0	(5.7)
	Thailand	414	(4.7)	402	(4.2)	**12**	(4.3)	405	(3.6)	396	(3.7)	**9**	(3.3)	-9	(7.7)	-6	(7.4)	-4	(5.4)

Note: Values that are statistically significant are indicated in bold (see Annex A3).
StatLink http://dx.doi.org/10.1787/888932343285

[Part 2/2]

Table V.5.9 **Performance of students who read fiction in PISA 2000 and 2009, by gender**
Results based on students' self-reports

	Girls																	
	PISA 2000						PISA 2009						Change between 2000 and 2009 (PISA 2009 – PISA 2000)					
	Students who read fiction		Students who do not read fiction		Difference (F-NF)		Students who read fiction		Students who do not read fiction		Difference (F-NF)		Students who read fiction		Students who do not read fiction		Difference (F-NF)	
	Mean score	S.E.	Mean score	S.E.	Score dif.	S.E.	Mean score	S.E.	Mean score	S.E.	Score dif.	S.E.	Mean score	S.E.	Mean score	S.E.	Score dif.	S.E.
OECD																		
Australia	576	(7.2)	527	(4.2)	**49**	(7.2)	569	(2.9)	502	(2.5)	**67**	(2.7)	-7	(9.2)	**-25**	(7.0)	**17**	(7.7)
Austria	531	(5.2)	499	(3.7)	**33**	(4.4)	m	m	m	m	m	m	m	m	m	m	m	m
Belgium	561	(6.4)	517	(5.0)	**44**	(6.0)	562	(3.5)	508	(2.9)	**54**	(3.6)	1	(8.8)	-9	(7.6)	10	(7.0)
Canada	578	(2.2)	535	(2.0)	**43**	(2.4)	565	(1.9)	516	(2.1)	**49**	(2.3)	**-13**	(5.7)	**-19**	(5.7)	6	(3.3)
Chile	429	(5.4)	420	(4.7)	**9**	(4.0)	470	(4.2)	457	(3.8)	**13**	(3.5)	**41**	(8.4)	**37**	(7.8)	4	(5.3)
Czech Republic	526	(3.3)	507	(3.1)	**19**	(3.8)	543	(4.4)	493	(3.2)	**50**	(4.6)	**17**	(7.4)	**-14**	(6.6)	**31**	(6.0)
Denmark	539	(3.8)	493	(3.4)	**46**	(4.8)	532	(3.8)	496	(2.8)	**36**	(4.3)	-6	(7.3)	4	(6.6)	-10	(6.5)
Finland	599	(2.7)	553	(3.9)	**46**	(4.5)	597	(3.0)	542	(2.9)	**54**	(3.9)	-2	(6.4)	-10	(6.9)	8	(5.9)
France	547	(3.7)	514	(2.9)	**34**	(4.4)	556	(4.3)	494	(3.8)	**62**	(5.3)	8	(7.5)	**-20**	(6.9)	**28**	(6.9)
Germany	538	(4.1)	490	(3.4)	**48**	(4.2)	554	(3.4)	498	(3.3)	**56**	(4.1)	**17**	(7.3)	8	(6.9)	9	(5.9)
Greece	508	(6.5)	488	(4.7)	**21**	(5.6)	532	(3.7)	495	(4.2)	**37**	(4.6)	**24**	(9.0)	7	(8.0)	**16**	(7.2)
Hungary	521	(5.6)	484	(4.7)	**37**	(5.6)	529	(5.2)	504	(3.5)	**25**	(5.0)	8	(9.1)	**21**	(7.7)	-13	(7.5)
Iceland	562	(3.9)	515	(2.4)	**48**	(4.5)	559	(2.9)	504	(2.4)	**55**	(3.8)	-3	(6.9)	-10	(6.0)	7	(5.9)
Ireland	572	(4.5)	526	(3.9)	**45**	(4.6)	559	(3.7)	495	(3.3)	**64**	(4.2)	-13	(7.6)	**-32**	(7.1)	**19**	(6.3)
Israel	476	(10.3)	461	(9.1)	14	(8.4)	510	(4.3)	489	(3.6)	**22**	(4.3)	**35**	(12.2)	**28**	(10.9)	7	(9.5)
Italy	520	(3.8)	500	(4.1)	**20**	(4.1)	531	(2.4)	492	(2.0)	**38**	(2.7)	10	(6.7)	-8	(6.7)	**18**	(4.9)
Japan	564	(5.7)	528	(5.5)	**37**	(3.9)	559	(4.6)	524	(4.1)	**35**	(4.4)	-6	(8.8)	-3	(8.5)	-2	(5.9)
Korea	553	(3.6)	522	(4.1)	**31**	(3.8)	565	(4.0)	551	(4.3)	**15**	(3.3)	12	(7.3)	**28**	(7.7)	**-16**	(5.0)
Luxembourg	m	m	m	m	m	m	530	(3.1)	467	(2.2)	**63**	(4.2)	m	m	m	m	m	m
Mexico	441	(4.3)	429	(4.2)	**12**	(3.6)	435	(2.6)	441	(2.2)	**-6**	(2.1)	-5	(7.0)	13	(6.8)	**-18**	(4.1)
Netherlands	m	m	m	m	m	m	550	(4.9)	510	(6.1)	**40**	(5.4)	m	m	m	m	m	m
New Zealand	577	(4.7)	537	(4.0)	**39**	(4.7)	569	(3.6)	517	(3.3)	**52**	(4.6)	-8	(7.7)	**-21**	(7.2)	**13**	(6.6)
Norway	561	(3.9)	513	(3.4)	**48**	(4.7)	558	(3.9)	511	(2.8)	**48**	(3.7)	-3	(7.4)	-2	(6.6)	-1	(5.9)
Poland	520	(8.6)	494	(5.0)	**26**	(7.5)	555	(4.1)	514	(2.9)	**42**	(3.8)	**35**	(10.7)	**20**	(7.6)	16	(8.4)
Portugal	490	(5.5)	479	(4.6)	**10**	(4.0)	525	(3.5)	497	(3.1)	**28**	(3.4)	**35**	(8.2)	**18**	(7.4)	**17**	(5.3)
Spain	525	(3.9)	497	(2.8)	**28**	(3.8)	525	(2.5)	478	(2.6)	**48**	(2.7)	0	(6.8)	**-19**	(6.3)	**20**	(4.7)
Sweden	558	(3.7)	517	(3.0)	**41**	(4.6)	556	(3.6)	493	(3.3)	**63**	(4.3)	-2	(7.1)	**-24**	(6.6)	**22**	(6.3)
Switzerland	532	(5.7)	495	(4.1)	**37**	(5.2)	553	(3.6)	498	(2.8)	**55**	(3.9)	**20**	(8.4)	3	(7.0)	**18**	(6.5)
United Kingdom	m	m	m	m	m	m	547	(3.8)	483	(3.0)	**64**	(4.0)	m	m	m	m	m	m
United States	541	(5.3)	513	(6.7)	**28**	(4.7)	537	(5.2)	493	(3.3)	**44**	(4.6)	-3	(8.9)	**-20**	(9.0)	**17**	(6.6)
OECD average-26	535	(1.0)	502	(0.9)	**33**	(1.0)	543	(0.7)	500	(0.6)	**42**	(0.8)	7	(5.1)	-2	(5.1)	**9**	(1.2)
Partners																		
Albania	386	(3.8)	376	(3.5)	**10**	(4.8)	421	(4.1)	412	(6.0)	9	(5.9)	**35**	(7.5)	**36**	(8.5)	-1	(7.6)
Argentina	456	(13.4)	438	(9.6)	**18**	(6.7)	414	(6.2)	422	(5.1)	-7	(5.7)	**-42**	(15.6)	-16	(11.9)	**-26**	(8.8)
Brazil	406	(3.5)	408	(4.4)	-2	(4.7)	423	(3.5)	432	(3.4)	**-9**	(3.9)	**17**	(7.0)	**24**	(7.4)	-7	(6.1)
Bulgaria	480	(6.9)	446	(6.9)	**35**	(5.8)	482	(8.3)	450	(5.1)	**31**	(7.9)	1	(11.9)	5	(9.9)	-3	(9.8)
Hong Kong-China	553	(4.3)	520	(3.6)	**33**	(4.1)	565	(3.3)	533	(3.2)	**32**	(3.8)	11	(7.3)	12	(6.9)	-1	(5.6)
Indonesia	388	(5.9)	378	(4.0)	**10**	(3.8)	424	(4.1)	413	(4.5)	**10**	(3.4)	**36**	(8.7)	**36**	(7.8)	0	(5.1)
Latvia	505	(6.7)	475	(5.4)	**30**	(5.6)	516	(4.1)	502	(3.3)	**14**	(4.1)	11	(9.3)	**28**	(8.0)	**-17**	(6.9)
Liechtenstein	529	(13.0)	485	(8.2)	**45**	(16.6)	542	(9.8)	502	(6.3)	**40**	(13.4)	13	(17.0)	17	(11.5)	-5	(21.4)
Peru	343	(6.0)	337	(5.5)	5	(5.2)	384	(4.7)	382	(6.4)	3	(4.6)	**42**	(9.1)	**44**	(9.8)	-3	(7.0)
Romania	436	(4.9)	436	(4.7)	1	(4.4)	453	(5.2)	441	(4.5)	**12**	(4.8)	17	(8.7)	6	(8.2)	11	(6.5)
Russian Federation	492	(4.3)	464	(4.7)	**28**	(3.3)	491	(3.4)	465	(4.8)	**26**	(4.5)	-1	(7.4)	1	(8.3)	-2	(5.6)
Thailand	454	(3.6)	441	(3.4)	**14**	(3.7)	441	(3.3)	429	(3.9)	**12**	(3.5)	-13	(7.0)	-11	(7.1)	-2	(5.1)

Note: Values that are statistically significant are indicated in bold (see Annex A3).
StatLink http://dx.doi.org/10.1787/888932343285

[Part 1/1]

Table V.5.10 **Diversity of reading materials in PISA 2000 and 2009, by gender**

Results based on students' self-reports

		PISA 2000						PISA 2009						Change between 2000 and 2009 (PISA 2009 – PISA 2000)					
		All students		Girls		Boys		All students		Girls		Boys		All students		Girls		Boys	
		Mean index	S.E.	Mean index	S.E.	Mean index	S.E.	Mean index	S.E.	Mean index	S.E.	Mean index	S.E.	Dif.	S.E.	Dif.	S.E.	Dif.	S.E.
OECD	Australia	0.00	(0.02)	0.00	(0.02)	0.00	(0.03)	-0.12	(0.01)	-0.06	(0.01)	-0.19	(0.02)	**-0.12**	(0.03)	**-0.06**	(0.03)	**-0.19**	(0.04)
	Austria	-0.03	(0.02)	0.00	(0.02)	-0.06	(0.02)	m	m	m	m	m	m	m	m	m	m	m	m
	Belgium	-0.06	(0.02)	0.01	(0.02)	-0.13	(0.02)	-0.08	(0.02)	-0.05	(0.02)	-0.12	(0.03)	-0.02	(0.03)	**-0.06**	(0.03)	0.01	(0.03)
	Canada	-0.01	(0.01)	0.07	(0.01)	-0.08	(0.01)	-0.11	(0.01)	0.01	(0.01)	-0.24	(0.02)	**-0.11**	(0.02)	**-0.06**	(0.02)	**-0.15**	(0.03)
	Chile	0.02	(0.02)	0.16	(0.03)	-0.15	(0.03)	-0.02	(0.02)	0.16	(0.02)	-0.19	(0.02)	-0.03	(0.03)	0.00	(0.03)	-0.04	(0.04)
	Czech Republic	0.01	(0.02)	0.11	(0.02)	-0.10	(0.03)	-0.16	(0.02)	0.00	(0.02)	-0.30	(0.02)	**-0.17**	(0.02)	**-0.11**	(0.02)	**-0.20**	(0.03)
	Denmark	0.49	(0.02)	0.59	(0.02)	0.40	(0.03)	0.07	(0.02)	0.15	(0.02)	-0.01	(0.03)	**-0.42**	(0.03)	**-0.44**	(0.03)	**-0.41**	(0.04)
	Finland	0.61	(0.02)	0.70	(0.02)	0.51	(0.02)	0.45	(0.02)	0.55	(0.02)	0.36	(0.02)	**-0.16**	(0.02)	**-0.15**	(0.03)	**-0.15**	(0.03)
	France	-0.01	(0.02)	-0.03	(0.02)	0.02	(0.03)	-0.07	(0.02)	-0.07	(0.02)	-0.07	(0.03)	**-0.06**	(0.03)	-0.04	(0.03)	**-0.09**	(0.04)
	Germany	-0.18	(0.02)	-0.10	(0.02)	-0.26	(0.03)	-0.18	(0.02)	-0.15	(0.02)	-0.20	(0.03)	0.00	(0.03)	**-0.06**	(0.02)	0.05	(0.04)
	Greece	-0.06	(0.02)	-0.11	(0.02)	-0.02	(0.03)	-0.32	(0.02)	-0.33	(0.02)	-0.32	(0.03)	**-0.26**	(0.03)	**-0.22**	(0.03)	**-0.30**	(0.04)
	Hungary	0.10	(0.02)	0.21	(0.02)	0.00	(0.04)	0.28	(0.02)	0.42	(0.03)	0.14	(0.03)	**0.17**	(0.03)	**0.21**	(0.04)	**0.13**	(0.05)
	Iceland	0.51	(0.01)	0.59	(0.02)	0.41	(0.02)	0.19	(0.02)	0.36	(0.02)	0.02	(0.03)	**-0.31**	(0.02)	**-0.23**	(0.03)	**-0.40**	(0.03)
	Ireland	-0.10	(0.02)	0.00	(0.02)	-0.20	(0.03)	-0.13	(0.02)	-0.06	(0.02)	-0.20	(0.03)	-0.03	(0.02)	**-0.06**	(0.03)	0.00	(0.04)
	Israel	0.14	(0.05)	0.27	(0.05)	-0.04	(0.06)	-0.08	(0.02)	0.17	(0.03)	-0.35	(0.04)	**-0.22**	(0.05)	-0.10	(0.06)	**-0.30**	(0.07)
	Italy	0.03	(0.02)	0.09	(0.02)	-0.02	(0.03)	-0.31	(0.01)	-0.22	(0.01)	-0.40	(0.01)	**-0.34**	(0.02)	**-0.31**	(0.02)	**-0.38**	(0.04)
	Japan	0.54	(0.02)	0.51	(0.02)	0.57	(0.02)	0.38	(0.02)	0.38	(0.02)	0.39	(0.02)	**-0.15**	(0.02)	**-0.13**	(0.03)	**-0.18**	(0.03)
	Korea	0.33	(0.02)	0.24	(0.02)	0.40	(0.03)	0.01	(0.02)	0.06	(0.03)	-0.03	(0.03)	**-0.32**	(0.03)	**-0.18**	(0.04)	**-0.44**	(0.04)
	Luxembourg	m	m	m	m	m	m	0.06	(0.02)	0.10	(0.02)	0.02	(0.02)	m	m	m	m	m	m
	Mexico	-0.05	(0.02)	-0.06	(0.03)	-0.04	(0.03)	-0.08	(0.01)	-0.06	(0.01)	-0.10	(0.01)	-0.03	(0.02)	0.00	(0.03)	-0.06	(0.03)
	Netherlands	m	m	m	m	m	m	-0.32	(0.04)	-0.16	(0.04)	-0.49	(0.05)	m	m	m	m	m	m
	New Zealand	0.16	(0.02)	0.15	(0.02)	0.16	(0.02)	0.05	(0.01)	0.13	(0.02)	-0.03	(0.02)	**-0.11**	(0.02)	-0.03	(0.03)	**-0.18**	(0.03)
	Norway	0.51	(0.02)	0.60	(0.02)	0.42	(0.03)	0.32	(0.02)	0.43	(0.03)	0.22	(0.03)	**-0.19**	(0.03)	**-0.18**	(0.04)	**-0.20**	(0.04)
	Poland	-0.06	(0.02)	0.05	(0.03)	-0.17	(0.03)	0.00	(0.02)	0.18	(0.02)	-0.19	(0.03)	**0.06**	(0.03)	**0.13**	(0.03)	-0.02	(0.04)
	Portugal	0.01	(0.02)	0.10	(0.02)	-0.09	(0.03)	-0.09	(0.01)	-0.05	(0.01)	-0.14	(0.02)	**-0.10**	(0.02)	**-0.15**	(0.03)	-0.05	(0.04)
	Spain	-0.15	(0.02)	-0.16	(0.02)	-0.15	(0.03)	-0.30	(0.01)	-0.28	(0.01)	-0.31	(0.02)	**-0.14**	(0.03)	**-0.13**	(0.03)	**-0.16**	(0.04)
	Sweden	0.29	(0.02)	0.37	(0.02)	0.21	(0.02)	-0.01	(0.02)	0.15	(0.02)	-0.17	(0.03)	**-0.30**	(0.03)	**-0.22**	(0.03)	**-0.39**	(0.04)
	Switzerland	0.06	(0.02)	0.13	(0.02)	0.00	(0.04)	0.15	(0.02)	0.20	(0.02)	0.09	(0.03)	**0.08**	(0.03)	**0.07**	(0.03)	**0.09**	(0.04)
	United Kingdom	m	m	m	m	m	m	-0.11	(0.02)	-0.02	(0.02)	-0.21	(0.02)	m	m	m	m	m	m
	United States	-0.16	(0.03)	-0.07	(0.03)	-0.26	(0.04)	-0.32	(0.02)	-0.24	(0.02)	-0.40	(0.03)	**-0.16**	(0.04)	**-0.17**	(0.04)	**-0.14**	(0.05)
	OECD average-26	0.11	(0.00)	0.17	(0.00)	0.05	(0.01)	-0.02	(0.00)	0.07	(0.00)	-0.10	(0.01)	**-0.13**	(0.01)	**-0.10**	(0.01)	**-0.16**	(0.01)
Partners	Albania	0.20	(0.03)	0.29	(0.03)	0.10	(0.04)	0.33	(0.03)	0.45	(0.03)	0.21	(0.03)	**0.13**	(0.04)	**0.16**	(0.04)	**0.11**	(0.05)
	Argentina	0.08	(0.05)	0.21	(0.05)	-0.08	(0.05)	0.07	(0.02)	0.20	(0.03)	-0.10	(0.03)	-0.02	(0.05)	-0.01	(0.06)	-0.01	(0.06)
	Brazil	0.20	(0.02)	0.40	(0.03)	-0.03	(0.03)	-0.05	(0.02)	0.12	(0.02)	-0.24	(0.02)	**-0.25**	(0.03)	**-0.29**	(0.03)	**-0.21**	(0.04)
	Bulgaria	0.35	(0.02)	0.56	(0.03)	0.15	(0.03)	0.03	(0.04)	0.23	(0.03)	-0.17	(0.05)	**-0.33**	(0.04)	**-0.32**	(0.04)	**-0.32**	(0.06)
	Hong Kong-China	0.57	(0.02)	0.57	(0.02)	0.57	(0.03)	0.46	(0.02)	0.48	(0.02)	0.45	(0.03)	**-0.11**	(0.02)	**-0.09**	(0.03)	**-0.12**	(0.04)
	Indonesia	0.12	(0.03)	0.22	(0.04)	0.01	(0.04)	0.60	(0.03)	0.71	(0.04)	0.49	(0.04)	**0.48**	(0.04)	**0.48**	(0.06)	**0.48**	(0.05)
	Latvia	0.17	(0.02)	0.31	(0.03)	0.01	(0.04)	0.13	(0.02)	0.30	(0.03)	-0.05	(0.03)	-0.04	(0.03)	-0.01	(0.04)	-0.06	(0.05)
	Liechtenstein	-0.07	(0.05)	-0.06	(0.07)	-0.06	(0.08)	0.04	(0.05)	0.06	(0.06)	0.01	(0.07)	0.11	(0.07)	0.12	(0.10)	0.07	(0.11)
	Peru	0.35	(0.03)	0.33	(0.05)	0.37	(0.03)	0.62	(0.02)	0.70	(0.02)	0.54	(0.03)	**0.27**	(0.03)	**0.37**	(0.05)	**0.17**	(0.04)
	Romania	0.02	(0.03)	0.06	(0.03)	-0.02	(0.04)	-0.08	(0.02)	0.04	(0.03)	-0.21	(0.03)	**-0.10**	(0.03)	-0.01	(0.04)	**-0.19**	(0.05)
	Russian Federation	0.60	(0.03)	0.80	(0.03)	0.40	(0.03)	0.27	(0.02)	0.40	(0.02)	0.13	(0.02)	**-0.33**	(0.03)	**-0.40**	(0.04)	**-0.27**	(0.04)
	Thailand	0.75	(0.03)	0.91	(0.03)	0.51	(0.04)	0.99	(0.02)	1.19	(0.02)	0.73	(0.03)	**0.25**	(0.04)	**0.28**	(0.04)	**0.21**	(0.05)

Note: Values that are statistically significant are indicated in bold (see Annex A3).

StatLink http://dx.doi.org/10.1787/888932343285

[Part 1/1]

Table V.5.11 Teacher-student relations in PISA 2000 and 2009

Percentage of students agreeing or strongly agreeing with the following statements

		PISA 2000						PISA 2009						Change between 2000 and 2009 (PISA 2009 – PISA 2000)					
		Most of my teachers really listen to what I have to say		If I need extra help, I will receive it from my teachers		Most of my teachers treat me fairly		Most of my teachers really listen to what I have to say		If I need extra help, I will receive it from my teachers		Most of my teachers treat me fairly		Most of my teachers really listen to what I have to say		If I need extra help, I will receive it from my teachers		Most of my teachers treat me fairly	
		%	S.E.	%	S.E.	%	S.E.	%	S.E.	%	S.E.	%	S.E.	% dif.	S.E.	% dif.	S.E.	% dif.	S.E.
OECD	Australia	71.7	(1.0)	84.3	(0.8)	82.7	(0.8)	71.4	(0.5)	84.2	(0.4)	84.6	(0.4)	-0.4	(1.1)	0.0	(0.9)	**1.9**	(0.8)
	Austria	55.5	(1.0)	59.6	(1.1)	75.0	(0.8)	m	m	m	m	m	m	m	m	m	m	m	m
	Belgium	68.3	(0.8)	77.7	(0.7)	81.8	(0.7)	67.3	(0.7)	84.1	(0.5)	85.8	(0.5)	-1.0	(1.0)	**6.4**	(0.9)	**4.0**	(0.9)
	Canada	70.5	(0.5)	87.4	(0.3)	80.8	(0.4)	74.0	(0.4)	89.5	(0.3)	88.0	(0.3)	**3.5**	(0.6)	**2.1**	(0.4)	**7.2**	(0.5)
	Chile	66.0	(1.1)	70.1	(0.9)	63.7	(1.0)	72.4	(0.8)	77.4	(0.8)	70.9	(0.9)	**6.5**	(1.4)	**7.3**	(1.2)	**7.2**	(1.3)
	Czech Republic	56.6	(1.1)	72.4	(1.1)	68.3	(1.0)	56.9	(0.9)	78.3	(0.7)	72.2	(0.7)	0.3	(1.4)	**5.9**	(1.3)	**3.9**	(1.2)
	Denmark	71.7	(0.9)	78.7	(0.8)	87.5	(0.7)	71.1	(0.8)	79.2	(0.8)	85.2	(0.6)	-0.6	(1.2)	0.5	(1.1)	**-2.3**	(0.9)
	Finland	64.7	(0.9)	82.5	(0.7)	75.2	(0.8)	62.7	(0.8)	84.2	(0.7)	79.8	(0.7)	-2.0	(1.2)	1.7	(1.0)	**4.6**	(1.0)
	France	61.7	(1.0)	75.9	(0.7)	72.7	(0.7)	61.7	(1.0)	79.8	(0.7)	88.3	(0.7)	0.0	(1.5)	**3.9**	(1.0)	**15.6**	(1.0)
	Germany	50.9	(1.0)	58.6	(1.0)	72.7	(0.8)	68.8	(0.8)	70.5	(0.9)	77.4	(0.8)	**17.9**	(1.3)	**11.9**	(1.4)	**4.7**	(1.1)
	Greece	64.8	(1.0)	61.5	(1.2)	64.7	(1.0)	62.2	(0.8)	63.0	(0.9)	65.0	(1.0)	**-2.6**	(1.2)	1.6	(1.5)	0.2	(1.4)
	Hungary	79.1	(0.7)	73.3	(0.9)	68.6	(0.9)	79.1	(0.9)	77.4	(0.8)	74.1	(0.9)	0.0	(1.2)	**4.1**	(1.2)	**5.6**	(1.2)
	Iceland	62.6	(0.7)	73.4	(0.8)	71.9	(0.8)	73.9	(0.8)	82.0	(0.7)	80.3	(0.8)	**11.3**	(1.1)	**8.6**	(1.0)	**8.4**	(1.1)
	Ireland	57.3	(1.0)	73.2	(0.8)	77.9	(0.8)	62.8	(1.0)	77.4	(0.9)	81.1	(0.8)	**5.5**	(1.4)	**4.2**	(1.2)	**3.1**	(1.1)
	Israel	62.2	(1.4)	71.4	(1.8)	72.2	(1.2)	68.0	(0.9)	70.2	(0.9)	79.6	(0.6)	**5.8**	(1.7)	-1.2	(2.0)	**7.5**	(1.4)
	Italy	70.9	(1.2)	73.1	(1.0)	63.6	(0.9)	62.3	(0.5)	76.7	(0.4)	79.1	(0.4)	**-8.5**	(1.3)	**3.6**	(1.1)	**15.5**	(1.0)
	Japan	49.8	(1.2)	64.2	(1.2)	69.3	(1.1)	63.0	(0.8)	63.5	(0.7)	74.4	(0.8)	**13.2**	(1.4)	-0.7	(1.4)	**5.0**	(1.3)
	Korea	40.7	(0.9)	76.4	(0.9)	66.4	(0.9)	57.2	(0.9)	83.3	(0.7)	75.3	(0.7)	**16.4**	(1.3)	**6.9**	(1.1)	**8.8**	(1.1)
	Luxembourg	m	m	m	m	m	m	63.2	(0.8)	72.2	(0.7)	78.0	(0.7)	m	m	m	m	m	m
	Mexico	85.1	(0.6)	78.8	(0.7)	65.3	(0.8)	76.9	(0.4)	78.4	(0.4)	74.7	(0.4)	**-8.2**	(0.7)	-0.4	(0.8)	**9.3**	(0.9)
	Netherlands	m	m	m	m	m	m	65.9	(0.9)	85.0	(0.8)	85.1	(0.8)	m	m	m	m	m	m
	New Zealand	67.7	(0.9)	82.2	(0.7)	82.2	(0.8)	72.6	(0.7)	87.4	(0.6)	86.3	(0.5)	**4.9**	(1.1)	**5.3**	(0.9)	**4.1**	(1.0)
	Norway	55.8	(1.3)	71.7	(0.9)	69.8	(1.0)	54.9	(0.9)	74.2	(0.9)	73.6	(0.7)	-0.9	(1.6)	**2.5**	(1.3)	**3.8**	(1.2)
	Poland	64.5	(1.0)	56.7	(1.0)	57.0	(1.2)	59.5	(0.8)	73.4	(0.8)	70.6	(0.8)	**-4.9**	(1.3)	**16.7**	(1.3)	**13.6**	(1.5)
	Portugal	75.4	(0.8)	76.9	(0.8)	83.8	(0.6)	81.9	(0.6)	89.8	(0.6)	81.5	(0.6)	**6.5**	(1.0)	**12.9**	(1.0)	**-2.3**	(0.9)
	Spain	63.4	(1.0)	67.5	(1.0)	83.9	(0.6)	67.5	(0.6)	68.5	(0.6)	79.3	(0.5)	**4.1**	(1.2)	1.0	(1.2)	**-4.6**	(0.8)
	Sweden	68.3	(1.1)	78.1	(0.9)	80.2	(0.8)	71.5	(0.9)	81.8	(0.9)	82.4	(0.6)	**3.2**	(1.4)	**3.7**	(1.3)	**2.2**	(1.0)
	Switzerland	67.0	(1.1)	77.7	(0.9)	78.7	(0.8)	70.4	(0.7)	82.3	(0.7)	83.0	(0.6)	**3.4**	(1.3)	**4.5**	(1.2)	**4.3**	(1.0)
	United Kingdom	m	m	m	m	m	m	69.3	(0.8)	88.5	(0.6)	83.4	(0.7)	m	m	m	m	m	m
	United States	70.8	(1.1)	82.2	(0.9)	82.2	(1.1)	73.6	(1.0)	88.4	(0.5)	88.6	(0.4)	2.8	(1.5)	**6.2**	(1.0)	**6.4**	(1.2)
	OECD average-26	64.9	(0.2)	74.1	(0.2)	74.0	(0.2)	67.8	(0.2)	78.7	(0.1)	79.3	(0.1)	**2.9**	(0.2)	**4.6**	(0.2)	**5.3**	(0.2)
Partners	Albania	73.7	(0.9)	76.1	(1.0)	85.0	(0.9)	89.5	(0.5)	91.9	(0.5)	94.0	(0.4)	**15.8**	(1.1)	**15.9**	(1.1)	**8.9**	(0.9)
	Argentina	65.3	(1.4)	69.4	(1.7)	73.7	(1.6)	73.0	(1.0)	67.7	(1.2)	79.5	(0.8)	**7.7**	(1.7)	-1.7	(2.1)	**5.8**	(1.7)
	Brazil	74.1	(1.0)	88.0	(0.7)	85.6	(0.7)	74.4	(0.8)	77.8	(0.7)	83.0	(0.6)	0.3	(1.2)	**-10.2**	(1.0)	**-2.6**	(0.9)
	Bulgaria	74.4	(0.8)	75.8	(1.0)	71.8	(0.9)	70.9	(1.1)	79.6	(0.7)	73.3	(1.1)	**-3.5**	(1.4)	**3.8**	(1.2)	1.5	(1.4)
	Hong Kong-China	66.7	(0.9)	85.4	(0.6)	69.4	(0.8)	66.8	(0.9)	88.7	(0.5)	81.8	(0.6)	0.1	(1.3)	**3.3**	(0.7)	**12.3**	(1.0)
	Indonesia	67.6	(1.1)	78.8	(0.7)	91.0	(0.6)	63.2	(0.9)	84.8	(0.7)	91.0	(0.4)	**-4.4**	(1.4)	**6.0**	(1.0)	-0.1	(0.7)
	Latvia	62.1	(1.5)	72.0	(1.2)	73.6	(1.2)	69.3	(0.9)	85.3	(0.7)	81.8	(0.8)	**7.3**	(1.7)	**13.4**	(1.4)	**8.2**	(1.5)
	Liechtenstein	61.3	(3.0)	74.6	(2.4)	81.1	(2.2)	66.4	(2.6)	77.7	(2.4)	74.6	(2.2)	5.1	(4.0)	3.1	(3.4)	**-6.5**	(3.1)
	Peru	78.6	(1.0)	78.1	(0.7)	79.8	(0.9)	82.1	(0.7)	84.7	(0.6)	82.7	(0.7)	**3.5**	(1.2)	**6.7**	(0.9)	**2.9**	(1.1)
	Romania	71.3	(1.1)	72.4	(1.0)	79.4	(0.9)	76.8	(0.9)	74.0	(0.9)	83.6	(0.7)	**5.5**	(1.4)	1.6	(1.3)	**4.2**	(1.1)
	Russian Federation	69.6	(0.8)	77.5	(1.0)	73.9	(1.0)	72.6	(0.7)	82.1	(0.7)	80.2	(0.8)	**2.9**	(1.0)	**4.6**	(1.2)	**6.3**	(1.3)
	Thailand	78.6	(0.7)	84.2	(0.5)	85.6	(0.9)	82.1	(0.6)	83.0	(0.5)	87.4	(0.5)	**3.5**	(1.0)	-1.2	(0.7)	1.8	(1.0)

Note: Values that are statistically significant are indicated in bold (see Annex A3).

StatLink http://dx.doi.org/10.1787/888932343285

[Part 1/2]
Table V.5.12 Disciplinary climate in PISA 2000 and 2009
Percentage of students reporting that the following happen "never or hardly ever" or "in some lessons"

		PISA 2000										PISA 2009									
		Students don't listen to what the teacher says		There is noise and disorder		The teacher has to wait a long time for the students to quieten down		Students cannot work well		Students don't start working for a long time after the lesson begins		Students don't listen to what the teacher says		There is noise and disorder		The teacher has to wait a long time for the students to quieten down		Students cannot work well		Students don't start working for a long time after the lesson begins	
		%	S.E.	%	S.E.	%	S.E.	%	S.E.	%	S.E.	%	S.E.	%	S.E.	%	S.E.	%	S.E.	%	S.E.
OECD	Australia	78.7	(0.9)	67.7	(1.1)	68.6	(1.0)	81.6	(1.0)	74.1	(0.9)	67.7	(0.7)	60.8	(0.7)	70.9	(0.7)	82.0	(0.5)	76.4	(0.6)
	Austria	78.1	(0.8)	81.1	(1.0)	68.5	(1.2)	78.8	(0.9)	70.8	(1.1)	m	m	m	m	m	m	m	m	m	m
	Belgium	75.9	(0.9)	62.9	(1.0)	64.6	(1.3)	85.0	(0.7)	68.8	(0.9)	71.7	(0.9)	62.9	(1.0)	67.7	(0.9)	84.6	(0.6)	71.3	(0.8)
	Canada	77.1	(0.4)	66.1	(0.5)	64.8	(0.6)	83.3	(0.3)	70.4	(0.5)	70.6	(0.6)	61.1	(0.6)	72.3	(0.6)	82.2	(0.5)	72.7	(0.6)
	Chile	73.0	(0.8)	51.0	(1.2)	59.4	(1.0)	77.1	(0.8)	66.3	(0.8)	73.6	(0.8)	62.9	(1.0)	65.0	(1.1)	81.5	(0.7)	70.1	(0.9)
	Czech Republic	73.9	(1.0)	74.0	(1.2)	67.7	(1.4)	82.7	(0.7)	78.8	(0.8)	63.2	(1.4)	66.0	(1.4)	67.6	(1.2)	75.3	(1.1)	70.2	(1.2)
	Denmark	80.3	(0.9)	65.6	(1.2)	72.3	(1.2)	82.8	(0.8)	77.2	(1.0)	71.7	(0.9)	65.2	(1.1)	78.1	(1.0)	88.1	(0.7)	81.9	(0.9)
	Finland	70.0	(0.9)	56.9	(1.1)	60.5	(1.2)	84.8	(0.6)	78.2	(0.8)	60.4	(1.0)	52.1	(1.1)	63.1	(1.0)	79.9	(0.8)	67.9	(1.0)
	France	72.1	(0.9)	56.8	(1.3)	64.4	(1.1)	84.8	(0.6)	62.6	(0.9)	64.3	(1.1)	56.2	(1.3)	64.2	(1.3)	76.3	(1.1)	62.5	(1.1)
	Germany	75.9	(0.8)	77.5	(1.1)	63.8	(1.1)	76.3	(0.7)	72.4	(0.8)	84.6	(0.7)	83.5	(0.8)	77.5	(0.9)	82.2	(0.8)	81.0	(0.7)
	Greece	70.3	(1.0)	53.1	(1.2)	56.8	(1.2)	59.9	(1.0)	65.2	(0.8)	55.2	(1.2)	58.4	(1.4)	62.5	(1.2)	56.3	(1.0)	65.4	(0.7)
	Hungary	77.5	(1.1)	76.4	(1.2)	65.7	(1.5)	74.3	(1.1)	83.3	(0.9)	70.5	(1.4)	70.9	(1.3)	68.9	(1.3)	79.5	(1.1)	78.1	(1.0)
	Iceland	80.0	(0.7)	71.5	(0.7)	66.2	(0.7)	83.6	(0.7)	80.0	(0.7)	74.1	(0.6)	66.9	(0.7)	73.1	(0.7)	83.6	(0.6)	80.8	(0.6)
	Ireland	74.9	(0.9)	73.7	(1.0)	70.8	(1.2)	83.4	(0.9)	74.8	(0.9)	63.7	(1.1)	64.6	(1.2)	69.9	(1.2)	80.8	(0.9)	75.1	(1.0)
	Israel	70.6	(1.9)	70.9	(2.0)	60.0	(2.3)	68.8	(1.2)	68.4	(2.1)	77.8	(0.8)	75.2	(0.9)	72.6	(0.9)	77.3	(0.8)	74.3	(0.8)
	Italy	64.5	(1.1)	53.9	(1.2)	51.4	(1.3)	77.8	(0.8)	70.7	(0.9)	66.0	(0.5)	68.0	(0.7)	69.8	(0.6)	81.2	(0.5)	73.7	(0.6)
	Japan	82.6	(1.2)	82.3	(1.6)	90.5	(0.9)	78.6	(1.1)	82.1	(1.2)	91.6	(0.5)	90.3	(0.7)	92.8	(0.5)	87.0	(0.5)	91.4	(0.6)
	Korea	67.9	(1.1)	70.6	(1.2)	82.5	(0.9)	78.7	(0.9)	77.1	(0.9)	89.9	(0.7)	77.2	(0.8)	87.8	(0.6)	90.3	(0.7)	87.4	(0.8)
	Luxembourg	m	m	m	m	m	m	m	m	m	m	59.6	(0.8)	65.3	(0.7)	64.2	(0.6)	71.4	(0.7)	64.2	(0.6)
	Mexico	80.4	(0.8)	74.9	(1.0)	71.0	(1.1)	82.4	(0.7)	80.5	(0.8)	79.1	(0.4)	73.3	(0.5)	79.1	(0.5)	83.2	(0.4)	76.5	(0.4)
	Netherlands	m	m	m	m	m	m	m	m	m	m	68.1	(0.9)	58.9	(1.1)	63.2	(1.0)	80.5	(1.0)	55.5	(1.1)
	New Zealand	76.4	(0.9)	67.5	(1.0)	66.5	(1.0)	77.8	(0.8)	73.6	(0.9)	67.6	(0.8)	61.3	(0.8)	68.3	(0.9)	82.1	(0.7)	74.1	(0.8)
	Norway	72.4	(1.0)	59.8	(1.3)	57.8	(1.6)	76.7	(0.9)	66.5	(1.2)	66.8	(0.8)	61.4	(1.1)	65.5	(0.9)	76.6	(0.9)	66.7	(1.0)
	Poland	79.8	(1.0)	81.0	(1.2)	73.3	(1.4)	86.1	(0.8)	79.8	(1.1)	67.4	(1.0)	74.1	(1.0)	73.7	(1.1)	79.4	(0.8)	79.5	(0.9)
	Portugal	79.4	(0.7)	75.6	(0.9)	74.8	(0.9)	80.1	(0.8)	75.1	(0.8)	78.3	(0.8)	75.5	(0.9)	79.6	(0.9)	86.5	(0.6)	79.4	(0.9)
	Spain	75.0	(0.9)	65.6	(1.3)	59.2	(1.5)	81.4	(0.8)	64.6	(1.0)	73.5	(0.7)	74.1	(0.7)	72.5	(0.6)	83.1	(0.5)	72.7	(0.7)
	Sweden	70.8	(0.9)	61.0	(1.3)	56.6	(1.3)	77.1	(0.9)	68.5	(1.1)	75.1	(1.0)	67.2	(1.1)	71.1	(1.1)	82.7	(0.7)	76.5	(1.0)
	Switzerland	81.6	(0.8)	81.5	(0.9)	72.3	(1.1)	81.3	(0.7)	76.8	(1.0)	72.4	(0.9)	73.8	(1.0)	74.2	(0.9)	81.0	(0.6)	75.8	(0.7)
	United Kingdom	m	m	m	m	m	m	m	m	m	m	73.0	(0.9)	68.4	(1.0)	73.8	(0.9)	85.6	(0.7)	81.2	(0.8)
	United States	73.8	(1.1)	70.2	(1.3)	72.5	(1.3)	81.5	(1.0)	74.9	(1.0)	75.5	(0.8)	72.0	(0.8)	78.9	(0.8)	87.1	(0.6)	81.6	(0.8)
	OECD average-26	75.2	(0.2)	68.0	(0.2)	66.7	(0.2)	79.5	(0.2)	73.5	(0.2)	72.0	(0.2)	68.3	(0.2)	72.6	(0.2)	81.2	(0.1)	75.5	(0.2)
Partners	Albania	89.6	(0.6)	92.4	(0.4)	87.6	(0.7)	84.8	(0.8)	85.0	(0.7)	88.7	(1.0)	88.0	(0.8)	86.1	(0.9)	86.7	(0.8)	88.2	(0.7)
	Argentina	66.0	(2.8)	51.5	(2.7)	55.5	(3.5)	75.0	(2.0)	61.6	(1.0)	66.9	(1.3)	57.0	(1.3)	61.9	(1.2)	73.9	(1.1)	65.5	(1.1)
	Brazil	70.5	(0.9)	58.2	(1.1)	63.2	(1.4)	75.2	(0.8)	60.3	(1.2)	75.3	(0.7)	59.8	(0.9)	66.6	(0.7)	75.9	(0.8)	62.9	(0.6)
	Bulgaria	70.3	(1.0)	74.9	(1.2)	65.6	(1.4)	79.8	(0.9)	74.1	(1.1)	69.0	(1.2)	72.2	(1.3)	73.4	(1.5)	75.5	(1.2)	76.5	(1.3)
	Hong Kong-China	72.2	(1.0)	78.9	(0.9)	79.0	(0.8)	71.0	(0.9)	66.0	(0.9)	87.2	(0.6)	87.9	(0.6)	89.4	(0.5)	88.0	(0.6)	86.2	(0.7)
	Indonesia	84.3	(0.9)	65.6	(1.2)	48.7	(1.1)	85.7	(0.8)	79.5	(0.9)	84.3	(0.8)	74.8	(0.9)	79.2	(0.9)	84.0	(0.8)	84.1	(0.8)
	Latvia	81.0	(1.0)	83.1	(1.0)	80.6	(1.1)	83.0	(0.9)	83.7	(1.0)	77.8	(1.0)	78.1	(1.2)	79.1	(1.1)	85.6	(0.8)	86.1	(0.8)
	Liechtenstein	85.1	(2.0)	89.9	(1.8)	74.6	(1.9)	78.9	(2.3)	84.8	(1.9)	70.8	(2.6)	81.1	(2.0)	75.8	(2.5)	79.4	(2.2)	80.2	(2.2)
	Peru	74.0	(0.9)	66.0	(1.1)	77.1	(1.0)	71.7	(0.9)	66.8	(1.1)	83.2	(0.7)	77.2	(0.8)	84.6	(0.7)	85.4	(0.6)	81.8	(0.8)
	Romania	80.6	(1.0)	83.9	(0.9)	80.3	(1.1)	79.1	(1.0)	79.0	(1.0)	88.6	(0.7)	89.3	(0.7)	88.5	(0.7)	88.5	(0.7)	86.6	(0.6)
	Russian Federation	83.7	(0.6)	87.2	(0.5)	80.8	(0.9)	83.0	(0.7)	86.3	(0.8)	81.0	(0.7)	86.0	(0.7)	85.3	(0.7)	84.8	(0.7)	88.6	(0.6)
	Thailand	87.2	(0.6)	68.5	(0.9)	80.5	(0.9)	85.1	(0.8)	89.2	(0.8)	90.5	(0.5)	85.3	(0.5)	86.4	(0.6)	91.3	(0.5)	91.4	(0.5)

Note: Values that are statistically significant are indicated in bold (see Annex A3).
StatLink http://dx.doi.org/10.1787/888932343285

[Part 2/2]
Disciplinary climate in PISA 2000 and 2009
Table V.5.12 *Percentage of students reporting that the following happen "never or hardly ever" or "in some lessons"*

		Change between 2000 and 2009 (PISA 2009 – PISA 2000)									
		Students don't listen to what the teacher says		There is noise and disorder		The teacher has to wait a long time for the students to quieten down		Students cannot work well		Students don't start working for a long time after the lesson begins	
		% dif.	S.E.	% dif.	S.E.	% dif.	S.E.	% dif.	S.E.	% dif.	S.E.
OECD	Australia	**-10.9**	(1.2)	**-6.9**	(1.3)	2.3	(1.2)	0.4	(1.1)	**2.3**	(1.1)
	Austria	m	m	m	m	m	m	m	m	m	m
	Belgium	**-4.2**	(1.3)	0.0	(1.4)	**3.2**	(1.6)	-0.4	(0.9)	**2.5**	(1.2)
	Canada	**-6.5**	(0.7)	**-4.9**	(0.8)	**7.4**	(0.8)	-1.1	(0.6)	**2.2**	(0.8)
	Chile	0.5	(1.2)	**11.9**	(1.5)	**5.7**	(1.5)	**4.4**	(1.0)	**3.8**	(1.2)
	Czech Republic	**-10.7**	(1.7)	**-7.9**	(1.8)	-0.1	(1.8)	**-7.3**	(1.3)	**-8.6**	(1.4)
	Denmark	**-8.6**	(1.3)	-0.5	(1.6)	**5.7**	(1.6)	**5.3**	(1.0)	**4.7**	(1.3)
	Finland	**-9.6**	(1.4)	**-4.8**	(1.6)	2.7	(1.5)	**-4.9**	(1.0)	**-10.3**	(1.3)
	France	**-7.7**	(1.4)	-0.6	(1.9)	-0.2	(1.7)	**-8.5**	(1.3)	-0.1	(1.4)
	Germany	**8.7**	(1.1)	**6.0**	(1.4)	**13.7**	(1.4)	**5.9**	(1.0)	**8.6**	(1.1)
	Greece	**-15.1**	(1.6)	**5.3**	(1.9)	**5.6**	(1.7)	**-3.7**	(1.4)	0.2	(1.1)
	Hungary	**-7.0**	(1.8)	**-5.5**	(1.8)	3.2	(1.9)	**5.2**	(1.6)	**-5.2**	(1.3)
	Iceland	**-6.0**	(0.9)	**-4.6**	(1.0)	**6.9**	(1.0)	-0.1	(0.9)	0.8	(0.9)
	Ireland	**-11.2**	(1.4)	**-9.1**	(1.6)	-1.0	(1.6)	**-2.5**	(1.2)	0.3	(1.4)
	Israel	**7.3**	(2.1)	4.3	(2.2)	**12.6**	(2.4)	**8.5**	(1.4)	**5.9**	(2.2)
	Italy	1.5	(1.2)	**14.1**	(1.4)	**18.4**	(1.4)	**3.4**	(0.9)	**3.0**	(1.0)
	Japan	**9.0**	(1.3)	**7.9**	(1.8)	**2.3**	(1.0)	**8.5**	(1.2)	**9.3**	(1.4)
	Korea	**22.0**	(1.3)	**6.7**	(1.4)	**5.3**	(1.1)	**11.6**	(1.2)	**10.3**	(1.2)
	Luxembourg	m	m	m	m	m	m	m	m	m	m
	Mexico	-1.3	(0.9)	-1.6	(1.2)	**8.1**	(1.2)	0.8	(0.8)	**-4.0**	(0.9)
	Netherlands	m	m	m	m	m	m	m	m	m	m
	New Zealand	**-8.8**	(1.2)	**-6.2**	(1.3)	1.8	(1.4)	**4.3**	(1.1)	0.5	(1.2)
	Norway	**-5.6**	(1.3)	1.6	(1.7)	**7.7**	(1.8)	0.0	(1.2)	0.2	(1.5)
	Poland	**-12.3**	(1.4)	**-6.9**	(1.6)	0.4	(1.8)	**-6.7**	(1.1)	-0.3	(1.4)
	Portugal	-1.2	(1.1)	0.0	(1.2)	**4.8**	(1.3)	**6.4**	(1.0)	**4.3**	(1.2)
	Spain	-1.5	(1.1)	**8.5**	(1.4)	**13.4**	(1.6)	1.7	(0.9)	**8.0**	(1.3)
	Sweden	**4.3**	(1.3)	**6.2**	(1.7)	**14.5**	(1.7)	**5.7**	(1.2)	**7.9**	(1.5)
	Switzerland	**-9.2**	(1.2)	**-7.7**	(1.3)	1.9	(1.4)	-0.3	(0.9)	-1.0	(1.2)
	United Kingdom	m	m	m	m	m	m	m	m	m	m
	United States	1.7	(1.3)	1.8	(1.6)	**6.4**	(1.5)	**5.7**	(1.1)	**6.7**	(1.3)
	OECD average-26	**-3.2**	(0.3)	0.3	(0.3)	**5.9**	(0.3)	**1.6**	(0.2)	**2.0**	(0.3)
Partners	Albania	-0.9	(1.1)	**-4.4**	(0.9)	-1.5	(1.2)	1.9	(1.1)	**3.3**	(1.0)
	Argentina	0.9	(3.1)	5.5	(3.0)	6.4	(3.7)	-1.1	(2.3)	**4.0**	(1.5)
	Brazil	**4.7**	(1.2)	1.6	(1.5)	**3.4**	(1.6)	0.6	(1.2)	2.5	(1.3)
	Bulgaria	-1.4	(1.5)	-2.7	(1.8)	**7.8**	(2.0)	**-4.4**	(1.5)	2.5	(1.7)
	Hong Kong-China	**15.0**	(1.2)	**9.1**	(1.1)	**10.4**	(1.0)	**17.0**	(1.1)	**20.2**	(1.1)
	Indonesia	0.0	(1.2)	**9.2**	(1.5)	**30.5**	(1.5)	-1.7	(1.1)	**4.5**	(1.2)
	Latvia	**-3.1**	(1.4)	**-5.1**	(1.5)	-1.5	(1.6)	**2.6**	(1.2)	2.4	(1.3)
	Liechtenstein	**-14.3**	(3.3)	**-8.9**	(2.7)	1.2	(3.2)	0.5	(3.1)	-4.6	(2.9)
	Peru	**9.2**	(1.2)	**11.3**	(1.3)	**7.6**	(1.2)	**13.7**	(1.0)	**15.0**	(1.4)
	Romania	**8.0**	(1.2)	**5.4**	(1.1)	**8.2**	(1.3)	**9.4**	(1.3)	**7.6**	(1.2)
	Russian Federation	**-2.7**	(0.9)	-1.2	(0.9)	**4.5**	(1.2)	1.8	(1.0)	**2.3**	(1.0)
	Thailand	**3.3**	(0.8)	**16.8**	(1.1)	**5.8**	(1.0)	**6.2**	(0.9)	**2.2**	(0.9)

Note: Values that are statistically significant are indicated in bold (see Annex A3).
StatLink http://dx.doi.org/10.1787/888932343285

ANNEX B2
SUBNATIONAL TABLES

[Part 1/1]

Table S.V.a Mean reading performance in PISA 2000, 2003, 2006 and 2009

	PISA 2000		PISA 2003		PISA 2006		PISA 2009		Change between 2000 and 2009 (PISA 2009 - PISA 2000)		
	Mean score	S.E.	Mean score	S.E.	Mean score	S.E.	Mean score	S.E.	Score dif.	S.E.	p-value
Adjudicated											
Belgium (Flemish Community)	532	(4.2)	530	(2.1)	525	(3.9)	519	(2.3)	**-14**	(6.9)	0.05
United Kingdom (Scotland)	526	(3.8)	516	(2.5)	499	(4.0)	500	(3.2)	**-25**	(7.0)	0.00
Non-adjudicated											
Belgium (French Community)	476	(7.2)	477	(5.0)	473	(5.0)	490	(4.2)	14	(9.7)	0.00

Note: Values that are statistically significant are indicated in bold (see Annex A3).
See Table V.2.1 for national data.

[Part 1/1]

Table S.V.b Percentage of students below Level 2 and at Level 5 and above on the reading scale in PISA 2000 and 2009

	Proficiency levels in PISA 2000				Proficiency levels in PISA 2009				Change between 2000 and 2009 (PISA 2009 – PISA 2000)			
	Below Level 2 (less than 407 score points)		Below Level 2 (less than 407 score points)		Below Level 2 (less than 407 score points)		Level 5 and above (from 626 score points)		Below Level 2 (less than 407 score points)		Level 5 and above (from 626 score points)	
	%	S.E.	%	S.E.	%	S.E.	%	S.E.	% dif.	S.E.	% dif.	S.E.
Adjudicated												
Belgium (Flemish Community)	11.6	(1.5)	15.6	(0.9)	13.4	(0.9)	12.5	(0.9)	1.7	(1.7)	**-3.1**	(1.3)
United Kingdom (Scotland)	12.3	(1.1)	15.3	(1.0)	16.3	(1.1)	9.2	(0.9)	**4.0**	(1.6)	**-6.1**	(1.4)
Non-adjudicated												
Belgium (French Community)	28.2	(2.7)	7.5	(0.9)	23.3	(1.6)	9.6	(0.9)	-4.9	(3.2)	2.1	**(1.3)**

Note: Values that are statistically significant are indicated in bold (see Annex A3).
See Table V.2.2 for national data.

[Part 1/2]

Table S.V.c Percentiles on the reading scale in PISA 2000 and 2009

	PISA 2000								PISA 2009							
	10th percentile		25th percentile		75th percentile		90th percentile		10th percentile		25th percentile		75th percentile		90th percentile	
	Score	S.E.	Score	S.E.	Score	S.E.	Score	S.E.	Score	S.E.	Score	S.E.	Score	S.E.	Score	S.E.
Adjudicated																
Belgium (Flemish Community)	396	(9.5)	476	(7.5)	601	(3.1)	644	(3.0)	390	(4.3)	453	(3.1)	589	(2.8)	636	(3.7)
United Kingdom (Scotland)	394	(6.4)	460	(4.8)	596	(4.1)	647	(4.0)	379	(4.9)	439	(3.6)	567	(3.5)	621	(4.9)
Non-adjudicated																
Belgium (French Community)	321	(11.8)	395	(10.4)	561	(5.6)	614	(4.6)	338	(8.8)	415	(6.7)	574	(4.1)	624	(3.8)

Note: Values that are statistically significant are indicated in bold (see Annex A3).
See Table V.2.3 for national data.

[Part 2/2]

Table S.V.c Percentiles on the reading scale in PISA 2000 and 2009

	Change in percentiles between PISA 2009 and PISA 2000							
	10th percentile		25th percentile		75th percentile		90th percentile	
	Score dif.	S.E.	Score dif.	S.E.	Score dif.	S.E.	Score dif.	S.E.
Adjudicated								
Belgium (Flemish Community)	-6	(11.5)	**-24**	(9.5)	-12	(6.5)	-9	(6.9)
United Kingdom (Scotland)	-16	(9.4)	**-21**	(7.8)	**-30**	(7.3)	**-26**	(8.0)
Non-adjudicated								
Belgium (French Community)	17	(15.5)	19	(13.3)	13	(8.5)	10	(7.7)

Note: Values that are statistically significant are indicated in bold (see Annex A3).
See Table V.2.3 for national data.

[Part 1/1]

Table S.V.d **Gender differences in reading performance in PISA 2000 and 2009**

	PISA 2000						PISA 2009						Change between 2000 and 2009 (PISA 2009 - PISA 2000)					
	Boys		Girls		Difference (B-G)		Boys		Girls		Difference (B-G)		Boys		Girls		Difference (B-G)	
	Mean score	S.E.	Mean score	S.E.	Mean score	S.E.	Mean score	S.E.	Mean score	S.E.	Mean score	S.E.	Score dif.	S.E.	Score dif.	S.E.	Score dif.	S.E.
Adjudicated																		
Belgium (Flemish Community)	516	(6.0)	551	(5.2)	**-35**	(7.6)	505	(3.0)	533	(3.3)	**-28**	(4.1)	-11	(9.5)	**-18**	(9.1)	7	(8.6)
United Kingdom (Scotland)	511	(4.4)	541	(4.3)	**-30**	(4.4)	488	(4.5)	512	(3.0)	**-24**	(4.1)	**-23**	(7.9)	**-29**	(7.2)	6	(6.1)
Non-adjudicated																		
Belgium (French Community)	460	(9.1)	495	(7.9)	**-35**	(9.7)	478	(6.2)	503	(4.5)	**-26**	(7.1)	18	(12.9)	9	(11.3)	9	(12.0)

Note: Values that are statistically significant are indicated in bold (see Annex A3).
See Table V.2.4 for national data.

[Part 1/1]

Table S.V.e **Percentage of boys below Level 2 and at Level 5 and above on the reading scale in PISA 2000 and 2009**

	Boys – Proficiency levels in PISA 2000				Boys – Proficiency levels in PISA 2009				Change between 2000 and 2009 (PISA 2009 – PISA 2000)			
	Below Level 2 (less than 407 score points)		Level 5 and above (from 626 score points)		Below Level 2 (less than 407 score points)		Level 5 and above (from 626 score points)		Below Level 2 (less than 407 score points)		Level 5 and above (from 626 score points)	
	%	S.E.	%	S.E.	%	S.E.	%	S.E.	% dif.	S.E.	% dif.	S.E.
Adjudicated												
Belgium (Flemish Community)	14.8	(1.9)	12.5	(1.4)	16.9	(1.1)	10.1	(1.1)	2.1	(2.2)	-2.3	(1.8)
United Kingdom (Scotland)	15.5	(1.5)	11.8	(1.2)	20.8	(1.6)	8.3	(1.3)	**5.3**	(2.2)	-3.5	(1.8)
Non-adjudicated												
Belgium (French Community)	33.7	(3.3)	6.4	(1.0)	27.2	(2.4)	8.7	(1.3)	-6.4	(4.1)	2.3	(1.6)

Note: Values that are statistically significant are indicated in bold (see Annex A3).
See Table V.2.5 for national data.

[Part 1/1]

Table S.V.f **Percentage of girls below Level 2 and at Level 5 and above on the reading scale in PISA 2000 and 2009**

	Girls – Proficiency levels in PISA 2000				Girls – Proficiency levels in PISA 2009				Change between 2000 and 2009 (PISA 2009 – PISA 2000)			
	Below Level 2 (less than 407 score points)		Level 5 and above (from 626 score points)		Below Level 2 (less than 407 score points)		Level 5 and above (from 626 score points)		Below Level 2 (less than 407 score points)		Level 5 and above (from 626 score points)	
	%	S.E.	%	S.E.	%	S.E.	%	S.E.	% dif.	S.E.	% dif.	S.E.
Adjudicated												
Belgium (Flemish Community)	8.0	(1.6)	19.4	(1.6)	9.7	(1.1)	15.0	(1.2)	1.7	(2.0)	**-4.4**	(2.0)
United Kingdom (Scotland)	8.6	(1.2)	19.0	(1.4)	11.8	(1.0)	10.0	(1.0)	3.2	(1.6)	**-9.0**	(1.7)
Non-adjudicated												
Belgium (French Community)	21.3	(2.9)	8.8	(1.5)	19.1	(1.7)	10.6	(1.0)	-2.2	(3.4)	1.8	(1.8)

Note: Values that are statistically significant are indicated in bold (see Annex A3).
See Table V.2.6 for national data.

[Part 1/1]
Table S.V.g Mean mathematics performance in PISA 2003, 2006 and 2009

	PISA 2003		PISA 2006		PISA 2009		Change between 2003 and 2009 (PISA 2009 - PISA 2003)		
	Mean score	S.E.	Mean score	S.E.	Mean score	S.E.	Score dif.	S.E.	p-value
Adjudicated									
Belgium (Flemish Community)	553	(2.1)	546	(3.7)	537	(3.1)	**-17**	(4.2)	0.00
Spain (Andalusia)	m	m	463	(4.2)	462	(5.2)	m	m	m
Spain (Aragon)	m	m	513	(4.5)	506	(5.2)	m	m	m
Spain (Asturias)	m	m	497	(4.9)	494	(4.6)	m	m	m
Spain (Basque Country)	502	(2.8)	501	(3.4)	510	(2.8)	8	(4.5)	0.07
Spain (Cantabria)	m	m	502	(2.6)	495	(5.0)	m	m	m
Spain (Castile and Leon)	503	(4.0)	515	(3.3)	514	(5.3)	11	(6.9)	0.11
Spain (Catalonia)	494	(4.7)	488	(5.2)	496	(6.0)	1	(7.9)	0.88
Spain (Galicia)	m	m	494	(4.1)	489	(4.3)	m	m	m
Spain (La Rioja)	m	m	525	(2.4)	504	(2.7)	m	m	m
Spain (Navarre)	m	m	515	(3.5)	511	(3.6)	m	m	m
United Kingdom (Scotland)	524	(2.3)	506	(3.6)	499	(3.3)	**-25**	(4.5)	0.00
Non-adjudicated									
Belgium (French Community)	498	(4.3)	490	(5.2)	488	(3.9)	-9	(6.1)	0.13
Belgium (German-Speaking Community)	515	(3.0)	514	(3.1)	517	(2.5)	2	(4.4)	0.63
Finland (Finnish Speaking)	m	m	549	(2.3)	541	(2.3)	m	m	m
Finland (Swedish Speaking)	m	m	533	(7.5)	527	(2.9)	m	m	m
Italy (Provincia Autonoma of Bolzano)	536	(4.8)	513	(1.8)	507	(3.2)	**-30**	(6.1)	0.00
Italy (Provincia Basilicata)	m	m	443	(5.0)	474	(4.4)	m	m	m
Italy (Provincia Campania)	m	m	436	(9.0)	447	(7.8)	m	m	m
Italy (Provincia Emilia Romagna)	m	m	494	(3.4)	503	(4.7)	m	m	m
Italy (Provincia Friuli Venezia Giulia)	m	m	513	(3.6)	510	(4.6)	m	m	m
Italy (Provincia Liguria)	m	m	473	(6.4)	491	(9.3)	m	m	m
Italy (Provincia Lombardia)	519	(7.3)	487	(6.6)	516	(5.6)	-4	(9.5)	0.71
Italy (Provincia Piemonte)	494	(4.9)	492	(4.8)	493	(6.0)	-1	(8.0)	0.89
Italy (Provincia Puglia)	m	m	435	(4.9)	488	(6.9)	m	m	m
Italy (Provincia Sardegna)	m	m	433	(6.7)	456	(5.2)	m	m	m
Italy (Provincia Sicilia)	m	m	423	(6.5)	450	(8.8)	m	m	m
Italy (Provincia Trento)	547	(3.0)	508	(2.3)	514	(2.5)	**-33**	(4.4)	0.00
Italy (Provincia Valle d'Aosta)	m	m	456	(5.8)	502	(2.3)	m	m	m
Italy (Provincia Veneto)	511	(5.5)	510	(6.2)	508	(5.6)	-3	(8.1)	0.71
United Kingdom (England)	507	(2.9)	495	(2.5)	493	(2.9)	**-14**	(4.6)	0.00
United Kingdom (Northern Ireland)	515	(2.8)	494	(2.8)	492	(3.1)	**-23**	(4.6)	0.00
United Kingdom (Wales)	498	(10.8)	484	(2.9)	472	(3.0)	**-26**	(11.4)	0.02

Note: Values that are statistically significant are indicated in bold (see Annex A3).
See Table V.3.1 for national data.

[Part 1/1]

Table S.V.h Percentage of students below Level 2 and at Level 5 and above on the mathematics scale in PISA 2003 and 2009

	Proficiency levels in PISA 2003				Proficiency levels in PISA 2009				Change between 2003 and 2009 (PISA 2009 – PISA 2003)			
	Below Level 2 (less than 420 score points)		Level 5 and above (from 607 score points)		Below Level 2 (less than 420 score points)		Level 5 and above (from 607 score points)		Below Level 2 (less than 420 score points)		Level 5 and above (from 607 score points)	
	%	S.E.	%	S.E.	%	S.E.	%	S.E.	% dif.	S.E.	% dif.	S.E.
Adjudicated												
Belgium (Flemish Community)	11.4	(0.6)	34.4	(1.0)	13.5	(0.9)	26.9	(1.2)	2.1	(1.1)	**-7.5**	(1.5)
Spain (Basque Country)	16.3	(0.9)	9.7	(0.8)	14.9	(1.0)	12.8	(0.8)	-1.4	(1.4)	**3.1**	(1.1)
Spain (Castile and Leon)	16.2	(1.6)	10.9	(1.3)	15.4	(1.7)	15.4	(1.8)	-0.8	(2.4)	**4.5**	(2.2)
Spain (Catalonia)	19.5	(1.9)	10.2	(1.3)	19.1	(2.2)	10.5	(1.7)	-0.4	(2.9)	0.3	(2.1)
United Kingdom (Scotland)	11.3	(0.9)	16.2	(0.9)	19.7	(1.3)	12.4	(1.0)	**8.4**	(1.6)	**-3.8**	(1.3)
Non-adjudicated												
Belgium (French Community)	23.2	(1.6)	16.2	(1.2)	26.1	(1.6)	12.4	(1.0)	2.9	(2.2)	**-3.8**	(1.6)
Belgium (German-Speaking Community)	17.7	(1.3)	19.2	(1.4)	15.2	(1.4)	15.7	(1.6)	-2.6	(1.9)	-3.5	(2.1)
Italy (Provincia Autonoma of Bolzano)	8.8	(1.0)	20.4	(1.8)	16.7	(1.4)	13.8	(0.9)	**7.9**	(1.8)	**-6.6**	(2.0)
Italy (Provincia Lombardia)	14.3	(2.6)	16.9	(2.3)	13.7	(1.9)	14.1	(1.7)	-0.6	(3.2)	-2.8	(2.9)
Italy (Provincia Piemonte)	18.9	(1.7)	9.1	(1.5)	21.5	(2.3)	10.1	(1.4)	2.6	(2.9)	1.1	(2.1)
Italy (Provincia Trento)	4.9	(0.9)	22.0	(1.7)	14.4	(1.3)	14.0	(1.1)	**9.5**	(1.6)	**-8.0**	(2.1)
Italy (Provincia Veneto)	14.4	(1.8)	12.5	(1.5)	15.9	(1.9)	12.8	(1.8)	1.5	(2.6)	0.4	(2.3)
United Kingdom (England)	18.4	(1.0)	15.0	(1.1)	19.8	(1.1)	9.9	(0.9)	1.4	(1.5)	**-5.1**	(1.4)
United Kingdom (Northern Ireland)	16.5	(1.1)	16.8	(1.1)	21.4	(1.3)	10.3	(1.0)	**4.9**	(1.7)	**-6.5**	(1.5)
United Kingdom (Wales)	19.6	(4.5)	10.4	(3.3)	26.2	(1.4)	5.0	(0.6)	6.6	(4.7)	-5.4	(3.3)

Note: Values that are statistically significant are indicated in bold (see Annex A3).
See Table V.3.2 for national data.

[Part 1/1]

Table S.V.i **Mean science performance in PISA 2006 and 2009**

	PISA 2006		PISA 2009		Change between 2006 and 2009 (PISA 2009 – PISA 2006)		
	Mean score	S.E.	%	S.E.	Score dif.	S.E.	p-value
Adjudicated							
Belgium (Flemish Community)	528	(3.4)	526	(2.9)	-2	(5.2)	0.74
Spain (Andalusia)	474	(4.0)	469	(5.3)	-4	(7.1)	0.53
Spain (Aragon)	513	(3.9)	505	(4.3)	-8	(6.4)	0.22
Spain (Asturias)	508	(4.9)	502	(4.9)	-7	(7.4)	0.36
Spain (Basque Country)	495	(3.5)	495	(2.5)	0	(5.0)	0.99
Spain (Cantabria)	509	(3.6)	500	(4.7)	-9	(6.4)	0.15
Spain (Castile and Leon)	520	(3.9)	516	(4.9)	-4	(6.8)	0.54
Spain (Catalonia)	491	(5.1)	497	(5.9)	6	(8.2)	0.47
Spain (Galicia)	504	(3.4)	506	(4.9)	2	(6.5)	0.80
Spain (La Rioja)	520	(2.3)	509	(2.6)	**-11**	(4.3)	0.01
Spain (Navarre)	511	(2.9)	509	(3.2)	-3	(5.1)	0.59
United Kingdom (Scotland)	515	(4.0)	514	(3.5)	-0	(5.9)	0.94
Non-adjudicated							
Belgium (French Community)	486	(4.3)	482	(4.2)	-4	(6.6)	0.58
Belgium (German-Speaking Community)	516	(2.9)	519	(2.8)	3	(4.8)	0.52
Finland (Finnish Speaking)	565	(2.1)	556	(2.5)	**-9**	(4.1)	0.03
Finland (Swedish Speaking)	531	(6.2)	528	(3.0)	-3	(7.3)	0.72
Italy (Provincia Autonoma of Bolzano)	526	(2.0)	513	(2.5)	**-13**	(4.1)	0.00
Italy (Provincia Basilicata)	451	(5.0)	466	(3.9)	**15**	(6.8)	0.02
Italy (Provincia Campania)	442	(5.9)	446	(6.8)	4	(9.3)	0.66
Italy (Provincia Emilia Romagna)	510	(3.7)	508	(4.8)	-2	(6.6)	0.80
Italy (Provincia Friuli Venezia Giulia)	533	(3.3)	524	(4.8)	-9	(6.3)	0.14
Italy (Provincia Liguria)	488	(6.7)	498	(9.9)	10	(12.2)	0.41
Italy (Provincia Lombardia)	499	(6.2)	526	(5.8)	**27**	(8.9)	0.00
Italy (Provincia Piemonte)	508	(4.8)	501	(5.2)	-7	(7.5)	0.37
Italy (Provincia Puglia)	447	(4.4)	490	(6.3)	**43**	(8.1)	0.00
Italy (Provincia Sardegna)	450	(6.3)	474	(4.5)	**25**	(8.1)	0.00
Italy (Provincia Sicilia)	433	(7.3)	451	(8.2)	18	(11.2)	0.11
Italy (Provincia Trento)	521	(2.0)	523	(3.6)	1	(4.9)	0.77
Italy (Provincia Valle d'Aosta)	470	(5.6)	521	(2.6)	**51**	(6.7)	0.00
Italy (Provincia Veneto)	524	(5.4)	518	(5.1)	-6	(7.8)	0.45
United Kingdom (England)	516	(2.7)	515	(3.0)	-1	(4.8)	0.88
United Kingdom (Northern Ireland)	508	(3.3)	511	(4.4)	3	(6.1)	0.59
United Kingdom (Wales)	505	(3.5)	496	(3.5)	-9	(5.6)	0.11

Note: Values that are statistically significant are indicated in bold (see Annex A3).
See Table V.3.4 for national data.

[Part 1/1]

Table S.V.j Mean mathematics performance in PISA 2003, 2006 and 2009

	Proficiency levels in PISA 2006				Proficiency levels in PISA 2009				Change between 2000 and 2009 (PISA 2009 - PISA 2000)			
	Below Level 2 (less than 410 score points)		Level 5 and above (from 633 score points)		Below Level 2 (less than 410 score points)		Level 5 and above (from 633 score points)		Below Level 2 (less than 410 score points)		Level 5 and above (from 633 score points)	
	%	S.E.	%	S.E.	%	S.E.	%	S.E.	% dif.	S.E.	% dif.	S.E.
Adjudicated												
Belgium (Flemish Community)	12.1	(1.2)	12.2	(0.8)	12.9	(1.0)	13.5	(1.1)	0.7	(1.5)	1.3	(1.4)
Spain (Andalusia)	23.4	(1.7)	2.9	(0.6)	23.8	(2.3)	2.4	(0.6)	0.4	(2.8)	-0.6	(0.8)
Spain (Aragon)	12.3	(1.4)	8.0	(0.9)	13.7	(1.5)	5.2	(1.0)	1.4	(2.0)	**-2.7**	(1.3)
Spain (Asturias)	12.4	(1.7)	5.7	(0.9)	16.4	(1.5)	6.3	(1.0)	4.1	(2.2)	0.5	(1.4)
Spain (Basque Country)	15.8	(1.2)	4.3	(0.6)	13.8	(1.0)	3.2	(0.5)	-2.0	(1.6)	-1.1	(0.8)
Spain (Cantabria)	12.6	(1.3)	6.8	(0.8)	16.2	(1.5)	6.2	(0.9)	3.6	(2.0)	-0.6	(1.2)
Spain (Castile and Leon)	8.8	(1.4)	7.6	(0.9)	11.5	(1.6)	7.9	(1.1)	2.7	(2.1)	0.3	(1.4)
Spain (Catalonia)	18.7	(1.8)	4.6	(0.8)	16.3	(1.9)	4.7	(1.0)	-2.4	(2.6)	0.1	(1.3)
Spain (Galicia)	14.2	(1.2)	6.7	(0.7)	13.4	(1.4)	5.6	(1.0)	-0.9	(1.8)	-1.1	(1.2)
Spain (La Rioja)	10.4	(0.9)	8.9	(1.1)	14.1	(1.3)	7.0	(1.0)	**3.7**	(1.6)	-1.9	(1.5)
Spain (Navarre)	13.6	(1.1)	8.5	(0.9)	12.7	(1.3)	6.0	(0.8)	-0.9	(1.7)	**-2.4**	(1.2)
United Kingdom (Scotland)	14.7	(1.2)	12.6	(1.0)	14.1	(1.0)	11.0	(1.0)	-0.6	(1.6)	-1.6	(1.4)
Non-adjudicated												
Belgium (French Community)	24.3	(1.8)	7.1	(0.9)	24.6	(1.5)	5.8	(0.7)	0.3	(2.4)	-1.3	(1.2)
Belgium (German-Speaking Community)	15.5	(1.2)	11.8	(1.1)	12.0	(1.2)	9.7	(1.1)	**-3.5**	(1.7)	-2.2	(1.6)
Finland (Finnish Speaking)	3.8	(0.5)	21.4	(0.8)	5.8	(0.5)	19.2	(1.0)	**2.0**	(0.7)	-2.1	(1.3)
Finland (Swedish Speaking)	9.4	(2.5)	11.4	(2.6)	8.9	(0.9)	10.9	(1.1)	-0.6	(2.6)	-0.5	(2.8)
Italy (Provincia Autonoma of Bolzano)	9.8	(0.8)	10.6	(0.7)	13.0	(0.9)	8.9	(0.9)	**3.2**	(1.2)	-1.7	(1.1)
Italy (Provincia Basilicata)	32.7	(2.4)	1.4	(0.4)	26.6	(2.1)	2.5	(0.5)	-6.1	(3.2)	1.1	(0.7)
Italy (Provincia Campania)	35.7	(3.0)	1.1	(0.5)	33.3	(2.6)	1.6	(0.5)	-2.4	(4.0)	0.5	(0.7)
Italy (Provincia Emilia Romagna)	15.5	(1.3)	8.7	(1.2)	16.0	(1.9)	9.3	(1.2)	0.5	(2.3)	0.6	(1.7)
Italy (Provincia Friuli Venezia Giulia)	7.8	(0.8)	11.1	(1.3)	11.1	(1.8)	11.3	(1.3)	3.3	(2.0)	0.2	(1.8)
Italy (Provincia Liguria)	21.3	(2.7)	5.6	(1.1)	17.5	(3.6)	6.6	(1.4)	-3.9	(4.5)	1.0	(1.7)
Italy (Provincia Lombardia)	18.0	(2.4)	6.8	(1.1)	10.9	(2.0)	10.5	(1.3)	**-7.0**	(3.1)	**3.7**	(1.7)
Italy (Provincia Piemonte)	14.4	(1.6)	7.7	(1.0)	16.9	(1.9)	6.7	(1.0)	2.5	(2.5)	-1.0	(1.4)
Italy (Provincia Puglia)	33.6	(2.2)	1.4	(0.5)	18.8	(2.1)	4.9	(1.2)	**-14.8**	(3.0)	**3.6**	(1.3)
Italy (Provincia Sardegna)	34.3	(2.9)	1.7	(0.6)	23.3	(1.9)	3.3	(0.7)	**-11.0**	(3.4)	1.5	(0.9)
Italy (Provincia Sicilia)	41.5	(3.2)	1.7	(0.6)	32.7	(3.5)	2.2	(0.8)	-8.8	(4.8)	0.5	(1.0)
Italy (Provincia Trento)	12.8	(0.7)	10.8	(1.2)	12.1	(1.7)	11.7	(1.1)	-0.7	(1.8)	0.9	(1.7)
Italy (Provincia Valle d'Aosta)	25.0	(2.6)	3.1	(0.9)	10.8	(1.0)	9.1	(1.0)	**-14.2**	(2.8)	**6.0**	(1.3)
Italy (Provincia Veneto)	10.8	(1.3)	10.4	(1.3)	11.7	(1.8)	9.0	(1.3)	0.9	(2.2)	-1.4	(1.8)
United Kingdom (England)	16.7	(0.9)	14.0	(0.7)	14.8	(1.0)	11.6	(0.9)	-1.9	(1.3)	**-2.4**	(1.1)
United Kingdom (Northern Ireland)	20.5	(1.1)	13.9	(1.0)	16.7	(1.7)	11.8	(1.1)	-3.8	(2.0)	-2.1	(1.5)
United Kingdom (Wales)	18.1	(1.1)	10.9	(0.9)	18.7	(1.4)	7.7	(0.7)	0.6	(1.7)	**-3.1**	(1.1)

Note: Values that are statistically significant are indicated in bold (see Annex A3).
See Table V.3.5 for national data.

[Part 1/1]

Table S.V.k Between- and within-school variance in reading performance in PISA 2000 and 2009

	PISA 2000			PISA 2009			Change between 2000 and 2009 (PISA 2009 – PISA 2000)					
	Total variance	Between-school variance	Within-school variance	Total variance	Between-school variance	Within-school variance	Total variance		Between-school variance		Within-school variance	
							Dif.	S.E.	Dif.	S.E.	Dif.	S.E.
Adjudicated												
Belgium (Flemish Community)	9309	8222	4247	8801	5499	4282	-508	(325)	-2723	(1837)	36	(267)
United Kingdom (Scotland)	9793	1221	8271	8872	1611	7668	-921	(421)	390	(460)	-603	(536)
Non-adjudicated												
Belgium (French Community)	12356	6396	5525	11905	6123	5672	-452	(410)	-272	(806)	147	(359)

Note: Values that are statistically significant are indicated in bold (see Annex A3).
See Table V.4.1 for national data.

[Part 1/1]

Table S.V.l Socio-economic background of students in PISA 2000 and 2009

	PISA 2000				PISA 2009				Change between 2000 and 2009 (PISA 2009 – PISA 2000)	
	PISA index of economic, social and cultural status		Variability in ESCS		PISA index of economic, social and cultural status		Variability in ESCS		PISA index of economic, social and cultural status	
	Mean	S.E.	S.D.	S.E.	Mean	S.E.	%	S.E.	Dif.	S.E.
Adjudicated										
Belgium (Flemish Community)	0.12	(0.03)	0.82	(0.02)	0.20	(0.02)	0.91	(0.01)	**0.07**	(0.03)
United Kingdom (Scotland)	0.20	(0.03)	0.79	(0.01)	0.19	(0.03)	0.81	(0.01)	-0.02	(0.04)
Non-adjudicated										
Belgium (French Community)	0.18	(0.04)	0.95	(0.02)	0.19	(0.04)	0.96	(0.02)	0.02	(0.05)

Note: Values that are statistically significant are indicated in bold (see Annex A3).
See Table V.4.2 for national data.

Table S.V.m [Part 1/3]
Relationship between reading performance and the PISA index of economic, social and cultural status (ESCS) in PISA 2000 and 2009

	PISA 2000					
	Overall association of ESCS[1]		Within-school association of ESCS[2]		Between-school association of ESCS[3]	
	Student-level score point difference associated with one unit of the ESCS	S.E.	Student-level score point difference associated with one unit of the student-level ESCS	S.E.	School-level score point difference associated with one unit of the school mean ESCS	S.E.
Adjudicated						
Belgium (Flemish Community)	42	(2.1)	10	(2.2)	178	(18.6)
United Kingdom (Scotland)	50	(2.5)	39	(2.8)	44	(7.7)
Non-adjudicated						
Belgium (French Community)	52	(2.1)	13	(2.9)	121	(9.6)

1. Single-level bivariate regression of reading performance on the ESCS: the slope is the regression coefficient for the ESCS
2. Two-level regression of reading performance on student ESCS and school mean ESCS: within-school slope for ESCS at the student level.
3. Two-level regression of reading performance on student ESCS and school mean ESCS: between-school slope for ESCS at the school level.

See Table V.4.3 for national data.

Table S.V.m [Part 2/3]
Relationship between reading performance and the PISA index of economic, social and cultural status (ESCS) in PISA 2000 and 2009

	PISA 2009					
	Overall association of ESCS[1]		Within-school association of ESCS[2]		Between-school association of ESCS[3]	
	Student-level score point difference associated with one unit of the ESCS	S.E.	Student-level score point difference associated with one unit of the student-level ESCS	S.E.	School-level score point difference associated with one unit of the school mean ESCS	S.E.
Adjudicated						
Belgium (Flemish Community)	41	(2.0)	11	(1.8)	108	(8.2)
United Kingdom (Scotland)	44	(2.3)	34	(2.8)	47	(6.5)
Non-adjudicated						
Belgium (French Community)	54	(2.8)	15	(2.1)	112	(8.4)

1. Single-level bivariate regression of reading performance on the ESCS: the slope is the regression coefficient for the ESCS
2. Two-level regression of reading performance on student ESCS and school mean ESCS: within-school slope for ESCS at the student level.
3. Two-level regression of reading performance on student ESCS and school mean ESCS: between-school slope for ESCS at the school level.

See Table V.4.3 for national data.

Table S.V.m [Part 3/3]
Relationship between reading performance and the PISA index of economic, social and cultural status (ESCS) in PISA 2000 and 2009

	Change between 2000 and 2009 (PISA 2009 – PISA 2000)					
	Overall association of ESCS[1]		Within-school association of ESCS[2]		Between-school association of ESCS[3]	
	Student-level score point difference associated with one unit of the ESCS	S.E.	Student-level score point difference associated with one unit of the student-level ESCS	S.E.	School-level score point difference associated with one unit of the school mean ESCS	S.E.
Adjudicated						
Belgium (Flemish Community)	-0.7	(2.9)	1.7	(2.8)	**-69.7**	(20.3)
United Kingdom (Scotland)	-5.9	(3.4)	-5.0	(4.0)	3.7	(10.1)
Non-adjudicated						
Belgium (French Community)	1.5	(3.5)	2.1	(3.6)	-9.2	(12.8)

1. Single-level bivariate regression of reading performance on the ESCS: the slope is the regression coefficient for the ESCS
2. Two-level regression of reading performance on student ESCS and school mean ESCS: within-school slope for ESCS at the student level.
3. Two-level regression of reading performance on student ESCS and school mean ESCS: between-school slope for ESCS at the school level.

See Table V.4.3 for national data.

[Part 1/1]

Table S.V.n Percentage of students and reading performance by immigrant status in PISA 2000 and 2009

	PISA 2000								PISA 2009								Change between 2000 and 2009 (PISA 2009 – PISA 2000)			
	Percentage of students with an immigrant background		Performance of native students		Performance of students with an immigrant background		Difference in performance between native students and students with an immigrant background		Percentage of students with an immigrant background		Performance of native students		Performance of students with an immigrant background		Difference in performance between native students and students with an immigrant background		Change in the percentage of student with an immigrant background		Change in the performance difference between native students and students with an immigrant background	
	%	S.E.	Mean score	S.E.	Mean score	S.E.	Score dif.	S.E.	%	S.E.	Mean score	S.E.	Mean score	S.E.	Score dif.	S.E.	% dif.	S.E.	Score dif.	S.E.
Adjudicated																				
Belgium (Flemish Community)	7.1	(1.3)	541	(3.3)	432	(14.4)	109	(13.6)	4.7	(0.7)	526	(2.7)	450	(7.8)	76	(8.8)	-2.4	(1.4)	**-33**	(16.2)
United Kingdom (Scotland)	2.2	(0.6)	528	(3.6)	495	(18.0)	33	(17.1)	1.4	(0.3)	503	(3.0)	529	(17.2)	-26	(16.7)	-0.8	(0.6)	**-59**	(23.9)
Non-adjudicated																				
Belgium (French Community)	18.3	(1.8)	495	(8.0)	409	(9.6)	86	(11.2)	13.6	(1.5)	508	(3.8)	456	(10.4)	52	(10.8)	**-4.7**	(2.3)	**-34**	(15.5)

Note: Values that are statistically significant are indicated in bold (see Annex A3).
See Table V.4.4 for national data.

[Part 1/1]

Table S.V.o Language spoken at home and reading performance in PISA 2000 and 2009

	PISA 2000								PISA 2009								Change between 2000 and 2009 (PISA 2009 - PISA 2000)			
	Percentage of students whose language spoken at home most of the time is DIFFERENT from the language of assessment		Performance of students whose language spoken at home most of the time is the SAME as the language of assessment		Performance of students whose language spoken at home most of the time is DIFFERENT from the language of assessment		Difference in the performance of students whose language spoken at home is the SAME and those whose language spoken at home is DIFFERENT from the language of assessment		Percentage of students whose language spoken at home most of the time is DIFFERENT from the language of assessment		Performance of students whose language spoken at home most of the time is the SAME as the language of assessment		Performance of students whose language spoken at home most of the time is DIFFERENT from the language of assessment		Difference in the performance of students whose language spoken at home is the SAME and those whose language spoken at home is DIFFERENT from the language of assessment		Change in the percentage of students whose language spoken at home most of the time is DIFFERENT from the language of assessment		Change in the performance difference between students whose language spoken at home is the SAME and those whose language spoken at home is DIFFERENT from the language of assessment	
	%	S.E.	Mean score	S.E.	Mean score	S.E.	Score dif.	S.E.	%	S.E.	Mean score	S.E.	Mean score	S.E.	Score dif.	S.E.	% dif.	S.E.	Score dif.	S.E.
Adjudicated																				
Belgium (Flemish Community)	33.8	(1.7)	543	(4.0)	522	(5.8)	108	(13.5)	24.9	(1.5)	530	(3.5)	513	(4.9)	17	(6.5)	**-8.9**	(2.2)	**-91**	(15.0)
United Kingdom (Scotland)	1.3	(0.4)	528	(3.7)	482	(14.5)	24	(15.2)	2.5	(0.4)	503	(3.0)	477	(18.5)	26	(18.1)	**1.2**	(0.5)	2	(23.7)
Non-adjudicated																				
Belgium (French Community)	9.2	(0.8)	491	(7.3)	399	(8.7)	81	(11.2)	17.7	(1.6)	506	(3.9)	427	(9.6)	79	(9.4)	**8.5**	(1.8)	-2	(14.6)

Note: Values that are statistically significant are indicated in bold (see Annex A3).
See Table V.4.5 for national data.

[Part 1/1]

Table S.V.p Between- and within-school variance in reading performance in PISA 2000 and 2009

	PISA 2000						PISA 2009						Change between 2000 and 2009 (PISA 2009 – PISA 2000)					
	All students		Girls		Boys		All students		Girls		Boys		All students		Girls		Boys	
	%	S.E.	%	S.E.	%	S.E.	%	S.E.	%	S.E.	%	S.E.	% dif.	S.E.	% dif.	S.E.	% dif.	S.E.
Adjudicated																		
Belgium (Flemish Community)	53.1	(1.4)	68.3	(1.3)	39.8	(1.8)	50.7	(1.0)	62.7	(1.3)	39.2	(1.3)	-2.5	(1.7)	**-5.6**	(1.8)	-0.6	(2.2)
United Kingdom (Scotland)	66.7	(1.1)	74.0	(1.4)	58.9	(1.4)	57.3	(1.3)	64.3	(1.5)	50.4	(1.8)	**-9.3**	(1.7)	**-9.7**	(2.1)	**-8.5**	(2.3)
Non-adjudicated																		
Belgium (French Community)	63.9	(1.1)	70.8	(1.2)	56.9	(1.8)	61.9	(1.0)	68.7	(1.4)	55.2	(1.4)	-2.0	(1.5)	-2.1	(1.8)	-1.6	(2.3)

Note: Values that are statistically significant are indicated in bold (see Annex A3).
See Table V.5.1 for national data.

[Part 1/1]

Table S.V.q Index of enjoyment of reading in PISA 2000 and 2009, by gender (results based on students' self-reports)

	PISA 2000						PISA 2009						Change between 2000 and 2009 (PISA 2009 – PISA 2000)					
	All students		Girls		Boys		All students		Girls		Boys		All students		Girls		Boys	
	Mean index	S.E.	Mean index	S.E.	Mean index	S.E.	Mean index	S.E.	Mean index	S.E.	Mean index	S.E.	Dif.	S.E.	Dif.	S.E.	Dif.	S.E.
Adjudicated																		
Belgium (Flemish Community)	-0.29	(0.02)	0.04	(0.03)	-0.57	(0.03)	-0.34	(0.02)	-0.05	(0.02)	-0.62	(0.03)	-0.05	(0.03)	**-0.08**	(0.04)	-0.04	(0.04)
United Kingdom (Scotland)	-0.06	(0.02)	0.16	(0.03)	-0.29	(0.03)	-0.15	(0.03)	0.08	(0.03)	-0.37	(0.04)	**-0.09**	(0.04)	-0.08	(0.05)	-0.08	(0.05)
Non-adjudicated																		
Belgium (French Community)	-0.10	(0.03)	0.15	(0.04)	-0.36	(0.04)	-0.02	(0.03)	0.21	(0.04)	-0.24	(0.03)	**0.09**	(0.04)	0.07	(0.05)	**0.12**	(0.05)

Note: Values that are statistically significant are indicated in bold (see Annex A3).
See Table V.5.2 for national data.

[Part 1/2]

Table S.V.r **Percentage of students who read diverse materials in PISA 2000 and 2009**
Percentage of students who reported that they read the following materials because they want to "several times a month" or "several times a week"

	PISA 2000										PISA 2009									
	Magazines		Comic books		Fiction (novels, narratives, stories)		Non-fiction books		Newspapers		Magazines		Comic books		Fiction (novels, narratives, stories)		Non-fiction books		Newspapers	
	%	S.E.	%	S.E.	%	S.E.	%	S.E.	%	S.E.	%	S.E.	%	S.E.	%	S.E.	%	S.E.	%	S.E.
Adjudicated																				
Belgium (Flemish Community)	74.1	(1.2)	39.0	(0.9)	19.6	(0.8)	13.8	(0.6)	53.2	(0.9)	67.3	(1.1)	31.1	(0.8)	19.2	(0.8)	12.1	(0.7)	54.7	(1.0)
United Kingdom (Scotland)	69.4	(1.0)	8.1	(0.5)	28.7	(1.3)	19.1	(0.8)	79.7	(0.8)	58.9	(1.1)	7.2	(0.5)	32.6	(1.3)	17.8	(0.8)	69.4	(1.0)
Non-adjudicated																				
Belgium (French Community)	60.2	(1.4)	37.4	(1.2)	22.3	(1.4)	19.4	(1.0)	37.0	(1.1)	64.3	(0.9)	33.0	(1.2)	26.5	(1.0)	15.8	(0.9)	44.9	(1.4)

Note: Values that are statistically significant are indicated in bold (see Annex A3).
See Table V.5.6 for national data.

[Part 2/2]

Table S.V.r **Percentage of students who read diverse materials in PISA 2000 and 2009**
Percentage of students who reported that they read the following materials because they want to "several times a month" or "several times a week"

	Change between 2000 and 2009 (PISA 2009 – PISA 2000)									
	Magazines		Comic books		Fiction (novels, narratives, stories)		Non-fiction books		Newspapers	
	% dif.	S.E.	% dif.	S.E.	% dif.	S.E.	% dif.	S.E.	% dif.	S.E.
Adjudicated										
Belgium (Flemish Community)	**-5.3**	(2.5)	**-7.1**	(1.5)	0.1	(1.3)	-1.3	(0.8)	2.5	(1.9)
United Kingdom (Scotland)	**-8.8**	(2.3)	-0.7	(0.5)	4.8	(3.3)	-0.7	(1.3)	**-8.2**	(1.9)
Non-adjudicated										
Belgium (French Community)	**8.3**	(3.0)	-1.7	(2.7)	**5.8**	(2.9)	-2.1	(1.7)	**10.4**	(3.1)

Note: Values that are statistically significant are indicated in bold (see Annex A3).
See Table V.5.6 for national data.

[Part 1/1]

Table S.V.s Relationship between reading performance and the PISA index of economic, social and cultural status (ESCS) in PISA 2000 and 2009

	PISA 2000						PISA 2009						Change between 2000 and 2009 (PISA 2009 – PISA 2000)					
	Students who read fiction		Students who do not read fiction		Difference (F-NF)		Students who read fiction		Students who do not read fiction		Difference (F-NF)		Students who read fiction		Students who do not read fiction		Difference (F-NF)	
	Mean score	S.E.	Mean score	S.E.	Mean score	S.E.	Mean score	S.E.	Mean score	S.E.	Mean score	S.E.	Score dif.	S.E.	Score dif.	S.E.	Score dif.	S.E.
Adjudicated																		
Belgium (Flemish Community)	581	(4.8)	524	(4.7)	**-57**	(4.6)	574	(4.4)	513	(2.2)	**-60**	(4.2)	-7	(8.1)	-10	(7.2)	-3	(6.2)
United Kingdom (Scotland)	569	(4.5)	511	(3.8)	**-58**	(4.8)	554	(4.0)	477	(2.9)	**-77**	(4.1)	-15	(7.8)	**-35**	(6.9)	**-20**	(6.3)
Non-adjudicated																		
Belgium (French Community)	515	(14.2)	475	(6.9)	**-41**	(11.3)	549	(4.3)	479	(4.5)	**-70**	(5.1)	**34**	(15.6)	4	(9.6)	**-30**	(12.4)

Note: Values that are statistically significant are indicated in bold (see Annex A3).
See Table V.5.8 for national data.

[Part 1/1]

Table S.V.t Teacher-student relations in PISA 2000 and 2009

Percentage of students agreeing or strongly agreeing with the following statements

	PISA 2000						PISA 2009						Change between 2000 and 2009 (PISA 2009 – PISA 2000)					
	Most of my teachers really listen to what I have to say		If I need extra help, I will receive it from my teachers		Most of my teachers treat me fairly		Most of my teachers really listen to what I have to say		If I need extra help, I will receive it from my teachers		Most of my teachers treat me fairly		Most of my teachers really listen to what I have to say		If I need extra help, I will receive it from my teachers		Most of my teachers treat me fairly	
	%	S.E.	%	S.E.	%	S.E.	%	S.E.	%	S.E.	%	S.E.	% dif.	S.E.	% dif.	S.E.	% dif.	S.E.
Adjudicated																		
Belgium (Flemish Community)	69.4	(1.0)	78.0	(1.0)	79.2	(0.9)	67.9	(0.9)	85.2	(0.8)	82.1	(0.8)	-1.5	(1.4)	**7.1**	(1.2)	**2.8**	(1.2)
United Kingdom (Scotland)	68.8	(1.2)	89.5	(0.8)	83.9	(0.8)	68.8	(1.1)	88.9	(0.7)	84.6	(0.7)	0.1	(1.7)	-0.6	(1.0)	0.7	(1.1)
Non-adjudicated																		
Belgium (French Community)	66.8	(1.3)	77.3	(0.9)	85.2	(0.9)	66.7	(1.0)	82.9	(0.7)	90.5	(0.6)	-0.1	(1.7)	**5.6**	(1.1)	**5.3**	(1.1)

Note: Values that are statistically significant are indicated in bold (see Annex A3).
See Table V.5.11 for national data.

[Part 1/2]

Table S.V.u **Disciplinary climate in PISA 2000 and 2009**

Percentage of students reporting that the following happen "never or hardly ever" or "in some lessons"

	PISA 2000										PISA 2009									
	Students don't listen to what the teacher says		There is noise and disorder		The teacher has to wait a long time for the students to quieten down		Students cannot work well		Students don't start working for a long time after the lesson begins		Students don't listen to what the teacher says		There is noise and disorder		The teacher has to wait a long time for the students to quieten down		Students cannot work well		Students don't start working for a long time after the lesson begins	
	%	S.E.	%	S.E.	%	S.E.	%	S.E.	%	S.E.	%	S.E.	%	S.E.	%	S.E.	%	S.E.	%	S.E.
Adjudicated																				
Belgium (Flemish Community)	77.9	(1.0)	67.2	(1.3)	64.7	(1.5)	86.0	(0.8)	72.4	(1.2)	65.3	(1.2)	63.8	(1.3)	65.3	(1.2)	85.5	(0.8)	73.1	(1.1)
United Kingdom (Scotland)	80.9	(1.0)	74.6	(1.2)	76.0	(1.4)	84.4	(0.8)	78.7	(0.9)	74.2	(1.0)	65.3	(1.3)	74.2	(1.0)	84.4	(0.9)	79.3	(1.0)
Non-adjudicated																				
Belgium (French Community)	73.4	(1.5)	57.4	(1.4)	64.4	(1.9)	83.7	(1.0)	64.2	(1.4)	70.6	(1.4)	61.6	(1.8)	70.6	(1.4)	83.6	(0.9)	68.9	(1.1)

Note: Values that are statistically significant are indicated in bold (see Annex A3).
See Table V.5.12 for national data.

[Part 2/2]

Table S.V.u **Disciplinary climate in PISA 2000 and 2009**

Percentage of students reporting that the following happen "never or hardly ever" or "in some lessons"

	Change between 2000 and 2009 (PISA 2009 – PISA 2000)									
	Students don't listen to what the teacher says		There is noise and disorder		The teacher has to wait a long time for the students to quieten down		Students cannot work well		Students don't start working for a long time after the lesson begins	
	% dif.	S.E.	% dif.	S.E.	% dif.	S.E.	% dif.	S.E.	% dif.	S.E.
Adjudicated										
Belgium (Flemish Community)	**-12.6**	(1.5)	-3.4	(1.8)	0.6	(1.9)	-0.5	(1.2)	0.8	(1.6)
United Kingdom (Scotland)	**-6.7**	(1.4)	**-9.3**	(1.7)	-1.9	(1.7)	0.0	(1.2)	0.6	(1.4)
Non-adjudicated										
Belgium (French Community)	-2.8	(2.1)	4.2	(2.3)	**6.3**	(2.3)	-0.1	(1.3)	**4.7**	(1.8)

Note: Values that are statistically significant are indicated in bold (see Annex A3).
See Table V.5.12 for national data.

Annex C

THE DEVELOPMENT AND IMPLEMENTATION OF PISA – A COLLABORATIVE EFFORT

INTRODUCTION

PISA is a collaborative effort, bringing together scientific expertise from the participating countries, steered jointly by their governments on the basis of shared, policy-driven interests.

A PISA Governing Board on which each country is represented determines, in the context of OECD objectives, the policy priorities for PISA and oversees adherence to these priorities during the implementation of the programme. This includes the setting of priorities for the development of indicators, for the establishment of the assessment instruments and for the reporting of the results.

Experts from participating countries also serve on working groups that are charged with linking policy objectives with the best internationally available technical expertise. By participating in these expert groups, countries ensure that the instruments are internationally valid and take into account the cultural and educational contexts in OECD Member countries, the assessment materials have strong measurement properties, and the instruments place an emphasis on authenticity and educational validity.

Through National Project Managers, participating countries implement PISA at the national level subject to the agreed administration procedures. National Project Managers play a vital role in ensuring that the implementation of the survey is of high quality, and verify and evaluate the survey results, analyses, reports and publications.

The design and implementation of the surveys, within the framework established by the PISA Governing Board, is the responsibility of external contractors. For PISA 2009, the questionnaire development was carried out by a consortium led by Cito International in partnership with the University of Twente. The development and implementation of the cognitive assessment and of the international options was carried out by a consortium led by the Australian Council for Educational Research (ACER). Other partners in this consortium include cApStAn Linguistic Quality Control in Belgium, the *Deutsches Institut für Internationale Pädagogische Forschung* (DIPF) in Germany, the National Institute for Educational Policy Research in Japan (NIER), the *Unité d'analyse des systèmes et des pratiques d'enseignement* (aSPe) in Belgium and WESTAT in the United States.

The OECD Secretariat has overall managerial responsibility for the programme, monitors its implementation on a day-to-day basis, acts as the secretariat for the PISA Governing Board, builds consensus among countries and serves as the interlocutor between the PISA Governing Board and the international consortium charged with the implementation of the activities. The OECD Secretariat also produces the indicators and analyses and prepares the international reports and publications in co-operation with the PISA consortium and in close consultation with Member countries both at the policy level (PISA Governing Board) and at the level of implementation (National Project Managers).

The following lists the members of the various PISA bodies and the individual experts and consultants who have contributed to PISA.

Members of the PISA Governing Board

Chair: Lorna Bertrand

OECD countries

Australia: Tony Zanderigo

Austria: Mark Német

Belgium: Christiane Blondin, Isabelle Erauw and Micheline Scheys

Canada: Pierre Brochu, Patrick Bussière and Tomasz Gluszynski

Chile: Leonor Cariola

Czech Republic: Jana Strakova

Denmark: Tine Bak

Estonia: Maie Kitsing

Finland: Jari Rajanen

France: Bruno Trosseille

Germany: Annemarie Klemm, Maximilian Müller-Härlin and Elfriede Ohrnberger

Greece: Panagiotis Kazantzis (1/7/05 – 31/03/10) Vassilia Hatzinikita (from 31/03/10)

Hungary: Benő Csapó

Iceland: Júlíus K. Björnsson

Ireland: Jude Cosgrove

Israel: Michal Beller

Italy: Piero Cipollone

Japan: Ryo Watanabe

Korea: Whan Sik Kim

Luxembourg: Michel Lanners

Mexico: Francisco Ciscomani

Netherlands: Paul van Oijen

New Zealand: Lynne Whitney

Norway: Anne-Berit Kavli

Poland: Stanislaw Drzazdzewski

Portugal: Carlos Pinto Ferreira

Slovak Republic: Julius Hauser, Romana Kanovska and Paulina Korsnakova

Slovenia: Andreja Barle Lakota

Spain: Carme Amorós Basté and Enrique Roca Cobo

Sweden: Anita Wester

Switzerland: Ariane Baechler Söderström and Heinz Rhyn

Turkey: Meral Alkan

United Kingdom: Lorna Bertrand and Mal Cooke

United States: Daniel McGrath and Eugene Owen

Observers

Albania: Ndricim Mehmeti

Argentina: Liliana Pascual

Azerbaijan: Talib Sharifov
Brazil: Joaquim José Soares Neto
Bulgaria: Neda Kristanova
Colombia: Margarita Peña
Croatia: Michelle Braš-Roth
Dubai (United Arab Emirates): Mariam Al Ali
Hong Kong-China: Esther Sui-chu Ho
Indonesia: Mansyur Ramli
Jordan: Khattab Mohammad Abulibdeh
Kazakhstan: Yermekov Nurmukhammed Turlynovich
Kyrgyz Republic: Inna Valkova
Latvia: Andris Kangro
Liechtenstein: Christian Nidegger
Lithuania: Rita Dukynaitė
Macao-China: Kwok-cheung Cheung
Montengegro: Zeljko Jacimovic
Panama: Arturo Rivera
Peru: Liliana Miranda Molina
Qatar: Adel Sayed
Romania: Roxana Mihail
Russian Federation: Galina Kovalyova
Serbia: Dragica Pavlovic Babic
Shanghai-China: Minxuan Zhang
Singapore: Low Khah Gek
Chinese Taipei: Chih-Wei Hue and Fou-Lai Lin
Thailand: Precharn Dechsri
Trinidad and Tobago: Harrilal Seecharan
Tunisia: Kameleddine Gaha
Uruguay: Andrés Peri

PISA 2009 National Project Managers

Albania: Alfonso Harizaj
Argentina: Antonio Gutiérrez
Australia: Sue Thomson
Austria: Ursula Schwantner
Azerbaijan: Emin Meherremov
Belgium: Ariane Baye and Inge De Meyer
Brazil: Sheyla Carvalho Lira
Bulgaria: Svetla Petrova
Canada: Pierre Brochu and Tamara Knighton
Chile: Ema Lagos
Chinese Taipei: Pi-Hsia Hung
Colombia: Francisco Ernesto Reyes
Croatia: Michelle Braš Roth
Czech Republic: Jana Paleckova
Denmark: Niels Egelund
Dubai (United Arab Emirates): Mariam Al Ali
Estonia: Gunda Tire
Finland: Jouni Välijärvi
France: Sylvie Fumel
Germany: Nina Jude and Eckhard Klieme
Greece: Panagiotis Kazantzis (from 1/7/05 to 18/11/08)
Chryssa Sofianopoulou (from 18/11/08)
Hong Kong-China: Esther Sui-chu Ho
Hungary: Ildikó Balázsi
Iceland: Almar Midvik Halldorsson
Indonesia: Burhanuddin Tola
Ireland: Rachel Perkins
Israel: Inbal Ron Kaplan and Joel Rapp
Italy: Laura Palmerio
Japan: Ryo Watanabe
Jordan: Khattab Mohammad Abulibdeh
Kazakhstan: Damitov Bazar Kabdoshevich
Korea: Kyung-Hee Kim
Kyrgyz Republic: Inna Valkova
Latvia: Andris Kangro
Liechtenstein: Christian Nidegger
Lithuania: Jolita Dudaitė
Luxembourg: Bettina Boehm
Macao-China: Kwok-cheung Cheung
Mexico: María-Antonieta Díaz-Gutiérrez
Montenegro: Verica Ivanovic
Netherlands: Erna Gille
New Zealand: Maree Telford
Norway: Marit Kjaernsli
Panama: Zoila Castillo
Peru: Liliana Miranda Molina
Poland: Michal Federowicz
Portugal: Anabela Serrão
Qatar: Asaad Tounakti
Romania: Silviu Cristian Mirescu
Russian Federation: Galina Kovalyova
Serbia: Dragica Pavlovic Babic
Shanghai-China: Jing Lu and MinXuan Zhang
Singapore: Chia Siang Hwa and Poon Chew Leng
Slovak Republic: Paulina Korsnakova
Slovenia: Mojca Straus
Spain: Lis Cercadillo
Sweden: Karl-Göran Karlsson
Switzerland: Christian Nidegger
Thailand: Sunee Klainin
Trinidad and Tobago: Harrilal Seecharan
Tunisia: Kameleddine Gaha
Turkey: Müfide Çaliskan
United Kingdom: Jenny Bradshaw and Mal Cooke
United States: Dana Kelly and Holly Xie
Uruguay: María Sánchez

OECD Secretariat

Andreas Schleicher (Overall co-ordination of PISA and partner country/economy relations)

Marilyn Achiron (Editorial support)

Marika Boiron (Editorial support)

Simone Bloem (Analytic services)

Francesca Borgonovi (Analytic services)

Niccolina Clements (Editorial support)

Michael Davidson (Project management and analytic services)

Juliet Evans (Administration and partner country/economy relations)

Miyako Ikeda (Analytic services)

Maciej Jakubowski (Analytic services)

Guillermo Montt (Analytic services)

Diana Morales (Administrative support)

Soojin Park (Analytic services)

Mebrak Tareke (Editorial support)

Sophie Vayssettes (Analytic services)

Elisabeth Villoutreix (Editorial support)

Karin Zimmer (Project management)

Pablo Zoido (Analytic services)

PISA Expert Groups for PISA 2009

Reading Expert Group

Irwin Kirsch (Education Testing Service, New Jersey, USA)

Sachiko Adachi (Nigata University, Japan)

Charles Alderson (Lancaster University, UK)

John de Jong (Language Testing Services, Netherlands)

John Guthrie (University of Maryland, USA)

Dominique Lafontaine (University of Liège, Belgium)

Minwoo Nam (Korea Institute of Curriculum and Evaluation)

Jean-François Rouet (University of Poitiers, France)

Wolfgang Schnotz (University of Koblenz-Landau, Germany)

Eduardo Vidal-Abarca (University of Valencia, Spain

Mathematics Expert Group

Jan de Lange (Chair) (Utrecht University, Netherlands)

Werner Blum (University of Kassel, Germany)

John Dossey (Illinois State University, USA)

Zbigniew Marciniak (University of Warsaw, Poland)

Mogens Niss (University of Roskilde, Denmark)

Yoshinori Shimizu (University of Tsukuba, Japan)

Science Expert Group

Rodger Bybee (Chair) (BSCS, Colorado Springs, USA)

Peter Fensham (Queensland University of Technology, Australia)

Svein Lie (University of Oslo, Norway)

Yasushi Ogura (National Institute for Educational Policy Research, Japan)

Manfred Prenzel (University of Kiel, Germany)

Andrée Tiberghien (University of Lyon, France)

Questionnaire Expert Group

Jaap Scheerens (Chair) (University of Twente, Netherlands

Pascal Bressoux (Pierre Mendès University, France)

Yin Cheong Cheng (Hong Kong Institute of Education, Hong Kong-China)

David Kaplan (University of Wisconsin – Madison, USA)

Eckhard Klieme (DIPF, Germany)

Henry Levin (Columbia University, USA)

Pirjo Linnakylä (University of Jyväskylä, Finland)

Ludger Wößmann (University of Munich, Germany)

PISA Technical Advisory Group

Keith Rust (Chair) (Westat, USA)

Ray Adams (ACER)

John de Jong (Language Testing Services, Netherlands)

Cees Glas (University of Twente, Netherlands)

Aletta Grisay (Consultant, Saint-Maurice, France)

David Kaplan (University of Wisconsin – Madison, USA)

Christian Monseur (University of Liège, Belgium)

Sophia Rabe-Hesketh (University of California – Berkeley, USA)

Thierry Rocher (Ministry of Education, France)

Norman Verhelst (CITO, Netherlands)

Kentaro Yamamoto (ETS, New Jersey, USA)

Rebecca Zwick (University of California – Santa Barbara, USA)

PISA 2009 Consortium for questionnaire development

Cito International

Johanna Kordes

Hans Kuhlemeier

Astrid Mols

Henk Moelands

José Noijons

University of Twente

Cees Glas

Khurrem Jehangir

Jaap Scheerens

PISA 2009 Consortium for the development and implementation of the cognitive assessment and international options

Australian Council for Educational Research

Ray Adams (Director of the PISA 2009 Consortium)

Susan Bates (Project administration)

Alla Berezner (Data management and analysis)

Yan Bibby (Data processing and analysis)

Esther Brakey (Administrative support)

Wei Buttress (Project administration and quality monitoring)

Renee Chow (Data processing and analysis)

Judith Cosgrove (Data processing and analysis and national centre support)

John Cresswell (Reporting and dissemination)

Alex Daraganov (Data processing and analysis)

Daniel Duckworth (Reading instruments and test development)

Kate Fitzgerald (Data processing and sampling)

Daniel Fullarton (IT services)

Eveline Gebhardt (Data processing and analysis)

Mee-Young Handayani (Data processing and analysis)

Elizabeth Hersbach (Quality assurance)

Sam Haldane (IT services and computer-based assessment)

Karin Hohlfield (Reading instruments and test development)

Jennifer Hong (Data processing and sampling)

Tony Huang (Project administration and IT services)

Madelaine Imber (Reading instruments and administrative support)

Nora Kovarcikova (Survey operations)

Winson Lam (IT services)

Tom Lumley (Print and electronic reading instruments and test development)

Greg Macaskill (Data management and processing and sampling)

Ron Martin (Science instruments and test development)

Barry McCrae (Electronic Reading Assessment manager, science instruments and test development)

Juliette Mendelovits (Print and electronic reading instruments and test development)

Martin Murphy (Field operations and sampling)

Thoa Nguyen (Data processing and analysis)

Penny Pearson (Administrative support)

Anna Plotka (Graphic design)

Alla Routitsky (Data management and processing)

Wolfram Schulz (Management and data analysis)

Dara Searle (Print and electronic reading instruments and test development)

Naoko Tabata (Survey operations)

Ross Turner (Management, mathematics instruments and test development)

Daniel Urbach (Data processing and analysis)

Eva Van de gaer (Data analysis)

Charlotte Waters (Project administration, data processing and analysis)

Maurice Walker (Electronic Reading Assessment and sampling)

Wahyu Wardono (Project administration and IT services)

Louise Wenn (Data processing and analysis)

Yan Wiwecka (IT services)

Westat

Eugene Brown (Weighting)

Fran Cohen (Weighting)

Susan Fuss (Sampling and weighting)

Amita Gopinath (Weighting)

Sheila Krawchuk (Sampling, weighting and quality monitoring)

Thanh Le (Sampling, weighting, and quality monitoring)

Jane Li (Sampling and weighting)

John Lopdell (Sampling and weighting)

Shawn Lu (Weighting)

Keith Rust (Director of the PISA Consortium for sampling and weighting)

William Wall (Weighting)

Erin Wilson (Sampling and weighting)

Marianne Winglee (Weighting)

Sergey Yagodin (Weighting)

The National Institute for Educational Research in Japan

Hidefumi Arimoto (Reading instruments and test development)

Hisashi Kawai (Reading instruments and test development)

cApStAn Linguistic Quality Control

Steve Dept (Translation and verification operations)

Andrea Ferrari (Translation and verification methodology)

Laura Wäyrynen (Verification management)

Unité d'analyse des systèmes et des pratiques d'enseignement (aSPe)

Ariane Baye (Print reading and electronic reading instruments and test development)

Casto Grana-Monteirin (Translation and verification)

Dominique Lafontaine (Member of the Reading Expert Group)

Christian Monseur (Data analysis and member of the TAG)

Anne Matoul (Translation and verification)

Patricia Schillings (Print reading and electronic reading instruments and test development)

Deutsches Institut für Internationale Pädagogische Forschung (DIPF)

Cordula Artelt (University of Bamberg) (Reading instruments and framework development)

Michel Dorochevsky (Softcon) (Software Development)

Frank Goldhammer (Electronic reading instruments and test development)

Dieter Heyer (Softcon) (Software Development)

Nina Jude (Electronic reading instruments and test development)

Eckhard Klieme (Project Co-Director at DIPF)

Holger Martin (Softcon) (Software Development)

Johannes Naumann (Electronic reading instruments and test development)

Jean-Paul Reeff (International Consultant)

Heiko Roelke (Project Co-Director at DIPF)

Wolfgang Schneider (University of Würzburg) (Reading instruments and framework development)

Petra Stanat (Humboldt University, Berlin) (Reading instruments and test development)

Britta Upsing (Electronic reading instruments and test development)

Other experts

Tobias Dörfler, (University of Bamberg) (Reading instrument development)

Tove Stjern Frønes (ILS, University of Oslo) (Reading instrument development)

Béatrice Halleux (Consultant, HallStat SPRL) (Translation/verification referee and French source development)

Øystein Jetne (ILS, University of Oslo) (Print reading and electronic reading instruments and test development)

Kees Lagerwaard (Institute for Educational Measurement of Netherlands) (Math instrument development)

Pirjo Linnakylä (University of Jyväskylä) (Reading instrument development)

Anne-Laure Monnier (Consultant, France) (French source development)

Jan Mejding (Danish Schoool of Education, University of Aarhus) (Print reading and electronic reading development)

Eva Kristin Narvhus (ILS, University of Oslo) (Print reading and electronic reading instruments, test instruments and test development)

Rolf V. Olsen (ILS, University of Oslo) (Science instrument development)

Robert Laurie (New Brunswick Department of Education, Canada) (Science instrument development)

Astrid Roe (ILS, University of Oslo) (Print reading and electronic reading instruments and test development)

Hanako Senuma (University of Tamagawa, Japan) (Math instrument development)

ORGANISATION FOR ECONOMIC CO-OPERATION AND DEVELOPMENT

The OECD is a unique forum where governments work together to address the economic, social and environmental challenges of globalisation. The OECD is also at the forefront of efforts to understand and to help governments respond to new developments and concerns, such as corporate governance, the information economy and the challenges of an ageing population. The Organisation provides a setting where governments can compare policy experiences, seek answers to common problems, identify good practice and work to co-ordinate domestic and international policies.

The OECD member countries are: Australia, Austria, Belgium, Canada, Chile, the Czech Republic, Denmark, Finland, France, Germany, Greece, Hungary, Iceland, Ireland, Israel, Italy, Japan, Korea, Luxembourg, Mexico, the Netherlands, New Zealand, Norway, Poland, Portugal, the Slovak Republic, Slovenia, Spain, Sweden, Switzerland, Turkey, the United Kingdom and the United States. The European Commission takes part in the work of the OECD.

OECD Publishing disseminates widely the results of the Organisation's statistics gathering and research on economic, social and environmental issues, as well as the conventions, guidelines and standards agreed by its members.

OECD PUBLISHING, 2, rue André-Pascal, 75775 PARIS CEDEX 16
(98 2010 11 1 P) ISBN 978-92-64-09149-8- No. 57733 2010